WILLIAM JAMES

William James, ca. 1893

WILLIAM JAMES

HIS LIFE AND THOUGHT

GERALD E. MYERS

YALE UNIVERSITY PRESS

NEW HAVEN AND LONDON

Designed by Sally Harris
and set in Meridien type by
The Composing Room of Michigan, Inc.
Printed in the United States of America by
Vail-Ballou Press, Binghamton, N.Y.

Library of Congress Cataloging-in-Publication Data

Myers, Gerald E. (Gerald Eugene), 1923–
    William James, his life and thought.

    Bibliography: p.
    Includes index.
    1. James, William, 1842–1910.   I. Title.
B945.J24M94 1986   191 [B]   85–26288
ISBN 0–300–03417–2

The paper in this book meets the guidelines for
permanence and durability of the Committee on
Production Guidelines for Book Longevity
of the Council on Library Resources.

10 9 8 7 6 5 4 3 2 1

All photographs are reproduced by permission of the Houghton Library, Harvard University.

Acknowledgment is made for permission to quote from the following:

Two letters from William James to Robert Underwood Johnson, by permission of the American Academy and Institute of Arts and Letters.

A letter from William James to Elizabeth Glendower Evans, by permission of the Schlesinger Library, Radcliffe College.

A letter from John Dewey to Scudder Klyce, by permission of the Center for Dewey Studies, Southern Illinois University at Carbondale.

Materials from the Ralph Barton Perry Papers, by permission of Bernard Perry and of the Harvard University Archives.

Materials from the William James Papers, by permission of Alexander R. James and of the Houghton Library, Harvard University.

Ralph Barton Perry, *The Thought and Character of William James* (Boston: Little, Brown and Company, 1935), by permission of the publisher.

TO CURT AND MARTHA

CONTENTS

PREFACE

My interest in William James began years ago when I was working through the ideas of G. E. Moore, Bertrand Russell, Ludwig Wittgenstein, Gilbert Ryle, and A. J. Ayer in the philosophy of mind. Since these philosophers explicitly and often implicitly referred to James as an influential predecessor, I turned to his writings for a historical perspective on contemporary arguments in philosophical psychology and to clarify the issues for myself. Much of my thinking in this area has been stimulated by the work of my undergraduate and graduate students who have written on Russell's *Analysis of Mind*, Wittgenstein's *Philosophical Investigations*, Ryle's *Concept of Mind*, and Ayer's *Origins of Pragmatism*, along with James's *Principles of Psychology* and related writings.

While I had no doubt about the importance of James's ideas or their relevance to current controversies over sensation, consciousness, introspection, will, emotion, and memory, I discovered that considerable uncertainty confronts his would-be interpreter. All great thinkers, including James, make interpreters of their readers; I found reading James both stimulating and baffling. It was not easy to determine the meaning of certain key concepts or the precise nature of a particular thesis or doctrine. The more carefully I studied his texts, the more intrigued I became by his ideas and the more convinced that an interpretive analysis of his philosophy of mind was needed.

The project of writing a modest-sized book on James's philosophy of psychology was repeatedly stalled, mainly because I could find no satisfactory way to confine an interpretive study to the psychology alone. Having undertaken to explain what James believed about consciousness, thought, imagination, reasoning, and perception, I was increasingly impressed, and consequently detoured, by the fact that his reflections in the philosophy of psychology were inextricably connected with his thoughts about epistemology, metaphysics, ethics, and religion. As long as I tried to confine his thought to the philosophy of mind, I seemed either to trivialize it by not acknowledging what connected it with other philosophical areas, or to desert my intention of explicating James rather than using his ideas merely as a base for my own conceptions of memory, consciousness, and cognition. Although I had often heard scholars in American philosophy say that a full-scale critical study of James was needed, I did not originally plan to attempt one. That I subsequently decided to do so is due to the fact that a respectful treatment of James's philosophy of mind—or of any other domain of his thought—requires a careful look at his entire philosophy.

I have tried to understand James throughout the remarkable range and variety of his thought, to comprehend the issues that occupied him, the claims that he made, and the difficulties and breakthroughs he encountered in making them. Particular arguments are viewed critically, texts are compared for consistency, changes of conviction are noted, and the obstacles that prevented facile solutions are examined. The book might have been subtitled "A Critical Study," but because of the amount of biographical material that appears, "His Life and Thought" seemed more appropriate. Criticisms of James's ideas are included to show those ideas in bolder relief, to underscore the richness of his thinking by revealing the thorny complexities of the problems he set for himself. I have taken criticisms only as far as necessary to illuminate the profundity and elusiveness of James's intentions. As an admirer of James but not his follower, I offer appraisals which are meant to throw light on his reflections; my own ideas appear as the honest response of one who has been deeply engaged with Jamesian arguments.

No case need be made for the continuing relevance of James's thought. The major event in contemporary Jamesian scholarship is the authoritative edition of his works, supervised by Frederick Burkhardt, General Editor, and Fredson Bowers, Textual Editor, now being published by Harvard University Press. To date, this edition consists of eleven titles in thirteen volumes, providing scholars with dependable texts as well as relevant manuscript and historical materials. Another important contribution is *William James: A Reference Guide* by Ignas K. Skrupskelis, who is also Associate Editor of the Harvard edition. His book covers the literature about James from 1868 through 1974; if updated it would require a lengthy list of additions, testimony to the uninterrupted interest in James.

In addition to studying the corpus of James's writings, I have tried to consult most of what has been published about him; an impressive amount of insightful scholarship exists, some in books but most in journal articles. Perhaps my most pronounced regret is that I could not respond more fully to specific contentions of those who have contributed to Jamesian scholarship. While my notes reflect some of my research in the secondary literature, certain deserving publications have doubtlessly gone unmentioned through inadvertence or accident, and I regret any such omissions. Because of its length alone, this book may be compared by some with Ralph Barton Perry's landmark study, *The Thought and Character of William James*, published in 1935. As with any work on James since then, this book owes much to Perry's. But whereas his two volumes presented James's life and thought sympathetically and uncritically through correspondence, historical sources, and summaries of James's doctrines, I have tried instead, through focusing upon James's writings, to give a more critical and interpretive analysis of his ideas.

Because my focus has been the analysis of what James himself said, I could not launch, without adding another volume or two, an examination of the many alleged influences on his thought. He obtained his conception of the main issues in psychology and philosophy from a long line of predecessors and contemporaries, and thus there are inevitable points of comparison. However, definitive influences are not easy to determine because James based his thinking on a core of steadfast convictions and tended to take from other thinkers only what harmonized with those convictions. What he found in the writers who he said had influenced his thought was less a discovery of something new than an echo of something he already believed. Compared to the influences of his father, Henry James, Sr., and of the French philosopher Charles Renouvier, what he and others attributed to other sources is considerably less significant. Given the focus of this book, however, this question is a side issue at best, and I mention it only to indicate why a discussion of influence does not figure more prominently here.

I have consulted extensively the voluminous collection of James papers in the Houghton Library at Harvard University and have drawn upon original manuscripts, diaries, notebooks, correspondence, and memoranda not only by William but by other members of the James family as well. While these items do not demand significant revisions in the interpretation of James's published works, they provide insights into his ponderings on important but stubborn problems and give a fuller sense of his intellectual motivations. A major reason for his perennial popularity is the fact that his life was fascinatingly intertwined with his thought. Unlike most academics, he brought a vivid personality to his ideas while assimilating those ideas to the expression of his personality. The Jamesian world of concepts is thus brought to life for the reader by a sense of personal drama.

William James was once America's foremost philosopher and psychologist, and some scholars claim that distinction for him even now. But he made contributions in so many fields—religion, psychical research, medicine, self-help therapies, the rights of animals, social and educational reforms, politics, the arts—that he belongs to nothing less than American cultural history. Students in a wide variety of disciplines other than philosophy and psychology have taken an interest in James. Much of this widespread interest is directed at the ways in which his life and thought intersected. As I expanded my initial inquiry beyond his philosophy of mind to all of his intellectual achievements, I felt that it was necessary to become better acquainted with biographical background in order to appreciate more fully how his ideas connected with his life.

The James family has attracted an exceptional amount of attention, and for good reason. Their lives touched those of an extraordinary number of illustrious persons; indeed, to look at this family is like opening a window upon an entire historical era. William's brother, Henry James, Jr., who is often considered America's greatest novelist and man of letters, outranks the rest of the family in the amount of attention received. Leon Edel's five-volume life of Henry James is indispensable reading for anyone interested not only in the novelist but in the entire James family. William's father, Henry James, Sr., has also received his share of attention, partly because he mixed with such contemporaries as Ralph Waldo Emerson and Thomas Carlyle, partly because his own religious ideas are interesting, but largely because of the alleged interactions between him and his children that challenge psychobiographers and psychohistorians. William's brilliant, invalid sister is the subject of Jean Strouse's *Alice James: A Biography;* along with *The Diary of Alice James,* edited with an introduction by Leon Edel, Strouse's biography is essential for understanding both Alice and her family. The biographical interest in William James has continued since Gay Wilson Allen's biography of him appeared in 1967. We now have Jacques Barzun's study, *A Stroll with William James;* a special issue of the Harvard Library Bulletin titled *A William James Renaissance: Four Essays by Young Scholars;* Daniel W. Bjork's book, *The Compromised Scientist: William James in the Development of American Psychology;* and, most recently, Howard M. Feinstein's *Becoming William James.*

In the first chapter and at various places throughout the book, I have added my voice to the chorus of opinions about the personality and character of William James and about his relationships with Henry, Alice, and the other family members. For biographical information, I examined relevant items in the Houghton Library and the Harvard Archives, including thousands of letters to and from the James family. I spent more time on this than was needed for a book which is only partly biographical, for I had built up a strong curiosity about the family. I have made the most use thus far of the correspondence between William and his wife, Alice (the "second" Alice James), which was not available to scholars until recently. I also use several letters of 1857–59 written by the teenaged William to a friend in New York City, Edgar Van Winkle. Perry was unaware of these when he composed his two-volume work, and although he reproduced the most important of these letters in his briefer version of 1948, he left their significance for understanding the young William largely unexplored.

In offering my impressions of the relationship between William and Henry, I refer to two items which as far as I know have gone undetected: a few lines by Henry that were appended to a letter from William to Van Winkle in 1858, and a first draft of William's letter of resignation from the National Institute of Arts and Letters in 1905; the final version of the letter has provoked considerable controversy in recent years. Also previously unknown, to my knowledge, is William's manuscript, "The Foreboding Meeting; or, The Artist's Fate," which is a fine example of his entertaining drawings and concerns an encounter with Ralph Waldo Emerson. The manuscript suggests the way James saw the relation of the poet and the philosopher, and calls to mind the opinion of Plato. The manuscript is reproduced in the illustration section and discussed in chapter 13.

Today, when there is a tendency for philosophies to be regarded as impersonal solutions to conceptual puzzles, we need to revive James's spirit, to respect the role and value of personal philosophies. Though his thought is no more immune to criticism than any other philosophical approach, James showed that the philosopher's personality can influence not only his social and political outlooks but also his philosophy of psychology and the foundations of his epistemology and metaphysics. There was always something personal at stake for James in formulating his theories; indeed, few other thinkers could provide a stimulating journey into as many subjects as James did. This book is a tribute to his greatness and an expression of appreciation for what I have gained through exploring his legacy.

I am especially grateful to the National Endowment for the Humanities for granting me a Fellowship for Independent Study and Research in 1981–82. Without the freedom from academic duties that this grant provided, my work for this book might never have been completed. I am also indebted to the Research Foundation of the City University of New York, which awarded me a summer grant in 1983 that permitted my final research in the Houghton Library and the Harvard Archives. I thank Queens College for a Mellon Fellowship in 1983–84, which reduced my teaching responsibilities so that I could further pursue the relationship between William and Henry James; and I hope to incorporate more on that subject in a future study.

The staff of the Paul Klapper Library of Queens College was especially helpful in my research. I must also thank the staffs of the Reading Room at the Houghton Library and of the Archives at Harvard University. My research also benefited from the kind help given by James MacDonald at the Connecticut College Library.

The friends and colleagues whom I must thank for assistance and encouragement include Frederick Burkhardt, Marshall Cohen, Abraham Edel, Eugene Fontinell, J. N. Jordan, Edward Madden, Frederick Purnell, Alan Rosenberg, and Ralph Sleeper. To John J. McDermott, who read the manuscript and helped to improve it, I am singularly grateful. Former students who have contributed to my ongoing interest in James and who have assisted in shaping my understanding of him are too numerous to name, but I thank them in their anonymity all the same.

For her confidence in this book and her encouragement of its development, I thank Marian Ash at Yale University Press. I am also grateful to Channing Hughes at the Press for his acumen in refining the manuscript into its completed form.

Finally, I must thank Mary Chiffriller, my research assistant, who not only supervised the manuscript through its completion but was a counselor and guide throughout. Her understanding of the content and aim of the book was indispensable, and her suggestions were especially useful as I structured chapter 1 and decided what of my research should be included there.

CHRONOLOGY OF THE LIFE
OF WILLIAM JAMES

1842	January 11. Born in New York City to Henry James, Sr., and Mary Walsh James.
1843	Henry James, Jr. (brother) born.
1845	Garth Wilkinson James (brother) born.
1846	Robertson James (brother) born.
1848	Alice James (sister) born.
1852–55	Attends school in New York City.
1855–58	Attends school and studies with private tutors in France and England.
1858–59	Lives in Newport, Rhode Island.
1859–60	Attends school and studies with private tutors in Germany and Switzerland.
1860–61	Studies painting with William Morris Hunt in Newport.
1861	Enters Lawrence Scientific School at Harvard.
1864	Enters Harvard Medical School. James family moves to Boston.
1865–66	Participates in research expedition to Brazil with Louis Agassiz.
1866	James family moves to 20 Quincy Street, Cambridge.
1867–68	Travels to Germany for study and recuperation from ill health.
1869	Receives M.D., Harvard.
1869–72	Suffers ill health and depression; recovers.
1872	Becomes instructor in physiology at Harvard.
1873	Becomes instructor in anatomy and physiology at Harvard.
1873–74	Suffers ill health; travels to Italy for recuperation.
1875	Teaches first psychology course at Harvard.
1876	Becomes assistant professor of physiology at Harvard.
1878	Marries Alice Howe Gibbens. Contracts to write *The Principles of Psychology*.

1879	Begins teaching philosophy.
1880	Becomes assistant professor of philosophy.
	Henry James III (son) born.
1882	Henry James, Sr., and Mary Walsh James die.
	William James, Jr. (son) born.
1884	Herman James (son) born.
1885	Becomes professor of philosophy.
	Herman James dies.
1886	Buys summer home in Chocorua, New Hampshire.
1887	Mary Margaret James (daughter) born.
1889	Becomes professor of psychology.
	Moves to 95 Irving Street, Cambridge.
1890	*The Principles of Psychology* published.
	Alexander Robertson James (son) born.
1892	Alice James (sister) dies.
1892–93	Travels with family in Europe.
	Succeeded by Hugo Münsterberg as director of the psychological laboratory at Harvard.
1897	*The Will to Believe, and Other Essays in Popular Philosophy* published.
1898	Announces pragmatism in a lecture, ''Philosophical Conceptions and Practical Results,'' at the University of California at Berkeley.
	Injures heart while hiking in Adirondacks.
1899	*Talks to Teachers* published.
1899–1901	Suffers ill health; travels to Europe for recuperation, mainly in Nauheim, Germany.
1901–02	Delivers Gifford Lectures, basis for *The Varieties of Religious Experience* (published in 1902), at the University of Edinburgh.
1903	Receives honorary LL.D. from Harvard.
1905	Travel in Greece.
	Attends Psychological Congress in Rome.
1906	Serves as visiting professor at Stanford University.
	Returns to Cambridge after San Francisco earthquake.
1907	*Pragmatism* published.
	Resigns from Harvard.
1908–09	Delivers Hibbert Lectures, basis for *A Pluralistic Universe* (published in 1909), at Oxford.
1909	*The Meaning of Truth* published.
1910	Seeks health cures in Europe.
	August 26. Dies in Chocorua.

CHRONOLOGY OF KEY WRITINGS

POSTHUMOUS PUBLICATIONS

WILLIAM JAMES

1 ❦ LIFE AND CAREER

ACHIEVEMENTS

When William James died on 26 August 1910 in his summer home in Cho-corua, New Hampshire, the tributes paid him were as varied as his contributions. John Dewey wrote: "By common consent he was far and away the greatest of American psychologists—it was a case of James first and no second. Were it not for the unreasoned admiration of men and things German, there would be no question, I think, that he was the greatest psychologist of his time in any country—perhaps of any time."[1] The Paris *Temps* called him "the most famous American philosopher since Emerson," a sentiment which Bertrand Russell echoed in describing James's death as a "personal loss by all who knew him" and citing him as "one of the most eminent, and probably the most widely known, of contemporary philosophers"; the *Boston Evening Transcript* lamented his death as "the removal of the greatest of contemporary Americans."[2] James was remembered as America's representative thinker, foremost psychologist, and preeminent philosopher, as well as its most influential writer on religion, psychical research, and self-help. It is sometimes said that James had few actual disciples, but his followers include countless people who have felt genuinely inspired and enriched by his writings.[3]

James's greatest achievement was to command professional and popular au-diences simultaneously. He was elected president of both the American Philosoph-ical and the American Psychological associations, and thousands of nonprofes-sionals showed up for his public lectures; this dual success must have been gratifying to a thinker whose philosophy of pragmatism taught that theory and practice are inevitably intertwined. We can understand why his colleagues responded to his discourses, but why did the educated public? Only a constellation of answers can suffice. He had a vibrant literary style—"game flavored as a hawk's wing," as a friend of his once said—which enabled him to communicate with the intellectually curious from every background. His audience may not always have comprehended

1

his meaning, but unlike most academics he secured their interest in trying to understand. He envisioned a universe conforming to what he called pluralistic pragmatism; the appeal of his theory was heightened by the language with which he described it: "To rationalists this describes a tramp and vagrant world, adrift in space, with neither elephant nor tortoise to plant the sole of its foot upon. It is a set of stars hurled into heaven without even a centre of gravity to pull against. . . . Such a world (say the rationalists) would not be *respectable,* philosophically. It is a trunk without a tag, a dog without a collar, in the eyes of most professors of philosophy."[4] But if the layman chortled when philosophy was served up in this fashion, Russell represented many a college professor in protesting James's formulation: "It is insinuating, gradual, imperceptible; it is like a bath with hot water running in so slowly that you don't know when to scream. If this comparison seems not worthy of the dignity of philosophy, I can only plead in extenuation that it is quite in the manner of William James."[5] James's professional audience sometimes thought that the popular appeal in his writings was excessive, and he himself sometimes agreed, though he never modified his style of presentation. No matter how abstruse the subject, James managed to quicken the reader's interest by injecting a personal or picturesque touch.

Whatever the popular or professional merits of James's texts, *The Principles of Psychology,* which appeared in 1890 after twelve years in the making, is undoubtedly his magnum opus. James was an established Harvard professor and a psychologist and philosopher with an international reputation when *Principles* was published, but the book alone guaranteed him permanent renown. Since psychology and philosophy were not distinctly separated in 1890, *Principles* is not only a textbook in experimental psychology but also a landmark contribution to the philosophy of psychology or the philosophy of mind. Discussions of the mind-body relationship and of free will, for instance, accompany explanations of brain functions and of physiological optics. *Principles,* a massive study that occupies two volumes and twenty-eight chapters, is absorbing for the philosopher and the psychologist alike. Russell called *Principles* "the most delightful and readable book on its subject," a sentiment that many modern thinkers still hold.[6]

Two years after the book's publication, James began to receive praise and honors for it; he wrote to his colleague, Josiah Royce: "I went to Padua last week to a Galileo anniversary. It was splendidly carried out, and great fun; and they gave all of us foreigners honorary degrees. I rather like being a doctor of the University of Padua, and shall feel more at home than hitherto in the 'Merchant of Venice.'"[7] James received honors and degrees from universities in Rome, Oxford, Durham, Geneva, Edinburgh, Copenhagen, Paris, Milan, Berlin, and Moscow, and in the United States from Harvard, Princeton, and Yale; he was elected an honorary member of the National Academy of Science, the American Association for the Advancement of Science, and the British Academy. But he was temperamentally not a joiner, and he tried to limit his affiliations to organizations that genuinely reflected his interests and contributions. Although gratified by the reception of *Principles* and by its success as a textbook (it was abridged to a single volume in 1892), James moved away from psychology to philosophy after its publication. He was not comfortable being designated America's first psychologist; toward the end of his life he wrote to Dickinson S. Miller, a friend who had composed a study of James's thought: "I'm sorry you stick so much to my psychological phase, which I care little for, now, and never cared much. This epistemological and metaphysical phase seems to me more original and important" (*LWJ,* 2:331−32). It was as if he had abandoned psychology after completing the best book in the field, as Russell would abandon mathematical logic after finishing *Principia Mathematica.* But one acquainted with the facts of James's earlier life might have predicted at the time that he would turn from psychology to other interests.

James's academic career at Harvard included a number of positions. In 1872 he began as an instructor in anatomy and physiology, his first position after receiving his M.D. from Harvard in 1869 and deciding not to enter medical practice. The following year he was appointed assistant professor of physiology. Three years later he taught his first philosophy courses, and was appointed assistant professor of philosophy in 1885. In 1889 he was named a professor of psychology, and in 1897 he returned to teaching philosophy until his retirement in 1907. This variety of titles reflects James's varied interests as his pursuits developed from medicine to anatomy and physiology to psychology and finally to philosophy.

Philosophy and religion, largely because of his father's influence, had interested James before he left the family household, and if philosophy had appeared a feasible way of making a living and if someone had encouraged him to try it, he might well have done so. He was, however, aware of the opportunities and prestige of a scientific career, which his father had emphasized when James had considered painting; in 1858, at the age of sixteen, James wrote to a friend that he liked mathematics and might consider engineering as a vocation. He soon decided that engineering was not an appropriate choice, however, and in a letter to his friend Edgar Van Winkle, he made what can be called his first philosophical statement, a reflection on possible careers. The letter reveals that James was a precocious lad already adept at philosophizing about life and examining the propositions which might justify an eventual lifestyle; it displays a flair for ideas and words that he had gained from an intellectual family whose internal conversations and lively debates have been emphasized by Jamesian biographers. Seriousness of purpose and fluency of thought and expression are clear in this excerpt:

> I want now to tell you plainly what I think. . . . The choice of profession torments everyone who begins life, but there is really no reason why it should; that is, there is no reason why it should if society was decently ordered. Everyone, I think, should do in society what he would do if left to himself, and I think I can prove it to you conclusively.
>
> In the first place, what ought to be everyone's object in life? To be as much use as possible. . . . But what is use? Analyse any useful invention, or the life of any useful man, and you will see that its or his use consists in some *pleasure,* mental or bodily, conferred upon humanity. . . .
>
> Suppose that food and clothing and shelter were *assured* to everyone. What

men would then be held in honour? Not only the constructors of bridges and tunnels, the inventors of steam engines and spinning jennies, but all those who afforded some pleasure to others, whether material or spiritual, and in such a state of society (which will soon come, I hope) every man would follow out his own tastes, and excel as much as possible in the particular line for which he was created. It is then the duty of everyone to do as much good as possible. . . .

But now let us see what our duty is. I have already said, I know not how many times, that it's *use*. Which of us would wish to go through life without leaving a trace behind to mark his passage. . . . Suppose we do nothing and die; we have swindled society. Nature, in giving us birth, had saddled us with a debt which we must pay off some time or other. I saw today at school a sentence of Rousseau which I agree with perfectly. "What are 10, 20, 30 years for an immortal being? Pleasure and pain both pass like shadows. Life is gone in an instant. In itself it is nothing. Its value depends upon the use to which you put it. The good which you have done is lasting and that alone,—and life is valuable only by that good!" It is hard to translate it into English, but that is the sense. By *good* I do not mean mere *force*, muscle, and sinew. . . . For what was our mind given us if not that we should employ it? We should, then, each in his own particular way, find out something new, something which without us could not be. . . .

Poets may be laughed at for being useless, impractical people. But suppose the author of the "Psalm of Life" had attempted to invent steam engines (for which I suppose he has no genius) in the hope of being useful, how much time would he have wasted and how much would we have lost! . . . Astronomy and natural history are of little *practical* use, and as such are not all important at the present day, but they afford inexpressible pleasure to those who are interested in them and therefore are useful. And I think that a man who was urged toward them by his tastes and who, wishing to be more useful, should make discoveries of little importance in practical branches would do very wrong.

I think now you will agree with me that everyone has his own particular use, and that he would be a traitor were he to abandon it for something else for which he had little taste. . . .

If I followed my taste and did what was most agreeable to me, I'll tell you what I would do. I would get a microscope and go out into the country, into the dear old woods and fields and ponds. There I would try to make as many discoveries as possible,—and I'll be kicked if I would not be more useful than if I'd laid out railroads by rules which others had made and which I have learned from them. If in the former case I do not vindicate my existence better than in the latter, then I'm no man. I'll tell you what I think I'll do. I'll be a farmer and do as much good in the natural history line as I can. . . .

In my first letters there was a great display of miserable prejudice against the French. I am heartily ashamed of it. I like the French more and more every day. Dear Ed, never give way to prejudice. Human nature is the same all over the world. Everywhere it has faults and everywhere it is good at heart.[8]

Despite this early defense of the poetic and philosophical way of life, James turned three years later to the study of chemistry at the Lawrence Scientific School at Harvard and after that to the pursuit of a Harvard M.D. which he received, after interruptions, in 1869. He seems to have had little enthusiasm for these programs and to have followed them out of a hope that by remaining at Harvard and living at home, he would eventually find a vocational opportunity in the vicinity, perhaps at Agassiz's museum. His studies for the medical degree were scarcely prompted by a desire to practice. Upon deciding in 1864 to study medicine, he wrote: "My first impressions are that there is much humbug therein, and that, with the exception of surgery, in which something positive is sometimes accomplished, a doctor does more by the moral effect of his presence on the patient and family, than by anything else. He also extracts money from them."[9] James described the informality and tentativeness of his quest for a medical degree in an interview years later. There were nine candidates at his degree examination, he remembered, facing as many professors; each professor sat at a small table before which was a vacant chair.

"We all sat down, and the examination began," said Professor James in telling the story. "Each professor questioned a student for ten minutes, then we all moved on to the next table, like a progressive euchre, you know. The whole examination was ended in an hour and a half. It happened that at my first table was a professor who had known my family for some time. We lived near each other in Cambridge. He asked me one question, something about the nerves at the base of the brain. I did what I could with it. 'Oh, well,' he said, 'That's all right; if you can answer that, you can answer anything. Now tell me, how's the folks?' and that," concluded Professor James, "was the extent of my doctor's examination."[10]

James's hunch that studying science at Harvard might lead to employment close to home was realized three years after Charles William Eliot, his former chemistry professor, was appointed Harvard's president in 1869. In 1872 Eliot invited James to be an instructor in anatomy and physiology.[11] Teaching in these fields was an excellent preparation for his movement into psychology and the writing of *Principles,* because the new experimental psychology was linked with physiology to such a degree that it was called physiological psychology. The position in anatomy and physiology enabled him to found a laboratory in physiological psychology, and Hugo Münsterberg was eventually hired to run the lab, freeing James to pursue philosophy. James published short reviews and notices before he was hired at Harvard; by 1874 he had written more than twenty such articles, and he produced as many more over the next two years. The subjects of these reviews ranged from books on science and the philosophy of science to a novel by Hermann Grimm and a book on the relevance to art and industry of a theory of color. They appeared mainly in *Nation, Atlantic Monthly,* and *North American Review.* During this period James was not writing technical treatises based on his instruction in physiology; rather, he was gearing up for the important philosophical and psychological essays he would begin in 1878. Although he taught physiology, his earliest publications indicate that his deeper interests lay elsewhere.

Nevertheless, it would be a mistake to ignore what James achieved while teaching in the 1870s. His positions in anatomy and physiology lent authority to his writings on physiological psychology and helped him to separate in his own mind biological, psychological, and philosophical issues. He was more than just a writer about psychology; he was a leading analyst in a discipline that was becoming increasingly linked with physiology. In 1875 he founded the world's first psychological laboratory, before those created by Wilhelm Wundt in Leipzig in 1879 and by G. Stanley Hall at Johns Hopkins in 1881.[12] James's and Münsterberg's experimental work laid the groundwork for a more ambitious laboratory and eventually a separate department of psychology, but it was itself of little scientific consequence. They investigated the vestibular sensitivity of frogs, and James and his students speculated as to whether the reflex actions of decapitated frogs were in any way purposeful, and whether the responses of the stump of a frog's amputated foot when acid was applied indicated that its spinal cord was stimulated by the acid. James's students performed many dissections, including the examination of sheeps' brains. One psychological apparatus used by James in the mid-1870s was an elementary device for measuring the speed of nerve force, according to Robert S. Harper.[13] Using electrical apparatus, students performed reaction-time experiments, such as the one described by Ralph Waldo Black:

> We would press a key the instant we saw a spark. I noticed my reactions seemed to take less time than the others and asked how we knew whether we were in reality responding to the spark or to the metallic sound of the contact. He stopped experimenting and I never knew whether I had raised a doubt in his mind or exposed the procedure, that is whether he was testing to see which we would respond to. He had some staples with a pin and a screw in each the width of the staple apart and we all stripped to the waist or rolled up our pant legs and he would try them on the skin to see if we felt the contact as one or two. He said I had the most insensible calves he ever saw and I thought perhaps they needed washing.[14]

James conducted experiments in hypnosis, automatic writing, and the sense of dizziness in deaf-mutes; in 1881–82 he reported that a significant number of deaf-mutes did not feel dizzy when rotated, supporting his hypothesis that the semicircular canals are involved in the feeling of movement rather than in hearing. But James did not feel suited to experimental work, and he questioned the importance of much of the work conducted in his own and in Wundt's laboratories. By 1878, when he stopped teaching physiology, he had already published his first—and some of his most important—essays in philosophy.[15] This was the first step toward his lobbying at Harvard for a psychological laboratory with a full-time director. He spearheaded the drive to raise the few thousand dollars needed to build the lab, which was completed in 1891, and a year later Hugo Münsterberg was hired as its director. Among those contributing to the fundraising campaign was Henry Adams, who donated two hundred dollars.

During his first two years of liberation from teaching physiology, James published articles that would form part of *Principles*. He wrote on features of the human intellect, the shortcomings of the theory that humans are mere automata, and the merits of his own nativistic theory of space-perception. At the same time, he was writing philosophical essays, confronting at the beginning of his career the question, What is Philosophy? He had declared in 1875 that philosophy could not boast of any stable achievements and that its value must lie somewhere other than in the solution of problems on the model of science. "The labors of philosophers have, however, been confined to deepening enormously the philosophic *consciousness*, and revealing more and more minutely and fully the import of metaphysical problems."[16] He meant that metaphysical issues are not objectively resolvable but are instead challenges to our emotional and moral character; if we apprehend their seriousness, they will compel us to take a stand by arousing our emotional and moral sentiments. No one can be a deep philosopher and be dispassionate, James thought; he wrote in an obituary notice for his friend Chauncey Wright: "The lack of emotional bias which left [Wright] contented with the mere principle of parsimony as a criterion of universal truth was really due to a defect in the active or impulsive part of his mental nature."[17] James did not deny that Wright was a genuine philosopher or that his exclusion of emotional preferences in seeking a consistency and unity of thought was an important challenge to the Jamesian concept of philosophy. But James held that a dispassionate approach such as Wright's lacked the depth of the great philosophies, the worldviews into which the very souls, temperaments, or moral and emotional propensities of the authors have been projected. As he expressed it in another 1875 essay, "What is this but saying that our opinions about the nature of things belong to our moral life?"[18]

This conception of philosophy, as a subjective opinion about the universe in which the hard facts of science and common sense are interpreted at a higher level where moral and emotional sentiments come into play, was fully conceived by James at the outset of his career as philosopher and psychologist. His writings in both fields take that conception as a starting point. The question of why individuals philosophize belongs to both philosophy and psychology, James thought, since both the philosopher's testimony and the psychologist's analysis are required to answer it. The philosopher says that his motive is the desire to attain as rational a conception of the world as possible, but he leaves the meaning of *rational* undetermined. He may say that what is rational is consistent and agrees with known facts, but a fuller definition must be provided by the psychologist. James identified the sentiment of rationality, or the experience of finding something to be rational, as a "feeling of the sufficiency of the present moment, of its absoluteness—this absence of all need to explain it, account for it or justify it. . . . As soon as we are enabled from any cause whatever to think of a thing with perfect fluency, that thing seems to us rational."[19]

When something strikes us as irrational, we feel blocked or interrupted; if something strikes us as rational, we feel a fluency of thought throughout our experience.

In our philosophizing we look for beliefs that strike us as rational because they afford us relief, fluency, or a satisfaction of the heart. Philosophers search for beliefs that are intellectually satisfying because they are emotionally so; James argued that the philosopher's emotional biases justifiably influence his choice of beliefs. James fortified this conviction with a Socratic insistence upon human ignorance in metaphysical, moral, and religious questions. The ultimate nature of philosophical concepts is not accessible to science, and therefore the only beliefs that we can acquire about such concepts will be uncertain and the result of our emotional biases. James thus dismissed theories—whether traditionally materialistic or more recently based, for example, on Darwinian ideas—which hold that we are entitled to believe only what is objectively or scientifically demonstrable. Legitimate beliefs about the nature of things need not be pressed upon us by observation and experience. To the contrary, James argued, "The knower is not simply a mirror . . . passively reflecting an order that he comes upon and finds simply existing. The knower is an actor. . . . He registers the truth which he helps to create. Mental interests . . . help to *make* the truth which they declare. In other words, there belongs to mind, from its birth upward, a spontaneity, a vote."[20] Subjectivity figures not only in the search for truth and in its definition but also in its creation.

These convictions led to such famous discussions as "The Dilemma of Determinism," "The Will to Believe," and finally "Philosophical Conceptions and Practical Results," in which James announced the philosophy of pragmatism. His beliefs also affected the way in which he treated psychology in *Principles* and elsewhere, because they caused him to deny that psychology can ever provide definitive answers. What is the nature of cognition? What is consciousness? Is emotion wholly physiological? Where do acts of will originate, and are they free? Does all knowledge originate from sense-experience? These questions begin in psychology but are delivered unanswered to philosophy, but philosophers cannot solve them either. All that philosophers can do—though we should not underestimate the subjective significance of the process—is to articulate the wider import of the problems and to blend intellectual and emotional considerations in an educated and sensitive position. The scientific inquiry into psychological issues spills over into the subjectivity of philosophy, but even at the outset psychology is tinged with subjectivity, for its investigations rely on introspection. James argued forcefully that introspection is indispensable for physiological psychology:

> Now, how are ideas [about brain function] to be understood or talked about without what introspection tells us of their formation from coalesced residua of motor and sensory feelings? In a word, brain physiologists would be still groping in Cimmerian darkness without the torch [of introspection] which psychology proper puts into their hands. The entire recent growth of their science may, in fact, be said to be a mere hypothetical schematization in material terms of the

laws which introspection long ago laid bare. . . . But whereas we directly see their [mental] process of combination in the mind, we only guess in the brain what it *may* be from fancied analogies with the mental phenomena. . . . Dr. Maudsley's bad temper about introspection is therefore not simply wrong, but monstrous. . . . His cerebral physiology is to a great extent a pure *a priori* attempt to make a diagram, as it were, out of fibres and cells, of phenomena whose existence is known to him only by subjective observation. . . . A bad psychology, too, will suggest an impossible physiology.[21]

As he crystallized his psychology throughout the 1880s, James played back and forth between introspective and physiological reports (whether factual or speculative). He sometimes based a conjecture about the brain's system on the stream of consciousness as it appeared to introspection, and at other times he hypothesized about features of the stream of consciousness that might have been overlooked through faulty introspection; he believed that apparently related cerebral events must possess analogous features. For example, if a mental sequence seems upon introspection to wax and wane, there may be an analogous process in the brain which is also a causal condition of the introspected experience. James emphasized the fallibility of introspection and almost never relied upon it alone to establish an important proposition, but he never questioned its indispensability. Accordingly, he defended the subjective method—the use of introspection in psychology and of one's preferences in philosophy—before he moved into the mature phase of his career. In trying to define philosophy and psychology, he was confident that both disciplines included an inescapable subjective element. Most of his later theorizing would revolve around that conviction.

During the 1890s James lectured and traveled as the author of *Principles*. After numerous family trips to Europe as a boy, he was multilingual and at home in other cultures; his continued visits to foreign countries in adulthood helped him to become recognized quickly by European intellectuals. At home and abroad he was known as the father of the James-Lange theory of emotion and as the author of many widely discussed theories. He responded in lectures and journals to criticisms of his nativistic conception of space and to questions about the mind-body dualism he had provisionally adopted in *Principles*. He was also in demand as the philosopher who had defended free will in "The Dilemma of Determinism," mounted a case for religious faith in "The Will to Believe" and "Human Immortality," taken philosophy to the public with lectures and essays such as "The Importance of Individuals" and "Is Life Worth Living?" and launched pluralistic pragmatism in "Philosophical Conceptions and Practical Results." A movement grew out of this lecture and James's successive writings on pragmatism. Defending pragmatism and attacking nineteenth-century absolute or monistic idealism was a major activity for James during the last twenty years of his life.

James's other interests included abnormal psychology, psychical research, and the mind-cure movements that arose as alternatives to orthodox medicine. He repeatedly confessed consternation that most scientists ignored the data upon which claims in these areas were made, and he was pleased to see the beginnings of a scientific abnormal psychology in the work of Pierre Janet, Alfred Binet, Josef Breuer, and Sigmund Freud. He was impressed by Janet's work on multiple personalities and discussed it in *Principles*, for it stressed the unconscious as a new area of research with many potential applications. Having suffered all his life from psychosomatic difficulties including eye strain, insomnia, backaches, and deep depressions, James hoped that reserves of energy might be discovered and tapped to relieve such miseries. There was evidence from experiments with hypnotism and mental suggestion that both mental and physical symptoms could sometimes be eliminated through mental techniques; such relief might result, he thought, if the unconscious were utilized in ways not then understood. He welcomed what were called at the time mind-cure and new thought advocates. Like Freud, who developed psychoanalysis because he saw that orthodox medicine had failed to find cures for hysterical illnesses, James encouraged every variety of research in abnormal psychology, hoping that self-help practices might thereby be shown to be effective as a cure for chronic melancholy, for example. James often attracted crowds at his lectures because he inspired optimism in his listeners, telling them that they had untapped reserves of energy which, if discovered, might help them to live more vigorously and enthusiastically.[22]

For James, research into telepathy, clairvoyance, mediumship, and even demonic possession was simply an extension of abnormal psychology. Such research might approach the unconscious through different types of experiments, revealing powers and properties that might otherwise go undetected. The British Society for Psychical Research was founded in 1882, and James became a member along with Edmund Gurney, Frederic W. H. Myers, and Henry Sidgwick. The interest in psychical research in this country owes much to James, who founded the American Society in 1884. Psychical research was without doubt one of his most controversial interests. He was already suspect in some circles because of his religious and metaphysical speculations and his preoccupations with abnormal psychology and with self-help programs that might involve experimenting with drugs, and his interest in psychical phenomena invited further criticism. He was himself dubious about the time and effort he had given to this endeavor, concluding in 1909, after twenty-five years of dedication to it, "I find myself believing that there is 'something in' these never ending reports of psychical phenomena, although I haven't yet the least positive notion of the something."[23] Despite the seeming impossibility of establishing definite hypotheses based on so-called experimental data, he continued to believe that such phenomena as occur in automatic writing and in medium-sittings support the idea that a person's subconscious can be directly related to the mental activities and forces of others.

Pursuing psychical research was one of James's many activities during the 1890s. When he was not beset with illness, he was teaching, traveling, lecturing, and publishing numerous articles and reviews. He spent time revising *Principles* for the abridged, one-volume edition that appeared in 1892, and he rethought some of the ideas in *Principles,* notably his claim that a state of consciousness is unique and indivisible. In fact, he was on his way to reformulating the concept of consciousness itself. His first major new book published in the 1890s was *The Will to Believe, and Other Essays in Popular Philosophy* (1897), a miscellaneous collection of earlier essays. Two years later he completed *Talks to Teachers on Psychology; and to Students on Some of Life's Ideals* (1899), a book that has not yet gone out of print. The first part of the book was based on lectures to teachers on the application of psychology to pedagogy, much of it a direct adaptation of *Principles* for the use of the classroom teacher; the second part was originally lectures to college students, especially women, and a good part was in the self-help vein.

Like James's other major books, *Talks* was successful in the United States and abroad, and it was translated into a variety of languages, including Russian. It pioneered an empirical and experimental approach to education and showed that a knowledge of the new psychology could be used by teachers at all stages of education, especially the primary grades. Its significance was characterized thus by Bird T. Baldwin:

> These *Talks,* together with his *Principles,* were the first books to make serious inroads on the scholastic faculty psychology, to establish the method of introspection on a scientific basis and to bring modern psychology into the school-room and apply it to the everyday problems of the aim of education, the pedagogical significance of instinct, play, habit, motor responses and suggestion, methods of arousing interest and developing voluntary attention, the necessity of routine, the need of effort, the transfer of learning, the value of discipline, methods of punishment, the meaning of marks, the evils of cramming, the methods of the recitation and methods of teaching, the limitations of object-teaching, the value of school-room observation, individual differences, the basis of moral training and the relation between teachers and pupils.[24]

The most distinctive feature of *Talks* is its application of physiological psychology to pedagogy. It contains a host of suggestions for engaging the attention and interest of the student, all of which are based on the idea that the student must be regarded to a considerable extent as a biological mechanism whose behavior the teacher must modify. The theoretical discussions in *Principles* about the biology of habit, instinct, memory, reasoning, and discrimination thus become relevant to the teacher's preparation. E. L. Thorndike, a professor at Columbia Teachers College who did as much as anyone to apply Jamesian psychology to education, wrote that *Talks* was a highly influential presentation of what "has since become known as Situation-Response psychology. I think it prepared the way for the factual studies of intelligence, learning and the like which have been so important in educational psychology in the last twenty-five years. The reasonable and modest behaviorism which James preached was very healthy, in my opinion, for psychology and for educational science."[25]

Thorndike's description of James's pedagogical behaviorism as modest is judicious, for James believed that there are definite limits to the biological and behavioral approach to education. In all the psychological and physiological discussion in *Talks,* a prominent theme is that the child is an autonomous being whom the teacher must respect profoundly. Cautioning against the mechanical uses of psychology for instruction, James emphasized the need for creative, flexible techniques of teaching, which he thought would probably be learned only through experience. He asserted that teachers must regard their pupils as little pieces of subtle machinery, yet "if in addition, you can also see him *sub specie boni,* and love him as well, you will be in the best possible position for becoming perfect teachers."[26] As an educator, James always stressed the worth of the individual and the justice of democratic principles.

James's achievements went far beyond the fields of psychology and philosophy; because of his moral, social, and political beliefs and activities, his life and thought have become an essential part of American intellectual history. His opposition to the imperialism he saw behind the Spanish-American and other wars, his concern for better care of the insane, his worry that minority rights were being trampled by society, his socialistic declarations in favor of a more equitable distribution of wealth, his attempts to protect experimental animals without endorsing antivivisectionist laws, his efforts to protect practitioners of alternative forms of medicine from the threat of restrictive statutes, and his fervent hope that American democracy and its respect for individuality would become a world model—all of this has made him a permanent figure in American history. Those characteristics in James that seem distinctly American were also present in his role as educator.

Like John Dewey, James valued education which keeps in touch with off-campus realities. He once declared that American higher education should be widely shared and should yield learned men of utmost efficiency. "Listlessness, apathy, dawdling, sauntering, the smoking of cigarettes and living on small sarcasms, the 'Harvard indifference,' in short, of which outsiders have so frequently complained, are the direct fruit of keeping these men too long from contact with the world of affairs to which they rightfully belong."[27] He supported a recommendation to reduce the course requirements for a Harvard degree so that students could join the real world more quickly. College should not be a clubhouse, he thought; book learning is not a solution to society's problems, and something more than success ought to be education's goal. He characterized Harvard as a place where "special students, scientific students, graduate students, poor students of the College, who make their living as they go" but who "seldom or never darken the doors of the Pudding or the Porcellian" attend only in the background, and only because "they have heard of [Harvard's] persistently atomistic constitution, of her tolerance of exceptionality and eccentricity, of her devotion to the principles of individual vocation and choice. . . . The true Harvard is the invisible Harvard in the souls of her more truth-seeking and independent and often very solitary sons."[28]

Curiously, James did not himself enjoy teaching. He often complained about preparing courses or the frustration of conveying his ideas to half-interested students, and he assessed his own teaching ability thus: "When I look back at my thirty-five years of teaching [at Harvard], I sometimes shudder at the thought of the bad instruction I have given."[29] William Neilson, a distinguished professor of English and once James's student, disagreed; although James may have seemed uninterested in delivering polished lectures—he sometimes left sentences unfinished, groped for the right word, or casually digressed from the main material—Neilson recalled that he and his fellow students nevertheless felt a part of something historically significant, of contemporary thought being developed before them. He commented also on the vivid and "spontaneous humanity" of James's presence.[30] Many anecdotes record students' responses to that humanity, conveyed through informality, modesty, and directness, and to James's references to an encyclopedic range of topics and readings. Dickinson S. Miller, a student of James's, testified: "His own reading was immense and systematic. No one has ever done justice to it, partly because he spoke with unaffected modesty of that side of his equipment."[31]

James offered his philosophy students the opportunity to participate in the process of philosophizing, to learn the Socratic respect for the process as much as the product. "What doctrines students take from their teachers are of little consequence provided they catch from them the living, philosophic attitude of mind, the independent, personal look at all the data of life, and the eagerness to harmonize them."[32] James conveyed a unique sense of the life in the ideas that occupied him. Sincerity, warmth, compassion, knowledge, and integrity colored his ideas and their expressions. One student who was grateful for those qualities was W. E. B. DuBois, who enrolled at Harvard in 1888. DuBois later wrote that he had attended Harvard out of a desire to probe for truth. "Eventually it landed me squarely in the arms of William James of Harvard, for which God be praised. . . . I was repeatedly a guest in the house of William James; he was my friend and guide to clear thinking."[33] For Theodore Roosevelt, Gertrude Stein, Walter Lippmann, Morris Cohen, E. L. Thorndike, E. B. Holt, and Ralph Barton Perry, the influence of James's personality and thought endured long beyond their student days, though Roosevelt was not favorably impressed. In a letter of 24 August 1917 to Henry James III, Dickinson Miller reported that James said to a colleague while on his way to one of the last lectures he gave at Harvard, "I have lectured so-and-so many years and yet here I am in trepidation on the way to my class." James may often have dreaded facing a classroom of students and believed that he was not a good teacher, but his students' accounts do not support that verdict. The undergraduates in his introductory class gave him a memorial cup at his final class, and his graduate students presented him with a silver-topped inkwell. James was as surprised as he was pleased.[34] His career of teaching physiology, psychology, and philosophy at Harvard—a career that carried a man just out of medical school to a reputation thirty-five years later as one of America's most prominent intellectuals—was one of his finest achievements.

James accomplished an astonishing amount both shortly before and after his resignation from Harvard in 1907. In this period when he attempted a philosophical synthesis of the multiple strains in his thought—psychical research, mind-cure hypotheses, the application of psychology to everyday life, pluralistic metaphysics, a pragmatic revision of the concepts of meaning and truth, a metaphysical revision of the mind-body dualism and of the concept of consciousness that had been presented in *Principles,* a reassertion of the merits of religious faith, and an appreciation of religious experience. The last subject was addressed in what has been called the most important treatise on religion by any American, *The Varieties of Religious Experience,* which was the published version of the Gifford Lectures on Natural Religion which James had delivered at the University of Edinburgh in 1902. The book is a study in human nature, specifically as it is revealed through the psychology of religious experience. Readers are entranced by the experiences and attitudes expressed by mystics and individuals of faith in the accounts quoted in James's book. *Varieties* served a further purpose in his thinking: it used recorded religious episodes as evidence that our personal experiences may be continuous with a wider experience from which we may obtain regenerative succor. The mystical occasions James studied supported his belief that experience and consciousness are not merely what ordinary psychology takes them to be.

In "Does 'Consciousness' Exist?" James set out to define experience and consciousness; this essay and a series on the same theme were published posthumously as *Essays in Radical Empiricism.* The main goal of James's metaphysics of radical empiricism was to eliminate mind-body dualism and the accompanying notion that consciousness is some sort of entity. He proposed to do this by employing pure experience as a primitive concept in terms of which the ideas of both mind and body could be reduced or redefined. *Essays in Radical Empiricism* is among the Jamesian writings still crucial to philosophers of many schools, who often pick up on special issues in the essays without embracing the whole Jamesian metaphysics. But James saw the notion of pure experience—if combined with the metaphysical claim that reality is not monistic but pluralistic experience(s) and with the pragmatic or epistemological claim that such concepts as knowledge, meaning, and truth must be understood as essentially concerned with the relations between experiences—as the key idea around which a truly contemporary philosophy could be constructed.

James was clearly working toward that end in *Pragmatism,* which came out of lectures at the Lowell Institute and at Columbia. In 1909 he published *The Meaning of Truth,* a sequel to *Pragmatism* and a reply to its critics. It is clear from these two works that pragmatism was not just a philosophical revision of traditional theories about the nature of truth, meaning, and knowledge; in James's hands it was connected with the defenses of radical empiricism, metaphysical pluralism, and religion. This connection is even clearer in *A Pluralistic Universe,* the published version of the Hibbert Lectures that James had delivered at Oxford. To be sure, James was highly productive in the last eight years of his life, and his final output has proved to be quite influential. The 1870s were a period of launching, the 1880s were devoted largely to preparing *Principles,* the 1890s were comparatively slight in production, but between 1902 and James's death in 1910, his creativity was phenomenal.

James also wrote many reviews and articles in these years, such as "The Moral

Equivalent of War'' and ''A Suggestion About Mysticism,'' which helped to form posthumous collections like *Memories and Studies* and *Collected Essays and Reviews*, volumes which include writings that span his entire career. Another important posthumous book is *Some Problems of Philosophy*. James envisaged this book as a technical, systematic, nonpopular treatment of essentially metaphysical issues; it might also serve as an introductory philosophy text. Although it is not certain that James would have approved of the book in the form it was given by Horace M. Kallen and Henry James III, it contains valuable analyses of such concepts as infinity and continuity, which have continued to interest philosophers of science as well as Jamesian scholars.

The variety of James's contributions helps us to understand why his influence has been so broad. Psychologists of virtually all schools have testified to that influence. Philosophers who are phenomenologists, analysts, existentialists, pragmatists, or positivists have found points of departure in James's work, as have scientists such as Niels Bohr and Wilder Penfield. Penfield, one of the twentieth century's leading researchers on the human brain, has written: ''As an undergraduate, majoring in philosophy at Princeton, I was much impressed by my reading of William James's *The Principles of Psychology*. That was, I suppose, the beginning of my curiosity about the brain and the mind of man.''[35] Historians, sociologists, political scientists— indeed, representatives of almost every discipline—have paid their respects to the Harvard philosopher. Not every reference to James is positive, nor did those who knew him always praise him or his thought. George Santayana, in declining an invitation to write a piece about James, observed: ''It is easier for me to take James seriously and sympathetically when I look at him as a historic figure, as a human apparition. If you force me to enter into his abstract doctrine, there is too much in it that seems to me blind and incoherent, in spite of profound justifications in many points underlying it, and what I could write on such a theme would either be too hostile and self-assertive, or else irrelevant.''[36]

Some critics miss a polished system in James's thought and lament his tendency to build indeterminately from bits and pieces. Alfred North Whitehead thought that James systematized more than his critics granted but that he preferred to ''assemble'' his philosophy in order not to sacrifice experience for the sake of a system. Whitehead wrote: ''In Western literature there are four great thinkers, whose services to civilized thought rest largely upon their achievements in philosophical assemblage; though each of them made important contributions to the structure of philosophic system. These men are Plato, Aristotle, Leibniz, and William James.''[37]

FAMILY

The question of influence in James's thought is complex, in part because he cited extensively an extraordinary range of literature; his reader naturally compares James's views with all of those he cited. Since he intentionally developed his own philosophy and psychology against a historical and contemporary backdrop, most of the problems he considered were inherited from others. Establishing definite influences upon James's conclusions is also complex because he went out of his way to credit other thinkers with the same views at every opportunity.

James's wife, Alice, and his son Henry James III believed he had been excessive in citing influences. For example, they felt that Charles S. Peirce was unappreciative of what James had done for him personally and professionally, and that James's attribution of influence to Peirce was superfluous and in fact inaccurate, simply another instance of James's naive generosity.[38] Peirce certainly supplied James with issues to ponder and ways to ponder them, but the major influences upon James were the French philosopher Charles Renouvier and William's father, Henry James, Sr.

It is often easier to espy influence than to explain its precise nature. Whether a son imitates his father or rebels against him, his behavior can be considered a reaction to the father's presence; thus, nothing in a son's behavior is parentally *un*influenced—a consequence so sweeping that any particular claim about a father's influence is diluted. There is no point in finding influences everywhere, and furthermore, it is exceedingly difficult to sort out the influences of family members; I therefore prefer to err on the side of caution in viewing James in the context of his family. Given the amount of attention that has been devoted to the Jameses, however, I want to describe the impressions I have gained from my own efforts to understand the family.

Henry James, Sr., was a colorful personality, a genuine character. All his life he was a man of leisure, having inherited an annual income of ten thousand dollars from his father, an earlier William James, who had immigrated from Ireland about 1790 and by the time of his death in 1832 had amassed three million dollars from business interests in upstate New York, including the opening of the Erie Canal. The elder William James was a devout, strong-willed Presbyterian and fathered Henry, Sr., in his third marriage. Although the relationship between father and son had tender moments, it was usually a stormy one; Henry, Sr., did not conform to his father's religious rigidities and ultimately had to contest William's will to insure his own share of the inheritance. At the age of thirteen he had a leg amputated after an accident. He was vigorously verbal, self-assured in his own religiosity, accustomed to considerable affluence, and devoted above all to family and God.

Long before William and Henry, Jr., became famous, Henry James, Sr., had established his own identity as a man of leisure who penetrated the literary and theological circles of America and England. Not long after William was born in 1842, he was shown by his doting father to Ralph Waldo Emerson, who was visiting the impressive James townhouse near Washington Square. Other notable visitors were Henry David Thoreau, Amos Bronson Alcott, Albert Brisbane, Horace Greeley, and William Cullen Bryant; when Henry, Sr., took his family to England, he introduced them to Thomas Carlyle, Alfred Lord Tennyson, and John Stuart Mill. He made a noticeable impression upon such luminaries not only because he was a man of means whose aim in traveling was a cultural exchange for himself and, in subsequent trips, a superior education for his children, but also because he spoke and wrote with an arresting style that befitted the iconoclastic American freethinker that he was. His personal way with language would also deeply impress his own children; for example, he once wrote:

> I will not attempt to state the year in which I was born, because it is not a fact embraced in my own knowledge, but content myself with saying instead, that the earliest event of my biographic consciousness is that of my having been carried out into the streets one night, in the arms of my negro nurse, to witness a grand illumination in honor of the treaty of peace then just signed with Great Britain. From this circumstance I infer of course that I was born before the year 1815, but it gives me no warrant to say just how long before. The net fact is that my historic consciousness, or my earliest self-recognition, dates from this municipal illumination in honor of peace. So far, however, as my share in that spectacle is concerned, I am free to say it was a failure. That is, the only impression left by the illumination upon my imagination was the contrast of the awful dark of the sky with the feeble glitter of the streets; as if the animus of the display had been, not to eclipse the darkness, but to make it visible. You, of course, may put what interpretation you choose upon the incident, but it seems to me rather emblematic of the intellect, that its earliest sensible formulations should thus be laid in "a horror of great darkness."[39]

Language was not simply used by Henry James, Sr.; it was wielded, and sometimes with a cutting edge as, for example, when he described Emerson as "an unsexed woman" because of his seeming innocence of evil.[40] Not only did the father's impulse to create unique formulations influence the son, but William also developed his father's penchant for identifying the shortcomings of those whom he most admired. Correspondence between William and his wife, Alice, reveals that his respect for his associates could be mingled with sharp criticism, sometimes directed less at their ideas than at their attitudes and personalities. In a letter of 31 January 1899 to Miller, for example, James characterized his colleague Josiah Royce thus: "He is the Rubens of philosophy. Richness, abundance, boldness, color, but a sharp contour never, and never any *perfection*. But isn't fertility better than perfection?" (*LWJ*, 2:86). James was not prone to criticizing others; to the contrary, he was usually silent if a good word could not be found. But like his father, he felt the need to balance exuberant praise with emphasis on some flaw. William and his father never overlooked the fact that no one deserves praise alone.

Everything in the demeanor of Henry James, Sr., emphasized his individuality. He felt rebellious tensions with his own father, and while he came to embrace religion as his father had originally desired, he did so on his own terms. Finding institutions stifling, he sought religious inspiration outside the mainstream, discovering it in two eighteenth-century figures, the Scottish theologian Robert Sandeman and the Swedish mystic Emanuel Swedenborg. He refashioned their ideas as he deemed necessary, so the religion that eventually satisfied him was largely of his own making.[41] The same is true of the religion of William James. As one of America's most eloquent spokesmen for the sanctity of individuality, he could not plod in predecessors' footsteps about religion or anything else—a trait he probably learned from his father.

As Jamesian biographers have emphasized, Henry James, Sr., was the patriarch of a tightly knit family, dependent upon one another for love and security. Leading his wife and five children—William, Henry, Jr., Wilkinson, Robertson, and Alice— to and from Europe, so that the children went from school to school, he seemed to have only a vaguely spiritual mission in his life. In proclaiming weightily about the nature of God and the universe, he treated his family as a captive audience. Because their father had no vocational identity, the children puzzled over his jovial statement that he was a philosopher or a seeker of truth; indeed, Garth Wilkinson (Wilky) once expressed envy of a playmate whose father had an identifiable job—as a stevedore.[42] Mary Walsh James was an equally devout, traditional mother who echoed her husband's spiritual words; there was probably an intense moral atmosphere in the James household. This mood was relieved by humor, banter, and worldly talk, for Henry James, Sr., encouraged his children to cultivate a variety of intellectual and cultural interests. Nevertheless, in his lonely role as a spiritual seeker, he depended upon the responses of his family, and he thus may have engendered an anxious and pensive environment. One Jamesian biographer has written: "The conflictful personality of James's father led the elder James to turn his family into an outpatient clinic for the overindulgence of papa."[43] The irresistibility of this viewpoint has given much of today's commentary on the Jameses a decided psychoanalytic flavor. We can never know whether this emphasis is justified, but the claim that the family was an unusually self-contained unit which interacted in the shadow of the father's spectacular words is supported by William's description of his brother, Henry, Jr.: "He's really, I won't say a Yankee, but a native of the James family, and has no other country."[44]

Henry James, Sr., was devoted to William and had high expectations for him, and the son responded affectionately and dutifully, if sometimes casually or carelessly. The father's influence is clear in the fact that William did not demonstrate emotional independence until his marriage in 1878, when he was thirty-six. In fact, his father first met Alice Howe Gibbens and promptly predicted that William would marry her. Though it took William two years to do so, there is no denying the canniness of his father's prediction. In time, that canniness was simply the manifestation of a character shared by father and son, for the parallels between their lives are striking. Both men married dutiful, strong wives and had four sons and a daughter. Both were restless, neurotic, and susceptible to depression, and both coped with these problems through moralizing, mystical speculation, humor, and a vague sense that there was a religious justification for all their self-exertions. As adults, both suffered from an emotional crisis (described by Henry, Sr., in Swedenborgian terminology as a *vastation,* today sometimes called an identity crisis) over their own worth. They were uncomfortable with institutions, preferring to be iconoclasts, a trait reflected in their language as well as in their values and ideals. William was perhaps as uneasy about being a professor at Harvard as his father would have been, and both men combined reverence and irreverence in a unique and charming way.

Interestingly, William was not self-conscious about the amount of influence his father had exerted in his life. Some awareness of that influence is evident in William's letter of 14 December 1882 to his dying father: "All my intellectual life I derive from you; and though we have often seemed at odds in the expression thereof, I'm sure there's a harmony somewhere, and that our strivings will combine. What my debt to you is goes beyond all my power of estimating,—so early, so penetrating and so constant has been the influence" (*LWJ,* 1:219). William appreciated his filial debt, particularly in his assumption of a moral, philosophical, and religious consciousness, but he felt himself to be largely different from his father. In a letter of 15 May 1868 to his friend Oliver Wendell Holmes, Jr., he wrote: "With Harry [Henry, Jr.] and my Dad I have a perfect sympathy 'personally,' but Harry's orbit and mine coincide but part way, and Father's and mine hardly at all, except in a general feeling of philanthropy in which we both indulge."[45] In his personality and thought, he considered himself in an orbit different from his father's, pointing out philosophical and religious differences between them. Correspondence and anecdotes suggest that William had little conscious awareness that he resembled his father.

In fact, James was skeptical about any automatic transfer of parental traits to children; in a letter of 1898 to a friend, Wincenty Lutoslawski, he observed: "I still doubt the mental influence of the parents on the offspring" (quoted in RBP, 2:213). In "The Divided Self" chapter of *The Varieties of Religious Experience,* he referred to the question of whether a personality that contains substantial inconsistency is inherited, but he offered no opinion of his own: "Heterogeneous personality has been explained as the result of inheritance—the traits of character of incompatible and antagonistic ancestors are supposed to be preserved alongside of each other. This explanation may pass for what it is worth—it certainly needs corroboration."[46] James preferred to believe that individuals define themselves rather than inherit their personalities, for this view was an essential part of his argument for free will. Despite the parallels between their lives, he judged that he and his father were vastly different persons and thinkers. James was not given to a psychoanalytic discussion of such differences, partly because he thought they were too obvious to require probing. The two men led different lives, had different things on their minds, and exhibited normal variations in personality.

Considerable attention has been given to the hypothesis that Henry James, Sr., by encouraging his son to pursue a scientific rather than an artistic career, was a significant factor in William's first identity crisis. The question is not one of influence, but rather whether the father "managed" his son's thinking to persuade him, perhaps against his actual preferences, to choose one career over another. William, who had considerable skill as a painter and draftsman, studied for a year, in the company of John La Farge and others, with William Morris Hunt in Newport, Rhode Island.

But at the end of that year, around the time that the Civil War erupted in 1861, he abandoned art and decided to enroll at Harvard's Lawrence Scientific School. This decision resulted from considerable scheming by Henry, Sr., who vigorously counseled William on the merits of the parental position in order to convince him to choose science rather than art as a vocation. Since the reasons for William's decision must be inferred, some biographers assume that his father's influence is the most likely cause. Furthermore, because William's first neurotic symptoms, such as inexplicable eye and digestive problems and anxiety, occurred at this time, it can be argued that father-son tensions were a critical factor in making William chronically depressed.[47]

The fragmentariness of the evidence casts doubt on this theory, as does the fact that the exchanges between father and son on the advisability of art as a career were amicable.[48] Henry, Sr., probably preferred not to repeat the father-son battles of his own youth, and although he wanted to influence William toward science, he exercised good humor and caution in that effort.[49] William approached the decision with surprising practicality for an eighteen-year-old. He said he would try art and determine whether he was good enough to succeed at it. Perry theorized that he probably decided against art as a career either because he lacked the motivation to continue it or because he concluded that his talent was too modest.[50] Letters from William to his father on the subject demonstrate his concern that in viewing art and spirituality as compatible he had not overlooked some crucial objection. He wrote in 1860: "My experience amounts to very little, but it is all I have to go upon; and I am sure that far from feeling myself degraded by my intercourse with art, I continually receive from it spiritual impressions the intensest and purest I know" (quoted in RBP, 1:199). As long as his father did not argue that art was an immoral vocation, he would give it a try.

Some scholars are struck by the fact that James's psychological problems, which would become prominent in his later life, seem to have begun in 1861 when he left Hunt's studio in Newport. Although this episode may have been his first sustained attack of neurasthenic symptoms, his deep concern (if not anxiety) about a suitable vocation was manifested at least four years earlier; in the 1858 letter to Van Winkle he worried about a career, and even during the previous year he had written to Van Winkle about what he might do with his life.[51] Those letters alone give the impression of a lad not far into his teens who was unusually intense and serious about how he might earn a living. He wrote that he "detested trade" and would like to become a doctor, but feared he could not stand operations and dissections. His distaste for a business career is even more evident in a letter of 18 December 1859 to Van Winkle, in which he said that Robertson and Wilky were already "destined for commerce"— when they were only thirteen and fourteen years old.[52] One wonders why verdicts about different family members' careers were delivered so early, why being "destined for commerce" was considered disgraceful, and why William feared such a destiny for himself.

It seems evident that William, at fifteen and perhaps earlier, was nervous about the future; his nervousness was characterized by a moral and immature religious earnestness, which he presumably learned from his father. One plausible psychiatric theory is that too intense a moral and religious upbringing results in an overpowering superego. Such a burden, if placed upon an already delicate constitution, might certainly prepare a child of ten or twelve to begin a lifetime of repeated crises and depressions when he must enter the competitive world. Such a development could happen even in the absence of hostility or tension between father and son. It seems reasonable to conjecture that a pervasive moral and religious atmosphere affected James's already fragile temperament and brought on his neurasthenia just when he had to choose a career. His struggles might well have been entirely internal, centered on anxieties about his own ability, involving no negative feelings toward his father. It is nevertheless possible that the way in which Henry, Sr., cast a theological spell over his children was also partly responsible. It is equally plausible that William's psychological problems were basically physiological, for he was never free of them as an adult, and a minor conflict could trigger his somatic reactions. This explanation is supported by the fact that all of his siblings were also neurotically susceptible, and that the tale of his grandfather William's family is a "dismal record of wasted talent, early deaths, broken homes, orphaned children" (Allen, 8). Whatever James suffered from ran in the family.

There is evidence that in 1856–57, when James was fourteen, he was unhappy at the Parisian school in which he was enrolled during a family trip abroad.[52] In addition to his desire to be with friends in America, he probably felt mounting anxiety that he was not receiving an adequate vocational preparation. The family's constant travel involved many uprootings, and the schools he attended sometimes impressed him as inferior to those in America; he may well have suspected that he could not rely on his father to plan his future. Because Henry, Sr., had no occupational identity, William's apprehension about his own future may have been heightened by the sense of a career vacuum in his family. The children realized that their father could be described as ineffectual; not only did he hold no position, but his sporadic lecturing and writing were offbeat and barely noticed. He was a family man with a private religious mission, possessing means and a few influential friends, and enjoyed an accessibility to men of letters. These achievements may have seemed minimal to William, whose affection for his father may have been mixed with concern that he himself might be ineffectual because he was unprepared, either by training or by talent, to earn a living. Something about the James family, he may have thought, distanced it from reality; although his father had not suffered from this because of his inheritance, William might not be so lucky.

The relationship between William and his brother Henry, Jr., whom many consider the more prominent James, has also been a continuing subject of discussion. In 1916 Rebecca West wrote that "one of [the brothers] grew up to write fiction as though it were philosophy and the other to write philosophy as though it were fiction."[53] William was a candid critic of Henry's literary style, but Henry let such criticism wash over him without leaving a trace of influence.

The most conspicuous feature of their relationship was the affection and loyalty with which they always regarded each other. Although separated all their adult lives—Henry had moved to England—they corresponded regularly, read carefully one another's writings, and periodically visited. Theirs was a curiously intimate although geographically removed relationship; despite their vastly different temperaments and lifestyles, they remained close through a correspondence voluminous enough to delight the most indefatigable biographer. Their exchanges from youth onward were a mixture of banter and seriousness. Although they occasionally reproached one another, each was usually considerate of the other's feelings to the point of delicacy and quick to defend the other in public. Upon William's death, Henry wrote to a friend, "I sit heavily stricken and in darkness—for from far back in dimmest childhood he had been my ideal Elder Brother. . . . His extinction changes the face of life for me—besides the mere missing of his inexhaustible company and personality, originality, the whole unspeakably vivid and beautiful presence of him" (quoted in Allen, 493). Had Henry died first, William's epitaphic words would certainly have been similar.

Just as William's relationship with his father has been said to have had its darker aspects, the brothers' relationship has been analyzed in recent years—notably by Leon Edel—as having been characterized by negative features. In his five-volume biography of Henry James, a work that must be consulted by any student of William's life and career, Edel portrays the relationship as similar to that of Jacob and Esau. Despite the fact that there were "neither deliberate acts of usurpation nor overt fraternal struggles" between William and Henry, Edel argues that they were nevertheless locked in a rivalry like that of the Old Testament brothers.[54] Edel offers various bits of evidence, including the tendency of the brothers to experience headaches or other psychosomatic problems, to argue that, notwithstanding their obvious fondness for each other, their relationship was an ambivalent one.[55] After reading Edel's study of Henry, with its wealth of information and insight about the James family and the two brothers in particular, it is easy to feel convinced that William and Henry, beneath the veneer of civility in their relationship, felt envy, jealousy, and disapproval of one another.

The Jacob-Esau theme gives us a richer picture of Henry, Jr., his relationship to William and to the rest of the family, the inner side that he was determined to keep hidden, and the ways in which his inner being had origins in family dynamics and outlets in his prolific writing. Since the story of Jacob and Esau tells how one brother tried to usurp the other's family position—and since Edel's interpretation of the relationship between the brothers focuses on the theme of usurpation—it is intriguing that the word *usurp* occurs in Henry's first written statement (hitherto unpublished) about his relationship with William. Henry's words were appended to a letter of January 1858 from William to Van Winkle; after thanking Van Winkle for having communicated his condolences, Henry, who had been suffering from typhus, continued:

I assure you I felt very much obliged to you for the former expressions and had sat down to write to you when Mr. Willy—(he quite merits that name now, in more respects than one) usurped my rights and took upon himself the performance of the duty I had exclusively deemed my own, inasmuch as you were so observant in your desires to that effect. However I hope that your . . . [the rest of the letter is lost].[56]

Whether this was sheer frivolity or rather a half-suppressed revelation of Henry's Jacoblike feeling toward an Esaulike brother, I will not guess. Through Edel's eyes it would seem a clear indication of Henry's mixed attitudes toward William. According to Edel, William was defensive toward Henry because their mother preferred Henry and because Henry settled early into a literary career while William fretted over his own late vocational start. Even if we wonder whether Edel overworks the Jacob-Esau theme, we may gradually accept the conjecture of a subconscious struggle for primacy as the purported evidence accumulates. In his final volume Edel brings his story to a climax, portraying William finally allowing his "hidden animus" for Henry to show only five years before his own death—and with a vengeance!

The scenario, according to Edel, took place in 1905, during a prolonged visit to America by Henry. "Henry James's incursion into the orbit of his elder brother, after a three-decade absence, revived the long-buried struggle for power that had existed between the two, ever since their nursery days in Washington Square. The infant Henry had made his original incursion by the very act of birth and caused William to flee instinctively from the threat to his dominion" (Edel, 5:294–95). During the same period, the National Institute of Arts and Letters, to which both Henry and William had been elected upon its founding in 1898, began to establish the American Academy of Arts and Letters, which was to have an even more select membership chosen from among existing Institute members. In February of 1905, on the second ballot, Henry was elected; in May, on the fourth ballot, William was elected. On 16 May, the Academy secretary, Robert Underwood Johnson, notified William of his election and requested him to accept it. Edel comments that William "seems to have brooded over the matter for a month" before replying, but in fact William did not arrive home from Europe until 11 June (only six days before seeing the letter and responding to Johnson). Since he was occupied with a family reunion and was preparing for Henry's visit on 16 June, it is surprising that he wrote his reply as early as he did—a reply which Edel believes showed a deep "hidden animus" toward Henry.[57] The letter which William wrote to decline membership in the Academy and to resign from the Institute, and which has caused much controversy, is as follows:

Cambridge
June 17, 1905

Dear Mr. Johnson
    Just back from three months in Europe, I find your letter of May 16th

awaiting me, with the very flattering news of my election into the Academy of Arts and Letters. I own that this reply gives me terrible searchings of the heart.

On the one hand the lust of distinction and the craving to be yoked in one social body with so many illustrious names tempt me to say "yes." On the other, bidding me say "no," there is my life-long practice of not letting my name figure where there is not some definite work doing in which I am willing to bear a share; and there is my life-long professorial habit of preaching against the world and its vanities.

I am not informed that this Academy has any very definite work cut out for it of the sort in which I could bear a useful part; and it suggests *tant soit peu* the notion of an organization for the mere purpose of distinguishing certain individuals (with their own connivance) and enabling them to say to the world at large "we are in and you are out." Ought a preacher against vanities to succumb to such a lure at the very first call? Ought he not rather to "refrain, renounce, abstain," even tho it seem a sour and ungenial act? On the whole it seems to me that for a philosopher with my pretensions to austerity and righteousness, the only consistent course is to give up this particular vanity, and treat myself as unworthy of the honour, which I assuredly am. And I am the more encouraged to this course by the fact that my younger and shallower and vainer brother is already in the Academy, and that if I were there too, the other families represented might think the James influence too rank and strong.

Let me go, then, I pray you, "release me and restore me to the ground." If you knew how greatly against the grain these duty-inspired lines are written, you would not deem me unfriendly or ungenial, but only a little cracked.

By the same token, I think that I ought to resign from the Institute (in which I have played so inactive a part) which act I herewith also perform.

Believe me, dear Mr. Johnson, with longing and regret, heroically yours,

WILLIAM JAMES[58]

It is startling that the question of William's true feelings toward Henry has become so intertwined with the interpretation of this particular letter. Edel, connecting the letter with William's criticisms of Henry's novels *The Golden Bowl* and *The American Scene*, reads it not as an ironic epistle but rather as a despicable attack on Henry; he says that irony was "William James's most characteristic mark. He used it constantly to put parents and brothers in their place (as in this instance), to annihilate friends and to vanquish enemies."[59] Edel is responsible for the controversy over the letter, not only because he has interpreted it in a way unfavorable to William, but also because he was the first to come upon it and used it as the final evidence for his Jacob-Esau theory. The letter betrayed William's animus toward Henry, Edel says, insofar as it pretended to decline the Academy's invitation in the guise of resisting vanity, even though William had previously accepted many comparable honors, including original membership in the Institute. Edel continues:

A deeper and more palpable reason existed than those he gave for his refusal to

accept election to the Academy. He had in effect articulated it by his characterization of his "younger brother." The Academy had elected Henry James—
"younger, shallower, vainer"—ahead of the older brother, who considered
himself wiser, more serious-minded, and without vanity. The letter seemed to
imply once again that it was impossible for Jacob and Esau to live under the
same roof, to be in the same room—or Academy—and occupy seats side by
side. The adult William admitted in his letter that his act was "sour" and
"ungenial." In fact he added a sentence, "If you knew how greatly against the
grain these duty-inspired lines are written, you would not deem me unfriendly
or ungenial, but only a little cracked." The philosopher of pragmatism sensed he
was committing—under some strange impulse—an irrational and inconsistent
act. Still, under the guise of modesty and consistency, he bowed himself out of
the American Academy of Arts and Letters and its parent, the Institute. (Edel,
5:299)

Our judgment of Edel's diagnosis must take into account an earlier version of
this letter which I discovered recently in the Houghton Library. The earlier version,
also dated 17 June, begins with the mistaken salutation "Dear Mr. Underwood." It
was probably this error which caused William to rewrite the letter, and perhaps
Henry himself called William's attention to the mistake.[60] The differences between
the two versions are minor but nonetheless interesting. The first draft reads, "the
desire to be yoked in one social bond," the final version, "the craving to be
yoked . . . "; the former says, "the only consistent course is to give up this honour,"
the latter changes it to " . . . to give up this particular vanity"; more interesting, the
unsent letter says, "by the fact that my younger and vainer brother is already in the
Academy," and the sent version, "by the fact that my younger and shallower and
vainer brother . . . " The unsent letter does not include the phrase "dear Mr. Johnson," which gives a special emphasis to the concluding line of the final version.[61]

Comparing the sent and unsent versions suggests that James quickly and impulsively wrote his resignation, not troubling even to check his correspondent's
name. He does not seem to have given the matter much thought, beyond what it took
to grace the letter with a bit of style. Upon discovering that he had mistakenly used
Johnson's middle name, he rewrote the letter, adding a few flourishes, all in the
direction of ironic or playful exaggeration. (Here I favor Jacques Barzun's and Lionel
Trilling's interpretation of the letter rather than Edel's.) In the rewriting he played
even more upon the idea of vanity, and in referring to Henry added "shallower" as a
further exaggeration. This indicates that the unsent version was not written in a
moment of pique, a mood of envy and hostility, even if it was penned quickly and
impulsively. When he rewrote it and had the chance to review what he had said, he
deliberately amplified the play between his own (feigned) modesty and Henry's
(equally feigned) vanity. There is no indication in the rewriting that he felt uncomfortable with anything he had said about Henry or with the way his letter might be
interpreted. No sense of guilt or reservation crops up between the first and second

versions, which seems to be evidence there was none; he was involved in a bit of literary jollity, though his resignation was in earnest, and he confidently assumed that his comments would be understood as such. The existence of the unsent version clearly shows that James did not send off the letter in an angry moment. This conclusion is further confirmed by his writing again on 26 June, in response to a second urging by Johnson to accept the Academy's invitation of membership: "On the contrary, your picture of the Academy's duties and functions rather makes me feel glad that I wrote promptly enough not to be too late with my declension of the honour. I am an unassimilable barbarian, and there is an end of the matter."[62]

Those who distrust the manifest message of James's resignation, regarding the letter as a transparent indication of fraternal rivalry, lean heavily on the fact that he declined this honor while accepting others. But his correspondence is filled with remarks befitting an outsider. He derived little satisfaction from belonging to elitist groups or from receiving unearned honors. He appreciated the streak of vanity in all of us and acknowledged that all philosophers, including himself, craved praise. But he accepted honors, usually reluctantly, only if the awarding institution was especially bent upon it, if accepting the award might benefit the institution, or if the honor was directly related to his professional achievements. He usually stressed the need for some practical work to be done before his name could be attached to a cause. Even when an award might seem to require no apology whatever, he often protested as he did in a letter to F. S. C. Schiller:

> I hope you are not serious about an Oxford degree for your humble servant. If you are, pray drop the thought! I am out of the race for all such vanities. Write me a degree on parchment and send it yourself—in any case it would be but your award!—and it will be cheaper and more veracious. I *had* to take the Edinburgh one, and accepted the Durham one to please my wife. Thank you, no coronation either. I am a poor New Hampshire rustic, in bad health, and long to get back, after four summers' absence, to my own cottage and children, and never come away again for lectures or degrees or anything else. It all depends on a man's age; and after sixty, if ever, one feels as if one ought to come to some sort of equilibrium with one's native environment, and by means of a regular life get one's small message to mankind on paper.[63]

This letter was written three years before his now notorious resignation from the Institute, and it sheds light upon James's frame of mind during the final decade of his life. Despite almost constant ill health, he managed by extraordinary feats of will to make the years preceding his death unusually productive. He often complained about interruptions in his writing, sometimes expressing the fear that he might not live to complete his philosophical projects. His notebooks reveal the intensity and single-mindedness with which he sought to master the ideas that did not fit easily with his metaphysics. If a lecture, degree, or honor was connected with that intense effort, or if it was related to some practical concern such as the care of the insane or the use of experimental animals, he might consider it. But empty honors only annoyed him, especially in his declining years, and it is wholly understandable that he would have regarded election to the Academy as an empty achievement.

When he originally accepted membership in the National Institute of Arts and Letters, along with his brother Henry and friends such as Henry Adams, he may have assumed that there was some purpose, perhaps even some practical work, to be achieved by the organization. But by 1905 the Institute had proved to be simply an honorary society, and the Academy promised to be merely the result of a few of those already honored selectively honoring themselves. Indeed, it is difficult not to sympathize with James in scorning the idea of the original members of the Academy— John Hay, William Dean Howells, E. C. Stedman, Augustus Saint-Gaudens, Edward McDowell, Mark Twain, and John La Farge—politicking among themselves to decide who might be worthy of joining them. James knew them all and undoubtedly felt, especially after his brother Henry and his friend Henry Adams had joined their ranks, that it was hardly a distinction for him to be officially linked with them; it was like being offered a national honor that actually came from the old neighborhood block. Furthermore, he saw his own achievements in philosophy and psychology as lying outside the fields—literature, sculpture, painting, and music—in which the Academy's founding members excelled. As someone who had long since abandoned painting for another kind of work, James may have felt that in the Academy's circles he was a fish out of water. In declining membership and resigning from the Institute, he was acting in a way consistent with his well-known intention to lend his name only where some purpose might be served. His grounds for resigning were clear, and he naturally expected that they would be taken at face value.[64]

One last detail about James's letter of resignation deserves mention. There is evidence that Henry was not happy about his own election to the Academy. Thinking that Henry Adams had lobbied on his behalf (actually it was John Hay who had logrolled for his election), Henry wrote to Adams: "I have written 1st to thank R. U. Johnson for crowning me with glory—& now I must thank *you* for guiding, straight to my unworthy & even slightly bewildered brow, his perhaps otherwise faltering or reluctant hand. Well, I am crowned—& I don't know that that makes much difference; but, still more, I am *amused,* & that very certainly does. . . . I hope you are thinking of our uniforms. But keep it cheap—think what Theodore [Roosevelt] will want."[65] Henry James would have been "amused" to be invited at last to join such great literary lights as John Hay and Theodore Roosevelt, especially if he assumed that heavy politicking within the Academy was responsible for his elevation to such distinguished company. While he consented to his own election, he probably mixed his amusement with deeper misgivings; while he was visiting William in Cambridge, he may have expressed those misgivings to his brother. He may even have contributed to William's resolve to resign from the Institute. In any event, if Henry was not keen about the organization, there is no reason to suppose that William's scorn of it reflected a personal animus toward Henry.

In fact, I have located nothing in my review of correspondence and family documents to suggest an underlying rivalry between the brothers. William's criticisms of Henry's novels were sometimes blunt, perhaps even off-target and insensitive, but they were always aboveboard.[66] What he thought on that score he simply put on the table for Henry to see, as he did with everyone, whether family or not. If he had critical observations to make, he generally found it impossible not to vent them. Repression was not among his talents, so there is no evidence that his literary criticisms were symptoms of antagonism toward his brother. If he had felt such antagonism, it would certainly have appeared in his most intimate letters to his wife, Alice, yet nothing like envy shows in those letters.

In 1882, William was in England when his father took fatally ill. Henry, Jr., and both Alice Jameses were among those at the bedside; in her letters to him, William's wife sometimes complained that Henry and Alice made her nervous. William responded in a letter of 31 January 1883, a month after his father's death, that his wife had made him "feel like flying instantly home to surround and protect you. Yes, Harry is a queer soul, so good, and yet so limited, as if he [had] taken an oath not to let himself out to more than half of his humanhood, in order to keep the other half from suffering, and had capped it with a determination not to give anyone else credit for the half he resolves not to use himself. Really it is not oath or resolve, but helplessness." William often used words like *helpless* and *powerless* within the family to characterize Henry, as in this letter of 29 July 1889 to his wife:

> Harry is as nice and simple and amicable as he can be. He has covered himself, like some marine crustacean, with all sorts of material growths, rich sea weeds and rigid barnacles and things, and lives hidden in the midst of his strange heavy alien manners and customs, but these are all but "protective resemblances," under which the same dear old good innocent and at bottom very powerless feeling Harry remains, caring for very little but his writing, and full of dutifulness and affection for all gentle things.

One looks in vain for a display of animus toward Henry in William's most confidential correspondence. Occasionally, he poked fun at his brother, as he did regularly toward everyone, including himself. He wrote to his friend Pauline Goldmark on 8 August 1908: "You may address me as 'Esq.,' now that I'm staying with my conventional-minded brother, who thinks that only tradesmen should be called Mister when written to." William was not the only member of the family to think that Henry, who seemed to epitomize civilized living in his English setting, was somehow removed from the real world. Their younger brother Robertson wrote in a letter to William on 4 April 1898, when he was himself recovering from depression and alcoholism in a sanatorium and feeling that the real world was all too close: "Poor Henry, how far away his world has been from the world of gross sensation in which some people live. Would that I could go and dwell away from the world of gross sensation." What William, Robertson, and others found baffling about Henry was his reclusiveness, his dedication to a lonely existence of writing, and his "helplessness." What William meant by this term is clear in a letter of 29 July 1889 to his wife Alice: "I am sorry to say that [Henry] is saving not a cent of money, so that my vision of him, paralyzed, in our spare room is stronger than ever. He seems quite helpless in that regard—of the Syracuse money [inherited from the grandfather's estate] some has gone for his and A[lice]'s current expenses of living."

William worried about money most of his life, especially while raising a family, and the letters between him and his wife reveal his fears about running out and her efforts to reduce domestic expenditures. Much of their correspondence until the final years focused upon monetary concerns, and William felt driven to lecture and publish beyond the Harvard campus in order to give his family something like the lifestyle that he himself had always enjoyed. He wrote to his wife on 1 August 1890 that he had just received a check for seventeen dollars from the Houghton Company, not from book sales but from the melting of old plates; he added this postscript: "With all outstanding bills paid, except 50 for my new coat and 7 for my Cheviot shirts, we have just 302 balance in the bank and I 15 in cash. I sent you fifty in cash day before yesterday." When money was involved and he felt unfairly treated, James could become extremely angry and aggressive.[67] A friend of James's once related that when James made a new acquaintance, he asked first the person's age and then his income; according to the friend, this anecdote "was almost literally true."[68]

William may well have worried (though perhaps not justifiably) about Henry's finances and seeming inability to save for old age. His recurrent vision of Henry ending up as a paralytic in William's house was probably more a reflection of his own anxieties than anything else. Interestingly, when Henry was partially paralyzed two months before his death on 28 February 1916, he was for a time in severe condition. However, "within twenty-four hours the patient had rallied and was calling for a thesaurus to discover the exact descriptive word for his condition. He didn't think 'paralytic' was right" (Edel, 5:543). William had been dead five years when this occurred, but Henry may have known of his brother's vision, remembered it, and reached for the thesaurus in order to thwart the prophecy.

In repeatedly imputing helplessness or powerlessness to his brother, William clearly meant more than financial impracticality. He had in mind a personality trait which contrasted prominently with his own; he saw in Henry a passivity, a willingness to let life come to him, whereas William viewed himself as meeting life head-on. Henry was the serene observer, William the restless doer. Henry once wrote to a troubled friend: "Don't think, don't feel, any more than you can help, don't conclude or decide—don't do anything but *wait*. . . . I am determined not to speak to you except with the voice of stoicism."[69] William, on the other hand, rejected Stoicism as being too passive and resigned. Referring to "the drab discolored way of stoic resignation to necessity" (*VRE*, 41), he condemned it for lacking the passion and emotional commitment that lead to corrective action. For William, Stoicism was a "do-nothing" attitude, taking a person into himself rather than on crusades to improve the world. We exist, he believed, to do rather than to be done unto; in calling Henry helpless, he must have thought that he and his brother differed radically. But it was not fraternal rivalry or hidden animus that led William to separate himself from Henry, but rather a genuine difference in philosophical attitudes. We need not assume that such a difference tarnished their fraternal affection.[70]

The place of the younger brothers in the James family has never been clear.

Garth Wilkinson and Robertson lived luckless lives compared to their famous siblings. Wilky was wounded in the Civil War while still in his teens; after the war he tried unsuccessfully to run a cotton plantation in Florida, married a woman whom his parents did not like, and died before he reached the age of forty. Robertson also served in the Civil War, then joined Wilky in the disastrous Florida business venture, and finally moved into a troubled existence of intermittent depressions and alcoholism. William and Henry always credited Robertson with literary and artistic talent, but given his problems it could hardly show.[71] Robertson's death preceded William's by only a few weeks, concluding a mostly unhappy life.

Perhaps some prejudicial treatment within the family is evident in William's comment in the 1859 letter to Van Winkle that "Wilky and Bobby are destined for commerce." William had already expressed unmitigated distaste for trade as a career, and it was apparent that Henry's temperament excluded a business life. Since their father probably would not have endorsed such a career enthusiastically, we can only conclude that to be destined for commerce was hardly high praise in the James household. Although vocations were generally determined earlier then than they are today, Wilky was only fourteen and Bob thirteen when the letter was written—tender ages at which to have one's fate sealed. We should not make too much of William's letter, but if it manifested a family attitude toward Wilky and Bob, labeling them as future businessmen in a home where the world of ideas was most valued, then the younger brothers may well have felt estranged while growing up. The few extant examples of Wilky's correspondence are rather pathetic. A letter of 27 April 1865, written to his father when Wilky was twenty, places a religious interpretation on Lincoln's assassination as his father might have done; he added that it was nearly midnight and he felt for his parents as "I did when you were nursing me in my bed in the summer of 1863 [after he was wounded in the war]." On 8 April 1868, at twenty-three, he wrote to his parents that "the day will come when I can with honor and satisfaction to myself and with profit to the family live once more in your midst . . . where I can get sympathy and instruction in what pertains to all things heady and hearty, by turning to my father, and a constant example of joy and affection and saintliness by turning to my Mother as all things that pertain to holy living and holy thinking." In 1878, upon the announcement of William's engagement to Alice Howe Gibbens, Wilky wrote to William: "It fills my soul with joy unutterable at the thought of what must be your contentment and happiness. . . . I should have been by this time deep in Hell if it had not been for my wife.—You have other qualities and other features of character which would save you *anyway*, but you have an intellectual force to your being, which must be very much helped and softened by the influence of love and all that it brings with it."[72]

The correspondence between Robertson and William was more extensive and clearly shows William's concern for his brother; Robertson's letters in turn display the family trait of keen interest in the details of each member's life. His relationship with William was clearly unsettled—sometimes he was grateful for his brother's help, sometimes not. In a letter of 3 March 1875, for instance, he reacted against

William's advice on how to cope with depression, saying: "I think the best thing we can do is simply to sit and exhaust all hell by *your patient thinking upon God*. This recourse to outward things won't last you long." Another letter expresses anger at William for believing stories about Robertson's alleged marital problems. When he was recuperating from alcoholism in 1897 at a sanatorium in Dansville, New York, where William had encouraged him to check in, he wrote: "I feel sure I will never meet father again in the Kingdom to come. I should not care to meet him unless his philosophy had grown more simple and more practical. *He* was always better than his metaphysics."[73] In 1909, when Robertson was residing in Concord and painting at Walden Pond, he wrote to William that his wife had brought home a copy of *The Meaning of Truth*, just published. In this letter he said that his parents "had the truth" not because they were Swedenborgians, and that William had it not because he was a pragmatist, but rather because they were all kind people. William's relationship with Robertson was difficult; not only did William have to meet his brother in a drunken condition occasionally, he often gave him money which, though intended to pay for essentials, went for alcohol instead. Throughout these difficulties, William maintained a patient, loyal concern for his brother.

It is not clear why Wilky and Robertson served in the Civil War when William and Henry, Jr., did not. Their father was adamantly against any of his sons enlisting. Henry, Jr., had a back problem which released him from the obligation, and William also had his share of health problems. Further, Wilky and Robertson were at school in Concord, where the abolitionist sentiment ran particularly high, so they were exposed to influences not playing upon their brothers. Although their parents were against their enlistment, the fact remains that they went to war and William and Henry, Jr., did not. Most likely, the combination of health problems and paternal opinion was responsible. Henry, Jr., apparently felt strong guilt over this, but there seems to be no evidence that William did. The onset of his neurasthenia coincided with the outbreak of the Civil War, so that the 1860s may have been a period of intense self-preoccupation for him, in which he was distanced from the war except when it touched him directly, as when Wilky was wounded. He may have been too deeply involved in saving himself emotionally to have entertained visions of saving his country. In any event, the differences between the two sets of brothers were dramatically illustrated when one pair went off to battle and the other pursued intellectual careers.[74]

Alice James has received much more attention than Wilky or Robertson, mainly because she more nearly matched William's and Henry's intellectual and literary gifts. Her remarkable diary, supplemented by correspondence and anecdotes, attests to her verbal genius and wit. A spinster and an invalid, almost constantly suffering from the psychosomatic disorders that plagued the Jameses, Alice can be seen as a paradigm of the Victorian woman's conflicts and sufferings in a patriarchal family and a male-dominated society. The prevailing theory is that William dominated and emotionally wounded Alice. Jean Strouse has written the definitive study of Alice James, which one reviewer has summarized thus: "Alice's relationships with the 'other' James brothers, Robertson and Garth Wilkinson, seem less important to her development. But William James emerges here as a stultifying influence, not at all the 'adorable' genius so revered in other biographical treatments."[75] That is indeed the portrait painted in Strouse's biography; William is seen as the prototypical domineering older brother, somewhat loutish to boot, who badly misunderstood Alice's sensitivities.

Through Strouse's eyes, William's domination of Alice was sexual and flirtatious and endured into adulthood. Given Alice's fragile health, neuroticism, and lack of romantic outlets, a seductive older brother could only add to her problems. Because this alleged flirtation existed until William's marriage in 1878 to Alice Howe Gibbens—the fact that she was a second Alice could hardly have helped—Strouse argues that "William's engagement and marriage precipitated Alice's 1878 breakdown not simply because it seemed a desertion, but also because it brought her face to face with familiar questions about love and what would happen to her without it" (Strouse, 184). According to Strouse, only Henry, Jr., treated Alice as an equal; the rest of the family patronized her and thus put her on the defensive. Strouse does not argue that William deliberately damaged his sister, for whom he obviously felt great love, but rather that his words and deeds were heedless in a way that was typical for a family living when the Jameses did. Strouse's interpretation agrees with Edel's: despite the banter and overt display of love (here between brother and sister), on its other side lurked hostility, jealousy, confusion, and anxiety. The relationship between Alice and William then becomes another piece in the family puzzle that strikes so many as being uniquely suited for psychoanalytic diagnosis. According to Strouse, William contributed to Alice's problems by being mercurial, inconsistent, and oddly insensitive.

> William had often praised his sister's letters as "inestimable," "splendid, noble, etc." (the "etc." undercutting what preceded it), and suggested she keep a record of her impressions of England more permanent than letters. He inevitably took back with his left hand the encouragement he gave with his right. "I am entirely certain that you've got a book inside of you about England," he wrote her in August 1890, "which will come out yet. Perhaps it's the source of all your recent trouble." And a year later he took up the topic again: "I do hope that you will leave some notes on life and english life which Harry can work in hereafter, so as to make the best book he ever wrote." (Strouse, 289)

I am less confident than Strouse about identifying instances of undercutting, as I am about the unqualified declarations that William's engagement precipitated Alice's breakdown and that his relationship with Alice was erotically flirtatious. These are plausible hypotheses, especially in the context of Strouse's carefully assembled evidence, but toned-down versions of the same hypotheses are equally plausible. Perhaps William's marriage contributed to Alice's breakdown; given her medical history, however, her condition may have been worsening for physical reasons around the time William made his marital decision. How flirtatious was the sister-brother relation? Can we be sure that the banter between Alice and William was as erotically motivated as Strouse depicts it? Verbal style may be a symptom of unconscious sentiment, but it is also a function of culture, upbringing, and the immediate environmental climate; in the household, the banter between Alice and William was more likely an attempt to be smart than to be sexy. The same caveat applies to the thesis that William unwittingly stultified Alice's development; though there may be some truth in it, we cannot be at all confident about such a conjecture.

Despite these reservations, I want to acknowledge that Strouse's book on Alice James contributes to the appreciation not only of Alice and her times but also of the entire James family. William, too, is seen more fully, especially in his relation to women, in Strouse's study. More successfully than any other writer, she has identified his tendency to relate to others through his own intense self-preoccupation and to leave an alien imprint on what began as an intimate gesture. Toward the end of his famous letter to Alice before her death, for example, he himself realized that what he intended as consolation might sound harsh and unsympathetic. "It may seem odd for me to talk to you in this cool way about your end; but, my dear little sister, if one has things present to one's mind, and I know they are present enough to *your* mind, why not speak them out?"[76] This sentiment may have contributed to the belief that William acted as a bully in his role as the eldest child. He had a habit of pressing his version of things upon others whether they wished to hear it or not. Strouse identifies William's self-absorption and interprets how it was conveyed to Alice. "He never ceased to offer her unsolicited advice and diagnoses, nor to treat her with condescending pity—perhaps in order to keep the greatest possible distance between himself and the 'neurotic' suffering that had so plagued his own earlier life" (Strouse, 256). A person need not be vain, unsympathetic, or arrogant to unsettle another's sensibilities; it is sometimes enough to be intensely self-preoccupied, and Strouse makes us aware that William may have had such an effect on Alice.

Strouse also comments on William's relationship with his wife, Alice Howe Gibbens. "In later years, he would see her as having saved his life. William's successful marriage probably contributed even more toward the 'cure' of his emotional troubles than his philosophical resolutions of the early 1870s did. His wife's calm practicality offset his fitful nervousness: she understood his moods, catered to his whims, protected him from the outside world and the cares of domesticity, and provided an order within which he was free to come and go as he pleased" (Strouse, 180). This assessment agrees with what others have written about their marriage. While Alice Gibbens may have held William together, however, he remained as seriously neurotic (though perhaps freer of suicidal impulses) after his marriage as he had been before it. His depressions and psychosomatic symptoms—problems with his eyes, back, digestion, and breathing, bad temper, boredom, moodiness, and fatigue—were a constant strain on his wife. Knowing the difficulties he caused her, he sometimes masked his suffering. On 21 May 1899 she wrote to Henry, Jr., that William had lain awake all night during a bad storm, that the wind had caused him cardiac disturbances, and that he had seen three doctors the next day who detected a heart murmur. But all this, Alice wrote, he had concealed from her. "Was ever man born of woman harder to take care of than William! Do you wonder that I want to get him away from all the frustration which wearies him more than work, and establish, if possible, a well-ordered life?" William found no cures before or after marriage, a fact that Alice emphasized when she wrote to a friend that "my husband has had a complete nervous break-down which naturally has aggravated all the cardiac symptoms."[77]

William was introduced to his wife in 1876 by his father, who recognized in the twenty-seven-year-old schoolteacher some of his own spouse's virtues. She was plain, mature, intelligent, strong, and without the pretensions of the rich and elite. Like her mother-in-law, she would be her family's emotional mainstay, supporting her husband in every way possible and acting as a paragon of devotion for her children. William would come to depend on her as his father had relied on his wife, and he made many testimonials to her angelic nature.[78] Both Henry, Sr., and William praised their wives' support, terming it *moral*. Strouse refers to a letter in which William wrote: "Alice Gibbens is an angel if ever there was one—I take her for her moral more than her intellectual qualities"; as Strouse points out, this passage recalls what Henry, Sr., once wrote to his wife, characterizing William as "much dearer to my heart for his moral worth than for his intellectual" (quoted in Strouse, 180). It would have been even more pointed had Henry, Sr., applied this description to his wife. Although William tended to develop his philosophy and psychology independently of Alice, he did converse with her about his lectures and writings. She wrote to him on 28 February 1893: "You know your good theory of music becoming harmful in so far as its appeal to the emotions bearing no fruit? I found myself resolving Saturday night, as I listened to Beethoven's Serenades . . . that I would no more offend you with black clothes, even if I do make a mountain of myself." They shared intimately their interests in religion, psychical research, and mind-cure experiments, and in these areas James was confident of Alice's intuition and good sense; for example, he occasionally asked for her judgment about the character and integrity of a professed psychic healer.

Those who study the James family have long been curious about the marital relationship between William and Alice, partly because their correspondence was locked in the Houghton Library with instructions from their heirs that it not be made available until the year 2022, a century after Alice's death. This restriction was recently rescinded, and I was permitted access to their correspondence, which comprises approximately fifteen hundred letters. Henry James III, their eldest son, left a memorandum dated 9 June 1936 with the correspondence. He states that when he originally proposed in 1921 to collect their letters, his mother was "frightened" (this reaction is not explained). She had already begun to sort out the letters in 1911, however, and she continued to do so until her death in 1922. Henry III then went through the correspondence, partly for use in Perry's book, and concluded that his mother had destroyed some of William's letters to her, especially those written prior to their marriage, for little of that correspondence remains. Henry reported that he himself destroyed a few of William's letters which were liable to misinterpretation, although none of them was significant. Of his mother's side of the correspondence, which he described as voluminous but of no special interest, he destroyed all but two bundles of letters selected at random. He saw no reason, he said, to publish the correspondence, since he and Perry had edited his father's papers so thoroughly; he did keep some of his mother's letters for himself, however.

In addition, Alice wrote diaries, some or all of which were shown to Gay Wilson Allen for his biography of William; although Allen occasionally refers to them, he does not suggest that they provided any fresh information. A letter of 29 May 1973 from Alexander R. James, then executor of the estate, is now included with the James Papers in the Houghton Library: "Of great regret to me, as well as others, my cousin J. S. R. James destroyed the diaries of Mrs. William James. I even had several which I had turned over to him for safekeeping." What we know, then, about the relationship between William and Alice is based upon anecdotes, fragments from Alice's no longer extant diaries, William's diaries (which are not very illuminating about the marriage), and a correspondence that, especially on Alice's side, was carefully selected by Alice herself and by her son Henry.

The recent surge of biographical interest in the James family is mainly the work of scholars with a flair for Freudian interpretation. Whatever the merits of such an emphasis, an unintended effect of this literature has been to create an image of William James as an enigmatic man, usually depressed or having a psychophysical crisis, who survived crises either by reclusive writing and introspective brooding or by traveling and who showed no understanding of the source of his symptoms. The image of the self-absorbed neurotic, though not strictly incorrect, is lopsided; what emerges from his letters to Alice and his diaries is the picture of an extremely busy and practical man who fulfilled many responsibilities and had a successful career. He enjoyed much of his life, traveling in Europe, attending concerts and the theater, visiting museums, hiking in the mountains, speaking before large and enthusiastic audiences, mixing with distinguished company, and fathering five children of whom he was understandably proud.

James's diaries attest to his full schedule during the academic year; he served on university committees, took care of departmental affairs, supervised dissertations, entertained students at home, and fulfilled endless social obligations. Far from being a cranky recluse, he followed daily routines in the outside world. His letters to Alice are often concerned with finances, since his salary was too small to maintain the lifestyle he had known before marriage. In 1890, for instance, he wrote to her that he had borrowed six hundred dollars from the bank to pay their taxes—when he was forty-eight and the well-known author of *Principles*. Two years earlier, he wrote a letter giving instructions for repairing the plumbing, complete with sketches he had drawn to help her. One letter complained, "I'm interrupted every moment by students come to fight about their marks," and another reported, "Last night, by the bye, we gave Santayana the degree of Ph.D. His thesis is simply an exquisite production."[79] The reader of hundreds of such letters begins to feel fatigue, not merely from reading but also from attempting to keep pace with the life of William James.

His letters to Alice afford glimpses of distinguished persons he met. When he was in Berlin, he wrote on 9 November 1882 that he had gone to the veterinary school to visit Hermann Munk, "the great brain vivisector" whose work he referred to in *Principles*. Although he could show James no animals, Munk was very cordial, "poured out a torrent of talk for 1½ hours," and introduced him to Benno Baginsky, whose studies of the semicircular canals especially interested James. (James himself had advanced the hypothesis that the canals function mainly for equilibrium.) Baginsky's torrent of words, he reported, was even more overwhelming than Munk's. "I never felt quite so helpless and small-boyish before, and am to this hour dizzy from the onslaught" (*LWJ*, 1:213–14). He recounted in letters from England that he had met persons whose names Alice would recognize, such as the neurophysiologist Hughlings Jackson, who was "one of the most peculiar men I ever saw in the way of modesty and delicacy. He gave me more of his reprints and I am to dine with him next week. . . . [Had] lunch at Seville Club with one Middlemore. A red-nosed unwholesome looking individual who ate at the same table with us as I learned afterwards to be my old foe Saintsbury. He was witty and carnal looking and very different from the Saintsbury of my imagination." He said of a dinner with Jackson and others: "After dinner we adjourned upstairs to the Grosvenor Galley which was lighted up expressly for us and saw Alma-Tadema's collected works and Alma himself explained them to some of us. There's something wrong about them."[80] In a letter of 28 June 1880 he described meeting two of his "heroes" in psychology, Alexander Bain and Shadworth Hodgson. Of Bain he said, "He is a little hickory nut of a Scotch man, standing to Hodgson about in the same relation as a snapping turtle to a splendid setter dog. He was genial and talkative enough in an utterly dogmatic and charmless way. No atmosphere in his mind, he looks like a very respectable little old family servant, does not read German, and altogether makes me glad to have seen once but never more." In his letters to Alice, he occasionally expressed criticism of others. He wrote of G. Stanley Hall, his former student and eventually the president of Clark University, "He's a queer creature and *positively avoided* asking me to contribute to his journal, about which he talked at great length." He wrote a day later, "He's the queerest mixture of bigness and pettiness I ever knew."[81]

James's numerous letters to Alice, some of which have been reproduced or described by biographers, provide a kind of travelogue of places he visited and people he encountered. On 9 December 1882 he wrote: "While lunching at the Club [in London] was the great [Thomas] Huxley's gray whiskered jaws moving at the table opposite mine. I wished I might have spoken to him, but 'twas not the thing." More important, their correspondence sheds light on their relationship. The vast number of letters they wrote to one another indicates how much they were apart. William often felt restless and needed to run off to New Hamshire or the Adirondacks, if not to Europe. His letters give the impression that he periodically needed to be alone, that any intimate relationship was fatiguing for him over time, and that he saw travel as a crucial means of coping with restlessness. It was well known to James's friends that he arranged a journey in the aftermath of each child's birth, and then wrote to Alice about his guilt for having done so. He was often absent, if only as far away as

Newport, on holidays such as Christmas, New Year's Day, and birthdays. Although he must have appreciated the difficulties his absence caused for his family, he seems to have been powerless to alter the habit. He wrote to Alice, in a letter of 16 September 1897 from the Adirondacks: "You wrote of the 'peace' that you now have, I being gone. How sad it is that two people who live but for each other should find so much 'peace' when parted. Yesterday afternoon I was haunted by the tho't of your pale face, transparent and beautiful in bed, after each of those childbirths, still turning to me and anxious to do something for me. Darling, I do not forget." On 4 July 1889 he wrote that he regretted his "three trips to Europe in 9 years with you always left behind—c'est pas trop fort."

James's flights from his family were escapes from human entanglements to nature, solitude, and mystical relief. He wrote on 14 August 1891, "I regard the Asheville [North Carolina] trip as strictly necessary for health—I don't know when I've felt such an inward weariness, but it will soon yield to novel mountain scenery. . . . I want not to hear of Psychology until October." After completing *Principles* in 1890, he was prone to serious neurotic difficulties. During that period he seldom felt the enthusiasm he had expressed in a letter to Alice, dated 3 August 1890, in which he had said that he hoped she would be with him for finishing the proofs of *Principles:* "We will have the greatest week together that we have ever had, or that *any* two hearts that beat as one have ever yet had." After completing *Principles* he sought solitude and scenery, and though he socialized in his travels, he did not crave company. In a letter of 11 August 1897, he wrote from Bar Harbor that he had been to a fireworks display and then, "believe it if you can of *me*—to a 'domino-party' at a country club, where as a spectator I got a weird impression, but withdrew at midnight *solas* and came to bed."[82]

The letters often reflect moodiness, tension, confusion, and the combination of approach and withdrawal that often occurs in stable yet feisty marriages. He wrote on 3 September 1890, after a tense parting:

> What a queer way to leave you ! What was it all about? How did it originate? Who began first? Etc. Etc.? All I know is that your level look into truth, your tender sensibility to discord, your absolute charity to me . . . are things which the moment I turn my back upon you, loom up much higher than Mount Washington has done it this afternoon. Darling, in all seriousness you have lifted me up out of lonely hell. . . . You have redeemed my life from destruction.

William often apologized to his wife for outbursts of temper before a parting, reiterated his love for her and his appreciation of her care and devotion, and expressed the hope that the trip was improving his nerves so that he would be easier to live with when he returned. Such marital problems are not surprising, given their precarious courtship between 1876 and their marriage in 1878. For a time, it looked as if the wedding would never happen. Some biographers have speculated that a puritanical streak in William may have caused him, as both a psychologist and an individual, to be uncomfortable about sex. But despite what he said about an antisexual instinct in *Principles* (2:437), I do not think he felt unusual sexual conflicts. He lived at a time when the subject of sex was more delicate than it is today, and his religious and moral beliefs probably affected his sexuality, but he does not seem to have been more inhibited than his average contemporary. In fact, there is ample evidence that he regarded sex as a natural outlet. Alice received her share of passionate love letters from him, and his affection for her apparently included an ardent sexual dimension. On 5 January 1883, five years after their wedding, he wrote to her: "I long to see and hear you and tell you 10,000 things. I really begin to think I'm becoming affectionate. I don't see why else I should have such thrills and convulsions at every mental image of your looks that sweeps over me."

William occasionally appears to have wanted more affection, passion, and sexual responsiveness from Alice, although it is difficult to know to what extent this was a problem. On 22 June 1880, for example, he wrote from England:

> At this distance, dear, you seem to me so unapproachable, so as you used to during those two winters of non-intercourse. You have been the same "wraith" to me. No longer solid; but insubstantial, trembling, and with a sort of crimson passion radiating from you and keeping me off.—
>
> Dear, how amusing this verbiage will seem to you. You don't seem to me all the time so, but today and yesterday. You change like a chameleon. And I suppose I to you. . . . I kissed your dear letter.

The first part of 1888 was apparently a period when William needed more warmth from Alice. On 15 February he wrote that he had spontaneously kissed Lizzy, their housemaid, and justified it by saying that he never kissed anyone spontaneously "but to repress which seems to me churlish and inhuman." In the spring he mentioned that he was reading Nicolas Restif, an eighteenth-century French novelist whose books, based on his own libertine existence, had earned him such titles as the Rousseau of the gutter and the Voltaire of the chambermaids. James wrote on 22 April: "Restif . . . beats Rousseau hollow. Only the imaginary is real. It is astonishing how a creature can have gone through life possessed of this one fever for women—and nothing else and gratified it like a stallion, and yet preserved the completely naive innocence of his heart as this cuss did." Because Alice seemed to take a dim view of such literature, James wrote a week later: "You needn't be afraid of bad influence . . . from 'those dirty autobiographies!' I wish that cleaner books had as much reality of life in them as the non-dirty parts of these. It is not for the dirt, but for the whole sense of reality of which the dirt is part that I find these books so renovating." His interest in Restif persisted, and he wrote on 1 May about "the mention of all those females. . . . As a piece of mental pathology it is a most invaluable document."

James was not sure whether he or Alice was responsible for the occasional tensions, but he was not given to detailed psychoanalytic diagnoses. Personal problems were really moral challenges, as he often said to Alice. On 3 October 1890 he wrote: "What is to become of us I don't know. But you shall see no more temper fits from me (*unless you are foolish yourself*) for I have achieved a moral victory over my low spirits and tendency to complain whilst I have been here [Cambridge] these days. . . . I have actually by steady force of will kept it down and at last got it under for a while and mean to fight it out on that line for the rest of my life, for I see that is my particular mission in the world." He sometimes complained that she was too reserved, and in a letter of 17 September 1901 he accused her of having a "delicate moral constitution" that was rooted in self-hatred. (This remark might be seen as a psychoanalytic diagnosis, but it was made only in passing.) He sometimes beseeched her to be more "sentimentally effusive" in her letters and to echo the tenderness of his letters. There is no evidence that James had romantic trysts, and it seems unlikely, despite the amount of time he spent away from Alice, that the lost part of the family correspondence would have revealed that he was romantically entangled with other women. But the following excerpt from a letter to Elizabeth Glendower Evans—a friend of his and Alice's and a correspondent with whom he exchanged ideas on religion and philosophy—suggests that he may have been subject, if only platonically, to extramarital attractions:

> You will be surprised at hearing from me at this distance; but at intervals all through the summer I have had stirrings of romantic appreciation of your character (which character grows upon me more and more and which I won't pretend to diagnosticate for your own self-elation) that have brought me to the verge of a letter to tell you the same—for why, when we feel most friendly towards a person, should we stay as dumb as a Boston Back Bay Fish?—but the letter has each time been post-poned till now. Yes! Elizabeth, there is that about you, a touch of—what shall I call it?—magnanimity, that makes the thought of your existence in the world and of your friendship and toleration very, very consoling and helpful when one is in certain sorts of spirits about oneself and life. I wish to say to you this, for it is literally true; but I will say no more, for you probably find this enough.[83]

Perhaps this letter indicates that there were moments when James felt that a woman other than Alice might provide greater warmth and comfort. Perhaps Alice even reminded him at times of his own mother, who had not only appeared to favor his brother Henry during their youth but had also been impatient with William's illnesses, believing them to be the hypochondriacal results of morbid self-preoccupation. In any event, no extramarital romance seems to have threatened their marriage, and William was as determined as Alice to keep the family intact through its stresses and strains. A great loyalty and affection clearly kept them together for the thirty-two years of their marriage. Alice's letters to William show that she was constantly concerned with his welfare and troubled by the doubt that she might be failing him somehow. Such concerns may have been unwarranted or even obsessive, suggesting that she shared William's neuroticism. Her behavior at the deathbed of Henry, Jr., in 1916 was described as hysterical, which may point to a character trait that might have contributed to tensions in the marriage.[84] But she was immensely strong and devoted as she supported a neurasthenic husband, raised four well-adjusted children, and grieved the loss of an infant son. Her voice in the family was prominent, independent, and firm, as the following excerpt from a letter to their children shows:

> My children, it is a mistake to cultivate friendships with people decidedly inferior to yourselves in social status. I used not to realize this, and I have suffered. The inferior either settles down into a parasite, or groans under the burden of obligations [conferred?], and which must increase; in either case he is likely to be on the look out for slights and neglect. This is my advice to you and your offspring: "Find your acquaintance among people more liberally educated, more able, more socially powerful, and more high-minded than yourselves; keep good company, and be *one of the number*, and let your friendships form themselves on the simple intercourse of every day life; do not hurry into them, but when you have made them, do your best to keep them. Grapple them to thy soul with hoops of steel. Quarreling and making it up is decidedly unsatisfactory . . . and remember that much of our happiness in this world depends on the amount of affection we are able to inspire.[85]

It is not clear whether William saw this postscript, and if he did whether it offended his democratic inclinations. He took his parental duties seriously and followed closely the progress of his children, Henry III, William, Jr., Margaret Mary, and Alexander. On 24 December 1882, when Henry III was only three and William, Jr., but an infant, he wrote to Alice: "About Harry especially do I feel responsible,—Willyam somehow seems to me more likely to take of himself." There may be a sentiment here, harking back to his relationship with Henry, Jr., to stimulate the thinking of psychobiographers. His advice to his children usually urged the use of willpower in cultivating useful habits and overcoming apathy and depression. In a letter to Henry III, dated 14 March 1893, he encouraged his son to study conscientiously, adding, "Meanwhile do your [darndest?] in *every* respect. Live *hard!*" On 15 June 1899, when William, Jr., was doing summer forestry work and apparently complaining about it, his father wrote that the job was an opportunity superior to what Harvard offered. A young man should experience the wilderness, he declared. He advised: "Never *grumble*. The grumbling habit grows like a weed. . . . The *Man of men* . . . keeps up the spirits of the crew by showing good cheer and turning things into a joke himself. . . . Cold nights, starvation, constipation (Carlyle says that the greatest enemy the immortal Roland had was constipation)—see them all *sub specie boni*." This sentiment, regularly declared to his children, became famous in "The Moral Equivalent of War," and it was essential in his own struggle to cope.

PERSONALITY

An amusing story has been told that Winifred Smith Rieber, portraitist of John Dewey, Albert Einstein, Thomas Mann, and Franz Boas, tried to paint a group picture of the Harvard philosophy department. The sittings occurred not long before James's retirement, and besides him the group included G. H. Palmer, Josiah Royce, Hugo

Münsterberg, and George Santayana. The painter had blocked in a preliminary sketch of the five on a large canvas prior to the actual sittings, but none of them liked her sketch. Royce was unwilling to occupy the focal point to which she had assigned him. Münsterberg, a much bulkier man than Royce, insisted on being seated front and center, but since this arrangement destroyed the picture's composition, Rieber simply eliminated him (while retaining his empty chair) from the finished portrait that hangs in Emerson Hall. Santayana excluded himself from the painting, saying, "Whatever metaphysical egotism may assert, one cannot vote to be created." The final product thus shows an attenuated department of James, Palmer, and Royce.

James is pictured in profile, although he had protested this position because he thought that one eye carries less authority than two. Compared to the others, he was easy to paint, reported Rieber, because he appreciated how an artist works and made no demands on her attention. "A fragile man, lightly bearded, James had a charming smile, a tranquil manner, an affable friendliness, and a flower pulled through his lapel. His clothes looked as if they had come freshly pressed from the cleaners; and his mind seemed to have blown in on a storm."[86] James was usually described as a short, wiry, intense, alert, masculine, and energetic man with striking blue eyes set beneath bushy brows. He customarily wore a Norfolk jacket or double-breasted blue coat, bright shirts, and flowing ties; his appearance was further brightened by an unusually broad grin.[87] The complexities and paradoxes of his character seemed to many observers a part of his immediate appearance; one could simultaneously see in him strength and fragility, joy and sadness, gregariousness and introversion, frivolity and seriousness. His domed forehead, receding hairline, and beard made him look like a sage, yet something impish in his manner suggested an eternal boyishness.

James defied pat descriptions, for he seemed always to reveal both sides of any dichotomy. For example, he has been described as a gentleman, but among his papers is this note to himself: "A 'gentleman' is a man who cares nothing for his life." He declared elsewhere: "The Prince of darkness may be a gentleman, as we are told he is, but, whatever the God of earth and heaven is, he can surely be no gentleman."[88] Moreover, James insured that he would not be remembered entirely as a gentleman when, for instance, he horrified his brother Henry by climbing a ladder and peeping over a wall in order to glimpse G. K. Chesterton in his garden.[89]

James was as curious about the variety of life's experiences as he was about Chesterton. His fondness for nature, for hiking in the Adirondacks and the White Mountains, and for traveling in scenic parts of England and Europe, is well known. He enjoyed exercise and the expenditure and renewal of physical energy. When he suffered heart damage from overexertion on a hiking trip in 1898, his zest was dulled not only by the malady itself but by being denied the exhilaration of his favorite mountain trails. He kept himself fully occupied with a range of other activities as well. Even in advanced middle age, he sometimes rose at 2:00 A.M. and wrote from 4:00 A.M. until dinner. He regularly dined at clubs with colleagues or friends in Boston and on lecture tours, for he was a friendly and gregarious philosopher.[90] When he was not working on a book or an article, writing to famous as well as unknown correspondents, or reading Tolstoy or Stevenson, two of his favorite authors, he might be looking at paintings in the museum, for he was especially devoted to the work of Manet. His diaries mention attendance at the opera, the theater, dance performances, and even, on 13 January 1907, a "Zionist meeting at Tremont Theatre. Wonderful Yiddish orator." He followed the political and social scene closely and was remarkably busy with the many causes he adopted.

There are many statements on record about his generosity. Students benefited from his offers of money, food, hospitality, and friendship. A notable example was his continuous financial and other aid to Peirce, which is described in their extensive correspondence. Although ill and often incapacitated toward the end of his life, James still struggled to raise funds for Peirce. He was a loyal friend to John Dewey as well; upon his retirement, he asked the Harvard philosophy department to recommend John Dewey, whom he admired as friend and colleague, as his successor. Despite the department's recommendation, however, President Eliot notified James that the appointment would have been "preposterous."[91]

A moody person, James was susceptible to sudden feelings of frustration and bursts of anger, but he seems never to have borne a grudge or created enemies, for he was as gentle as he was generous. In one of his earliest publications, a review in 1865 of a book by Thomas Huxley, he lamented the savagery of Huxley's attacks on others and the fact that "people go to Prof. Huxley's lecture room with somewhat of the same spirit as that with which they would flock to a prize fight."[92] James was not unlike the affectionate dog of which he wrote, "He makes on me the impression of an angel hid in a cloud. He longs to do good" (quoted in Compton, 85). Helen Keller wrote that James visited her and Anne Sullivan when Keller was a young girl at the Perkins Institution for the Blind in South Boston. Comparing him to Plato and to Francis Bacon, she recalled in 1929 that he had brought her an ostrich feather. " 'I thought,' he said, 'you would like the feather, it is soft and light and caressing' " (quoted in Compton, 127). The creative touch in this gesture was another of James's trademarks.

James disliked routine, placid conformity, and a plodding approach to life; he preferred the spontaneous, novel, and surprising even if it entailed some anxiety. He tried to create each day anew, to endow even the minor details of his existence with an artistic flavor. Life was enjoyable as long as its variety could be appreciated. The need to put his own imprint on everything permeated his posture, gestures, clothing, voice—and especially his language. He lived in and for his words, which were his most valued artistic tool.

In 1907 he wrote to his brother Henry about a visit to New York City, and his words expressed his usual gusto:

> The first impression of New York, if you stay there not more than 36 hours, which has been my limit for twenty years past, is one of repulsion at the clangor, disorder, and permanent earthquake conditions. But this time, installed as I was at the Harvard Club (44th St.) in the centre of the cyclone, I caught the pulse of

the machine, took up the rhythm, and vibrated *mit,* and found it simply magnificent. I'm surprised at you, Henry, not having been more enthusiastic, but perhaps that superbly powerful and beautiful subway was not opened when you were there. It is an *entirely* new New York, in soul as well as in body, from the old one, which looks like a village in retrospect. The courage, the heaven-sealing audacity of it all, and the *lightness* withal, as if there was nothing that was not easy, and the great pulses and bounds of progress, so many in directions all simultaneous that the coordination is indefinitely future, give a kind of *drumming background* of life that I never felt before. I'm sure that once *in* that movement, and at home, all other places would seem insipid.[93]

Over the years an astonishing number of people have collected examples of James's phrasings, as others have treasured the sayings of Voltaire or Nietzsche. Henry James III recalled that his father liked a directness and "folk-arty" boldness of expression.

He also disliked style that makes an affectation of learning and therewith desiccates and often obscures the thought. [Herbert] Spencer said: "Evolution is an integration of matter and concomitant dissipation of motion; during which the matter passes from an indefinite, incoherent homogeneity to a definite coherent heterogeneity; and during which the retained motion undergoes a parallel transformation." "This," remarked my father, stirring up the minds of his students, "might be translated: 'Evolution is a change from a no-howish, untalkaboutable, all-alikeness to a somehowish and in general talkaboutable not-all-alikeness by continuous stick-to-getherations and something-elsifications.'"[94]

Another criticism of Spencer typified James's down-to-earth philosophy:

The case of Herbert Spencer's system is much to the point here. Rationalists feel his fearful array of insufficiencies. His dry schoolmaster temperament, the hurdy-gurdy monotony of him, his preference for cheap makeshifts in argument, his lack of education even in mechanical principles, and in general the vagueness of all his fundamental ideas, his whole system wooden, as if knocked together out of cracked hemlock boards—and yet the half of England wants to bury him in Westminster Abbey. (*Pragmatism,* 25–26)

William Allan Neilson, a professor of English at Harvard, characterized James's literary style as better than Stevenson's (whom James admired), praising it for the "absence of all sophistication, with a touch of audacity in the use of a native idiom, and the suffusion of a spontaneous humor. . . . It has been one of the minor glories of the Harvard Department of Philosophy that it contained more men who could write with distinction than any other department in the University. Their colleagues in English have been fain to acknowledge the claim with humility,—and it is with keen regret that they see this superiority diminished by the transference of William James to the ranks of the *emeriti.*"[95] James wanted to avoid not only the inherent tendency of philosophy to become ethereal and abstract, but his own weakness of writing from the misty heights of noble sentiment. He always countered with a dash of humor or an earthy turn of phrase. In technical discussions, he often introduced such locutions as "he has at last got the mystery of cognition where, to use a vulgar phrase, 'the wool is short' " or "I fornicate with that unclean thing [the will-to-believe], my adversaries may think, whereas your genuine truth-lovers must discourse in Huxleyan heroics, and feel as if truth ought to bring eventual messages of death to all our satisfactions."[96] Apperception was a favorite topic in psychology, but the tedious accounts of it—including one theorist's ability to distinguish sixteen different types—vexed James considerably.

> There are as many types of apperception as there are possible ways in which an incoming experience may be reacted on by an individual mind. A little while ago, at Buffalo, I was the guest of a lady who, a fortnight before, had taken her seven-year-old boy for the first time to Niagara Falls. The child silently glared at the phenomenon until his mother, supposing him struck speechless by its sublimity, said, "Well, my boy, what do you think of it?" to which, "Is that the kind of spray I spray my nose with?" was the boy's only reply. That was his mode of apperceiving the spectacle. You may claim this as a particular type, and call it by the Greek name of rhinotherapeutical apperception, if you like; and if you do, you will hardly be more trivial or artificial than are some of the authors of the books. (*Talks,* 97–98)

James's contemporaries appreciated the unexpected humor in his conversations and found him responsive to their own wit. The philosopher Samuel Alexander recalled that James was greatly amused by a story told at dinner at Oxford about the French law of divorce, that when a train stopped at a railway station the porters would call out, "Vingt minutes d'arrêt pour le divorce."[97] James punctuated his arguments with anecdotes or aphorisms that made his point more vivid. In a notebook dated 1863, he recorded one such aphorism for future use: "Advice of an old farmer to a young one: Never, never, by all means never, get into debt. But if you do, let it be for manure." In discussing unconscious inference, James said that Wundt and Helmholtz might have been so dismayed by Robert Hartmann's "excessive and riotous applications" of their principle as to alter their own defense of it. "It would be natural to feel towards him as the sailor in the story felt towards the horse who got his foot in the stirrup,—'If you're going to get on, I must get off' " (*Principles,* 2:169). To illustrate that hypotheses that do not imply special consequences should not be honored, he wrote: "When the Irishman's admirers ran him along to the place of banquet in a sedan chair with no bottom, he said, 'Faith, if it wasn't for the honor of the thing, I might as well have come on foot' " (*Pragmatism,* 112).

It is important to remember that fun and laughter were a large part of James's personality. He saw humor as a captured insight and considered the humorousness of things a dimension as real as their weight and color. Joking was nature's safety valve, relieving internal pressure, but it was also a recognition of the need to heed both the gravely serious and the comical or ridiculous. An intellectual and moral sensitivity devoid of wit, no matter how admirable it might be otherwise, was for James sadly deficient. To cultivate and respect the laughable around us, he thought, is to have an accurate perspective on the world and on ourselves, yielding a proper blend of modesty and self-regard.

But James was a complicated individual; depression alternated with laughter, and an inner loneliness counterbalanced his social charm. He felt isolated from his colleagues because of his interest in mind-cures, psychical research, and religion, areas which were suspect in the eyes of his academic friends. His sense of restlessness and rootlessness began with his frequent travels and changes in schools as a young-ster and continued into his Harvard career; he never felt at home as the newly arrived Irishman among the Boston Brahmins.[98] In addition, he felt an intellectual and personal alienation which he expressed late in life: "So deadly is their intellectual respectability that we can't converse about certain subjects at all. . . . I have num-bered my dearest friends persons thus inhibited intellectually, with whom I would gladly have been able to talk freely about certain interests of mine, certain authors, say, as Bernard Shaw, Edward Carpenter, H. G. Wells, but it wouldn't do, it made them too uncomfortable, they wouldn't play, I had to be silent."[99] Much of James's writing, correspondence, and travel may have been a creative compensation for the intellectual solitude he felt throughout his life.

Many scholars are intrigued by the intersection between James's thought and his experience, between his philosophy and his life. Whereas some academics can separate their work from their personal lives, James could not. He was the best instantiation of his own doctrine that philosophies are the expressions of tempera-ment, that a person's philosophy is the index to his innermost character. His attitude toward philosophy was always ambivalent; he once said, "Philosophy is a queer thing—at once the most sublime and yet the most contemptible of human occupa-tions" (quoted in RBP, 2:376). In his Hegelian moments, he believed in such para-doxical formulations. Ambivalence is necessary, he thought, for an accurate re-sponse to the nature of things. Philosophizing was sometimes tedious, sometimes enjoyable. In 1908, two years before his death, he wrote to Henri Bergson: "Why should life be so short? I wish that you and I and Strong and Flournoy and [William] McDougall and [James] Ward could live on some mountain-top for a month, to-gether, and whenever we got tired of philosophizing calm our minds by taking refuge in the scenery" (quoted in RBP, 2:628).

James's philosophy was an old-fashioned philosophy of life. It was not pri-marily logical analysis, the solution of puzzles, or the clarification of concepts from some related field such as art, religion, or physics; it included these functions, but it was considerably more. His philosophy integrated multiple beliefs into a systematic outlook which provided him with practical guidelines for conducting his daily exis-tence. Thus conceived, philosophy was a subject for the man of all seasons, a pursuit for all moods. One could philosophize light-heartedly, professionally, socially, conversationally; but one could also philosophize in the face of personal crises, as James did in 1870, at the age of twenty-eight.

During that year he was deeply depressed, at times on the verge of suicide. Looking back on that episode, he wrote to his friend B. P. Blood on 28 June 1896: "I take it that no man is educated who has never dallied with the thought of suicide." His diary for this period shows his concern about whether a fundamental pessimism can be avoided. It can be avoided, James thought, if one's moral interests are real rather than illusory; but they cannot be real if there is no free will, because there is no sense in holding that we ought to do what we cannot do. This issue seems to have been one over which he alternated between hope and despair. On 30 April 1870 he recorded in his diary that he had been reading the French philosopher Charles Renouvier.

> I think that yesterday was a crisis in my life. I finished the first part of Renouvier's second *Essais* and see no reason why his definition of free will—"the sustaining of a thought *because I choose to* when I might have other thoughts"— need be the definition of an illusion. At any rate, I will assume for the present— until next year—that it is no illusion. My first act of free will shall be to believe in free will.[100]

James emerged from the depression, although he would suffer from neurotic difficulties throughout his career. The intersection between philosophy (arguing for free will) and life (pulling out of a severe depression) has been doubted by those who believe that a philosophical issue is not powerful enough to cause or resolve an emotional crisis. Critics of the idea of such an intersection argue that physical or psychological causes, more potent than philosophical uncertainties, are what intensify or alleviate severe depressions. According to such critics, what one thinks and says philosophically is more a symptom than a cause.[101] But James would have argued that the important consideration is not whether a physical, psychological, or philosophical condition is a cause or a symptom, but whether the whole constellation of a severe depression, which may include elements of all three categories, can be significantly altered by improving the philosophical condition. James has in fact become a paradigm (resembling Bertrand Russell and Ludwig Wittgenstein in this respect) of the way the philosophical component of one's personality can interact dynamically with the other components. James asserted that reading Renouvier helped him to appreciate the force that philosophical ideas and claims can have upon personality.

After Henry James, Sr., Renouvier was the single most influential figure in James's life. Perry wrote: "That Renouvier was the greatest individual influence upon the development of James's thought cannot be doubted. Renouvier's phenomenalism, his pluralism, his fideism, his moralism, and his theism were all congenial to James's mind, and in them James found support and confirmation. On the other hand, he dissented from Renouvier's intellectualism, from his monadism, and from certain of his speculative extravagances."[102] James discovered in Renouvier a systematic outlook which contained practical guidelines for conduct—exactly what he wanted and needed in his own philosophy. Renouvier connected elements of pluralism, moralism, phenomenalism, fideism, and theism in a way that appealed to James. Renouvier's weltanschauung was lofty and inspiring because of all that it incorporated; his philosophy had a solid center.

Renouvier's definition of freedom—the sustaining of a thought because one chooses to—had a special power for James, leading him to assert that his first act of free will was to believe in free will. Because James was at the time very depressed and needed to hear a powerful voice declare that free will can be demonstrated within oneself, his reading of Renouvier probably did help James to overcome his mental crisis, as he claimed it did. This case was not the only time that philosophizing helped James out of a depression; in fact, he continuously fought his emotional battles with thoughts and words, with philosophy. His was a talking cure, but of a different variety from the psychoanalysts.

The philosophy James used in 1870 to combat depression was not simply the acceptance of a definition of freedom and a willingness to act upon it; the entire Renouvierian "atmosphere of mind and ideas" appealed to him and lent authority to his decision about free will. James's distinctive ideas are traceable not only to his predisposition to believe in them, but also to the confidence he gained from reading Renouvier. Although he later diverged from the French thinker on metaphysical issues, and although Renouvier's influence naturally receded in time, James never again encountered a thinker who had formulated a point of view so close to his own. On 27 June 1880 he wrote to his wife that the English philosopher Shadworth Hodgson (who some say was almost as influential on James as Renouvier) had called Renouvier the most important philosophical writer of the period. "You can't think how it pleaseth me to have this evidence that I have not been a fool in sticking so to R[enouvier]."

A philosophical idea was not necessarily the exclusive cause of James's recovery; in fact, he also credited Goethe and Wordsworth with contributing to it, so we know that he was not lured into a pat explanation. But James seems to have altered his depressed state, at least in part, by inducing in himself the assumption that free will exists. He accomplished this act of will without any self-diagnosis of the cause of his depression and suicidal tendencies. He never suggested that he had identified the precise cause of his crisis; he did not blame it on a past failure to believe in free will, or on the family dynamics of his childhood. (Could he witness contemporary efforts to explain his succession of psychosomatic illnesses in terms of childhood conflicts, he would certainly be resistant to such explanations—as he was throughout his life.)

According to most commentators, James was chronically introspective, a trait which connected naturally with his use of introspection as a psychologist. His was indeed an introspective personality insofar as he was moody and self-preoccupied, often worrying about his health or living in the internal world of ideas that is the lot of most thinkers and writers. But there are two important respects in which he was not introspective. First, he did not try to manage negative feelings by paying them introspective attention. Whereas some therapists contend that troublesome feelings are best handled by intense scrutiny, James counseled otherwise. In "The Gospel of Relaxation" he wrote: "One hearty laugh together will bring enemies into a closer communion of heart than hours spent on both sides in inward wrestling with the mental demon of uncharitable feeling. To wrestle with a bad feeling only pins our attention on it, and keeps it still fastened in the mind; whereas if we act as if from some better feeling, the old bad feeling soon folds its tent like an Arab and silently steals away" (*Talks*, 118). James thus agreed with those who fear that morbidity may result from introspective dwelling on one's feelings and states of mind. Negative states of consciousness, he claimed, are more effectively dissipated by strategic behavior than by introspective scrutiny.

Second, James did not practice introspective self-diagnosis or self-analysis as Freud did, for example, in *The Interpretation of Dreams*. One of the most remarkable aspects of James's numerous references to his own problems is that he never attempted a sustained introspective analysis of their underlying causes. His diaries and correspondence mention his being depressed, fatigued, out of sorts, and tense, but he never ventured sophisticated causal explanations. In this regard he set an example for himself early in life; in 1868 he wrote to his friend Oliver Wendell Holmes, Jr.: "You have a far more logical and orderly mode of thinking than I . . . and whenever we have been together I have somehow been conscious of a reaction against the ascendancy of this over my ruder processes—a reaction caused by some subtle deviltry of egotism and jealousy, whose causes are *untraceable* by myself."[103] James was to an extent an introspectionist in psychology, but he seldom used introspection to discover the causes of his own psychic states, nor did he advocate any systematic method by which people could locate the causes of their psychological troubles; he seems to have thought that the causes are always mainly untraceable.

The concept of causality was an elusive one according to the Jamesian philosophy of science; for that matter, it seems to have been problematic in practice as well. In his reflections on his 1865 trip to the Amazon he wrote:

> To me the peculiar feature which at all times of the day and everywhere made itself felt was the sadness and solemnity produced by the flood of sun and the inextricable variety of vegetable forms, elements which one would suspect beforehand to have a gay and cheerful effect on the observer. On those side views at dawn when the forests used to reveal themselves standing as if painted, the soberness was particularly striking—whereas in our climate there always seemed to me something exhilarating about the "jocund morn."
>
> It strikes me suddenly that my black spectacles may have had something to do with it.[104]

James certainly had a self-awareness and a literary talent for expressing it. Perry characterized the following passage from a letter from James to his wife as an "unusual bit of self-analysis" (RBP, 2:699).

I have often thought that the best way to define a man's character would be to seek out the particular mental or moral attitude in which, when it came upon him, he felt himself most deeply and intensely active and alive. At such moments there is a voice inside which speaks and says: "*This* is the real me!" . . . Now as well as I can describe it, this characteristic attitude in me always involves an element of active tension, of holding my own, as it were, and trusting outward things to perform their part so as to make it a full harmony, but without any *guaranty* that they will. Make it a guaranty—and the attitude immediately becomes to my consciousness stagnant and stingless. Take away the guaranty, and I feel . . . a sort of deep enthusiastic bliss, of bitter willingness to do and suffer anything, which translates itself physically by a kind of stinging pain inside my breast-bone (don't smile at this—it is to me an essential element of the whole thing!), and which, although it is a mere mood of emotion to which I can give no form in words, authenticates itself to me as the deepest principle of all active and theoretic determination which I possess. (*LWJ*, 1:199–200)

This passage is typical of Jamesian introspective descriptions and, in its translation of emotional properties into physical ones, is what one would expect from the author of the James-Lange theory of emotion (see chapter 8). But it scarcely qualifies as a subtle piece of self-analysis, for it is more descriptive than analytical; as a contribution to self-knowledge in terms of uncovering important causal connections, it is very modest indeed. James was skillful in rendering his feelings into words or in recording his habits and mannerisms, but he was oddly uninterested in self-analysis. He could be aware of his tendency to be silent in his father's presence, to feel relief when away from his wife, to dread being alone, to be assertive toward younger siblings, to dislike exact disciplines such as formal logic, to escape whenever he became a parent, to be endlessly neurotic—yet he was not motivated even to speculate about the psychological causes of these phenomena, much less to seek those causes out introspectively. This feature of James's personality is undoubtedly what some scholars mean when discussing his innocence of himself or his lack of interest in self-analysis. From such studies as those of Edel, Strouse, and Allen, one gets the impression that, when it came to understanding the psychological causes for his behavior and that of people close to him, James was like a blind man engaged in target practice.

Nevertheless, he always sought practical remedies for his so-called psychosomatic illnesses. He traveled to Europe for the baths and hydrotherapy treatments, put himself in the care of various doctors, and experimented with all sorts of medications—in short, he was prepared to do almost anything that promised any degree of alleviation. In a letter of 12 September 1912(?) to Henry III, James Jackson Putnam, a doctor and a friend of James, described James's difficulties with fatigue and backache: "I well recall his telling, more than once, of his experiments in the treatment of his weak back, for which he used galvanism daily with his invariable faith, and which he would sometimes "bully" but must sometimes give in to. He became, like myself, considerably interested in Dr. H. P. Bowditch's new ventures in physiology." James often reported to his wife such incidents as having to relieve his backache by sleeping naked on the floor, waking up at 4:00 A.M. because of the pain, and facing the next day exhausted. His correspondence is full of exchanges about how to relieve various illnesses through medication, diet, exercise, hypnotism, or mind-cure. Neither he nor Alice felt inhibited about using any remedy that worked. In 1882, for instance, Alice took opium for attacks of pain and nausea.

Both James's lack of interest in possible psychological causes for his difficulties and his ceaseless quest for remedies suggest that he presumed the causes to be physiological. Something was wrong with his body, and he was ready to correct it with whatever medicine or physiology could offer.[105] As his diaries and correspondence show, he was also prepared to combat illness through consultations with mediums and hypnotists, as well as whatever mind-curists and psychical researchers had to offer. In a letter of 29 March 1888 he wrote to Alice, "I will send you a mind-cure-theosophist book by one Mulford. . . . Pray read it if you can and tell me what is in it when we meet." He and Alice sat with a Boston medium, either together or separately; they were not always seeking relief from illness, but they seem to have thought that they might benefit from the sittings. They met with a mind-curist, a Mrs. Newman, during 1907, from whom James sought relief for his chronic heart condition. As his angina worsened, he also had a series of consultations with a Christian Scientist, L. G. Strang, less than a year before his death from the heart condition in August 1910.

James had no doubt about the physical nature of his ailments. His visits to mind-curists, Christian Scientists, and psychics did not mean that he judged his problems to be primarily psychological in origin. Indeed, in his unpublished 1896 Lowell Lectures on exceptional mental states, he wrote: "Poor hysterics! First treated as victims of sexual trouble . . . then of moral perversity and mendacity . . . then of imagination . . . honest disease not thought of."[106] His were legitimate diseases, but they might be alleviated by the power of changes in consciousness that alternative forms of treatment could provide. Even if the causes were physiological, the remedies might be psychological insofar as they did not directly alter the body as do drugs or surgery.

James did not believe that he could improve his health through self-diagnosis or self-analysis along psychoanalytic lines. He distrusted Freud's dream symbolism, so he did not attempt reflections on his own dreams and fantasies.[107] He thought the unconscious was a reality that could be tapped for reserves of strength, but he did not believe that the causes of his bad health lurked there. Such concepts, even if wielded by a professional, did not appeal to him. Dwelling on boyhood experiences and family politics in order to gain a better understanding of himself was not something to which he was drawn. His brother Henry wrote that William "professed amazement, and even occasionally impatience, at my reach of reminiscence—liking as he did to brush away old moral scraps in favour of new rather than to hoard and so complacently exhibit them."[108]

Lumping James's health problems into the single psychosomatic category would have outraged his sense of accuracy. Angina and backaches are one thing, depression and apathy quite another. He held, for instance, that depression is more philosophical and less medical than angina. Certain kinds of depression intensify or diminish simply in response to the ideas or beliefs which happen to occupy the mind. When James looked back at notes made during his depressions of 1869–70 and sent a page of them for Alice to read, he said, "This you see was written years ago when I was going through the pessimistic crisis."[109] He clearly thought that a pessimistic crisis was different from a medical one. In calling his despondency a pessimistic crisis, he may have supposed that he had identified its main cause. Whatever its causes, he may have reasoned, the despondency was a state of mind that felt as if it would evaporate if he were somehow able to reject philosophical pessimism. The very character of his despondency may have suggested to him that by an act of will he might succeed in overcoming it, that by exercising moral strength he could alleviate the crisis.

A remarkable feature of James's correspondence with his wife is the recurrence of the word *moral,* which he invested with a variety of simultaneous meanings. He sometimes used the word to describe a memorable experience:

> I had a great crisis as I lay in bed. . . . A sort of moral revolution passed through me . . . and the dear sacred Switzerland whose mountains, trees and grass and water are . . . *honest* . . . all got mixed up into my mood; and in one torrent of adoration for them, for you, and for virtue, I rose towards the window to look at the scene . . . mountain . . . milky way . . . big stars. . . . I actually wept aloud for I thought it was *you.* . . . I had one of those moral thunderstorms that go all through you and give you such relief. I hope you'll write me if you have one.[110]

Here the meaning of *moral* is clearly connected with *morale,* for the experience described was the weathering of another crisis and the relief of recovering a healthy morale. Sometimes, as here, the opposite of *moral* is not *immoral* but *demoralized.* For James, to be demoralized was to be in a pessimistic crisis, incapable of finding a single reason to make him want again to continue with life. Sometimes he was saved from such a crisis by a sudden wave of feeling, the rescue resulting from forces outside his control. A similar "moral thunderstorm," though one not involving a crisis, occurred when James was camping on Mount Marcy in the Adirondacks, during the hiking trip that led to his weakened heart condition. He was awake most of the night while his companions slept, being in a state of "spiritual alertness" during what became a "regular Walpurgis Nacht." In a letter of 9 July 1898 he described the experience thus:

> I spent a good deal of [the night] in the woods, where the streaming moonlight

lit up things in a magical checkered play, and it seemed as if the Gods of all the nature-mythologies were holding an indescribable meeting in my breast with the moral Gods of the inner life. The two kinds of Gods have nothing in common—the Edinburgh lectures [*Varieties*] made quite a hitch ahead. . . . The intense significance of some sort, of the whole scene, if one could only *tell* the significance. . . . I can't find a single word for all that significance, and don't know what it was significant of, so there it remains, a mere boulder of *impression*. (*LWJ*, 2:76–77)

These experiences had a moral dimension by reviving morale, but their significance always remained impressionistic. They were James's closest approximations of mystical experiences, suggesting profound meanings too elusive for even the poetic phrase to capture. They were also moral in that they revived the moral will, the determination to perform one's duties as conscience dictated. Even if they fell short of yielding specific moral illuminations, they supplied the entire enterprise of morality with a mystical formulation and confidence.

In his letters to Alice, James often referred to moral victories or triumphs of will over what he took to be weaknesses of character. His apologies to her for intemperate words and behavior were often accompanied by reassurances that he had won a moral battle over his nerves, tensions, or anxieties. He knew what it was like to use willpower to regain self-control when nerves or fears threatened to engulf it. Struck by this sort of moral battle, some scholars have echoed Elizabeth Hardwick's characterization of James as a hero.[111] That the life worth living must contain an element of heroism was affirmed by James at sixteen, in a letter to Van Winkle dated 1 March 1858: "You and I must fight the good fight of faith and be heroes in the strife." He also found this idea in Renouvier; while one should request help wherever available, it is ultimately up to oneself. The challenge in alleviating nerves, anxieties, fears, and depressions is less finding the nexus of causes underlying them than battling them as they appear. It is less important to diagnose their origins than it is to vanquish them through creating future-oriented incentives.

James fought his battles largely through what he called acts of thought. He resolved the issue of free will by making his first act one of believing in free will. Philosophy for him consisted of acts of thought, but it also involved information, reasoning, argument, and assessment. Nevertheless, he thought that on the major issues in metaphysics, morals, religion, and self-help, there comes a point when one must perform an act of thought and decide where to place one's belief. For James, philosophy at its grandest was an interpretation of the entire world, of everything from the glory of the Milky Way to the degradation of an attack of nerves. In 1903 James wrote to a friend, "I actually dread to die until I have settled the Universe's hash in one more book" (quoted in Allen, 437). He wove the concepts of space, time, causality, and being into a philosophical interpretation of the universe that was also a creative response to it, by which he could live as he thought he ought to live.

James's philosophy was unusually and deliberately personal. He meant it to reflect both the universe and himself, because he could not believe that the former could exist independent of individual selves. Yet his philosophy is not the product of an introspective self-analysis but is rather the outward projection of his personality upon the world. His philosophy was the spontaneous and immediate expression of his personality, for all to witness. In James, personality and philosophy are inextricably connected. Philosophizing brought him closer to himself while affording relief from the preoccupation with self; it was an expression of the inner achieved by focusing outward. The consciousness that came to life in his philosophizing could be described as he described his summer home in Chocorua: "Oh, it is the most delightful house you ever saw; it has fourteen doors, all opening outwards" (quoted in Allen, 286). Philosophy lured the inner self outward and toward the future. In so doing it served a moral purpose, at times even won a moral victory; it revealed what human consciousness can achieve from its own resources—but that is the subject of the next chapter.

2 ❧ CONSCIOUSNESS

MIND AND BODY

James has often been called an introspective psychologist, but he was also a
representative of physiological psychology, which had been developing rapidly in
Europe. The movement of psychology away from philosophy and toward the laboratory resulted from its new alliance with physiology, which promised to illuminate
the study of perception, emotion, thought, memory, attention, will, and association
through discoveries about functions of the central nervous system. A striking feature
of James's *Principles of Psychology* is its abundant references to continental and British
research in human physiology; as a result, the book continues to be the classic—and
most interesting—source for understanding the rise of nineteenth-century physiological psychology. James has sometimes been called a behaviorist, with justification
to the extent that he identified the varieties of consciousness with their functions and
sometimes identified emotions with their manifestations. But unlike B. F. Skinner's
concept of psychology today, physiological psychology in James's day required
going "under the skin." Whereas Skinner and other contemporary behaviorists view
psychology as independent of physiology and see its central job as correlating sched-
ules of reinforcement with their behavioral effects, James saw its task as improving
our knowledge of mind-body relationships by drawing upon the new science of
human physiology.

James's very definition of psychology reveals its subject matter to be the relation
between mind and body: it is "the Science of Mental Life, both of its phenomena,
feelings, desires, cognitions, reasonings, etc. and their [physiological] conditions."[1]
Both psychology and common sense assume Descartes's view that there are mental
events, such as thoughts and feelings, and physical ones, such as those in the brain
and other parts of the body; between these types of occurrences, it is further assumed, important cognitive and causal relations obtain. James would insert "as-

54

sume" here because he believed that any science, including psychology, begins with uncritically assumed data which, if philosophically examined and interpreted, may be understood quite differently. Thus, after declaring his intention to suppose, with scientific psychology, that "the uniform correlation of brain-states with mind-states is a law of nature," he explained that this was not a materialistic thesis, because even if the coming to pass of mind-states depends upon brain-states, the nature of mind-states is not necessarily explained by such dependence.[2] Although the brain seems to be a necessary condition of the mind's existence, there are perhaps forms of life, different from the human, for which consciousness survives apart from the particularities of the body. When writing as a metaphysician, James professed to believe such possibilities.[3] The distinction between mental and physical states is itself suspect, he suggested in asides and footnotes in *Principles* while (unphilosophically) employing the distinction along Cartesian lines as demanded by psychology and common sense. In 1904 he wrote a famous essay, "Does 'Consciousness' Exist?" which announced his abandonment of Cartesian dualism or of any ultimate distinction between mind and body, making it clear that he had adopted a provisional dualism in *Principles* on behalf of a new effort, a textbook in which psychology was at last presented as a natural science.[4] While the laboratory psychologist must believe that there are two distinct occurrences—a person's feeling of elation and something occurring in his brain—he is not thereby committed to the Cartesian idea that the elation is in some philosophical sense "mental" and the brain-state "physical." On the contrary, he may hold that both occurrences, while distinct, are of the same type, perhaps physical. Because Cartesian dualism so dominated both common sense and the climate of scientific psychology, James knew that it would have been a strategic error to write a textbook that explicitly argued for the rejection of such dualism. The result would have been too distracting and controversial, and instead of producing a pioneering work in scientific psychology, he would at best have added to a continuing debate in the philosophy of mind.

Principles can be viewed as a logical step toward a metaphysics that interprets psychology more deeply than common sense can. Such a metaphysics requires collecting the scattered data of psychologists into a systematic picture which will present the metaphysician with an adequate body of materials for his interpretation. Although James had crystallized favorite ideas before beginning *Principles*—the doctrine that subjective interests and preferences are part of what justify beliefs, for example—he seems to have become increasingly confident, as he surveyed psychology during the twelve years required to complete *Principles*, about the nature of the problems bequeathed to philosophy by psychology and about his own philosophical responses to those problems. For instance, none of the actual or foreseeable achievements of psychology could in his eyes satisfactorily explain how mind and body relate, nor could they prove a materialistic theory of mind which asserts that humans are merely conscious automata. James was justified in asserting that he had overlooked nothing in psychological research which might contradict his contentions that "the relations of a mind to its own brain are of a unique and utterly mysterious sort'' (*Principles,* 1:216) and that, in the absence of sound empirical evidence, to urge materialism ''on purely *a priori* and *quasi*-metaphysical grounds, is an *unwarrantable impertinence in the present state of psychology*'' (*Principles,* 1:138). It had been evident since Hume that the concept of causality belonged to philosophy, so psychology could articulate only tentatively a causal relation between mind and body. Moreover, as Descartes's critics had declared long before, the ways that mind and body interact causally are not easily investigated. Psychologists can correlate happenings in the mind with those in the body and can assume such correlations to be bona fide causal connections, but understanding the meaning of these connections demands philosophical analysis. James believed that the *how* of any causal interaction between mind and body defies scientific identification, and thus that the philosopher ought to speculate for himself about the nature of the mind-body relation.

At the commonsense level, which James urged psychologists to respect, he supposed that mind and body do interact, although he knew that it is always harder to convince the materialist that mind is a causal agency than to persuade the mentalist that the body is a causal entity.[5] Who can doubt that a knock on the head can cause changes in consciousness? But many doubt whether a change in consciousness, such as depression, causes anything at all, whether other emotions or physiological changes.[6] Such people find it difficult to believe that causality can be anything but physical, and judge that states of consciousness are incidental byproducts of physical occurrences, comparable to the transient sparks produced by a welding operation but not comparable to the welding process itself. James replied that this epiphenomenalistic or ''conscious automata'' theory of mental states is ''impertinent'' in that it is pressed in the absence of evidence. Further, he offered a counterargument that consciousness is primarily a selecting agency, directing its attention to what is most interesting. The idea of consciousness as a selective agency suggests that consciousness exists to do some work. The brain is a delicate, unstable organ, and it is plausible that it requires the assistance of consciousness for survival and better environmental adjustments. Moreover, to accept evolutionary theory in a Darwinian era was not to conclude that a person's interests are merely bodily, aimed at survival as an absolute goal; what we commonly call human interests are functions of human intelligence and consciousness, and it is sometimes in the interest of a particular consciousness not to survive. Against the claims of materialism or epiphenomenalism, James asserted that consciousness exists because it has things to do, that it is a ''*fighter for ends,* of which many, but for its presence, would not be ends at all.''[7]

Indeed, James supposed, if at the commonsense level we must deny the influence of mind upon body, then we must also renounce any conviction that we are ever in control of our own lives. Much of his thought about the mind-body relation is an argument against theoretical challenges to the ordinary view that our states of consciousness sometimes—and sometimes deliberately—control our bodies. Unless our decisions, beliefs, feelings, and concentrations are causally efficacious, our lives are the effects only of bodily mechanics; yet disproving the epiphenomenalistic theory is impossible. Someone declares that his desire to get well caused him to recover, but his physician doubts the claim, attributing the recovery to chemistry and dismissing the desire to improve as inconsequential. Though the patient argues his case, he can never produce proof. If all claims that the mind affects the body are thus dismissed, the ordinary conviction that we are at least somewhat in control of our lives evaporates. If we side with the patient against the metaphysical physician who holds stoutly to the epiphenomenalistic notion that causes never include states of consciousness, we must, like James, support our commonsense perceptions with the most persuasive philosophical arguments we can summon. The dramatic tone of James's words in defending mental causality fits naturally with his championing a heartfelt belief. "But the whole feeling of reality, the whole sting and excitement of our voluntary life, depends on our sense that in it things are *really being decided* from one moment to another, and that it is not the dull rattling off of a chain that was forged innumerable ages ago" (*Principles*, 1:453). A good deal of the excitement in James's writings occurs where he nurtures (or abandons) by philosophical argument some belief that is precious to common sense.

In 1898, eight years after publication of *Principles*, James argued for the plausibility of immortality, urging that the brain does not produce but only transmits consciousness; consciousness may be dependent upon the brain not for its existence but only for being channeled or filtered in the ways to which we are accustomed. Despite whatever appearance the mind gives of being wholly at the body's mercy, then, it may live its own life apart from the body, although without the brain it is no longer capable of manifesting itself in familiar ways. "And when finally a brain stops acting altogether, or decays, that special stream of consciousness would still be intact; and in that more real world with which, even whilst here, it was continuous, the consciousness might, in ways unknown to us, continue still."[8] The fact that the mind exists in a temporary condition of dependence upon the brain—as far as ordinary experience reveals—need not mean, James suggested, that the mind is permanently subservient in all respects to its associated body. We are therefore free, if we wish, to use reason and imagination to support the speculation that the mind outlives the body.

James did not believe mind and body to be the distinct entities they may seem to be; whatever differences we ascertain between them can be interpreted, he thought, not as differences between two radically opposed entities, but as dissimilarities within what he called pure experience. He held that there is only one basic phenomenon, experience itself, and that the distinctions we ordinarily draw between mind and body fall within experience; such distinctions do not arise from two substances, mind and body, but rather from the particular ways in which experience has been arranged: if arranged in one fashion it appears as mind, if in another, as body. The idea that mind and body are merely varying aspects of pure experience is the centerpiece of the radical empiricism which James introduced in 1904, six years before his death. But the idea had been attractive to him even some years prior to the completion of *Principles*, and it was responsible for the doubts about Cartesian dualism sprinkled throughout that book.[9] We find in his writings, therefore, the claims that mind and body interact, that they are not radically opposed entities, and that the mind may outlive the body. It was hardly easy to make these claims mutually consistent, but James was dedicated to doing so throughout his career. Among his pronouncements about consciousness, many appear to be consistent with one but not all of these claims.

CONSCIOUSNESS

In his early writings and in *Principles*, James typically referred to consciousness as if it were an agency with distinct properties; as the phrase "fighter for ends" suggests, he was especially given to characterizing it in causal terms and ascribing to it certain capacities that might be attributed more appropriately to persons. "But consciousness itself is not merely intelligent in [a merely hypothetical sense]. It is *intelligent intelligence*. It seems both to supply the means and the standard by which they are measured. It not only *serves* a final purpose, but *brings* a final purpose— posits, declares it. This purpose is not a mere hypothesis—'*if* survival is to occur, then brain must so perform,' etc.—but an imperative decree: 'Survival *shall* occur, and, therefore, brain *must* so perform.' "[10] We can of course read such locutions as indirect and eloquent ways of saying that persons have purposes, but we would thus minimize any significance that might be attached to James's fondness for the word *consciousness*. In the absence of more explicit explanation, the reader understandably wonders whether James once believed that we have purposes only because we are endowed with a consciousness with a variety of its own remarkable properties. He repeatedly credited consciousness with taking an interest in something, attending to something, decreeing this, choosing that, selecting one thing, preferring another— so anxious was he to establish the efficacy of consciousness and therefore the vulnerability of materialism.[11]

That James saw consciousness as an entity is evident in many of his questions: Is consciousness composed of parts? Does any consciousness contain smaller bits of consciousness? Does consciousness include unperceived mental units of some sort? In raising these questions he was examining the tradition that just as physical things or processes are composed of smaller physical ones, so are mental states or processes formed of smaller mental ones. James broke from this tradition, reasoning that subjective states are not like physical ones in this regard. Whereas green and red light can combine to produce yellow, the consciousness or sensation of green obviously cannot combine with the awareness of red to yield the consciousness of yellow. There can be combinations and permutations in brain processes that cause what occurs in consciousness, but states of consciousness themselves, unlike brain processes, are not combinable. James concluded that

> there *are* no unperceived units of mind-stuff preceding and composing the full consciousness. The latter is itself an immediate psychic fact and bears an immediate relation to the neural state which is its unconditional accompaniment. Did

each neural shock give rise to its own psychic shock, and the psychic shocks then combine, it would be impossible to understand why severing one part of the central nervous system from another should break up the integrity of consciousness. The cut has nothing to do with the psychic world. (*Principles*, 1:157)

It is the essence of consciousness, he urged, to appear as it really is; *esse est sentiri* (to be is to be sensed). The taste of lemonade, for instance, is what it appears to be, a unique taste that cannot be separated into the taste of lemon and the taste of sugar. States of consciousness, James argued, are like the taste of lemonade, unique and not divisible into smaller units.

James defended this position in "The Mind-Stuff Theory," chapter 6 of *Principles*; in the process he commented on the concept of the unconscious. The so-called mind-stuff theory, which maintained that mental states are compounds of smaller mental units (mind-stuff), conceded that we are generally unaware of the smaller elements, being conscious only of the total result (the taste of lemonade or the color yellow, for example). Mind-stuff was said to exist unconsciously in our experience while contributing to the total result. James considered ten proofs or arguments for the mind-stuff theory and rebutted each, thus supporting a negative answer to the question: Do unconscious mental states exist? At the end of James's chapter 6 the reader has the impression that nothing mental or experienced can occur at an unconscious level, because the *to be* of consciousness is *to be sensed*, and therefore no mental elements are unconscious components of any state of consciousness. But this impression is corrected later in *Principles* (notably in chapters 8, 9, and 11), because there were at least two ways in which James thought mental or subjective states can occur unconsciously. We can be unconscious of experiences when we fail to attend to them. "Our insensibility to habitual noises, etc., whilst awake, proves that we can neglect to attend to that which we nevertheless feel."[12] Something can be mental, subjective, or experienced and yet elude consciousness; it can be felt yet be excluded from attention or consciousness. Being felt insures that it is a mental or psychic event and not merely a physiological occurrence not yet translated to the psychological level. However, we may insist that if something is felt then it must, if only minimally, register in consciousness. James agreed. But for all practical purposes, it is ignored by one's conscious attention to such an extent that it is virtually unconscious.

The second way that mental states can exist unconsciously is illustrated by cases of abnormal psychology. In hysterical blindness, for example, the patient sees at an unconscious level what he cannot see consciously. "Binet has found the hand of his patients unconsciously writing down words which their eyes were vainly endeavoring to 'see,' i.e., to bring to the upper consciousness. Their submerged consciousness was of course seeing them, or the hand could not have written as it did. Colors are similarly perceived by the subconscious self, which the hysterically color-blind eyes cannot bring to the normal consciousness" (*Principles*, 1:206). In such cases a splitting of consciousness occurs, a situation difficult to describe. James followed Pierre Janet in calling the waking person who cannot see consciously what is nevertheless seen unconsciously, the *primary* personality or consciousness; continuing to assume that nothing is experienced wholly unconsciously, Janet and James called the submerged or subconscious viewer who does see it, the *secondary* (*tertiary,* etc.) personality. Although something may be experienced unconsciously by the primary personality, it must be consciously experienced by someone, a secondary personality in the same body. Cases of multiple personalities or splittings of consciousness associated with a single human body do in fact occur, but nothing that is experienced can fail to be noticed by at least one consciousness. No mental state can occur that is not in some consciousness; nothing can be experienced at an unconscious level that does not register in the consciousness of someone else. James writes in "The Stream of Thought," chapter 9 of *Principles,* that any state of consciousness or anything experienced must belong to a personal consciousness, even if it is claimed in some context to be experienced unconsciously.

The Janet-James interpretation of unconscious mental events differs sharply from the Freudian concept of the unconscious; Freud, who explicitly opposed his own view to Janet's, saw the unconscious as an impersonal realm in which opposing mental forces are in conflict. In the Freudian scheme what occurs in someone's unconscious need not be in the consciousness of someone else. The idea that an item experienced unconsciously must be conscious to a secondary or subconscious self struck Freud as paradoxical. "Anyone who tried to push the argument further and to conclude from it that one's own hidden processes belonged actually to a second *consciousness* would be faced with the concept of a consciousness of which one knew nothing, of an 'unconscious consciousness'—and this would scarcely be preferable to the assumption of an 'unconscious mental.' "[13] Could James have replied, he would presumably have denied such a paradox, insisting that the secondary consciousness is indeed not known or recognized by the primary, but knows or recognizes itself in the way that any of us is acquainted with our own consciousness. Thus the notion of a secondary or subconscious personality does not saddle us with an unintelligible "unconscious consciousness." James would have shifted the burden of proof upon Freud, as many others have, by asking what can be the point of calling something both unconscious and mental if it is not felt or experienced to some degree, that is, if it is not impressed upon someone's consciousness at least a little bit.

The exact status of James's concept of consciousness in the years before he introduced radical empiricism is difficult to determine. In addition to suggesting that consciousness was an entity, he contrasted it with physical processes, attributing to it distinct properties which might be sufficient to challenge materialism. Mental states (also called feelings and thoughts in *Principles*) have five major characteristics: they belong to a personal consciousness, are always changing, are sensibly continuous, intentionally have objects other than themselves, and always favor some objects over others. Together with the property of not being composed of parts or elements, for which James argues in "The Stream of Thought," these characteristics appear to distinguish consciousness from anything physical. Things in the physical world may be constantly changing or sensibly continuous without appearing to be so, but for consciousness, because its *to be* is *to be sensed,* these characteristics appear to be what they really are.

James believed at times that consciousness, unlike ordinary physical things or processes, displays a special unity which connects with the *esse est sentiri* nature of mental states; if a mental state is not divisible into parts, then it is a unified complex. James was drawn to the idea that the only thing which in itself exhibits genuine unity is consciousness or a mental state. "In physical nature, it is universally agreed, a multitude of facts always remain the multitude they were and appear as one fact only when a mind comes upon the scene and so views them, as when H–O–H appears as 'water' to a human spectator."[14] The mind can hold many things together in a synthetic unity; it is "obvious that if things are to be thought in relation, they must be thought together, and in one *something,* be that something ego, psychosis, state of consciousness, or whatever you please" (*Principles,* 1:277). Consequently, the reader of *Principles* and other of James's works easily gains the impression that consciousness, as an indivisible unity, a continuous "stream," and so on, is an entity or a process that is one side of a Cartesian dualism. Consciousness seems to be completely different from anything physical.

But James was far from confident about the nature of consciousness or about giving it a Cartesian interpretation, as indicated throughout *Principles* in asides, parenthetical remarks, and footnotes; before the work was completed in 1890, he had become increasingly doubtful about a philosophical opposition of consciousness to everything physical. In "The Consciousness of Self," chapter 10 of *Principles,* for example, he insisted that whatever his introspections disclosed was always permeated with bodily or physiological aspects to such a degree that he believed that only physiological occurrences such as heartbeats or temperature changes are ever felt. Because introspective analysis is delicate and fallible, we cannot be at all certain of its conclusions, yet "if the dim portions which I cannot yet define should prove to be like unto those distinct portions in me, and I like other men, *it would follow that our entire feeling of spiritual activity, or what commonly passes by that name, is really a feeling of bodily activities whose exact nature is by most men overlooked.*"[15] James came to question the idea of an irreducible difference between consciousness as a spiritual (that is, purely nonphysical) activity and physical or physiological activities, largely because his introspection never conclusively showed that anything purely nonphysiological ever occurs. As far as introspection can determine, anything "mental" appears physiological—a point James recalled in his writings on radical empiricism, where he argued that consciousness and physical things are less heterogeneous than is commonly assumed.[16]

James's second reason for abandoning a Cartesian concept of consciousness is connected with the impossibility of proving that nonphysiological events occur, although considerable sorting of the texts is required before the connection can be made confidently. This reason relates to James's change of heart on the compounding of consciousness and thereby on the *esse est sentiri* doctrine of states of consciousness. In insisting that states of consciousness, unlike physical things, cannot combine into more complex ones, he wrote: "The physical lemonade contains both the lemon and the sugar, but its taste does not contain their tastes, for if there are any two things which are certainly *not* present in the taste of lemonade, those are the lemon-sour on the one hand and the sugar-sweet on the other. These tastes are absent utterly" (*Principles*, 1:158n). But in 1895 he wrote: "In a glass of lemonade we can taste both the lemon and sugar at once. In a major chord our ear can single out the *c, e, g,* and *c'*, if it has once become acquainted with these notes apart. And so on through the whole field of our experience, whether conceptual or sensible."[17] What prompted James to change his mind was his realization that in at least some states of consciousness there is an inner complexity that is decipherable introspectively. Whereas in *Principles* he had let their complexity reside in their plural cognitive function, in 1895 he appreciated "better now than then that my proposal to designate mental states merely by their cognitive function leads to a somewhat strained way of talking of dreams and reveries, and to quite an unnatural way of talking of some emotional states" (*CER*, 399). The reference here to emotional states is significant, because in the 1884 essay "What Is an Emotion?" he had analyzed certain emotions into simpler elements: "The immense number of *parts* modified in each emotion is what makes it so difficult for us to reproduce in cold blood the total and integral expression of any one of them" (*CER*, 252; italics mine). James acknowledged here that emotional states have parts (although in 1884 his statement might have been seen as merely a lapse); in an announced change of position in 1895, he deliberately surrendered the *esse est sentiri* doctrine and agreed that some mental states can be introspectively dissected into constituent mental elements. And if mental states can be made up of smaller parts of the same sort of "stuff," they resemble in this respect physical things. Further, if those mental elements cannot be definitively introspected as nonphysiological, then the Cartesian concept of consciousness becomes less defensible—a realization evident in James's thought subsequent to *Principles*.

His later ideas about consciousness resulted from a combination of introspection and argument. He became increasingly confident that no distinct entity, process, or state called consciousness is introspectable. Explicitly denying G. E. Moore's claim that the consciousness of blue can be introspectively distinguished from the actual color, James wrote: "*Experience, I believe, has no such inner duplicity; and the separation of it into consciousness and content comes, not by way of subtraction, but by way of addition*—the addition, to a given concrete piece of it, of other sets of experiences, in connection with which severally its use or function may be of two different kinds."[18] Consciousness is not an entity or something introspectable, but rather the way in which experiences function in relation to one another. We can talk about thoughts as conscious, for instance, but we must not suppose them to be composed of something called consciousness; thought are not introspectively found to be different from physical entities, and to ascribe consciousness to them suggests that they have a cognitive function. The doubts expressed in *Principles* about Cartesian dualism are transformed into definite convictions in the metaphysics of radical empiricism.

James declared, "It is very difficult, or even absolutely impossible, to know solely by intimate examination [introspection] whether certain phenomena are of a physical nature—occupying space, etc.—or whether they are of a purely psychical and inner nature."[19] This inability of introspection to mark an immediately felt distinction between the psychical and the physical points to the fact that no distinction can be drawn between them; any such distinction is only functional.

The inability of introspection to make a sharp division between the psychical and the physical, or between consciousness and its nonconscious objects, was in one respect welcomed by James. It agreed with his temperamental opposition to intellectual dualisms, dichotomies, and alleged discontinuities in nature and experience. He preferred to believe that nature abhors a discontinuity, and wherever he found a philosopher creating one he sought to replace it with a concept that would reinstate continuity; for example, he was prepared to invoke evolutionary theory on appropriate occasions. The failure of introspection to support the discontinuity introduced by Cartesian dualism cleared the way for radical empiricism and the notion that the distinction between consciousness and nonconscious or physical things can be conceived in terms of elements that are themselves neither conscious nor physical. These elements, called pure experiences, are neutral with respect to being either mental or physical. The last decade of James's life was largely devoted to developing arguments for the thesis that pure experience is a more basic or primitive concept than consciousness.

James's task of reconciling his later doctrine that nothing is literally designated by consciousness with other trends in his thought was not easy. It seems inevitable that the concept of consciousness was doomed to an ambiguous status in his philosophy. It can be argued that the later notion of pure experiences presupposes that of consciousness, and that pure experiences, far from being neutral occurrences, are described in terms of conscious sensations. As Bertrand Russell remarked, James almost gave away his case for a primary neutralism: "The phrase 'pure experience' . . . points to a lingering influence of idealism. 'Experience,' like 'consciousness,' must be a product, not part of the primary stuff of the world."[20] We might agree with James that introspection does not reveal something called consciousness within experience, yet simultaneously insist that experiences are precisely part of what is meant by being conscious; if so, it is tempting, on introspective evidence, to see a radical distinction between what it is to have an experience and what it is to be a physical thing. The original question of whether consciousness presents us with a Cartesian dichotomy becomes a question of whether that dichotomy is sustained by the fact that experiences occur. However we answer such questions, it is evident that James never adequately explained how the concepts of consciousness and experience connect. Nor did he explain, despite what he may have implied at times, whether anything is gained by understanding an experience as conscious. The project of his later metaphysics—to analyze consciousness in terms of a neutral notion of pure experience—thus remains a hazy one.

The attempt to understand what James really believed about the nature of consciousness is complicated further by his opposition to materialism and his defense of religion and its message that mind ultimately triumphs over matter. If introspection cannot reveal once and for all the existence of the nonphysical, or at least of something sufficiently unusual to replace former notions of the mental or the spiritual, then an escape from materialism can only be managed through philosophical argument, to which much of James's writing was devoted. In seeking to make immortality plausible, for instance, he argued that despite appearances consciousness may depend upon the brain not for its existence but only for its ordinary manifestations in our everyday experience. The brain may not produce but merely transmit consciousness, and when the brain dies consciousness may endure. "Consciousness in this process does not have to be generated *de novo* in a vast number of places. It exists already, behind the scenes, coeval with the world."[21] James used Gustav Fechner's notion of threshold in describing the brain as a kind of dam or threshold whose height may vary such that when it is elevated consciousness is diminished, and when it is lowered consciousness is widened enormously. "We need only suppose the continuity of our consciousness with a mother sea, to allow for exceptional waves occasionally pouring over the dam. Of course the causes of these odd lowerings of the brain's threshold still remain a mystery on any terms" (*WTB*, 27). He wrote later in the same work: "The amount of possible consciousness seems to be governed by no law analogous to that of the so-called conservation of energy in the material world" (*WTB*, 41). Such statements, which occur throughout James's later writings, recall his forceful formulations in *Principles* of consciousness as a fighter for ends or the director of energies.

If we try to make such statements consistent with James's denial of Cartesian dualism, and of consciousness as something distinct, by interpreting them according to his radical empiricism, our attempt will be fraught with the difficulties surrounding the idea of pure experience. It is hard for the reader not to get the impression that James's pure experiences are really free-floating bits of consciousness that function independently of the human brain or other physical influences. Whether the phenomenon is called experience or consciousness, James's testimonial words to it lead us irresistibly to view it not merely as a function but as something with an inherent nature, by which it is a causal agent that produces effects, including whatever he supposed it to achieve on its own without the aid of the brain. James wanted to hold that in one way consciousness does not exist, but that in another way it does; yet he was never able, even to his own satisfaction, to define the two ways clearly enough to show that they are consistent rather than contradictory.

INTROSPECTION

The natural sciences depend upon sense-perception, whereas psychology, it was commonly assumed in James's time, relies upon introspection as its distinct method of inquiry. James tempered this assumption by requiring psychology to supplement its introspections with experimental or laboratory techniques, but introspection was for him always an indispensable investigative tool for psychological studies. He spent little effort defining introspection: "The word introspection need hardly be defined—it means, of course, the looking into our own minds and reporting what we there discover."[22] He addressed immediately the sorts of things that introspection can be claimed to disclose, and with what degree of certainty or uncertainty. James's "introspection" resembles John Locke's "reflection," which is defined as "the perception of the operations of our own mind within us" or as "that notice which the mind takes of its own operations."[23] James did not confine introspective disclosures to mental operations (nor did Locke, in fact, insofar as he included "passions" such as satisfaction and uneasiness under "mental operations"), yet he agreed with Locke that introspection is a form of observation, and what is observed, as long as we adhere to commonsense dualism, is always internal to the mind.

In urging his subjects to introspect, the psychologist, according to James, encourages them to observe their own states of mind and to notice as carefully as possible the features of those states. Introspection takes practice as well as considerable concentration, because inner states succeed each other rapidly and often blend in a way that makes it difficult to distinguish them. Accordingly, James's concept of introspection, like Locke's, is directly analogous to sense-perception; the objects of introspective observation are "inner," or in the mind—as long as dualism is retained—whereas the objects of sense-perception are "outer," external to the mind. Like sense-perception, introspection is fallible and can at times be troublesome and difficult, yet *the difficulty is simply that of all observation of whatever kind* (*Principles*, 1:191). Introspection as observation surely occurs, but it can be argued that the word is often taken to mean something other than observation and that, for the goal of self-knowledge, introspection as observation may be less useful than introspection differently conceived. The literature on the topic suggests that the concept of introspection is polymorphic, referring to a wide variety of activities. If the case could be made here, we might be persuaded that some of these senses of introspection are more important than observation is for self-knowledge.[24]

James himself recognized an essential feature of introspection as observation that points to an inherent weakness in the claims sometimes made about it. Agreeing with Franz Brentano, he emphasized

the difference between the immediate *feltness* of a feeling, and its perception by a subsequent reflective act [introspection]. But which mode of consciousness of it is that which the psychologist must depend on? If to *have* feelings or thoughts in their immediacy were enough, babies in the cradle would be psychologists, and infallible ones. But the psychologist must not only *have* his mental states in their absolute veritableness, he must report them and write about them, name them, classify and compare them and trace their relations to other things. . . . And as in the naming, classifying, and knowing of things in general we are notoriously fallible, why not also here? [Auguste] Comte is quite right in laying stress on the fact that a feeling, to be named, judged, or perceived, must be already past. No subjective state, whilst present, is its own object; its object is always something else.[25]

James either construed introspection as observation with a classifying report of what was observed or conceived of observation as including classification. In either case, introspection involves naming and classifying, not merely having an experience of some kind. For example, the feeling of jealousy (the mere "having" it) is registered to a preintrospective awareness, but to introspect it, we must conceptualize it through naming and classifying. The possibility of error always haunts introspection; while a mistake may not attend the *feltness* of jealousy, we can always go wrong in conceptualizing it.

The distinction between preintrospective and introspective awareness is important not only in showing how error can permeate the latter. Introspection as observation is a studied scrutiny of an existent form of awareness; we cannot introspect stumps, but we can introspect our perceptual awareness of stumps. To introspect jealousy is to introspect an existent feeling of jealousy. In short, introspective awareness presupposes an awareness upon which the introspection is directed. That this often occurs, sometimes with little risk of error in the reporting, sometimes with great risk, is undeniable. Again, if we made the case here, we might be persuaded that we do not obtain as much distinct information from introspection superimposed upon an anterior awareness as James and traditional introspective psychology supposed. We can sometimes tell the doctor, after we have introspected on a pain in the knee, more precisely where the pain is located. But in the main, introspection is so parasitic upon the existent awareness that it can do little more than register what is already in that awareness—a dependence which severely undermines the importance of introspection as observation. Oddly, despite everything he examined that might exhibit the fallibility and difficulty of introspection, James seems never to have considered that introspection may be doomed to reiterating what is already present in preintrospective awareness; this oversight raises important questions about James's own introspections, especially as discussed in such chapters of *Principles* as "The Stream of Thought" and "The Consciousness of Self."

The distinction between preintrospective and introspective awareness does not itself imply any inability of introspection to observe a state of consciousness while it occurs, but James believed that introspection is always subsequent to the object it observes; that is, introspection is really immediate retrospection. His point that naming and classifying are part of what we call introspective observation meant, he believed, that the time required to classify any preintrospective awareness (the mere *feltness* of a feeling or sensation) will force the report of what is felt to occur later than the sensation itself; thus, if the report is part of the introspective observation, such observation must always be later than the event reported. We might reply that this distinction only confuses a report of an observation with the observation itself and urge that the introspective observation and the observed mental state may in fact happen simultaneously. We might presume that we can experience and observe the same inner state at a single stroke, as when we say "I feel tired" or "I feel angry." But this presumption is an illusion, James held: "The present conscious state, when I say 'I feel tired,' is not the direct state of tire; when I say 'I feel angry,' it is not the direct state of anger. It is the state of *saying-I-feel-tired*, of *saying-I-feel-angry*, entirely different matters, so different that the fatigue and anger apparently included in them are considerable modifications of the fatigue and anger directly felt the previous instant. The act of naming them has momentarily detracted from their force."[26] In general, he agreed, the two states are sufficiently continuous to make an erroneous introspective report unlikely, but the truth of the report involves an empirical hypothesis and cannot be decided on a priori or self-evident grounds.

James evidently assumed that any conceptualization, whether a verbal utterance or not, occupies some time, and that when it is completed the conceptualized mental state has already slipped into the immediate past. But why cannot a preconceptualizing, introspective observation precede the conceptualization, allowing us both to compare the two by testing the adequacy of the conceptualization, and to hold that the observed mental state and the introspective observing of it can occur simultaneously? James never accepted Comte's claim that the observational process necessarily alters the mental state being scrutinized; he was content to maintain simply that mental states have certain peculiarities which make it hard to see them as they are. Because each mental state is a phase or "pulse" (temporary wavelet) in a stream of consciousness, any one pulse has already been succeeded by another in the onrushing stream by the time we can train introspective attention upon it. Thus even a preconceptualizing introspective look is inevitably tardy. James apparently concluded that introspective observation occurs as retrospection, that one can still observe (rather like an afterimage) something that has just happened. His concept of the *now* as a *specious present*, according to which the just-past is apprehended in an extended present rather than remembered from a more remote past, permits him to speak of things in the just-past as still observed or immediately retrospected—a process which differs from what we ordinarily mean by memory or recollection. This concept allowed James to hold that the way a mental state felt or registered to preintrospective awareness can be checked against the introspective observation (and report) of it as just-past in testing for observational accuracy. And this comparison can be made without requiring that the mental state and the introspective observing of it be absolutely simultaneous. We may not want to adopt this notion of introspective observation for ourselves, but it clearly functions coherently in James's scheme.

Since James is often called an introspective psychologist, it is important to avoid thinking that he accepted even his own introspections uncritically; to the contrary, he always insisted upon the fragility and elusiveness of the introspective process.

However it may be with such strong feelings as doubt or anger, about weaker feelings, and about the *relations to each other,* of all feelings, we find ourselves in continual error and uncertainty so soon as we are called on to name and class, and not merely to feel. Who can be sure of the exact *order* of his feelings when they are excessively rapid? Who can be sure, in his sensible perception of a chair, how much comes from the eye and how much is supplied out of the previous knowledge of the mind? Who can compare with precision the *quantities* of disparate feelings even where the feelings are very much alike? For instance, where an object is felt now against the back and now against the cheek, which feeling is most extensive? Who can be sure that two given feelings are or are not exactly the same? Who can tell which is briefer or longer than the other when both occupy but an instant of time? Who knows, of many actions, for what motive they were done, or if for any motive at all? Who can enumerate all the distinct ingredients of such a complicated feeling as *anger?* And who can tell offhand whether or no a perception of *distance* be a compound or a simple state of mind? The whole mind-stuff controversy would stop if we could decide conclusively by introspection that what seem to us elementary feelings are really elementary and not compound. (*Principles*, 1:191)

In addition to checking the accuracy of introspective reports by comparing the way a mental state felt or registered to a preintrospective awareness with the immediately subsequent introspective report of it, there were, James emphasized, new techniques for testing introspective reporting, techniques that no longer relied upon the introspections of single individuals but could be employed instead by teams of psychologists in the laboratory. Without describing details which would be of little help to those unfamiliar with experimental psychology, he summarized the areas in which introspective observation could be checked and supplemented by experimental methods:

The principal fields of experimentation so far have been: 1) the connection of conscious states with their physical conditions, including the whole of brain-physiology, and the recent minutely cultivated physiology of the sense-organs, together with what is technically known as "psycho-physics," or the laws of correlation between sensations and the outward stimuli by which they are aroused; 2) the analysis of space-perception into its sensational elements; 3) the measurement of the *duration* of the simplest mental processes; 4) that of the *accuracy of reproduction* in the memory of sensible experiences and of intervals of space and time; 5) that of the manner in which simple mental states *influence each other*, call each other up, or inhibit each other's reproduction; that of the *number of facts* which consciousness can simultaneously discern; finally, 6) that of the elementary laws of oblivescence and retention. It must be said that in some of these fields the results have as yet borne little theoretic fruit commensurate with the great labor expended in their acquisition. But facts are facts, and if we only get enough of them they are sure to combine. (*Principles*, 1:193)

The kind of introspective psychology that interested James placed experimental controls upon introspective reports in order to check their accuracy and to determine their physiological conditions and correlates. But this psychology also maintained its traditional role by exploring the way consciousness appears to itself and the way states of mind appear to introspection, to whatever degree of accuracy objectively possible. We are all cognizant to some degree of our passing mental states, but James believed that we can understand them more richly and comprehensively through introspective observation; we can improve our subjective grasp of our states of mind, however they compare to nonmental realities, by focusing our introspective attention upon them. Introspective observation is important partly for identifying a mental state, such as remembering, which can then be correlated with its causal conditions in the brain, but it is valuable also for revealing the easily overlooked details of the remembering itself. In the latter function introspection seems to be left to its own devices; how can it be checked by nonintrospective techniques? If a mental state is introspected as panic that improves or worsens, what kind of external control can check the accuracy of that perception?

For the most part, James agreed that as we become more acutely aware of what a mental state is like, our introspection can be checked only by another. He defined "the psychologist's fallacy" as the idea that an external observer such as a psychologist has a grasp of a subject's state of mind that is superior to the subject's own introspection of that state.

> The mental state is aware of itself only from within; it grasps what we call its own content, and nothing more. The psychologist, on the contrary, is aware of it from without, and knows its relations with all sorts of other things. . . . We must avoid substituting what we know the consciousness *is*, for what it is a consciousness *of*, and counting its outward, and so to speak physical, relations with other facts of the world, in among the objects of which we set it down as aware. Crude as such a confusion of standpoints seems to be when abstractly stated, it is nevertheless a snare into which no psychologist has kept himself at all times from falling, and which forms almost the entire stock-in-trade of certain schools. (*Principles*, 1:197)

What a mental state is can be known only from within, by introspection, and our direct acquaintance with it through introspection must not be confused with the knowledge an external observer may have *about* it. In seeking to improve our acquaintance with our own mental states, we learn that some introspections are more faithful to the character of those states than are others, so that to a significant extent the introspective procedure is self-corrective.

We learn, for instance, that our own introspective observations and reports can suffer because we are often content with a "vocabulary of outward things," and as a result we neglect what is present in an introspected mental state. We describe our feelings and sensations through references to outward things; we speak of feeling dizzy "like a top spinning around and around" or of having a visual sensation that is "the color of an orange." This dependence upon the physical environment for our vocabulary enables us to convey the character of an experience, but it can also lead us, because of a lack of adequate subjective terminology, to ignore the potentially introspectable nuances and shadings of our experiences. The lack of a descriptive word can cause us unwittingly to overlook what is subjectively present, and we thus neglect what might be familiar to all of us if we had grown up with the appropriate words. "It is hard to focus our attention on the nameless, and so there results a certain vacuousness in the descriptive parts of most psychologies."[27] Even worse, because our language imitates the environment, we may suppose that our consciousness imitates it also. We easily err in judging that the contents of consciousness, like the objects in the external world, are independent, identical throughout time, recurrent, and even mobile. As a result, "the continuous flow of the mental stream is sacrificed, and in its place an atomism, a brickbat plan of construction, is preached, for the existence of which no good introspective grounds can be brought forward, and out of which presently grow all sorts of paradoxes and contradictions, the heritage of woe of students of the mind" (*Principles*, 1:196).

Former introspections can thus be faulty by neglecting nameless subjective nuances of our experience that are in fact introspectable and by attributing characteristics to our experience that belong rather to objects in the physical environment. James asserted as an introspectable fact that characteristics other than those of the environment belong to our experiences. Introspections can thus correct other introspections. James employed yet another way of supporting or supplementing introspective reports. Even when he seems to have been satisfied with what his own introspective observations disclosed, he often added a further argument, usually in the form of an analogy between what occurs or is believed to occur in the brain and what actually or supposedly occurs within consciousness. For example, he held that in any experience consciousness will show itself, upon introspection, to be in continuous change, so that each introspectable state is experienced as unique, ephemeral, quickly succeeded by the next state. He asked anyone who doubted this theory to consider that there must be a basic resemblance between the stream of consciousness and the stream of cerebral events which correlate with or determine what occurs in consciousness. He then proposed that "every sensation corresponds to some cerebral action. For an identical sensation to recur it would have to occur the second time *in an unmodified brain.* But as this, strictly speaking, is a physiological impossibility, so is an unmodified feeling an impossibility" (*Principles*, 1:232–33). Consequently, each introspectable state of consciousness must be unique and ephemeral, and often the conclusion drawn from an analogy between mind and brain seems more powerful than what introspective observation yields. James usually wrote as if the argument by analogy corroborated introspection, but it sometimes seems that the reverse is true.[28] In any event, a distinct feature of James's psychology is his manner of reaching conclusions about consciousness by comparing it with what is known or speculated to be the nature of cerebral activity, and vice versa. Discussing alternately the brain and consciousness was justified, he believed, by the natural assumption that they are like two sides of the same coin. In support of this method of argument he wrote:

The present writer recalls how in 1869, when still a medical student, he began to write an essay showing how almost every one who speculated about brain-processes illicitly interpolated into his account of them links derived from the entirely heterogeneous universe of Feeling. Spencer, Hodgson . . . [Henry] Maudsley, [J. G.] Lockhart, [Jacob] Clarke, Bain, Dr. [William] Carpenter, and other authors were cited as having been guilty of the confusion. The writing was soon stopped because he perceived that the view which he was upholding against these authors was a pure conception, with no proofs to be adduced of its reality. Later it seemed to him that whatever *proofs* existed really told in favor of their view. (*Principles*, 1:130–31n)

Given his conviction that introspection as observation is delicate and fallible and that arguments by analogy often support introspective reports, it is not surprising that James's own introspections were typically formulated in terms that make it difficult to know whether the reports are literal or metaphorical, literal or elaborative. If we accept James's idea that an introspective or subjective language encounters that difficulty at the outset, then it can be argued that all introspective reporting poses the problem of how to check it for literal accuracy. It is thus somewhat perplexing that he was unconcerned about sorting the literal from the elaborative elements in his subjective verbal renderings of the felt qualities of his experiences. As a result, his introspective descriptions imperceptibly blend what in his view are direct or literal protocols with formulations which elaborate them or which are irresistibly suggested or implied by them. One of the most interesting questions raised by any program of introspective observation is the status of elaborative introspective language: if such language is not a direct and literal report of what is introspectively observed, then how can we be confident in its assertions?

Consider the following example from James's own introspections: "The acts of attending, assenting, negating, making an effort, are felt as movements of something in the head. . . . My brain appears to me as if all shot across with lines of direction, of which I have become conscious as my attention has shifted from one sense-organ to another, in passing to successive outer things, or in following trains of varying sense-ideas" (*Principles*, 1:300). Like Locke, James held that mental acts are introspectively observable, and therefore any straightforward verbal report of them is literal. But are we to suppose that the descriptions *"felt as* movements . . . in the head" and *"as if* all shot across with lines of direction" (italics mine) are equally direct, literal reports of what is introspectively observed? Should we not be suspicious that introspective license is being indulged here, that the words convey considerably more than can be established by introspective observation? As compared with "I am aware of a headache" and "I now feel a tension in the throat"—formulations without locutions like "feel as" or "appear as if," which may indicate a departure from literal reporting— the descriptions arousing our suspicions seem a step or two removed from what is directly revealed to inner observation. We might characterize such descriptions as that which is "immediately suggested" by, or which represents an "immediate and natural elaboration" of, what is directly introspected, but we must then ask, as James did not, what these expressions mean and how they apply to introspected experience. The status of those elaborative elements that are smuggled into descriptions claimed to be literal introspective protocols ought to be a top priority for any devotee of introspection. Although James did not choose to address the topic, the question of how the elaborative relates to the literal in his introspective formulations is an interesting one.[29]

It is a standard reaction, then, to confront James's introspective reporting by querying in each case the extent to which it is literal or elaborative. At times in the next section, where we examine certain introspective claims made by James, we will assume the appropriateness of a skeptical reaction rather than explicitly holding the claim up to methodological scrutiny. There is hardly an important introspective passage in James's psychology that does not provoke such a reaction if approached in a skeptical spirit. Our main interest will be less to disentangle the literal from the elaborative in his reports than to ascertain how plausible such reports are at the outset.[30]

INTROSPECTION AND CONSCIOUSNESS

An advocate of introspective psychology will assert that such particular judgments as "I feel sad" and "I like you" often express truths about ourselves that we learn by introspectively observing our states of consciousness; in addition he may maintain, like James, that introspection as observation informs us of important characteristics of all conscious states or of consciousness itself. Whereas a single introspective observation may suffice to warrant saying "I feel sad," James concluded that something more than isolated introspection is required for substantiating the five general features he attributed to consciousness (see p. 60). He was committed to this conclusion by refusing to resolve any general philosophical proposition by appeal to introspection.[31] Consequently, making a case for each of the five characteristics of consciousness demanded certain arguments that either supplemented or virtually replaced introspection. The tendency of mental states to be part of a personal consciousness, for example, depends at least as much on the arguments and the analysis of the concepts involved as upon direct introspective observations. James's view of two of the five characteristics, change and continuity, is more intertwined with introspective observations. While venturing an assessment of the claim that constant change and sensible continuity are pervasive properties of consciousness, we can also comment further on consciousness and introspection.

It is a popular assumption that James asserted consciousness to be in constant change and believed that this change is proved by feeling and introspection. Not only does he say explicitly, "Within each personal consciousness thought is always changing," but he thought it natural to suppose also that change is a corollary of continuity.[32] Moreover, change is repeatedly cited as a condition for sustained mental acts: *"No one can possibly attend continuously to an object that does not change"*; "A field of consciousness, however complex, is never analyzed unless some of its ingredients have changed"; and "The components of an absolutely changeless group of not-elsewhere-occurring attributes could never be discriminated" (*Principles*, 1:421, 1:495, 1:503). Together with his pronouncements on change in his later metaphysics, these statements lead to the logical conclusion that change is as essential and pervasive a feature of reality and experience as is continuity. While this conclusion is surely correct in a sense, it is interesting to compare it with what James wrote about change as introspected.

He quoted Hodgson's testimony that experience is a sequence of *differents*, that our mental states, as felt or introspected, are a procession in which each state differs from the others. James accepted this theory insofar as we find ourselves now seeing, then hearing, now reasoning, then willing, now expecting, then recollecting.

> But all these are complex states. The aim of science is always to reduce complexity to simplicity; and in psychological science we have the celebrated "theory of *ideas*" which . . . seeks to show how this is all the resultant effect of variations in the *combination* of certain simple elements of consciousness that always remain the same. These mental atoms or molecules are what Locke called "simple ideas." It is enough that certain philosophers have thought they could see under the dissolving-view-appearance of the mind elementary facts of *any* sort that remained unchanged amid the flow. (*Principles*, 1:230)

If Locke and others who held that beneath the appearance of change lies a world of unchanging mental atoms ("ideas") are to be refuted, can that refutation be accomplished through introspection? A common interpretation of James assumes that his answer was yes, whereas in fact it was no.

For one thing, he noted that some states of mind have duration or "stand still" for a time and thus are not at every moment introspected as being superseded by a new mental state. On its face, then, consciousness does not seem to be always changing; since these "standing still" states of consciousness are relatively complex ones of the sort that Locke analyzed into more elementary constituents, however, it remains to be asked whether there is any reason to believe that such elementary and unchanging constituents exist. In James's interpretation of Locke's theory of simple ideas or elementary constituents, complex states of consciousness such as reasoning or recollecting are composed of simpler elements or sensations that can recur without loss of identity in subsequent, different complex states. James vehemently opposed this view, holding that its only support comes from alleged introspective evidence; Locke claimed that the same color green recurs, the same tone is heard again, the same bitterness is tasted again, suggesting that the basic units of consciousness are nuggets of sensation which endure self-identical in whatever complex mental states they help to constitute.

James opposed this position. "The change which I have more particularly in view is that which takes place in sensible intervals of time [not at every moment]; and the result on which I wish to lay stress is this, that *no state once gone can recur and be identical with what it was before*" (*Principles*, 1:230). To bolster his position, with its repudiation of Lockean simple ideas or elementary units of consciousness, James found it necessary to cast doubt upon introspective evidence. He argued that only objects recur in full identity and that no two sensations, however much they resemble each other, can be correctly judged as the same. It is nothing more than our inclination, based on apparent introspective findings, to call two similar sensations the same that lends any credence to Locke's theory.

> This is what makes off-hand testimony about the subjective identity of different sensations well-nigh worthless as a proof of the fact. The entire history of Sensation is a commentary on our inability to tell whether two sensations received apart are exactly alike. What appeals to our attention far more than the absolute quality or quantity of a given sensation is its *ratio* to whatever other sensations we may have at the same time. When everything is dark a somewhat less dark sensation makes us see an object white. Helmholtz calculates that the white marble painted in a picture representing an architectural view by moonlight is, when seen by daylight, from ten to twenty thousand times brighter than the real moonlit marble would be.
>
> Such a difference as this could never have been *sensibly* learned; it had to be inferred from a series of indirect considerations. There are facts which make us believe that our sensibility is altering all the time, so that the same object cannot easily give us the same sensation over again. . . . To these indirect presumptions that our sensations . . . are always undergoing an essential change, must be added another presumption, based on what must happen in the brain. Every sensation corresponds to some cerebral action. (*Principles*, 1:232)

In James's view, then, we have every reason to trust introspection to show consciousness altering its sequential states at periodic intervals: now we remember, then we anticipate, and so on. Nor does this constant change imply that we are experiencing an introspectable change in consciousness at every moment; the "inner scene" need not resemble a constant and frantic tumble of fresh events. On the other hand, we cannot trust those introspections that seemingly prove the existence of Lockean elemental ideas or sensations, supposed somehow to constitute as unchanging things the complex conscious states that appear to change. The point of attributing change to consciousness, James believed, is to recognize that every state of consciousness or introspectable experience is unique in being unrepeatable. There is an inevitable change from one state to the next, for each must differ from the other, and sameness, strictly speaking, has no place in subjectivity. Introspection had been mistakenly employed to deny this change on behalf of Lockean theory, but it is just as surely the case, James argued, that introspection is ineffective for demonstrating his own position. To accomplish this, he insisted that arguments and considerations that cannot be sensibly (introspectively) learned, pertaining to the nature of sensations and their dependence upon brain physiology, must replace introspection.

Although James argued at a familiar and nontheoretical level that both change and continuity characterize consciousness, the case for continuity reads rather differently from that for change when his discussion moves to a more theoretical and difficult plane. Introspection is crucial throughout his account of consciousness as continuous. What does it mean to say that within each personal experience consciousness feels continuous? Where there is a time gap such as occurs during sleep or anesthesia, the later consciousness "feels as if" it belongs together with the consciousness before the time gap or interruption in consciousness. If this were a sustained study of introspection, we would need to consider further the phrase "feels as if," but because James explained the sense of continuity over a time gap as due more to inference than to introspective observation, we can focus instead on the proposition that the successive changes in the quality of consciousness are never absolutely abrupt. He needed to demonstrate the truth of this proposition in order to uphold his celebrated thesis that "consciousness . . . does not appear to itself chopped up in bits. . . . It is nothing jointed; it flows. A 'river' or a 'stream' are the metaphors by which it is most naturally described. *In talking of it hereafter, let us call it the stream of thought, of consciousness, of subjective life"* (*Principles*, 1:239).

The introspective impression that consciousness makes upon itself is that of a continuous stream; to put it another way, if we introspectively observe the sequential contents of our own experience, then the term *stream of consciousness* will seem effective in conveying the subjective side of experience. Like all metaphors, stream of consciousness quickly becomes a dead metaphor as it is absorbed into the literal part of our language, so that it refers for James to a feature of consciousness that is literally introspectable. But can we adhere to the stream concept while conceding that our experiences undergo real interruptions such as loud explosions, sudden shocks, and startling appearances? James replied by asserting that this question rests partly on a confusion and partly on a superficial introspective viewpoint.

> The confusion is between the thoughts themselves [states of consciousness], taken as subjective facts, and the things of which they are aware. . . . The things are discrete and discontinuous; they do pass before us in a train or chain, making often explosive appearances and rending each other in twain. But their comings and goings and contrasts no more break the flow of the thought that thinks them than they break the time and the space in which they lie. A silence may be broken by a thunder-clap, and we may be so stunned and confused for a moment by the shock as to give no instant account to ourselves of what has happened. But that very confusion is a mental state, and a state that passes us straight over from the silence to the sound. The transition between the thought of one object and the thought of another is no more a break in the *thought* than a joint in a bamboo is a break in the wood. It is a part of the *consciousness* as much as the joint is a part of the bamboo.
>
> The superficial introspective view is the overlooking, even when the things are contrasted with each other most violently, of the large amount of affinity that may still remain between the thoughts by whose means they are cognized. Into the awareness of the thunder itself the awareness of the previous silence creeps and continues; for what we hear when the thunder crashes is not thunder *pure*, but thunder-breaking-upon-silence-and-contrasting-with-

it. . . . The *feeling* of the thunder is also a feeling of the silence as just gone. . . . Here, again, language works against our perceptions of the truth. We name our thoughts simply, each after its thing, as if each knew its own thing and nothing else. What each really knows is clearly the thing it is named for, with dimly perhaps a thousand other things. It ought to be named after all of them, but it never is. Some of them are always things known a moment ago more clearly; others are things to be known more clearly a moment hence. Our own bodily position, attitude, condition, is one of the things of which *some* awareness, however inattentive, invariably accompanies the knowledge of whatever else we know. (*Principles*, 1:240–241)

Characteristically, James supplemented this rationale with an appeal to brain physiology to solidify his argument for the continuity of consciousness, but the main support for the view is clearly introspective. Introspective observation is cited on behalf of numerous "discoveries" about the nature of subjective experience. For example, all our subjective experience can be sorted into stationary moments, which James picturesquely called *perchings,* and transitional moments, which he called (continuing the bird analogy) *flights.* The former include enduring images and sensations; the latter, which include relations, tendencies, and feelings, contribute an easily overlooked continuity to experience. Furthermore, things that occupy our interest, such as vivid images and sensations, are introspectively found to be at the center of a *field* of attention, but the center is *fringed* in a manner that guarantees an experiential continuity between the contents at the center and the adjoining fringe contents extending to the extreme periphery of our field of attention. Another of introspection's "discoveries" is thought without language, a concept important to James because it shows that a process of thinking can flow continuously without being retarded, fixed, or halted by discrete words or images of words. Upon describing an array of introspective disclosures, all of which fortify his thesis, James declared: "This is all I have to say about the sensible continuity and unity of our thought as contrasted with the apparent discreteness of the words, images, and other means by which it seems to be carried on. Between all their substantive elements there is 'transitive' consciousness, and the words and images are 'fringed,' and not as discrete as to a careless [introspective] view they seem."[33]

There seems to be a possible conflict in James's position here. Quite clearly, he meant that the mass of introspective details produces transitive elements or a continuity in consciousness that we often overlook, sometimes causing us to conclude mistakenly that consciousness is not continuous. But if consciousness can feel *dis*continuous, how does that feeling square with his assertion that it is in the nature of consciousness to feel unbroken? "Consciousness, then, does not appear to itself chopped up in bits. Such words as 'chain' or 'train' do not describe it fitly as it presents itself in the first instance. It is nothing jointed; it flows" (*Principles*, 1:239). To avoid a contradiction here, we must interpret "appear" in this context to mean "feel" as distinguished from "is believed to be." Thus James's claim is that consciousness is never felt to be chopped up or discontinuous, but because of sloppy introspective observations we can easily overlook the transitive or connecting details in our experiences and then mistakenly infer that consciousness can occur in a jointed fashion. This theory requires our distinguishing between the preintrospective feeling distinctive of consciousness and the subsequent introspective observation and report of that feeling; as we have seen, there is ample room for error in the latter activity. Accordingly, if we accurately and introspectively observe the preintrospective feeling of consciousness, we will inevitably observe its streamlike character.[34]

James's claims about consciousness had been denied by certain of his predecessors. Sometimes appealing to introspection, sometimes to speculative arguments about the function of the brain, they judged that what can be subjectively observed displays in fact a discontinuous appearance. Bain asserted: "The stream of thought is not a continuous current, but a series of distinct ideas, more or less rapid in their succession; the rapidity being measurable by the number that pass through the mind in a given time."[35] Even if the stream appears to be continuous, someone like Bain was free to argue that this continuity is only illusory; consciousness is really disjointed, comparable to a "moving" picture, an illusion created by a sufficiently rapid series of stills. When Pierce read James's "Stream of Thought" chapter in *Principles*, he commented that consciousness need not *be* continuous merely because it *feels* so.[36] Although James certainly supposed introspection to be fallible, he was prepared to answer Peirce's query by declaring that for preintrospective feeling or consciousness the *esse est sentiri* doctrine indeed holds. There is no point in suggesting that consciousness may *mis*appear to itself, for if such a possibility is entertained, then there is no place where knowledge can even begin.

If it is objected that there are abrupt breaks in consciousness that show it not to be streamlike, James replied that the objection stems from a superficial approach to introspection and a resultant confusion. He clearly conceded that the objects of consciousness are often *dis*continuous, so that the things we experience often occur in a jointed rather than a stream-like fashion. This concession may surprise some readers who had assumed that the stream-of-consciousness notion implies that what we experience is a continuous stream filled with all sorts of discriminable items. It is a natural assumption, in trying to grasp the stream-of-consciousness idea, that what we introspectively observe in the succession of our own experiences is itself a stream even though it contains discriminable, discrete, and therefore discontinuous items. But James's concession plainly shows that the continuity has been removed from the introspected state to the introspective observing of it, the watching consciousness (which he sometimes called *thought*). He appears to have concluded that, whereas the objects of introspective observation admittedly can be discontinuous, the introspecting consciousness nevertheless monitors the passing scenes continuously.

But how is this continuity established? By introspection or preintrospective feeling, one might answer, supposing this to be the answer given in "The Stream of Thought." James's meaning seems clearest wherever he refers to consciousness as appearing to itself. For example: "Such consciousness as this, whatever it be for the onlooking psychologist, is for itself unbroken. It *feels* unbroken" (*Principles,* 1:238). But this answer to our question of how we know that consciousness is continuous when its objects are not prompts further questions. James had charged traditional psychologists with having overlooked the continuity of consciousness because they had ignored important relations, transitions, or "flights" that connect successive experiences, but these all belong to the objects of consciousness rather than to the bare monitoring consciousness itself. If these psychologists had introspected more assiduously the contents of their experiences, he claimed, they would have realized that continuity rather than atomicity characterizes the sequence of experiences. All his instructions for locating what traditional psychology introspectively omitted apply to the objects of consciousness rather than to consciousness itself. But if the objects are now conceded to be discontinuous, then of what use are James's directions for locating relations and transitions? These relations no longer bestow an essential continuity on the contents of consciousness, for any continuity is attributed instead to consciousness itself, considered as something apart from content.

Evidently, if we argue that we know consciousness itself to be streamlike because it feels so, but that the objects of consciousness are not streamlike because they do not feel so, then we have taken consciousness to be introspectively discriminable. But in *Principles,* as in his later metaphysics, James obviously doubted this conclusion. "All people unhesitatingly believe that they feel themselves thinking, and that they distinguish the mental state as an inward activity or passion, from all the objects with which it may cognitively deal. *I regard this belief as the most fundamental of all the postulates of Psychology,* and shall discard all curious inquiries about its certainty as too metaphysical for the scope of this book" (*Principles,* 1:185). Only after *Principles* did James address the philosophical task of showing how suspect this "postulate" of psychology really is. In "The Consciousness of Self" chapter he wrote that, while the distinction between consciousness and its objects is accepted by virtually everyone, yet "the deeper grounds for this discrimination may possibly be hard to find" (*Principles,* 1:297). Oddly, he seems to have doubted even in *Principles,* as he did later, the very proposition upon which the stream of consciousness depended—that consciousness can be isolated for introspection and can be seen as essentially continuous in a way not displayed by its objects. He later abandoned Cartesian dualism and a theory of consciousness which he had officially but reservedly adopted in *Principles,* but it is strange that he argued for the stream-of-consciousness doctrine, which was a lifelong commitment, on the premise that consciousness can on its own exhibit to introspection a streamlike character, when the premise itself was something he apparently doubted strongly even as he was strenuously advocating it.

This doubt became official in the 1904 essay "Does 'Consciousness' Exist?" where James denied Moore's claim that when "we try to fix our attention upon consciousness and to see *what,* distinctly, it is, it seems to vanish. . . . When we try to introspect the sensation of blue, all we can see is the blue; the other element [consciousness] is as if it were diaphanous. Yet it *can* be distinguished, if we look attentively enough, and know that there is something to look for."[37] To the contrary, James replied, *"Experience . . . has no such inner duplicity"* of consciousness and content, and this statement finalized the prior doubts in *Principles*. His conclusion was evidently reached not by a complicated argument but by his finally deciding that his introspections could not isolate anything that might be called consciousness which had a nature of its own different from that of its content. I believe he was right and Moore was wrong on this issue, but if there is indeed no consciousness to be introspected apart from its content, James's whole case in *Principles* for the stream-of-consciousness doctrine has been discarded, and, unlike Cartesian dualism, the stream of consciousness was not something he was ever prepared to renounce.

James does not seem to have acknowledged anywhere these problems for his view, but he was persuaded after *Principles* that if he conceptualized things in terms of experiences rather than consciousness and its content, he could retain for experiences what he had formerly claimed for consciousness, including continuity. Instead of analyzing an experience like seeing a star into the seeing or consciousness and its content (the multiple visual sensations that occur), he seems to have proposed the reverse, collapsing the distinction between consciousness and content into the simple experience. The initial motive for doing so was simply to admit the failure of introspection to reveal anything designated by "consciousness." "Being conscious" does not then refer to something discernible within an experience but is merely a generic expression for registering the fact that an experience occurs. Seeing, hearing, feeling, tasting, and smelling are all ways of being conscious, but within the experience of hearing, for instance, there is no element of consciousness. To hear is to be conscious, to have an experience.

Placing the philosophical focus on having an experience instead of on consciousness as distinguished from content has the immediate advantage of focusing on something with which we can all agree—obviously we all have experiences. Among the motives that led James in his later metaphysics to the idea of pure experience, which replaced any opposition or duality in which consciousness might wrongly be supposed to stand for something else, was the belief that "an experience" designates an occurrence that is unitary by nature—and we know this just by having experiences. An experience is the most basic unit of psychological life, that with which an analysis of everything else can begin. It permits us to analyze what happens within it (its qualities, possibly including continuity) and outside it (its relations, possibly including continuity with its predecessor and successor). It is an experience, after all, that we introspect to see whether it includes consciousness, discovering that it does not. This fact alone proves that an experience is logically a more basic concept than consciousness.

The foregoing discussion represents James's mature thinking, although there is some risk of misrepresentation in that it rests upon an overall familiarity with his views rather than upon reading a specific text. (Various textual passages are cited in chapter 11 to support my interpretation.) Not only did James analyze consciousness in terms of what it is to have an experience, but in his later metaphysics of radical empiricism he even sought to analyze the commonsense notion of having an experience in terms of a metaphysical concept of pure experience. Consequently, whether he was eventually successful in retaining the stream-of-consciousness doctrine, by recasting it as a *stream of experience* and retaining the experiential data that originally led him to the doctrine but that he now conceptualized in terms of experience instead of consciousness, depends upon how we judge the metaphysics of radical empiricism and its key concept of pure experience.

We must agree with James that consciousness is not introspectable and that we should therefore explicate it in terms of having an experience rather than vice versa. We should try, as he did after *Principles,* to locate the stream-like character not in a questionable consciousness but in the states that constitute an unquestionable experience. James refused in *Principles* to attribute continuity to the objects of consciousness, and these objects seem to constitute in toto an experience (which is admitted to have no further element of consciousness). Thus, if the stream-of-consciousness doctrine is to be preserved, either a revised view of the content of consciousness or a reworked concept of experience must be provided. He seems in his thinking after *Principles* to have changed his mind and to have found the stream in the content of experience, which he had formerly called the content of consciousness. Because he still relied upon the term *consciousness* long after his rejection of it as an introspectable entity, James burdened his reader with trying to determine whether the project of recasting consciousness in terms of experience was consistently executed. But while fully conceding the difficulties of discovering the proper conceptualization of it, he was always confident that continuity as well as other characteristics are essential aspects of what we introspect and experience. We can overlook or neglect the continuity, but if we introspect carefully, we will find it, however perplexed we are about verbalizing it and the ways we recognize it.

3 ❧ SENSATION AND PERCEPTION

SENSATION

Despite the priority that sensation, as a special mode of consciousness, enjoyed in traditional psychology, James waited until chapter 17, the beginning of the second volume of *Principles*, to give it special attention. This discussion follows chapters that treat such concepts as memory, time, association, discrimination, attention, and conception; it begins: "After inner perception, outer perception!" This declaration may puzzle the reader who has noticed that James has already said much about sensation and that outer and inner perception are both prominent concerns in the first volume. But James explained at length that he chose not to begin *Principles* with a chapter on sensation, defying precedent, because he wanted to emphasize the difference between his view and that of his predecessors. (In his *Psychology*, the abridged version of *Principles* that appeared in 1892, he started with sensation, remarking, "I have obeyed custom and put that subject first, although by no means persuaded that such order intrinsically is the best" [iv*n*].)

Sensations (or their objects, if *sensation* is taken to mean a special mode of consciousness or cognitive experience) include, for example, hotness, loudness, dizziness, pain, sexual arousal, and satiation. An influential philosophical tradition, James believed, had treated sensations unfairly. "Plato's earlier pupils used to admit Sensation's existence, grudgingly, but they trampled it in the dust as something corporeal, non-cognitive, and vile" (*Principles*, 2:9). Platonists taught that sensations lack the clarity of thought, and Kantians later held that sensations without concepts are blind; the history of philosophy, it seemed to James, thus amounted to an endorsement of reason or thought at the expense of sensation. The philosophical tendency had been to classify all sensations as akin to headaches, ringings in the ears, spots before the eyes—merely subjective effects that are cognitively worthless unless interpreted or diagnosed (that is, subjected to reason). James's philosophical convictions were offended by writings such as this: "Sense is a kind of dull, confused, and

81

stupid perception obtruded upon the soul from without, whereby it perceives the alterations and motions within its own body . . . but does not clearly comprehend what they are . . . being intended by nature, as Plotinus speaks, not so properly for *knowledge* as for use *of the body* . . . very different from the energies of the noetical part, . . . which are free, clear, serene, satisfactory, and awakened cogitations. That is to say, knowledge."[1] This opinion struck James as complacent and pretentious high-mindedness that often lurked behind the distrust of anything bodily, including sensations. It was only fitting that physiological psychology, which appreciated the perceptual details of the laboratory, should consider more seriously the lowly sensations exiled from the purity of the philosopher's study.

James insisted that sensations can be vague and confused, and in explicating the stream of consciousness he claimed to have reinstated the vague to its proper place in human experience.[2] Like Francis Galton and T. H. Huxley, but unlike Hume and Berkeley, he held that sensations and images need not be distinct or clearly formed but can occur as objective blurs or vaguenesses. To the extent that they vaguely yet incipiently connect us with objective realities, they can even be given the traditional name *confused perceptions*. It was important, James believed, to realize that vagueness often characterizes our feelings and sensations; introspective psychology, to be accurate, must acknowledge this vagueness, and at the level of sensation and feeling— the "guts" of experience—vagueness is usually the harbinger of something further to be detected, the promise of a potential discovery. Vague sounds, if they challenge us to move closer to their origins, may be replaced by the clear and distinct sounds of two men arguing on the street below; indistinct, intermittent odors are succeeded, when we open the basement door, by the clearly recognizable smell of leaking sulfuric acid. Sensations can thus be vague or distinct; confusion, vagueness, and indistinctness are certainly not the trademarks of all sensations. That some are indiscernible, or are like headaches or ringings in the ears, hardly means that all are confused perceptions or merely subjective effects.

A major point in James's theory is that sensations are cognitive. The awareness of pain such as toothache, for example, he treated as a case of "knowledge-by-acquaintance"; toothache is something that one can know only by being acquainted with it through experience. Knowledge of someone else's toothache is at best "knowledge-by-description"; although we can know that certain descriptions apply to another's toothache, we can never know its intimate detail or quality. It is "just as wonderful for a state of mind to be a 'sensation' and know a simple pain as it is for it to be a thought and know a system of related things."[3] (James sometimes meant by *sensation* a cognitive state of mind and at other times the object cognized, in this case the pain.) Whereas the mental state that knows the toothache is intellectually simpler than one that knows a mathematical theorem, it is no less wonderful in its being cognitive. We should not contrast sensing and thinking, as traditional philosophy did, by insisting that the former functions noncognitively. The thesis that sensations are cognitive was also a theory about the objects of sensing, sensations such as colors, sounds, and odors, but this theory is not easily interpreted.

In stating that sensation is cognitive, James was arguing against the notion that colors or sounds are merely subjective effects produced by things external. He was denying Arthur Schopenhauer's assertion that "sensation is through and through subjective, that is, inside of the organism and under the skin," as well as that of his contemporary, G. T. Ladd, who wrote: "Sensations . . . are psychical states *whose place*—so far as they can be said to have one—*is the mind.* The transference of these sensations from mere mental states to physical processes located in the periphery of the body, or to qualities of things projected in space external to the body, is a mental act."[4] James thought all experiental evidence opposed this view of sensations. Who can deny that seeming to be objective (seeming to be external, a part of what we call the real world) is a property of sensations? The blue of the sky, the ring of the bell, the fragrance of the rose certainly appear to be external realities in the spatial environment that we share, and are thus different from the reveries, dreams, fancies, and other occurrences normally considered to be confined to private experience. There is no evidence for the hypothesis that such sensations as colors and sounds seem to be external and objective only because by an unconscious mental act we project them from their actual occurrences within us into the space outside us.

What is known as James's *nativism* enters into his thinking here. The characteristics of externality and objectivity are native to sensations, are original or built-in features of sensations rather than acquired properties.[5] His theory of space is nativistic in its claim that spatiality is an inborn property of sensations which does not come from any mental act or other agent. In the heyday of introspective psychology and the initial years of physiological psychology, it was important to search out the multiple properties of sensations. It was fashionable for James to devote the early chapters of *Psychology* to the intensity of sensation, the effects of color contrast, the qualities of sounds, the sense of pressure, sensations of motion over surfaces, and the sensibility of the semicircular canals in the ears. His study of sensations revealed conclusively, he thought, that "seeming to be in real space" is generally true of sensations; from our first experiences as infants, our initial experiences dominated by sensations, we certainly feel ourselves face-to-face with a real, objective world. We do not begin our lives with internal sensations that seem cut off from the surrounding reality; to the contrary, "Our earliest, most instinctive, least developed kind of consciousness is the objective kind; and only as reflection becomes developed do we become aware of an inner world at all" (*Principles,* 2:32). Until we have good reason to doubt what seems to be true of our sensations—which James believed would never happen—we are wholly justified in accepting sensory evidence that sensation acquaints us not with the merely internal or subjective but with the real world.

If sensations, taken as cognized objects such as colors and sounds, are part of the objective world, then they may—despite the neo-Kantian tradition which holds that they are inherently chaotic until an order is imposed upon them by the mind—have inherent principles of order. James wrote in "Discrimination and Comparison," chapter 13 of *Principles,* that a baby's first experience of the world is felt "all as one great blooming, buzzing confusion." In chapter 17, "Sensation," he elaborated on one meaning of the phrase "blooming, buzzing confusion":

> *The first sensation which an infant gets is for him the Universe.* And the universe which he later comes to know is nothing but an amplification and an implication of that first simple germ which, by accretion on the one hand and intussusception on the other, has grown so big and complex and articulate that its first estate is unrememberable. In his dumb awakening to the consciousness of *something there,* a mere *this* as yet (or something for which even the term *this* would perhaps be too discriminative, and the intellectual acknowledgment of which would be better expressed by the bare interjection 'lo!'), the infant encounters an object in which (though it be given in a pure sensation) all the 'categories of the understanding' are contained. *It has objectivity, unity, substantiality, causality, in the full sense in which any later object or system of objects has these things.* Here the young knower meets and greets his world; and the miracle of knowledge bursts forth, as Voltaire says, as much in the infant's lower sensation as in the highest achievement of a Newton's brain. (*Principles,* 2:8)

Life begins as the experiencing of sensations that can be called a buzzing confusion as long as they remain sensations only, not yet adding up to the perception of order in the world. It is a busy confusion; the baby is besieged by new sensations from all sides, and the confusion buzzes with reverberations produced in the baby's body by the impinging environment; his awareness of his own body is like the awareness of a constant hum or buzz. Yet those first sensations are a blooming confusion because they are quickly organized into the perception of the regularities of nature, of its objects and their properties. The baby learns to perceive the world maturely not because its little mind imposes an order upon the initial welter of sensations, but rather because the sensations gradually disclose what they already contain—objectivity, unity, causality, and substantiality. The baby needs no assistance from reason or thought to perceive sensations as ordered; nor do adults use reason to move from confused to distinct perception. To correct the traditional views that downgrade sensation, James suggested that we think of the baby's original sensations as related to its mature perceptions just as the acorn is related to the oak.

The Jamesian claim that sensation is cognitive eliminates the hoary philosophical puzzle of how we ever come to know an objective, public world when the origins of such knowledge are sensations that are private and internal. But James never came to grips with the difficulties that philosophers have always met when arguing that sensations are part of an objective, public reality. Since the character of a color or sound seems to depend as much upon the condition of the percipient as upon anything perceived, it is tempting to suppose that sensations exist only subsequent to the stimulation of the percipient's sensory apparatus. As pain is a consequence of being cut, so may the sensation of seeing a pink book be a consequence of visual stimulation. In that case, the visual sensation cannot precede the visual stimulation any more than the pain can precede being cut. Two people look at the same book, but one, wearing pink glasses, sees a pink one, and the other, wearing blue, sees a blue one. How can the pink that one sees and the blue that the other sees both be in the same space? How can they both be objective constituents of the same public environment? Are we prepared to assign sounds, tastes, tactile data, and smells an existence apart from our experiences of them? James recommended that we picture the perceptual world as blooming out of infantile sensations, much as the oak tree develops from the acorn. One of the problems of this analogy, which James sometimes conceded, is that sensations, unlike acorns, are relatively ephemeral and are thus not capable of the continuous existence required for the alleged process of blooming or development.

James was aware of such objections but did not come to grips with them, largely because he was impatient with such traditional epistemological perplexities. He sought a metaphysics that would either dissolve such puzzles or reduce their importance, and as a result he developed a metaphysical system under the names of radical empiricism, pure experience, and the pluralistic universe. The seeds of the later metaphysics are clearly discernible in *Principles* and exhibit some of the vulnerabilities of his subsequent theories. The chief difficulty in his treatment of sensations is that he never decided whether they are, as a class of cognized objects, ephemeral qualities of individual experience or stable, enduring things which, like everyday physical objects, continue to exist even if absent from anyone's experience. The difficulty emerges from the formulations to which James was drawn in explaining how he not only avoided the rationalistic or idealistic contempt for sensations but also the error of the empiricist or sensationalist school, namely, the tendency to treat sensations as durable elements.

A recurrent theme in James's account of sensation, and one that impressed his contemporaries, is that sensations, if interpreted in a certain way, are abstractions rarely if ever found in adult experience.[6] If they are interpreted as pure sensations (what Hume meant by "simple impressions" and Locke by "simple ideas")—discrete, isolated qualities such as a pink patch or a soft tone, which are alleged to occur unmodified by the context in which one experiences them—then they are mere abstractions which we approach or approximate by analyzing our experiences, conceptually stripping them down to their sensory cores. Part of what we mean by sensation is the first experiential event to result from some event in the brain. The causal sequence of events involved in vision begins with light waves stimulating the eyes; the optic nerve is then affected, other brain events follow, and at some point the sensation or experience of sight comes into existence. In its first, pristine moments, before past experience or present conditions can modify or affect it, before it can be named or conceptualized, it is a sensation pure and simple. But pure sensations elude adult experience because adults automatically name and classify sensations, contaminating their purity almost immediately.[7]

James believed that although we may never have absolutely pure sensations as adults, we may occasionally find close approximations. "Such anaesthetics as chloroform, nitrous oxide, etc., sometimes bring about transient lapses even more total, in which numerical discrimination especially seems gone; for one sees light and hears sound, but whether one or many lights and sounds is quite impossible to tell" (*Principles*, 1:147). In drowsy or drug-induced states, our discriminative and analytical powers may be sufficiently dulled to permit sensations to be experienced in almost pure form. James had more than a passing interest in such out-of-the-way experiences, not merely because he had an adventurer's enjoyment of the unfamiliar, but more because a genuinely mystical conception of sensation ran through his philosophy. He believed that even ordinary acquaintance with sensations shows that they are richly endowed, despite the rationalists' argument to the contrary, with all the "categories of the understanding." James thought of sensations as remedies for the ill moments when reason goes astray. For instance, if the intellect cannot understand how multiplicity and heterogeneity can also be unity, the paradox can be solved, James thought, by consulting sensations, which all display a peculiar "unity-in-manyness."[8] A musical chord illustrates the point: despite its internal detail and variety, it nevertheless sounds as a single unity.

But unusual experiences, including those of drug-induced alterations of consciousness, may yield even more clues about the fugitive properties of sensations. James seems always to have supposed (explicitly in *Essays in Radical Empiricism, A Pluralistic Universe,* and *Some Problems of Philosophy*) that the innermost nature of reality is discovered through acquaintance with the details of sensation. He appears to have thought that awareness of pure sensations wholly untainted by human thought, memory, or expectation could bring an understanding of reality more accurate than any information gained through science or common sense. Oddly enough, although he is remembered for his opposition to philosophical dualisms, James was always prepared to oppose sensing to thinking and to champion the former as the source of the profoundest insights into the differences between appearance and reality. In a candid declaration of his philosophic faith, James wrote:

> If the aim of philosophy were the taking full possession of all reality by the mind, then nothing short of the whole of immediate perceptual experience could be the subject-matter of philosophy, for only in such experience is reality intimately and concretely found. But the philosopher, although he is unable as a finite being to compass more than a few passing moments of such experience, is yet able to extend his knowledge beyond such moments by the ideal symbol of the other moments. . . . But the concepts by which he does this, being thin extracts from perception, are always insufficient representatives thereof, and, although they yield wider information, must never be treated after the rationalistic fashion, as if they gave a deeper quality of truth. *The deeper features of reality are found only in perceptual experience.* Here alone do we acquaint ourselves with continuity, or the immersion of one thing in another, here alone with self, with substance, with qualities, with activity in its various modes, with time, with cause, with change, with novelty, with tendency, and with freedom. Against all such features of reality the method of conceptual translation, when

candidly and critically followed out, can only raise its *non possumus*, and brand them as unreal or absurd. (*SPP*, 97; first italics mine)

With these lines in mind, we can appreciate James's inclination to equate reality with sensation and his assertion that "sensations are the stable rock, the *terminus a quo* and the *terminus ad quem* of thought" (*Principles*, 2:7). There is a basic vacillation in his writing about sensations; on the one hand he wanted to regard sensations as realities, but on the other hand he wanted to dissociate himself from the Lockean or Humean concept of sensation as elemental. Because of his *esse est sentiri* doctrine and its denial that simple mental states can constitute more complex ones, James did not regard states of consciousness, including sensations, as analogous to elements in physics or chemistry; they do not endure or enter into combinations with other elements, which led James to state: "Locke's pupils seek to do the impossible with sensations, and against them we must once again insist that sensations 'clustered together' cannot build up our more intellectual states of mind" (*Principles*, 2:9).

Because pure sensations rarely if ever occur in adult life, and because sensations cannot be considered mental elements analogous to physical ones, James urged that in routine experience sensations are abstractions of fuller experiences, experiential limits which the laboratory psychologist may approach in his analyses. Jamesian commentators therefore point to this passage: "The 'simple impression' of Hume, the 'simple idea' of Locke are both abstractions, never realized in experience. Experience, from the very first, presents us with concreted objects, vaguely continuous with the rest of the world which envelops them in space and time" (*Principles*, 1:147). James vigorously asserted that psychologists ought to begin with a study of the perception of full-bodied objects rather than of isolated sensations. He thus set an example for current theorists of sense-perception who combat sense-datum hypotheses and foundationalist accounts of empirical knowledge; in this respect his work supports both common sense and modern philosophy of perception.

We can understand why James held that as adults we ordinarily describe our perceptions of objects rather than the simple impressions or isolated sensations of traditional empiricism; we can understand also why he contended, in league with empiricism, that our infantile experience begins in the form of isolated sensations. What may be difficult to grasp is why, in view of his developmental (acorn-oak) concept of perceptual knowledge, James thought he could deny the elemental character of sensations. That sensations are not elements capable of enduring or of combining into larger complexes is the official thesis of *Principles*; this assertion may seem to be merely a commonsense statement, yet if we construe empirical knowledge as a development of sensations (as James did), it is difficult not to understand sensations as the elements of which the perceptual world is constituted. How can a metaphysics that rests so completely upon the concept of sensation avoid seeing sensations as elements? That dilemma was never resolved in James's philosophizing.

The dilemma was manifested, for example, in his discussions of the idea that sensations can combine into more complex forms. The official claim of Jamesian psychology is that sensations cannot fuse; former psychological explanations of such fusion are replaced by James's hypothesis that a specific sensation is the first psychic event to follow required events in the brain. If there is any reason to invoke fusion to explain sense-perception, James supposes the fusion to be a process in the brain rather than a psychological one.

> Probably everyone will agree that the best way of formulating all such facts [that when two objects act together the sensation which either would give alone becomes a different sensation] is physiological: it must be that the cerebral process of the first sensation is reinforced or otherwise altered by the other current which comes in. No one, surely, will prefer a psychological explanation *here*. Well, it seems to me that *all* cases of mental reaction to a plurality of stimuli must be like these cases, and that the physiological formulation is everywhere the simplest and the best. When simultaneous red and green light make us see yellow, when three notes of the scale make us hear a chord, it is not because the sensations of red and of green and of each of the three notes enter the mind as such, and there "combine" . . . into the yellow and the chord, it is because the larger sum of light-waves and of air-waves arouses new cortical processes, to which the yellow and the chord directly correspond. Even when the sensible qualities of things enter into the objects of our highest thinking, it is surely the same. Their several *sensations* do not continue to exist there tucked away. They are *replaced* by the higher thought which, although a different psychic unit from them, knows the same sensible qualities which they know. (*Principles*, 2:30).

That statement is part and parcel of the *esse est sentiri* doctrine, but despite James's repeated appeal to it in *Principles*, he had difficulty in always adhering to it. His account of how the perception of space is acquired seems at crucial places to desert the official view of *Principles* and to claim instead that sensations can fuse. He may have intended his loose allusions to the coalescence of sensations to imply a more accurate reference to the brain events that occur just prior to the occurrence of a sensation; if so, a fusion of cerebral events may be responsible for the unique character of subsequent but unfused sensations. Yet in his discussion of the perception of objects he wrote, "In this *coalescence in a 'thing*,' one of the coalescing sensations is held to *be* the thing, the other sensations are taken for its more or less accidental *properties*, or modes of appearance" (*Principles*, 2:184). This statement seems to conflict with the *esse est sentiri* doctrine of *Principles* and its denial of the traditional view that sensations are elemental phenomena. This doctrine led James to assert: "We ought to talk of the association of *objects*, not of the association of *ideas* [sensations]. And so far as association stands for a *cause*, it is between *processes in the brain*."[9] It thus seems a contradiction for him to dismiss the belief that an object perceived as a complete unity could never have appeared otherwise: "But this is an erroneous view, the undeniable fact being that *any number of impressions, from any number of sensory sources, falling simultaneously on a mind* WHICH HAS NOT YET EXPERIENCED THEM SEPARATELY, *will fuse into a single and undivided object for that mind*" (*Principles*, 1:488).

If by *impressions* James meant physiological sensory data that are below the threshold of consciousness, then the fusion alluded to is physiological, consistent with his philosophy of sensation. He seems to have had a physiological interpretation in mind, for the above passage occurs immediately before the description of a baby's experience as "one great blooming, buzzing confusion." Even though the baby's experience receives sensory data from separate sense-modalities and through distinct nerves, its experience is assumed to feel like one big confusion rather than many. Throughout our lives, James held, "our location of all things in one space is due to the fact that the original extents or bignesses of all the sensations which came to our notice at once, coalesced together into one and the same space. There is no other reason than this why 'the hand I touch and see coincides spatially with the hand I immediately feel.'"[10] Although he did not make the point specifically here, James evidently supposed, by taking infantile experience as an illustration, that the coalescence of sensory data to which he referred is prepsychological; the infant, too young for its interests and preferences to be causal conditions, simply responds to sensory fields as organized through coalescing processes in the brain. Thus interpreted, the Jamesian thesis that sensations cannot fuse remains intact, as does the doctrine that any coalescence of sensory data is physiological rather than psychological.

However, if we move from infantile to adult experience and, as James always insisted, include psychological influences such as preference, interest, desire, expectation, and belief among the conditions for a given coalescence of sensory data, then it is hard to understand how anything but sensations could coalesce as a result of desire, expectation, and so forth. James's theory of sense-perception asserts that the way we perceive an object, taking some properties and not others as its real ones, is due partly to our frame of mind, beliefs, preferences, and interests.[11] It remains a question, therefore, whether James was always faithful, in analyzing adult sense-perception, to the claim that coalescence is entirely physiological. The issue is clearly important in James's philosophy of psychology, connecting with his theories of sense-perception and its objects. If his final position was that physical objects are systems of sensations, then his arguments (in "The Mind-Stuff Theory," chapter 6 of *Principles*, for example) against the idea that sensations can coalesce are in his final conclusions either abandoned or suspended.[12] I base this interpretation primarily on the fact that James essentially renounced, after *Principles*, the doctrine that sensations cannot coalesce. When he jettisoned this doctrine, he also gave up the basic motive for thinking that sensations cannot fuse. And even in *Principles* he may have unwittingly hinted at this change of doctrine: "The law is that all things fuse that *can* fuse, and nothing separates except what must."(Principles, 1:488). When he came to believe that mental states can be parts of larger ones, he was in essence asserting that mental phenomena, including sensations, can coalesce into more complex mental configurations.

SENSATION AND PERCEPTION

Throughout the history of the philosophy of sense-perception it has been debated whether sensing is one kind of mental phenomenon and perceiving another.

Psychology textbooks often define sensing as merely the experiencing of sensations and characterize perceiving as something more complex than sensing, namely, the interpretation of sensations, the recognition of what they signify. For example, the successive sounds of a coded message (for example, in Morse code) can be sensed by someone who does not understand the code, but they are not perceived in the sense of being understood or recognized; the sounds are heard but their meanings are not. Words such as *hear, see, touch,* and *smell* are thus ambiguous because they can refer either to sensing or to perceiving. Moreover, some theorists claim that the distinction between sensing and perceiving is sometimes introspectable; hearing the sounds with their meanings may *feel* different from hearing only the sounds. If this distinction is valid, then the claim that sensing and perceiving are different mental states seems true.

James was prepared to distinguish between sensing and perceiving but not to allow the distinction to run afoul of his *esse est sentiri* doctrine of mental states and its implication that one state cannot be a constituent of another. He therefore opposed the traditional idea that sensing is the core of every perception, that every perception contains a constituent sensing, or that perception is a complex mental state in which sensations are crucial substates. "Once more we find ourselves driven to admit that when qualities of an object impress our sense and we thereupon perceive the object, the sensation as such of those qualities does not still exist inside of the perception and form a constituent thereof. The sensation is one thing and the perception another, and neither can take place at the same time with the other, because their cerebral conditions are not the same. They may *resemble* each other, but in no respect are they identical states of mind" (*Principles,* 2:81–82). James wanted to avoid treating perception as if it included sensing. He summed up his position—now sometimes called the Percept Theory—by asserting: "The perception is one state of mind or nothing— as I have already so often said."[13]

But the reader, while cognizant that James wanted to avoid a theory implying that any mental state can be part of another mental state, may be puzzled about the passage quoted above is consistent with what was declared earlier:

> *The words Sensation and Perception* do not carry very definitely discriminated meanings in popular speech, and in Psychology also their meanings run into each other. Both of them name processes in which we cognize an objective world. . . . Perception always involves Sensation as a portion of itself; and Sensation in turn never takes place in adult life without Perception also being there. They are therefore names for different cognitive *functions,* not for different sorts of mental *fact.* The nearer the object cognized comes to being a simple quality like "hot," "cold," "red," "noise," "pain," apprehended irrelatively to other things, the more the state of mind approaches pure sensation. The fuller of relations the object is, on the contrary; the more it is something classed, located, measured, compared, assigned to a function, etc., etc.; the more unreservedly

do we call the state of mind a perception, and the relatively smaller is the part in it which sensation plays.

Sensation, then, so long as we take the analytic point of view, differs from Perception only in the extreme simplicity of its object or content. Its function is that of mere *acquaintance* with a fact. Perception's function, on the other hand, is knowledge *about* a fact; and this knowledge admits of numberless degrees of complication. (*Principles*, 2:1–2)

Here perception is said always to include sensation, but it is contrasted with sensation not as a different mental state, but only in *functional* terms. Above, on the other hand, we found him writing that sensation is not a constituent of perception; while it may resemble perception at times, the two states of mind are in no respect identical. Inconsistencies in James's psychology of sense-perception should not strike us as incredible. Many fine philosophers have stumbled into traps when discussing sensation and perception, so it would not be unprecedented if James's theory, too, fell short of being fully coherent. Further, he does not seem to have thought extensively about the philosophical complexities of sense-perception either before or during the early writing of *Principles*. Whereas he had tested his ideas earlier on such topics as space, time, habit, emotion, will, consciousness, and the subjective method in philosophy, much of what he asserted about sense-perception was probably crystallized just before *Principles* was completed. The 1885 essay "On the Function of Cognition" is his only excursion into epistemology prior to *Principles*, but it is less relevant to James's psychology of perception than to his subsequently developed pragmatism. Unlike much of *Principles*, four of the first five chapters of the second volume are not based on earlier journal articles. There is evidence that "The Perception of Reality" was a difficult chapter for James to work out, and that "The Perception of 'Things'" was composed under pressure, possibly long after "Sensation" was thought out. (The latter two chapters are the ones that seem to conflict in their comparison between sensation and perception.)[14] Most important, it was ultimately impossible for James to finalize his thinking about the nature of sensation and perception until he formulated his metaphysics of radical empiricism during the last decade of his life. In certain respects, then, we must wait until we examine his later metaphysics (chapters 10–11) before we can gain a genuine overview of his philosophy of sense-perception.

I do not think that James was guilty of making contradictory claims in *Principles* about the relation between sensation and perception. In "Sensation" he declares that sensation and perception are not different sorts of mental phenomena; by this he meant in part, I think, that even in situations where a theorist might justifiably want to assert that both sensing and perceiving occur (for example, deciphering a series of sound-messages), we cannot introspectively detect two distinct states of mind, much less one (sensing) within the other (perceiving). It is difficult to quarrel with James on this point. There is an innocuous sense in which it can be said that we both sense the sounds and perceive their meanings, but it is an introspectable fact that we can detect only one state of mind at a time. Rather than maintain that two mental states occur simultaneously, it is less misleading to express the matter by saying that one state of mind functions in both a sensing and a perceiving manner. In adult life virtually all perceptual states of mind function in both ways at once, a situation sometimes expressed misleadingly by saying that sensation is invariably accompanied by perception, and vice versa.

Consequently, in situations where it has been traditional to assert that both sensing and perceiving occur, James argued that in fact only one mental state occurs, to which we can assign both sensing and perceiving. This view squares with what he wrote in "The Perception of 'Things'": sensation and perception, while perhaps resembling each other, are always distinct, separate mental states. James meant that sensing, taken by itself and not assumed to be a part of any perception, *can* be introspectively contrasted in function with a state of mind which combines both sensing and perceiving. That is, sensing which is assumed to be a part of perceiving cannot be distinguished from the perceiving, but sensing which is at the outset assumed to exist apart from any perception can be thus distinguished. Although rare in adult life, as James admitted when he acknowledged that sensation is invariably accompanied by perception, sensing occasionally occurs as a phenomenon that differs from perceiving. If we recall that the distinction between sensation and perception was construed by James as merely a difference in the complexity of what is apprehended, and that sensing acquaints us with a more limited perceptual object than does perception, it is easy to understand sensing as a mental state different from perceiving. James gives the following examples:

> If we look at an isolated printed word and repeat it long enough, it ends by assuming an entirely unnatural aspect. Let the reader try this with any word on this page. He will soon begin to wonder if it can possibly be the word he has been using all his life with that meaning. It stares at him from the paper like a glass eye, with no speculation in it. Its body is indeed there, but the soul is fled. It is reduced, by this new way of attending to it, to its sensational nudity. We never before attended to [sensed] it in this way, but habitually got it clad with its meaning the moment we caught sight of it, and rapidly passed from it to the other words of the phrase. We apprehended [perceived] it, in short, with a cloud of associates, and thus perceiving it, we felt [perceived] it quite otherwise than as we feel [sense] it now divested and alone. . . .
>
> The same thing occurs when we turn a painting bottom upward. We lose much of its meaning, but, to compensate for the loss, we feel [sense] more freshly the value of the mere tints and shadings, and become aware of any lack of purely sensible [sensed] harmony or balance which they may show. . . . We get it as a naked sensation and not as part of a familiar object perceived. (*Principles*, 2:80–81)

Although consistent, the Jamesian account of sensation and perception may be inadequate, vulnerable to readily apparent objections. One difficulty in this account arises over James's contention that, although sensing seems to be a distinct mental state that is part of perceiving, in fact only the perceiving, an indivisible state of mind, occurs. The initial plausibility of this contention stems not from any special insight into the nature of perception but rather from our general inclination to conclude, because we use the idiom "states of mind" no matter what the circumstances, that we can be in only one state of mind at any time. The importance of this inclination can be dismissed, however, simply by putting aside the locution "states of mind" and asking instead whether, in a case of perceiving, we can detect anything relevant other than sensing. If we can, then James's theory does not stand, for it implies by its requirement of a single state of mind that we cannot.

When we hear the rustling of a bird in the brush, we can both detect the sounds in our ears (which can be sensed, in James's terminology, that is, focused upon without regard to sensory context) and infer that something else may be occurring, that a bird in the brush is producing the sounds. When we confidently make such a judgment, we say we *hear* a bird in the brush; this hearing, as distinguished from merely sensing the sounds without regard for what they signify, is what is meant by saying that we *perceive* a bird in the brush.[15] Some theorists believe that the difference between sensing and perceiving, thus defined, is detectable in audition and the other senses but is difficult if not impossible in vision. Curiously, James himself supplied two examples from vision (the printed word and the upside-down painting), a fact that prompts us to reconsider our criticism of his position. Another example makes the difference between sensation and perception more emphatic.

> In many cases it is easy to compare the psychic results of the sensational with those of the perceptive process. We then see a marked difference in the way in which the impressed portions of the object are felt, in consequence of being cognized along with the reproduced portion, in the higher state of mind. Their sensible quality changes under our very eye. Take . . . *Pas de lieu Rhône que nous:* one may read this over and over again without recognizing the sounds to be identical with those of the words *paddle your own canoe.* As we seize the English meaning the sound itself appears to change. Verbal sounds are usually perceived with their meaning at the moment of being heard. Sometimes, however, the associative irradiations are inhibited for a few moments (the mind being preoccupied with other thoughts) whilst the words linger on the ear as mere echoes of acoustic sensation. Then, usually, their interpretation suddenly occurs. But at that moment one may often surprise a change in the very *feel* of the word. (*Principles,* 2:80)

This is surely a fine description of how sensing and perceiving can be introspectively distinguished, of how perceiving, as an additional process of making judgments or recognizing meanings, can distinctly alter the character of what is being sensed. Thus, our first objection to James's position—which we provisionally interpreted to imply that despite all our inclinations both sensing and perceiving cannot occur simultaneously, one within the other—is invalidated; indeed, James insisted that sensation and perception can on occasion be clearly distinguished. His basic claim in *Principles* (subsequently abandoned) that one mental state cannot include another remains intact; the admission that sensing and perceiving can occur simultaneously and can be distinguished does not contradict that claim. The two processes can occur alongside each other, just as we can hear and see something at the same time. The sole criticism to which James seems susceptible, then, is that his speaking of perception as a unitary state of mind which excludes sensing is somewhat misleading; his terminology might imply that perceiving is never simultaneously distinguishable from sensing, but he clearly never intended that implication.

A second, more telling difficulty with James's account of sensation and perception pertains to his idea that they differ only in the degree of complexity of what is apprehended (*"Sensation . . . differs from Perception only in the extreme simplicity of its object or content"*). The narrower one's sensory apprehension of something, the more one approaches a pure sensation; but as the context is noticed, one moves from sensing to perceiving. For James, the distinction between the two processes was always one of degree. While they differ in the amount of complexity registered to consciousness, they are equally cognitive of an independent, external reality. James discerned that a theory about the "cognitive dumbness" of sensations can result in a wrongheaded philosophy of perception, one that mistakenly contrasts perception (a process in contact with things around us) with everything nameable as sensation (a process in touch only with phenomena in some philosophically invented place such as "one's own mind"). He insisted that sensation, when it is regarded as part of perception, is an integral part of our acquaintance with nonmental realities and thus should not be separated from its context and assigned a subjective status.

But some phenomena nameable as sensations are not part of perception; such sensations are not contrasted with perception simply by being more narrowly focused. Sensations include ringings in the ears, spots before the eyes, and sinking feelings in the stomach. In calling these sensations, we mean that they are bodily states that depend upon appropriate physiological stimulation. When that stimulation ceases, so do the sensations. They are not part of the external environment, not even when we apprehend them in full context. Ringings in the ears are not buzzing confusions that bloom into perceptions when understood in context. James's distinction between perception and sensation works for some cases but not for those sensations that are bodily states occurring only during a definite period of physiological stimulation. It is in this regard that we *perceive* the ringing of the telephone, while we *sense* the ringing in our ears. Thus not all sensations are rudimentary, about-to-bloom perceptions.

It may be erroneous, James argued, to lift a sensation conceptually out of context and then assert that it is merely a subjective occurrence in one's mind. Yet ringings in the ears and spots before the eyes seem—partly because no one else can find the ringings and spots in the same space—to qualify as internal occurrences. Those theorists who take such internal phenomena as the paradigm of sensations will conclude that all sensations are subjective, merely internal processes. The main argument for this view is that all such sensations are products of a uniform kind of physiological stimulation and thus cannot be conceived as existing apart from that stimulation. Ringing in the ears is not part of the objective environment, independent of the bodily condition of the person experiencing them; likewise, some argue, the ringing of the telephone does not belong to the objective environment.

James preferred to remain with common sense in supposing that most sensations are external realities and that ringings in the ears, for example, are the exception. Such a belief was required by his thesis that sensations are cognitive. But given James's emphatic denial that sensations are subjective, his reader must wonder on what criterion the ringings in the ears qualify as subjective. Because he thought the "new psychology" ought to discover the bodily (especially the cerebral) conditions of mental states, he offered hypotheses about the conditions underlying sensations and perceptions. He sometimes based his physiological hunches on the results of introspection; at other times he based his introspection on physiological evidence. When distinguishing sensations and perceptions from thoughts and images, he used introspection to make the initial distinction that thoughts are not experienced as physically present, whereas images, as Hume held, are experienced as pale copies of sensations; he then sought physiological explanations for the introspectable differences between them.[16]

The trouble, however, is that introspection can hardly be a definitive arbiter of which sensations are subjective and which are objective, since illusory and hallucinatory sensations can often seem external. Physiological explanations presuppose some method of distinguishing subjective and objective sensations; they cannot be invoked for establishing that distinction, because it is precisely that distinction which they are brought in to explain. In his concern in volume 2 of *Principles* with introspective identification of mental states and with suggesting the nature of their bodily conditions, James seems simply to have forgotten to make explicit his assumption that the distinction between subjective and objective sensations is made by common sense. We learn to distinguish the two categories of sensation, and the process of learning involves more than introspection and less than physiological expertise. Nothing in James's distinction between sensation and perception (as a difference in complexity of the sensory field) expresses what is actually involved when we learn to separate subjective sensations from objective ones. Not all sensations are equally cognitive and objective; James was well aware of this but somehow never incorporated it into his theory of sensation and perception.

A related topic is the status of perceptual objects and the question of how we perceive them. James's opinions on this subject prior, roughly, to 1904 (the year of the first essay in radical empiricism, "Does 'Consciousness' Exist?") must be reinterpreted in terms of the metaphysics developed during the last decade of his life (see chapter 11). In "The Perception of 'Things,' " he expressed a basic thesis from which he never deviated: "Every concrete particular thing is a conflux of sensible qualities" (*Principles*, 2:78). Sensible qualities, called the objects of sensation when the experience of sensing is called sensation, include the traditional primary and secondary qualities, including images, sounds, colors, tactile data, fragrances, shapes, sizes, and so on.[17] James always adhered to the Berkeleyan and Humean conception that physical objects are constituted of sensible qualities, although he tried to improve upon their theories by endowing the qualities that make up an object with greater system and unity. His position in *Principles* was essentially the one formulated later in "Some Metaphysical Problems": "Berkeley's criticism of 'matter' was consequently absolutely pragmatistic. Matter is known as our sensations of colour, figure, hardness, and the like. They are the cash-value of the term. The difference matter makes to us by truly being is that we then get such sensations; by not being, is that we lack them. These sensations then are its sole meaning. Berkeley doesn't deny matter, then; he simply tells us what it consists of. It is a true name for just so much in the way of sensations."[18]

A main difficulty for James's theory of how we perceive the external world results directly from his adoption in *Principles* of a dualistic epistemology in which he was unable to remain confident. He reasoned, in traditional fashion, that perceptions (as states of mind) have their own content and are thus inner pictures of the objects perceived. "So when I get, as now, a brown eye-picture with lines not parallel, and with angles unlike, and call it my big solid rectangular walnut library-table, that picture is not the table. It is not even like the table as the table is for vision, when rightly seen. It is a distorted perceptive view of three of the sides of what I mentally *perceive* (more or less) in its totality and undistorted shape" (*Principles*, 2:78). The perennial problem for this theory of perception—sometimes called representationalism because the mental picture-contents of the perceivings are said to represent the perceived object—is to show how, if all perceivings are pictures, we can ever go beyond the pictures to the objects themselves and make a comparison between the perceivings and the perceived. The difficulty is aggravated in James's philosophy of perception because the "real" object perceived is something arbitrary. "But what are things? Nothing . . . but special groups of sensible qualities. . . . [The mind] chooses [for practical and aesthetic reasons] certain of the sensations to represent the thing most *truly*, and considers the rest as its appearances."[19] But if the object of perception is just a "conflux of sensible qualities" and the decision about which sensible qualities are real is an arbitrary one, then any commonsense concept of a real object has been eliminated. Instead of the real objects of either science or common sense, the Jamesian universe provides an indefinite array of sensible qualities from which to select, depending upon our interests and pragmatic concerns, what is reality and what mere appearance.

James welcomed this consequence and did not regard it as an embarrassment. Its emphasis upon sensations and sensible qualities clearly adumbrates the concept of pure experience in the later metaphysics of radical empiricism, as does its idea that perceptual knowledge is largely a function of interest and will—the concept I call subjective pragmatism in James's philosophy after *Principles*.[20] In trying to reconcile this line of thinking with common sense during his final years, he experienced much

confusion and embarrassment (see chapter 11), as he had when he sought to combine epistemological dualism (mental perceivings duplicating the features of the
perceived objects) with the hypothesis that objects of perception are simply confluxes of sensible qualities. *Principles* often displays a lack of confidence in the epistemological dualism adopted largely for strategic reasons specific to a pioneering
textbook in psychology. For example, James's discussion of "the genesis of the
elementary mental categories" has doubtlessly puzzled many readers. He focuses on
elementary sensations—feelings of personal activity, emotions, ideas of time and
space and number, and ideas of difference and resemblance, for example—and
describes them as "mental affections" or "ways of knowing." The question occupying James here was whether these elementary ways of knowing objects originate
more from experience or from the human organism's structure, especially its cerebral makeup. James questions the notion that the external world has gradually been
duplicated by the mind; he cites the fact that secondary qualities (colors, sounds,
tastes, etc.) are generally agreed to depend more upon the stimulated brain than
upon environmental stimuli:

> Why may it not have been so of the original elements of consciousness, sensa-
> tion, time, space, resemblance, difference, and outer relations? Why may not
> they have come into being by the back-door method, by such physical processes
> [as cerebral ones] . . . than in that of the 'sensible presence' of objects? Why
> may they not . . . be pure *idiosyncrasies,* spontaneous variations, fitted by good
> luck . . . to take cognizance of objects . . . without being in any intelligible
> sense immediate derivatives from them? I think we shall find this view gain
> more and more plausibility as we proceed.[21]

What bedeviled James's efforts in his later years to make his theory feasible even
in his own eyes was his determination to follow Berkeley in construing the objects of
perception to be of the same stuff of which our experiences are made, namely,
sensations. He thought that concepts as well as sensations are involved in our
perception of physical objects, but this view only complicated matters further. For
one thing, it was one step toward the goal of establishing a relation between perceived objects and introspectable experience: "Reproduced sights and contacts tied
together with the present situation in the unity of a *thing* with a name, these are the
complex objective stuff out of which my actually perceived table is made" (*Principles,*
2:78). In addition to present sensations, images and concepts aroused by memory
and past experience contribute not only to the perceiving but, apparently, to the
"complex objective stuff" of which the perceived table is made—not an easy idea to
absorb! To include concepts was not really a qualification of the analysis of perceived
objects into sensations, because, as he later put it, concepts and sensations "are made
of the same kind of stuff, and melt into each other" (*SPP,* 107). There were permanent uncertainties and occasional expressions of defeat in the effort to make the
theory work, but the irresistible drift of James's thought was toward the construction
of the perceived world out of sensations.

He wrestled repeatedly with the question of how the properties of physical objects, as normally conceived, can be reformulated as properties of sensations or sensible qualities (see chapter 11). Stickiness and roughness are sensible qualities or the objects of sensing experiences; but stickiness or roughness, as the *felt* qualities of sensation, cannot be seriously considered independent of the experience or an inherent feature of perceived objects.[22] To think they can is like supposing that the taste is in the candy or the pain is in the knife. How can colors, sounds, tastes, or smells be the essential properties of perceived objects, when these qualities vary with the conditions of observation while the objects are assumed to remain the same from every perspective? We suppose that our porch furniture is constantly what it is even though we are accustomed to changes in its appearance (its sensible qualities) with changing light, alterations in the atmosphere, modifications in our perceptual condition, and so on. The primary qualities of shape, size, and distance also vary with the conditions of observation and, according to James, are assumed by most psychologists to be dependent upon our memories and expectations.[23] How, then, can the relative stability of perceived objects be achieved from the comparative volatility of sensible qualities or sensations? Despite his efforts, James never succeeded in answering this question (see chapter 11).

James never really acknowledged the question of what is the ultimate source of organization in the sensible flux of experience. In upgrading sensation from the status to which he thought neo-Kantian idealism had consigned it, James stressed the putative belief that the infant's initial world of sensations contains all the categories of the understanding, all the principles required to give it shape and order. Yet he also wrote: "In other words, *all brain-processes are such as give rise to what we may call* FIGURED *consciousness*" (*Principles*, 2:82). By attributing unity and structure ("figured" consciousness, that is, sensible qualities occurring as figured objects) to processes in the brain, he seems to have denied that this unity results from sensations, which had previously received credit for it. There is some wavering in *Principles* between basing the structure of consciousness either on sensations, considered as autonomous entities, or on physiology. But this hesitation should not surprise us. James knew well enough the tensions in his own thought, the reasons for his uncertainties and vacillations, but he was willing to tackle them in public view. James would have been sympathetic with Ryle's confession about his own treatment of the philosophical problem of perception: "I shall not unravel the whole tangle, for the simple reason that I do not know how to do it. There are patches in it, and important ones where I feel like a bluebottle in a spider's web. I buzz but I do not get clear."[24]

IMAGINATION

James rarely treated imagination independently of his theorizing about sensation.[25] He thought of images, in accordance with tradition, as copies of sensations in the absence of the original stimuli. Following Locke's dictum that "the mind can frame unto itself no one new simple idea," James asserted that no image can be formed of any sensation not stimulated by an external source.[26] People born deaf and blind can never imagine what distinguishes sound and sight. Imagination is the capacity to make literal copies of original sensations and to produce images which are novel combinations of elements from different originals.[27] Afterimages, those sense-experiences that continue after an external stimulus has ceased, are sensations, not imaginings. The "most immediate phenomena of imagination would seem to be those tardier images . . . coercive hauntings of the mind by echoes of unusual experiences for hours after the latter have taken place. The phenomena ordinarily ascribed to imagination, however, are those mental pictures of possible sensible experiences, to which the ordinary processes of associative thought give rise" (*Principles,* 2:44–45). When mental pictures are not recollections but are of "data freely combined," they are instances of imagination in the usual sense of the word.

James took up a question still of interest today: Is the neural process underlying imagination only a "milder degree" of that underlying the original sensation? Another question is integrally connected with the first: Can peripheral sense-organs be excited by imagination or only by external stimuli? If currents can run forward into the brain and discharge into the muscular system, can they also be made by an act of imagination to run backwards—for example, from the optical centers of the brain to an excitement of the peripheral sense-organ, the retina? This phenomenon seems to occur when, by "mental acts" alone, we cause sensations in our bodies. For instance, tingling sensations in the toe seem to result just from concentrating upon it, irritating sensations in the hand just from imagining it severely burned.

James's approach to these questions is a fine example of his psychological method. That method, which he claimed characterized psychology as a natural science, is two-staged: one first identifies introspectively the relevant details of a state of consciousness, then seeks the physiological cause of that state. This cause is tentatively established by combining what ordinary introspection suggests as the physiological cause with what we know about the mechanics of the brain and the central nervous system.

> If I may judge from my own experience, all feelings of this sort [bodily changes apparently produced by mere imagining] are consecutive upon motor currents invading the skin and producing contraction of the muscles there, the muscles whose contraction gives "goose-flesh" when it takes place on an extensive scale. I never get a *feeling* in the skin, however strongly I *imagine* it, until some actual condition of the skin itself has occurred. The truth seems to be that the cases where peripheral sense-organs are directly excited in consequence of imagination are exceptional rarities, if they exist at all. *In common cases of imagination it would seem more natural to suppose that the seat of the process is purely cerebral, and that the sense-organ is left out.* (*Principles,* 2:69–70)

Two further reasons for this conclusion reinforce it in cases of ordinary imagining. The first, taken from physiology, shows that currents do in fact ordinarily flow forward to the brain, and thus cases in which they flow backward to peripheral sense-organs are comparatively rare. Second, there is a distinct introspectable difference between merely imagined events and those actually sensed or felt. "It is hardly possible to confound the liveliest image of fancy with the weakest real sensation. The felt object has a plastic reality and outwardness which the imagined object wholly lacks. Moreover, as [Gustav] Fechner says, in imagination the attention feels as if drawn backwards to the brain; in sensation (even of after-images) it is directed forward towards the sense-organ" (*Principles*, 2:70). But the issue is complex and difficult to resolve sharply. Certain experimenters held that they had learned to summon subjective visual sensations at will, and, further, that not all properties (notably in negative afterimages) could be derived from the initial stimulation of a peripheral sense-organ.[28] In such cases the current seems to flow backwards, from brain to sense-organ. Moreover, the subjective difference between imagining and sensing is sometimes indistinct, particularly when the sensation is barely perceptible. In hearing a distant clock, our imagination may reproduce the rhythm and sound of the strokes even after the chiming has stopped, and thus we may be unable to say which was really the last stroke. "Certain violin-players take advantage of this in diminuendo terminations. After the pianissimo has been reached they continue to bow as if still playing but are careful not to touch the strings. The listener hears in imagination a degree of sound fainter still than the preceding pianissimo" (*Principles*, 2:71–72). Given the ambiguity of experimental results and the less-than-absolute introspectable differences between sensation and imagination, James tentatively concluded that the cortical processes underlying the two probably differ not in locality but rather in intensity. Brain states normally require peripheral sense-organ stimulation to produce sensations; mere imagining, lacking that sort of stimulation, ordinarily yields a noticeably different conscious state. But if given a strange new intensity, the brain may send its currents backwards, resulting in a state of consciousness indistinguishable from a sensation.[29] Whatever the physiological facts, James seems to have described the subjective facts correctly here. He was also correct in emphasizing the importance of introspective data in testing rival physiological hypotheses. Without such data there is nothing to explain; what is to be explained physiologically, James insisted, are variations in experience and not, as others have argued, merely other physiological states or behavioral responses.

Hume had raised another question about the relation between imagination and sensation in declaring that images are adequate copies of sensations. He held that "whatever is true of the one must be acknowledged concerning the other" and that "as a strong impression must necessarily have a determinate quantity and quality, the case must be the same with its copy or representative."[30] James replied that the "slightest introspective glance" refutes this theory and that "Hume surely had images of his own works without seeing distinctly every word and letter upon the pages which floated before his mind's eye" (*Principles*, 2:46). In emphasizing the vagueness of most imagery, James was not denying Hume's claim that images must have their own determinate properties but rather his claim that images are always detailed, adequate copies of original impressions or sensations. In support of his argument James cited T. H. Huxley's account of generic images. When the images of six different faces are registered on the same photographic plate, each for a sixth of the time needed for a portrait, the result emphasizes those features shared by the faces and leaves vague the differing features. Huxley called this image *generic*, as distinguished from *specific* images, and held that much of our imagery is generic. He identified generic images with "abstract ideas," but here James dissented. The use of an image to represent a whole class of things, he observed, is clearly different from any intrinsic property of the image; accordingly, generic images cannot be equated with abstract ideas even though they may be used to represent classes of things. Further, any specific and distinct image may be so used; generic images are not privileged in this way. The issue between Locke and Berkeley over abstract ideas, James suggested, was perhaps due in part to variations in the human capacity to enjoy sharp, vivid imagery; a major portion of the chapter on imagination reviews the extent to which individuals differ in their ability to make or have images.

James, though himself a poor visualizer, never doubted the common occurrence of images. Apart from his phenomenalism and radical empiricism, he was in general an ontologist unworried about Occam's razor; he asserted that imaginary objects exist, although their existence is different from that of real things.[31] Very much the introspective psychologist in discussing images, he was highly interested in the descriptions used in trying to communicate imaginations and was never dismayed by the odd things we occasionally ask or say in assuming that images are a type of entity. For example, some people apparently depend for imaginative experiences more upon motor impulses or muscular feelings than upon visual or auditory stimuli. They empathize bodily but inwardly in imaging movements, their own or others'. James was intrigued by a Professor Stricker of Vienna, who fit this description. "In thinking of a soldier marching, for example, it is as if he were helping the image to march by marching himself in his rear. And if he suppresses this sympathetic feeling in his own legs, and concentrates all his attention on the imagined soldier, the latter becomes, as it were, paralyzed."[32] Stricker also claimed an ability, after practice, to make his "eye-movements 'act vicariously' for his leg-movements in imagining men walking" (*Principles,* 2:63n). Ludwig Wittgenstein made numerous references to *Principles,* and it is perhaps James's discussion of Stricker that led him to ask, "When I see the picture of a galloping horse—do I merely *know* that this is the kind of movement meant? Is it superstition to think I *see* the horse galloping in the picture?—And does my visual impression gallop too?"[33] Such funny questions naturally arise if we accept the existence of images as private pictures, special kinds of entities. We can argue, however, against the reification of images on the grounds that we may seem to see images without actually doing so. Just because we seem to see someone in a dream, it does not follow that we really see anything, even an image resembling the person. If what distinguishes imaginary experiences is just that we seem to see or hear things without in fact seeing or hearing anything at all, then we can dispense with the idea that we actually see or hear images in imaginative experiences.

But this argument confronts various difficulties. What about mirror images, for example? Reflections or mirror images are publicly witnessable and in this respect are unlike the images of dreams and reveries; yet, like such images, they are intangible, unlike ordinary objects. They may not be "entities" in some important sense of the word, but they are surely occurrences. Once that is acknowledged, why worry about admitting images in dreams and reveries as bona fide occurrences? As James's own review of the literature demonstrates, psychologists have investigated the properties of such images under varying conditions. Their experiments yield limited behavioral information, mostly useless for predicting and controlling behavior. Nevertheless, for those interested in the subjective details of imaginative experiences and in how we may encourage or inhibit imaging in our own experience, the investigations reviewed by James are valuable.

Subjectively, what is remarkable about imaginings are their occasionally vivid, sensationlike character and borderline nature. For example, upon seeing a photo of a deceased relative, some individuals suddenly seem to smell vividly the flowers at the funeral and claim to have an actual sensation of fragrance, an experience virtually indistinguishable from their olfactory experience at the funeral. That is, a fragrance is really present and does not merely seem to be; the sensation may be comparable to a toothache felt when there is no actual defect in the tooth. There are also borderline cases where one is uncertain whether a fragrance is actually present and then decides affirmatively or negatively, depending on whether the experience was sufficiently vivid to overcome the feeling that it was illusory. The philosophical issue of whether we really or only seemingly apprehend images is, in actual practice, the problem of resolving borderline cases, deciding whether the experience is sufficiently like an actual sensation. Most people have no doubt about images in vivid experiences; they decide either that the experience is so sensationlike that they really do sense something, or that only an image resembling a sensation is in fact present. In actual practice, whether one merely seems to sense something or really does is decided by introspection or retrospection. Our experiences can puzzle us, and introspection or retrospection is often held to be decisive—if fallible—in these cases. We may decide that an introspective judgment was erroneous, but only another introspective judgment can lead us to that decision.

Curiously, James's major claim on behalf of imagination occurs not in "Imagination," chapter 18 of *Principles,* but in "Attention" and "Discrimination and Comparison," chapters 11 and 13. This claim concerns the alleged role of imagination in attending to something, perceiving something, and discriminating aspects of what is attended to and perceived. James apparently formulated it after reflecting on experiments by Hermann Helmholtz and Ewald Hering. Helmholtz said that his experiments showed that, in visually fixating something, our attention can function independently, without coincidental accommodation of our eyes, to bring previously unnoticed details into view. Hering concluded from his investigations that we can disperse our attention between central and marginal objects, the bulk of it obviously on the former.[34] James interpreted Hering to mean that our attention to marginal objects in our usual field of vision is, as Helmholtz said in a different context, voluntary and not identifiable with muscular changes in our eyes. Attending to something thus seems a distinctly psychological activity, different from any physiological or muscular one.[35]

James discussed attention further in his hypothesis about the nature of what psychologists call the perceptual set. He found a clue to this concept in pondering Hering's experiments, in which subjects succeeded at dispersing their attention to marginal objects or pictures in their fields of vision.

> *The effort to attend to the marginal region of the picture consists in nothing more nor less than the effort to form as clear an idea as is possible of what is there portrayed.* The idea is to come to the help of the sensation and make it more distinct. It comes with effort, and such a mode of coming is the remaining part of what we know as our attention's "strain" under the circumstances. Let us show how universally present in our acts of attention, this reinforcing imagination, this inward reproduction, this anticipatory thinking of the thing we attend to, is. (*Principles,* 1:438–39)

When we expect to perceive something, our expectation takes the form of imagining the expected thing and influences the actual perception, sometimes causing us to think mistakenly that we are perceiving what we expected. Perceptual attention thus involves imagining or "inward reproduction" and facilitates perceptual recognition and discrimination. "In looking for any object in a room, for a book in a library, for example, we detect it the more readily if, in addition to merely knowing its name, etc., we carry in our mind a distinct image of its appearance" (*Principles,* 1:504).

As James emphasized, we often think we perceive what we expected to perceive. It is probably also true that our imagining what we expect to see often influences not only what we think we see but also our ability to focus on it, to study perceptual details. But James exaggerated his case in trying to explain how the effort to disperse attention, assumed to be a psychological and not a physiological effort, is identical with the effort to imagine what one expects to perceive. The capacity to make images of something is only one of countless factors that may cause us to attend perceptually to it. We don't need anticipatory imaginings to make daily and attentive recognitions of our family members, although such anticipation may assist us in recognizing a friend not seen for many years. Although he expressed it ambiguously, James meant that we often imagine that we see what we were set or expected to see; this phenomenon often happens in strange perceptual experiences treated by abnormal psychology, a subject in which he was vitally interested.[36] In pondering Helmholtz and Hering, James was tempted into giving a fuller description than necessary of attending (dispersing attention). If attending is not the physical accommodation of the sense-organs, what is it? In the tradition of British empiricism he asked: Is it a mental activity that can be described? James, in that tradition, answered that we can describe what we imagine just as we can describe what we perceive. He was thus tempted to blend the more introspectively elusive activity of attending with that of imagining. But the two activities are hardly identical: it may be difficult to attend to what we are imagining, and perhaps impossible to imagine what we are attending to. The imagination may help us to attend to something, as James claimed, but that joining of activities appears to be an occasional phenomenon rather than a routine technique.

The topic of imagination and images was important for James throughout his psychology. Without covering every facet of it, I have tried to explain the proximity of imagination to sensation in James's thought and how the properties of images were for James as interesting a subject for study as were those of sensation.[37]

SPECIAL ISSUES

In perception the mind meets an object that is in part a product of the mind, but in sensation, James insisted, the mind can encounter sensible qualities or objects untainted by mental activity. All perception is acquired or learned, and we contribute through the learned processes and their accompanying physiological conditions to the character of what we perceive. But sensation provides brute, unlearned acquaintance with extramental realities—or so James believed, though he was forced to argue the point with those who disagreed. Whereas he defended sensations as relational terms exhibiting intrinsic sensory content, "the only reals for the neo-Hegelian writers appear to be *relations,* relations without terms." Such writers assert that "the relation of sensations to each other is something belonging to their essence, and that no one of them has an absolute content."[38] The challenge confronting James was the psychological doctrine that the intrinsic qualities of sensations are always modified by our habit of comparing them; whereas he was delighted, in his pragmatic account of perceptual knowledge, to declare that the trail of the human serpent is everywhere, he was also anxious to protect sensations from the slightest human influence.

Psychologists point to certain phenomena that show how sensations are modified by contrast and comparison; James needed to show that these accounts did not refute his claim that sensations can display themselves without modification. For example, the color and brightness of one object will generally affect the color and brightness of another that is seen either simultaneously or immediately afterwards. If a bright object is placed in an even brighter context, it will appear darker; if placed in a darker context, it will appear brighter. One explanation for such phenomena, adopted by Helmholtz, attributes the contrast to a "deception of judgment": we neglect the details of sensations because we are more interested in objects. This theory has a complicated consequence for Helmholtz's psychological hypothesis. The change in brightness through contrast is only apparent, for there is no actual change in either the sensory stimulation or the sensation; through the initial neglect of sensory details a faulty judgment is made, which causes a faulty interpretation of the unchanged sensation, producing a changed *awareness* of the brightness. Opposed to this was Hering's physiological explanation, according to which both the neural process and the sensation are changed through contrast. James sided with Hering, persuaded that his experiments were more conclusive.[39] The advantage of Hering's hypothesis in James's eyes was that sensations were considered the immediate results of cerebral activity, so that what actually changes is not the sensation but rather its causal conditions (including those in the brain). In keeping with his *esse est sentiri* principle and its implications that sensations cannot be enduring elements, James held that no one sensation is modified by contrast; rather, the physiological conditions in the first instance produce one sensation, and new conditions produce a second, different sensation. Both sensations can be said to display their intrinsic characters unaffected by human comparison or by their own relations of contrast. Indeed, James asked, instead of thinking of the relations of sensations as being alien ideas that modify the sensations, "is it not manifest that the relations are part of the 'content' of consciousness . . . just as much as the sensations are?" (*Principles*, 2:28).

James discussed other interesting phenomena. A small amount of skin immersed in hot water will experience a less intense sensation of heat than will a larger amount, even though the water's temperature is kept the same. Heat cannot be distinguished from touch when applied to a minute portion of skin through a small hole in a card. These examples show the need for a certain extensity as well as intensity in the stimulus if a certain sensation is to occur; inversely, a certain intensity in the stimulus is needed to produce greater extensity in the sensation, as when a whole room seems to expand or contract as we increase or diminish its illumination. "It is not easy," James remarked, "to explain any of these results as illusions of judgment due to the inference of a wrong objective cause for the sensation which we got" (*Principles*, 2:29). Another sensation that cannot be explained away is known as *colored hearing*, in which visual sensations are accompanied by distinct auditory ones so intimately that colors seem almost to contain sounds. This is an instance not of sensations being modified by their relations or by our reaction to them, but of the tendency of sense-organs in league with the central nervous system to interact and produce different sensations from those produced by a single sense-organ. The modifications are physiological and occur prior to the sensations thus produced; to the extent that he could appeal to experimental evidence on behalf of the physiological explanation, James could shore up his claim that sensations occur pristinely and are ephemeral events, not events that endure and are modified by our comparisons and judgments. Far from proving that sensations are modifiable, the phenomena just described merely "show us that the *same real thing* may give us quite different sensations when the conditions alter, and that we must be careful which one to select as the thing's truest representative" (*Principles*, 2:28). James's commitment here to an epistemological dualism between sensations and physical objects clearly conflicts with his doctrine that real objects are simply confluxes of sensible qualities. The objects here are not equated with sensible qualities (sometimes called sensations, sometimes objects of sensation) but are assumed to be their causes.

James concluded that physiological conditions can be such that they can suffice, without the help of psychological explanations, to explain why certain sensations occur as they do. But there are more complex cases, including illusions, where psychological hypotheses are necessary. Even in these cases, however, the sensation is what it is, according to James, because the illusion is always caused by what is inferred, not by what is immediately given. *"The so-called 'fallacy of the senses' of which the ancient sceptics made so much account, is not fallacy of the senses proper, but rather of the intellect, which interprets wrongly what the senses give"* (*Principles*, 2:86). James cites an example said to date from Aristotle: if one crosses two fingers and rolls a pea or other small object between them, it will seem double.

> Professor Croom Robertson [editor of *Mind*] has given the clearest analysis of this illusion. He observes that if the object be brought into contact first with the forefinger and next with the second finger, the two contacts seem to come in at different points of space. The forefinger-touch seems higher, though the finger is really lower; the second-finger-touch seems lower, though the finger is really higher. "We perceive the contacts as double because we refer them to two distinct parts of space." The touched sides of the two fingers are normally not together in space, and customarily never do touch one thing; the one thing which now touches them, therefore, seems in two places, i.e. seems two things.[40]

Whether the Robertson-James explanation is adequate is not evident at first glance. It claims that we perceive the contacts as double "because we refer them to two distinct parts of space," but if this is based on introspective evidence, it runs counter to my own introspections, which disclose no such process of referring the contacts to two different places. It would be surprising if the alleged referral occurs "unconsciously," for James was generally unsympathetic to the idea that sense-perception uses unconscious judgment or inferences.[41] He probably meant that we tend to perceive what we expect to perceive, and since we habitually expect (because of past experience) to perceive the two fingers in two distinct places, we perceive illusorily the one object that touches both to be itself two things in two distinct places. The process of referral, if conceived simply as the operation of a perceptual habit, can then be construed as a physiological and behavioral set. Thus nothing more than reference to a process of learning or to past experience is involved in saying that such illusions need both a physiological and a psychological explanation.

James was surely correct in concluding with most psychologists that numerous illusions illustrate that *"whilst part of what we perceive comes through our senses from the object before us, another part (and it may be the larger part) always comes . . . out of our own head"* (*Principles*, 2:103). If, while looking in the dark for my dog, I come upon a box that suddenly looks like the dog, my experience is sensibly explained as resulting in large part from my expectation; what I perceived came largely "out of my own head." Yet we must be wary, as James did not sufficiently advise us, of supposing that *whenever* the box appears to be a dog, whether the cause be in the brain or in the mind, the experience arises from a prior expectation, belief, or idea. A set of conditions, including the state of my eyes and the character of the light but not my expectations and habits, may sometimes adequately explain why the box looks like a dog. Some illusions can, like elementary cases of color and brightness contrast, be physiologically based. This is an incidental observation, however, for James's main point was that the character of sensations is often the product of an individual's psychology (beliefs, expectations, habits, etc.) in combination with his physiology. Despite the opposed claims of Thomas Reid and Hermann Helmholtz, he declared, the sensations we normally expect from certain stimuli or objects can be replaced by sensations that result from our interpretation of those stimuli, or by what we take those sensations to signify. One sensation is not necessarily modified into another as a result of perceptual interpretation, but interpretation can be one condition under which certain unexpected sensations, ordinarily called illusions, occur.

But did James mean that new sensations are always the products of modifications in the perceptual conditions and are never modifiable once they exist? Despite his insistence upon the ephemeral nature of sensations, he intended, in denying the elemental or atomistic character that some predecessors had attributed to sensations, to avoid the opposite extreme of considering sensations so short-lived and fragile that nothing can happen to them except a quick death. He believed (supported by common sense) that our attitudes can alter present situations. For instance, he held that we can distinguish between sensing and perceiving; he also wrote: "I went out . . . and found that the snow just fallen had a very odd look, different from the common appearance of snow. I presently called it a 'micaceous' look; and it seemed to me as if, the moment I did so, the difference grew more distinct and fixed than it was before. . . . I think some such effect as this on our way of feeling a difference will be very generally admitted to follow from naming the terms between which it obtains" (*Principles*, 1:512). If the appearance of snow is modifiable simply by naming it, it must be even more susceptible to alteration by strong moods, beliefs, or desires. While sensations cannot function as psychic atoms that recur indefinitely (James ascribed the view that they can to Locke and his followers), they can linger long enough to be interesting subjects of introspective study and thus to be alterable by both physical and psychological influences.

James never theorized about *how* a sensation is changed by giving it a name or adopting a special attitude toward it. He repeatedly scorned in *Principles* the theory that changes in sensations are achieved by addition or subtraction of other sensations (regarded as manipulable mind-stuff). The modification of sensations by attitudes was either a brute, inexplicable fact or the result of cerebral mechanisms; James favored the second explanation in his psychology, and he would presumably have recommended it as the sole alternative to surrendering all efforts at finding an explanation. He always preferred in *Principles* a physiological explanation over a psychological one that assumed sensations to be measurable quantities.

James was an outspoken admirer of the nineteenth-century philosopher and psychologist Gustav T. Fechner in many respects, but he was an unsympathetic critic of Fechner's psychophysics—widely acclaimed to be his greatest achievement in psychology.

> In 1860, Professor G. T. Fechner of Leipzig, a man of great learning and subtlety of mind, published two volumes entitled "Psychophysik," devoted to establishing and explaining a law called by him the psychophysic law, which he considered to express the deepest and most elementary relation between the mental and the physical worlds. It is a formula for the connection between the amount of our sensations and the amount of their outward causes. Its simplest expression is, that when we pass from one sensation to a stronger one of the same kind, the sensations increase proportionally to the logarithms of their exciting causes. Fechner's book was the starting point of a new department of literature, which it would be perhaps impossible to match for the qualities of thoroughness and subtlety, but of which, in the humble opinion of the present writer, the proper psychological outcome is just *nothing*. (*Principles*, 1:533–34)

James then quoted liberally from Wilhelm Wundt, who supported the verdict that Fechner—by having improved upon the work of his predecessor, Ernst H. Weber, in showing that the psychophysical "law" allegedly holds for all sensations—had taken the first step toward making mental magnitudes subject to exact measurement. It was certain, Wundt believed, that the increase of the stimulus required to cause an increase in the sensation is expressible as a constant ratio to the total stimulus; future research was needed to refine the measurements. In a discussion that covers a good deal of technical detail, James addressed the assumption that sensations can be measured numerically, pointing out several difficulties. Fechner's "method of just-discernible differences," for instance, assumes that we can add to and subtract from sensations incrementally, but, as James observed, we do not always know whether anything has been added to or taken from a sensation. Another Fechnerian method assumed that in a long series of experiments we will make some true and false judgments in comparing two sensations; Fechner used this method "to ascertain his own power of discriminating differences of weight, recording no less than 24,576 separate judgments, and computing as a result that his discrimination for the same relative increase of weight was less good in the neighborhood of 500 than of 300 grams, but that after 500 grams it improved up to 3000, which was the highest weight he experimented with" (*Principles*, 1:541). James also assessed methods used by other researchers, and he pointed to the discrepancies in results from different laboratories.

In James's interpretation, Fechner's psychophysics assumed that the just-perceptible increment of a sensation is the *sensation-unit*, that all sensations are composites of such units, and that the stimulation of this unit by a constant fractional increase of the stimulus is explained by the ultimate "law" that connects the "quantities" of sensations logarithmically to the quantities of other stimuli. But, James declared, all these assumptions are precarious. The experience which the experiments supposedly find is not an "enlarged sensation" but rather the subject's *judg-*

ment that a sensation has been enlarged. "Fechner tacitly if not openly assumes that such a *judgment of increase* consists in the simple fact that an *increased number* of sensation-units are present to the mind; and that the judgment is thus itself a quantitatively bigger mental thing when it judges large differences . . . than when it judges small ones. But these ideas are really absurd. . . . It has no meaning to talk about one judgment bigger than another" (*Principles,* 1:546). Further, James argued, the contention that sensations are sums of sensation-units is introspectively suspect, because one's sensation of scarlet, for example, does not seem to contain a sensation of pink. If we speak of a sensible quality as twice or thrice what it was, we must not think of it as a compound object that truly has parts; we mean instead that "if we were to arrange the various possible degrees of the quality in a scale of serial increase, the *distance, interval,* or *difference* between the stronger and the weaker specimen before us would seem about as great as that between the weaker one and the beginning of the scale. *It is these* RELATIONS, *these* DISTANCES, which we are *measuring and not the composition of the qualities themselves,* as Fechner thinks" (*Principles,* 1:546). James objected further that Fechner gratuitously presumed that equally perceptible additions to sensations are equally great; for all we know, a small addition to a small sensation might be as perceptible as a large addition to a large sensation. James concluded that Weber's "law," which Fechner had refined, was physiological in nature. Its main point is that there seems to be a loss of effect in the transition from stimulus to sensation, an event James believed might be explained biologically. "Weber's law would thus be a sort of *law of friction* in the neural machine. . . . The latest, and probably the most 'real,' hypothesis is that of Ebbinghaus, who supposes that the intensity of sensation depends on the *number* of neural molecules which are disintegrated in the unit of time."[42]

James had various reasons for preferring physiological explanations of sensations. His theorizing about sensation had several aims: the analysis of how we routinely perceive the world; the identification of the ultimate data of empirical knowledge; the illumination of such processes as perceptual discrimination and imagination; the attempted replacement (in the metaphysics of radical empiricism) of a psychophysical dualism with a theory that equated reality with sensations; a demonstration that the products of human intellect always fail to capture reality "right and entire"; and an explanation of illusions, delusions, hallucinations, and the sensations involved in abnormal experiences.

A number of unusual experiences involving peculiar sensation and perception interested James: hysterical blindness, which is not total blindness at all; alterations in sensations caused by drugs such as nitrous oxide; changes in sensibility caused by disruptions in one's sense of self; perceptual susceptibilities in hypnotism; the way in which mediums sense and perceive; the experiences of persons who have lost a limb; the sensation of dizziness in deaf-mutes; the illusion of successfully willing movement in an anesthetized part of the body; and the sensations that attend melancholy and depression, something James knew from his own experience.[43] If these unusual experiences and the sensations that characterize them are composed of smaller sensible qualities and can be augmented or diminished by the addition or subtraction of sensation-units, then how would one set out to trace their causes? According to the sensation-unit theory, the process by which sensations assume their character is exceedingly elusive; sensations combine in psychologically mysterious ways to produce new sensations. On the other hand, if sensations result from physiological events, their causes become fathomable, and for this reason also James preferred to explain sensations physiologically in his psychology, though not so evidently in metaphysics. Perhaps one can sometimes fight off the sensations of an attack of melancholy through an exertion of moral will, but if not, there is hope, James believed, that the main causes are physiological and can be isolated. Some sensations may help to reveal what is happening within the body. The physiological explanation, unlike the psychological, may help us to understand the underlying causes of sensations in abnormal experiences. Where it is important, for coping and recovery, to get at the causes, the physiological hypothesis offers hope of success—certainly a motivating factor in James's thinking.

James's choice of a physiological over a psychological/metaphysical explanation (the mind-stuff theory) figured in his position on an issue that gained some notoriety because it involved him in a debate with F. H. Bradley. In *Principles* James argued (in agreement with Carl Stumpf) that our perception of the qualitative difference between things, the "shock" of difference, is an unanalyzable mental event, as is our perception of a simple resemblance between things; he also asserted that the relation of resemblance is itself ultimate and unanalyzable. Although the discussion of this issue occurs in chapter 13, "Discrimination and Comparison," there is a significant footnote reference to it in chapter 6, "The Mind-Stuff Theory." The recurrent issue is whether mental states can be conceived as mixtures or compounds of other mental states, and James argued in *Principles* and elsewhere—until he changed his position in 1895 in "The Knowing of Things Together"—that they cannot be so conceived. Whereas the physical lemonade contains both lemon and sugar, the *taste-sensation* of lemonade does not contain discernible parts of lemon-sour and sugar-sweet. "These tastes are absent utterly. The entirely new taste which is present *resembles,* it is true, both those tastes; but in chapter XIII we shall see that resemblance cannot always be held to involve partial identity" (*Principles,* 1:158n). The claim that resemblance can be ultimate and not analyzable into identity was connected in James's mind with the denial of the mind-stuff theory, and with his own *esse est sentiri* doctrine of mental states. If resemblance between things necessarily implied that they were identical in certain respects, then it would follow, because the taste of lemonade resembles lemon-sour and sugar-sweet, that an identical sensation common to the lemonade taste, the lemon-sour, and the sugar-sweet must be present in all three. In that case, the mind-stuff theory would triumph over the *esse est sentiri* doctrine.

James believed that there are cases where resemblance presupposes an underlying identity but also cases in which this relation is not true. To establish the latter cases would be sufficient to prove that resemblance does not necessarily entail identity; if this claim was granted, then any a priori argument for the mind-stuff theory collapses. When two lines differ in length, for example, it is plausible to say that their difference can be canceled by adding a certain length *l* to the shorter one; we can then say that in our perception of the original difference we were cognizant of the presence of *l* in one line and its absence in the other. When *l* is added to the shorter line, we are aware of the presence of *l* in both, showing that *l* is the identity upon which the perceived resemblance depends. If all resemblances were like this, James's claim that resemblance can be a primitive relation would not hold. But he asserted that not all are.

> Is right equal to left with something added? Is blue yellow *plus* something? If so, *plus* what? So long as we stick to *verifiable* psychology, *we are forced to admit that differences of simple* KIND *form an irreducible sort of relation* between some of the elements of our experience, and forced to deny that differential discrimination can everywhere be reduced to the mere ascertainment that elements present in one fact, in another fail to exist. The perception that an element exists in one thing and does not exist in another and the perception of qualitative differences are, in short, entirely disconnected mental functions. (*Principles*, 1:493–94)

Bradley, in arguing that resemblance is always based upon partial identity, criticized James's examples and claims in "Discrimination and Comparison." James replied that what Bradley had isolated in his criticisms was not essential to James's viewpoint; in my judgment, Bradley's theory rested upon a premise that simply placed him and James at an impasse.[44] According to Bradley, James presented this choice: either resemblance exists only between what is simple, or the difference between two objects consists of two things, identity in certain respects and nonidentity in others. Bradley argued:

> Now I wish to point out at once that this alternative seems incomplete. A man may be sure that resemblance between what is quite simple is quite unmeaning; and yet he need not believe that the one alternative to "simple" is "composite," if "composite" means made up of separable parts. The view that sameness and difference are everywhere inseparable aspects most certainly exists. But its existence is not included in the dilemma in which the argument exists. And, in the second place, while holding resemblance, not indeed to *be*, but to be based always on, partial identity, *one need not in consequence hold that this identity is explicit*. If, that is, in things before my mind, which seem to me like, *I do not distinguish, and perhaps could not specify*, the identical point, *this does not prove that no perceptible identity is there*. But on these false assumptions Professor James's whole conclusion seems to rest. (*Collected Essays*, 1:287–88; italics mine)

This passage gives an impression of what the dispute was like. Bradley's first point, like his other criticisms of James's position, turns on the notion of simple and composite things, but James considered this point unimportant. "Can it be the word 'simple' which has caused all the trouble?—for . . . in my book I did heedlessly use the expression 'simple resemblance' in one place. But I never meant to imply that the simplest phenomenon of resistance might not seem . . . to curdle and swim with inner complexity" (*CER*, 341). Bradley's second point, representing the fundamental premise of his position, was the claim that perceptual identity is present even where it cannot be discerned. James had made it reasonably clear in *Principles* that he was writing on psychology and was therefore concerned only with discernible distinctions; he responded to Bradley's argument: "The usual English name for that sort of identity between two things which you cannot abstract or distinguish from their differences is their 'resemblance.' . . . I never meant to go beyond psychology; and on that relatively superficial plane I now confidently greet Mr. Bradley, no longer as the foe which by a mere verbal ambiguity he has seemed, but as a powerful and welcome ally" (*CER*, 340–41). Quite obviously, he and Bradley were at an impasse.

For both thinkers, although probably for different reasons, the issue was a serious one with many ramifications. To James's way of thinking, sensations are what really exist; their vibrancy contrasts with the "pallid" and sometimes "sickly" preoccupations of the intellect feeding upon itself. Sensations arouse our belief in reality: they are coercive in their power to occupy our attention, lively and pungent, stimulating to our will, capable of creating emotional interest, congruous with unity and permanence, and relatively independent of other causes.[45] We live for, with, through, and by our sensations. Particularly in a philosopher's life, the pleasant sensation is an oasis in a desert of dry reflections; for James the visual sensations afforded by standing atop Mount Marcy in the Adirondacks were a soothing relief from weeks of pondering the intricacies of sense-perception. When metaphysically equated with reality, sensations must be conceived to be as they seem to be, to have the absolute natures they appear to have, for unlike human conceptions they are neither inherently suspect nor vulnerable to the skeptical reversals of a restless intellect. They always appear as they are, with no discrepancy between appearance and reality. We may never be exempt from the possibility of erroneously reporting or classifying a sensation—sensory acquaintance may or may not constitute knowledge (see chapter 10)—but the error is in our response and not in the sensation. Thus if resemblance is something sensed, experienced as a "shock" at the level of a sensation, then James urges that we accept it at face value, not letting the skeptical voice of speculative reason persuade us, despite its appearance, that resemblance is really a case of disguised identity. To be so persuaded would be tantamount to holding all sensations hostage and surrendering completely to skepticism. Something of the sort was at stake in James's dispute with Bradley.[46]

One final issue concerns the relation of sensation and consciousness to space. James wanted to believe, in accordance with his nativistic theses that sensations are cognitive and that their cognitions are innate rather than learned, that such qualities as spatial distance are sensible; yet he acknowledged that, like distance, they are in certain respects subject to a learning process.

Our whole optical education indeed is largely taken up with assigning their proper distances to the objects of our retinal sensations. An infant will grasp at the moon. . . . In the much quoted case of the "young gentleman who was born blind" and who was "couched" for the cataract by Mr. Chesselden, it is reported of the patient that "when he first saw, he was so far from making any judgment about distances, that he thought all objects whatever touched his eyes (as he expressed it) as what he felt did his skin." And other patients born blind, but relieved by surgical operation, have been described as bringing their hand close to their eyes to feel for the objects which they at first saw, and only gradually stretching out their hand when they found that no contact occurred. Many have concluded from these facts that our earliest visual objects must seem in immediate contact with our eyes. (*Principles,* 2:36–37)

James had a ready reply for the objection that this phenomenon contradicts his thesis that distance is a sensation or sensible quality. It does not follow from the fact that the baby first reaches for the moon, or that the blind person given sight reaches for an object at the site of his own eyes, that distance is not a sensory datum. All that these responses imply, James insisted, is that such individuals have not yet learned the manual or tactile distance of the objects at that visual distance.[47] We must learn to coordinate the spatial data of the different senses just as we learn to estimate or measure more exactly spatial data which originally seem vague. There is no contradiction between the Jamesian theses that phenomena such as spatial distance are given immediately as sensible qualities and that a learning process is required to refine their initial vagueness into more precise formulations.

In his discussion of sensation James reiterated what he had said in chapter 8, "The Relations of Mind to Other Things": that it makes no sense to ascribe spatial position to consciousness itself.[48] He meant that sensation, taken as sensing or a state of consciousness, cannot intelligibly be said to be here or there, or even to seem to be. As long as we say that consciousness (or sensing) occurs, we are forced to admit that its relation to space is a mystery. This admission provoked James to try, in his final years, to eliminate the psychophysical dualism that sets the stage for the mystery. If sensation is taken to mean the sensible qualities or immediate objects of the sensing experiences, we must acknowledge another subtlety. The sensible qualities in our initial experience, while natively spatial in the sense of having inborn spatial qualities, do not enjoy a definite spatial position. An example, James thought, is our original visual sense of movement, which he believed to be produced by any image passing over the retina. "Originally, however, this sensation is definitely referred neither to the object nor to the eyes. Such definite reference grows up later, and obeys certain simple laws" (*Principles,* 2:88). Sensations originally come with their own places, but places not distinguished at the outset. It is misleading to conceive of sensations as things in space, because they *"bring* space and all its plans to our intellect, and do not derive it thence" (*Principles,* 2:35).

4 ❧ SPACE

NATIVISM AND SPACE-PERCEPTION

One of James's earliest articles is "The Spatial Quale" (1879), which announced a theory of space-perception that was later amplified in various essays and in the longest chapter of *The Principles of Psychology*.[1] Some contemporary thinkers, however, may subscribe to Josiah Royce's reaction to the 1879 essay. Calling the topic of space the most puzzling of all, Royce wrote to James:

> But the space problem, who shall master it? What is needed is, I think, this:— Some one must master the whole science of geometry in its latest forms as well as in its long history. Then this same man must have complete control over physiological psychology. Then he must master all the uses that have been made of space-science as an aid to other sciences . . . and so come to see the true connection of geometry and logic. . . . Then he must have control of the philosophic literature about space from Zeno of Elea to Kant and the present day. On the basis of all this he must write a special treatise, say on the "Properties of Space," which shall develop the principles of a new philosophic science—a synthesis of all the previous material, an elaborate account of what is empirical in our knowledge and application of space-properties. Give me ten years and nothing to hinder, and I will undertake that work myself. But I have neither the time nor the material.[2]

Despite the amount of attention he gave to the subject, James never saw his task in developing a theory of space-perception in such ambitious terms. He wrote more about space-*perception* than about space itself, and he wrote as a psychologist, not as a physicist or a philosopher of physics. He does not discuss whether space is euclidean, whether it is absolute or relative (though he seems at places to suggest, without discussion or argument, that it is absolute), or whether certain technical relations hold between time and space. He concentrated instead on the following questions:

How do we originally apprehend space? How is the system called real space created and understood? How is distance or the third dimension perceived? And what role does the intellect play in space perception?[3]

James's basic thesis was that all sensations have a spatial dimension. For example, sensations of sight, touch, sound, and pain display *voluminousness* or *extensity*. "We call the reverberations of a thunderstorm more voluminous than the squeaking of a slate-pencil; the entrance into a warm bath gives our skin a more massive feeling than the prick of a pin; a little neuralgic pain, fine as a cobweb, in the face, seems less extensive than the heavy soreness of a boil or the vast discomfort of a colic or a lumbago; and a solitary star looks smaller than the noonday sky" (*Principles*, 2:134). There is no sensation, James argued, lacking extensity, and acquaintance with this feature is our original acquaintance with space. Using Wundt's distinction, James called his theory of space-perception nativistic rather than genetic, meaning that this primitive feature of extensity is a datum of experience, not something of which we learn to become aware through experience. We no more learn a capacity to perceive this spatial dimension than we learn to apprehend redness or loudness. Just as redness and loudness are experiential data, sensed or intuited qualities of our experiences, so is extensity a sui generis, immediately sensed quality of all our sensations. Our initial acquaintance with space, compared with our later, more sophisticated knowledge of it, is vague. The originally apprehended extensity runs equally in all directions, since no measurements or comparisons have been made; surface has not been distinguished from depth, for example. But our more sophisticated knowledge of space is founded upon our acquaintance with the primitive spatial dimension of sensations. Nativism holds that, while sophisticated knowledge of space is learned and conceptual, such knowledge presupposes an unlearned, sensory awareness of space.

James's nativism was opposed to theories of space-perception which try to derive space from nonspatial elements. Such empiricists as Herbert Spencer, Thomas Brown, Alexander Bain, and John Stuart Mill had defended an ontology which included only unextended feelings and time as original elements. They argued that retinal sensations, for example, which are originally in our experience, do not possess extension; this feature occurs only later, through processes of association. Extensity is born from certain muscular feelings; the sweep and movement of our eyes creates our sense of extensity or vastness. After birth it is associated with nonspatial retinal sensations; colors are seen next to, outside of, or beyond each other. But, the empiricists argued, the eye requires the assistance of the muscular feelings involved in moving the head to see colors in such relations. According to this argument, then, space is not found in elementary sensations. As Bain put it, space as a quality of experience "has no other origin and no other meaning than the *association* of these different [nonspatial] motor and sensitive effects."[4]

James dissented, holding that association has no power to produce or create anything; its only capacity is connecting things originated in other ways. How, he asked, can association generate space from totally nonspatial elements? It seemed obvious enough that no persuasive answer could be invented here. On introspective grounds, he rejected the "mental chemistry," appealed to by James Mill and John Stuart Mill, which allegedly creates space out of time and unextended feelings.[5] For similar reasons he saw nativism as squarely opposed to the Kantian theory that space is generated from the mind's internal resources. According to Kant, sensation alone never informs us of an external world. Schopenhauer, who James thought was the most eloquent spokesman for the theory, had said:

> For sensation of every sort is and remains a process in the organism itself. As such it is limited to the territory inside the skin and can never, accordingly, *per se* contain anything that lies outside the skin or outside ourselves. . . . The feeling in the hand, even with different contacts and positions, is something far too uniform and poor in content for it to be possible to construct out of *it* the idea of Space with its three dimensions. . . . This is only possible through Space, Time, Causality . . . being performed in the Intellect itself . . . from whence it again follows that the perception of the external world is essentially an intellectual process, a work of the Understanding, *to which sensation furnishes merely the occasion,* and the data to be interpreted in each particular case."[6]

James noted, in response, that he was unaware of any such "Kantian machine-shop" in his own mental processes. Further, he believed that sensations *do* inform us about an external world. Accordingly, he saw no reason in the putative nature of sensations for denying that space as a feature of the external world is given in sensation.

James charged that both the empiricists, with their concept of association, and the Kantians, with their concept of a priori mental machinery, had given accounts of space-perception which either had no supporting evidence or could not be tested experimentally. The empiricists and the Kantians maintained that association or certain other processes of the mind itself are responsible for space-perception, yet no one has shown that spatial appearance can be produced from nonspatial elements. James's abandonment of psychological wheelwork in favor of a physiological account of space-perception, and his assertion that sensations have the properties they seem to have, provide an explanation of space closer to the facts and common sense than that of the empiricists or the Kantians. Recent research seems to support James's nativism. Neurophysiologists have shown that the ability of humans and certain animals to locate objects spatially is due to binocular nerve cells in the visual cortex.[7] We can sometimes judge distance from the visual image of one eye by using indirect cues, but this determination is not as accurate or as immediate as the "powerful sensation of stereopsis," the visual sensation we know when looking at stereoscopic slides or three-dimensional movies.[8] Things that are invisible monocularly will stand out vividly when seen stereoscopically. James argued that this phenomenon appears to be neurophysiological, due only to the eyes and brain, not requiring psychological explanations that involve mind-set, unconscious inferences, or association. Stereoscopic vision depends entirely upon the horizontal disparity between the two retinal images, and binocular apprehension of depth does not require prior recognition of form, "suggesting that the disparity information is processed by the brain fairly early in visual perception."[9] If learning or experience is needed for depth perception, the only learner is the brain itself.[10] Nativism, taken as the theory that spatial dimensions are experiential data acquired without the help of psychological processes, is thus the contemporary position that James anticipated.

SPACE AND SENSATION

James included in his theory of nativism two claims which are hardly defensible. The first claim is that spatial relations such as up and down are sensations; the second is that knowledge of space develops from acquaintance with the primordial extensity which allegedly characterizes all sensations: "*Rightness and leftness, upness and downness, are again pure sensations* differing specifically from each other, and generically from everything else" (*Principles*, 2:150).

The problem with the first claim concerns the definition of a sensation and brings into question James's statement that no sharp distinction exists between sensation and perception. He meant that if a distinction is made between the psychological states of sensing and perceiving, there is no clear-cut introspective way of distinguishing them; no psychological device can help us know which state we are in. But he also meant, more controversially, that there is no definite conceptual distinction between sensation and perception; accordingly, they cannot be sharply contrasting "ways of knowing." Sensation was for James an acquaintance with the external environment, less complex and rich than perception. But he considered both states to be direct acquaintance with things beyond one's own body. This view was deliberately opposed to the conception of sensation, espoused by Schopenhauer and others, that sensation is a process in the body itself and "can never contain anything that lies outside the skin."[11]

In declaring the fundamentals of space to be sensations, James included figures, lines, and angles. A square, a circle, and a triangle are as immediately different to the eye as are red and blue. Horizontal and vertical lines differ as directly as do acute and obtuse angles. Distance is a "simple sensation—the sensation of a line joining the two distant points; lengthen the line, you alter the feeling and with it the distance felt" (*Principles*, 2:148). Spatial relations are sensations and as such can be indicated or pointed to but not described. "We can only point and say *here* is right and *there* is left, just as we should say *this* is red and *that* is blue."[12] James's claim is that apprehending a spatial relation, like noticing a color, is having a certain sensation. This claim is stronger than the claim that a specific sensation is just a condition for noticing a color or a spatial relation.

Debating whether spatial relations are sensations is confusing, because the definition of a sensation is unclear. Schopenhauer held that sensations—which include headaches, hallucinations, and other processes that are dependent upon physiological stimulation and do not exist objectively independent of such stimulation—do not include figures, lines, and angles. But James thought that sensations, insofar as they include what is directly and immediately apprehended without hesitation or inference, are at least like simple spatial relations. In ordinary circumstances we apply spatial terms instantly, without hesitation or inference. Because spatial relations seem to be a given as much as are headaches, James was tempted to call them sensations and to conclude that sensing is an immediate way of coming to know external things. However, if objective relations are to be kept distinct from sensations like headaches and hallucinations, it is less confusing to say that such relations are not sensations but that they are noticed and recognized just as directly and immediately as sensations. To avoid confusing the category of *the given* with that of *sensation,* we need to concede that some things that are not sensations are recognized unhesitatingly and noninferentially.

James assumed that we can unhesitatingly and noninferentially apply a linguistic label to something perceptually recognized because what is recognized has a sensory character that seizes our attention so that ignoring it or mistaking it is virtually impossible. A loud noise, a striking blue, a stabbing headache are obvious examples. We do not hesitate in calling a noise loud or a headache stabbing; their sensory natures make the epithets appropriate. We can focus on these phenomena and study them introspectively. It is because sensations so often command our attention that we describe them unhesitatingly and noninferentially. This conclusion can lead imperceptibly to the assumption that whatever can be identified noninferentially must be a sensation—including spatial relations.

But this assumption is erroneous. Given a grasp of the concepts of up and down or left and right, we can identify immediately, without hesitation or inference, instances of such relations. We see these instances so directly that we may find ourselves saying that we not only see directly the terms of the relation, but also the relation itself. We fancy that the relation, because of its own peculiar sensory nature, forces itself upon our attention. But spatial relations have no sensory nature to focus on or study introspectively. We can see directly that a rock is to the left of a tree, but we cannot see a separate, isolable *to-the-left-of.* This relation and *to-the-right-of* do not differ as do loud and faint noises or mild and stabbing headaches. *Above* does not gleam above, nor does *below* perceptually bristle below. Spatial relations lack the sensuous marks of sensations. The concepts of the given, of spatial relations, and of sensations must be allowed their proper distinctness.

It would be extraordinary to have sensations and yet overlook or ignore their prominent features. If we notice a loud noise or a stabbing pain, it would be peculiar not to be aware of the loudness or the stabs. But the case is not the same with spatial relations. We can be intensely attentive to two things without registering that one is above or to the left of the other. The spatial relation is there before us in full view, yet our attention bypasses it, which would be unusual if it were a sensation.

SPACES AND SPACE

The second troublesome claim of James's nativistic theory of space is that our everyday apprehension of space is a development of a prior acquaintance with space-as-sensation. He moved from the thesis that all sensations possess a vague quale of spatiality to the claim that the "primordial largenesses which the sensations yield must be *measured and subdivided* by consciousness, and *added* together, before they can form by their synthesis what we know as the real Space of the objective world" (*Principles,* 2:145). The "primordial largenesses" here are the spatial properties of sensations which prompt us to talk of *big* noises, *heavy* odors, or *minute* tastes. Our descriptions of sensations, in borrowing from the vocabulary of the physical environment, always include a spatial dimension. This dimension originally occurs in a vague and unordered form; it is a primitive extensity not yet measured or otherwise defined; an example is the ocular vastness of an empty blue sky. These unordered extensities, which according to James are sensations and our original experiences of space, are subsequently arranged into one surrounding spatial world by a "complicated set of intellectual acts" (*Principles,* 2:145–46).

The problem, as James and others saw it, is to explain how we get from the disconnected spaces of sight, smell, taste, and touch to the single, ordered space of everyday experience. James's solution is highly intricate, requiring the longest chapter of *Principles* for its exposition. According to this solution, human experience begins with sensations which have a spatial bigness or extensity (retinal, cutaneous, olfactory). The original vastness of each sensation is eventually subdivided by our discriminative attention, which arises in response to our developing interest in the environment. The motion of impressions over sensory surfaces is important in learning to discriminate and to divide the primitive extensities of spatial perception.[13] But the subdivisions remain chaotically related to each other until we reduce them to a "common measure." We have no way of directly comparing the spaces of different sense-modalities, so some device is required for coordinating, for example, the extensity of a tooth cavity as it feels to the tongue and to the finger.

The device, James theorized, is *superposition,* which yields "exact equivalences and common measures. . . . Could we not superpose one part of our skin upon another, or one object on both parts, we should hardly succeed in coming to that knowledge of our own form which we possess. The original differences of bigness of our different parts would remain vaguely inoperative, and we should have no certainty as to how much lip was equivalent to so much forehead, how much finger to so much back" (*Principles,* 2:177). The spatiality of the felt or seen length of some part of the body, when that part is touched by the palm and fingers, is compared directly to the felt or seen spatiality of the palm and fingers. Allegedly, the two spatialities will seem either equal or discrepant in length, and this direct comparison of sensed spatial extensities affords a common measure from which more exact measurements of sensations can proceed on a common scale. A blind person is said to use this technique for obtaining a spatial conception of himself; by superposing bodily parts and tracing lines on different parts by the same movements, he eventually reduces all the felt differences of his bodily dimensions to a common scale.[14]

James subscribed to the familiar thesis that the "real" magnitude is chosen from among the various candidates by our practical and aesthetic interests.[15] The real size of a tree, for example, is not the sight-space from far away or close up but the one from a short distance, which enables us to discriminate the greatest variety of details in the tree's appearance. Without this interest, we have no motive for our usual determination of the tree's actual size. James theorized that the sense of touch enjoys a special status in our choice of what is real among our space-perceptions. Just as we reduce sight-sensations to a common scale, we must reduce sensations of different modalities to a homogeneous method of comparison. How do we compare the spaces experienced by sight, sound, taste, smell, and touch? Joseph Jastrow had speculated that "the striking disparities between our visual and other space-perceptions can only be explained by the tendency to interpret all dimensions into their *visual equivalents.*"[16] James agreed that some interpretation into a sensory equivalent is required, but he conceived the equivalent as one of touch rather than sight. Sight-spaces tend to reduce to touch-spaces, he argued, because of the "far greater constancy of felt over seen magnitudes" and the "greater practical interest which the sense of touch possesses for our lives. Sight is only a sort of anticipatory touch" (*Principles,* 2:180). When touch and sight conflict, touch reveals what is real among our space-percepts.

We must take another step to get from our first sensations of space to the one surrounding, common space, the real space in which we live and move. James said that we discriminate original spatial sensations into subdivisions, compare those subdivisions, and reduce their dimensions to a common scale. But how do we move from these subdivided spaces to the one space of everyday life? *"How are the various sense-spaces added together into a consolidated and unitary continuum?"* (*Principles,* 2:181).

James's theory emphasizes the chaotic nature of our first spatial experiences. Things are not originally experienced as inside, outside, or alongside each other, or as spatially continuous or discontinuous. Each spatial experience is initially like a world unto itself, exhibiting no apparent relation to any other. For instance, the felt magnitude of a tooth cavity originally has no spatial relation to the rest of the world, and we must mature considerably before we acquire a sense of its real size, its relation to other things. The same applies to all first perceptions of space. There is no reason that our early perceptions should be related to each other in one space-world. Experiments show that the connections between sense-modalities are quite flexible. For example, though we visually displace objects to the left when looking at them from the right through prismatic glasses, we make a rapid motor adjustment and within an hour or so can accurately and unhesitatingly locate the object manually.[17] This example illustrates the looseness of connection between different space-perceptions and reflects the original chaos of our space-experiences.

> The primitive chaos thus subsists to a great degree through life so far as our immediate sensibility goes. We feel our various objects and their bignesses, together or in succession; but so soon as it is a question of the order and relations of many of them at once our intuitive apprehension remains to the very end

most vague and incomplete. . . . Nevertheless *throughout all this confusion we conceive of a world spread out in a perfectly fixed and orderly fashion, and we believe in its existence. The question is: How do this conception and this belief arise? How is the chaos smoothed and straightened out?* (*Principles*, 2:183)

James's answer is difficult to interpret confidently, provoking questions at every turn. I think he intended the following: If we grant the nativistic claim that space is a feature of our first sensation, a curious historical allegiance is established. Berkeley, who in James's judgment was wrong to deny that distance is an original perceptual datum, is now commended for having understood the part played by the intellect in sense-perception. Berkeley appreciated—as Kant did not—the existence of spaces and the problem of harmonizing them into one spatial system. "The essence of the Kantian contention is that there are not *spaces*, but *Space*—one infinite continuous *unit*—and that our knowledge of *this* cannot be a piecemeal sensational affair, produced by summation and abstraction. To which the obvious reply is that, if any known thing bears on its front the *appearance* of piecemeal construction and abstraction, it is this very notion of the infinite unitary space of the world. It is a *notion*, if ever there was one; and no intuition."[18] James vigorously objected to the Kantian view that our perception of the external world is essentially an intellectual process and claimed to find no such "Kantian machine-shop" in his own mental processes. But in explaining how we get from originally unordered spaces to one system or continuum of space, he himself resorted to two basic, albeit unconscious, intellectual acts.

The first such act is to collect the different "places" of simultaneous data of touch, sound, sight, etc., into one place and then to regard those data as constituting a single entity. "*Whatever sensible data can be attended to together we locate together. Their several extents seem one extent. The place at which each appears is held to be the same with the place at which the others appear. They become, in short, so many properties of* ONE AND THE SAME REAL THING. This is the first and great commandment, the fundamental 'act' by which our world gets spatially arranged" (*Principles*, 2:183–84). Presumably, this is James's version of a phenomenalistic account of how we construct physical things out of sense-data. His version emphasizes the role of *place* (a feeling or coalescence of different spaces) in the construction of material objects. He makes an important qualification: "*the sense-data whose spaces coalesce into one are yielded by different sense-organs*" (*Principles*, 2:184). This qualification is necessary because data from different sense-modalities can be observed simultaneously, whereas impressions on the same sense-receptor interfere with each other and must be attended to successively. A cookie is a thing constructed from its taste-at-a-place, its fragrance-at-a-place, and its feel-at-a-place. We make these different but simultaneous cases of *at-a-place* coalesce into one place, where we point to indicate the cookie. In one act, we create both the cookie as a physical thing and its place. James thought that constructing a physical thing at one place from different sense-data at different places was the first step from spaces to *space itself*.[19]

The second and consummatory step involves the different sense-data of a single sense-organ. We cannot attend very well to different visual impressions at the same time; they tend to interfere with each other, so that if one visual impression is noticed, others are displaced entirely or at least to the periphery of consciousness. "Hence *we do not locate them in each other's spaces, but arrange them in a serial order of exteriority, each alongside of the rest, in a space larger than that which any one sensation brings.* This larger space, however, is an object of conception rather than of direct intuition, and bears all the marks of being constructed piecemeal by the mind" (*Principles*, 2:185). Suppose, for example, that we are looking at a cookie before us and think of our whole impression as a visual field. If we then raise our gaze to a jar behind the cookie, the first visual field is replaced by another, although some objects may be common to both. The two visual fields, unlike data of different sense-organs, cannot be viewed simultaneously, only successively; they are comparable to adjoining or juxtaposed objects having adjoining or juxtaposed places. "They must be out- and alongside each other, and we conceive that their juxtaposed spaces must make a larger space" (*Principles*, 2:185). James asserts that our successive visual fields, whose respective spaces cannot coalesce because they cannot be viewed simultaneously, are spatial regions lying alongside each other seriatim. We thus acquire the notion of a "space larger than that which any one sensation brings," a single spatial system or continuum incorporating the different spaces of particular sensations. This continuum is conceived, not perceived. Since James called this larger space an object of conception, he must have supposed a single system or continuum of space.[20]

CONSTRUCTING SPACE

The fundamental act by which James said the spaces of sensations become the space of things is problematic. We supposedly tend to locate together those heterogeneous sensible data which are apprehended simultaneously. *"Their several extents seem one extent. The place at which each appears is held to be the same with the place at which the others appear. They become, in short, so many properties of* ONE AND THE SAME REAL THING.*"*[21] In this fundamental act, not only do the different *extents* of colors or sounds somehow fuse into one complex (a "thing"), but their *places* also fuse into one place for that complex. Such coalescence of sensation is initially responsible for the transition from spaces to space, from sensations to physical things.

But do sensations in fact coalesce, or do they only seem to do so? James believed that they only seem to; he ascribed the fusion to a perceptual act motivated by an instinctive desire for unity and simplicity. (The words "seem" and "held to be the same" occur prominently in the passage just cited.) Fusion, according to James, is not an intrinsic property of sensations (as we interpreted Jamesian theory in the preceding chapter) but rather an appearance generated by an instinctive perceptual act. Despite his dislike of Kantian mental machine-shops which compensate for the allegedly weak powers of sensations, and his own insistence that introspection reveals no experience of mentally creating space, James believed in an act that creates the illusion of a single continuum of space.[22] The extents of different but simultaneous sensations seem to fuse into the extent of one thing, and their places seem to coalesce into the one place where we locate that thing. There is no transition from real spaces to real space but only to the appearance of a single space. Although James emphasized, in his account of the second mental act by which spaces become space, that the spatial continuum (which is larger than the space of any given sensation) is a piecemeal construction and not an intuition, it seems plausible at first to interpret him as believing it to exist externally. The spatial continuum may be knowable only by construction and in piecemeal fashion, but it isn't necessarily fictive. Yet if the basis of our construction is an illusion, then it is not feasible that the spatial continuum actually exists. If James did suppose that a spatial system actually corresponds to the illusion we construct piecemeal—and his writing is strangely inexplicit on this point—then his own account of how we move from the spaces of sensations to the concept of a larger, continuous space undermines that very supposition.[23]

The theory of sensation-fusion—which we will assume can be interpreted consistently with the assertion that sensations themselves do not literally fuse, although the antecedent events in the brain may do so—is designed to get us from separate, spatially unrelated spaces of different sensations to a single space. But how can the spatial features of sensations even *seem* to fuse or coalesce, if not in an already apprehended larger space? How can the concepts of *at a place* and *spatial extent* be grasped without *in space,* and how can the latter concept be derived from the former ones? The places of colors or sounds cannot appear to coalesce unless they were once discerned as spatially separate, in a space where their locations were apprehended as different. The theory of coalescence, far from showing how a spatial environment containing discrete locations is constructed from originally unrelated places of particular sensations, actually presupposes that spatial environment. The same presupposition is necessary for the putative fusion of the spatial extents of sensations; unless the apparent shapes, sizes, or volumes of colors or sounds have already been observed as discrete but relatable within a common space-setting, they cannot be perceived as fusing. Without the common space-setting, how could spatial fusion of sensations be detectable? If fusion is not detectable, then the theory of coalescence ceases to be relevant; if the supposed fusion is not empirically based, there is nothing in perceptual experience (James's court of appeal) with which to explain the move from spaces to space. At best, the theory of sensation-fusion leaves the ''how'' of this move a speculative mystery. James had just the opposite intent.

The second act by which space is supposedly perceived also prompts questions. James held that because different impressions on the same sense-organ cannot be noticed simultaneously, we tend not to fuse their places but rather to *''arrange them in a serial order of exteriority, each alongside of the rest, in a space larger than that which any one sensation brings.* The larger space, however, is an object of conception rather than of direct intuition, and bears all the marks of being constructed piecemeal by the mind" (*Principles*, 2:185). This process is an act of sensation-*fission* as far as space is concerned. But what guides this act of arrangement in a serial, external order? James does not account for the properties of sensation responsible for our arranging colors and sounds in the external relations that we commonly encounter. More important, the second act faces the difficulty that any space larger than that of a simple sensation is conceived, not sensed or intuited; accordingly, when two or more colors are instinctively arranged serially in a larger space, that space is merely conceived. The theory is designed to explain the appearance of a larger space or the fact that we arrange sensations serially and externally in a space-setting that we seem to perceive literally. But how can arranging sensations in a merely conceived space begin to explain that appearance? The theory claims that we construct not only the space extending beyond the range of our biggest telescope, but also the smallest portion of that single space which is *"larger than that which any one sensation brings."* But what meaning can we attach to the declaration that sense-impressions, which vibrantly affect the same sense-organ and vigorously resist simultaneous notice and spatial coalescence, are consequently arranged by us in a space that is merely conceived? It would be more natural to suppose that they are somehow fitted into an equally vibrant spatial setting where they at least appear to be immediately witnessed in their external spatial relations. The theory again presupposes what it sets out to demonstrate—a space in which sensations can be serially arranged. To the extent that it substitutes a conceived for a perceived space, the theory is inconsistent with what it seems to presuppose.

The source of these difficulties is the nativistic twofold thesis that all sensations are spatial and that ordinary perception of things in space evolves from our initial acquaintance with the spaces of sensations. To question the first part of the thesis would require a discussion more prolix than critically significant.[24] What is unquestionably suspect is the second part of the thesis, the view that commonplace perception of spatial relations gradually emerges from an original chaos of disconnected spaces characterizing our earliest sensations. James's metaphysical picture is neatly conveyed in the philosophical example of a dental cavity and the discrepancies between how large it feels and how large it looks and measures: "The space of the tooth-sensibility is thus really a little world by itself, which can only become congruent with the outer space world by farther experiences which shall alter its bulk, identify its directions, fuse its margins, and finally imbed it as a definite part within a definite whole."[25] James was not content to write that with experience we learn and tend to remember the sorts of perceptual discrepancies that occur when the same thing is perceived differently. Instead he wrote as if the "little world" of the cavity and its spatial extent as defined by the tongue is some kind of primitive material which, through the influence of subsequent experiences, we "alter," "fuse," and "imbed" within the common spatial continuum we call the one real space. This metaphysical picture of our sensations as little worlds with their own spaces provokes an epistemological query: How do we escape from those little worlds into the one big one?

To reject James's metaphysical picture, and consequently to avoid grappling with the query, we must insist that we do not begin our perceptual lives trapped in tiny sensation-worlds. The dental cavity is part of the one world, and we learn that our perceptual judgments about its size and shape vary with the conditions of perceiving it. Rather than gradually constructing a single world out of our different perceptions, we compare those perceptions, already understanding them as part of such a world. Without the public *it* we would have no reason to be aware of any discrepancy between how the cavity feels to the tongue, how it feels to the finger, and how it looks in the mirror. Observed discrepancies presuppose things like cavities as common reference points, which already constitute what we call the one world.[26]

When James considered space a reality and not simply a conceptual system, he thought of it as perceptible, though constructed by us in the way that phenomenalists believe physical things to be constructed. Just as colors, smells, and sounds are combined into the complexes we know as material entities, so, James believed, are the places and extents of sensations altered, fused, and imbedded into one complex which we know as the spatial continuum. James pictured space as a single, smooth place resulting from the fusing of all hard lines that demarcated the places of first sensations, the homogeneous union of a colossal coalescence, the place *in* which (rather than merely *at* which) all material things and processes are located.

This theory of space can tempt anyone who starts from nativistic or phenomenalistic premises. If we begin from the differently perceived extents and places of a cavity and then try to accommodate them within such common notions as same place, one space, and spatial continuum, it seems natural to picture the extents and places of sensations somehow fusing or coalescing into a smoothed-out continuum. This continuum is entirely homogeneous because it has eliminated any intrinsic difference of place and thus allows continuous movement through it; differences of place are only temporary indicators of the occurrence of events. James conceived of the felt place and the mirrored place of the cavity somehow melting into a single place, respecting the fact that we ordinarily say that we see and feel something in the same place. His concept of *the same place* has no intrinsic identity, for it can be identified only relative to other entities and places, such that it imperceptibly melts into the next place, creating a continuum or dense series of places. The one space is thus a dense series of fused places that are intrinsically indistinguishable and that radiate in every direction from the starting point, the dental cavity.[27]

The basic incoherence in this depiction is the notion of place-fusion. We know what it is for things to fuse or coalesce, but where they do nothing occurs that could be called place-fusion. If two things melt into one at a new place altogether, then the former places have evaporated with their former occupants; if one melts into the other at its original place, then one place has evaporated in favor of the other. Places can be changed, created, or evaporated—but it makes no sense to say they can be mixed. A place can be occupied by a mixture, but it is not itself mixed like its occupant. The concept is inviting only when, like James, we theorize that we live in a single space which is the commingling of alleged phenomena like the space of sight and the space of sound. Perhaps it then seems plausible that there are such phenomena as the place of touch and the place of pain that can somehow mix, with differences melted down.[28]

Unlike other philosophers, James did not argue for originally experienced, separate spatial worlds of sight or sound on the grounds that they are allegedly inconsistent and cannot without metaphysical qualifications be accommodated to a single system of public space. Nor did he regard the space of our first sensations to be like the spaces of dreams and hallucinations, which require a philosophical explanation of their relation to real space. He did not appeal to the concept of private experience, which says that the space of our initial experiences is private to each of us and which generates the problem of how public space develops. What led him to the image of separate spatial worlds of sensations was his general concept of what a sensation is.

His definition of a sensation was the immediate psychic effect of a nerve process. Pure sensations or experiences owe their character to the nerve processes that cause them but not to psychological factors or to any learning process.[29] The evidence, James argued, indicates that the *qualia* of sensations are due to physiological causes, including the condition of parts of the body they are connected with.[30] We can discover by introspection the extensity of any present sensation. Since there is no reason to ascribe the mere extensity or voluminousness of the sensation to psychological factors such as suggestion, association, or any learning process (here James parted company notably with Wundt and Helmholtz, among others), we can safely conclude that the same kind of vague extensity characterized our original sensations, since they could not have been the effect of learning.[31] When we focus our introspective attention on the extensity of the blue sky, we can also notice that this sky may be experienced by itself, disconnected from other things and localities, isolated from the rest of space. This isolation, we may infer, is true also of our original sensations. Added to these considerations is what James called the "Psychologist's Fallacy," references to which occur throughout *Principles*.[32] A typical psychologist, James held, would call the reverielike staring at the blue sky not an experience or sensation disconnected from the rest of reality but an actual viewing of some part of real space. James replied that such a psychologist commits the fallacy of neglecting the subjective or intrinsic nature of the experience, which is identifiable introspectively as disconnected, and mistakenly insists that the sensation be described as connected. Respecting the subjective nature of sensations or experiences and avoiding the psychologist's fallacy are two motivations that led James to picture our lives as commencing in sensations that separate into different spatial worlds.

But why was James drawn to the theory of sensation-fusion (and -fission) to connect those worlds? This concept was not his invention; the notion of synesthesia or complicated perception (the idea of colored sounds, for example) was well established in psychology.[33] Why he resorted to sensation-fusion in explaining the genesis of our common conception of space, however, is puzzling. Not only were there difficulties in the theory of place-fusion, but James could have chosen a more natural, commonsense explanation. Suppose we believe that our original sensations or immediate experiences are what he conceived them to be, and suppose we avoid the psychologist's fallacy and refuse to surrender the introspective descriptions that underline the subjective disconnectedness of our first sensations from the rest of space. This position is entirely compatible with the fact that the experiences are actually connected with the rest of space and that perceptual learning is in part a process of realizing how our perceptions connect within a space that is gradually found to be continuous (in the ordinary sense of the word). Rather than try to construct space by a theory about the peculiar dynamics of original sensations (fusion and fission of spaces), and insist that an original extensity is the material from which later perceptions evolve, we can easily explain our perceptual learning from infantile experience on by referring to a spatial system that is already there. Perhaps James actually questioned the reality of space, though he offers no arguments toward that end; his arguments are directed rather toward establishing the chronology of our perception of space. His theory of place-fusion is especially puzzling in light of the passages where he criticizes Kant, Wundt, and Helmholtz for downgrading sensations and crediting intellectual acts for our ordered perception of space.[34] James set out as a crusader on behalf of sensations, prepared to demonstrate that all the categories exist in the sensuous manifold, that no psychic combinations or syntheses are necessary to illuminate the blindness of sensations. Yet in his own construction of space, sensations are not self-sufficient and require exactly what he derided in his opponents' theories—intellectual hocus-pocus, or what he called the two basic mental acts by which space is arrived at. There are certainly important differences between James and antinativists, but his prominently advertised resolve to champion sensations in his theory of space faltered noticeably.

Why did James take such a complicated, metaphysical route when confronted by the psychological question of how we perceive space? The answer here connects with his deeply felt conviction that the profoundest truths are disclosed in sense-perception.[35] He may have meant by this that the nature of reality, including space, can be disclosed to one who attends carefully and reflectively to his own sensations. James attempted to model a system of space on what we seem to find within our experiences of space, which may explain why sensations rather than behavior and motor-learning play the dominant role in his theory of space-perception. He thought that we come closer to understanding space by heeding what it is like to hear or feel or see something than by registering how spatial relations are established through pacing off a distance or placing one thing between others.

Thinking along these lines can help us see what motivated James in his treatment of space and eliminate much of the puzzlement and uncertainty of our interpretive efforts, but the objections to his theory of space-construction remain. For James the space that is real, that antedates any human perceptual construct and resembles our experience of space, is an unmeasured *vastness* that our original sensation of extensity or unordered vastness models in miniature. The space that does not antedate our construction of it is the ordered, measured space of common experience, of geometry and physics.[36] (James may have judged the latter space to be merely conceptual; if so, our objections still stand.) The space conceived in physics is a configuration carved out of the initial vastness, just as an order is carved out of the extensity or vastness that features every sensation through processes of measuring and adding. James thus insisted upon the evolution of ordinary space-perception out of sensed vastness as if it were a kind of primitive material. Seen in this light, James did not falter so much after all in championing sensations, for his two intellectual acts (however *ex cathedra* they may seem) were invoked to explain not real space or preexistent vastness but only the ordered determinations of it, the space of common experience and science. The idea of real space as an indeterminate vastness appealed to the mystic in James; the attendant notion that our usual concept of space-as-order is somewhat artificial in comparison anticipates his alliance with Bergsonian anti-intellectualism.[37] Of all topics, space may have been the one first to incline James toward his eventual metaphysics of radical empiricism, pluralistic universe, and mysticism.

James thought he had established the nature and genesis of *ordered space*, but how did he establish his picture of real space as an indeterminate vastness? He never claims to know this vastness. Like any space "larger than that which any one sensation brings," the vastness of real space may be, as far as human knowledge is concerned, simply a concept. We can believe in it but can never establish its existence or nonexistence. It is a metaphysical theory toward which we can muster attitudes of belief or disbelief after adding the pragmatist's test question: What difference does it make one way or the other? The issue lies beyond the bounds of significant evidence, and we must seek an answer to this query unless we are content with indecision and paralysis of belief. James was prepared to argue that his view of real space as an indeterminate vastness was the view that most adequately portrayed a world that strongly appeals to both heart and mind.[38]

VASTNESS

When James said, "Space is really an indeterminate vastness," what did he mean? Because his treatment of this topic is minimal, we must conjecture somewhat. Some clues are found in writings later than *Principles*. In 1895 he wrote that although our original intuition of space is a single field of view and our original intuition of time is only a few seconds, "yet by an ideal piecing together and construction we frame the notions of immensity and eternity, and suppose dated events and located things therein, of whose actual intervals we grasp no distinct idea."[39] Not only is the concept of ordered space constructed of space-intuitions, so is the concept of sheer immensity or vastness. In his final years James insisted, consistent with his earlier psychology, that there is "no really inherent order, but it is we who project order into the world by selecting objects and tracing relations so as to gratify our intellectual interest. We *carve out* order by leaving the disorderly parts out; and the world is conceived thus after the analogy of a forest or a block of marble from which parks or statues may be produced by eliminating irrelevant trees or chips of stone."[40] Here, more explicitly than in *Principles* (or in *Psychology*), is the thesis that we carve out a spatial order, in line with practical and subjective interests, from an original, unstructured vastness that is itself only conceived and not experienced. Such a spatial order is presumably that of physics, for the space of physics appears to be carved out of a vastness that is imagined to resemble, save for its astronomic dimensions, the voluminousness of a single sensation. This account is James's nativistic explanation of how scientific space is supposed to develop from intuited spaces.

Returning to our question, what more can be said about space-as-vastness? For James there was no doubt about the intelligibility of the concept, which is defined simply as an indefinitely larger version of what qualifies any sensation; he claimed credit in his psychology for tracing the idea to the impression from which it derives its meaning. Only after the earlier psychology did James refer to space as a receptacle. Space, in the theory of radical empiricism, is the source of shared or common experience. "Whatever differing contents our minds may eventually fill a place with, the place itself is a numerically identical content of the two minds, a piece of common property in which, through which, and over which they join. The receptacle of certain of our experiences being thus common, the experiences themselves might some day become common also."[41] In the course of showing how pragmatism treats the old question of the one and the many, he wrote: "But add our sensations and bodily actions, and the union mounts to a much higher grade. Our *audita et visa* and our acts fall into those receptacles of time and place in which each event finds its date and place."[42] These isolated passages suggest that James subscribed to absolute space as defined by Newton: "Absolute space in its own nature, without relation to anything external, remains always similar and immovable. Relative space is some movable dimension or measure of the absolute spaces."[43] Relative space, which James apparently considered to be the space of physics, was for Newton and apparently for James merely a measure of absolute space—which in James's case is sheer vastness.

James's intent in holding that space is really vastness might seem essentially skeptical, a denial of our ability to determine the properties of space-in-itself; to say that space is an indeterminate vastness is in effect to confess that we don't know what it really is. I believe, however, that he actually considered real space (vastness) to be akin to our experience of it (voluminousness), a view true to his principle that the "deeper features of reality are found only in perceptual experience" (*SPP*, 97). With space, as with other "deeper features of reality," sense-perception is not merely a register of what appears but is rather the indispensable clue to what *is*. Given his view about the relation of physics to reality, he might have agreed with Bertrand Russell that the physicist need not speculate about the "concrete character of the processes with which he deals" and that his "only legitimate attitude about the physical world seems to be one of complete agnosticism as regards all but its mathematical properties."[44] But James held that metaphysics is speculative in a way that physics is not, and although metaphysical speculations are beliefs and not knowledge, sense-perception gives both a basis for some beliefs over others and an insight into the concrete processes speculated about. James's belief that voluminousness is a feature of every sensation supports his conclusion that there is a space beyond present sensations whose concrete character resembles sensed voluminousness, although on such a grand scale that it deserves to be called vastness.

James's silence on the physics of space probably stemmed from a conviction that the speculations and hypotheses of physics were at best "order-carvings" out of something spatially more primitive and were confined to Newton's relative space or Kant's phenomenal realm. By contrast, William Kingdon Clifford wrote:

I hold in fact

(1) that small portions of space are in fact of a nature analogous to little hills on a surface which is on the average flat; namely, that the ordinary laws of geometry are not valid in them.

(2) that this property of being curved or distorted is continually being passed on from one portion of space to another after the manner of a wave.

(3) that this variation of the curvature of space is what really happens in that phenomenon which we call the motion of matter, whether ponderable or etherial.

(4) that in the physical world nothing else takes place but this variation, subject (possibly) to the law of continuity.[45]

Nothing like this appears in James's writings on space. Instead he focuses on whether space, as conceived in physics, has properties unlike those of sense-perception; he does, however, make some passing remarks about the concepts of infinity and continuity.[46] This silence is surprising since James, though concentrating on the *perception* of space, was nevertheless concerned with the extent to which sense-perception acquaints us with reality.[47] As early as the writing of *Principles*, James may already have been so persuaded of the metaphysics that later allied him with Bergson—in particular of the doctrine that conceptual systems, including those of natural science, are distortions of reality despite their practical utility—that he had no interest in comparing his own account of space-perception with physical theories about the nature of space itself. He might even have agreed with this modern opinion: "It seems quite certain that no general philosophical accounts of space and time are likely to prove adequate for the total range of scientific speculation. Space and time, like the conception of an environment, may turn out to be related closely to the details of development of a particular theory."[48] But James would add that any leading physical theory is nothing more than a superior way of ordering what is in itself an indeterminate vastness. His reason for this verdict appears to be merely his preference for the view that clues to metaphysics are often found less in scientific theory than in sensory experience.

Did James mean empty space when he spoke of vastness, and if so, did he mean that it is something perceptible? Did he picture vastness as what a man centered in a sphere of pure air might apprehend? James J. Gibson has considered what this experience might be like, noting that although a person in this condition could move his eyes, there would be nothing upon which to fixate. He could see color, but only a film-color, unpositioned in depth and vague in distance. What he saw could not be described as near or far, flat or three-dimensional. In an atmosphere free of everything, devoid of texture, shape, and horizontal and vertical axes, "The observer might as well be in absolute darkness so far as he can *see* anything. . . . What an observer would perceive in a space of air would not be space but the nearest thing to no perception at all. The suggestion is that *visual* space, unlike abstract geometrical space, is perceived only by virtue of what fills it."[49] On this point James was equally emphatic. We cannot intuit empty time or empty space, that is, an extension wholly lacking sensible content. For James, awareness of change is always a condition for the perception of something in time and space.[50] The perception of space and time is impossible without the perception of something happening in it. James was explicitly opposed to the notion of an empty space that is perceptible, so he did not conceive vastness on such a model.

But to hold that space is perceptible only amid changing occurrences does not imply that it is in any sense physical or that it is merely an order of physical objects, as the so-called relational theory of space holds. To say that space is not perceptible in isolation is comparable to considering it a sort of container, like the space of a box. Einstein put it clearly: "By a natural extension of 'box space' one can arrive at the concept of an independent (absolute) space, unlimited in extent, in which all material objects are contained. Then a material object not situated in space is simply inconceivable; on the other hand, in the framework of this concept formation it is quite conceivable that an empty space may exist."[51] Einstein described the empty space or container theory as "logically more daring" than the concept of space as the "positional quality of the world of material objects," which makes space without a material object inconceivable. Yet it is the more daring concept which surrendered to Einstein's own relativistic theory because, he says, this theory replaced the concept of the physical thing by that of the *field*. He concluded: "That which constitutes the spatial character of reality is then simply the four-dimensionality of the field. There is then no 'empty' space, that is, there is no space without a field" (xvi).

James would have welcomed the collapse of material objects into fields, a theory which agrees precisely with the spirit of radical empiricism; in fact, he himself employed the term *field*.[52] He might even have dissociated himself from the container theory of space, or at least the versions of it rejected by Einstein and other leading physicists. But by characterizing space-as-vastness as an indefinitely larger replica of the voluminousness of sensations, he seems committed to something like the concept of box space. For James, sensed voluminousness was an indeterminate, three-dimensional extensity that is occupied or filled. "Loud sounds have a certain enormousness of feeling. It is impossible to conceive of the explosion of a cannon as filling a small space. In general sounds seem to occupy all the room between us and their source (*Principles*, 2:136). The surrounding vastness that resembles this voluminousness is likewise occupied or filled. Further, both sensed and real space, in James's view, must always be larger than their occupants. Space cannot be completely occupied or filled, for the place occupied by an object is not identifiable without the object; if space could be completely filled, a totally occupied space would become a place rather than that space in which places are identified. James pictured his real space or vastness as a sort of box space so inexhaustible that, no matter how extended or large its occupants, it would always be related to them as a container. This conclusion is inescapable if space-as-perceived is taken as our model. But the occupants may not be physical things, according to radical empiricism, since physical things reduce to sensations; the ultimate occupants of spatial vastness must be sensations and feelings. James may have been thinking of this concept of space, the vastness in which sensations and feelings can be spatially related, when he made mystical references to a "mother-sea" in his final years.[53] Because of James's reticence on the topic, there is little more that can be said about his concept of real space, the space with which sensation acquaints us.

PLACE

The concept of place has been discussed previously but we need to address three fresh issues: Is place or position an experiential given? Does place differ with the different sense-modalities? How can two people know that they apprehend the same place?

The Perception of Place

Einstein wrote: "Now as to the concept of space, it seems that this was preceded by the psychologically simpler concept of place. Place is first of all a (small) portion of the earth's surface identified by a name" (Jammer, xiii). By contrast, James believed that space is the psychologically simpler concept. As three-dimensional voluminousness, space is an intrinsic feature of a single sensation. But position or place, he argued, is by definition a relative matter. Awareness of a single point, for example, cannot convey awareness of its being at a certain place. "*Only when a second point is felt to arise can the first one acquire a determination of up, down, right or left, and these determinations are all relative to that second point.* . . . Position has nothing *intrinsic* about it. . . . Although a feeling of absolute bigness may, *a feeling of place cannot possibly form an immanent element in any single isolated sensation.*"[54] Place, unlike space, cannot be a quale of a sensation. For James, as for nineteenth-century psychology, explaining the nature of place-perception and of what is involved in localizing sensations was thus a major problem.

James subscribed, with his own emendations, to what in the history of psychology is called the local sign theory.[55] The theory is usually associated with Rudolph Lotze, but James, despite his great appreciation of Lotze, barely mentions him in his own formulation of the theory. Given that place is not intrinsic to sensations, the local sign theory tries to explain our localizing sensations at definite places, especially in or on our own bodies. Psychologists had offered rival hypotheses about the different qualities of sensations that might indicate position. James sought an account of how in sensation something can function as a sign of position by evoking consciousness of the different points related to it: "the position of a point is not only revealed, but created, by the existence of the other points to which it stands in determinate *relations*" (*Principles*, 2:158). Unlike some predecessors, James looked for an explanation not within the introspectable items of consciousness but in the nervous system, and the notion of subjective association of feelings or sensations is replaced by a law of habit that governs the nervous system—although "local sign" still refers to a specific quality of feeling. Consider how a stomach sensation is localized: "When the epigastrium is heavily pressed, when certain muscles contract, etc., the stomach is squeezed, and its peculiar *local sign* awakes in consciousness simultaneously with the *local signs* of the other squeezed parts. There is also a sensation of total vastness aroused by the combined irritation, and *somewhere* in this the stomach feeling seems to lie (*Principles*, 2:158; first italics mine). According to this theory, when one of the nerve centers responsible for a local sign-feeling is later excited, the local sign-feelings of the neighboring nerve centers are aroused in a pattern resembling that of the first occasion. Subjectively, this experience registers as a feeling of stomach-vastness in which diaphragmatic and epigastric sensations are localized according to the position of the nerve centers of which the sensations are local signs.[56]

James offered a psychophysical isomorphism whereby what is consciously experienced (pain in the stomach) is explained as a reflection of a spatially analogous pattern of neural events. He hypothesized a neural mechanism to explain how one local sign-feeling clusters with others into a spatial pattern within which we position the different feelings. But his theory fails at a critical point. Though it states the necessary conditions for witnessing place or position, it omits the sufficient conditions. One can be aware of things, including the spatial relations of simultaneous sensations, without being aware of their respective places. Merely being aware of a cluster of points does not entail noticing their places. Our attention might overlook their places, being drawn instead to their pattern or colors. While it may be a necessary condition if a point's place is to be noticed that at least one other point also be noticed, it is not, as James believed, a sufficient condition.

What makes us notice place or position? This was the sort of question that nineteenth-century psychologists were asking. James answered that we are aware of space simply by the fact that it's *there*, part of the sensation. But just as Hume remarked that existence has no impression, James had to admit that there is no impression of place. The fact that space is simply "there" cannot *make* us witness the place of something; space for James is thus unlike pain, color, or even spatial relations like up and down. He resorted therefore to a complicated combination of physiology and psychology to formulate a process equivalent to our noticing the place of something. But that process, a pattern of neural events causing an accompanying pattern of local sign-feelings, does not necessitate our noticing the *positions* of what we observe. It is tempting to go beyond James's conditions and invoke a special act of attention, suggesting that if we attend in a certain way, we will notice places and positions. But we are sometimes aware of a thing's position without any hint that a special act of attention is involved. Our awareness of its place may be totally effortless and automatic, and the idea of an act of attention is strained.

The trouble stems from seeking a universal answer to the question of what *makes* us notice the place of something. The answer can range from "Because I see it" or "Because I happened to recall . . ." to "Because my eye twitched at just that moment." As an across-the-board answer to this question, the local-sign theory, like any other theory, is bound to fail. But given the intimate connection between the concepts of place and space, it is tempting to defend the nativistic incorporation of place within sensation. Still, explanatory efforts such as the different versions of the local sign theory, despite their failure to answer the question, may illuminate the necessary physiological and psychological conditions for place-perception.[57]

Place and Sense Modalities

How do we know that the place where we see something is the same place where we touch or taste it? Common sense assumes the existence of a public space that is the same system both for different persons and for the different senses of the same person. But that assumption may be precarious if each sense-modality is autonomous and if, when discrepancies occur between the places where we see and touch something, our decision in favor of one sense-modality over the other is arbitrary. Without a nonarbitrary formulation of places identical for the different senses, the imagined fabric of a common space beings to pull apart. The history of studies on space-perception from Locke and Berkeley to the present illustrates the difficulty of unifying the senses spatially; Jastrow made sight the arbiter of sensory conflicts, but James appealed instead to touch.[58] Such debates between psychologists hardly bolster confidence in the commonsense view of a common space.[59]

The uncertainties and complexities presented by the literature can provoke this picture: at one moment we visually apprehend something at a place, at another moment tactually or aurally. It is as if we view the world alternately by alternate sensory systems, and where conflict occurs one system is arbitrarily declared correct. Thus simultaneous perceptual identification through different senses may be at best an illusion. Philosophers ask how we can be sure that two people's percepts are at the same place; the same question applies, at a deeper level perhaps, to the percepts of a single person. James explicitly asked the former question but not the latter. He tried to show that places which seem the same to the different sense-modalities originate through "coalescence," and he argued that where conflict occurs, touch prevails. If asked whether an individual's touch and sight percepts are at the same place, he would probably have said exactly what he said about the sameness of location of two people's percepts: "If they be not identically where mine are, they must be proved to be positively somewhere else. But no other location can be assigned for them, so their place must be what it seems to be, the same."[60] If the question is not practical and experimentally resolvable, it is pointless.

But a philosophical doubt can arise that cannot be relieved by practical reminders; such a doubt can be encouraged by (though certainly not implied by) the way nativism is formulated and defended. Nativistic formulations of place-perception such as James's may make us think of place as something given to each sense-modality, such that we passively register the places to which our sensations (taken together) belong. We are then led to the idea that our judgments of where something is are passively made in accordance with what is given to the separate systems of the sense-modalities. If we then picture each sense-modality as a spatial world unto itself and reject James's doctrine of coalescence as a way of relating them, we may conclude that a judgment of place or position always accords with a single sense-modality system. When we judge that a box seen on a table is in the same place that we feel it, we assume that our judgment accords with one sense-system but not both; one overrides the other, since the place of touch is one thing and the place of sight another. If they seem sometimes to meet, that is only because we judge, without realizing it, in favor of one rather than the other.

This schema of place-perception, while neither implied nor intended by James, can easily be read into his nativism, especially if his theory of place-fusion is discarded, leaving the different sense-modalities in a state of isolation from one another. Nativists seem to encourage this schema because they attempt to explain the sameness of place for different senses at the level of sensation, in terms of the postulated dynamics of sensations and their interactions. The way to correct this schema is not specific practical reminders but a different theoretical picture. The correct picture brings back into view the person who judges where things are. The complicated learning process that enables us to correlate sight and touch at the same place must be emphasized; this process involves movement, making allowances for error, and recalling how appearances can deceive and does not define space-perception as occurring entirely at the level of sensation. In the corrected picture, the person is rescued from the separate conduits of the sense-modalities, each transmitting its own recorded place. Given the learning required for correlation of data from the different senses, a person can make accurate judgments about sameness of place, judgments that are fair to each sense-modality. Sometimes one sense overrides another, as happens in separating reality from hallucinations, but there is no reason to believe that one always overrides the others.

Public Places

G. E. Moore and A. J. Ayer have wondered whether James succeeded in establishing a system of public or common space.[61] Both cite a passage in which James discusses whether two minds have anything in common:

Yes, they certainly have *Space* in common. On pragmatic principles we are obliged to predicate sameness whenever we can predicate no assignable point of difference. . . . But there is no test discoverable, so far as I know, by which it can be shown that the place occupied by your percept of Memorial Hall differs from the place occupied by mine. The percepts themselves may be shown to differ; but if each of us be asked to point out where his percept is, we point to an identical spot. All the relations, whether geometrical or causal, of the Hall originate or terminate in that spot wherein our hands meet. . . . "There" for me means where I place my finger. If you do not feel my finger's contact to be "there" in *my* sense, when I place it on your body, where then do you feel it?[62]

Ayer and Moore question whether James succeeded here in establishing the sameness of place for the percepts of different people; if he did not, then each individual seems trapped in his own spatial system of percepts. Both critics point out questions that arise when we press the distinction—which James did not want to allow—between physical space and perceptual space (Moore's "sense field") or between the way physical things occupy space and the way percepts do. Moore meets James's challenge by offering two reasons why the place one person feels in touching another's body may not be the same place the touched person feels. The place where one person feels the contact can be argued to be in his sense-field or perceptual space, and where the other person feels it is in a different sense-field. Further, what one feels in touching may differ greatly from what the other feels in being touched. How, Moore asks, can two such different feelings be simultaneously in the same place?[63] Although our percepts may seem to be in the same place, there are reasons to doubt that they really are. Ayer points out that if two people's percepts differ, as James agreed they will, then how can they be in exactly the same place, however much they seem to be? While there might be a distinction between the ways physical objects and percepts or sense-data occupy space, James did not explore this possibility and, strangely, did not appear sensitive to the objection that Ayer describes.[64] Moore and Ayer call attention to serious problems for James's reliance on pragmatic common sense in arguing that what we perceive together occurs at the same place. The philosophy of space in *Principles* recurs in the metaphysics of radical empiricism and is a significant anticipation of James's phenomenalism. It seems impossible to reconcile phenomenalism and common sense as an analysis either of objects or of space, as Ayer and Moore assert in their critical objections to James's effort to effect that reconciliation.

DISTANCE

Berkeley argued in his *New Theory of Vision* (1709) that a difference in the distance of a point can make no difference in its retinal image, because "distance being a line directed endwise to the eye, it projects only one point in the fund of the eye—which point remains invariably the same, whether the distance be longer or shorter." He concluded that distance "of itself and immediately" cannot be seen, that it is not a visual sensation but rather something "suggested" by past experience and by the sense of touch. Retinal sensations lack depth or third-dimensionality, and the concepts of volume and distance must therefore be derived from something other than visual sensations alone.[65]

James denied Berkeley's theory, offering instead his own thesis in *Principles* that all objects of sensation are voluminous in three dimensions. He appealed to introspective experience for his disagreement with Berkeley:

> It is impossible to lie on one's back on a hill, to let the empty abyss of blue fill one's whole visual field, and to sink deeper and deeper into the merely sensational mode of consciousness regarding it, without feeling that an indeterminate, palpitating, circling depth is as indefeasibly one of its attributes as its breadth. We may artificially exaggerate this sensation of depth. Rise and look from the hill-top at the distant view; represent to yourself as vividly as possible the distance of the uttermost horizon; and then *with inverted head* look at the same. There will be a startling increase in the perspective, a most sensible recession of the maximum distance; and as you raise the head you can actually see the horizon-line again draw near. (*Principles*, 2:212–13)

The visual field is always a volume unit, and distance or depth is given as an immediate quale of the sense-field, but the estimation or measurement of the distance is not given. This, James agreed with Berkeley, results from experience and learning but not from the quality of a momentary sensation. Moreover, the relative sizes of the three dimensions of a visual field can be shown to be functions of each other. "If we plunge our head into a wash-basin, the felt nearness of the bottom makes us feel the lateral expanse to be small. If, on the contrary, we are on a mountain-top, the distance of the horizon carries with it in our judgment a proportionate height and length in the mountain-chains that bound it to our view" (*Principles*, 2:213–14). The relative dynamics of the three dimensions can actually be experienced. Reid, in accordance with Berkeley's philosophy, assumed that a fictive species (called Idomenians), possessing only the sense of sight, would live in a two-dimensional world differing in absurd-sounding ways from our normal world. James emphatically disagreed. An Idomenian, provided he had our intellectual powers, could, even with eyeballs made immovable, acquire our usual conception of the external world. James explained this belief with a thesis central to the physiological aspects of his discussion of space-perception: he argued that the movement through parts of our bodies of impressions produced by external objects—and not, as popularly supposed, by our own muscular movements—are sufficient for perceiving space. With Reid's Idomenian, "the *same object*, by alternately covering in its lateral movements different parts of his retina, would determine the mutual equivalencies of the first two dimensions of the field of view; and by exciting the physiological cause of his perception of depth in various degrees, it would establish a scale of equivalency between the first two and the third."[66] In the imagined situation the visual sense alone is sufficient to excite the sensation of depth in the Idomenian's experience. This argument sustains James's claim that depth or distance is an optical sensation.[67]

On the basis of James's introspective descriptions of the sort quoted above, we can perhaps concur that distance is a sensation insofar as its properties depend upon physiological stimulation and insofar as it can be an immediate object of introspective scrutiny. We may agree also that just as the changes from loud to soft or from pink to red qualify as sensations, so do perceptible changes from near to far or from deep to shallow. James illuminated unsuspected issues in Berkeley's belief that distance cannot be a visual datum. James's introspective examples may enable us to connect more adequately the concept of distance with our own perceptual experiences.

But the concept of sensation is not clear-cut, and declarations that something is or is not a sensation tend to be revised or qualified when, amid the complications of experiment and debate, some additional condition is set for its application. Hence, just when the reader might suppose James to have clinched his argument for distance as an optical sensation, he introduced a new consideration from Reid and Helmholtz which proves more troublesome to rebut. Helmholtz wrote: "No elements in our perception can be sensational which may be overcome or reversed by factors of demonstrably experimental origin. Whatever can be overcome by suggestions of experience must be regarded as itself a product of experience and custom. If we follow this rule it will appear that only *qualities* are sensational, whilst almost all *spatial* attributes are results of habit and experience."[68] Helmholtz in effect added a condition for sensation that James had not considered thus far in arguing that distance is a sensation. To this point *sensation* has meant "the mental affection that follows most immediately upon the stimulation of the sense-tract. Its antecedent is directly physical, no psychic links, no acts of memory, inference, or associational intervening."[69] But Reid and Helmholtz considered a sensation anything that cannot be overcome or reversed by suggestion or experience. James freely admitted that what he called sensations can be overcome by what we know or expect. "Our mental knowledge of the fact that human faces are always convex overpowers them, and we directly perceive the nose to be nearer to us than the cheek instead of farther off" (*Principles,* 2:217). Reid, Wundt, and Helmholtz concluded that distance is not simply a visual sensation but is rather a product of learning and suggestion from past experience.

Though James mentions his disagreement in "The Perception of Space," he defers his rebuttal in *Principles* until the next chapter, "The Perception of Reality." His main contention in this debate is that distance sensations—which would have been the immediate effects of visual processes and thus clearly sensations, but are overcome by what we know and expect—have been altered by an unsuspected process of association.[70] Presented with Helmholtz's modification of the concept of sensation, James was compelled to supplement introspective evidence with complicated hypothesizing. How introspection and theorizing can combine to provide an interpretation of distance as an optical sensation remains uncertain. This problem may have been on James's mind in 1887 (the year he published the essay "The Perception of Space," which became the chapter in *Principles*) when he wrote to Carl Stumpf: "Space is really a direfully difficult subject! The third dimension bothers me very much still."[71] Given that he mentioned to Stumpf that the essay had actually been composed as early as 1880, he appears never to have been satisfied that he had established distance as a sensation neatly and firmly by his own introspections in concert with appropriate theory.

MOTION, ILLUSIONS, AND PHYSIOLOGY

There is an extraordinary richness of detail in the chapter on space-perception in *Principles*. James makes many references to psychological literature, both historical and contemporary, including compact summaries with critical comments on the technical aspects of relevant experiments. Many of the footnotes are whole topics in themselves; one, for example, alludes to James's own unpublished experiments aimed at discovering the conditions for spatial discrimination on sensitive surfaces such as the skin.[72] We are overwhelmed by information ranging from flies and frogs to humans, from joints and surfaces to brains, from Kant and Mill to Münsterberg. A reader of the condensed chapter in *Psychology* would not suspect that its sixteen pages are little more than a footnote to the original chapter in *Principles*. From this wealth of information, three topics stand out as particularly important: motion, illusion, and physiology.

Motion

James's thesis is that motion is a sensation.[73] But, he wrote, "*the feeling of motion* has generally been assumed by physiologists to be impossible until the positions of *terminus a quo* and *terminus ad quem* are severally cognized, and the successive occupancies of these positions by the moving body are perceived to be separated by a distinct interval of time" (*Principles*, 2:170). According to this theory, the cognition of motion is always an inference, never a sensation; James countered that it is "*experimentally* certain that we have the feeling of motion given us as a direct and simple *sensation*" (first italics mine). He does claim that motion is a quale of sensation not on introspective but rather on experimental grounds.

What we see when looking directly at the second hand of a watch differs from what we see when we look away for a moment, then look back to see that the hand is in another position, and accordingly infer that it has moved. In the first instance we are immediately aware of its motion as a sensation. This example helps us to understand James's thesis. But is the thesis experimentally certain? James gives an example to demonstrate that it is: if you press the two points of a compass against your arm an inch apart such that they are felt as only one impression, and if you then move a pencil point a tenth of an inch along the skin within that inch of space, you will notice the motion as well as its direction. We cannot argue that the perception of the motion is derived from an initial awareness of its beginning and ending points and the successive occupancies by the pencil of positions between the two, since we had already established that the two points were undiscriminable.[74] Sigmund Exner's experiment also proved that "movement is a primitive form of sensibility, by showing it to be much more delicate than our sense of succession in time" (*Principles*, 2:172). Exner made two electric sparks appear in quick succession and asked observers to determine which appeared first; his results showed that a determination is impossible if the temporal interval is reduced to 0.044 seconds. But if the sparks are spatially juxtaposed so closely that their irradiation circles overlap, the flashing is perceived as if it were the motion of a single spark from the first place to the second, and the interval can be reduced to 0.015 seconds before it is impossible to detect whether the motion begins on the left or on the right.

What did such experiments in the new laboratories of the nineteenth century indicate to James? In this instance, he said that it is "thus certain that our sense of movement, being so much more delicate than our sense of position, cannot possibly be derived from it" (*Principles*, 2:172). If it is maintained that motion is not a sensation because, to return to an earlier example, the second-hand does not continuously move but rather jumps from position to position, then James is correct in saying that our introspection refutes that claim conclusively. Or if it is insisted that we do not really comprehend the concept of motion-as-sensation, then, like Hume and James, we can argue that our introspection of the "impression" refutes that claim also. But suppose it is hypothesized that experiments or arguments show that "a body is in motion if it is in a series of adjoining places at successive times. That is all that motion is. . . . Now this means that we can give an analysis of motion solely in terms of the concepts of shape, size, position and duration. It is not a new primitive concept."[75] Introspective examination does not meet this challenge; the claim is not meant to conflict with anything we can introspect, but as a theoretical assertion it requires experiment and argument to decide its merits. If it is suggested (as James said was the case in nineteenth-century psychology) that the awareness of position is more basic than that of *motion* and that the latter is theoretically derivable from the former, then the experiments James cited are critical in deciding the issue. The experiments that support James not only help us to understand the debate more fully, but also provide ingenious support for a commonsense assumption: however complex the conditions for perceiving motion, seeing our finger move as we write is as ultimate a fact as can be desired. It is not a cinematic illusion or the result of unconsciously apprehending the finger in a series of positions. To this extent (though the whole question can be revived by attaching a new condition for using the term *sensation*) James argues convincingly that motion is a sensation.

Illusions

In his chapter on space-perception James provides illustrations of those optical illusions that occur in most psychology textbooks. James is motivated by two particular questions in his discussion of illusion: How much is psychology, beyond physiological factors, needed to explain illusions, and are illusions exceptions to the nativistic theory of space-perception? Despite the claims of Joseph Delboeuf and Wilhelm Wundt, James argued that alleged "feelings of muscular innervation" are not needed to explain why small angles can appear proportionally larger than larger ones.[76] Whenever possible James sided with Hering on the first question in replacing psychological explanations that refer to "feelings" with physiological ones.

Illusions threaten the nativistic thesis because they "overcome," as Helmholtz put it, the spatial sensations that ought to occur if the nativist is correct. Illusions demonstrate that a stimulus, without any alteration, can give rise to alternating or conflicting perceptions. James summarized the antinativist use of illusions: "Surely, if form and length were originally retinal sensations, retinal rectangles ought not to become acute or obtuse, and lines ought not to alter their relative lengths as they do" (*Principles*, 2:257). He replied that retinal spatial impressions, though they can be ambiguous with respect to their stimulus, may still be considered sensations—especially if their ambiguity can be explained consistently with their nature as sensations. According to his explanation, illusions result from an "imagined seeing" that momentarily *replaces* the sensation that occurs when the illusion is not perceived. As a nativist, James asserted that sensed space is the "stuff" wherein all spatial discriminations are made. He summarized his thesis in the debate with Helmholtz on the significance of illusions: "*Measurement implies a stuff to measure. Retinal sensations give the stuff; objective things form the yard-stick; motion does the measuring operation*" (*Principles*, 2:267). The suspect assumption here is that a recurrent "stuff," not identical with public or ordered space, is what we discriminate and measure. Yet it is this metaphysical thesis that James defended in his lengthy treatment of the technical details of perceptual illusions.

James fully agreed that sensations can be overcome or transformed, ignored or suppressed. He noted that in looking at things at a distance, we can become aware of the suppression of sensed elements in our visual field and of the consequent diminution of the field. In a footnote he remarked: "The shrinkage and expansion of the absolute space-value of the total optical sensation remains to my mind the most obscure part of the whole subject. It is a real optical sensation, seeming introspectively to have nothing to do with locomotor or other suggestions. It is easy to say that 'the intellect produces it,' but what does that mean? The investigator who will throw light on this one point will probably clear up other difficulties as well" (*Principles*, 2:269–70). Even the sensed vastness of the visual field is subject to fluctuations of expansion and shrinkage. This argument, though important for technical issues in the psychology of space-perception, seems inconsistent with the *esse est sentiri* doctrine of sensation. If sensations can be transformed, ignored, and suppressed, then their properties, including defining ones, need not be evident to consciousness. The idea of suppression suggests that sensations are elusive and dynamic, such that one can sometimes overcome another. In his treatment of illusions, James was not entirely successful at replacing psychological with physiological explanations. Relations between felt sensations, as well as those between nerve currents, are both needed to explain illusions and the fact that certain sensations replace others.

Physiology

Much of the detail in James's chapter on space-perception is physiological. This emphasis accords with his aim of writing a textbook that presents psychology as a natural science concerned with the correlations that obtain between conscious states and their physiological conditions. Most of the detail is from reports of other investigators, and James examined it carefully before using it to support traditional theories in philosophical psychology.

For example, he argued that the resemblance between a conscious state and its anatomical condition cannot be used to explain why the conscious state occurs as it does. A correlation is conceded in cases where there is no resemblance; a nonred brain-state is a condition of seeing red, but only by a spatial and temporal juxtaposition with the conscious state. "But in the matter of *spatial* feeling, where the retinal patch that produces a triangle in the mind is itself a triangle, etc., it looks at first sight as if the sensation might be a direct cognition of its own condition."[77] Were this claim true, however, the perception would be of a multitude of impressions instead of a single continuous extent if the condition cognized were, for example, the stimulation of the numerous optical nerve termini. And the immediately preceding brain-state is certainly not triangular. Only in the case of space, James argued, does an organic condition, the retinal impression, resemble a conscious state, the awareness of a triangle. James quoted Thomas Brown's rejection of the explanation that the shape of the space is perceived by the shape of the "nervous expansion affected." "If this alone were necessary, we should have square inches and half inches, and various other forms, rectilinear and curvilinear, of fragrance and sound" (*Principles*, 2:144–45). At the same time, the philosophical thrust of James's use of physiological detail was to bring the human percipient and the external world as close together as possible. Physiological psychology, he believed, was destined to eliminate much of the psychological machinery that in earlier theories had served as an intermediary between the world and our cognition of it. Wherever possible, James invoked physiology to show that sensation, conceived as the immediate effect of bodily events, contained all the categories of the understanding. This physiological emphasis is most evident in his account of space-perception, but the attempt to justify it was problematic and in the end required some concessions.

James cited a great amount of physiological detail to exhibit the kinesthetic basis of much space-perception. He frequently credited predecessors with having fathered the idea of kinesthetic space-perception; according to Boring, the investigations of A. Goldscheider, to whom James attributed his own views, were largely responsible for the interest in kinesthesis and movement in late-nineteenth-century psychology.[78] Kinesthesis was especially important in introspective psychology, and "the Wundtian school reduced all space perception to a consciousness of movement" (Boring, 533). But Boring does not mention that James and Wundt were opposed about the role of kinesthesis in space-perception. James argued repeatedly in *Principles* that our sense of space is a product of the retina, not of muscular movements, and this position was crucial to his defense of nativism. In citing Goldscheider, James held that our perception of space and movement results more from the articular surfaces, or surfaces of the joints, than from the muscles used in movement. Many psychologists maintained that the contraction of the muscles causing the eyeball to rotate is chiefly responsible for our perception of extent, but James concluded instead that the sensitive surfaces of our joints are *"the starting point of the impressions by which the movements of our members are immediately perceived"* (*Principles*, 2:193). Consequently, the articular surfaces, including that of the retina, are the *fons et origo* of space- and movement-perception.[79] Kinesthesis, in James's theory of space-perception, does not include sensory impressions accompanying such movements as rotating the eyeball; the term refers instead to the more "passive" motion, when the eye is at rest, of an impression across its sensitive surface; that motion is enough to create a sensation of extensity and movement. This physiological evidence supports the nativistic thesis that space-as-sensation is given; we do not create it from the muscular activity of our movements.

James includes other details; he discusses critically the classical studies, in the 1830s, by Sir Charles Wheatstone, who invented the stereoscope and investigated binocular parallax and retinal disparity. James refers briefly to the semicircular canals, whose function had interested him for years, and their role in "defining the points of the compass and the direction of distant spots, in the blind as in us. We *start* towards them by feelings of this sort; and so many directions, so many different feeling-starts."[80] He made no significant contributions to the physiology of space-perception, for he reviewed more than contributed to its literature. But his review is extraordinarily comprehensive, and its massive accumulation of physiological details provides a fascinating argument for James's nativistic theory of space-perception.[81]

5 ♫ TIME

THE SPECIOUS PRESENT

James's theory of time-perception is essentially a theory about the specious present.[1] He begins by considering how the present or the present moment is to be understood. If we mean by such expressions an instant without duration, an instantaneous point in time, then there is nothing to match this concept in our experience. No such strict present can be perceived; to be identified, any temporal moment, no matter how brief, must endure for some time. When we try, James said, to attend to the present moment, "one of the most baffling experiences occurs. Where is it, this present? It has melted in our grasp, fled ere we could touch it, gone in the instant of becoming" (*Principles,* 1:608). Whenever we try to identify the strictly present moment, it is already past, succeeded by another.

The only sort of present that is perceptible, James concluded, is specious, in the sense that it is not strictly present but is rather a constant slipping into the past while yielding to the future. There is no perceptible present free of past and future; if we do not recognize this feature of present experience, James said, it is because we have not understood the specious nature of the present; time comprises an unceasing succession of moments with no sharp distinction between past, present, and future. The specious or enduring present is *duration,* not to be confused with mere temporal succession. Time-as-duration and time-as-succession are different concepts, a difference explained by the idea of the specious present. James's theory declares that time-as-duration, time-as-succession, and simultaneity are different, as are the ways by which we become aware of them.

For James, all perception begins with *wholes* or complexes or units, which can be understood in terms of their elements and their mutual relations. A simple sensation, for example, is an abstraction, not an original perceptual datum.[2] James's doctrine is vividly illustrated by the concept of the specious present or time-as-duration, because duration is defined as a block or unit within which time-as-succession becomes perceivable.

> The unit of composition of our perception of time is a *duration,* with a bow and a stern, as it were—a rearward- and a forward-looking end. It is only as parts of this *duration-block* that the relation of succession of one end to the other is perceived. We do not first feel one end and then feel the other after it, and from the perception of the succession infer an interval of time between, but we seem to feel the interval of time as a whole, with its two ends embedded in it. The experience is from the outset a synthetic datum, not a simple one; and to sensible perception its elements are inseparable, although attention looking back may easily decompose the experience, and distinguish its beginning from its end. (*Principles,* 1:609–10)

Time is thus analogous to space, since spatial relations are apprehended within the originally perceived unit of a certain extensity. The Jamesian theory holds that specific temporal and spatial relations are identified within an already apprehended context of a temporal and a spatial *muchness.*[3]

James cited Wilhelm Volkmann and James Ward in support of his contention that, because a succession of ideas is not in itself an idea of succession, the awareness of succession must be more than merely registering the fact that a succession has occurred in one's perception.[4] Although James tended wherever possible to explain mental states by their physiological (usually cerebral) correlates, in this instance he advocated an intermediary psychological account. He differed with Helmholtz, who had written that the only case where mental states copy physical ones and where

> our perceptions can truly correspond with outer reality is that of the *time-succession* of phenomena. Simultaneity, succession, and the regular return of simultaneity or succession, can obtain as well in sensations as in outer events. Events, like our perceptions of them, take place in time, so that the time-relations of the latter can furnish a true copy of those of the former. The sensation of the thunder follows the sensation of the lightning just as the sonorous convulsing of the air by the electric discharge reaches the observer's place later than that of the luminiferous ether.[5]

James disagreed, arguing that the mere succession of events does not constitute the perceptual awareness of that succession. Even if the succession of the thunder upon the lightning is copied in the brain and in experience, we are not necessarily aware of that succession. A theory of time-perception must locate the missing condition, which for James is a special feature of the specious present. In being aware of the specious present (the short duration or interval), James argued, we are aware simultaneously of its beginning and end. This condition is required for our awareness of succession within that block; without a simultaneous awareness of beginning and end, we are left with a mere sequence of perceptions that does not amount to a perception of sequence. If asked why simultaneous awareness of the first and last phases of the specious present insures awareness of the succession within it, James would have answered somewhat elusively by concurring with Volkmann's antithesis: "If idea A follows idea B, consciousness simply exchanges one for another. That B *comes after A* is for our consciousness a non-existent fact; for this *after* is given neither in B nor in A; and no third idea has been supposed. . . . If A and B are to be represented as *occurring in succession* they must be *simultaneously represented;* if we are to think of them as one after the other, we must *think* them both at once."[6]

But why must we accept the premise that if idea A follows idea B, consciousness merely exchanges one for the other? The answer of Volkmann and James seems implicit in their reasoning that a temporal relation resembles a spatial one insofar as identifying the relation requires simultaneous awareness of the terms related. To see that A is above B, we must see both A and B at once; to hear B after A, we must hear both B and A at once. The specious present allows exactly such simultaneity to occur. Experiments had determined, James said, that the specious present for the average person is approximately twelve seconds—the length of time that most people can, in a single act of attention, clearly perceive an ongoing process.[7] A considerable succession can be perceived within a twelve-second specious present. A sentence or a melody of that length, if James is right, can be apprehended all at once within what deserves to be called the present moment; the first word or note of the twelve-second interval is heard now, as are the intervening and the final ones. The fact that one word or note precedes another is recognized during the enduring *now,* and thus the before-after relation is given within the present moment. The first moment of the specious present is apprehended simultaneously with the last. Any moment earlier than the first moment of the specious present can only be recollected or conceived, since it is no longer part of our awareness. The just-past, contained within the before-after relation and included within the specious present, is still part of our awareness and is therefore contrasted with the remembered past. The Jamesian concept not only allows but requires that the initial and final phases of the specious present be perceived simultaneously, and the intervening temporal relations are made noticeable within and because of those terminal boundaries.

There are two immediate objections to this theory. We can deny the premise that if idea A follows idea B, consciousness merely exchanges one for another, without the idea of succession. The elusive assumption here is that the perceived interval or duration (the specious present), like a spatial relation, is thought to be identifiable only if its respective terms are identified. One can be said to perceive something complex if, in addition to identifying it and its collective properties correctly, one is aware of all or most of its details. A blind man who builds a picture of a toy that he handles perceives the toy at some point, although he does not perceive it all at once. Likewise, we can—and constantly do—build a perception of a duration or time interval on the basis of perceived successions, although there is no moment when we perceive the interval all at once. There is no reason to assume—contrary to James's theory—that we merely exchange A for B and neglect the idea of *after* when we perceive that A is followed by B but do not perceive A and B simultaneously. For example, if a minute elapses between A's disappearance and B's appearance, we can surely perceive that B follows A, although we do not perceive them simultaneously. Individual temporal relations can be perceived seriatim, resulting in the perception of duration even though no simultaneous perception of events occurs. James's assumption then seems not only groundless but mistaken. Durations do not resemble spatial relations, as the theory requires.

A second objection is that simultaneity itself suffers the same logical fate assigned to succession. If A and B are perceived simultaneously within the specious present, is this because simultaneity, like succession, can only be perceived within a unit of time whose initial and final phases are simultaneously perceived? If so, then this perception of simultaneity necessitates a larger, more inclusive unit of time whose initial and final phases must be perceived simultaneously, and so on in an infinite regress. If, to avoid this regress, we allow a relation of simultaneity to be perceived without presupposing another simultaneity, why not grant the same privilege to succession, since the two concepts seem to have the same logical footing? The Jamesian will reply that it is only simultaneity within the specious present whose perception depends upon the simultaneous perception of the beginning and end of the interval; the theory is not intended to apply to simultaneity in general. But since the perception of simultaneity between the initial and final phases of the specious present is just as much in the present as is any perceived simultaneity within the specious present, what entitles James to select the perception of one such relation as being causally dependent upon the perception of another? The inference here appears to be gratuitous.

TIME AND SENSATION

Although he titled his chapter "The Perception of Time" in *Principles*, James was anxious to show that time is sensed; "The Sense of Time" in the abbreviated *Psychology* is clearly a more apt chapter title. He used expressions like "sense of time," "sensation of duration," "intuition of duration," and "feeling of time."[8] He sought to prove that time is a datum of experience, something apprehended immediately and directly. Of course, units such as hours, days, and years are not experiential data but are rather determined inferentially, with the aid of measurements and calculations; the concept of a year is not the concept of a temporal datum but of a temporal construct. James wanted to show that we have a concept of a temporal datum, that *"the original paragon and prototype of all conceived times is the specious present, the short duration of which we are immediately and incessantly sensible"* (*Principles*, 1:631).

In urging that time can be a sensation, James was defending not only a theory of time-perception but also the concept of knowledge by acquaintance. He believed that a mode of awareness called sensing can acquaint us with things differently from perception. He emphasized that the distinction between sensation and perception is not sharp. Perceiving is more complex than sensing and involves awareness of the relations surrounding the objects sensed; it is thus knowledge about rather than acquaintance.[9] In claiming that the distinction was not sharp, James stressed his objections to earlier philosophies of psychology which, he believed, downgraded the cognitive role of sensation by considering sensation and perception either as radically different states of mind or as having radically different objects. But, James thought, sensing is not intrinsically different from perceiving, nor is it somehow subjective in a way that perceiving is not. James meant that when we sense something, the nature of our sensing is due only to the nature of the object sensed, not to the influence of past experience, our inferences and expectations, or observed relations of the object. If any of these factors is relevant, then we perceive rather than sense the object. Sensing, being acquainted with the object directly and immediately, is less complex psychologically than perception, but it is knowledge insofar as it makes us aware of what something is like.[10]

According to James, introspection reveals that temporal intervals short enough to qualify as the specious present are sensed, intuited, and directly known. He explicitly denied that "empty" time can be sensed, saying that time cannot be apprehended as an abstract entity, but only as an accompaniment or a dimension of some process.[11] Introspection thus reveals an awareness of intervals short enough to allow simultaneous awareness of the first and final moments of those intervals and simultaneous awareness of the succession of intervening moments. Introspection supposedly reveals the passage of time within an apprehended, delimited interval; since the interval itself is not in temporal movement, it seems that our awareness of a time that moves is due to an awareness of a time that stands still.[12] Because James believed that a twelve-second specious present is a constant, built-in feature of our temporal consciousness, he wrote that although the content of this interval is in continuous flux, "the specious present, the intuited duration, stands permanent, like the rainbow on the waterfall, with its own quality unchanged by the events that stream through it" (*Principles*, 1:630). He claimed that we can introspectively analyze the specious present into smaller intervals or bits of time, that "subdividing the time by *beats of sensation* aids our accurate knowledge of the amount of it that elapses" (*Principles*, 1:619). Time, experienced as duration, is a sensation which can be subdivided into shorter interval-sensations, and James cited Exner's report that intervals as short as 0.002 seconds can be heard.[13] James sometimes referred to the twelve-second maximum span as the specious present, sometimes as the *nucleus* of a slightly longer specious present.

Upon introspection, there is one sweeping objection to the Jamesian theory: we do not literally observe time at all. Speaking colloquially about perceiving time hardly commits us to the notion that time is something that can be heard or seen. Sight is rarely if ever identified as a time-sense; traditionally, the apprehension of time has been called inner or internal perception.[14] James discussed time-perception almost exclusively in terms of audition: "Hearing is the sense by which the subdivision of durations is most sharply made. Almost all the experimental work on the time-sense has been done by means of strokes of sound. How long a series of sounds, then, can we group in the mind so as not to confound it with a longer or a shorter series?" (*Principles*, 1:611). But is time literally heard? Where James was most emphatic about time as a sensation, one is tempted to interpret it as an auditory sensation. But although he made no explicit statement on this issue, I think he made the commonsense assumption that the only proper objects of hearing are sounds, and that only in a metaphoric sense do we "hear" time. The time-sense apprehends not groups of sounds but groups of a few seconds and is therefore a sui generis intuition. Time may be called a sensation, not because it is apprehended via any of the sense organs, but simply because it is direct and immediate and owes its nature exclusively to the nature of what is intuited; it is inseparably connected with the apprehension of sensations such as sounds, and its occurrence is therefore explicable physiologically like other sensations. According to this interpretation, our time-sense, while never operative apart from the sensing of phenomena, acquaints us with a specious present that is the inevitable accompaniment of our apprehending those phenomena. Time, therefore, is something separate which we observe by intuiting or sensing.

But we can easily object that time is not something independent which can be intuited or sensed. A condition for our sensing or intuiting something is that the nature of our sensing or intuiting is due to the nature of the sensed object alone; in another formulation, descriptions of the object and of our sensory awareness of it are the same. (This condition does not apply to certain uses of *perceive* or *observe;* we can, for example, perceive (observe) a red book but fail to notice its redness.) Our appeal to introspection shows that we can be aware of a ping, then a brief silence, and then a bang, without necessarily being aware that the ping occurred before the bang. If, however, *before* and *after* function like characteristics such as *red,* then a sensible or intuitive awareness of all the sensory details of the situation necessitates an awareness that the ping happened before the bang. But the latter awareness need not result from the former, suggesting that *before* and *after* differ logically from *red.* Further, if *before* and *after* did function like *red,* then a single fact—X occurs before Y—would require a different sensory awareness from the awareness needed to be reported by "Y occurs after X." Our appeal to introspection thus reveals that temporal relations are not sensory items discriminable apart from the terms they relate. These relations alone do not correspond to any sensory experience; in Hume's language, we cannot find an impression of *before* and *after,* any more than we can for *existence.* It is more complex to teach *before* and *after* than it is to teach *red* or *shrill,* because the former terms do not refer to sensations; it is impossible to locate a sensory experience corresponding to such terms. Temporal concepts, like similarity, must be distinguished, therefore, from concepts of sensation.[15]

James not only invoked introspection for his claim that experienced time is a sensation or intuition, but he also called upon Mach's argument that "we must have a real *sensation* of time—how otherwise should we identify two entirely different airs as being played in the same 'time'? How distinguished in memory the first stroke of the clock from the second, unless to each there clove its special time-sensation, which revived with it?"[16] But the Mach-James argument mistakenly assumes that when we identify two tunes as being in the same time or distinguish two qualitatively similar strokes of the clock as earlier and later, there is a special sensation by which we make such identifications and distinctions. Different factors on different occasions may cause us to note that two melodies share the same rhythm or that one clock-stroke preceded the other, but there is in experience no recurrent sense responsible for our noticing such facts. It is a mistake to argue, as Mach and James did, that there must be an identifiable time-sensation. Identifying or noticing a temporal relation between events need not require the awareness of the relation as something distinct, with its own sensory character, as the referents of *red* and *shrill* have distinct sensory natures. Time, whether taken as succession or duration, is not something which introspective analysis shows to be a sensation or intuition.[17]

THE PASSAGE OF TIME

There was for James an intimate connection between the concepts of consciousness and time, for his elaboration of consciousness as a stream includes many references to the "felt continuity" that makes successive experiences into a single stream. Most of "The Stream of Thought" in *Principles* is devoted to factors such as relations, tendencies, and fringes that are responsible for the felt continuity of experience, but there is little reference to time in this chapter.[18] There is, however, one relevant observation here that is fortified by subsequent writings: while a single experience has *time-parts*, these actually "melt into each other like dissolving views" (*Principles*, 1:279). If time is not continuous, then neither is consciousness.

To say that time is experienced as continuous is apparently also to say that it is passing or flowing; yet despite the emphasis James placed on the continuity and connectedness of consciousness, he provided no in-depth account of what it is like to experience the passage or flow of time. He may have thought that his careful description of our experience of the specious present was such an account, but the specious present is a constant interval which is not itself in flow. The content of the specious present is in "constant flux, events dawning into its forward end as fast as they fade out of its rearward one, and each of them changing its time-coefficient, [but] . . . specious present, the intuited duration, stands permanent, like the rainbow on the waterfall, with its own quality unchanged by the events that stream through it" (*Principles*, 1:630). Thus, the temporal awareness of the specious present is an awareness of time standing still, contrasted with the flow of the events it contains. The time-flow accompanying the flow of these events is never described. While James gave copious descriptions of the conditions for grasping the flow of events and for registering the duration of the specious present, he said little about the perception of time's passage.

James pondered at some length in "The Perception of Time" the factors responsible for a stretch of time seeming to pass slowly or quickly and for the same span seeming shorter as we grow older. But such cases, as he himself observed, are usually instances of our estimating time lapses instead of intuiting them.[19] They are occasions for judging that time has gone quickly or slowly, not for discovering how time is felt or intuited. James's law of time's discrete flow explains the fact that we tend to grasp the passage of time rhythmically, through pulses or beats.[20] But this discrete flow is not the continuous flow of time, as we know it introspectively, before it is cut or counted in rhythmic pulses.

James came closest to explaining our intuition of continuous time in a passage discussing why a span of time can seem excessively tedious. Although he had denied a pure experience of empty time, he wrote:

> [Tedium] comes about whenever, from the relative emptiness of content of a tract of time, we grow attentive to the passage of the time itself. Expecting, and being ready for, a new impression to succeed; when it fails to come, we get an empty time instead of it; and such experiences, ceaselessly renewed, make us most formidably aware of the extent of the mere time itself. . . . All because you attend so closely to the mere feeling of the time *per se,* and because your attention to that is susceptible of such fine-grained successive subdivision . . . *stimulation* is the indispensable requisite for pleasure in an experience, and the feeling of bare time is the least stimulating experience we can have. The sensation of tedium is a *protest,* says Volkmann, against the entire present. (*Principles,* 1:626)

In this purported account of a direct experience of the passage of time—an experience which accompanies the awareness of some process or other, since according to James no experience of time completely in itself is possible—the awareness of temporal passage so prevails over awareness of the accompanying process that tedium is produced. Let us focus on James's remark that attention to time in itself is "susceptible of such fine-grained subdivision."

We must ask whether this remark is a deeper report of what James elsewhere called the experience of time's continuity. Is the experience of temporal continuity in fact analyzable into awareness of temporal "fine-grained subdivisions"? In 1895, five years after the publication of *Principles,* James wrote:

> The smallest effective pulse of consciousness, whatever else it may be consciousness of, is also consciousness of passing time. The tiniest feeling that we can possibly have involves for future reflection two sub-feelings, one earlier and one later, and a sense of their continuous procession. . . . The passing moment is the only thing that ever concretely was or is or shall be; and, in the phenomenon of elementary memory [memory of what has just occurred] whose function is to apprehend it, earlier and later are present to each other in an experience that feels either only on condition of feeling both together.[21]

Whenever we immediately focus (retrospect, reflect, introspect) on the just-passed moment, we always find that it contains an earlier and a later moment. So the passing moment, however brief, is itself analyzable into two successive moments, and passage of time is conceived as something following something else. But does mere succession guarantee continuity? This query may have prompted James to add "and a sense of their continuous procession" to the passage quoted above. But what proceeds continuously? Is it just a succession of indefinite moments, or rather the succession of specious presents that contain successions of shorter moments? Among James's unpublished notes, undated but evidently written after 1904, is the following entry: "The 'processional' character of our own experience gives the familiar feeling of 'more' and of its *sensible* verification or rebuke—in time and space."[22] In light of James's other discussions of the concept of *more,* the entry suggests that in experiencing the processional nature of time, we experience what we can only vaguely describe as the unfolding or developing of something that is more than the present, a datum of experience that we learn to call the appearance of the future. This interpretation may explain why James included "a sense of continuous procession" in the passage discussed above.

Why didn't James simply declare the experience of time's passing to be sui generis and unanalyzable, like other instances of immediate awareness or knowledge-by-acquaintance? He never explicitly endorsed this statement, although we may argue from textual evidence that it was his implicit conviction all along. For example, he wrote: "All *felt* times coexist and overlap or compenetrate each other."[23] This statement suggests that the experience of times melting into or overlapping each other is sui generis and unanalyzable, incapable of explication to anyone who has not shared it; but the problem remains—which is not solved by simply declaring the experience to be sui generis—of trying to grasp what *times* refers to, what temporal things are alleged to "coexist and overlap or compenetrate each other." This description indicates that James demanded more than mere succession to insure temporal continuity; separate moments must be more than merely adjacent, they must overlap and compenetrate.

But what are the "*felt* times" that melt together to give us the sense of time's passage? Unlike Kant, James held that, just as there are given spaces but not one space, so are there given times but not one time. This conviction may explain James's reluctance to use Bergson's formulation, "that which flows throughout the intervals, namely real time."[24] James and Bergson agreed that time is continuous, but James avoided such expressions as "the flow of real time," because he thought both that real time is a construct and not an experiential datum, and that there is no introspective or other evidence for concluding that a single something called time is perceived to move, pass, or flow.[25] It thus appears that the only alternative is to construe the passage of time as the special connections between given times. James's problem then resembles that of his opponents on the topic of space, who had to construct space from nonspatial elements; James was forced to construct flow from nonflowing elements.[26]

When the specious present is conceived as an unchanging block of time analyzable into "fine-grained successive subdivisions," the resulting picture is a time line choked with minute successions but having no flow. If each subdivision is what James meant by a felt time, then on his account each overlaps or compenetrates with the next, generating a flow that is more than mere succession.[27] But this argument plainly confuses the relations of succession and compenetration. If felt moment M occurs before felt moment N, and we are aware that N succeeds M, we register the succession of two distinct moments, which cannot then be identified as melting, overlapping, or compenetrating. Though our successive experiences may be continuous by compenetrating, as James argued, the temporal line of those experiences is not necessarily continuous in the same way. How can temporal flow be generated from temporal succession? Is it possible to avoid a theory which makes temporal continuity only an illusion, created by the rapid succession of nonflowing subdivisions of the specious present, each called a *time*, which, taken together, constitute the processional nature of experience?[28]

The task seems a hopeless one. If the passage of time is not sui generis, a unique experiential datum, then it is either a myth or an illusion. James, when he turned his phenomenological eye to the experiences that people refer to as witnessing the flow of time, found only "successive subdivisions" but no flow within them. He was preoccupied in *Principles* with contemporary laboratory studies of how humans register time intervals and the relevance of the specious present to such studies. In his later metaphysics the concept of time's passage received little attention in the recurrent discussions of the continuity of experience.[29] His preoccupation with deciphering time's "fine-grained" structure, to the neglect of its flowing nature, is further suggested by the fact that there is no sustained discussion of the intrinsic direction or "arrow" which is often said to characterize the passage of time.[30] We might have expected James, in his radical empiricistic period when he tested his concepts in terms of pure experience, to offer an engaging disquisition on the experience of time's irreversible flow, its constant movement forward. It would be typical for him to explore, for instance, whether "the intrinsic direction of time" is exemplified in experience. He may have considered his view to be implicit in his description of the specious present. On the other hand, he may have thought the important concept related to a construct rather than an experiential datum, perhaps for the same reason that he avoided Bergson's reference to the flow of real time.

I am not suggesting that the passage or flow of time is actually an experiential datum; my objection throughout has been that time is not something intuitable, but rather a measure of processes than cannot in itself be measured. Time is not a sensation and can have no flow to be intuited. But since James clearly believed in the continuity of time as a part of his belief in the general continuity of consciousness or experience, we naturally expect him to elaborate what the awareness of time's passage is like.[31] His theory of time-perception, including the specious present, makes it difficult if not impossible to provide an adequate account of the continuous temporal flow which we would expect to characterize the continuity of experience he asserts. It seems paradoxical that his phenomenological emphasis on reporting the perception of time in itself stressed time's fine-grained or granular nature. James provides no protocol to demonstrate that time can be a flow without granular divisions; his readers are left with an unsubstantiated belief that the continuity of such a flow is a constant property of human awareness.

TIME AND REALITY

James's early interest in the reality of time and space is suggested in a letter of 1880 to Renouvier: "If time and space are not *in se*, do we not need an enveloping ego to make continuous the times and spaces, not necessarily consistent, of the partial egos?" (*LWJ*, 1:207–08). Four years later he wrote in another letter to Renouvier: "Consciousness is *felt*. . . . It is as continuous, as space and time are. And I am willing to admit that it is not a *chose en soi*, for this reason, if you like, any more than they."[32] Like his theorizing on space, James's discussion of time emphasizes the certainty of pluralism, of *times*, and the uncertainty of monism, of *time*, as a thing-in-itself, a single system or reality. If times and spaces do not themselves connect into a larger unity, and if time and space do not refer to antecedent unities that are such things-in-themselves, then James's argument that an enveloping ego constitutes a larger unity seems unfounded. The psychology of time and space, in what it fails to achieve, points us to theology or metaphysics.

Having identified the experience of time, the sort of temporal consciousness that gives "cash value" to the concept of time, James turned to the psychologist's second task—identifying the cerebral or physiological conditions of temporal consciousness. The relation between mind and brain, always a conjecture and never a direct perception for James, is intriguing in the perception of time. After recapitulating the efforts of psychologists to explain why we apprehend events in a time-order at all, he himself was satisfied in simply formulating the psychophysical law governing our awareness of time.[33] Because of the "summation of stimuli" principle governing the nervous system, according to which the effect of each stimulus fades rather than instantly vanishes, James believed that the relevant brain processes may be describable. *"There is at every moment a cumulation of brain-processes overlapping each other, of which the fainter ones are the dying phases of processes which but shortly previous were active in a maximal degree"* (*Principles*, 1:635). The amount of overlapping is said to determine the specific duration-awareness, while the specific brain processes determine the particular succession of events filling the duration. This principle, James thought, is the psychophysical law governing time-cognition; he offered no further explanation of it. If we accept this account of the brain conditions underlying the intuition of time, what does it tell us about the subjectivity or objectivity of that intuition? Is the intuition of duration merely an awareness of one feature of consciousness, or is it an awareness of a property of external events? It is difficult to find a consistent answer in James's writings.

The problem is aggravated if we ask whether James's theory of time-consciousness includes anything but a causal relation between mind and brain. In his dissent from Helmholtz, James argued that even if simultaneity and succession in our sensations both result from brain events, our awareness of them is not simply equivalent to their presence in a sensation; a succession of ideas is not the same as the idea of succession. It is possible to read the final section of the chapter "The Perception of Time," on the brain's role in time-perception, as enlarging the dispute with Helmholtz and therefore emphasizing the dissimilarity between extramental processes (including brain events) and sensations in the intuition of time; according to this interpretation, this section supports James's insistence that there is no simple correspondence between mind and brain. But this reading would be a mistake, although the error is clear only when we look beyond this chapter in *Principles*. In the final chapter, "Necessary Truths and the Effects of Experience," James wrote: *"Time-and-space relations,* however, *are* impressed from without—for two outer things at least the evolutionary psychologist must believe to resemble our thoughts of them, these are the time and space in which the objects lie. *The time-and-space-relations between things do stamp copies of themselves within."*[34] James agreed with Helmholtz here, declaring that the sensation of lightning before thunder is due to a corresponding before-after process in the brain, which in turn is presumably due to a before-after process in the sky. James does not explain how we know this correspondence, nor does he address the Lockean view that we cannot possibly know it.[35] But his conviction is definite here, though it was not in the chapter on time-perception.

If we could know that our sensation of time-succession at least occasionally duplicates a feature of the world beyond our consciousness, we would have a reason to say that our sensation of time directly acquaints us with a characteristic of the external world. This conclusion seems to be what James intended in the final chapter of *Principles,* and it corresponds with his emphatic belief, as against neo-Kantians and others, that sensation puts us in touch at the outset with an extrasubjective reality. The conclusion harmonizes as well with the natural realism of common sense, which James defended repeatedly during the period of radical empiricism, when he was charged with succumbing to Berkeleyan idealism.[36] It hardly seems possible to construct a public world out of what we experience, if intuited time is only subjective, like a headache. We need a time-order that matches experience with reality; James declared time-awareness to be objective at the outset: "Our *audita et visa* and our acts fall into those receptacles of time and space in which each event finds its date and place."[37] Such remarks suggest a real time-order with which our intuitions of time at least sometimes correspond.

But other remarks rule out a definitive interpretation of James's view on the subjectivity or objectivity of the intuition of time. In the 1904 essay "A World of Pure Experience," he asserts that our minds have space in common but makes no mention of time. It may have struck him that it is much easier to indicate a common space than a common time, since we can point to the place where a thing is; if two people see it there, then it occupies a common place for them. But to show that our time-perceptions are shared, we are forced into a different procedure. In addition to James's apparent reluctance to follow Bergson in talking of "the flow of *real* time," there are other important issues in his essay on Bergson. Bergson charged that the mathematical treatment of time places undue emphasis on the moment and neglects "that which flows throughout the intervals, namely real time."[38] James endorsed Bergson's accusation, but his conclusion diverges from Bergson's insofar as he regards all talk of real time as a distortion of what actually occurs in sensible reality (sensation or intuition). "With such a definition we escape wholly from the turbid privacy of sense. But do we not also escape from sense-reality altogether?"[39] The notion of one objective, evenly flowing time, by which we arrange our private temporal intuitions on a common scale, is a practical necessity but is nevertheless called an artifice.[40] In another important essay, where the connection between James's psychology and his pragmatism is manifest, he wrote: "We assume for certain purposes one 'objective' time that *aequabiliter fluit*, but we don't livingly believe in or realize any such equally-flowing time. 'Space' is a less vague notion."[41] If, however, there is no concept of objective time adequate to our experience, no standard or procedure by which to check and correct our temporal intuitions, then temporal intuitions seem doomed to mere subjectivity. To deny an evenly flowing, objective time contradicts James's doctrine that sensations, including temporal ones, acquaint us with realities beyond our own consciousness.

James did not deny objective time altogether, but only the notion of "one equally-flowing time," which is hardly a fashionable notion nowadays. Perhaps he believed that there are processes with inherent temporal lengths which can be called objective times. If our perceptions of those processes match the processes themselves in their temporal respects, then our intuitions of time are objective; if not, our intuitions are reverie or fantasy.[42] There are objective times as well as subjective ones, but the notion of a single, overarching Time remains an artifice, no matter what convenience it affords.If our concern is for the accuracy of our sensation of time rather than the introspective feel of it, we can check our sensation against the duration of an event as measured by a clock and then describe our sense of duration as the length of time occupied by the event. Accuracy involves measurement, which for James was extrinsic to the nature of temporal intuition. Using a clock to check on the accuracy of intuited time, therefore, does not compromise the nativistic notion of the priority of intuited over clocked time. I think James intended this interpretation, which allows both a commonsense view of how we class intuited times as objective or subjective (depending upon how well they match the clocked durations of perceived processes) and a denial of a single objective time-order comprising the objective times of public processes.

James clearly reconsidered until the end his concept of the continuity of time. He often declared confidently that time is continuous and is experienced as such; the more-than-casual reader might justifiably take this declaration to be a basic and unshakable part of James's theory. But there is textual evidence to the contrary. In a late essay he wrote: "Our world, being strung along in time and space, has *temporal and spatial unity*. But time and space relate things by determinately sundering them, so it is hard to say whether the world ought more to be called 'one' or 'many' in this spatial or temporal regard" (*SPP*, 127–28). James's concern here is that his defense of pluralism may be menaced by *too much* spatial or temporal unity. Temporal relations can be as fairly judged to sunder as to unite the things they relate, as easily to interrupt as to continue the flow of events.

James once wrote in a course syllabus: "Zeno's argument conclusive. Continuity is only an ideal construction. In actual experience, there are 'thresholds,' and change is always by finite increments."[43] Based on the syllabus and students' notes, Perry describes the course as James's most comprehensive statement of his philosophy.[44] James was rethinking the concept of continuity in terms of Peirce's tychism, or doctrine that things arise by chance. Though time and space may be infinite, the "inanity" of such a hypothesis, according to James, leads to philosophies like "pansychistic idealism."[45] All that can be concluded on this score, James believed, is that finite space and time are probabilities only. James wrote in the same syllabus: "Pragmatically, infinity means that more may come, infinitesimal means that something is lost, has sunk below the pragmatic threshold. 'Experience,' swinging between the two infinites, is thus most naturally describable in pluralistic or tychistic terms." James's agreement with Peirce's tychism seems to mean that genuine continuity is only an ideal construct; in actual experience we must settle for the perception of endurance, change, and growth by finite increments instead of by absolutely smooth or continuous progressions. Abstract space and time, conceived as infinite, may feature genuine continuity, but the finite space and time of experience do not.

Imputing such a view to James may seem unthinkable, but it is supported also by James's writing on the concept of *more*. He noted briefly in his discussion of space that there are "relations of muchness and littleness between times, numbers, intensities, and qualities, as well as spaces," and that we experience a sui generis sensation of *more* whenever we register one of those relations.[46] In original or native intuiting of space, we confront both a mere voluminousness or spatial muchness and a sensation of *more*, which may be called a fringe sensation because it surrounds or extends beyond the voluminousness at the center of attention. When we measure precisely the voluminousness or expanse before us, we distinctly connect the *more* on the fringe with the central focus of attention. This idea yields a somewhat different description of time-awareness from what we have entertained thus far. In intuiting the specious present, we are aware of both a temporal muchness and a sensation of *more*. But does this *more* connect smoothly and continuously with the temporal muchness at the center of our attention? James seems to have thought in his later years that the connection is relatively discontinuous, made in finite increments as he believed Peirce's tychism required. He had said in *Principles* that we measure rhythmically our original sensation of time through beats and pulses; perhaps this method clarifies the temporal *more* through distinct, discontinuous intervals. This idea consorts with James's evolutionary nativism, a belief that the sophisticated perception and knowledge of time, space, and objects evolves from the original sensation of time, which is "private and vague."[47] But the main evidence for suggesting that James thought the temporal *more* is discontinuously assimilated to the apprehended *now*—which is in itself just a temporal muchness—occurs in a passage from *Some*

Problems of Philosophy that Whitehead singled out for approval in *Process and Reality:* "We either perceive nothing, or something already there in sensible amount. This fact is what in psychology is known as the law of the 'threshold.' Either your experience is of no content, of no change, or it is of a perceptible amount of content or change. Your acquaintance with reality grows literally by buds or drops of perception. Intellectually and on reflection you can divide these into components, but as immediately given, they come totally or not at all."[48]

These buds or drops of perception are the finite increments by which the temporal *more* is assimilated to the temporal muchness that is the focus of the present moment. James called this concept his discontinuity theory, according to which every bit of matter is increased or decreased by finite quantities, as are "any amounts of time, space, change, etc., which we might assume would be composed of a finite number of minimal amounts of time, space, and change" (*SPP*, 154). We will consider the argument that James used against Russell's attempt to find a mathematical continuum in experience in chapter 11; it is enough for now to mention that such an argument is involved in defending the view of "real processes of change no longer as being continuous, but as taking place by finite not infinitesimal steps, like the successive drops by which a cask of water is filled, when whole drops fall into it at once or nothing. This is the radically pluralist, empiricist, or perceptualist position" (*SPP*, 172). The philosopher with whom James identified in holding that everything actual exists atomistically, or in "limited amounts," was Renouvier.[49]

This glimpse of the radically pluralist metaphysics is sufficient to show that the later philosophy of James rejects any attempt to locate a continuum in experience by some concept of continuous time. But how is this view compatible with James's statements, even in his later philosophy, about the stream of consciousness and the continuity of sensible experience?[50] James seems to say that the continuity of experience remains a fact, as he had always declared, but one which cannot be adequately conceptualized. The atomization of time, space, and matter, and the rejection of conceptualizing the actual in terms of a mathematical infinite and continuum, accord with Renouvier. The buds, drops, and finite increments of perception dovetail with Peirce's tychism. Bergson's influence is not seen in a concept of real time that provides the desired continuity for experience, but rather in the anti-intellectualism that declares the immediate awareness of the "sensible flux or reality" to be ineffable, incapable of being adequately conceptualized. James's final doctrine is that we know, directly or by acquaintance, that the stream of sensation is continuous, though we cannot formulate its nature. Genuine continuity is not found in experience insofar as it can never be shown to be instantiated. No philosopher, according to James, can smooth out the discontinuity inevitably produced by conceptualization of experience through a concept of real time. We must avoid easy or casual readings of Jamesian pronouncements like this: "The great continua of time, space, and self envelop everything, betwixt them, and flow together without interfering."[51]

We must not, however, interpret James as denying the reality of time; such a denial would be nonsense in his eyes. Time truly exists insofar as there are times, but there is no concept of real time which can adequately encompass the times of sensation or sensible experience. James was also prepared to say that everything happens *in* time, though this statement does not commit us to a single, overarching time. For instance, he labeled the idea of a timeless mind a gratuitous fiction, suggesting that we cannot grasp the notion of a mind to which all time is simultaneously present. "And is not the notion of eternity being given at a stroke to omniscience only just another way of whacking upon us the block-universe, and of denying that possibilities exist?—just the point to be proved. To say that time is an illusory appearance is only a roundabout manner of saying there is no real plurality, and that the frame of things is an absolute unit. Admit plurality, and time may be its form."[52] That times are real and belong to the world's process, and that everything exists in some time, is essential to James's final metaphysics.

But a scientific or developed metaphysical theory of time is largely irrelevant to the Jamesian ontology, for James held that conceptual formulations necessarily distort the qualities of the sensations, including the temporal, which they are designed to convey. This belief connects with another credo: "Individuality is founded in feeling; and the recesses of feeling, the darker, blinder strata of character, are the only places in the world in which we catch real fact in the making. . . . Compared with this world of living individualized feelings, the world of generalized objects which the intellect contemplates is without solidity or life."[53] Some philosophers have said that to be real is to be rational, others that it is to be perceived, or to be in a public space and time. For James, however, to be real is to be an experience or to be like an experience in nature:

> *As soon as we deal with private and personal phenomena as such, we deal with realities in the completest sense of the term.* . . . What we think of may be enormous—the cosmic times and spaces, for example—whereas the inner state may be the most fugitive and paltry activity of mind. Yet the cosmic objects, so far as experience yields them, are but ideal pictures of something whose existence we do not inwardly possess but only point at outwardly, while the inner state is our very experience itself; its reality and that of our experience are one. . . . It is of the *kind* to which all realities whatsoever must belong.[54]

The references to times are consistent with Jamesian pluralism. One can infer from this type of obiter dictum that a sophisticated concept of time is almost certainly beyond all connection with Jamesian reality.

The only time we know, the overlapping times of immediate experience, resists any attempt at adequate formulation. James believed that we can obtain a few propositions—time is a sensation, it is intuited, it is continuous, and it accompanies every sensation—but such statements struck him as paltry information about the "immediate experience" in which he found his own model for reality. If we try to explain how time is continuous, to conceptualize it in words, we fall into contradictions. How do we feel from one specious present to the next? How is time's flow intuited? According to James's final metaphysics, there is no adequate reply to these questions. No formulation will work. Though James criticized traditional rationalism for considering sensations to be "dumb," he himself concluded that knowledge-by-acquaintance is equally dumb. Perhaps he held this view all along, which would explain why so little phenomenology of time's flow occurs in his writings. If we try to conceive how a succession of subjective or objective times coalesces into a continuous stream, we are doomed to failure. Neither metaphysics nor science can help. If we adhere to the pragmatic demand for "cash-value" concepts, we can only imagine the coalescence of times by the analogy of how we experience but cannot formulate those phenomena. Each experience, which includes a *more,* connects with a larger reality that makes times continuous.[55] We can understand that a larger experience may provide continuity of times and spaces, but we cannot comprehend scientific and metaphysical attempts to effect such continuity through a concept of time that distorts our picture of what experience is like.

James's account of time-perception in *Principles* is still a locus classicus for anyone investigating the history of the topic. As on every psychological issue, James used an amazing amount of information from the laboratories and studies of others as an immensely rich background against which to sketch his own argument. But his account is more than a source for the historian of psychology and the philosophy of psychology, it is also an enlightening discussion for anyone who reflects on what it is to experience time. We may agree or disagree with the account, but we cannot afford to ignore it. The concept of the specious present is a basic consideration for almost all subsequent discussions of time, and though James may not have invented the concept, no one is more responsible than he for its sturdy popularity. The idea of the specious present helps clarify "the present moment" and the past-present-future distinction within the *now.* It suggests how an immediately past event can be said to be presently apprehended, when it would be odd to say it is remembered; or how an event coming to be is in a way both future and present.

James's theorizing on time is a valuable starting point for modern dialogues between philosophers and psychologists. In sorting and explaining different experiences for which time is significant, the psychologist will probably turn to concepts that will excite the philosopher's need to clarify. More than anything else, the value of James's ruminations on time lies in his effort to search out the subtle relations between the concept of time and the deeper recesses of experience that are accessible only to sensitive introspection. Even where the original philosophical suggestion may lead to an absolute dead end, James's writings can be a stimulating occasion for our own philosophizing. Even when we cannot credit him with providing the answers we formulate, he is often responsible for suggesting the questions that get us started—and that accomplishment can be the greatest contribution a philosopher can offer.

6 ✣ MEMORY

The chapter on time-perception in *Principles* is followed by one on memory, for James saw an important connection between the two psychological processes. Some writers had spoken of the just-past, or the most recent moments of the specious present, as objects of primary memory, but James thought this an odd use of the term *memory;* we do not usually describe someone as *remembering* something that occurred only a second ago. Although the occurrence is a past event, it is, according to the theory of the specious present, part of a single, continuing act of attention that is still occurring. James considered any moment later than the first moment of the current specious present to be part of our current awareness; any earlier moment is *remembered.* Memory, like anticipation, focuses our attention beyond the limits of the specious present.[1]

Even if we accept James's statement of the relation of memory to time-perception and the specious present, we must consider critically his further characterization of memory: "Memory proper, or secondary memory as it might be styled, is the knowledge of a former state of mind after it has already once dropped from consciousness; or rather *it is the knowledge of an event, or fact,* of which meantime we have not been thinking, *with the additional consciousness that we have thought or experienced it before*" (*Principles,* 1:648). This definition reflects the fact that we claim to remember only what we have experienced, that "I remember X" implies "I experienced X." But remembering X does not require remembering that I experienced X. We usually recall our experience of an event along with the recall of the event itself, but it is neither a sufficient nor a necessary condition for doing so. Exceptions are easy to imagine: if I am busy and hurried, I may suddenly remember that my wallet was left in the office without recalling actually leaving the wallet behind. We do not remember something that we did not experience, but we need not remember that we experienced it in order to remember it. Thus, the "additional consciousness" demanded by James's definition of memory is unwarranted.[2]

Because "I remember X" implies "I experienced X," it is not possible to remember something that we did not perceive or feel. This criterion for memory is compatible with a phenomenon that is an occasional and interesting feature of memory. The phenomenon has been called primary positive afterimage, and James described it as follows: "If we open our eyes instantaneously upon a scene, and then shroud them in complete darkness, it will be as if we saw the scene in ghostly light throughout the dark screen. We can read off details in it which were unnoticed whilst the eyes were open" (*Principles,* 1:645). Certain afterimages endure such that we can notice for the first time details of a scene that we did not notice while actually perceiving it a few seconds before. This feature is not restricted to immediate after-images but can belong also to remembered images much further distant in time. We may suddenly recall in surprising vividness a scene of some months ago and, in inspecting our recollection, discover details that went totally unnoticed when we actually perceived the scene. If it is agreed that we did not experience those details previously, then we cannot be said to remember them; rather, in a curious sort of memory-experience, we initially notice details from a past scene only later. The past is recovered in such a memory-experience by being *perceived* rather than remembered. But questions arise about this curious capacity of memory-experience, which is not memory proper.[3]

It is tempting to say that in noticing for the first time certain details of a past scene we are perceiving a present complex image, a memory-experience that we inspect when we discover those originally unnoticed details. James never doubted the virtual omnipresence of images in his account of memory and of experience generally; modern skeptics, who question the reality of images as distinct entities or processes, would consider him the worst of introspectors. He supposed that one necessary condition of remembering is "the revival in the mind of an image or copy of the original event" (*Principles,* 1:649). But this condition is not sufficient, for an image or duplicate of a past event is not necessarily a memory. We may have an image that resembles someone we have never seen or met and thus cannot possibly remember. Further, as James pointed out, to suppose that the mere presence of an image is sufficient for recollection presents the problem of explaining how we recall what did *not* happen.[4] Although images are not sufficient, they are necessary for remembering, according to James, especially in the experience of positive after-images in which features of a past event are noticed for the first time.[5]

As James suggested, we can, in remembering, perceive previously unnoticed details of a past event; but Ryle argues convincingly that images as distinct realities are more questionable than we may realize.[6] In any event, we should not rest our case on the assumption that when we notice in recollection something unnoticed in the original scene, we are inspecting an image literally present to our attention. Images such as afterimages, or those in dreams and hallucinations, are as real as the distinct images we see in mirrors. But when we use the term *image* to describe what we are aware of in recollection, the actual presence of the image is questionable. In remembering or imagining, all that is certain about our experience is that we feel *as if* we see an image of something. We can describe in great detail and with full confidence what we feel as if we see, hear, or smell. Although such a feeling seems impossible unless we are inspecting a current image, in reporting our introspection conscientiously, we often cannot locate a definite image such as an afterimage or mirror image. We may therefore doubt that any image exists, yet feel unable to declare confidently that no image is present, because we suspect that what accounts for our detailed and confident report of what we seem to be aware of may be an image so filmy or watery that it does not register as a distinct thing. We may ascribe to images properties that will make them elusive to introspective detection, thus confirming that not all memories and imaginings are clear-cut images, undermining any conviction that an image is being apprehended as an object whose configuration can be drawn.

Our introspections do not necessarily endorse the requirement, in James's definition of memory, of a distinct image of the past, regardless of whether what is recalled was noticed before or is noticed for the first time. All that we can definitely assert about the experience is that we feel as if we have an image of the past. This sort of description may strike some as perverse, especially those who believe that feeling as if they see something from the past is the result of actually seeing in the present an image of the past. But let the intrepid introspector beware! If asked whether a memory-experience makes us feel as if we see an image of the past or rather as if we see the past itself, some people will give one answer, some the other. But even if introspection leaves us sincerely convinced that there is no definite image of the past involved in remembering something, memory is nevertheless an intense, vital experience yielding vivid and accurate reports of what we recall, very much as if we were perceiving the past itself. It may seem that the experience ought to contain psychological ingredients such as images or present perceptions which can be used to explain its *as if* character, but no such ingredients can be uncovered that are relevant or essential to remembering. We are thus left with an experience which is aptly described by saying that we feel as if we perceived the past, without being able to locate any specific characteristics of the memory-experience to explain why it lends itself to that *as if* report.

James's theory of memory is a heroic effort to uncover the essential psychological ingredients of any memory-experience; he saw his task as revealing the complex factors that constitute the experience of remembering. He sought to explain why a memory-experience typically makes us feel as if we perceive the past. But that effort is fraught with difficulties. For example, James moved on to observations about the required image in memory. One condition is that the image "be *expressly referred to the past,* thought as *in the past*" (*Principles,* 1:650). Having said that the mere occurrence of an image does not necessarily constitute a memory, he appears to have concluded that images do not intrinsically refer to an original in the past, but are somehow referred to or thought in the past by the rememberer. The rememberer must respond in some way to the image before it becomes a memory-image, one that carries his attention to the past. This response, James believed, can be described in plain detail. Since remembered events are conceived and not perceived, and are always at least somewhat removed in time, their recall must proceed in part symbolically. "So that if we wish to think of a particular past epoch, we must think of a name or other symbol, or else of certain concrete events, associated therewithal. Both must be thought of, to think the past epoch adequately."[7] The indispensable reference to the past is thus accomplished by thinking of both the name of the remembered item and associations. Together with referring the remembered event to our own past, these processes constitute a memory.

The psychological picture of remembering is, however, still incomplete. James returned to the image component, declaring it to be more complex than he had indicated in introducing it. The image in memory is not as simple as ordinary images. (Here James agrees, though for different reasons, with part of my criticism above.) It is rather a "very complex representation, that of the fact to be recalled *plus* its associates, the whole forming one 'object' . . . and demanding probably a vastly more intricate brain-process than that on which any simple sensorial image depends" (*Principles*, 1:651). James had explained earlier in *Principles*, in "The Stream of Thought," that the term *object* is to be understood as the object of thought or memory; he sought to avoid an oversimplified picture of what actually occurs when we think of or remember something reasonably complex. Giving an example, James asked what is the mind's object when we assert, "Columbus discovered America in 1492." Most people, he thought, will reply "Columbus," or "America," or perhaps "discovery of America," defining in their response the topic or subject of the assertion. But these answers are a fraction of the total complex object conveyed by the whole sentence. If we want to experience what it is like to think of or remember such a complex object, we "must reproduce the thought as it was uttered, with every word fringed and the whole sentence bathed in that original halo of obscure relations, which, like an horizon, then spread about its meaning" (*Principles*, 1:275–76). He drew upon the doctrine that verbal meaning is not exclusively a dictionary definition, but consists of psychic *fringes* or overtones around our use of words; we can literally experience these fringes, which contribute to the genuine complexity of most objects of remembering.[8]

Remembering involves a "feeling of belief" in its complex object; James's comments about this belief are both curious and significant: "All the elements of this object may be known to other states of belief; nor is there in the particular combination of them as they appear in memory anything so peculiar as to lead us to oppose the latter to other sorts of thought as something altogether *sui generis*, needing a special faculty to account for it" (*Principles*, 1:652). The object of remembering is not different from the objects of other mental states such as imagining, and there is no special faculty of memory which constructs the complex memory-object. Any represented object which "is connected either mediately or immediately with our present sensations or emotional activities tends to be believed in as a reality" (*Principles*, 1:652). If we merely imagine something as past, its aura of unreality arises because it does not connect entirely with our psychic present and hence does not arouse the feeling or emotion of belief. The object of memory, which does arouse such belief, differs only in this respect from a merely imagined object; moreover, it arouses belief not because it has been formed by a distinct faculty of memory but because it is connected with our psychic present. The only faculties needed to explain how the object of memory is formed are perception, imagination, comparison, and reasoning. "The objects of any of these faculties may awaken belief or fail to awaken it; *the object of memory is only an object imagined in the past* (usually very completely imagined there) to which the emotion of belief adheres."[9]

This is a curious analysis of remembering in that it professes to decipher so many connections between so many ingredients, and in a manner apt to bewilder our own impressions of remembering. But it is significant in that it illustrates the introspective tradition in psychology; James could easily cite illustrious predecessors in English and European psychology as contributors to this sort of analysis of mental states. James's analysis is significant also in its denial of memory as sui generis and in its argument that memory can be analyzed into a complex of imagination, belief, perception, and thought. He included also the feelings of "warmth and intimacy" that accompany the object of recollection and contribute to our belief that it really represents the past.[10] The dissection of memory-states into a complex of mental activities—a process which eliminates the conception of memory as an isolated faculty—can be viewed as a promising flourish of Occam's razor in psychology (although James did not generally respect the razor). James's theory of memory is a fine example of how introspective analysis, supplemented by argument and by research and speculation in physiology, was intended to determine the psychological events that constitute a mental state.[11]

But if I protest that my own introspections fail to disclose the experiential complex into which James analyzed memory, I enter into the kind of dispute that has plagued introspective psychology—differing verdicts by different introspectors. Despite my regard for James's powers of introspection and the ingenuity of his supporting arguments, I sometimes find the experience of remembering elusive or intractable to the effort to identify a set of psychological ingredients that constitute it. I can apparently recollect something accurately and vividly, yet be unable to identify with any confidence the Jamesian ingredients—images, objects, feelings, perceptions, and thoughts. A critic might suppose that my description of an experience of recollecting, which seems to include no such components, is not really an experience but rather a *disposition* on my part to describe in detail what I recall. According to this criticism, my disposition or ability to recount what I recall may be confused with an allegedly elusive experience of remembering, but my ability to recount the past is not an experience at all.

But memory as mere disposition is illustrated by an ability to travel a familiar route or to recite historical dates—occasions that are not normally conceived as memory-experiences but rather as manifestations of something learned and not forgotten. But when we build up recollections of an exciting event, we are involved in a current experience of considerable richness. The recollection itself may be exciting and pleasant. It has a definite character which makes us feel as if we see or hear the remembered event. The nature of our memory-experience of something is not the same as seeing it or seeing a picture or a mirror image of it; we feel *as if* we see it or an image of it. The disposition or ability to recount what we remember seems to be the result of the memory-experience. Without memory-experience, our ability to recount the past ceases; while the experience continues, it generates our choice of verbal reports. The act of reporting is dependent upon memory-experience, but that experience is not describable in terms of specific psychological ingredients. If we recall seeing something, then we *believe* that we saw it. But belief here is dispositional; we are disposed to answer affirmatively if asked whether we believe that we saw it. But belief is not an introspectable occurrence in the memory-experience we report; it is a consequence of the memory-experience, not a moment in it.

Remembering is something that happens, an experience or series of events that we can attend to; it is by no means ineffable, and it does not collapse into a complex of other happenings such as imagining or perceiving. Ayer concludes his own reflections on James's theory of memory: "To speak of a 'feeling' of memory, which is *sui generis,* is not very satisfactory, but I confess that I do not know what else there is to say" (247). Remembering is a sui generis activity or experience in that it cannot be analyzed into a more basic formulation. Other psychological factors may accompany and embellish remembering—imagining, believing, doubting, and feeling, for example—but they do not constitute remembering itself. We can articulate what it is like to remember, but we cannot, through such articulation, provide the concept of memory to someone who has never himself remembered anything. Without the experience, no amount of description of others' memory-experiences can tell him what memory is. Although I agree with Ayer that remembering is sui generis, I am puzzled by the fact that he finds this conclusion "not very satisfactory." If, like James, he thinks it would be more satisfactory to discover that memory could be analyzed completely into other psychological activities or experiences, his reasoning is unclear, unless he relies on the familiar but unpersuasive argument that a simpler picture is better than a more complex one. To admit the sui generis nature of memory does not imply that memory is ineffable or mysterious. We can describe our experiences of remembering and of seeing red things, and neither the remembering nor the redness is mysterious. For the person who has never seen anything red or remembered anything at all, and who thus cannot grasp remembering and redness, these concepts represent not a mystery but a deprivation. If the world includes rememberings and red things, then any theory that accounts for their existence must, to that extent, be entirely satisfactory.

THE UNCONSCIOUS

Theories of memory are theories of consciousness, and at some point theorists must ask whether unconscious memory states occur. James reasoned that not all mental states can be recalled, since *"for a state of mind to survive in memory it must have endured for a certain length of time"* (*Principles,* 1:643). Some mental states (the flights or transitive states, said to correspond to prepositions and conjunctions, that James discusses in "The Stream of Thought") occur so fleetingly that they are elusive both to introspection and to memory. What we recall are the *perchings* or substantive mental states that endure for the required minimum of time. These mental states are most influential, simply because they can be recalled.

But James did not deny the possible influence of a mental state too rapid to be remembered: "Such a state, though absolutely unremembered, might at its own moment determine the transition of our thinking in a vital way, and decide our action irrevocably. But the *idea* of it could not *afterwards* determine transition and action, its content could not be conceived as one of the mind's permanent meanings" (*Principles*, 1:644–45). Mental states that exist too briefly to be identified introspectively or remembered may nonetheless be unconscious causes of feeling or conduct. James thought the evidence for such mental states comes from introspection and from pathology. We can learn to introspect more carefully than we normally do, discovering more detail in our mental states than we had suspected. At the same time, we become aware of limits to introspective analysis; some aspects of mental states evaporate too quickly to be adequately detected, and too much is occurring for it all to be registered simultaneously. We can be aware that more is occurring than we can consciously register, without having any clear idea of what that more is like. Introspection therefore supports the claim that some mental states or their details can occur without being remembered. This view seemingly conflicts with James's *esse est sentiri* doctrine of mental states: "for the essence of feeling is to be felt and as a psychic existent *feels,* so it must *be.*"[12]

James was impressed by the evidence from pathology for the existence of unconscious states; he cited the works of Hippolyte Bernheim, Alfred Binet, Edmund Gurney, and Jules and Pierre Janet on the unconscious perception found in hysterics. Patients suffering from hysterical blindness may not be able to see something consciously but can, through automatic writing, give an accurate description of it. Pains that might be consciously unnoticed are remembered (and complained about) when the hysteric is put into a hypnotic trance. James himself observed an interesting case: "In a perfectly healthy young man who can write with the planchette, I lately found the hand to be entirely anesthetic during the writing act; I could prick it severely without the Subject knowing the fact. The *writing on the planchette,* however, accused me in strong terms of hurting the hand. Pricks on the *other* (non-writing) hand, meanwhile, which awakened strong protest from the young man's vocal organs, were denied to exist by the self which made the planchette go" (*Principles,* 1:208). The hypothesis of Gurney and Janet appealed to James (though not, incidentally, to Freud); they asserted that a mental state which may be unconscious to oneself is consciously noticed by another self.[13] Each of us, according to this view, actually or potentially has several selves within the same body. When James denied the unconscious, as in chapters 6 and 7 of *Principles,* he denied only that mental states can occur entirely unnoticed by any self whatever. But he agreed that mental states occur unconsciously in what we regard as our normal, waking selves. Some states may be recalled in memory, at least those which have endured long enough for the secondary or tertiary self to witness. James thus reconciled the apparent conflict between holding that the *to be* of a mental state is *to be felt* and that such a state can occur unconsciously. The identity of an unconscious state still resides in how it is felt or experienced, but the self that feels or experiences it is not the normal, expected one, but rather a secondary, submerged center of consciousness. The *esse est sentiri* doctrine of mental states does not seem worth preserving, however, given James's own testimony to the difficulties and errors of introspection. Although the existence of burns or headaches may plausibly be held to consist in how these conditions feel, this claim is implausible when extended to the whole range of mental states, including complex ones, such as intentions, expectations, emotions, and beliefs, whose identity is not easily determined introspectively. In these cases the feeling may at best be a clue to the identity of the mental state, falling far short of being its equivalent. Faced with a choice, I believe in the existence of unconscious mental states rather than the *esse est sentiri* thesis. James seems to have thought that with the aid of Gurney's notion of multiple selves, he could have it both ways.

He envisaged two types of unconscious mental states that must elude memory: those that even under normal conditions occur rapidly, or occur when our attention is distracted, and are thus not consciously registered or introspected; and those that, in more pathological contexts, cannot be noted by the normal self but may be experienced by a secondary or more submerged self. But the admission of unconscious mental states that are normal and relevant to pathology, and that can causally influence us in ways not accessible to our introspection, hardly approaches Freudianism. There is no system of the unconscious in James as there is in Freud. Moreover, James offers no theory of repression as the agent of forgetting and no theory of infantile amnesia. Unlike Freud, James rarely mentioned unconscious memories; given his analysis of remembering, he apparently concluded that an unconscious memory is too exotic a concept to be considered. Certainly, nothing resembling Freud's idea of unconscious memory systems occurs in James.[14]

Compared to psychoanalytic theory, James's theory of memory may appear spare to the point of being shallow. But any adequate theory of memory must agree with James that mental states which occur unconsciously, and are thereby unavailable to memory, may nonetheless cause us to feel and act in certain ways. Many biochemical and physiological events, of which we are routinely unconscious, occur constantly in our bodies and influence our feelings and actions. But many psychologists balk at the suggestion that there are unconscious moods, perceptions, sensations, and feelings which do likewise. Such critics insist that the concept of an unconscious headache, for example, is incoherent. Yet if our heartbeat can be present in or absent from our consciousness without altering its nature as a heartbeat, so, it seems, can mental states such as emotions, perceptions, and feelings. Our emotions and perceptions do not always coincide exactly with what we are conscious of. We need not conclude that an emotion or perception, just at the point where it extends beyond our awareness, must have altered its nature, either by ceasing to exist entirely or by lapsing into something physiological. Since nature abhors sharp dividing lines, the hypothesis of continuity warrants the belief that mental states can exist on either side of the line of consciousness and can sometimes cross it, without radical alteration of character. Subjective states that elude memory but may be causally significant include both the unremembered—once consciously known but subsequently forgotten—and the unrememberable—never consciously known.

THE CONDITIONS OF MEMORY

In remembering, two factors require causal explanation: first, the retention of what is remembered, and second, the recollection or actual recall. Traditional associationists such as James Mill were right, James said, in arguing that recollection proceeds by association. (For example, the best way to remember a forgotten name may be to list consciously its associates.) James concluded that the machinery of recall is the same as the machinery of association, which is described as "the elementary law of habit in the nerve-centers."[15]

Retention is also explained physiologically. Unlike recall, it is not an experience or episode but a disposition. To say that we retain a memory of something is only to say that we are disposed to recall or recollect it in appropriate circumstances. The physiological basis for that disposition is an organization of neural paths which function according to elementary principles of association. Subjective associations in memory result from counterpart associations in the nerve cells of the brain. James wanted to contrast the purely physical nature of retention with the mental or experiential character of recall, and to show that retention is

> no mysterious storing up of an idea in an unconscious state. It is not a fact of the mental order at all. It is a purely physical phenomenon . . . the presence of these "paths" . . . in the finest recesses of the brain's tissue. The recall or recollection, on the other hand, is a *psycho-physical* phenomenon, with both a bodily and a mental side. The bodily side is the functional excitement of the tracts and paths in question; the mental side is the conscious vision of the past occurrence, and the belief that we experienced it before" (*Principles*, 1:655).

James's discussion of memory is another fine example of psychology, as he defined it, at work. First, using introspection supplemented by experiment and argument, we identify more exactly than does common sense or casual inspection the mental phenomenon of remembering. The complex of ingredients that constitute recollecting is analyzed introspectively and thus identified more clearly and comprehensively. Second, the mental state of recollecting is correlated with its physiological, especially its cerebral, conditions. James was forced into much speculation in order to perform this second task of his psychology, and he offered a substantial amount of argument, in place of experimental evidence, to support his guesses. He discussed critically what might be called a trace or engram theory. Suppose that something in the brain, a brain-path or molecule, is the organic condition underlying the thought or memory of a past event. A trace theory might assert that reexciting that condition is sufficient to effect the recall of the event; if we reactivate the proper trace, the proper memory results. But James insisted that the original excitement of the condition and its reexcitement produce two different conscious states that may have nothing relevant in common. Memory always requires that anything remembered must be in a context of associates; nothing can be recalled independently of such a context. Nothing can summon itself on its own to our memory; we require a context or setting, consisting of associates of a past event, in order to recall the event. Reexcitement of the organic condition underlying recall of an event is not sufficient for recall of the event. The cerebral paths between the organic conditions that underlie the event and those that underlie its context must also be excited. The cerebral context underlying the retention of the event is thus the system of brain-paths between the two sets of underlying organic conditions.

James concluded: "The only hypothesis, in short, to which the facts of inward experience give countenance is that *the brain-tracts excited by the event proper, and those excited in its recall, are in part different from each other*. If we could revive the past event without any associates we should exclude the possibility of memory, and simply dream that we were undergoing the experience as if for the first time" (*Principles*, 1:657). Introspective analysis of any recollection reveals the omnipresent condition of associates occurring; something must exist in the brain corresponding to that condition. James's discussion is another instance of his use of introspective analysis to suggest hypotheses about the brain functions that underlie introspected experience. When an introspective psychologist clarifies the elements and relations constituting an experience such as remembering, his result is tantamount to a description of the structure of the physiological conditions for that experience.

Given today's continuing research in the physiology of memory, and the apparent lack of consensus about the material basis of memory, James's speculations may even be correct. At least he avoided gross oversimplification in his hypothesizing. Like Bergson, for instance, he emphasized the distinction between perception and memory and hypothesized an underlying distinction in brain-processes. Just because a given portion of the brain is activated when we experience an event, we should not assume that recalling the event depends merely upon reactivating that portion of the brain. Believing memory to be something other than a cerebral function, Bergson wrote, "When we pass from . . . perception to memory, we definitely abandon matter for spirit."[16] James, however, continued the search for memory's cerebral conditions. Much has been learned about the physiology of memory since James's day. For example, Wilder Penfield has evoked memories in subjects by applying electrodes to the cerebral cortex, though he has renounced his earlier theory that memory is recorded in the cortex.[17] He is convinced that at least one side of the hippocampus is necessary for memory retention, and that synaptic facilitation is likely established by each original experience such that "permanent facilitation could guide a subsequent stream of neuronal impulses activated by the electric current of the electrodes even years later."[18] Penfield is inclined toward a dualism of mind and brain; among his reasons he stresses that no brain mechanism has been located to explain belief and decision: "There is no place in the cerebral cortex where electrical stimulation will cause a patient to believe or to decide" (77). The mind, not the brain, must then be the source of belief and decision, the agent of deliberate observation and direction. Penfield believes that the mind has no *memory* of its own, for all the evidence seems to indicate that memory is a function of the brain.[19] His reading of the data sides with James and against Bergson on the issue. Penfield's freeing of belief from brain dependence would appear to complicate James's account of how memory and brain connect, given his inclusion of belief as an essential ingredient in any experience of recollection. If Penfield is right, belief is independent of brain functioning, whereas memory is not.

Considerable publicity was given in the 1960s to the search for the so-called "memory molecule," and investigators discussed the possibility of transferring learning from animal to animal. Today that kind of thinking seems to have subsided, largely because more is being learned about the ways in which synaptic mechanisms contribute to both remembering and forgetting, the ways in which alterations in the cerebral cortex affect memory, and the role of nuclear RNA in neurons and glia in learning. Even in the 1960s, when the biology of memory was a preeminent topic, some investigators thought that the material basis of memory lay elsewhere. Heinz Von Foerster, for instance, wrote:

> At issue is an important property of the functioning of our nervous system. We call it "memory." In looking for mechanisms that can be made responsible for this property, I strongly suggested that we not look upon this system as if it were a recording device. Instead, I have proposed looking at this system as if it were a computer whose internal organization changes as a result of its interaction with an environment that possesses some order. The changes of the internal organization of this computer take place in such a way that some constraints in the environment which are responsible for its orderliness are mapped into the computer's structure. This homomorphism "environment-system" reveals itself as "memory" and permits the system to function as an inductive inference computer.[20]

Von Foerster suggests that instead of thinking of the brain as if it were a "storehouse or a gigantic table," a place where memory is recorded, we ought to compare it to a computer's memory that works "without a record kept." If James could reenter the discussion, he might find this theory closer to his own speculations about the cerebral conditions of memory than are the theories of memory molecules, physical traces, and records in the brain. Indeed, he might even revise his discussion of brain-paths to describe them as more akin to circuits than to physical parts of the brain.[21] In any case, the complicated story of the physiological basis of memory is hardly complete. Whatever its outcome, there is one serious difficulty in James's theory of memory.

This difficulty is not specific to physiology, not some defect in James's concept of how the brain works, but rather pertains to the attempt to explain remembering simply through putative associations in the brain. It is certainly plausible to claim that the arousal of certain associations in the brain is a necessary condition for recalling something. "If we could revive the past event without any associates we should exclude the possibility of memory, and simply dream that we were undergoing the experience as if for the first time. Whenever, in fact, the recalled event does appear without a definite setting, it is hard to distinguish it from a mere creation of fancy. But in proportion as its image lingers and recalls associates which gradually become more definite, it grows more and more distinctly into a remembered thing" (*Principles*, 2:657–58). James thought there is subjective evidence for the cerebral underpinnings of recollection. Subjectively, the main difference between merely dreaming or imagining something and remembering it, he believed, seems to be a difference between the absence and presence in the mind of items associated with the remembered thing. We may have a brief experience, for instance, which we describe as momentarily dreaming or imagining the vague details of a car accident, but as past associations accrue to this, the experience becomes one of recalling the vivid details of an actual accident. Introduction of the associations, James concluded, accounts for that change in experience, and he hypothesized that causal counterparts of those associations occur in the brain. But not all recollection, subjectively considered, fits the Jamesian model of associations that accumulate until the dawning of recall occurs. We may easily recall two or three notes of a melody but labor lengthily to remember their associates, or we may have to recall something else associated with the few remembered notes before we can remember the whole melody. We can thus seem to recall something immediately, before or without associates, and we may need to recall certain items before the associates come to mind. There are cases, then, when recollection is a condition of association, not vice versa. If we hypothesized from such subjective evidence about underlying conditions in the brain, we might reasonably suppose, contradicting James, that some specific memory trace in the brain, which underlies the recall, must be activated and in turn activates the cerebral associates that are responsible for our consciously remembering the associated items. We should then postulate a memory center in the brain which is a necessary condition for the arousal of brain associates, not vice versa.

James wrote as if he thought that associations in the brain are not only necessary but also sufficient conditions for remembering, as if he believed that for every recall there is a critical mass of associations in the brain. Given just that complex of associations, nothing else is required for conscious recollection. This situation may be an empirical possibility, but why should we credit it with any probability at all? To ask the kind of question that James himself liked to pose, why should associations in the brain yield anything but associations in the mind? Why should we accept James's claim that they yield memory as well? How can memories be generated from events that are always the cerebral counterparts of associations and never of memories? James's only reasons for claiming that such generation occurs is that it seems, subjectively, to happen that way and that remembering is not sui generis. According to his argument, there is no special feature of our experience described by the verb *recall* or *remember*, whereas there is for *associate* and similar terms. Whenever we are said to remember, we always find not only elements of belief, images, and so on, but also a complex of associations. Subjectively, associations always seem to accrete until they become a recollection. James urged that a similar process occurs cerebrally.

But if, as I have argued, remembering is sui generis, so that there is an experiential difference between recollecting and apprehending associations, then the difficulty remains. How can associations combine to constitute a memory? James himself agreed that a succession of ideas is not the same as an idea of succession.[22] Can a setting of associations be the same as the idea or memory of a setting of associations? At the very least, the Jamesian account must be modified to hold, not that associations literally accrete into a memory-experience, but that such accretion is a sufficient condition for the distinct, additional experience of recollecting. If we grant that the subjective facts are as James described them, that a study of our memory-experiences reveals associations as the only psychological causes of those experiences, we will find that the experience of recalling something follows an awareness of certain associations. Is it then reasonable to hypothesize, as James did, that a process in the brain both underlies and resembles the subjective process of conscious associations generating a conscious memory? A necessary ingredient is missing from James's physiological account: there must be something in the brain corresponding to the actual experience of recall. It is not enough to appeal to a sufficient number of associative paths in the brain that correspond causally to consciously apprehended associations, for these paths can at best constitute only the sufficient conditions for a recollection, not the recollection itself. The recalling is a distinct episode requiring a cerebral counterpart, perhaps some part of the brain being turned on by the activated paths of association. But James's speculative theory of the brain's underpinning of memory cannot include a specific place or mechanism for recall, because he viewed recall as only a complex of beliefs, images, and perceptions, triggered by a set of associations. Consequently, his theory settles for a system of associative paths in the brain as the mechanism of memory. It delineates the sufficient conditions—the associate paths—but not that for which they are sufficient—the cerebral process that underlies and corresponds to the conscious recollection itself. Whether formulated psychologically or physiologically, an accretion of associations is in itself just an accretion of associations, not at all like a memory.[23]

REMEMBERING AND FORGETTING

The search for the cerebral basis of memory was, for James, an essential part of psychology, which sought both to identify introspectively various states of consciousness and to correlate such states with their physiological conditions. In the case of memory, James had an additional reason for wanting to locate those conditions, however speculatively. He agreed with an unidentified correspondent's assessment: "Memory seems to me the most physical of intellectual powers. Bodily ease and freshness have much to do with it."[24] Remembering seems plainly dependent upon bodily condition. James elaborated upon the familiar fact that the capacity for remembering deteriorates with physical aging. If the evidence points to the dependence of memory upon brain-paths, it seems reasonable to suppose that a superior memory capacity results largely from the number and persistence of those brain-paths. The retentive nature of memory is more physiological, more brain-rooted, than is normally assumed.[25]

We hypothesize first, James argued, that the persistence or permanence of brain-paths is a physiological property of the relevant brain tissue, a part of one's genetic endowment; this persistence or permanence is the physiological retentiveness underlying long-term memory. James's concept of memory was largely physiological: "Some minds are like wax under a seal—no impression, however disconnected with others, is wiped out. Others, like a jelly, vibrate to every touch, but under usual conditions retain no permanent mark" (*Principles,* 1:659–60). The persistence of paths of association, upon which all remembering depends, are thus determined almost completely by physiological factors, and no amount of training or exercise can improve the capacity for remembering.

A modern psychologist, Carl Hovland, writes: "The first experimental attack on this problem was made by the American psychologist, William James. He determined to find out whether practicing the memorization of poetry really improved memorizing ability."[26] The results of James's self-experiment are given in the chapter on memory in *Principles.* He undertook to determine whether strenuous daily practice in learning one kind of poetry by heart can improve one's general ability to remember, as measured by the resulting time required to memorize an entirely different kind of poetry. Wondering whether the training effect of the first exercise would be transferred to the second, James devoted eight days to memorizing 158 lines of Victor Hugo's *Satyr;* the total time to achieve the memorization was 131 minutes, 10 seconds. He then spent twenty-odd minutes a day for thirty-eight days memorizing the first book of *Paradise Lost.* The test was to determine whether the training on Milton's poetry would shorten the time needed to memorize another 158 lines of Hugo's poem; in fact it took twenty minutes longer. This result confirmed James's hypothesis that general memory capacity cannot be improved by training; if it could, memory training on one task would likely shorten the time needed to cement a memory in a different task. James acknowledged the homespun nature of his self-experiment, volunteering that he had been "perceptibly fagged" with additional work during his second memorizing of Hugo, which might explain the slower rate of learning.[27] Nevertheless, on the basis of what others reported—including some of his students whom he persuaded to repeat his own experiment—he continued to assert the unchangeability of the native ability to remember. Hovland offers no devastating refutation of James here, settling for a caveat:

James' study was not ideally set up as an experiment and was therefore not conclusive, although it did set other investigators to studying the problem. We question whether James' learning was representative of all learning. We do not know that the first 158 lines were equal in difficulty to the second. We wonder whether James' physical condition was the same at the two times. (He himself says he was fagged out by other work at the time of the second learning.) We note that the effect of practice itself was not separated from transfer of training proper.[28]

But to hold that the general capacity for remembering is an unchangeable physiological trait is not to assert all improvement in remembering is impossible. For memory is due not only to the persistence of brain-paths but to their number as well. If the recall of something depends upon a given path, then the more such paths there are, the greater the probability of triggering the recall. If we can create more such cerebral routes in our brains, we will insure greater retentiveness. And we can increase the number of paths, James urged, by consciously forming as many associations as possible. "The 'secret of a good memory' is thus the secret of forming diverse and multiple associations with every fact we care to retain. But this forming of associations with a fact, what is it but *thinking about* the fact as much as possible? . . . *The one who* THINKS *over his experiences most,* and weaves them into systematic relations with each other, *will be the one with the best memory.*"[29] James realized that his claim does not stand without qualification. More recent experiments have shown that memorization succeeds if outlandish associations are avoided.[30] James presumably meant to obviate this difficulty by his reference to associations that are "woven" into "systematic relations." Associations that establish a systematic rapport with the fact to be remembered will not include the outlandish or farfetched. James was also aware of the objection that if too many associations are established with the fact to be remembered, the resulting interference or distraction may cause forgetting instead of remembering. "There are cases where too many paths, leading to too diverse associates, block each other's way, and all that the mind gets along with its object is a fringe of felt familiarity or sense that there *are* associates" (*Principles,* 1:673).

James makes a distinction between recognition and remembering. The latter is normally assumed to be a necessary condition of the former; one cannot recognize what one does not remember. On the other hand, we might argue that we can sometimes remember what we do not recognize; for example, we might remember someone without being able to recognize him. James drew a distinction that may strike the reader as odd; we can sometimes recognize something without remembering it. He thus rejected the normal assumption that remembering is a necessary condition of recognition. He cited Spencer in claiming that it is a misuse of the word *remember* to say, for instance, that we remember that fire burns, that the sun shines, or that we have two hands.[31] Some things are so familiar that it would be a strange use of the word to say they are remembered. If when someone mentioned our name we were to announce that we remembered it, our announcement would seem to be either a joke or a bizarre remark. James thought also that the word *remember* should not be applied to those experiences in which too many associations occur and "block each other's way, and all that the mind gets along with its object is a fringe of felt familiarity or sense that there are associates" (*Principles*, 1:673). As introspective proof of his claim, he gave a vivid autobiographical account of a return visit to a slaughterhouse. The associations aroused by the return were so intense and diverse that, though he recognized the place and some of its details, his mind was locked into the present assault of those associations, preventing any actual remembering of what his first visit had been like. The associations permitted only recognition; although the place seemed familiar, that familiarity blocked the remembering. This insight explains the déjà vu experience, which James thought results from associations that distract the mind, permitting only indistinct references to the past. The result is an overpowering sense of familiarity and recognition which falls short of remembering. Returning to his original claim, James argued that remembering a specific fact is improved by multiplying our associations with it, as long as the associations are not too numerous and their quality not outlandish or farfetched.

Discussions of memory typically refer to the pioneering work of Hermann Ebbinghaus, whose daily experimental labors for more than two years culminated in a classic publication in 1885.[32] Ebbinghaus tested the rates of learning and forgetting of random lists of nonsense syllables, which were chosen because they had no prior associations. The number of repetitions required for rote learning of a list yielded the measure of difficulty. After a subject learned the list, it was put aside for a time; Ebbinghaus discovered that a good deal of forgetting occurred in the first five minutes after the list had been laid aside. His measurements demonstrated that forgetting not only occurs much more rapidly in the first moments than in later ones, but that the rate of forgetting is calculable. Half of a list is forgotten within the first thirty minutes, two-thirds at the end of eight hours, but only four-fifths at the end of a month.[33] The curve representing the process of forgetting might even be said to indicate a "law of the mind." But despite his respect for this finding, James was more impressed by two other discoveries by Ebbinghaus.

The first is that the effect of the initial learning experience is never totally lost. No matter how long ago we learned a poem, no matter how poor our ability to recite it now, "yet the first learning will still show its lingering effects in the abridgment of the time required for learning it again" (*Talks*, 100). Ebbinghaus confirmed what James believed about the unconscious element in memory: things we cannot consciously recall can nevertheless influence our conscious memories and thoughts. "We are different for once having learned them. The resistances in our systems of brain-paths are altered. Our apprehensions are quickened. Our conclusions from certain premises are probably not just what they would be if those modifications were not there. The latter influence the whole margin of our consciousness, even though their products, not being distinctly reproducible, do not directly figure at the focus of the field" (*Talks*, 100). Herein, James urged, lies a practical lesson for teachers: do not treat a student who says he knows the answer but for some reason cannot articulate it as you would one who is totally ignorant of the answer. The student with forgotten learning may have something that the other has not, for such learning sometimes shows its effect. "Be patient, then, and sympathetic with the type of mind that cuts a poor figure in examinations. It may, in the long examination which life sets us, come out in the end in better shape than the glib and ready reproducer, its passions being deeper, its purposes more worthy, its combining power less commonplace, and its total mental output consequently more important" (*Talks,* 100). James characteristically located a moral in the technical details of a psychological hypothesis. He never wrote a systematic treatise on practical ethics, because he had expressed his ethical views in his psychology. He was mainly interested in psychological hypotheses and experiments that had pragmatic significance, those that contained lessons for living. The combined moral lessons that James found in psychology form a sizable body of practical ethics.

The second finding of Ebbinghaus that especially struck James concerns the association of ideas. Psychologists had debated the mode of association, wondering whether one idea can be related to another only if they are temporally contiguous, or whether ideas more remote from each other can be directly related in association. According to James, Ebbinghaus's experiments on remembering and forgetting showed conclusively that "an idea is not only 'associated' directly with the one that follows it, and with the rest *through that,* but that it is *directly* associated with *all* that are near it, though in unequal degrees" (*Principles,* 1:677). Suppose different syllables are represented by a number series. Ebbinghaus claimed to have shown that syllables as much as seven digits apart can be directly associated. James concluded from Ebbinghaus's report that association-in-consciousness may occur only between temporally contiguous ideas, but that association-in-memory or association in the brain need not be so limited. Ebbinghaus seemed to have shown that "association is subtler than consciousness, and that a nerve-process may, without producing consciousness, be effective in the same way in which consciousness would have seemed to be effective if it had been there" (*Principles,* 1:678). This point about the association of ideas clearly converges with the conclusion that the unconscious element in memory is remarkably influential. (James seems at some times to have meant a physiological and at others a psychological unconsciousness, but he always stressed the enduring effects of prior learning.)

It is interesting to compare James's view to contemporary evaluations of Ebbinghaus's investigations. Irvin Rock has focused upon Ebbinghaus's view that repetition is essential to rote learning—a natural conclusion, given the astonishing number of repetitions Ebbinghaus subjected himself to in memorizing list upon list of nonsense syllables. According to Rock, Ebbinghaus held that a single experience, without repetition, of two contiguous items establishes only a weak or partial connection between the two in the nervous system.[34] Repetition supposedly solidifies the neural connection such that a subject, upon presentation of the one item, will respond to the other. Using nonsense syllables and methods like those of Ebbinghaus, Rock tested the hypothesis that repetition is *not* essential to the formation of associations, that subjects should be able to learn items they have never experienced just as easily as items they have experienced but not learned or remembered. He concluded, on the basis of extensive experimentation, that the theory inherited from Ebbinghaus is in fact faulty; people form associations on one trial, learning and memory occur within a single experience, and repetition is essential not for forming neural and conscious connections but only for strengthening already established connections (Rock, 145–46). Repeating material already learned (sometimes called *overlearning*) certainly tends to inhibit forgetting. Rock suggests that such repetition does not help us to learn or remember as such, but is rather a device to represent for our attention items not learned or remembered earlier. What hinders remembering is interference; if we try to remember many details, attention to one interferes with attention to the others, and thus we are never able to learn or remember the details from which we were originally distracted. Interference may also explain forgetting. Benton Underwood has found that if a subject is given one list of syllables to memorize, he will forget only 20 percent, but if given two lists to learn, he will forget 60 percent on both. Forgetting has been increased by 40 percent, "and we must conclude that the reason is *interference* of one list with the other."[35] Repetition thus facilitates both learning and recall by reducing the amount of interference.

James, I think, would have found this theory acceptable. He certainly considered repetition to be essential for improving memory of particular facts and things (though not for improving basic memory capacity, which he believed is unchangeable). All possible improvement of memory, he concluded, consists in the improvement of habitual ways of noticing or recording particular facts or things.[36] Repetition plays an important role in this sort of improvement. I think James would have accepted Rock's claim that repetition strengthens but does not originally form connections; after all, he himself had noted that too much repetition causes interference, such that we can recognize something but not remember it.[37] In assessing memory techniques, James warned against trying to improve memory by "hammering in" what is to be remembered, repeating it again and again. He always emphasized, when commenting on how to improve recollection, that the art of remembering is the art of thinking. When we aim to fix something new in our own mind or a pupil's, "our conscious effort should not be so much to *impress* and *retain* it as to *connect* it with something else already there. The connecting *is* the thinking; and, if we attend clearly to the connection, the connected thing will certainly be likely to remain within recall" (*Talks*, 101–02). He emphasized that analysis of things, making a thoughtful connection of their properties and relations, will help to insure their remaining in memory. James would have been sympathetic to this statement by a modern psychologist: "Tentatively, therefore, we are justified in assuming that our memories are limited by the number of units or symbols we must master, and not by the amount of information that these symbols represent. Thus it is helpful to organize material intelligently before we try to memorize it. The process of organization enables us to package the same total amount of information into far fewer symbols, and so eases the task of remembering."[38] James came close to saying the same thing in his chapter on memory in *Talks to Teachers*. As usual, a practical tip attends the theorizing. Cramming is judged to be a bad memory technique, not to be recommended to students. The attempt to "hammer in" information intensely just before an examination does not work as well as continuous study, because cramming does not permit adequate connecting and associating. In short, it is too mechanical, too thoughtless.[39]

Before leaving the topic of memory, James noted the selective nature of most remembering. "Selection is the very keel on which our mental ship is built. And in this case of memory its utility is obvious. If we remembered everything, we should on most occasions be as ill off as if we remembered nothing" (*Principles*, 1:680). We cannot always identify the causes of this selectivity; nor can we always explain why we fail to recall what we try to, or why what ostensibly fails to interest us succeeds in being recalled. Conscious interest and intention explain some but not all memories. Yet for a general treatment of memory, it is not enough to mention only such factors as contiguity, repetition, and association. On many occasions the selective nature of recollecting, determined by interest and deliberate intention, explains a specific remembering. As James observed, we can sometimes set our memory to retain something for a precise period of time, then let it drop, perhaps forever, out of memory.[40]

James applauded the investigations of Ebbinghaus and others, and he never doubted the illumination gained from laboratory studies. But such studies were nevertheless bound, in his opinion, to remain fragmentary as explanations. It is difficult to study a mental faculty like memory in isolation from other faculties, dispositions, and traits.[41] In life, he insisted, our memory usually serves some interest, some concern, perhaps a true passion. Passionate interest can sometimes mobilize the memory for a specific task. "This preponderance of interest, of passion, in determining the results of a human being's working life, obtains throughout. No elementary measurement, capable of being performed in a laboratory, can throw any light on the actual efficiency of the subject; for the vital thing about him, his emotional and moral energy and doggedness, can be measured by no single experiment, and becomes known only by the total results in the long run" (*Talks*, 97). James made an important connection between memory and intelligence by equating the art of memory with the art of thinking and by asserting that the condition for good memory is often the ability to organize logically the material to be remembered. But teachers must beware, he warned, of relying on pedantic measurements of memory in evaluating the intellectual worth of their pupils. They must look rather to total performance, remembering that measurements "can give us useful information only when we combine them with observations made without brass instruments, upon the total demeanor of the measured individual, by teachers with eyes in their heads and common sense, and some feeling for the concrete facts of human nature in their hearts" (*Talks*, 98).

James added that we should speak not as if there were a single faculty called memory, but rather as if there were many memories. People differ in their capacities for visual, tactile, muscular, and auditory memory. "We have, then, not so much a faculty of memory as many faculties of memory. We have as many as we have systems of objects habitually thought of in connection with each other."[42] It is difficult, if not impossible, to generalize about all systems of memory. But James believed that the most general condition governing forgetting and remembering in all memory-modalities is subjective interest. Whether muscular or visual, auditory or tactile, we remember for the most part what interests us.

7 ❧ ATTENTION AND WILL

THE PSYCHOLOGY OF ATTENTION

In discussing memory, James said that attention to something will facilitate recollection of it. But what is *attention?* He thought that the British empiricists—Locke, Hume, Hartley, the Mills, and Spencer—had largely ignored this question, because they were committed to explaining higher mental functions, including attention, as derivative of more primitive, experiential data. One therefore had to turn to German psychology for information about what occurs when a person selectively attends to something. James's complaint that attention had been ignored by psychologists has been reiterated in our own time. As introspective psychology declined and a combination of behaviorism and positivism became the prevalent theory in academic psychology during the first half of the twentieth century, the concept of attention—which was often considered the peculiar offspring of introspective psychology—ceased to figure prominently in the literature. By the 1970s, however, the concept was resurrected, and today's psychologists have reasserted its importance for professional psychology.[1]

Today's reader must anticipate a certain amount of archaic and uninteresting detail in the chapter on attention in *Principles.* A specialized interest is needed to endure James's extensive reviews of experimental research, conducted primarily in German laboratories, and his speculations about the physiological processes thought to cause different varieties of attention. Yet Donald Broadbent, a modern psychologist who has helped to revive the concept of attention, argues that James's chapter is still a valuable source of information and insight. For example, James contends that voluntary attention, unlike involuntary attention, cannot be continuous because it requires an alternation of attention and inattention. Broadbent considers this observation "a remark of great insight, as is the whole of James's chapter." He later writes, "A work such as that of William James points out repeatedly the facts which are painfully restated in our different and unfamiliar terms. . . . It is striking to compare James's statements about attention, made on the basis of everyday observation and introspection, with the theory of filtered information flow set out in this book, and based on artificial experiments. The great value of the traditional approach is that it points out a phenomenon of importance and does not allow it to be forgotten."[2] The main disadvantage of the traditional approach, Broadbent suggests, is its reliance upon everyday rather than scientific concepts; its language is vague and susceptible to misinterpretation. But whatever his shortcomings, James emphasized the importance of attention, a topic as philosophical as it is psychological.

James raises three major philosophical questions in his treatment of attention. The first is whether attending is a mental or a physical activity, whether an analysis of attention supports a Cartesian dualism. This question has been rediscovered in modern philosophy and debated along the lines of James's discussions.[3] The second question is whether attention can be a free rather than a forced activity, and the third is whether an essential connection exists between attention and will. The third question requires our looking at James's treatment of habit, instinct, and effort, or what we might call his theory of motivation. But first we must review the ways in which attention, as James saw it, is significant for psychology.

Herbert Spencer, the last representative of British empiricism, had conceptualized human experience as a passive response to a given external order. James alleged that Spencer had described perceptual experience as the mere presence to the senses of an external world, the percipient being "absolutely passive clay upon which 'experience' rains down" (*Principles*, 1:403). James had attacked this conception years before writing *Principles*, and throughout his career he insisted that we are capable of active contributions to the make-up of our own experience.[4] Unlike Kant, he did not construe those contributions in terms of a complicated mental machinery but settled instead for a simpler explanation involving interest and attention. He would have endorsed enthusiastically today's critics of standard stimulus-response theories, who argue that what is occurring in the black box must figure also in the explanation. The properties of experiences must be registered as well as those of stimulus and response in order to explain the nature of those experiences. "Millions of items of the outward order are present to my senses which never properly enter into my experience. Why? Because they have no *interest* for me. *My experience is what I agree to attend to.* Only those items which I *notice* shape my mind—without selective interest, experience is an utter chaos. Interest alone gives accent and emphasis, light and shade, background and foreground—intelligible perspective, in a word" (*Principles*, 1:402). Our interest and attention make our experiences more than they are made by them. The nature of an experience is not merely a function of presented stimuli but is also the result of our interests, which lead us to attend to things in a specialized manner. James was fond of saying that attention is a highly selective process and that we tend to experience what we select from all available presented stimuli.

Everyone, James said, knows what it is like to attend or to pay heed to something, even though we may disagree about the best formulation of it. Attending is essentially a focusing or concentrating of consciousness. "It implies withdrawal from some things in order to deal effectively with others, and is a condition which has a real opposite in the confused, dazed, scatter-brained state which in French is called *distraction,* and *Zerstreutheit* in German" (*Principles,* 1:404). When this state of vacancy or inattention is broken and something particular comes to the fore of our consciousness, we say that our attention has been awakened. This description of attention suffices for psychological purposes. One question has always engaged psychologists and philosophers: How many things can we attend to simultaneously? The real question for James and others was less how many things we can attend to at once than whether we can ever attend to more than one thing at a time. The unity of the soul or of consciousness seemed to many theorists to conflict with the notion that attentive consciousness can be devoted to many things, suggesting a priori reasons for denying that we can heed more than one thing at the same moment. A hypothesis that appeared on the one hand to be testable seemed doomed by a priori arguments on the other hand. Although the question might well appear answerable on the basis of introspective tests, it was never resolved to everyone's satisfaction by such tests. Introspective psychology heightened the interest in the question by being unable to resolve it.

James would not have agreed that experiments had failed to resolve the issue of simultaneous attention. He mentioned the demonstrated abilities of individuals to "double the mind" by simultaneously performing two easy and heterogeneous operations, for example, reciting a poem while making arithmetical calculations on paper. The evidence indicated, he thought, that attention may, though it need not, oscillate between the two activities. If the question is really how many "disconnected systems or processes of conception can go on simultaneously, the answer is, *not easily more than one, unless the processes are very habitual; but then two, or even three, without very much oscillation of attention"* (*Principles,* 1:409). But if the processes are less automatic or more homogeneous, an increasingly rapid oscillation of attention is demanded. But one problem running throughout James's discussion is the difficulty of specifying what counts as a single or simultaneous act of attention. Does the blink of an eye terminate a visual heeding, the notice of a new sound represent the beginning of a new attentiveness? Without specific guidelines, we are bound to feel uncertain whether a subtle oscillation of attention occurs within one act of attention or signals the onset of another. James seems not to have appreciated this difficulty, for he never mentioned the methodological dilemma it posed for the introspective experiments on attention during the late nineteenth century. James did seek to clarify the concept of a present moment in his treatment of the specious present (see chapter 5). But the present moment is not the same as a single act of attention, for if the present moment is taken as the specious present, then many successive acts of attention can occur within it. Although James attempted to specify, in his notion of the specious present, what counts as a single experience within which temporal succession is simultaneously perceived, this concept is unrelated to that of a single act of attention. Yet the two concepts were presupposed to be identical

in nineteenth-century psychology. It is not surprising, then, that experimental conclusions on this issue—including James's—were uncertain or vague.[5]

Nevertheless, certain observations about simultaneous or virtually simultaneous attending are intriguing. For instance, attention to one sensation tends to
interfere with the awareness of another, such that a surgeon may see blood flow
before he cuts the skin or a blacksmith may see sparks before he sees his hammer
strike the iron. The expectant attention, focusing upon one sensation, can displace
other sensations so that they appear later. It is difficult, therefore, to notice the exact
moment of two dissimilar sensations which do not engage our attention equally.
Exner and Wundt designed experiments to obtain more precise information about
virtually simultaneous heeding. Exner tried to determine how attention must be set
in order to notice the interval and correct order of sensations occurring a short
interval apart. He discovered, according to James, that two techniques of attending
are available. When the sensations are alike, such as two similar sounds, we can wait
for the one that occurs first. Exner's introspections disclosed that he noticed the first
sound, then identified or classified it slightly later while remembering it; if the
interval between the sounds was large enough, he might notice the second but not be
able to identify it clearly. If the interval was too short, however, the two sounds could
not be distinguished at all. The second technique is to prepare our attention for a
certain kind of impression, then to recall after its occurrence whether it came before
or after another, virtually simultaneous impression. This device is most convenient
in judging dissimilar impressions, but Exner declared that it tends to yield uncertain
or wrong judgments. The impression for which attention is not prepared is usually
hard to recall, and we are inclined always to judge that the expected impression
occurs first. Exner observed an exception, however, for in his experiments "from
touch to sight it often seemed to me as if the impression for which the attention was
not prepared were there already when the other came."[6] When two signals at a very
short interval are identified, they are simply noticed as the same signal twice, with no
distinction of priority. But Exner's experiments required that each of two signals be
associated with a different moment of time, so that in the subject's memory each
might be distinguished by its temporal position relative to the other.[7] James added:
"It is the simplest possible case of two discrepant concepts simultaneously occupying
the mind" (*Principles*, 1:410), by which he meant that the most simple example of
simultaneous heeding occurs when we remember simultaneously two things that
did not occur simultaneously.

Wundt studied what happens when signals or impressions are perceived as
simultaneous. If two signals really occur simultaneously and do not differ much in
strength or intensity, then we have little difficulty dividing our attention between
them at one time. According to Wundt's findings, we tend to want to make our
reaction coincide with an anticipated stimulus or signal. "We seek to make our own
feelings of touch and innervation [muscular contraction] objectively *contempo-
raneous with the signal* which we hear; and experience shows that in many cases we
approximately succeed. In these cases we have a distinct consciousness of hearing

the signal, reacting upon it, and feeling our reaction take place,—all at one and the same moment."[8] Wundt observed that it is generally difficult and often impossible to reduce our reaction time such that we experience the signal and our reaction to it as simultaneous:

> The comparative infrequency with which the reaction-time can be made thus to disappear shows how hard it is, when our attention is intense, to keep it fixed even on *two* different ideas at once. . . . One always tried to bring the ideas into a certain connection, to grasp them as components of a certain complex representation. Thus in the experiments in question, it has often seemed to me that I produced by my own recording movement the sound which the ball made in dropping on the board.[9]

Although he granted that attention can be divided between two simultaneous impressions, Wundt concluded that when attention is concentrated or when impressions are not simultaneous, we tend either to focus on one thing at the expense of others or to apprehend two or more things as aspects of one seeming composite object. Like other contemporary psychologists, he emphasized that the distorting influence of intense attention can make our reaction appear to precede the signal.

There were several reasons for the interest in such experiments in late-nineteenth-century psychology and philosophy. Attention seemed to be a subjective activity affecting our perception of things and thus worth investigating. Understanding its nature and function is still crucial for deciding among materialistic, epiphenomenalistic, and dualistic theories of the mind. That the ability to heed or concentrate appears autonomous and voluntary complicates any effort to explain human experience simply by stimulus and response. Experiments on attention were thought to be fine examples of what psychologists ought to be doing—investigating the contents and workings of the mind. Psychologists such as Wundt and Exner showed that aspects of consciousness can be altered by the activity of heeding and determined the conditions under which attention can occur effectively. Introspection seemed invaluable as a direct access to the contents of awareness, and thus psychology was distinct from the other sciences, which relied on sense-perception rather than introspection. Newly designed experiments were safeguards for checking and improving the indispensable yet fallible process of introspecting. Wundt and Exner brought introspective psychology into the laboratory, succeeding, for instance, in checking the judgments of their experimental subjects about simultaneous attention. Struck by the systematic correlation between the subjective reports of attentive subjects and the conditions under which those reports were made, they believed that they were pioneering a new science. Wundt wrote: "Although my own experiments extend over many years (with interruptions), they are not even yet numerous enough to exhaust the subject—still, they bring out the principal laws which the attention follows under such conditions."[10] James disputed Wundt's claim; he acknowledged the promise of experimental psychology and insisted that it must develop in the laboratory into a genuine science, but at the same time he complained about the tedium of German psychology, its immersion in monotonous details, and its failure to uncover even a single elementary law.[11] It is easy to be skeptical of James's optimistic pronouncements on the scientific future of psychology, given his private reservations about the value of what experiments had revealed and given his conviction that many urgent psychological issues are in part philosophical and thus cannot be resolved in the laboratory. For James, the main contribution of experimental research on attention was its confirmation of the importance of a concept he had long favored.

Psychological investigations assume at the outset an everyday understanding of attention, but before the varieties of attending can be classified or its characteristic effects catalogued, experimental data must be sorted through. Even the question of whether heeding is an activity depends on introspective testing. James's introspections showed that attending can be an activity or "a sort of action" (*Principles*, 1:415). Those of E. B. Titchener revealed that attention is not an activity at all but a state of affective consciousness.[12] This issue points up the difficulty of elaborating the everyday meaning of psychological concepts, in the hope of winning the approval of one's colleagues, before the experimental scene has been reviewed. James took care to supply his readers with the data from which he constructed his own answer to the question of what attention is. Heeding, he thought, is either immediate or derived, immediate when the stimulus or object is interesting or compelling in itself, derived when the stimulus or object is interesting by association with something immediately interesting. He contrasted passive or reflexive heeding with the active or voluntary variety: "*Voluntary attention is always derived;* we never make an *effort* to attend to an object except for the sake of some *remote* interest which the effort will serve."[13] If we find an object intrinsically or immediately intriguing, then, since it is absurd to conceive of making an effort to attend to something that has already engaged our attention, our attending must be passive or involuntary. But this claim conflicts with our everyday supposition that we voluntarily heed things that are intrinsically interesting. Each time we stand before a favorite painting in a museum, our attending is certainly voluntary. James requires that some effort must be built into any voluntary attending, but upon reflection such a requirement seems gratuitous. To ignore this objection might lead us, as it seems to have led James, to the bizarre conclusion that aesthetic enjoyment results entirely from our attention's being seized and is never the result of our attention's being voluntarily, deliberately directed.[14]

James and many of his contemporaries were impressed by the way attention can alter our perceptions, experiences, and attitudes. "Suffice it . . . that each of us literally *chooses,* by his way of attending to things, what sort of a universe he shall appear to himself to inhabit" (*Principles,* 1:424). How the world appears to us is a function of how we attend to it, how we select some features for notice and others for exclusion. James did not suppose that we always choose freely what we heed, and he considered one of the main achievements of attention involuntary. Attending instinctively and involuntarily fragments the wholes or complexes that we originally experience. Our perceptions first come to us in blocks, in James's view (which was explicitly opposed to the psychic atomism of the British empiricists), and the parts and details of those blocks appear only to successive acts of heeding. Attending carves a detailed, fragmented world from the continuous flux of unities or wholes that originally confront us. Our motives for this dissection of the flux are instinctual and practical; we need to fragment the original flow of gestalten in order to survive and to control our environment. Attention evolved as an indispensable instrument for coping with our surroundings; without it we could never perceive a world of discrete objects as we do. James was therefore being literal when he said that we choose, through what we heed, the kind of world we seem to inhabit.[15] James warned against the misinterpretation of conceiving of attention as an activity that either creates or analyzes things. "Attention *creates* no idea; an idea must already be there before we can attend to it. Attention only fixes and retains."[16] A survey of the experimental data and literature shows that attending is both uncreative and un-analytical. "The attention *per se* does not distinguish and analyze and relate. The most we can say is that it is a condition of our doing so" (*Principles*, 1:426). If we attend to two adjacent colors, for example, we may succeed in seeing them more clearly and distinctly. Whereas our heeding is a condition of that success, it is not itself responsible, if James was correct, for discriminating and comparing the two colors. Some other faculty or human ability must be credited with that accomplishment.[17]

Since attending is so important throughout human experience, psychologists and philosophers have naturally pondered when and how it is voluntary. Much of our heeding happens independently of our volitions; we may find ourselves wondering why we attend to certain things. In describing typical causes or motives of our heeding, James referred to J. F. Herbart's once-famous concept of apperception. Herbart, who succeeded to Kant's chair in philosophy at Königsberg in 1803, used Leibniz's term *apperception* to designate the process by which we typically notice or recognize something.[18] According to Herbart, we heed an object, sensation, or idea because of our established mental complex of memories and associations. Our interest in the objects of our attention results from this complex, which Herbart called the apperceiving mass. "Apperceptive attention may be plainly observed in very small children when, hearing the speech of their elders, as yet unintelligible to them, they suddenly catch a single known word here and there, and repeat it to themselves."[19] James offered the example of a faint tapping, uninteresting in itself, which suddenly arrests the hearer's attention when her apperceiving mass causes her to recognize it as her lover's signal on the windowpane.[20] James believed that Herbart's concept was an important contribution to traditional accounts of association and was helpful in explaining the causes of heeding, especially of passive heeding. Herbart's theory also helps to explain how voluntary attention can be sustained. But James distinguished apperception from attention more sharply than did Herbart; he made the distinction more clearly in *Talks to Teachers* than in *Principles*. In referring to attention as the concentration of consciousness, he wrote: "This concentrated type of attention is an elementary faculty: it is one of the things that might be ascertained and measured by exercises in the laboratory" (*Talks,* 85). On the other hand, apperception is "nothing more than the act of taking a thing into the mind. It corresponds to nothing peculiar or elementary in psychology, being only one of the innumerable results of the psychological process of association of ideas" (*Talks,* 109). James viewed apperception as an association of ideas; it can theoretically be assimilated, he thought, into a dynamic or mechanical model of the brain. In short, apperception is a mechanical cerebral function, not a distinct psychological act that can be introspected or identified as such in laboratory studies.

James took his exploration of the connection between apperception and attention in several directions. He assumed that active or volitional heeding is characterized by a determined effort. Introspection shows, he claimed, that one of the most difficult tasks we can undertake is to maintain such effort, to sustain an act of voluntary heeding. In fact, any instance of deliberate attending is really an ongoing succession of efforts to keep the object of attention in the forefront of consciousness. He insisted on a position, endorsed in our own time by Broadbent, that voluntary attending cannot be maintained continuously. In fact, if we attend to an unchanging visual or auditory object, it will become invisible or inaudible.[21] For support, James cited the experiments of Helmholtz, especially those that displayed the phenomenon of retinal rivalry. Helmholtz showed that it is difficult to attend simultaneously to both the left and right pictures in a stereoscopic slide; instead, our attention alternates between them or simultaneously notices only parts of each. He described the severe limits of what he could deliberately heed, remarking that we inherently tend to wander to new things; if we want to sustain our attention we may have to ask ourselves fresh questions about our object in order to create renewed interest in it.[22] James applauded the development of this technique as an insight of immense practical significance; he thought the procedure should be recommended to teachers and students, as usual setting out the practical applications of the theoretical work of psychology.[23] Helmholtz's suggestion works, James thought, because in generating new interest in the heeded object by asking new questions about it, we fuel the processes of apperception, adding to the associations that can focus our attention on the heeded object. Voluntary attention thus exploits apperceptive processes, which are equally effective with active and passive attention.

A fairly obvious objection to the Helmholtz-James theory appears to be supported by experimental evidence. Just as an increased number of associations can lead our attention to the heeded object, so can they lure our attention from it. Recent investigations suggest that the inferior cognitive performances of schizophrenic patients sometimes result from impairment in attention—a conclusion different from earlier ones that attributed this poor performance to an inability to think abstractly or to form concepts.[24] Norman Cameron's studies, for instance, show that schizophrenics can formulate concepts well enough, but that their concepts are based either upon irrelevant, peripheral properties of the heeded object or task or upon highly personal associations. One of Cameron's patients grouped together such objects as knife, fork, and fountain-pen, explaining that "you go to the fountain to drink after you have eaten your dinner and the water has to be piped out.'' Another patient, asked to assemble wooden blocks according to size, shape, and color, responded by concentrating on insignificant details like scratches and irregularities in the blocks. ''Cameron suggested that the schizophrenic patient suffered, not from impoverishment in concept formation, but rather from an over-abundance of loose concepts of his own making. He referred to the schizophrenic patient's 'inability to preserve conceptual boundaries' and put forward the term *overinclusive* to describe this feature of schizophrenic thinking.''[25] The Helmholtz-James theory fails to provide for the overinclusiveness that can accompany the accumulation of mental associations. The theory offers no psychological account of how relevance is recognized, how the relevant connections between a heeded object and its associations are sustained in attention, or how attending mainly to pertinent details distinguishes genius. However, in his efforts to show that volition can help attention, James included the apperceptive technique of adding associations that will rekindle interest in the heeded object only as one of a number of recommendations for varying circumstances.

James did not believe that piling up associations will by itself always sustain attention, so he offered another remedy for mind-wandering. ''If attention be the reproduction of the sensation from within, the habit of reading not merely with the ear, but of articulating to one's self the words seen or heard, ought to deepen one's attention to the latter. Experience shows that this is the case. I can keep my wandering mind a great deal more closely upon a conversation or a lecture if I actively re-echo to myself the words than if I simply hear them'' (*Principles*, 1:447). James appealed to this new description of attention as the reproduction of sensation to explain why repeating words to oneself tends to focus attention on them. He seems not to have worried about the apparent contradiction between this description and his claim that attending is not a creative or analytic activity; he meant, I think, not to redefine attending but rather to describe a process that occurs in experiences of attending. James was convinced that there are close ties between sensation, imagination, and attention. When he connected the introspectable experience of attending with its physiological conditions, he emphasized two processes: first, the accommodation or adjustment of the sense-organs, and secondly, a complicated bodily state involving muscular adjustments, certain brain-states, and messages from the brain to various parts of the body. These two processes correspond, respectively, to the psychological act of attending to something and the expectation of or preparation for that attending. Relying upon the research of many investigators, James concluded that voluntary attention involves both a preparation or expectancy and a disposition to ignore other things. He concluded also that imagining beforehand what will be attended to is an important if not essential feature of our expectant attentiveness. Wundt had shown that prior imagination of an object facilitates attention to it when presented—and that this imagining can make us think we see the thing before it is presented—prompting James to comment: ''The peculiar theoretic interest of these experiments lies in their *showing expectant attention and sensation to be continuous or identical processes, since they may have identical motor effects''* (*Principles*, 1:429). Because James compared imagination and sensation, it was incumbent upon him to connect expectant attentiveness, which he construed as expectant imagining, with sensation—both subjectively and physiologically.

James was overly enthusiastic in accepting the judgments of experimenters such as Exner, Wundt, and George Lewes and in concluding that expectant attentiveness "always partly consists of the creation of an imaginary duplicate of the object in the mind, which shall stand ready to receive the outward impression as if in a matrix."[26] This claim is exaggerated, for our efforts to attend to something are sometimes unaccompanied by any imaginary duplicate. Nevertheless, prior imagining is often a feature of expectant attentiveness and usually facilitates attention to and recognition of the anticipated object. It is interesting to consider his reasons for the hyperbolic claim that a "reinforcing imagination" is universally present in attention. He seems to have reasoned as follows: if imagining is always an introspectable factor in attentively anticipating something, then we have a theoretical explanation for practical suggestions for sustaining our attention. At the experiential level we know that our imagination can, by reproducing the sounds of words, help make them clearer and more distinct, and thus prolong our attention to them. If imagination and sensation connect so well subjectively, they must be closely associated physiologically as well. James thought that the evidence of introspective psychology substantiated the hypothesis that expectant attention or anticipatory imagination and sensation are continuous or identical physiological processes. Introspective details were important to James in identifying as fully as possible the states of consciousness of attention, emotion, imagination, and memory. But he considered such details important also because they provide clues for identifying the physiological processes with which those states of consciousness are supposedly correlated. He never doubted that introspection, which is indispensable for illuminating our subjective states, also provides an idea of what happens in our bodies when we remember, feel emotion, or attend.

According to this interpretation, *Principles* represents traditional psychophysical parallelism, a theory that bodily processes, which either cause of accompany subjective experiences, match in substantial detail those experiences. Time-reaction experiments on attention showed, James thought, that we tend to answer a question more quickly if we have directed our advance attention toward the answer rather than the question. In such experiments, James observed, the subject always knew at least generally what kind of question he would be asked, or

> the *sphere within which* his possible answer lay. In turning his attention, therefore, from the outset towards the answer, those brain-processes in him which were connected with this entire "sphere" were kept sub-excited, and the question could then discharge with a minimum amount of lost time that particular answer out of the "sphere" which belonged especially to it. When, on the contrary, the attention was kept looking towards the question exclusively and

averted from the possible reply, all this preliminary sub-excitement of motor tracts failed to occur, and the entire process of answering had to be gone through with *after* the question was heard. No wonder that the time was prolonged. It is a beautiful example of the summation of stimuli.[27]

James envisaged a close parallel between introspectable experience and its bodily "seat," notable here in the way that *sphere* is used for both. *Principles* is redolent of such examples. Wundt had argued that it takes a certain time for something to impress itself upon us while we wait attentively; when it does, our attention adapts to it with respect to both its intensity and its quality. James commented: "The natural way of conceiving all this is under the symbolic form of a brain-cell played upon from two directions. Whilst the object excites it from without, other brain-cells, or perhaps spiritual forces, arouse it from within. The latter influence is the 'adaptation' of the attention. *The plenary energy of the brain-cell demands the co-operation of both factors:* not when merely present, but when both present and attended to, is the object fully perceived" (*Principles*, 1:441).

In light of this sort of reasoning, it is easy to interpret *Principles* as a defense of traditional psychophysical parallelism. But a curious aspect of this parallelism, together with other considerations, forces an important qualification of this interpretation. James's speculations about the physiological correlations of states of consciousness give the impression that he did not cite actual or hypothetical facts about the brain or nervous system merely to locate the physiological causes of conscious states; rather, he often viewed physiological processes as models for understanding states of consciousness. In discussing the stream of thought, he sought to explain how intention connects with linguistic meaning: "Nothing is easier than to symbolize all these facts in terms of brain-action" (*Principles*, 1:257). If we consider a state of consciousness in terms of a conceptual framework taken from biology, James suggested, we may get a superior picture of its nature. The biological perspective is sometimes urged as a corrective to a view that he thought is mistaken; for example, he argued that identical sensations, as theorized by Locke, cannot recur because every sensation corresponds to some brain-state, and brain-states are continually changing.[28] He invoked the biological perspective for rounding out a description of conscious experiences, filling in details perhaps inaccessible to introspection. Although the experiences associated with purposeful thinking may not disclose anything persistent to introspection, James argued: "Physiologically considered, we must suppose that a purpose means the persistent activity of certain rather definite brain-processes throughout the whole course of thought" (*Principles*, 1:583). Speculation about the details of those brain-processes is often tantamount in James's writings to speculation about what is happening within associated experiences. (This reading certainly conflicts with the *esse est sentiri* doctrine of states of consciousness, but both views, contradictory as they are, seem present in *Principles*.)

According to James's psychophysical parallelism, introspection affords clues about what is occurring in parallel brain-processes, and vice versa. Following

James's development of this two-way information flow, one almost forgets that both mental and physical processes are involved; it often seems as if only one process were being described, sometimes in mental and sometimes in physical terms. Perhaps James's doubts about psychophysical parallelism, hinted at now and then in *Principles* and later aired officially in the radical empiricism, arose from a realization that James was himself inclined to forget that two processes were allegedly involved. His earliest vision of an alternative to psychophysical dualism may have occurred at the moment he sensed that he had construed mind-body parallelism so tightly and intimately—it was after all easy to interchange mental and physical descriptions of experiences—that there was actually just one process involved. In *Principles* he was officially a spokesman for dualism and for psychophysical parallelism, but unofficially he was unhappy with any form of dualism and eventually developed the metaphysics of radical empiricism as an alternative. In writing on attention, for example, he seems to have thought that the language of introspection and that of physiology may actually refer to only one process—and here the psychological discussion of attention begins to merge with the philosophical.

PHILOSOPHICAL QUESTIONS

James took as a starting point his experiential finding that heeding is a phenomenon that can be introspected, dated, and described; he classified it alternately under activities and feelings.[29] In defining attention, he tried to convey fully its phenomenological content; he described the subjective effects of being perceptually attentive thus: "The result is a more or less massive organic feeling that attention is going on. This organic feeling comes . . . to be contrasted with that of the objects which it accompanies, and regarded as peculiarly ours, whilst the objects form the not-me. We treat it as a sense of our *own activity,* although it comes in to us from our organs after they are accommodated."[30] There are other ways of describing the introspectable details: "As our hands may hold a bit of wood and a knife, and yet do naught with either; so our mind may simply be aware of a thing's existence, and yet neither attend to it nor discriminate it, neither locate nor count nor compare nor like nor dislike nor deduce it, nor recognize it articulately as having been met with before. At the same time we know that, instead of staring at it in this entranced and senseless way, we may rally our activity in a moment, and locate, class, compare, count, and judge it" (*Principles,* 1:481–82). We can get a better grasp of what heeding is like if we reflect on how it differs from mere awareness.

Another feature of attending is that when we concentrate intensely on a spot of color, for example, the color may seem to come closer and to become more vivid and distinct, and its surroundings may appear to blur; such changes definitely seem to be our own doing. As James and Fechner emphasized, the intensification of an object's appearance as a result of concentrated attending does not usually confuse our perceptual judgment. There are changes in vividness and distinctness, but as Fechner said, "A gray paper appears to us no lighter, the pendulum-beat of a clock no louder, no matter how much we increase the strain of our attention upon them. No one, by doing this, can make the gray paper look white, or the stroke of the pendulum sound like the blow of a strong hammer—everyone, on the contrary, feels the increase as that of his own conscious activity turned upon the thing."[31] We are aware of changes in the amount or degree of our attentiveness, itself an important introspectable detail.

Attendings certainly occur, but it is not possible to provide a philosophical analysis or reduction of the concept of attention more basic than what James and others have said. There are no elementary or primitive concepts in terms of which attention can be analyzed; as James said, certain psychological terms such as *attend* and *believe* are, like color-words, not expressible in other, more basic concepts. One must experience attending to know what it is like, just as one must see the color blue to understand what it is.

Having rallied behind the notion that attending is an elementary psychological activity which can only be known experientially, James had to decide whether the activity of attending is mental or physiological. Does the phenomenon of heeding support Cartesian dualism? James's answer was somewhat complex, not a simple yes or no. Because he characterized attending as an organic feeling caused by the muscular adaptations of the sense-organs, it might seem that he leaned toward materialism or physicalism.[32] But in that characterization, James was referring to involuntary attention that results from sensory stimulation, so we must ask whether an intellectual heeding is purely mental or at least partly physiological. In "The Consciousness of Self" James declared that the most intellectual exercises have physiological aspects; this statement holds for intellectual attending. His judgment that attending is not purely mental (that is, without important bodily events) was based upon extravagant introspections, the reports of which amuse as they instruct. He cited Fechner as having been the first to illuminate introspectively the bodily feelings that seem to be vital aspects of intellectual attentiveness. Fechner had described the "straining" of attention as a feeling which, when directed toward presented objects, is felt to be forward; when recalling something by intellectual attention, we have a sense not of straining our attention forward but of retracting it backward. James agreed: "In myself the 'backward retraction' which is felt during attention to ideas of memory, etc., seems to be principally constituted by the feeling of an actual rolling outwards and upwards of the eyeballs, such as occurs in sleep, and is the exact opposite of their behavior when we look at a physical thing."[33]

In their introspective efforts, Fechner and James both concluded that the central feeling of attending (intellectual or sensory) is essentially connected with bodily processes. It is typical of James's thinking throughout *Principles* to conclude that all mental activities seem, upon introspection, to require physiological involvements. His treatment of attention parallels his famous theory that emotions are always bodily commotions. But he did not hold that introspection conclusively establishes a necessary connection between mental activity and bodily events. His chapter on attention implicitly supports this reading, although he usually focused upon the question of whether attention is ever given freely; explicit textual evidence for this reading occurs in the chapter on the consciousness of self. In summarizing his introspections about what it is like to be intimately aware of oneself, he wrote that what "is most vividly felt turns out to consist for the most part of a collection of cephalic movements of 'adjustments' which, for want of attention and reflection, usually fail to be perceived and classed as what they are; that over and above these there is an obscurer feeling of something more; but whether it be of fainter physiological processes, or of nothing objective at all, but rather of subjectivity as such, of thought become 'its own object,' must at present remain an open question" (*Principles*, 1:305). This idea recurs throughout *Principles*, either explicitly or implicitly, and can be taken to be the book's official position. Introspection, when carefully performed, reveals more bodily involvement within mental activity than was appreciated by traditional psychology and philosophy. That idea does not necessarily imply, however, that bodily events wholly constitute any mental activity, much less every such activity. James asserted that attending, thinking, feeling, and remembering may have purely mental, nonphysical components, but that he could not support that belief with adequate grounds. Introspection yields no decisive answers; while we use it to locate relevant physiological detail accompanying mental activities, it alone is not a means of deciding whether such detail is essential to those mental activities. We sometimes seem through introspection to detect something more than bodily processes, but whether we in fact do remains unclear. In the end, James saw the question of whether the feeling or experience of attending contains a purely mental or totally nonphysical element as a nonexperimental question.[34] If we allow for "experiments in the imagination," then it is better to say that James thought the question could not be resolved in the laboratory. Remarks in the chapters on consciousness of self and emotion suggest that he conducted experiments in the imagination in this way: he noted introspectively how, for example, terror feels, then asked his imagination to decide whether the emotion could occur and feel as it did if there were no increase in blood pressure or heart palpitations. His imagination responded negatively. But when he asked it to decide whether there is anything purely mental in the emotion of terror, the response merely sent him back to his original introspections, which only suggested the presence of a nonphysical element. When he construed the question of whether attending is a purely mental activity as the question of whether the feeling or experience is constituted by bodily events, it ceased to be a laboratory problem, although it continued to be a haunting issue to be grappled with philosophically.

Though he never clearly stated it, James supposed that the question of whether attending is ever purely mental can be construed as an experimental question when attending is conceived less in its subjective role as a feeling and more in its objective function as an achievement. Consider, for instance, his remarks on experiments by Helmholtz and Hering pertaining to peripheral or marginal heeding. James was intrigued by the fact that these investigations indicated that a subject can learn to attend to a marginal object without moving his eyes. This finding suggested that marginal attention need not involve the musculature of the eyes or the usual accom-modations of the sense-organs, leading the experimenters to ask whether any bodily processes are involved. But Helmholtz concluded: "In this respect, then, our atten-tion is quite independent of the position and accommodation of the eyes, and of any known alteration in these organs; and free to direct itself by a conscious and volun-tary effort upon any selected portion of a dark and undifferenced field of view. This is one of the most important observations for a future theory of attention."[35] But Hering interpreted his own experiments as showing that we must, while attending to a marginal or peripheral object, also keep our attention riveted on what is centrally or directly heeded; if we permit our primary heeding to relax, even for an instant, our eyes move toward the marginal object and marginal attention ceases. Agreeing with Hering, James wrote: "Accommodation exists here, then, as it does elsewhere, and without it we should lose a part of our sense of attentive activity. In fact, the *strain* of that activity (which is remarkably great in the experiment) is due in part to unusually strong contractions of the muscles needed to keep the eyeballs still, which produces unwonted feelings of pressure in those organs."[36] A fuller explanation, Hering said, would list the muscular and bodily processes involved in expectant attentiveness, which contributes also to peripheral noticing. James considered these experiments to be examples of what the new psychology could achieve—the improvement of introspection under controlled conditions, its use in identifying with greater specific-ity the character of our experiences, and the experimental determination of the bodily processes that are conditions or correlates of these experiences. In agreeing with Hering and, to a point, with Helmholtz, James judged that the phenomenon of peripheral attention, which might seem to require no bodily input, can be shown experimentally to depend on a number of physiological factors. Whether attending is purely mental appears to have been, in James's mind, a question to be resolved in the laboratory. Psychologists can test, for example, whether marginal attending can occur when a subject is deprived of certain physiological input. Another question entirely is whether attending could continue even if all of its bodily content (though not bodily causes) were eliminated. James believed that certain bodily processes are needed for attention to succeed, but he was not as certain whether the felt character of attending always includes the feeling of bodily processes. When generalized be-yond a particular reference to attention, the question of whether attending is mental must be answered affirmatively—this is the official position of *Principles*. But before commenting further, we must ask whether attending is ever done freely.

Among James's formulations of the question was this: Is voluntary attention a resultant or a force?[37] He never doubted that some heedings are voluntary, in the everyday sense of the word. But the heedings we ordinarily think of as voluntary may also be effects of presented stimuli. James conceded the prevailing opinion that immediate sensorial attention, such as visual fixation on a bright color, is not itself a cause but is rather an effect produced by the colored stimulus. However, in a qualify-ing note he added that attending might be more than merely an effort, might instead be the cause of the adjustment of the eyes, a view supported by Hering. Although such a case could be made, James chose not to press it: "I do not here insist on this, because it is hard to tell whether the attention or the movement comes first (Hering's reasons . . . seem to me ambiguous), and because, even if the attention to the object comes first, it may be a mere effect of stimulus and association. Mach's theory that the *will to look* is the *space-feeling itself* may be compared with Hering's in this place" (*Principles*, 1:449n). Not only sensorial attention, but any experience of attending which does not include voluntary effort, is easily conceived as an effect. "In fact it is only to the *effort to attend*, not to the mere *attending*, that we are seriously tempted to ascribe spontaneous power. We think we can make more of it *if we will*. . . . But even here it is possible to conceive the facts mechanically and to regard the effort as a mere effect" (*Principles*, 1:451). James raised the question of whether attention is ever a cause rather than an effect; the issue is whether attending is ever a spontaneous power or is ever really subject to our command. An act of attending is free either if it is a spontaneous cause, not merely an effect, or, somewhat differently, if the cause of the attending is simply our willing to do it. Though not all philosophers accept this way of formulating the question of whether something is done freely, it was James's conception of the question.

Like all professional philosophers, James witnessed interminable debates about whether humans have free will; he concluded that neither experiment nor argument would ever end the debate. He realized that he ultimately could not convince a philosophical opponent of his own belief in free will or, in the present context, free attention. But the difficulty was not merely answering his opponents' skepticism, it was also silencing the skeptical voice within himself; for James, neither argument nor experiment did the trick. Reflection and observation helped to define the issue, but they did not provide definite proof that free will exists. Consider, for instance, the feeling of effort in straining our attention to something and the natural inclination to call the attention voluntary. As James noted, such thinkers as F. H. Bradley and Theodore Lipps argued that the feeling of effort may be only an inefficacious accompaniment of bodily processes, contributing no more to the resultant attention than the pain in one's finger, when hit by a hammer, contributes to the hammer's weight.[38] The attendings we ordinarily call voluntary, even those that involve a feeling of effort, can all be explained simply as the effects of what has preceded, not free in James's sense of the word. "The feeling of effort certainly *may* be an inert accompaniment and not the active element which it seems. No measurements are as yet performed (it is safe to say none ever will be performed) which can show that it contributes energy to the result. We *may* then regard attention as a superfluity, or a 'Luxus,' and dogmatize against its causal function with no feeling in our hearts but one of pride that we are applying Occam's razor to an entity that has multiplied itself 'beyond necessity'" (*Principles*, 1:452–53). If neither argument nor experience can decide the matter, what remains to be done? Should we discard the problem as trivial or pointless, or somehow keep it alive with some "feeling in our hearts"?

Admitting that he was prejudiced in favor of the idea that, since nature had introduced effortful feelings, they must exist for a purpose, James recognized the obligation to spell out the advantage of his view over his opponents'. Jamesian pragmatism was already at work in *Principles,* although its public articulation and development were still years away. Despite the popular notion that American pragmatism advocated the submission of philosophical quarrels to experimental procedures for arbitration, James's pragmatic maxim, when applied to the perennial problems of philosophy, does not require that they be experimentally resolvable; instead, it instructs us to compare the implications of opposed solutions to a problem so that, even though we are unable to test those implications, we can still see what is at stake between the rival solutions. There are three steps involved in applying his pragmatic maxim; first, we compare two opposed positions by tracing out and contrasting their consequences; second, we ask ourselves which set of consequences we prefer; and third, we choose or deliberately opt for our preference. This subjective pragmatism makes the final determination depend upon a process of subjective evaluation followed by an act of choice. James approached those problems of philosophy that seem to outlive all argument and experiment with such subjective pragmatism. This technique cannot objectively settle philosophical debates, but it can help us find a rationale for making up our mind when objective guidelines fail. James's answer to the question of whether attention is ever free, is ever a force rather than a mere effect, is a particularly apt example of his use of the pragmatic maxim.

What would be implied, James asked, if the effort to heed were an original force instead of a mere effect? He answered:

> It would deepen and prolong the stay in consciousness of innumerable ideas which else would fade more quickly away. The delay thus gained might not be more than a second in duration—but that second might be *critical;* for in the constant rising and falling of considerations in the mind, where two associated systems of them are nearly in equilibrium it is often a matter of but a second more or less of attention at the outset, whether one system shall gain force to occupy the field and develop itself, and exclude the other, or be excluded itself by the other. When developed, it may make us act; and that act may seal our doom." (*Principles,* 1:453)

If attention can be a spontaneous force, then we can use it to retain ideas, plans, cautions, or contingencies in the forefront of our consciousness to guide our conduct. For James, to hold that attention is a genuine force was to conceive of it as something we can use at will for our own purposes; this hypothesis seemed superior to mechanism, the rival hypothesis which, as he construed it, maintains that mechanical and physical phenomena matter and that consciousness does not. If this theory is true, then whatever happens in our consciousness and conduct is merely the mechanical result of a causal chain, not something that can be effected by our own willful attention. Our everyday sense of being able to affect our consciousness and conduct through acts of attention becomes an illusion. Given these contrasting consequences, James had no doubt about which hypothesis was preferable, but since he considered his reasons ethical and therefore inappropriate for discussion in a psychology textbook, he deferred further argument until the chapter on will, in the second volume of *Principles*, where he described the connections between will and attention.

ATTENTION AND WILL

James believed that there is an essential connection between our ability to heed and our capacity to will. In addition to the chapter on will in *Principles*, several other writings contribute to our understanding of his views on action and motivation. Few subjects interested James more than that of the human will; it is given substantial treatment not only in *Principles* but also in *Psychology* and *Talks to Teachers*. The celebrated essay "The Dilemma of Determinism" (1884) must be mentioned in studying James's conception of the will. That conception appears throughout his work, partly because the will has been prominent in traditional philosophy and psychology, partly because it had personal significance for James. Throughout life he had problems of health, professional achievement, and personal motivation; to cope he had repeatedly to summon the support of an occasionally flagging willpower.[39] Far from being a largely academic issue, the will was an extraordinarily poignant topic for him. Nowhere did he betray more zeal in harmonizing the disclosures of introspective psychology with the discoveries of physiology than in his search for an understanding of the will.

Will and voluntary action are allied concepts, and the first point that James made about them is that neither a willed nor a voluntary act can occur without having once been performed involuntarily: "When a particular movement, having once occurred in a random, reflex, or involuntary way, has left an image of itself in the memory, then the movement can be desired again, proposed as an end, and deliberately willed. But it is impossible to see how it could be willed before" (*Principles*, 2:487). This statement is an astonishing exaggeration if it implies that every voluntary act must have an identical and involuntary precedent; surely no one would make such a claim unless possessed by a peculiar definition of *voluntary*. But James believed that something must guide our movements when they occur in a series amounting to an act. He noted the case of an anesthetized boy who had feelings only in his right eye and left ear and was thus deprived of the kinesthetic sensations that condition awareness of the limbs; the boy mistakenly insisted, when his eye was shut, that he was opening and closing his hand, which was in fact being held in a fixed position by the experimenter. This and other examples show, James declared, that "absolute need of *guiding sensations* of some kind for the successful carrying out of a concatenated series of movements" (*Principles*, 2:490). We must know where we are in a chain of movements in order to will cogently what the next link ought to be, and this demands "informing" sensations of some sort. The opened eye was a prerequisite not only for the boy's knowing whether his hand was moving or fixed, but also for all of his voluntary movements. James reported an experiment of his own, in which he hypnotized two subjects such that each had an arm and hand anesthetized without being paralyzed; they could write their names while looking but not when their eyes were closed. James concluded: *"Whether or no there be anything else in the mind at the moment when we consciously will a certain act, a mental conception made up of memory-images of those sensations, defining which special act it is, must be there"* (*Principles*, 2:492). In uncomplicated voluntary acts, James claimed, merely the appropriate kinesthetic ideas of sensations suffice for carrying us through the series of movements constituting such acts. (His thesis is illustrated by the way professional dancers rely on an almost exclusively kinesthetic memory in repeated performances.) But the reader may be disconcerted by the claim that every voluntary act must be guided by a mental component of memory-images. Despite his phrasing, I think James intended to hold that only partial memory of what goes into an act's performance is required; that memory might be located in the nerves and muscles. Indeed, he argued at the conclusion of the chapter on will for a mentalistic concept of volition.

In contending that some voluntary acts involve nothing more than kinesthetic memory, James dissented from the excessive "mentalism" that he attributed to traditional psychology; his emphasis on the role in human action of the kinesthetic sensations aroused in tendons, ligaments, and especially articular surfaces, was meant to remedy the excesses of former theorizing by citing relevant discoveries in physiology. The spirit of Darwin was at work in James's thinking throughout *Principles* and all of his writings, particularly in his treatment of volition and his construing human action as a continuum from reflex to habitual movement to deliberate action. This continuum is insured by the fact, as he conceived it, that voluntary behavior is originally derived and indecipherable from reflex, involuntary movements.[40] Much of what we call voluntary action is habitual or automatic, so it is hardly surprising that the chapters on habit and will in *Principles* echo each other. James was immensely interested in determining how a theory of habit can assist our practical efforts to acquire good habits and to lose bad ones; he came to believe that lessons in behavior modification can be derived from the hypothesis, supported by the new psychology, that habitual patterning is ultimately a property of matter, to be studied by physicists. This theory explains the physiological tendency of the nervous system to pattern habitually, a tendency which underlies psychological habit. The philosophy of habit, he said, declares that our nervous system develops according to the modes in which it has been exercised; one consequence of this development is the simplification of movement through habit, as illustrated by an activity like playing the piano. The practiced pianist relies on habit to perform more accurately, more rapidly, and with less fatigue. Each muscular contraction occurring in its appointed order in the smooth execution of an habitual action is caused not by "a thought or a perception, but [by] the *sensation occasioned by the muscular contraction just finished"* (*Principles*, 1:115). Studies of habit and volition show, James believed, that sensation (which, he argued, had been scorned in the Kantian and idealistic traditions) can effectively guide and direct action; to be aware of this attribute of sensation is to correct the excessive mentalism of earlier psychologies and philosophies, which had assumed that every voluntary or intelligent act must be directed by an antecedent plan, thought, or blueprint in the mind.

Other lessons were suggested to James by the original proximity of voluntary and reflexive behavior and by the fact that kinesthetic images, for example, can be quite effective in controlling action. One lesson pertains to the psychophysical nature of effort in volition, another to the plausibility of ideo-motor action. The feeling of effort was supposed by many to be a hallmark of voluntary behavior, so it was a natural subject of investigation for the new psychology of the laboratory. All psychologists agreed that sensations such as color and sound are psychological effects or counterparts of the *afferent* nervous system, that is, the incoming system of nerve-conduction by which the effects of external stimuli are transmitted from sense-organs to the center. But some major thinkers, including Johannes Müller, Alexander Bain, Hughlings Jackson, and Wilhelm Wundt, had contended that some feelings of effort are distinctly connected not with the afferent but with the *efferent* or outgoing nervous system, by which central impulses discharge outwardly, for instance, in the muscles. Jackson wrote: "Sensations, in the sense of mental states, arise, I submit, during energizing of motor as well as of sensory nerve processes—with the outgoing as well as with the ingoing current."[41] Wundt, in distinguishing the feeling of force exerted from the feeling of movement effected, named the former *Innervationsgefühl* (feelings of innervation).[42] Before he began *Principles*, James had argued against such feelings, maintaining that all sensations are connected with the afferent nervous system, and it was on this issue that he thought he had made one of his few important contributions to the mainstream of scientific psychology.[43]

James denied, then, that there ever occur feelings which distinctly accompany the discharge of motor cells into motor fibers, or that any so-called feelings of effort or of muscular exertion can be explained as a feeling that accompanies outgoing currents in the nervous system. He asserted that the "feeling of *muscular* energy put forth is a complex *afferent* sensation coming from the tense muscles, the strained ligaments, squeezed joints, fixed chest, closed glottis, contracted brow, clenched jaws, etc. etc." ("The Feeling of Effort," 4). His inclusion of "complex" here, he said, signified the presence of a mental effort as well; he was not advocating a purely materialistic analysis of the special feeling of muscular exertion. Among the arguments for James's theory rather than those of Wundt and others was one connected with the hypothesis that kinesthetic images or memory suffices for the initiation of certain actions. This argument holds that nature and psychology obey a law of parsimony; consciousness will disappear from processes in which it has become useless, and if a single feeling rather than several will accomplish a given end, our consciousness will fix on the one and desert the others. If, as is often the case, the kinesthetic image (afferent feeling) of a movement suffices to initiate and control that movement, the other feelings of innervation, which hypothetically parallel the outgoing currents, are superfluous and consciousness ceases to notice them. Even if there had been such feelings, James argued, nature would have recognized their supernumerary character and at some point made the efferent system insentient. Another argument echoes Hume's point that when we will an action, we are not conscious of the physiological processes between the moment of willing and the execution of the action. But if efferent feelings occurred, they would inform us of the outgoing process that extends from the brain through the motor system to perform the action. Our introspective ignorance of such matters is in itself a confirmation that no such feelings exist. While not itself conclusive, the introspective evidence indicates, James said, that the feeling of effort, the sense of force exerted, owes its character to physiological factors such as tense muscles and rubbed joints. The feeling of effort seems like a sensory product of these factors, but there is nothing in its felt character that suggests that it is a by-product of the efferent system.

Why did James care so much to establish his side of this issue? It seemed more consistent with his theory that kinesthetic sensations, which are retained as the effects of movements, are sufficient to cause those movements in the future, so that additional feelings of innervation are superfluous. Since the job of psychology was to correlate the introspectable and the physiological as clearly and accurately as possible, it was important to weigh carefully the evidence about innervation feelings and the likenesses and differences between the afferent and efferent systems. The giants of the profession had endorsed the idea that the efferent system has its sentient aspect; James, convinced from 1880 onward that they were mistaken, naturally wanted to set the record straight and thus to make a place for himself in the history of psychology. Physiological speculations had become an exciting part of psychology, a fact particularly evident in James's discussion of volition.[44] Although most of this discussion is of mainly historical interest, occasionally someone resurrects James's thoughts on physiology as well as on psychology and philosophy. The physiologist W. B. Cannon, a younger contemporary of James and a celebrated opponent of James's theory of emotion, wrote shortly after James's death that Sir Charles Sherrington had been impressed by James's "law of forward conduction" formulated in the chapter on will in *Principles*. Sherrington and others saw this law as an important valvelike conception of the nervous system, emphasizing that nerve impulses enter by sensory pathways, exit by motor pathways, and are irreversible in direction; this model has been said to illuminate the significance of the central nervous system in effecting the motor expressions of sensory stimuli.[45] But James had another reason for considering sentience to be totally a product of the afferent system: this idea increased the plausibility of the theory of ideo-motor action and its associated thesis that the will is exerted upon mental rather than physical objects.

The term *ideo-motor action*, James stated, originated with W. B. Carpenter, author of *Human Physiology* and *Mental Physiology*, books often cited by James; the theory of ideo-motor action claims that once an idea occupies the mind it will, unless obstructed, seek expression in action.[46] James praised Rudolph Lotze and Charles Renouvier for persuading him of the theory; from James's notes we know that he was reading both thinkers before 1870, so he must have adopted the theory long before he began *Principles*.[47] Perry provides a succinct summary of the theory: "The work of conscious volition is done when the idea is instated. In order thus to perform any specific act such as *a*, it is necessary to instate the idea of *a* which is left in the mind as the result of a previous performance of *a*; and, feelings of innervation having been dismissed, this idea is held to consist of a reproduction of the (kinesthetic) sensations aroused by the original bodily movements" (RBP, 2:88). The theory of ideo-motor action—which in effect maintains that any idea, once it occupies consciousness, will translate itself into action or overt behavior—is a generalization from the limited cases where such items as kinesthetic sensations or ideas can by themselves produce behavior. The concept of ideo-motor action is part and parcel of James's well-known conviction that consciousness is dynamic, impulsive, and naturally disposed to manifest itself in public activity. If an action occurs because nothing more than the idea of it occurs, James's belief in the original similarity of voluntary and reflex action seems to be confirmed; there is a smooth transition from idea to behavior that requires no act of will or effort whatsoever. In Lotze's words, "All the acts of our daily life happen in this wise: Our standing up, walking, talking, all this never demands a distinct impulse of the will, but is adequately brought about by the pure flux of thought."[48] To remember this, James suggested, is to avoid the excessive mentalism of former psychologies, which saw the presence of "willfulness" in every volitional act; on the other hand, some aspects of ideo-motor action point away from automatism or materialism and toward something like traditional mentalism.

Every idea that represents an act will translate itself into that act unless something stands in its way; that barrier can be an "antagonistic or inhibiting" idea. As long as the idea of dining out tonight occupies our mind, we shall edge closer and closer to doing so; if the inhibiting idea of its expensiveness also enters our head, however, the original idea will need help to be expressed in behavior. In cases of conflict between ideas or blockage of an original idea, the help we provide is an "express fiat" or an "act of mental consent" (*Principles*, 2:526). Even something seemingly as physical as muscular exertion can be made complex by the mental element of willing or consenting that a particular act be done; James assumed that all of us are acquainted with this complexity in our everyday lives. If pressed to clarify this notion of an act of consent or a mental volition, James could only have referred the questioner back to his own experience. "The reader's own consciousness tells him of course what these words of mine denote. And I freely confess that I am impotent to carry the analysis of the matter any farther, or to explain in other terms of what this consent consists. It seems a subjective experience *sui generis*, which we can designate but not define" (*Principles*, 2:568). Jamesian psychology is replete with sui generis experiences whose verbal designation can be understood only by those who have had such experiences. His introspective certainty about such experiences was one source of his discontent with traditional associationism, a school of psychology which robbed experiences of their sui generis character by analyzing them instead as products of ideas associated in various ways. Volition, for instance, was defined as the association of ideas of muscular motion with ideas of the pleasures which such motion causes.[49] Although James agreed with the associationists in using the mechanistic language of struggle and inhibition, he differed with them when his introspections disclosed a phenomenon that could not be analyzed into something else— and one such phenomenon was volition. Mental willing—not to be confused with physical exertion or activity—is demonstrated by abnormal cases, such as paralysis or amputation; an act of willing certainly occurs in the patient's consciousness, although there is no corresponding action in his body. James discussed, for instance, how amputees differed in ability to will a change of position in their missing limbs; some thought they could accomplish it by an effort of will, others willed but without success, and a few declared that they could not manage even the act of will, much less the resultant illusion of a missing limb changing position.[50] Beyond any doubt, he concluded, mental and physical exertion are distinguishable in these and in more normal situations.

Although nothing further can help the reader to understand what is meant by an act of will if he does not already grasp the concept, James offers introspective description to illuminate the effort that is often a part of volition. Consider a person suffering from aphasia, who tries or wills to say something. Typically, James said, he forms an image of the words he wants to utter, consents to their utterance, opens his mouth but hears himself making wrong sounds, then becomes angry and frustrated; clearly his will is operative despite his lack of success. A paralytic may will to move his arm by imagining the sensation of the required muscular effort and by resolving (consenting) to make such an imagining happen; despite his success in summoning the images, however, he experiences the bitter disappointment of finding his arm still motionless. These examples demonstrate, James believed, that effortful willing is a process of making some idea, thought, or image dominate consciousness. When thoughts or ideas prevail without effort, they do so because of the mechanical principles that govern interest and association. But volition involving effort is more complicated and demands that additional factor of attention. *"The essential achievement of the will . . . when it is most 'voluntary' is to ATTEND to a difficult object and hold it fast before the mind."*[51] The paralytic succeeds in willing to raise his arm as soon as he stabilizes in his mind the idea of doing so; he experiences the difficulty, necessitating effort, of keeping his attention fixed on that idea. The thought or image of moving his arm proves hard to maintain, and trying to will the arm to move is the same process as trying to keep his attention focused upon that thought or image. He wills it when he succeeds in sustaining his attention on the thought, and that act of will occurs even though the raising of the arm is frustrated. In this way James joined attention and volition, viewing the act of attending as the core element in willing with effort to do something.

Sometimes James wrote as if heeding and willing were identical: *"The only resistance which our will can possibly experience is the resistance which such an idea offers to being attended to at all.* To attend to it is the volitional act, and the only inward volitional act which we ever perform" (*Principles,* 2:567). In insisting that the drama of a will in conflict is an exclusively mental drama, he seemed to suggest that the element of fiat or consent is identical with the successful maintenance of an idea in the forefront of attention: "Consent to the idea's undivided presence, this is effort's sole achievement. . . . The idea to be consented to must be kept from flickering and going out. It must be held steadily before the mind until it *fills* the mind. Such filling of the mind by an idea . . . *is* consent to the idea and to the fact which the idea represents" (*Principles*, 2:564). (James thought this account applies paradigmatically to the chronic drunkard who refuses to admit that he is one; if he could focus his attention, each time he is tempted by a drink, on the idea that he is a drunkard if he takes the drink, that idea might prevail over its rival which impels him to continue his habit.) Although such filling of the mind by an idea is consent or fiat because it "carries the man and his will with it," the element of resolve or consent may occur even when a thought fails to occupy the attention fully; we consent on occasion to things to which we partially or hardly pay attention. In cases of conflict and temptation, we try to fix our attention more fully on the thought that we think deserves our moral allegiance: "The effort to *attend* is therefore only a part of what the word 'will' covers; it covers also the effort to *consent* to something to which our attention is not quite complete. . . . So that although attention is the first and fundamental thing in volition, *express consent to the reality of what is attended to* is often an additional and quite distinct phenomenon involved" (*Principles*, 2:568). An act of will can involve an effort to attend to a difficult idea, and this effort can to some extent be introspectively described. It can also require an "express consent" (resolve, decision, fiat) or effort to consent to the attending that is needed; this effort, unlike the effort to attend, is a familiar aspect of our experience but defies further introspective analysis. The fact that some acts of will incorporate these two elements is itself discovered through introspective analysis, as are the four distinct mental phenomena involved: attending, the effort to attend, consenting or deciding, and the effort to consent or decide. I emphasize *mental* because James, in his treatment of attention and will, seems to have been a zealous dualist and not the reluctant or apologetic one that he sometimes professed to be. He stressed the need to distinguish mental from physical effort, pure volitional effort from muscular exertion; in addition, he advanced a proposition about the will which tilted him even further toward mentalism.[52]

This mentalistic proposition is that an act of will, while directly changing our relation to our thoughts or ideas, does not directly change our relation to our body. Willing is accomplished when an idea is stabilized for attention; this process is entirely mental, a fait accompli before the physiological events leading up to the willed act occur. *"The essential achievement of the will . . . is to ATTEND to a difficult object and hold it fast before the mind.* The so-doing *is* the *fiat;* and it is a mere physiological incident that when the object is thus attended to, immediate motor consequences should ensue" (*Principles*, 2:561). Hence, "volition is a psychic or moral fact pure and simple, and is absolutely completed when the stable state of the idea is there. The supervention of motion is a supernumerary phenomenon depending on executive ganglia whose function lies outside the mind" (*Principles*, 2:560). To take an example of James's, suppose that we try to summon the willpower to get out of bed on a winter morning; we may do so by trying to fix our attention on an appropriate but difficult idea—let us say the thought of a delicious cup of coffee—which would not be difficult to focus on except for the thought of the discomfort of leaving a warm bed. At last we stabilize the image of the coffee in our mind, and before we realize it we are on the way to the kitchen. The willing, on James's theory, stopped as soon as the idea of the coffee was firmly fixed in our attention; at that time the idea caused ideo-motor action in the brain, which in turn caused us to leave the bed and move to the kitchen. Willing is therefore confined to working with our own thoughts, ideas, or images; their interaction with our physiology will determine whether the willed act occurs. All ideas are impulsive, but whether they are effective in causing motor or behavioral results depends upon such factors as the existence of competing ideas and defective responses in the body's system. We are certainly the causes of our willed acts, but James believed that we are only indirect causes, since what we do directly is to bring an idea into the focus of attention, which may stimulate the brain to cause action. Ideas directly cause changes in our bodies. James claimed that the nexus between ideas and ganglia is inscrutable: "For the mysterious tie between the thought and the motor centres next comes into play, and in a way which we cannot even guess at, the obedience of the bodily organs follows as a matter of course."[53] The mystery in which the whole mind-body relationship is enveloped is one that psychology cannot hope to penetrate, one about which philosophy can only guess. At the same time, this account of where an act of willing begins and ends is a response to Hume's comment that, although we say we cause our arms to rise when we will to raise them, we are ignorant of what happens in the body between the time of our willing and the time when our arms ascend. James's view shows that we can know what we will without having to know what bodily effects are produced by the ideas made operative by fixing them in attention. In conjunction with the insistence that phenomena such as making an effort to attend are mental, the claim that willing is confined to the mental realm of thoughts, ideas, and images, gives the impression that James was an unapologetic dualist.

This impression is strongly reinforced by his thoughts on the freedom of the will, although he repeated the cautionary remarks of "The Consciousness of Self," chapter 10 in *Principles,* in the chapter on will. After giving overwhelming reasons for a clear-cut distinction between mental and physical activities, and between pure volition and muscular exercise, James qualified his earlier show of confidence by declaring that no amount of introspective evidence shows conclusively that purely non-physical activities exist.

> I do not *fully* understand how we come to our unshakable belief that thinking exists as a special kind of immaterial process alongside of the material processes of the world. It is certain, however, that only by *postulating* such thinking do we make things currently intelligible; and it is certain that no psychologist has as yet denied the *fact* of thinking, the utmost that has been denied being its dynamic power. But if we postulate the fact of thinking at all, I believe that we must postulate its power as well. . . . If we admit, therefore, that our thoughts *exist,* we ought to admit that they exist after the fashion in which they appear, as things, namely, that supervene upon each other, sometimes with effort and sometimes with ease; the only questions being, is the effort where it exists a

fixed function of the *object,* which the latter imposes on the thought? or is it such an independent "variable" that with a constant object more or less of it may be made? (*Principles,* 2:570–71).

Even if introspection leaves mind-body dualism uncertain, the hypothesis of dualism is superior in explanatory power to materialism or epiphenomenalism. This contention—that "only by *postulating* such thinking do we make things currently intelligible"—seems either gratuitous or misleading, since the choice between dualism and materialism is made not on the basis of explanatory or predictive power, but for reasons that are essentially metaphysical and ethical. Indeed, the question of whether the human will is ever free is the same question about attention; James's solution of the problem of free will in *Principles* is a simple and deliberate repetition of the solution offered for the problem of free attention. "As we said in Chapter XI ["Attention"], the operation of free effort, if it existed, could only be to hold some one idea, object, or part of an object, a little longer or a little more intensely before the mind. Amongst the alternatives which present themselves as *genuine possibles,* it would thus make one effective. And although such quickening of one idea might be *morally* and *historically momentous,* yet, if considered *dynamically,* it would be an operation amongst those physiological infinitesimals which calculation must forever neglect" (*Principles,* 2:576–77). The difference that free will represents is the same difference that free attention makes; there are occasions when, without being caused to do it, we can sustain an idea that would otherwise vanish, allowing us to act morally or heroically. Because there is no proof that attending and willing are purely immaterial—the claim that they are is only a postulate—there is no proof that they ever occur freely, spontaneously, or without being caused. Although psychologists are to be applauded for deepening the considerations that surround the problem of free will, emphasizing the connections between will and attention, and experimentally demonstrating that certain acts of will and certain acts of muscular effort are not identical, they must be content finally to surrender the issue to philosophy.

When philosophers take up the issue, they must compare the reasons for and against free will. This process may culminate in our being inclined one way or the other, but the debate continues, and there will be intelligent opposition no matter which side one takes. Philosophical reflection and debate can unsettle our commitment to our own position, and James realized that no amount of reasoning can result in an unequivocal answer to the question of what we should believe. We seek a definitive reason or thought that will produce a permanent belief. It is the philosopher's job, after weighing arguments and keeping moral and logical considerations in mind, to recognize the limits of philosophical reflection and debate and to appreciate when a decision rather than a line of reasoning is called for. To that end, he seeks reasons or arguments sufficient to determine his choice of what to believe. For the choosing of a belief is an act, and there comes that point when the philosopher yearns for a single consideration that will produce that act and thus bring the examination of reasons to term.

James, after comparing arguments for and against free will, found his definitive reason in the writings of the French philosopher Charles Renouvier.[54] The connection between attention and will had been formulated by Renouvier, who defined free will as the "sustaining of a thought *because I choose to* when I might have other thoughts." This statement suggested to James that if the will is free, then it ought to assert that it is, so that "my first act of free will shall be to believe in free will."[55] He understood that the power of such reasoning to motivate an act of belief might dissipate, so he was obliged either to rehearse the reasoning again or to find new arguments. He moved on to fresh reasons in "The Dilemma of Determinism," which was composed while key sections of *Principles* were being written, including the chapters on the stream of thought, the consciousness of self, emotion, and the will. Still, the chapter on the will in *Principles,* which refers to the "Dilemma" essay, by no means abandons Renouvier's influence.

> If, meanwhile, the will *be* undetermined, it would seem only fitting that the belief in its indetermination should be voluntarily chosen from amongst other possible beliefs. Freedom's first deed should be to affirm itself. We ought never to hope for any other method of getting at the truth if indeterminism be a fact. Doubt of this particular truth will therefore probably be open to us to the end of time, and the utmost that a believer in free-will can *ever* do will be to show that the deterministic arguments are not coercive. That they are seductive, I am the last to deny; nor do I deny that effort may be needed to keep the faith in freedom, when they press upon it, upright in the mind.[56]

James's psychology emphasizes what it is like to will freely, and the connection between attention and will is pointed out and developed. Because psychologists cannot decide the issue of free will, James emphasizes also what is psychologically involved in coming to a decision about that issue. In "The Dilemma of Determinism" and other places, he focuses on the metaphysical and ethical implications of the free will hypothesis, and the concepts of indeterminism, novelty, chance, pluralism, activity, and morality come to the fore. If free will is ever a fact, James argued, then the universe cannot be so monistic or of a single block that it fails to permit the indeterminism and chance that result from the occasional unpredictability of human action. Ours must be a universe in which the parts are real forces, not always to be explained in terms of the whole. In spelling out what was metaphysically at stake in the choices between determinism and indeterminism, James recognized as his opponents both materialists such as T. H. Huxley and W. K. Clifford and neo-Hegelians like Josiah Royce and Francis Bradley, who attributed ultimate reality to the absolute or the whole and to that alone. James believed that human activity makes a difference in what the future becomes, and that one of the most important ways in which it does so is the occasional triumph of moral good over moral evil. Determinism is caught in a dilemma, one horn of which is pessimism, the other subjectivism, a fact that can be appreciated when we consider how determinists must judge an evil act such as a hideous murder. Since they claim that everything happens in a theoretically predictable way according to natural laws, the murder had to occur, unless nature broke down or some law of physics collapsed; the event, however evil, must have been inevitable—a view James saw as unacceptably pessimistic. To avoid this horn of the dilemma one must adopt subjectivism, the attitude that what really counts is less the objective world, where murders take place, than our subjective responses to that world. Subjectivists are tempted to excuse the murder and its inevitability because it awakens noble and exquisite sensitivities in us. But, said James, such an attitude "wrenches my personal instincts in quite as violent a way. It falsifies the simple objectivity of their deliverance. . . . It transforms life from a tragic reality into an insincere melodramatic exhibition."[57] That murder is evil is an objective fact, James argued, and no kind of sensitivity of subjective response can make it otherwise; we need, therefore, to muster support for our belief that a better moral world can be achieved and that we have the freedom of will with which to achieve it. Moral and metaphysical reflections along these lines, which do not belong to psychology, are required to discern what differences are made if indeterminism rather than determinism is chosen.[58]

If our main concerns here were moral and metaphysical, we should have to examine James's ideas at length, but our topic is the philosophy of psychology. Whereas in many respects James admirably formulated the issue of free will— indeed philosophers and nonphilosophers have generated a huge literature in response to his formulation—he was unduly anxious to make the issue a metaphysical one. He ought to have said more about the commonsense conviction that free will is an attribute of the human race; this conviction leads us to determine whether someone decided of his own free will to act in a certain way. Common sense does not suggest that we can always make the determination, but there are times when we have overwhelming evidence that a person decided freely (in any appropriate sense of the word) to act as he did. If we still entertain a doubt that free will exists, it is the kind of reservation that nothing can reassure. James made this sort of doubt respectable, giving it a central importance in his philosophy. Despite the criticisms, sometimes exceedingly harsh, to which his writings on free will have been subjected, his reasoning about metaphysical doubt in "The Dilemma of Determinism" and elsewhere makes good sense. He succeeded in defining the differences implied by determinism and indeterminism, and he gave a vivid and powerful account of why he preferred the implications of indeterminism. Even if his reasons do not convince us, they make a formidable case. Unfortunately, his turning the question of free will into a metaphysical one preoccupies us with what is insoluble and makes us subordinate our thinking about the actual problems of responsibility and behavior to an enraptured fascination with the entire cosmos. Those whose chief interest is either a close analysis of the concepts involved in philosophizing about free will or a better comprehension of the conditions that allow freedom of will and of action are understandably put off by the Jamesian rhetoric, which seems at times to descend as if from the mountaintop.

As much as James sought to join attention and will, he conceded that the act of deciding (consenting, resolving, fiat) and the effort to decide cannot be simply identified with the act of attending. In the first place, we can introspectively distinguish the two acts; further, James observed, we must make an effort to consent to something to which our attention is not yet fixed. Despite all that he said about the efficacy of consciousness, the ideo-motor action theory, and its attribution of causal powers to ideas, James understood that we may initiate acts of decision or willing that need not be caused by ideas or anything else.[59] James was correct in distinguishing willing from attending, both because the two acts are introspectively and conceptually distinct and because such a distinction is consistent with his exhortations, to himself and others, to exert the moral will as strenuously as possible.

One can easily appreciate the everyday basis for linking attention and will or for being tempted into a theory of ideo-motor action, for we all remember occasions when we accomplished a difficult task by focusing our attention on it and not allowing distractions to interfere. But the connection between the attending, the willing, and the acting is much too loose for the theory of ideo-motor action to be built upon it. There is no basis for James's contention that the action of will upon behavior is always through the intermediary of ideas. We are less likely to cause an act by first fixing our attention on an idea of it than we are by deciding to do it without being aware that any act of attention or crucial idea is involved. Even if we agree with James that the connection between will and body is perplexing, nothing is gained by positing a connection between ideas and body; such a connection does not answer Hume's objection that we are ignorant of the bodily processes occurring in an act of will. None of these reservations detract, however, from the fact that James's theorizing on the overlap between will and attention has been permanently stimulating; as is often true of his philosophical psychology, professionals and non-professionals alike have found in it a fund of practical insights for their own lives.[60]

WILL AND MOTIVATION

The chapter on will in *Principles* includes brief sections on deliberation, various kinds of decision, good and bad varieties of will, and pleasure and pain as motives for behavior. These topics are important in James's exposition of what can be roughly called his theory of motivation. He equated motives with reasons, introducing the concept in a discussion designed to elicit the introspective details of deliberating before acting: "The reinforcing and inhibiting ideas meanwhile are termed the *reasons* or *motives* by which the decision is brought about" (*Principles*, 2:528). He pictured the process of deliberation as one in which we have centrally in mind a complex idea that includes a possible course of action as well as the reasons that reinforce the tendency to follow that course; in addition to this foreground idea there is a fringe or background in our consciousness, of which we are only dimly aware and which includes ideas that may inhibit the impulse to follow the course. Only when the dynamic interplay between foreground and background ideas is resolved does the deliberation cease and the action begin. The in specific motives that reinforce or inhibit vary specific circumstances, but James believed that certain motives are usually present, one of which is the impatience of the deliberative state: we seek to relieve the tension of hesitation through the outlet that action represents. Another frequent motive is dread of the irrevocable, and a third is the impulse to persist in a decision already made.[61]

We need to ask whether James considered the unconscious a factor in motivation. How unconscious is the fringe or background, and how conscious are we of the three general motives just identified? James did not himself raise these questions, although such chapters in *Principles* as "The Mind-Stuff Theory" and "The Relations of Minds to Other Things" indicate his keen interest in the question of whether mental states can be unconscious. I think he would have answered that the fringe or background field of motives (ideas or thoughts) can be as unconscious as we desire, in that we may ignore or fail to attend to their presence. The three motives or impulses can be both conscious dispositions to behave in certain ways and qualities of experience that are usually but not necessarily conscious. James's protests against the unconscious in chapters 6 and 8 were directed toward the unconscious "ideas" of traditional associationism; he clearly accepted the notion of sensations to which we remain oblivious. Thus his conceptions of motive, fringe, and impulse can feasibly operate in what Freudians call the preconscious or in what many refer to simply as the unconscious.[62] Notwithstanding the introspective tendency in James's reflections on motivation, and his inclination to focus on experiences of conscious internal conflict (rather than on Freud's energized "ideas," which confront each other on a battlefield that is permanently out of sight), James certainly assumed that we are sometimes motivated by unconscious mental states. He sided with Pierre Janet's analysis of multiple personality, which asserted that what is unconscious to one personality in a given body is conscious to another, subconscious personality in the same body, so that no mental state can exist apart from the experience of some personality. In addition, he rejected a depersonalized unconscious that can be understood only through psychoanalytic interpretation; he was thus clearly opposed to the Freudian notion of the unconscious, although he never made it a topic for careful study.[63] For James, the mind was not always a clear area for introspection to explore; abnormal psychology showed abundantly that consciousness can split mysteriously into several personalities, each shut off from the other at the conscious level, all cohabiting the same body and able to exert subtle and subliminal effects on each other. Introspective testimony about a person's motivations was no more taken at face value by James than it was by Freud. James argued that cases of abnormal psychology such as split personality and hysteria "prove one thing conclusively, namely, that *we must never take a person's testimony, however sincere, that he felt nothing, as proof positive that no feeling has been there*" (*Principles*, 1:211). It is not coincidental that he followed the chapter on will with one on hypnotism; he was interested not only in how much a person's will can be compromised by the power of the hypnotist, but also in how to interpret the hypnotic state itself. The fact that the senses can be anesthetized in odd ways, such that a hypnotized person will see something but be unable to realize consciously that he has seen it, and the fact that a person will obey posthypnotic instructions while completely unaware of having been so instructed, demonstrate that the relation between consciousness and subconsciousness is hard to fathom. James's conclusions were mainly tentative; he surmised that portions of consciousness can somehow split into subpersonalities, that even in the hypnotic state the subject is not a mere puppet, and that the hypnotic state is not just a condition produced by suggestion but is rather a genuinely neurotic trance.[64] James took a serious interest in psychical research and in the ways that our ideas and actions may be influenced by psychical phenomena. He clearly saw human motivation as a complex issue indeed, and he welcomed any technique that promised to illuminate it better than his introspection did.

One can make psychoanalytic statements without endorsing psychoanalysis, so it is not surprising to find them in James's psychology. His examples, which he never sought to systematize theoretically, stand on their own merits in his text. In "The Consciousness of Self" he wrote: "It is one of the strangest laws of our nature that many things which we are well satisfied with in ourselves disgust us when seen in others. With another man's bodily 'hoggishness' hardly anyone has any sympathy;—almost as little with his cupidity, his social vanity and eagerness, his jealousy, his despotism, and his pride" (*Principles*, 1:314). This psychological fact, reinforced by moral education, motivates us to judge ourselves as we have been prone to judge others. In the same chapter James stated that human nature virtually compels people to pray; his explanation, resembling the modern notion of sublimation, is that we have an innate impulse to belong not only to a social but to an ideal world of some sort.[65] James's explanation of selfishness denied the claim that "Each of us is animated by a *direct feeling of regard for his own pure principle of individual existence.*" (*Principles*, 1:318). This suggestion that selfishness rests ultimately upon an ontological emotion or desire to protect the bare fact of being an "I" was superseded in James's account: "To have a self that I can *care for*, nature must first present me with some *object* interesting enough to make me instinctively wish to appropriate it for its *own* sake, and out of it to manufacture one of those material, social, or spiritual selves [that each of us is]" (*Principles*, 1:319). The concept of instinct is basic to James's thoughts on motivation and is virtually omnipresent in his writings. Whereas Freud finally settled on two instincts, eros and thanatos, James outlined some forty of them, including pugnacity, emulation, curiosity, modesty, jealousy, secretiveness, sadism, constructiveness, acquisitiveness, and sympathy.[66] He resisted the attempts of traditional associationism to reduce the list of instincts to a primitive few and their associations; in keeping with his nativistic psychology, he professed an inability to understand how, unless blind impulses in certain directions were innately present, any association of ideas could possibly propel us in those directions. He did not define instinct, as some do, as an unmodifiable tendency to behave in a certain way, for he thought that what are usually classified as instincts are neither unalterable nor invariable and that many are transient. Instinct is a tendency to behave in ways that appear to be means to an end, but without foresight of the ends or the benefit of prior learning. Whereas some of his contemporaries took a dim view of human instincts, some believing that they indicate a deranged constitution, James assumed that we can learn to live with them and even to alter their influence upon us.

The depth of James's psychology is evident in his comments, similar to recent discussions of introjection and identification, about childhood motivation:

> Another element seems to be a peculiar sense of power in stretching one's own personality so as to include that of a strange person. In young children this instinct often knows no bounds. For a few months in one of my children's third year, he literally hardly ever appeared in his own person. It was always, 'Play I am So-and-so, and you are So-and-so, and the chair is such a thing, and then we'll do this and that.' If you called him by his name, H., you invariably got the reply, 'I'm not H., I'm a hyena, or a horse-car,' or whatever the feigned object might be. He outwore this impulse after a time; but while it lasted, it had every appearance of being the automatic result of ideas, often suggested by perceptions, working out irresistible motor effects.[67]

Explanations involving concepts like the oedipal conflict or the libido are absent; in discussing cases of obsessive behavior, for example, James seems to have been uninterested in speculations about its causes. What interested him about a person who obsessively washed his hands was that, although the man knew his hands were not dirty, he could not rid himself of the idea that they were, so he kept returning to the washstand; he was not intellectually deluded, yet he could not will the idea out of consciousness. Beyond remarking that most of us are potential victims of this sort of malady because the line between normal and abnormal is indiscernible, James did not venture an explanation of the man's behavior. His general inclination was to explain compulsive behavior as the result of habit, instinct, or physiological or hereditary causes, and he saw no reason to posit traumatic events in early life or monumental acts of repression as causes.

The index to *Principles* does not contain *sex* as a separate item; conventional wisdom has it that James was a somewhat prim spokesman for Victorian morals and mores.[68] Whatever his personal attitude, he clearly numbered sex as one of a host of instincts, something to be enjoyed but not to be enslaved by, a challenge on occasion to the strength of the moral will. There is no doubt that he was totally opposed to a libido theory of human nature. Roback cited James's marginal notes in his copy of Charles Mercier's *Sanity and Insanity*. Mercier had written: "She desires to injure herself for the sake of injuring herself, in order to satisfy her sexual instinct of self-sacrifice. *Self-sacrifice for self-sacrifice sake*, whether it take the form of unsweetened tea, of monastic vows, or of a cut throat, is *always of sexual origin*" (James's italics). At this passage, Roback said, James added "the emphatic mark of disagreement or surprise. It is evident that James, who seemed eager to follow Mercier's classification of what were later called 'psychoses,' was stunned at the connection between self-sacrifice (suicide) and sex activity" (Roback, 87–88). If James, like some other men of science, was indeed stunned, it was probably less from prudery than from coming upon an explanation so confidently made upon so little evidence. While granting that the excitement of sexual arousal is second only to that of fury, James also recognized what he called the *anti-sexual instinct*, an impulse to seek privacy and to be repulsed by the idea of intimate contact; this instinct, he believed, may contribute to sexual inhibitions and irregularities. "[Sexual] details are a little unpleasant to discuss, but they show so beautifully the correctness of the general principles in the light of which our review has been made, that it was impossible to pass them over unremarked."[69] Unpleasant or not, the details did not completely escape him; he was aware, for instance, of what some call the ambivalence of love and sexual attachment. "The passion of love may be called a monomania to which all of us are subject, however otherwise sane. It can coexist with contempt and even hatred for the 'object' which inspires it" (*Principles*, 2:543). Sexual behavior can also be compulsive, and it seems neither to be motivated normally nor to yield the usual rewards: "A man may lead a life of incessant love-making or sexual indulgence, though what spurs him thereto seems rather to be suggestions and notions of possibility than any overweening strength in his affections or lusts. He may even be physically impotent all the while" (*Principles*, 2:541). The cause for this behavior is either physiological, James assumed, or located in the power of some idea, but he gave no psychological account of how the idea acquires that power. Some students of psychology may think the last word on James and sex is his letter of 5 December 1899 to Havelock Ellis: "I have just been reading your *Affirmations*. I think you too indulgent to that monster of meanness, Casanova, but there are splendid pages in your chapter on St. Francis." Others may think that "The Consciousness of Self" provides the definitive statement of James's thoughts on sex: "I am often confronted by the necessity of standing by one of my empirical selves and relinquishing the rest. Not that I would not, if I could, be both handsome and fat and well-dressed, and a great athlete, and make a million a year, be a wit, a *bon-vivant*, and a lady-killer, as well as a philosopher; a philanthropist, statesman, warrior, and African explorer, as well as a 'tone-poet' and saint. But the thing is simply impossible. . . . The philosopher and the lady-killer could not well keep house in the same tenement of clay" (*Principles*, 1:309–10).

Human motivation is so complex, James believed, that no single factor, whether it be sex, will to power, or pleasure and pain, can explain it. Nineteenth-century thinkers such as Leslie Stephen, Herbert Spencer, and Alexander Bain had advanced the theory that pleasure and pain are the springs of action. James suspected that the admitted lure of the theory might be due to a mistaken equation of a pleasant act with an act of pursuing a pleasure, or of anticipated pleasure with the pleasure of achievement. If our impulse to act is frustrated, we feel displeasure, and if we carry out the impulse, we feel relief or pleasure. But, James urged, to infer that the motive of the act is the expectancy of pleasure, or that we act for the sake of the pleasure gained, ignores the fact that the impulse is a thing in itself, and the pleasure of achievement is the result and not the cause of the impulse. For support James turned to Hume: "Though the satisfaction of these passions gives us enjoyment, yet the prospect of this enjoyment is not the cause of the passions but, on the contrary, the passion is antecedent to the enjoyment, and without the former the latter could never possibly exist."[70] James included pleasure and pain, both felt and anticipated, as important motives of human action, but did not consider them the exclusive ones. Things can move us even though they neither give nor promise us pleasure. Interest may attract our attention and bend our will, and once something seizes our interest, it may induce us to move toward pain and away from pleasure. The ideo-motor theory of action contradicts the pleasure-pain theory of motivation, for habitual acts clearly do not result from thoughts about pleasure and pain. "As I do not breathe for the pleasure of breathing, but simply find that I *am* breathing, so I do not write for the pleasure of writing, but simply because I have once begun, and being in a state of intellectual excitement, which keeps venting itself in that way, find that I *am* writing still" (*Principles*, 2:553). If we always sought the pleasant and avoided the painful we might be better off, but to do so we would have to be much simpler in nature than we are; not only are we motivated habitually by ideas, we are sometimes victimized by them, a realization that prompted James's reflections on the healthiness of will.

A healthy will does not allow impulsive ideas to lead to action too rapidly or too slowly. The person with an explosive will cannot inhibit the power of his ideas that lead to drinking or carousing, and the person with an obstructed will cannot break the logjam of ideas that inhibits impulses to action. Due to his neurasthenia and his efforts to overcome it, James often wrote about the health and sickness of the human psyche; thus the chapter on the will in *Principles* is elaborated by virtually everything else he wrote. In theoretically connecting will and attention, he tried to find practical ways to become a healthy rather than a sick soul. The chapters on habit, will, and attention in *Principles* form a sort of manual for improving the psychological and moral dimensions of life. James thought, however, that there are limits to what can be expected of sheer willpower; it may not be possible in every situation to will the energy needed to persevere. "In general, whether a given idea shall be a live idea depends more on the person into whose mind it is injected than on the idea itself."[71] James thought we eventually need help from somewhere else, and he gave a mystical interpretation of such regenerative experience.[72] Characteristically, after describing what psychology reveals about our motivations, he felt compelled to suggest what it cannot reveal. He believed that the saving energy without which we might even lose the will to live is the subject not of psychology, physiology, or philosophy, but of religion, mysticism, and mystery. He concludes *Principles*: "And the more sincerely one seeks to trace the actual course of *psychogenesis*, the steps by which as a race we may have come by the peculiar mental attributes which we possess, the more clearly one perceives 'the slowly gathering twilight close in utter night.'"[73]

8 ⚛ EMOTION

No theory of the will or of motivation is complete without an account of emotion, since it is a common assumption that emotions motivate action and incline the will; indeed, James's chapter on emotions is placed between those on instinct and on the will in *Principles*. This chapter developed ideas originally presented in 1884 in the essay "What Is an Emotion?" James made a third statement in 1894 in the essay "The Physical Basis of Emotion."[1] James remarked in an 1888 letter to Renouvier that "What the Will Effects" had provoked more response than all of his other articles together.[2] If he could survey his literary output from today's perspective, however, he would probably see more response to his writings on emotion than to those on any other topic in psychology. Today's psychology textbooks may ignore James's work in other areas, at best incorporating a quotation about habit or instinct, but they rarely fail to present the essentials of his theory of emotion. There are, however, major discrepancies between what James said he meant and what critical readers think he meant. For whatever reason, his theorizing on emotion has commanded more interest than any of his other psychological contributions.

To match our interpretation with James's intent, we should begin with his opening remarks in "What Is an Emotion?" Physiologists, he said, had explored the cognitive and volitional roles of the brain but had ignored its connections with aesthetic and emotional experience. An important issue for the new physiological psychology was thus left hanging; is the "bodily seat" of emotions found in special centers in the brain or in motor and sensory processes? If the former, then the prevailing theory of cerebral functioning was contradicted; James thus tried to make a case for the idea that emotions are caused by sensory and motor processes of the same sort that underlie our perceptual experiences. The theory that no special centers in the brain are required for emotions was consistent with his earlier denial of efferent feelings in "The Feeling of Effort," and he thus chose to construe emotions, like perceptions, as products of afferent bodily processes.[3] In "What Is an Emotion?" James hoped to show that an already existing and relatively simple model of the brain can accommodate emotions. "But although this seems to be the chief result of the arguments I am to urge, I should say that they were not originally framed for the sake of any such result. They grew out of fragmentary introspective observations, and it was only when these had already combined into a theory that the thought of the simplification the theory might bring to cerebral physiology occurred to me, and made it seem more important than before."[4] In his earliest discussions of emotion, then, he explicitly stated that his chief triumph was in the domain of brain theory; indeed, identifying the physical conditions of states of consciousness was emphasized in the first pages of *Principles* as an essential task of the new psychology. For organizational reasons, the chapter on emotions in *Principles* does not begin with the same emphasis upon brain physiology—it opens instead with a statement that the close connections between instinct and emotion often make them impossible to distinguish—but the same physiological point eventually occurs: "If the neural process underlying emotional consciousness be what I have now sought to prove it, the physiology of the brain becomes a simpler matter than has been hitherto supposed. Sensational, associational, and motor elements are all that the organ need contain."[5]

The issue that dominated James's thinking was to define emotion. He was impatient with traditional psychology, from Descartes onward, which he said was content to describe and classify the varieties of emotion. Some writers bored him with their copious descriptions of the objects and circumstances that might cause different emotions, and others, especially authors of German psychology textbooks, tired him by characterizing emotions through an endless series of synonyms; for example, hatred is antipathy, animosity, resentment, aversion, dislike, spite, and so on. Traditional psychology was dull, compared to fiction and poetry, in its treatment of emotion; it did not succeed in being a science of the subject, nor did it illuminate emotion at the commonsense level.

> But as far as "scientific psychology" of the emotions goes, I may have been surfeited by too much reading of classic works on the subject, but I should as lief read verbal descriptions of the shapes of the rocks on a New Hampshire farm as toil through them again. They give one nowhere a central point of view, or a deductive or generative principle. They distinguish and refine and specify *in infinitum* without ever getting on to another logical level. Whereas the beauty of all truly scientific work is to get to ever deeper levels. Is there no way out from this level of individual description in the case of the emotions? I believe there is a way out, but I fear that few will take it.[6]

The way out was to hypothesize a generalized definition of emotion, and in pursuing such a definition James paid little or no attention to other issues and questions. He did not develop anything like a psychoanalytic account of such emotions as guilt, anxiety, jealousy, or hostility. Psychoanalytic observations occur aphoristically here and there, but nothing approaching a systematic depth-psychology of emotions can be found in James. Nor was he concerned, as many predecessors had been, with working out subtle relations between emotions or trying to define one in terms of others; to do so would have doomed his discussion to the merely descriptive level. Although he was obliged to say something about the relation of an emotion to its object or context, he was unconcerned about the technical matters that have been studied by recent philosophers.[7] Nor does James explain systematically the motivational role of any emotion, how, for example, the emotion attached to the need to achieve keeps a person in pursuit of some goal. However, he had great interest in the overlap between instincts and emotions, and his contentions on this topic provide the outlines of a motivational theory of emotion.

Emotions and instincts are sometimes indistinct in that what elicits an instinctive reaction, such as an impulse to strike back after being hit, also provokes the emotional response of anger or rage; the two blend into a characteristic, unitary reaction. In general, James held, emotional responses terminate in the body whereas instinctive ones extend into the environment; there are times, for example, when we fear something without doing anything to it. The class of emotional impulses is larger than that of instinctive ones, their stimuli are more numerous and their symptoms or expressions more internal and elusive to identify; nevertheless, he insisted that the physiological basis of both is the same. The intimate connections between instinct and emotion suggested to thinkers like Darwin and Spencer that a science of emotion might be furthered through inquiries into the genesis of emotions. James, too, advocated the idea that behaviors associated with or expressive of emotions can be understood genetically.

> Some movements of expression can be accounted for as *weakened repetitions of movements which formerly* (when they were stronger) *were of utility to the subject.* Others are similarly weakened repetitions of movements which under other conditions were *physiologically necessary effects.* Of the latter reactions the respiratory disturbances in anger and fear might be taken as examples—organic reminiscences . . . of the blowings of the man making a series of combative efforts, of the pantings of one in precipitate flight. Such at least is a suggestion made by Mr. Spencer which has found approval. (*Principles,* 2:478)

Spencer was the first to suggest that other behaviors indicative of fear and anger are explicable as arousals of formerly useful acts. Anger is often manifested in such movements as gnashing of the teeth and dilation of the eyes and nostrils, behaviors that were once useful for survival and still occur in emotional moments when similarities between present and ancient occasions reexcite them, even though their former utility has been long lost. One of Darwin's hypotheses claims that the snarl or sneer is a vestigial behavior from the days when our ancestors had large canine teeth and, like dogs, bared them for attack; similarly, he theorized that we open our mouths in astonishment because humans were once accustomed to doing so when listening intensely and quickly catching their breath before vigorous bodily effort. We distend our nostrils when angry, Spencer said, because our forefathers did so during combat, when "their mouth was filled up by a part of an antagonist's body that had been seized (!)" (*Principles*, 2:479). We tremble in fear because fear warms the blood; we laugh intermittently because doing so counteracts the anemia caused in the brain by the action of an amusing stimulus upon the vaso-motor nerves; we compress our lips when resolving to do something because tightly closing the mouth retains air in the lungs during physical exertion; the tendency to caress when feeling tender emotion is traceable to the high blood pressure of sexual intercourse and its consequent palpitations; and the "effusion of tears is explained by this author and by Darwin to be a blood-withdrawing agency" to relieve the brain of the blood pressure caused by the stimulating occasion.[8]

Somewhat surprisingly, James ticked off these examples of genetic explanations of emotions without specific criticisms, although he expressed some reservation. He clearly wanted to advance the psychology of emotion beyond individual reporting of experience and subjective comparison of feelings, and thus efforts to explain the origin of emotions in the manner of Darwin and Spencer were to be encouraged. But although he did not criticize the evolutionists, he had misgivings nonetheless. Though definitely siding with Darwin and against Lamarck about whether traits acquired in one generation are transmitted to successive ones, he nevertheless saw limitations of evolutionistic thinking. "No more if we take ancestral experiences into account than if we limit ourselves to those of the individual after birth, can we believe that the couplings of terms within the mind are simple copies of corresponding couplings impressed upon it by the environment" (*Principles*, 2:688). This conclusion is more emphatically true, he said, of emotional and aesthetic matters. In their application to emotions, the closing words of *Principles* are especially resonant: "And the more sincerely one seeks to trace the actual course of *psychogenesis*, the steps by which as a race we may have come by the peculiar mental attributes which we possess, the more clearly one perceives 'the slowly gathering twilight close in utter night'" (2:688). The importance which Darwin and Spencer ascribed to instinct and innate capacities leads to another genetic explanation, unrelated to natural history and inherited experience, based on physiology. James's theory stressed the physiological rather than ancestral origins of emotions. He objected to Spencer's idea that instincts are formed initially by the multiplication of experiences or by associations. One of James's quarrels with traditional associationism was that he believed certain emotions and instinctive reactions, such as desire and acquisitiveness, to be primitive, innate, or nativistic to the human psyche and therefore not the products of other elements associated in special ways. He did not deny that many instincts may have originated in human evolution; sympathy, maternal love, and the anger that attends pugnacity or the hunting instinct are all instinctive emotions traceable to ancestral experience.[9]

In "The Moral Equivalent of War" James wrote: "Our ancestors have bred pugnacity into our bone and marrow, and thousands of years of peace won't breed it out of us."[10] But unless evolutionary explanations could part company with associationistic analyses of emotions, James chose to separate himself from both. James's view, compatible with if not directly implied by Darwinian theory, was that the human race did not start as a tabula rasa any more than today's infant does. The innate capacities of the brain and nervous system are as important as ancestral experience in explaining the range of human emotion. The fear of high places, James suggested, is a peculiarity of the nervous system and, like the love of music or the propensity for seasickness, has no teleological significance as an instinct that evolution has selected for survival.[11] Merely because an emotion is classified as instinctive does not mean that it originated from a multiplication of experiences in the race; its origin may rather be physiological. After offering examples of emotional reactions (bodily responses) that might be residues of actions that were once teleological, James added:

> The reader will himself have felt how conjectural and fallible in some of the instances the explanation is—there remain many reactions which cannot so be explained at all, and these we must write down for the present as purely idiopathic effects of the stimulus. Amongst these are the effects on the viscera and internal glands, the dryness of the mouth and diarrhea and nausea of fear, the liver-disturbances which sometimes produce jaundice after excessive rage . . . the gaping of expectancy, the "lump in the throat" of grief, the tickling there and the swallowing of embarrassment. . . . It seems as if even the changes of blood-pressure and heart-beat during emotional excitement might, instead of being teleologically determined, prove to be purely mechanical or physiological outpourings through the easiest drainage-channels—the pneumogastrics and sympathetic nerves happening under ordinary circumstances to be such channels. (*Principles*, 2:482)

Darwin had explained certain bodily expressions of emotion by a principle of antithesis; if a specific stimulus caused a specific set of movements, then an opposite stimulus would cause an opposite set of movements, even though these might have no utility whatever. James commented: "It is in this wise that Darwin explains the expression of impotence, raised eyebrows, and shrugged shoulders, dropped arms and open palms, as being the antithesis of the frowning brow, the thrown-back shoulders, and clenched fists of rage, which is the emotion of power. No doubt a certain number of movements can be formulated under this law; but whether it expresses a *causal* principle is more than doubtful. It has been by most critics considered the least successful of Darwin's speculations on this subject" (*Principles*, 2:484). James also warned against Spencer's tendency to suppose that bodily expressions of emotion are always derived from some useful role in ancient acts; we should not assume, for instance, that each facial muscle is uniquely expressive of a certain emotion.[12] The muscular activities connected with any emotion are so variable and pathological, he concluded, that they can hardly be explained by inherited habit or former utility; for example, trembling that occurs in terror and other excitements is pathological and cannot be explained teleologically. Although James brought to the new psychology much of what the evolutionists claimed about instincts and somewhat less of what they claimed about emotions, he detected definite limits to their contribution on either subject. The gaps in their explanations might be filled by information from physiology. Indeed, physiology was James's focus in "What Is an Emotion?" and in "The Physical Basis of Emotion" his first and last theoretical statements on the subject; physiological considerations likewise dominate the chapter on emotions in *Principles*. However helpful the explanations offered by Darwin and Spencer, they failed to answer the question, What is an emotion? To formulate an adequate answer, we must understand what is happening when we undergo emotional excitement, what the emotion consists of, to what extent it is physiological, and the kind of cerebral and nervous-system model that will explain its occurrence.[13]

THE JAMES-LANGE THEORY OF EMOTION

James first defined emotion in the 1884 essay "What Is an Emotion?" In the chapter on emotions in *Principles* he acknowledged a similar definition by a Danish thinker, C. G. Lange, and in 1894 he wrote: "Professor Lange of Copenhagen and the present writer published, independently of each other, the same theory of emotional consciousness," now known as the James-Lange theory of emotion.[14] Although James differed with Lange on certain details, they agreed on the essentials of what constitutes an emotion; both asserted that it is "the effect of the organic changes, muscular and visceral, of which the so-called 'expression' of the emotion consists. It is thus not a primary feeling, directly aroused by the exciting object or thought, but a secondary feeling indirectly aroused; the primary effect being the organic changes in question, which are immediate reflexes following upon the presence of the object."[15] This is the nerve of the theory as stated in 1894 and is the major point urged in both the 1884 essay and the chapter in *Principles*. Although his emphasis and formulation changed significantly between the earliest and the latest discussions of emotion—the changes have indeed baffled and even annoyed James's commentators—he adhered to basically the same theory throughout.[16]

To understand the theory, we must appreciate not only what it asserts but also what it denies—the existence of "bodiless" emotions. Consider the emotion of fright caused by perceiving an approaching emu. According to common sense and traditional psychology, James said, the perception of the emu causes a pure, primary feeling of fright—pure in that it is purely mental and independent of physiological events, primary in that it is the initial or direct effect of the perception. Any associated physical changes, such as running, sweating, heightened blood-pressure, palpitations, or trembling, are called the expressions or effects of the bodiless emotion of fright. Our common sense presumes that fright, considered as an exclusively mental or nonbodily state of consciousness whose nature is given to introspection, was immediately brought into existence by the perception of the emu and then gave rise to the bodily effects or expressions. All emotions are likewise ghostly intermediaries between our perception and our bodily reactions. The James-Lange theory denied this presumption of common sense and traditional psychology, objecting vigorously to the idea that an emotion is a ghostly intermediary.

> Our natural way of thinking about these standard emotions is that the mental perception of some fact excites the mental affection called emotion, and that this latter state of mind gives rise to the bodily expression. My thesis on the contrary is that *the bodily changes follow directly the PERCEPTION of the exciting fact, and that our feeling of the same changes as they occur is the emotion.* Common sense says, we lose our fortune, are sorry and weep; we meet a bear, are frightened and run; we are insulted by a rival, are angry and strike. The hypothesis here to be defended says that this order of sequence is incorrect, that the one mental state is not immediately induced by the others, that the bodily manifestations must first be interposed between, and that the more rational statement is that we feel sorry because we cry, angry because we strike, afraid because we tremble, and not that we cry, strike, or tremble, because we are sorry, angry, or fearful, as the case may be. Without the bodily states following on the perception, the latter would be purely cognitive in form, pale, colourless, destitute of emotional warmth. We might then see the bear, and judge it best to run, receive the insult and deem it right to strike, but we could not actually *feel* afraid or angry.[17]

Let us focus on the assertion that the emotion of fright is the feeling of the bodily or organic changes immediately caused by perceiving the emu. The emotion consists of bodily elements, James argued; its felt nature is due to felt bodily events, and the felt emotion cannot occur until those events are caused by the perception. This is the core of the James-Lange theory of emotion and is what James repeated when he defended the theory. He denied the concept of the ghostly intermediary, claiming instead that an emotion is the immediately subsequent feeling of bodily changes provoked by the exciting perception. James himself termed this idea his theory's vital point:

> If we fancy some strong emotion, and then try to abstract from our consciousness of it all the feelings of its characteristic bodily symptoms, we find that we have nothing left behind, no ''mind-stuff'' out of which the emotion can be constituted, and that a cold and neutral state of intellectual perception is all that remains. It is true, that although most people, when asked, say that their introspection verifies this statement, some persist in saying theirs does not. . . . I cannot help thinking that all who rightly apprehend this problem will agree with the proposition above laid down. . . . Can one fancy the state of rage and picture no ebullition of it in the chest, no flushing of the face, no dilatation of the nostrils, no clenching of the teeth, no impulse to vigorous action, but in their stead limp muscles, calm breathing, and a placid face? The present writer, for one, certainly cannot. . . . In like manner of grief: what would it be without its tears, its sobs, its suffocation of the heart, its pang in the breast-bone? . . . A purely disembodied human emotion is a nonentity. I do not say that it is a

contradiction in the nature of things; or that pure spirits are necessarily condemned to cold intellectual lives; but I say that for *us*, emotion dissociated from all bodily feeling is inconceivable. The more closely I scrutinise my states, the more persuaded I become, that whatever moods, affections, and passions I have, are in very truth constituted by, and made up of, those bodily changes we ordinarily call their expression or consequence; and the more it seems to me that if I were to become corporeally anaesthetic, I should be excluded from the life of the affections, harsh and tender alike, and drag out an existence of merely cognitive or intellectual form.[18]

What numerous commentators have found confusing is James's saying in the same breath that an emotion *is* a bodily commotion of some sort and that each emotion has its own characteristic bodily *nature*. Many critics assumed that he meant the latter concept as his main point and seized upon it for quarrel.[19] He had invited this quarrel by seemingly equating fright with running and trembling, or grief with weeping and pangs in the breast-bone; many critics responded that one can be paralyzed with fear and be unable to run or tremble, or be transfixed with grief such that neither weeping nor pangs occur. James had in fact criticized Lange for oversimplifying the physical symptoms to which grief is susceptible and had emphasized that elaborate descriptions of emotions in terms of their physical manifestations was tedious; he clearly thought his critics' quarrel with him was insubstantial.[20] He agreed that, although there may be general correlations between felt emotions and their physical symptoms in specific societies and individuals, too much variation occurs to permit one emotion to be equated with one class of bodily manifestations. He took the blame for having evoked this critical response:

> I think that all the force of such objections lies in the slapdash brevity of the language used, of which I admit that my own text set a bad example when it said "we are all frightened because we run." Yet let the word "run" but stand for what it was meant to stand for, namely, for many other movements in us, of which invisible visceral ones seem by far the most essential. . . . Whatever the fear may be in such a case, it is not constituted by the voluntary act.[21]

In the 1894 essay James thus abandoned his striking formulation of the 1884 essay and *Principles* as having been slapdash; he never really believed that we are frightened because we run or are sorry because we cry, nor that any given emotion can be identified in terms of a specific act or bodily symptom. Nevertheless, he maintained the core of the James-Lange theory, the claim that a felt emotion is some feeling of bodily, organic change, whether or not it is a chronic or even identifiable symptom of the emotion. James consistently denied that emotions such as anger, jealousy, and grief, which commonly exhibit physical symptoms and are perceivable as bodily commotions, are ghostly or bodiless; he arrived at this conclusion by introspection and experiment in imagination. Introspection often allows us to identify the relevant bodily features of an emotion, but such features are sometimes elusive; it is only natural, James thought, that bodily changes, however elusive they are to introspection, are felt in experiencing the emotion. A bodiless emotion would involve nothing to be felt, but James believed that every actual emotion has felt objects or contents, organic changes occurring within the body.

James's discussion of emotion illustrates his concept of the new psychology as a cooperative enterprise between introspection and physiology. In answering the objection that the theory implies that voluntary, cold-blooded arousal of the bodily manifestations of an emotion ought to arouse the emotion itself—an implication contradicted by ordinary experience—James urged his readers to appreciate how complex emotions are. "The immense number of parts modified in each emotion is what makes it so difficult for us to reproduce in cold blood the total and integral expression of any one of them. We may catch the trick with the voluntary muscles, but fail with the skin, glands, heart, and other viscera. Just as an artificially initiated sneeze lacks something of the reality, so the attempt to imitate an emotion in the absence of its normal instigating cause is apt to be rather 'hollow.' "[22] (In admitting this, James did not overlook the fact that we can, by our own volition, develop sadness by moping around or joy by creative activity; this fact partly prompted the striking formulation that we do not cry because we are sad, but rather the reverse.) In any emotional experience an extraordinary variety of bodily changes occurs, and James believed that "every one of the bodily changes, whatsoever it be, is *felt*, acutely or obscurely, the moment it occurs. If the reader has never paid attention to this matter, he will be both interested and astonished to learn how many different local bodily feelings he can detect in himself as characteristic of his various emotional moods."[23] The opportunities are enormous for introspectively discovering or clarifying the physiological details that contribute to an emotional experience. Introspection itself testifies to this fact, and James thought that skeptics could be reassured by reading physiology.

> But not even a Darwin has exhaustively enumerated *all* the bodily affections characteristic of any one of the standard emotions. More and more, as physiology advances, we begin to discern how almost infinitely numerous and subtle they must be. The researches of Mosso with the plethysmograph have shown that not only the heart, but the entire circulatory system, forms a sort of soundingboard, which every change of our consciousness, however slight, may make reverberate. Hardly a sensation comes to us without sending waves of alternate constriction and dilatation down the arteries of our arms. The blood-vessels of the abdomen act reciprocally with those of the more outward parts. The bladder and bowels, the glands of the mouth, throat, and skin, and the liver, are known to be affected gravely in certain severe emotions, and are unquestionably affected transiently when the emotions are of a lighter sort. . . . And what is really equally prominent, but less likely to be admitted until special attention is drawn to the fact, is the continuous cooperation of the voluntary muscles in our emotional states. Even when no change of outward attitude is

produced, their inward tension alters to suit each varying mood, and is felt as a difference of tone or of strain. In depression the flexors tend to prevail; in elation or belligerent excitement the extensors take the lead. And the various permutations and combinations of which these organic activities are susceptible, make it abstractly possible that no shade of emotion, however slight, should be without a bodily reverberation as unique, when taken in its totality, as is the mental mood itself.[24]

This passage indicates that James thought the new psychologist could work back and forth between physiology and introspection. With the development of laboratory psychology, physiological findings were valuable for checking the introspective reports of subjects; for example, an investigator could discover the discrepancies that might occur between what was actually in a subject's visual field from what only seemed to the subject to be there. Physiological facts could thus guide introspection, causing the introspector to look for what he might never have supposed was there. James often appealed to physiology to confirm conclusions which careful introspection suggested but which were not appreciated by careless introspectors or were questioned by those unconvinced of the reliability of introspection. He made such appeals, for example, to defend his theories of the stream of consciousness and of emotion. Conversely, a physiological claim—that the flexors are involved in the emotion of depression, for example—could be checked out introspectively. James argued by analogy when discussing mind-body relations, contending, for instance, that because the brain displays a process of continuous modification, so should the experience that accompanies that process in the brain; or, because introspection reveals prominent features within consciousness, so should the bodily process that accompanies it. In explaining his grounds for connecting emotion with afferent rather than efferent nerve currents, he wrote: "[The theory of emotion] assumes (what probably every one assumes) that there must be a process of some sort in the nerve-centres for emotion, and it simply defines that process to consist of afferent currents. It does this on no general theoretic ground, but *because of the introspective appearances exclusively.*"[25] Although James appealed to mind-body analogies when they made sense to him, he often rejected them when used by others if they failed to agree with his own convictions.

> We do, it is true, but follow a natural analogy when we say . . . that the former direction of consciousness [outward] ought to be mediated by outgoing nerve-currents, and the latter [inward] by currents passing in. But is not this analogy a mere superficial fancy, which reflection shows to have no basis in any existing knowledge of what such currents can or cannot bring to pass? We surely know too little of the psycho-physic relation to warrant us in insisting that the similarity of direction of two physical currents makes it impossible that they should bring a certain inner contrast about.[26]

When James and his fellow psychologists alternated between physiology and introspection, developing biological models by analogy to what introspection seemed to find within consciousness and vice versa, there was often controversy about which analogies were relevant. A recurrent objection to James's theory was that it implied that a perceived object produces by itself an emotion in the perceiver; this can hardly be the case, critics argued, since emotions depend upon our mental state as well. A hunter who wants to find a bear will be delighted upon seeing one, but someone surprised to see a bear and afraid that it will attack is frightened. James's reply is somewhat cryptic and difficult to evaluate. He evidently thought that his theory could accommodate the objection, and he apparently believed, though his reasons are unclear, that whether we hunt or flee the bear, our reaction is at bottom instinctive.[27] After granting to his critics that the mental idea produced by the perception of the bear is as important as the bear itself, he declared that the truly important question is this: "Does the emotional excitement which follows the idea follow it immediately, or secondarily, and as a consequence of the 'diffusive wave' of impulses aroused?"[28] After entertaining the merits of the objection to his theory, he returned to this critical question. If the emotion follows immediately upon the idea's occurrence, it is purely mental, whereas if it follows secondarily as the result of a diffusive wave of organic changes, then there are bodily changes that both cause and constitute the emotion, as his theory claims. He sometimes seems to have been less interested in what causes an emotion than in what an emotion is; whenever pressed by criticism of the James-Lange hypothesis, he insisted that the "nerve" of the theory, that emotion consists of bodily commotion, remains intact. Whatever the causal or epistemological relations between the emotion and its object, the experience of emotion must be immediately preceded by bodily changes that can be identified, at least theoretically, as the "stuff" of the experience.

The most important criticisms of the James-Lange theory are directed at its claim that an emotion is a bodily commotion. One argument points to the variety of bodily symptoms or constituents of any specific emotion. One critic stated that the actions connected with emotions tend to become alike in proportion to their intensity; people weep from excessive joy; trembling and paling accompany excesses of hope as well as fear. James responded: "Do not the subject's feelings also then tend to become alike, if considered in themselves apart from all their differing intellectual contexts? My theory maintains that they should do so; and such reminiscences of extreme emotion as I possess rather seem to confirm than to invalidate such a view."[29] This reply seems somewhat obscure. Despite the presence of pallor and trembling in both extreme hope and extreme fear, and their resemblance in intensity of excitement, the two emotions retain a striking distinctness in feeling. It is not plain why the James-Lange theory is committed, as James asserted here, to the thesis that the feelings in such cases are alike. There seems to be some confusion in his concepts of emotion and feeling; if these are adequately distinguished, perhaps we can understand how extreme fear and hope may resemble each other in bodily commotion but still feel very different. In considering the critical hypothesis that there is less inconstancy between symptoms and emotions in "motived" emotions (those caused by identifiable motives) than in "unmotived" ones (induced, for example, by drugs), James responded: "I cannot regard this argument as fatal to Lange's and my theory so long as we remain in such real ignorance as to what the subjective variations of our emotions actually are. Exacter observation, both introspective and symptomatic, might well show in 'motived' emotions also just the amount of inconstancy that the theory demands."[30] It seems odd that he appealed here to the "real ignorance" that attends our knowledge of our own emotional states, whereas he disposed of another objection by invoking his "reminiscences" of his own emotional experiences. At the very least, James might have provided more introspective evidence from his own experience to help his readers understand his confidence that emotions vary neatly with their bodily symptoms. Even this confidence seemed to falter at times, as when he pondered how the symptoms of the same emotion may vary from one person to another. "The natural reply is that the bodily variations are within limits, and that the symptoms of the angers and of the fears of different men still preserve enough *functional* resemblance, to say the very least, in the midst of their diversity to lead us to call them by identical names. Surely there *is* no definite affection of 'anger' in an 'entitative' sense."[31] Although we may agree that emotions are not recurrent psychic entities, the idea that a functional resemblance between bodily symptoms is sufficient cause to ascribe anger to different persons deserts the introspectable criterion James had used thus far for identifying emotions. A functional resemblance can be conceived only in terms of behavior, and once we make the move from introspection to behavior, we are confronted by two possibly conflicting methods of determining what sort of emotional experience a person is undergoing. James did not give this problem the attention it deserved.

That he resorted to a concept of functional resemblance, stressed the bodily character of emotion, and declared that we are sad because we cry, has supported the interpretation that James's theory of emotion was behavioristic.[32] His view may seem to be that emotions are the effects of behavior (especially if all relevant bodily symptoms count as behavior) but never its causes. His admittedly "slapdash" formulations invite such an interpretation, as do some of his most careful statements, especially those which conceive of emotions as merely the "tag-ends" of physiological disturbances. He corrected his earlier statement that we are sad because we cry or afraid because we run, observing that running does not in fact produce fear but rather exhilaration. His theory of emotion was never intended, despite some misleading language, to deny the commonsense conviction that fear causes running and sadness causes crying. James meant rather that, until internal bodily changes occur that are causally connected with running or crying, no emotion of fear or sorrow will occur; the emotion is then the direct cause of the running or crying. (I remind the reader that my idea of what James "really" believed here is based upon the revisions that are found in the 1894 essay "The Physical Basis of Emotion.") Given James's insistence that consciousness is inherently impulsive and that ideas or states of consciousness, unless inhibited, are always translated into behavior, it would have been inconsistent with his basic convictions to have denied causality to emotions by downgrading them to mere epiphenomena. In connecting emotion with instinct, he meant not only to corroborate but to deepen the commonsense assumption that human behavior is constantly the effect of human emotion.

James's theory recognized—an important point in its favor, he believed—that emotion is not in direct contact with the mind either in its origin or in its elimination. "An emotion of fear, for example, or surprise, is not a direct effect of the object's presence on the mind, but an effect of that still earlier effect, the bodily commotion which the object suddenly excites."[33] Before an emotion reaches the mind, its intermediary of bodily commotion must occur; if the emotion is to be avoided, its intermediary must be displaced. Those commentators who sensed behaviorism in the declaration that we don't cry because we are sad but that we are sad because we cry, were not entirely wrong. In addition to James's endorsement of everyday observations that depressed behavior can produce the emotion of depression, or that energetic behavior can yield energetic emotions, he was an early advocate of behavior modification as a strategy for coping with threatening emotions. This technique was a natural correlate of the James-Lange theory, he thought; if an emotion consists of internal commotion, it will naturally intensify if the commotion is allowed to intensify, for example, by giving vent to tears or shutting out the world. We ought then to pay less attention to what we feel than to what we do and express. "If we only check a cowardly impulse in time . . . or if we only *don't* strike the blow . . . our feelings themselves will presently be the calmer and better, with no particular guidance from us on their own account. . . . By regulating the action, which is under the more direct control of the will, we can indirectly regulate the feeling, which is not."[34] To become cheerful, for instance, we should stand, sit, walk, and speak cheerfully, and "to feel brave, act as if we *were* brave, use all our will to that end, and a courage-fit will very likely replace the fit of fear."[35] James's underlying concept of emotion is ambivalent in that it considers emotion essential to the human condition but denies it the spiritual status accorded to the will and other mental faculties. He quoted from a contemporary inspirational book to support his belief that emotions are better ignored because they are not the "indicators of your spiritual state, but are merely the indicators of your temperament or of your present physical condition."[36] One practical implication of the James-Lange theory is that we can induce a desired emotion by acting so as to produce the needed bodily stirrings, and can eliminate an unwanted emotion by acting so as to dispel the bodily stirrings already there. James did not recommend an introspective scrutiny of emotions as a method of modifying them but instead advised behavior as the effective means. "To wrestle with a bad feeling only pins our attention on it, and keeps it still fastened in the mind: whereas, if we act as if from some better feeling, the old bad feeling soon folds its tent like an Arab, and silently steals away" (*Talks,* 133). Current debates about the merits of behavior modification, introspection as a tool in therapy, and psychoanalytic efforts to treat the emotions, are important for a comprehensive assessment of James's recommendations for dealing with the turbulence of emotion.

James's behavioristic strategy for coping with emotion was not so exaggerated that it led him to conclude that a person's inner life is unimportant. Indeed, in a reference to Freud he acknowledged that the treatment of a neurotic requires an understanding of that person's inner experience, which is difficult for the patient to communicate to others.[37] Like Freud, he understood that morbid emotion obstructs both action and thought and that a doctor must have a sense of what the patient suffers from such emotion. But for James the remedy lay primarily in action, and his confidence in this method was due to his confidence that he knew what emotions are: "In the unhealthy-minded, apart from all sorts of old regrets, ambitions checked by shames and aspirations obstructed by timidities, it consists mainly of bodily discomforts not distinctly localized by the sufferer, but breeding a general self-mistrust and sense that things are not as they should be with him. . . . In the healthy-minded, on the contrary, there are no fears or shames to discover; and the sensations that pour in from the organism only help to swell the general vital sense of security and readiness for anything that may turn up" (*Talks*, 134–35). Morbid emotions are basically "bodily discomforts not distinctly localized" by the sufferer, which can cause malaise and general self-distrust. Like psychoanalysts, James worried about remedies such as alcohol and drugs which treat only the symptoms and not the causes and are therefore only temporarily effective. It never occurred to him, however, that the psychoanalytic process ought to be adopted. Besides disliking Freudian symbolism and dream interpretation, he suspected that a clinical practice emphasizing conscious focus upon morbid states will only contribute further to the morbidity.[38] Unlike some of his critics, James did not believe that all emotions are intentional in the sense of being directed toward an object; that is, not all emotions, especially morbid or pathological ones, resemble the fear *of a bear*, the joy *of a birth*, or the anger *at someone*.

> The best proof that the immediate cause of emotion is a physical effect on the nerves is furnished by those *pathological cases in which the emotion is objectless*. One of the chief merits, in fact, of the view which I propose seems to me that we can so easily formulate by its means pathological cases and normal cases under a common scheme. In every asylum we find examples of absolutely unmotivated fear, anger, melancholy, or conceit. . . . A friend who has had occasional attacks of this most distressing of all maladies [dread or morbid fear] tells me that in his case the whole drama seems to centre about the region of the heart and respiratory apparatus, that his main effort during the attacks is to get control of his inspiration and to slow his heart, and that the moment he attains to breathing deeply and to holding himself erect, the dread, *ipso facto*, seems to depart.[39]

Acquaintance with or knowledge of the "feel" of an emotion, whether by the sufferer or by a doctor, can eventually provide clues about which physiological occurrences in the sufferer can be altered to modify the distressing emotion. The essential remedy is doing something to remove the bodily discomforts, vaguely sensed, that breed the emotional malaise and to avoid being preoccupied with the peculiar, often debilitating "feel" of the emotion. James wrote enthusiastically, and with a touch of naïveté, about the training and exercise of the human body. He applauded the new interest in tennis, hiking, skating, and bicycling by American women, guessing that such activities would improve them morally and psychologically.

> The strength of the British Empire lies in the strength of character of the individual Englishman, taken all alone by himself. And that strength, I am persuaded, is perennially nourished and kept up by nothing so much as by the national worship, in which all classes meet, of athletic outdoor life and sport . . . that blessed internal peace and confidence, that *acquiescentia in seipso*, as Spinoza used to call it, that wells up from every part of the body of a muscularly well-trained human being, and soaks the indwelling soul of him with satisfaction, is, quite apart from every consideration of its mechanical utility, an element of spiritual hygiene of supreme significance. (*Talks*, 135–37)

James did not mention people who cannot pull themselves up by their own bootstraps and achieve cheerfulness through positive posturing, top athletes who take drugs to mask chronic depression, or sedentary types who are constantly and insultingly blissful. While his message is obviously sensible to an extent, its limitations are equally obvious, and his hope that the "bottled lightning," the inner tension and turbulence he saw in so many Americans, might be released by relaxing the superego through physical exercise, is an exaggeration of an otherwise useful point.[40] The tendency to embrace a generalization on the basis of homely bits of evidence is clear also in James's observations on repression. Consistent with the James-Lange theory, he conceived of the repression, or the denial of expression, of an emotion as destroying the emotion; theoretically, the emotion is nothing more than its bodily expression. "Refuse to express a passion, and it dies" was a law for James to which there were no exceptions; he explained alleged counterexamples, such as the effects of suppressing tears or the calming results that follow a frank expression of anger, as showing not that an emotion can exist or even intensify while its bodily expressions are repressed, but rather that in particular individuals certain repressions or expressions produce certain results. He supposed that when repression occurs, the nerve-currents may be forced into other paths, the effects of which can, he admitted, occasionally be worse. "When we teach children to repress their emotions, it is not that they may *feel* more, quite the reverse. It is that they *think* more! for to a certain extent whatever nerve-currents are diverted from the regions below, must swell the activity of the thought-tracts of the brain."[41] In light of the evidence therapists cite today to show that repression, rather than destroying emotion, buries it in the unconscious, where it nags, irritates, and finally becomes strong enough to demand outlet, we seek something less brusque than James's explanation of repression. But the fact that he mentioned repression at all indicates the extraordinary richness of his psychology.

Although James was ambivalent about emotion—forced to be realistic about its part in the human condition, but reluctant to admit it to the inner circle of spirituality—we should not underestimate his positive attitude toward the life of emotion. While he omitted references to emotion in his account of the innermost self and regarded many emotions as enslavers or torturers, on the other hand he recognized their indispensable and beneficial role in human existence and built emotion into the origin, method, and goal of philosophy itself. The kind of philosophy that most infuriated him was what he judged to be cold, abstract, and disconnected altogether from passion and desire. Whereas some philosophers might converse about the purely cerebral aspects of their work, James spoke of the cravings, passions, and emotions that incite us to philosophize and to accept one school of thought over another. Indeed, his highly controversial doctrine held that it is sometimes rational and legitimate to permit desires and emotions to be influential in our philosophical commitments. "Nothing could be more absurd than to hope for the definitive triumph of any philosophy which should refuse to legitimate, and to legitimate in an emphatic manner, the more powerful of our emotional and practical tendencies."[42] With characteristic eloquence James gave feeling to thought and thought to feeling. He expressed a positive attitude toward emotion in "The Dilemma of Determinism" as well, arguing that indeterminism, chance, and freedom of the will are based upon the emotion of regret or remorse. If determinism is true, if what happens must happen no matter how evil or calamitous it is, then our regret that it occurs is pointless.[43] The fact that we feel remorse indicates that at least some unfortunate events might have been avoided, different choices might have been made. Whatever the merits of the argument, it rests upon the belief that emotions have an important role, that they can display genuine utility. He made the same point in "The Gospel of Relaxation":

> Prudence and duty and self-regard, emotions of ambition and emotions of anxiety, have, of course, a needful part to play in our lives. But confine them as far as possible to the occasions when you are making your general resolutions and deciding on your plans of campaign, and keep them out of the details. When once a decision is reached and execution is the order of the day, dismiss absolutely all responsibility and care about the outcome. *Unclamp*, in a word, your intellectual and practical machinery, and let it run free; and the service it will do you will be twice as good. (*Talks*, 144)

Emotions are appropriate if they encourage the free, uninhibited flow of thought and action, but not if they linger too long and clog the works, which is likely to occur if we fix our attention upon them. Even anxiety, worrisome as it is, can function profitably in a person's motivation, but it becomes an evil in the soul when it remains too long because of our brooding attachment to it. James's ambivalence in his attitude toward emotions results not as much from a distrust of emotions themselves as from a distrust of our tendency to become preoccupied with them to the point that thought and action are inhibited.

Two issues remain in our discussion of the James-Lange theory, the first concerning James's physiological hypothesis, the second involving his proof of the theory. In his own judgment the theory's main significance is physiological, because it permits the retention of a simpler brain-theory than some thinkers supposed possible. James believed that emotions correspond simply to processes in the motor and sensory centers, without needing any special, separate centers in the brain. The James-Lange theory is consistent with this simple concept of the brain because it conceives of the emotional process in the motor-sensory system not as unique or sui generis but as similar to ordinary perception.[44]

> An object falls on a sense-organ, affects a cortical part, and is perceived; or else the latter, excited inwardly, gives rise to an idea of the same object. Quick as a flash, the reflex currents pass down through their preordained channels, alter the condition of muscle, skin, and viscus; and these alterations, perceived, like the original object, in as many portions of the cortex, combine with it in consciousness and transform it from an object-simply-apprehended into an object-emotionally-felt. No new principles have to be invoked, nothing postulated beyond the ordinary reflex circuits, and the local centres admitted in one shape or another by all to exist.[45]

James's is sometimes called the "peripheral theory" because it states that what happens throughout the limbs or periphery of the body contributes to the nature of the experienced emotion, in contrast to the "centralized theory" that the nature of an emotion is due rather to a centralized system in the brain such as the thalamus. Since James admitted that emotions can occur normally despite peripheral anesthesia or when muscular and movement capacities are neutralized, and are thus dependent upon visceral processes, it would be more accurate to call it the "visceral theory" of emotion.[46] The centralized theory is usually associated with W. B. Cannon, a physiologist and Harvard colleague of James; according to Cannon, experiments showed that emotional behavior can be induced in animals whose visceral input has been eliminated and that such behavior is dependent upon centralized processes in the brain. Even today there is uncertainty as to whether evidence supports or refutes the James-Lange theory, perhaps because the formulation of the theory is vague or because there is initial disagreement about what emotions are and how to interpret subjective reports of them. Further, the physiological findings of experiments often do not neatly support one model rather than another. Some psychologists believe that James, whether right or wrong, moved the psychology of emotion in the proper direction by stressing its biological connection and suggesting ways of investigating that connection. Others conclude that trying to settle the James-Lange debate by attempting to locate a physiological basis for differentiating emotions has proved to be largely a failure, and still others point to ways in which some aspects of the James-Lange theory can be salvaged. Significantly, no one is prepared to defend the theory exactly as its authors stated it. Could James visit today's laboratories, he would probably agree that his theorizing about the physiology of emotion cannot be proved experimentally. The major reason why few psychologists claim explicitly to have refuted it is the assumption that, given its susceptibility to multiple interpretations and, more important, its insusceptibility to testing and observation as it was formulated, it should be considered an honorable if vague step in the history of the psychology of emotion.[47]

James emphasized the difficulty of putting the James-Lange theory to the test. "A case of complete internal and external corporeal anaesthesia, without motor alteration or alteration of intelligence except emotional apathy, would afford, if not a crucial test, at least a strong presumption, in favour of the truth of the view . . . whilst the persistence of strong emotional feeling in such a case would completely overthrow our case."[48] But it would be almost miraculous if such a case occurred; nothing like an ideal test case could be cited from the medical literature. James was intrigued by Ludwig Strümpell's investigation of a fifteen-year-old shoemaker's apprentice who was totally anesthetic inside and out, save for one eye and one ear, and who was said to have exhibited shame when soiling his bed and grief on another occasion. James wrote to Strümpell inquiring whether there was any certainty that the boy really experienced grief and shame. Strümpell replied that, although he had not studied his patient with any idea that a theory like James's might be at stake, he was convinced that the anesthetic boy had experienced not only grief and shame but anger and fear as well; he added that, while this condition was evidence against the James-Lange hypothesis, it did not decisively refute the theory, because his patient suffered from a centrally conditioned anesthesia (as in hysterics) which might permit him to experience more than was apparent. James regretted that Strümpell had not engaged the boy in introspective questioning of a sort that might have shed light on whether, in addition to behaving as if he experienced the emotions, he really experienced them. James expressed the hope that if another such case ever recurred, the patient would be carefully interrogated about his inward emotional states. "And if it then turned out that the patient recognized explicitly the same mood of feeling known under those names in his former normal state, my theory would of course fall. It is, however, to me incredible that the patient should have an *identical* feeling, for the dropping out of the organic sounding-board would necessarily diminish its volume in some way."[49] The last sentence alone suggests how difficult it would be for a critic to show to James's satisfaction that his theory had been refuted.

James returned to the issue of testability in "The Physical Basis of Emotion," reasserting confidence in his theory on the basis of studies he had not known when writing "What Is an Emotion?" or the chapter on emotions in *Principles*. Dr. Paul Sollier had examined a patient whose condition seemed to offer an opportunity for testing the James-Lange thesis. The patient was a forty-four-year-old man whose anesthesia affected cutaneous and mucous surfaces, the entire muscular sense, feelings of hunger and satiety, all needs of defecation and micturition, and the senses of taste, smell, and most of sight. Hearing alone was almost normal, but reflexes and physiognomical expression were lacking and locomotion almost impossible. When interrogated, the patient said he did not feel alive; nothing interested him or gave him pleasure, and he showed no reaction when told that he might be cured. Sollier reported: "Nothing surprises or astonishes him. His state of apathy, of indifference, of extreme emotionlessness, has developed slowly *pari passu* with the anaesthesia. His case realizes, therefore, as completely as possible the experiment desiderated by W. James."[50] But Sollier observed that the patient sometimes wished that his wife would leave his room and occasionally feared that his daughter had died, so he was not entirely without emotion, and his case thus did not prove James's theory. Sollier also induced anesthesia, sometimes visceral and sometimes peripheral or both simultaneously, through hypnotism. James interpreted his results thus: complete peripheral anesthesia eliminated movement altogether; adding visceral anesthesia caused the patient to say she no longer felt alive; when totally anesthetic she no longer reacted feelingly to hallucinations and delusions, and if the deadness was made less complete she said she felt not the normal emotion but perhaps a pain in the head or stomach when something was told to her. If the anesthesia was exclusively peripheral, the emotion occurred almost normally, whereas if it was solely visceral, the emotion was eliminated almost as much as with total anesthesia; occasionally a slight motor reaction occurred during visceral anesthesia when an exciting idea was suggested to the patient. James was cautious in his use of Sollier's work to support his own view, pointing out that what Sollier's hypnotized patient reported may have been partly due to the suggestions of the hypnotist-experimenter, and that in the case of the forty-four-year-old male patient, "inemotivity" may have been caused not merely by the anesthesia but by neural lesions. Nevertheless, he concluded, "If many cases like those of M. Sollier should be found by other observers, I think that Professor Lange's theory and mine ought no longer to be treated as a heresy, but might become the orthodox belief. That part, if there be any, of emotional feeling which is not of afferent origin should be admitted to be insignificant, and the name 'emotion' should be suffered to connote organic excitement as the distinctive feature of the state."[51]

James referred to a distinction between feeling and emotion, something he was anxious to respect while developing his theory of emotion. He declared, despite his equating emotions with bodily or organic processes, that his theory is not a version of materialism, and this contention naturally involves the distinction between emotion and feeling. There are crucial ambiguities in the James-Lange thesis, which are due partly to the notion of dissimilarity between feeling and emotion, partly to a vacillation in James's reiterations of his theory.

FEELING, EMOTION, AND MATERIALISM

Santayana commented in his review of *Principles* that James's battles were with a metaphysical psychology, that the most striking feature of his psychology was the tendency everywhere to substitute a physiological for a mental explanation, and that at times he outdid the materialists themselves. "He has applied the principle of the total and immediate dependence of mind on matter to several fields in which we are still accustomed only to metaphysical or psychological hypotheses."[52] Nowhere does this assessment seem more true than in the chapter on emotions in *Principles*, where James asserted that an emotion is merely a commotion inside one's body; that moods, affections, and passions are constituted by or made up of bodily processes.[53] Despite expressions of doubt, James adopted in *Principles* a mind-body dualism; he also pressed for the view of consciousness as a fighter for its own ends (which presumably are not identical with the brain's) and insisted upon the freedom of attention and will from what we ordinarily consider to be bodily constraints. We must wonder then whether he was disposed to downgrade emotions in his mental hierarchy by construing them as purely physical. This possibility is all the more surprising given his lifelong dislike of materialism and mechanism; indeed he continued in *Principles*: "Let not this view [of emotion] be called materialistic. It is neither more nor less materialistic than any other view which says that our emotions are conditioned by nervous processes" (2:453). He then observed that some philosophers might pronounce his view materialistic merely because it made emotions contingent on afferent impulses or the incoming currents associated with sensations; philosophical prejudice, he remarked, accorded a low status to sensations, as compared with thought and will.

> But our emotions must always be *inwardly* what they are, whatever be the physiological ground of their apparition. If they are deep, pure, worthy, spiritual facts on any conceivable theory of their physiological source, they remain no less deep, pure, spiritual, and worthy of regard on this present sensational theory. They carry their own inner measure of worth with them; and it is just as logical to use the present theory of the emotions for proving that sensational processes need not be vile and material, as to use their vileness and materiality as a proof that such a theory cannot be true.[54]

Despite this statement that the James-Lange theory of emotion is not materialistic, James's supporting argument is somewhat half-hearted and inclined to shift the burden of doubt to the critic; the effort that went into his defense of the freedom of will does not appear here, so the doubt about his underlying attitude toward emotions lingers. Whatever the complications attending his assessment of the value of emotion, however, he was sincere in his denial that it is materialistic, though some interpretive reconstruction is required to see this sincerity clearly. James knew when he denied materialism what he had declared in "The Consciousness of Self" chapter, almost a thousand pages earlier: introspection cannot prove that we are ever aware of anything nonbodily in the way it can show that we are aware of bodily things; nor, on the other hand, can it demonstrate that we are *not* aware of nonbodily things.[55] Introspection can be used in combination with arguments to support or to undermine certain viewpoints, but alone it is powerless to prove or refute, for example, the James-Lange hypothesis. "The only way coercively to *dis*prove it, however, would be to take some emotion, and then exhibit qualities of feeling in it which should be *demonstrably* additional to all those which could possibly be derived from the organs affected at the time. But to detect with certainty such purely spiritual qualities of feeling would obviously be a task beyond human power" (*Principles,* 2:455). There may be purely mental or nonbodily aspects of emotional experience that are inaccessible to introspection, so the introspective evidence that points to the James-Lange theory cannot prove materialism. But if the introspective evidence that points to the theory also points to materialism, is not the theory committed, despite James's demurrer, to materialism? The question is not whether the uncertainties of introspection make materialism uncertain, but whether the alleged truth of the James-Lange theory necessitates materialism.

The only suggestion of an answer to this query in James's discussions of emotion is his cryptic statement denying any commitment to materialism; a fuller grasp of his thinking on this issue thus depends upon our building an interpretation from comments made elsewhere. We may begin to understand why he believed that materialism was not implied by the James-Lange theory if we focus on a characteristic formulation of the theory. When we are emotionally stirred, the theory holds that bodily changes are occurring in us and *"our feeling of the same* [bodily] *changes as they occur is the emotion"* (*Principles,* 2:449). James thus stated that an emotion is identical not with bodily changes but with the feeling of such changes. This notion suggests the interpretation that there are two distinct elements in any emotion, the bodily events or commotion and a feeling of them; whether the feeling is bodily or nonbodily remains an open question. By *feeling* James clearly meant the broad sense of any act or state of consciousness, not the narrow sense of a specific feeling such as disappointment. The issue of materialism thus becomes the issue of whether consciousness or awareness is reducible to bodily occurrences.[56] James's argument throughout *Principles* and throughout his career was that the issue of emotion is decidedly philosophical and cannot be resolved by psychologists, because the questions and considerations involved cannot be adequately answered by introspection, observation, or experiment. James's psychological theory of emotion was never intended to answer the philosophical question, What is the nature of (all) consciousness? To formulate an answer would require arguing philosophically the pros and cons of a materialistic theory of consciousness and then applying the conclusion to the kind of consciousness (feeling) that occurs in experiencing emotion. This sort of reasoning was responsible for James's denial that the James-Lange theory implies materialism, and for his declaring: "In my own mind the theory has no philosophic implications whatever of a general sort. It assumes (what probably every one assumes) that there must be a process of some sort in the nerve-centres for emotion, and it simply defines that process to consist of afferent currents. It does this on no general theoretic grounds, but because of the introspective appearances exclusively."[57]

In equating an emotion with the feeling or consciousness of bodily changes, James reasoned that any state of awareness requires some content or object; in grief and jealousy, for example, the content is bodily changes, which we can introspect. To ask what an emotion is involves asking *what* is being felt; if we rule out disembodied emotions on introspective grounds, the only likely candidate is physiological commotion. Internal bodily events are the materials or objects for consciousness to focus upon when an emotion is experienced. James may have thought that the concept of a disembodied emotion, besides violating what our introspection indicates, makes no provision for an object of consciousness; a purely disembodied emotion would be a thing feeding on itself, a state of consciousness with nothing to be conscious of—not an intelligible idea. He may even have supposed that something is gained by equating emotions with "*how* certain processes in our body feel to us.*" This equation suggests that bodily events are not merely the causes of emotional feeling or awareness but are also felt objects, just as the sharpness of an object causes a feeling or consciousness of sharpness but also exists as a felt property of the object. By this formulation, knowing that we feel jealous entails knowing not only the quality of the feeling but also how associated, unspecified bodily events feel. James may have thought this idea was part of the James-Lange theory; it is a purely metaphysical proposition that seems impossible to test. It implies that emotions provide one way of being acquainted with the inside of our bodies, that emotional consciousness informs us of the inner aspect of some physical occurrences, an aspect which cannot be seen, heard, or handled, but only felt.[58]

James's main reason for denying that the theory is materialistic was probably that it conceives of emotions as akin to sensations, products of the afferent nervous system; whether sensations are mental or physical is a metaphysical and not a psychological question. The bodily changes involved in an emotional experience are all felt; that is, they are the objects of emotional consciousness in the guise of bodily sensations. James was fond of chiding philosophical tradition for downgrading sensations, and in his denial of materialism he was delighted to join the metaphysical fate of emotions with that of sensations. His subsequent metaphysics of radical empiricism, designed to replace traditional mind-body dualism, treated sensations not as mental or physical entities but rather as primitive, neutral elements which, when arranged in certain configurations, become mental or physical complexes. Radical empiricism resembles Berkeley's idealistic interpretation of sensations, and we can thus appreciate why, with this later metaphysics already in view, he would have objected to a materialistic interpretation of sensation and emotion. Perhaps he did not say more about his rationale for disowning materialism in his discussion of emotion because, having asserted that emotions closely resemble sensations, he assumed his readers would understand that the status of emotions, like that of sensations, is a metaphysical rather than a psychological issue. On this reading, the James-Lange theory states that emotion is the feeling of bodily sensations, and unless one is already philosophically prejudiced, this theory implies neither materialism nor any other metaphysical doctrine.

I wish to dispel the confusion that has always plagued attempts to understand the James-Lange theory, a confusion that results form the fact that James's formulations of the theory sometimes suggest that emotions are identical with certain bodily events (seemingly a materialistic theory) but at other times suggest that emotions are the effects of bodily processes (seemingly a dualistic theory).

James himself may have vacillated between the two, but in the end his commitment was to the latter position. A letter of 30 September 1884 to Renouvier makes this plain:

> From what you say I fear you may not have caught the precise meaning of my emotion theory. I don't mean that the emotion is the *perception* of bodily changes *as such*, but only that the bodily changes give us a feeling, which is the emotion. We can, it is true, partly analyze this feeling; if we could totally analyze it into local bodily feelings its emotional character would probably change. After all, what my theory has in view is only the determination of the particular nerve process which emotion accompanies. We are bound to suppose that there is *some* such nerve process accompanying every emotion. Now all I say is that the nerve process is the incoming currents, produced by the reflex movements which the perception of the exciting cause engenders. I feel sure that some part of our emotions is covered by this account; whether the *whole* of them is so covered is a question about which I am still doubtful.[59]

James made it clear that emotions are not bodily events but are rather the effects of bodily events, leaving open the question of whether, as effects, they are physical or nonphysical. He clearly meant that the objects of emotional awareness are bodily sensations and not the bodily events themselves. He repeated the point made originally in "What Is an Emotion?" that the force of his theory is mainly physiological, and he insisted that the afferent nervous system is the cause of both sensations and emotions. James's letter to Renouvier betrays some uncertainty about how to describe the feeling that an emotion is said to be; on the one hand, he held in *Principles* that a feeling is simple, indivisible, and unanalyzable; on the other hand, when emphasizing the introspectable bodily changes that contribute to emotional feeling, he characterized feeling as complex and analyzable. His proposition that the feeling of emotion can be only partly analyzed without changing character is an unpromising compromise which was perhaps symptomatic of James's failure to decide whether an emotional feeling is merely a complex of bodily sensations or is rather a consciousness of such sensations. If it is the former, it can be analyzed; if the latter, it cannot. James never made this point clear in his publications, and possibly not to himself.

The specific concept of feeling, connoting a single feeling such as disappointment rather than all states of consciousness together, was treated hesitantly by James. His account in *Principles* refers to "the subtler emotions" (the moral, intellectual, and aesthetic feelings), which had been called cerebral by some; James countered that these emotions, too, are comparable to sensations and are thus connected with the afferent nervous system; even in intellectual and moral rapture a bodily reverberation of some sort occurs.[60] It is hard to resist the conclusion, he thought, that quieter feelings or subtler emotions, which are not characterized by detectable commotions, nevertheless involve minimal bodily stirrings, of which we are scarcely conscious, that are responsible for the felt quality of the experience, the fact that the experience is tinged with some feeling or emotion instead of being "coldly or blood-lessly cognitive." He believed also that introspection could do valuable work with feelings and emotions, that it could be trained to discriminate an indefinite number of them and in so doing could discover their bodily locations or at least indicate their probable bodily sources.[61] To this extent, then, the quiet feeling of having done a good job, for example, is no exception to the James-Lange rule that something bodily is involved in emotion. But in *Principles* James stopped short of this claim, admitting that some feelings, distinguished from both localized feelings and turbulent emo-tions, may be entirely unrelated to specific processes in the body or related only to the cerebral area (and not to the visceral, as demanded by the James-Lange theory). "If there *be* such a thing as a purely spiritual emotion, I should be inclined to restrict it to this cerebral sense of abundance and ease, this feeling . . . of unimpeded and not overstrained activity of thought. . . . It is a fine and serene but not an excited state of consciousness" (*Principles*, 2:477). James was emphatic in "The Physical Basis of Emotion," where he replied to the objection that by conceding the possible exemp-tion of feelings he had undermined his own theory: "Such objections are a complete *ignoratio elenchi*, addressed to some imaginary theory with which my own, as I myself understand it, has nothing whatever to do, all that I have ever maintained being the dependence on incoming currents of the *emotional seizure* or *Affect*" (*CER*, 361). James concluded, then, that introspection shows at least some feelings to be detached from any specific bodily source or location; insofar as the James-Lange theory depends upon introspection, it apparently applies to all emotions but not to all feelings. But given the fallibility of introspection, James thought, we cannot say for sure that the theory does or does not cover all feelings. If feelings do occur that cannot be accommodated to the James-Lange hypothesis, they would make a mate-rialistic theory of consciousness even more problematic—a consequence that would hardly have displeased James.

James had good reason for denying that the James-Lange theory is materialistic, and despite an occasional failure to explain his intentions clearly, he propounded a concept of emotion that was consistent with his lifelong antimaterialistic bias.[62] He believed that the merits of Cartesian dualism or of materialism—and indeed of all metaphysical systems—must be debated at the philosophical rather than psycholog-ical level. This belief is widely shared by philosophers today; a substantial body of opinion still favors the Jamesian proposition that the mind-body problem is not scientific but metaphysical. We must pay attention as well to what neurophysiology tells us, for example, but that information must be evaluated philosophically before the perennial question can be answered. James thought that a psychological theory of emotion could not in itself select the most adequate philosophy of mind, and he came to believe that the most significant consequence of the James-Lange theory is the vindication of a certain physiological model. The experimental verdict on this issue would probably disappoint him, since it fails to prove his physiological theory of emotion. "What Is an Emotion?" led to an astonishing amount of experimentation and literature, so that 1884 can be considered the year when the concept of emotion was ushered into the modern era.

James asked about emotion at a time when philosophers and psychologists were more concerned with thoughts, images, and judgments. Such topics are now out of fashion because psychologists find them experimentally unproductive and philosophers consider them conceptually pointless. The psychologist interested in discovering the conditions of anxiety, for example, has a good idea of what he is investigating and wants to avoid disputes about how to define it. The philosopher, noting the variety of things that *anxiety* names in everyday language, despairs of finding a single definition and thus urges us to move beyond definitions to other questions. While there are sound reasons for the contemporary attitude, there nevertheless comes a point in the discussion of emotion when we must ask what is meant by *emotion*. Without necessarily sinking into definitional quarreling, the discussion can profit from James's contributions to the topic. His observations are extraordinarily rich, taking into account a surprising number of historical and contemporary considerations in three or four relatively compact essays. He suggested more than he proved, but it is striking that he was aware of such a great variety of things that needed to be suggested in the first place; indeed, there are few bases in current discussions of emotion that James did not touch.

Consider, for example, the objection that the James-Lange hypothesis defines the character of an emotion totally by certain events in the body, when in fact many emotions are conventionally and socially determined. Not only is a soldier's shame sometimes due to his violating a cardinal military rule, but calling it shame rather than embarrassment is a function of convention. James responded: "Most of the objects of civilised men's emotions are things to which it would be preposterous to suppose their nervous systems connately adapted. Most occasions of shame and many insults are purely conventional, and vary with the social environment. The same is true of many matters of dread and of desire, and of many occasions of melancholy and regret."[63] But he thought that this observation was no objection to his theory of emotion, because perceptions and behavior that are conventionally or otherwise conditioned are simply part of the general input that triggers the bodily commotion which must occur before the emotion can; only the latter point is required by the James-Lange theory. Any causal account of the events leading up to the bodily stirrings when we experience an emotion can be given consistently with the James-Lange theory, which mandates only that the bodily stirrings and awareness of them are the necessary and sufficient conditions of the emotion.

Although he was primarily presenting a theory of emotion, James was himself dissatisfied with the amount he said about feelings. He mentioned in the two-page preface to *Psychology* that he regretted "to have been unable to supply chapters [in *Principles*] on pleasure and pain, aesthetics, and the moral sense," chapters in which he would undoubtedly have tried to cover the range of feelings in depth. Feelings puzzled him, extant theories about them left him frustrated, and, as Perry tells us, he sought a "solution in the physiology of the nervous system. He went into the subject with his customary thoroughness, read extensively, prepared an exhaustive bibliography, drew up fifteen 'facts which every theory must keep account of,' corresponded with dentists regarding the painfulness of teeth and gums, and collected pamphlets" (RBP, 2:127–28). He eventually broached the subject in "The Physical Basis of Emotion," but his suggestions there are fragmentary; pleasantness and unpleasantness are called the "tone" of sensations, as are products of afferent currents, consistent with the physiological model of the James-Lange theory. There are also milder, "secondary" feelings such as acceptance and intolerability, which are reactions to primary feelings and are thus also traceable to the afferent system. Finally, James raised the question of whether liking and disliking are, as some critics had contended, a third sort of feeling which is not due to the afferent system and therefore not on a par with sensation. He decided that liking and disliking, like acceptance and intolerability, are delicate reactions to the primary feelings (pleasantness and unpleasantness) and can thus be assimilated into the complex process of incoming currents of the nervous system.

James readily conceded the difficulty of supporting his claim; he was unable to cite any better evidence than the anesthetic studied by Sollier. The fragmentary character of James's thoughts on feeling is obvious, and he openly regretted his inability to collect them into a fuller theoretical account that would also incorporate the feelings that contribute to aesthetic sensibility and the moral sense. He wanted to determine whether liking and disliking, or the so-called feelings of aesthetic and moral types, are actual feelings or only attitudes. Not all attitudes are necessarily feelings, and some attitudes about feelings may not themselves be feelings. Whatever the answer, this question should be analyzed before any assessment of James's remarks on feelings is attempted. Part of the problem arises from the continuum from sensation to emotion to feeling, as well as from feeling to attitudes, thoughts, and cognitions.

If James had worked out more clearly the link between emotion and feeling, he might have avoided the unfortunate confusion not only in his elaboration of the James-Lange theory, but in his very formulation of it. The theory, he said, is that an emotion is the feeling of bodily changes in oneself. In disclaiming disembodied emotions, he believed that bodily sensations are the object of the feeling, and that the quality of emotional feeling is due, perhaps exclusively, to that object. His confusion lies in thinking that if there is a feeling of anger, there must be an object, a complex of bodily sensations localized in the visceral area, and a subjective feeling of that object. If there were no such duality between subjective feeling and internal object, James thought we would be left with only a disembodied feeling. To save the theory, he was forced to construe all causes other than internal bodily events—for example, habits, expectations, judgments, and preferences—as always participating in the production of those bodily events, but never in a reaction to those bodily occurrences that produce the resultant feeling of anger. We ordinarily suppose that a person's feeling is often the result of how his personality reacts to what is happening, including the organic changes in his own body. A feeling of anger, as it is ordinarily understood, is a simple introspectable feeling, complete in itself, without any object of the sort that James's theory requires. That James fell into this confusion is indicated by his shift from saying that changes in the body are ingredients in feeling to saying that they are only the causes of it.[64] To claim that they are ingredients suggests that they or their associated sensations are objects felt when one is angry, whereas to hold merely that they are among the introspectable causes of our anger makes the feeling an effect that requires no peculiar object because it alone is describable as a feeling *of anger*. James's formulations make us think that he did not escape this confusion entirely, and that its source may be his use of *feeling* to mean alternately any state of awareness and some specific state. When he insisted that bodily changes or their associated sensations are felt as an essential part of any emotion, he may have confused, for example, *awareness* of heartbeats with the *feeling* of anger, and then concluded that heartbeats are the objects of anger. But if this confusion is clarified, then the feeling of anger can exist alongside awareness of internal commotion; there may be causes of feeling other than the commotion. The only thing that is felt is the feeling itself; when the object of an angry feeling is a particular person, no other object can be found within our experience or our body. I cannot agree with James that a feeling of anger is analyzable; feelings cannot be dissected into parts, ingredients, or elements. We can analyze their causes, objects, or significance, but not feelings themselves. Indeed, throughout most of *Principles* James claimed that feelings are *not* analyzable, so his discussion of emotion sometimes diverges from his prevailing opinion.

9 ❧ THOUGHT

THINKING

We can move from emotion to thought either by contrasting them, citing the adage that heart and head collide, or by likening them, arguing that emotion is cognitive and cognition emotive. James did both. He urged the submission of emotion to sober thought when required by moral and rational constraints, but he also asserted the need of reason to surrender to emotion on the unusual occasions when to do so is the rational and moral alternative. We may do better, for instance, by following the emotion of our will to live than by accepting the doctor's diagnosis of terminal illness; likewise, it may profit us to be drawn to religion by emotional rather than intellectual motives. Emotion and thought can be regarded as siblings which, though capable of mutual hostility, enjoy a common birthsite. There is a Hegelian suggestion in James's philosophy that feeling, sensation, and thought are primordially related, gradually emerging from an originally shared cocoon into separate identities. James wrote in his notes: "Thought with something given in it, that is the primordial irreducible datum. . . . The dim duality is given from the start, the faintest sensation has it, and need not wait for the mind to come and apply any 'category' to it. In other words I can see no radical distinction between sensation and thought like what the Kantian school sets up. All is sensation or all is thought, as you please to call it."[1] This idea is repeated throughout James's philosophical psychology and is supported by his endorsement of such declarations as this: "The faculty of judgment is itself a sort of sensibility, for it is the faculty of feeling the relations among our ideas; and to feel relations is to feel."[2] Given this attitude, we can understand why James decided to use either *feeling* or *thought* to designate every mental or conscious state.

Our concern in this chapter, however, is with thought as specific kinds of mental activity. Gilbert Ryle touches on the issue in asking what Rodin's *Thinker* is engaged in.[3] What is going on when a person is thinking? James never supposed that we can identify some single or sui generis activity called thinking, for a variety of happenings

242

may count as thinking. He never asked simply, What is thinking? as he did, What is an emotion?[4] We need to determine what James believed are the most important features of the activities we lump together under *thinking*. This project provokes queries and considerations about the objects of thought and about language and meaning. After addressing these topics, we should have a comprehensive view of James's concept of thought, in its narrower sense of a certain range of mental activities.

In his psychology of thinking James sought to identify introspectively both the internal conditions generally present when thinking occurs and the specific causes in the brain of those conditions. Thinking is a process that takes time, and introspecting it requires diligent monitoring over a long period. Much of what James said about thinking concerns what happens between the initial and terminal moments of a given process of thinking. This is not to deny that one can "think in a flash," but James assumed that "instantaneous" thinking is less susceptible to introspective description than is "process" thinking. In voluntary thinking, for instance, there is some topic to which our attention keeps returning, often a problem or

> a gap we cannot yet fill with a definite picture, word, or phrase. . . . Whatever may be the images and phrases that pass before us, we feel their relation to this aching gap. To fill it up is our thought's destiny. Some bring us nearer to that consummation. Some the gap negates as quite irrelevant. Each swims in a felt fringe of relations of which the aforesaid gap is the term. Or instead of a definite gap we may merely carry a mood of interest about with us. Then, however vague the mood, it will still act in the same way, throwing a mantle of felt affinity over such representations, entering the mind, as suit it, and tingeing with the feeling of tediousness or discord all those with which it has no concern. (*Principles*, 1:259)

An example fitting this description is the attempt to recall a name, during which a gap (the absence of the forgotten name) is intensely active in our consciousness.

> A sort of wraith of the name is in it, beckoning us in a given direction, making us at moments tingle with the sense of our closeness, and then letting us sink back without the longed-for term. . . . And the gap of one word does not feel like the gap of another, all empty of content as both might seem necessarily to be when described as gaps. When I vainly try to recall the name of Spalding, my consciousness is far removed from what it is when I vainly try to recall the name of Bowles. . . . The feeling of an absence is *toto coelo* other than the absence of a feeling. It is an intense feeling. The rhythm of a lost word may be there without a sound to clothe it. . . . Every one must know the tantalizing effect of the blank rhythm of some forgotten verse, restlessly dancing in one's mind, striving to be filled out with words. (*Principles*, 1:251–52)

If fifty persons are requested to describe the thinking process when they try to recall a name, the result will be fifty introspective reports each differing strikingly from the others. Moreover, many of the reports will testify to the difficulty of putting the felt details of the process into words at all, acknowledging that only when they had made the effort themselves did they appreciate the special genius of James's descriptions. James sought to describe those features of his experience that could be expected to occur in everyone else's, given the differences in introspective reporting from one person to the next. Those common features include a procession of images, words, and ideas which may pass through consciousness with incredible speed or linger in the attention, sometimes disappearing and reappearing repeatedly. A second feature is the "fringe" of relations with which each image or word is surrounded. When we are engaged in thinking, a particular word, phrase, image, or sensation may dominate our consciousness, but it is always surrounded by other mental material; no item of introspective attention is ever completely isolated. How to describe this phenomenon is not obvious, but James represented it to himself as a projection on an internal screen such that, in spatial terms, any item in introspective focus will be entirely surrounded by other ideas, words, and images in an unfocused fringe or cluster of associates. This fringe, James thought, is introspectable, although not as clearly and distinctly as is the item at the center of attention. We know abstractly that the item around which our thinking revolves radiates in all directions to connected ideas and images; further, we can introspectively "see" those connections in that we can introspect, if only dimly, how the central item is related to its fringe. James is known for his proclivity toward metaphoric and imagistic language for describing experience, but if we recognize our ability to use introspection as a type of observation, to project the content of consciousness onto an inner screen and thus to spatialize this content, James's descriptions become a literal account of the center and the fringe of thinking.

Another feature of thinking is that which gives it momentum and direction. In the example of trying to recall a name, he identified it as the feeling of a gap or absence, a sense of something definite but elusive which tantalizes and goads us into further efforts to recall and which also indicates whether our guesses at the name are warm or cold, thus supplying a direction, even if frustratingly vague, for our thinking. This feeling of direction has a definite character, so that upon recurrence it is familiar and recognizable. Nevertheless, we cannot describe the feeling while we are still searching for the lost name, because the desired description needs to include that name. We want to describe it as "the feeling we have when we try to recall the name *Bowles*" but cannot do so until *Bowles* is remembered; while struggling to remember, we are deprived of a good description for our feeling. James warned against concluding that without a definite name there is no definite feeling; he insisted instead that introspection outstrips the act of naming in finding differences between states of consciousness and of thought.

Some thinking is admittedly fueled or given direction without our control; when thought sweeps along as something observed rather than initiated, James assigned it mechanical causes. In such cases of involuntary thinking, which include certain reveries and musings, he hypothesized that one event in the process of thinking can arouse another without any association of ideas, simply from associations in the brain. He retained his faith in association while rejecting the atomistic ideas of British empiricism: *"psychic* contiguity, similarity, etc., are derivatives of a single profounder kind of fact" (*Principles,* 1:566), the dynamic interplay between states of the brain rather than between Lockean ideas. That a specific thought or feeling seems to arouse another involuntarily is explained by a law of association of cerebral events: *"When two elementary brain-processes have been active together or in immediate succession, one of them, on reoccurring, tends to propagate its excitement into the other"* (*Principles,* 1:566). One criticism of traditional associationism is that directed thinking cannot be ascribed to the "blindly mechanical interplay of purposeless elements."[5] While James enthusiastically agreed with this criticism of the attempt by traditional associationism to explain all thinking, his own theory allowed that some involuntary thinking can show direction, explicable in terms of physiological association in the brain. Even thinking without volition or control may display a remarkable progression from the confrontation of a problem to its partial or full resolution. At the same time, James characteristically believed that some thinking is voluntary and not mechanical; what and how we think can result not only from cerebral causes, but also from our deliberately attending to one mental item rather than another in the thought process. *"The effects of interested attention and volition* remain. These activities seem to hold fast to certain elements, and by emphasizing them and dwelling on them, to make their associates the only ones which are evoked. *This* is the point at which an anti-mechanical psychology must, if anywhere, make its stand in dealing with association" (*Principles,* 1:594). James denied that we can spontaneously create thoughts and argued that we are limited to emphasizing or reinforcing one thought over another among those that have already been put before consciousness by the associative machinery of the brain. Through such emphasis we introduce our interests and values into the causal chain, redirecting and rearranging the train of associations and thus exhibiting the capacity of thinking to influence indirectly its own cerebral conditions.

In voluntary thinking we think toward a certain end, which in itself influences the psychology and physiology of the thought process. Having a purpose involves the persistent activity of a specific set of brain processes during a particular thought process; when we take a special interest in one idea or image correlating with the brain's main activity, that act feeds back to the brain itself, with both psychological and physiological effects. The mechanism of this feedback was indecipherable for James; if the introspectable evidence for the claim that subjective interest and attention affect the brain had been challenged, he could only have offered feedback as a postulate.[6] Although he never developed it, he did make a suggestion about the alleged causal relation, one that is also pertinent to assessments of traditional associationism:

> If we call Z the brain-tract of general interest, then, if the object *abc* turns up, and *b* has more associations with Z than have either *a* or *c*, *b* will become the object's interesting, pivotal portion, and will call up its own associates exclusively. For the *energy of* b's *brain-tract* [my italics] will be augmented by Z's activity—an

activity which, from lack of previous connection between Z and *a* or *c*, does not influence *a* or *c*. If, for instance, I think of Paris whilst I am *hungry*, I shall not improbably find that its *restaurants* have become the pivot of my thought. (*Principles*, 1:583–84)

"Energy of *b*'s brain-tract" indicates that James assumed physiological association to work through some process of energizing and that taking an interest in Paris energized something in the brain that caused him to think of restaurants. By contrast, Kurt Lewin, a critic of traditional associationism, claimed in 1922 that mere association cannot be the cause of a mental event. "The experimental investigation of habit formation [association] has shown that the couplings caused by habit never supply as such the motor of a mental event. . . . Rather in all cases certain mental *energies* originating, as a rule, in the pressure of will or needs, i.e., mental systems *under stress* are the necessary conditions of mental events."[7] James might have agreed with Lewin's claim, extended to physical events as well, without significantly altering his own accounts of thinking and association. "Hartley accordingly suggested habit as a sufficient explanation of all connections of our thoughts, and in so doing planted himself squarely upon the properly psychological aspect of the problem of connection, and sought to treat both rational and irrational connections from a single point of view" (*Principles*, 1:553). If Hartley's view were modified toward Lewin's so that association is combined with systems under stress and with independent energy charges upon which association is contingent, James's position would need little revision. The variety of ways in which our thoughts coexist with and succeed each other ("all this magical, imponderable streaming") is important for both psychology and philosophy. "It has furthermore challenged the race of philosophers to banish something of the mystery by formulating the process in simpler terms. The problem which the philosophers have set themselves is that of ascertaining *principles of connection* between the thoughts which thus appear to sprout one out of the other, whereby their peculiar succession or coexistence may be explained" (*Principles*, 1:550–51). James speculated that the simplest, most powerful explanation is the law expressing how associations in the brain occur, but he complicated this law by adding that associations can be influenced by deliberate intervention on our part. The bold suggestion of a "simpler" explanation in terms of brain physiology must be substantially retrenched when Cartesian dualism is reinstated.

James was careful to furnish the reader with the complications that challenge his theory, conceding that its desired simplicity might not survive the challenge. For example, suppose that the thought of the moon summons the thought of a football, which in turn summons the thought of a railroad magnate. (Such strange paths of thinking are not unusual, James thought.) This association can be explained thus: the rotundity of the moon "broke away" from the moon's other attributes and was associated with "elasticity, leathery integument, swift mobility in obedience to human caprice." The latter broke away and was associated with the railroad czar. James agreed that we can only speculate why one item in the brain's processes breaks away and another does not, or even how such a process can be formulated physiologically. "Possibly a minuter insight into the laws of neural action will some-day clear the matter up; possibly neural laws will not suffice, and we shall need to invoke a dynamic reaction of the form of consciousness upon its content" (*Principles,* 1:580–81). The complications are more apparent in James's discussion of the factors responsible for association in thinking, which include recentness, habit, vividness, similarity, and emotional congruity. This last factor is illustrated by the fact that the same thing does not arouse the same associations when we are cheerful as when we are despondent. Translating the play of brain upon mind and of mind upon brain, along with the interplay between the factors that condition association, into physio-logical terms is a formidable task. James made claims that add to the difficulty; for instance, he declared without citing experimental evidence that it had been shown that simple qualities fail to remind us of similar ones. "The thought of one shade of blue does not remind us of that of another shade of blue, etc., unless indeed we have in mind some general purpose like naming the tint, when we should naturally think of other blues of the scale, through 'mixed association' of purpose, names, and tints, together. But there is no elementary tendency of pure qualities to awaken their similars in the mind" (*Principles,* 1:579). Despite the complications of finding a simple base in the brain for the bewildering variety of our associations, James remained convinced that some simplification had been achieved. Connections be-tween thoughts are at bottom connections between brain processes and can thus be explained mechanically, but a nonmechanical element occurs whenever we deliber-ately take an interest in some part of the mental content, fix attention upon it, and thereby impart an energy to that mental part, which in turn imparts an energy in the brain and affects the course of associations there. Compared to classical associa-tionism, with its dynamics of ideas as well as cerebral processes, James saw this theory as more orderly, less mythological, and more promising scientifically. The chapters in *Principles* on association, discrimination and comparison, and reasoning, which advance this concept of thought, were written before 1880 or were based upon articles written that early. During 1878–1880, James was formulating basic convictions that would endure through his life; among them was the belief that the process of thinking can be explained by purely physiological principles of association in combination with the thinker's acts of intervention through attention, will, and taking interest, acts that play back upon the brain itself. When he began *Principles* James had already formulated the belief that the thinker's subjective interests have an impact everywhere, from physiology to metaphysics.

THOUGHT AND OBJECT

James spoke of the need to distinguish adequately between an act of thinking and its object, declaring that the failure to do so was widespread enough to be called the psychologist's fallacy.[8] This fallacy often takes the form of assuming that an analysis of the object of thought is an analysis of thinking itself; James pointed to the overwhelming distinction that *"however complex the object may be, the thought of it is one individual state of consciousness"* (*Principles*, 1:276). He accused traditional associationism of committing the psychologist's fallacy in supposing that thought must contain various elements because its object does, an assumption leading to the mistaken Lockean doctrine that complex states of consciousness can be analyzed into simpler elements or ideas. According to James, introspection reveals instead that no matter how many things figure in thought's object, the act or experience of thinking is *"a single pulse of subjectivity, a single psychosis, feeling, or state of mind."*[9] The thought of a pack of cards on the table, for instance, does not break down into a thought of the cards and a thought of a table, for it is a different "subjective phenomenon" from either of these, a thought of "the-pack-of-cards-is-on-the-table."[10] He further stressed the difference between thought and its object: "[Thought] has no opprobrious connotation such as 'feeling' has, and it immediately suggests the omnipresence of cognition (or reference to an object other than the mental state itself), which we shall soon see to be of the mental life's essence" (*Principles*, 1:186). Thought is said to be intentional because it is directed upon an object distinct from itself.

What is the mind's object when thinking of the statement "Columbus discovered America in 1492"? It is misleading to answer, as most people do, "Columbus," "America," or "the discovery of America," because none of these answers represents the entire object of thought but only its "substantive kernel or nucleus." They are the topic or subject of discourse in that they are what the entire thought is *about*, but the whole thought's object would be better expressed as "Columbus-discovered-America-in-1492." Corresponding to this expression is an undivided experience or act of thinking referred to by the same words. The character of this act is introspectable: "If we wish to *feel* that idiosyncrasy we must reproduce the thought as it was uttered, with every word fringed and the whole sentence bathed in that original halo of obscure relations which, like an horizon, then spread about its meaning" (*Principles*, 1:275–76). Because of the inadequacy of everyday language for catching introspective nuances, we can achieve linguistic precision only by describing the experience of thinking with the same words used to describe its object; given James's hints of what that experience feels like, however, he must have supposed that it contains more than what a simple or literal understanding of those words can convey. From the perspective of conceptualization and language, much of what introspection discloses about acts of thinking is vague.[11] The same balance of precision and vagueness exists in the object of thought:

> The object of every thought, then, is neither more nor less than all that the thought thinks, exactly as the thought thinks it, however complicated the matter, and however symbolic the manner of the thinking may be. It is needless to say that memory can seldom accurately reproduce such an object, when once it has passed from before the mind. It either makes too little or too much of it. Its best plan is to repeat the verbal sentence, if there was one, in which the object was expressed. But for inarticulate thoughts there was not even this recourse,

and introspection must confess that the task exceeds her powers. The mass of our thinking vanishes for ever, beyond hope of recovery, and psychology only gathers up a few of the crumbs that fall from the feast. (*Principles,* 1:276)

In addition to the difficulty of trying to distinguish with linguistic precision between the act of thinking and its object, Perry discerned another obstacle for that distinction, which stems from James's wavering in *Principles* between his official defense of mind-body dualism and his private hope that such dualism could be replaced by the radical empiricism that he would propose during the final decade of his life. James was not prepared to explain the difference between thought and its object, partly because the two seem to match perfectly when verbalized, and partly because the distinction between thinking and the corresponding brain process is tenuous. After quoting James's statement (*Principles,* 1:234) that "the *knower* is in every case a unique pulse of thought corresponding to a unique reaction of the brain upon its conditions," Perry then observed: "If it be asked, then, what room there is for thought as a separate item between the cerebral pulsation and the thought's object, there appears to be no clear answer in the *Principles*" (RBP, 2:74). As it stands, Perry's reasoning is too cryptic, but he seems to have meant to reflect James's own doubts that a purely mental activity of thinking can be distinguished. James clearly expressed this doubt in "The Consciousness of Self," asserting that his own intro- spection characterized mental acts of assenting, negating, attending, and making an effort as felt movements in the head; as far as he could tell, all such inner activities are physiological and have no purely mental or spiritual element.[12] But he did not equate felt movements in the head with the brain processes underlying them; even if the introspection of thinking is of physiological processes, those processes are sepa- rate events occurring between their cerebral conditions and their objects. Thinking may then consist in distinctive activities whose bodily features can be felt but which are not identical with the events in the brain upon which they depend.[13]

But this is not the end of the matter, as Perry understood. James declared that if everything inner is indeed physiological, then

it would follow that *all* that is experienced is, strictly considered, *objective;* that this objective falls asunder into two contrasted parts, one realized as 'Self,' the other as 'not-Self;' and that over and above these parts there *is* nothing save the fact that they are known, the fact of the stream being there as the indispensable subjective condition of their being experienced at all. But this *condition* of the experience is not one of the things *experienced* at the moment; this knowing is not immediately *known.* It is only known in subsequent reflection. Instead, then, of the stream of thought being one of *con*-sciousness, thinking its own existence along with whatever else it thinks . . . it might be better called a stream of *Scious*ness pure and simple, thinking objects of some of which it makes what it calls a 'Me,' and only aware of its 'pure' Self in an abstract, hypothetic or conceptual way. Each 'section' of the stream would then be a bit of sciousness or knowledge of this sort, including and contemplating its 'me' and its 'not-me' as objects . . . but not yet including or contemplating its own subjective being. The sciousness in question would be the *Thinker*, and the existence of this thinker would be given to us rather as a logical postulate than as that direct inner perception of spiritual activity which we naturally believe ourselves to have. (*Principles*, 1:304)

James intended to continue assuming that we have direct awareness of the process of thinking as such, but he was nonetheless skeptical and considered the issue more suitable for metaphysics. In fact he made an unkept promise to offer metaphysical reflections about it in the concluding chapter of *Principles*.[14] We are thus confronted by a critical issue of interpretation: if James was seriously skeptical about the distinction between thinking and its object and about whether we are directly aware of acts of thinking, then his fascinating introspective descriptions of acts of thinking must be discarded as strange illusions.

We can, however, interpret James's expressed skepticism so that it does not conflict outrageously with his own assiduous introspections about the stream of thinking. If everything inner and introspectable is indeed physiological, then no mind-body distinction, no distinction between thoughts-as-mental and things-as-physical, can ever be given to introspection. Because everything is objective (subjectivity being lost if everything is physical), the knower-known and thinker-object distinctions fall within the objective. But there is nothing in the relation between knower and known, or between thinker and object, that enables the knower to know that he knows or the thinker to know that he thinks, because the knowing is not immediately known, but known only in subsequent reflection. Even the best and quickest introspection is retrospection, but the retrospective moment of knowledge is also related to the moment it knows without any immediate knowledge of itself, and so on ad infinitum. Any momentary knower or thinker is incapable of immediate knowledge or self-awareness, and we can register that fact by calling such a knower a "*scious*ness." How a person can know without knowing that he knows is a difficult question, the answer to which cannot be found introspectively but is a matter for pragmatically argued postulation.

This interpretation is compatible with James's introspective descriptions of his own experiences of thinking, in which the distinction between thought and its object is apparent; in fact, James never suggested that he was aware of any incompatibility. He offered a convoluted argument to show that although a stream of thought can be known introspectively (retrospectively), no phase of that stream can be sufficiently self-aware to declare its own intrinsic nature. If we assume that everything experienced is physiological, basing that assumption on what introspection seems to prove, then the distinction between thinker and object or between knower and known cannot be defined by a bodily/nonbodily dichotomy. But other important differences between an act of thinking and its object may be available to introspection, and James (with due respect to Perry) gave instances of such. The most important difference for James was that in thinking we can be aware both of the complexity of our object and of the undivided nature of the act of thinking it; each case of thinking "feels the total object in a unitary way. This is what I mean by denying that in the thought any parts can be found corresponding to the object's parts."[15] He did, however, doubt the claim that to be aware of the undivided unity of the act of thinking is to know that it differs metaphysically from its object in the way that mind and body, for example, have been conceived as radically different kinds of entities. Perry asserted that as long as James vacillated on the issue of mind-body dualism and groped for the later metaphysics of radical empiricism, he was unable in *Principles* to decide whether thinking and its object differ in kind as well as in introspectable detail. But James never called into question either the actual or the introspectable distinction between thought and object, which he tried to convey in "The Stream of Thought" and "The Consciousness of Self."[16]

It is still not clear what James meant by the object of thinking. The two chapters in *Principles* upon which we have focused were meant to show that thinking involves a cerebral condition, an act (experience) of thinking, and an object. In some cases there is an entity in the environment which corresponds to the object of thought, but in others—in thinking of the King of America, for example—there is no entity corresponding to the object of thought. Accordingly, the object of thought is not some entity in the environment. James sometimes called the object the total idea present to the mind in thinking; he repeated his point from "The Stream of Thought" in the chapter on will: "The reader who has made himself acquainted with Chapter IX will always understand, when he hears of many ideas simultaneously present to the mind and acting upon each other, that what is really meant is a mind with one idea before it, of many objects, purposes, reasons, motives, related to each other."[17] The object of thought is always a single idea, and whatever complexity it has is explained by multiplicity-in-unity rather than by multiple ideas; although James sometimes slipped into talk about ideas, he usually avoided the plural whenever it might be mistakenly interpreted to mean Lockean ideas that can combine or recur. The object or idea of thought is a synthesis of multiple elements, but these elements are not mental or psychological units corresponding to traditional definitions of ideas; rather, they are concepts (sometimes called conceptions) which have been combined into a single idea or object of thought.

Concepts were one of James's favorite topics, crucial to many of his doctrines, including anti-intellectualism and the thesis that reality and concepts are incommensurable. He always characterized concepts or conceptions as Platonic or Aristotelian entities that are abstract, eternally the same, and independent (he sometimes qualified this feature in Aristotelian fashion); together they constitute systems which are different from sensations and perceptions but capable of a Platonic intermingling with them. We acquire empirical concepts by abstracting partial aspects from the whole context gained through perception; a priori concepts such as logical and mathematical ones result from the mind's operations on other concepts or ideal objects. These operations include judging, comparing, predicating, subsuming, and constructing, which are sufficient to accomplish the synthesis into a single object of thought. James believed the motive for thinking, reasoning, and forming a particular object of thought is our wish to satisfy a subjective interest. He called attention in *Principles* to what he had said in 1879 about the nature of concepts or conceptions: "What is a *conception*? It is a *teleological instrument*. It is a partial aspect of a thing which *for our purpose* we regard as its essential aspect, as the representative of the entire thing. . . . But the essence, the ground of conception, varies with the end in view. . . . This shows that the whole doctrine of essential characters is intimately bound up with a teleological view of the world."[18] A conception, then, is an ideal object of thought, a concept or combination of concepts discovered or created by the mind, a representation of things real and imaginary, and a teleological instrument.

James stated that reference to an object (the "intentionality" of thought) by a mental state is the essence of mental life. The proposition that all thought displays intentionality is usually taken to mean that all thinking is *of* or *about* something; one never merely thinks without an object. The nature and cause of this intentionality or property of reference are only vaguely discussed in *Principles*.[19] We can speculate that James viewed intentionality as an introspectable feature of the act of thinking itself, or as a property of the object of thinking, or as neither of these but something else. The last possibility is suggested by James's comments in "The Stream of Thought" about signs of direction in thought and the role of intention in thinking. He may have believed that felt mental transitions, which lead from one idea or image to another and are called feelings of direction, themselves provide the reference or intentionality of thinking; when we say that our thought *refers to* something, we are describing a felt relation or transition between ideas or images. *Reference* is thus identified with a change in consciousness that is felt to have a certain direction. An immediate question is whether the reference precedes this sense of direction in thought. James may have seen the solution in *intention:*

> And has the reader never asked himself what kind of a mental fact is his *intention of saying a thing* before he has said it? It is an entirely definite intention, distinct from all other intentions, an absolutely distinct state of consciousness. . . . How much of it consists of definite sensorial images, either of words or things? Hardly anything! . . . It has therefore a nature of its own of the most positive sort, and yet what can we say about it without using words that belong to the later mental facts that replace it? The intention *to-say-so-and-so* is the only name it can receive. One may admit that a good third of our psychic life consists in these rapid premonitory perspective views of schemes of thought not yet articulate. (*Principles*, 1:253)

A case can be made for attributing to James the idea that intention underlies the intentionality of thought, but no such explanation actually appears in *Principles*.

About the time he was composing the chapters in *Principles* most relevant to the concept of thought, James specifically raised this question: " 'How *can* a thought refer to, intend, or signify any particular reality outside of itself?' . . . What is meant by saying that the thought *stands for* or *represents* that reality, or indeed any reality at all?"[20] Anticipating an objection like that which Wittgenstein would raise years later, James added that reference is not based on any resemblance between a thought and what it represents or refers to.[21] He acknowledged being attracted to Royce's answer, which he regarded as an attempted proof of idealism, but in the end he rejected it in favor of a solution that agreed with his own pragmatism and radical empiricism. In 1895 he returned to the issue of intentionality or objective reference, although more to explicate a pragmatic, experiential account of knowledge and truth than to make a detailed analysis of thinking. He set the problem thus: What does it mean to think or know that there are tigers in India?

> Most men would answer that what we mean by knowing the tigers is having them, however absent in body, become in some way present to our thought; or that our knowledge of them is known as presence of our thought to them. A great mystery is usually made of this peculiar presence in absence; and the scholastic philosophy, which is only common sense grown pedant, would explain it as a peculiar kind of existence, called *intentional inexistence,* of the tigers in our mind. At the very least, people would say that what we mean by knowing the tigers is mentally *pointing* towards them as we sit here.[22]

But how is the metaphor of pointing to be understood? In a sense, our thought points, or bears a relation, to India as it does not, say, to Canada; it is almost as if we can introspectively trace that relation from the mind outward in the direction of India rather than elsewhere. Although the evidence is not sufficient to draw a conclusion, James may have conjectured in *Principles* that a literal grounding for the metaphor might be found somewhere in introspection. By 1895, however, he had arrived at a different conclusion which he said traversed the assumptions of common sense, scholasticism, and traditional epistemology.

> The pointing of our thought to the tigers is known simply and solely as a procession of mental associates and motor consequences that follow on the thought, and that would lead harmoniously, if followed out, into some ideal or real context, or even into the immediate presence of the tiger. It is known as our rejection of a jaguar, if that beast were shown us as a tiger. . . . It is known as our ability to utter all sorts of propositions which don't contradict other propositions that are true of the real tiger. It is even known, if we take the tigers very seriously, as actions of ours which may terminate in directly intuited ti-gers . . . if we took a voyage to India. . . . In all this there is no self-transcenden-cy in our mental images taken by themselves. They are one physical fact; the tigers are another; and their pointing to the tigers is a perfectly commonplace physical relation. . . . The ideas and the tiger are in themselves as loose and separate, to use Hume's language, as any two things can be. . . . There is no special inner mystery, but only an outer chain of physical or mental intermedi-aries connecting thought and thing. *To know an object is here to lead to it through a context which the world supplies.*[23]

James's final account of objective reference, formulated five years after the publication of *Principles*, is a far cry from any mentalistic or phenomenological interpretations suggested by that work. He gives a straightforward behavioral explanation of intentionality (referring, pointing, intending). Thinking of tigers in India is only a disposition to believe in certain ways; if what we think of is true, our behavior will lead to fulfilled expectations, and if not, our actions will result in surprise or frustration. This viewpoint, familiar in twentieth-century philosophy, is perhaps most influentially expressed by Gilbert Ryle in *The Concept of Mind*. A number of criticisms have been leveled against this formulation. For example, it seems that we can know *now* that we are thinking of tigers in India, but if thinking of them is equated with a behavioral sequence or a disposition to one, then how can we know what we are thinking until the sequence or the disposition is manifested? James did not consider this objection; indeed, the only difficulties he acknowledged were internal obstacles encountered in weaving the concept of intentionality along with others into a new and visionary metaphysics. James uses physicalistic language to describe thought: "mental images" are characterized as "physical fact," with no suggestion of inner, psychological mystery, and the relation of thought to referent is equated with a series of actions that connect in the physical world the thought with the thing to which it points. Intentionality is neither an introspectable feature of thinking nor a property of its object, but is rather a connection made by physical actions. Although James moved after *Principles* to a metaphysics congenial to religion, psychical research, and personal vision, he was also intensifying the physiological analysis of thinking begun in *Principles* and adopting a more overtly behavioristic account of it than given there. This development was logical given James's aim to destroy mind-body dualism; one side of the attack had to concentrate on eliminating mentalism, and a successful physicalistic analysis of the intentionality of thought represented a major victory. What remained in rejecting materialism was an explication of physicalism that eliminates the other side of the original dualism— something the metaphysics of radical empiricism was meant to accomplish. James returned to the topic of intentionality in subsequent writings, but the doctrine remained the same; intentionality not only harmonized with his final metaphysical convictions, it actually facilitated their articulation and defense.[24]

In rejecting the contention that intentionality and self-transcendency are introspectable properties of thought and in advocating a behavioral analysis of them, James anticipated subsequent developments in psychology; introspective psychology gave way to behaviorism, and the concept of intentionality occurred only occasionally, receiving short shrift or being explained along Jamesian lines. Although problems beset a behavioristic account of the relation of thought to its object, James was correct in claiming that objective reference is not introspectable in the way that sensation or feeling is. In view of the wealth of subjective detail that James's introspections of thinking uncovered, it is surprising that he found nothing with which to identify objective reference or intentionality, that he failed to locate the reference of thinking to its object in a felt impulse or tendency to say or do something. What is it to think *of* someone? To answer that it is an introspective awareness of a felt impulse to telephone the person or to smile at her image would seem to be in the spirit of Jamesian introspective psychology, but James instead opted for a vigorous statement of behaviorism and physicalism.

But if intentionality can be thus disposed of, why not the object of thought also? Experiences of thinking do not display introspectable objects. Insofar as the object of thought is composed of abstract concepts and is a total idea or ideal object, it should not be introspectable as are sensations, images, and feelings, which are sensuous rather than abstract and retain some of the characteristics of perception. Yet James, in "The Stream of Thought," for example, appears to base the distinction between thought and its object upon introspection; presumably the ideal object is identified introspectively in the ways it differs from the act of thinking. A philosopher who wants nonintrospectable objects of thought in his ontology may argue that they are intuited, inspected, or otherwise apprehended in their abstractness by the mind's eye; or that they are postulated in order to make sense of the thinking experience, perhaps because whenever a thought is explicitly formulated, some reference to its object is inescapable.[25]

James seems to have based the distinction between thinking and its object upon introspection, but he did not conceive of the object itself as introspectable; his certainty that we know thinking has objects is thus less clear than it appeared originally. In the analogous case of intentionality, he took the behaviorist's route, dissolving the property into a series of behaviors. It is not clear why the same fate was not accorded to the objects of thought, collapsing them into patterns and relations of behavior and thus demystifying them. Curiously, for all his doubts and skepticisms, James never questioned Platonic or Aristotelian realism and its abstract entities, nor did he address the problem of how the Platonic world of concepts and eternal verities can be related to introspection and perception. A more powerful account than James's is needed to persuade us that the distinction between thought and its object truly exists. If the object were construed as verbal or imagistic, the distinction would be more evident and defensible, but James's account of thinking did not permit that sort of interpretation.

THOUGHT AND LANGUAGE

That the mind has its objects, as the senses have theirs, seemed obvious to James, and he assumed that the move from pointing to images as examples of such objects to asserting the existence of ideal, abstract entities was a small one. He would have been surprised by the claim that images are not mental objects, since he took it for granted that introspection can study images with remarkable results. He complimented Francis Galton's work on mental imagery, published in 1880, as marking "an era in descriptive Psychology" and quoted liberally from Galton's introspective investigations.[26] The things we imagine, dream, fantasize, or hallucinate are objects of a sort and cannot be dismissed as unreal or nonexistent. "To the generally philosophic mind . . . they still have existence, though not the same existence, as the real things. *As* objects of fancy, *as* errors, *as* occupants of dreamland, etc., they are in their way as indefeasible parts of life . . . as the realities are in their way" (*Principles*, 2:291). Philosophers may legitimately debate the ontological status of such things as the drunkard's pink elephant, but James argued that something in the drunkard's experience is responsible for calling the pink elephant an imaginary object. If the object of thought can be abstract rather than imagelike, and if it is not introspectable, how can we be aware of it? This problem does not arise for feelings, sensations, and images, which are all introspectable, nor would it if the object of thinking, however abstract or conceptual, were identified with words or the images of words.

Although words and images of words are part of the mental procession witnessed during a process of thinking, James believed that they are not the objects of thought in the sense of being what is meant. When these objects are equated with meanings, the spoken, written, or imagined word is not the meaning but is rather its vehicle, its medium of expression, or its occasion.

> When we read . . . is it true that there is nothing more in our minds than the words themselves as they pass? What then is the meaning of the words which we think we understand as we read? What makes that meaning different in one phrase from what it is in the other? "Who?" "When?" "Where?" Is the difference of felt meaning in these interrogatives nothing more than their differences of sound? And is it not (just like the difference of sound itself) known and understood in an affection of consciousness correlative to it, though so impalpable to direct examination? (*Principles*, 1:252)

Meaning, or difference in meaning, is different from either words or images and is not accessible to direct examination or introspective analysis; it can only be felt or intuited. James thought that the meanings of words are mental accompaniments of the words, notable as feelings of direction which lead our thinking toward other words, images, or actions; meanings differ from images and words in that they are flights rather than perchings. Unlike images, they occur in the fringe of awareness and are thus only dimly intuited, minimally describable as "bare images of logical movement" (*Principles*, 1:253). Meanings so construed have the power to give movement or progression to thinking, something that cannot occur as long as awareness centers on a word or image. The consciousness of our thinking, as it sweeps along too rapidly to allow each member of the accompanying verbal sequence to be discretely noticed, is the consciousness of meanings, mental occurrences in the fringe that are retrospectively describable as feelings of direction and logical movement.

This is an important part of James's definition of thinking. When we think, we are to a great extent caught up in the sweep of our states of consciousness, vividly aware of images or words present until displaced by others, but also continuously aware, although less vividly and on the fringes of the words and images, of a felt direction of thought movement in thinking. *"The sense of our meaning is an entirely peculiar element of thought.* It is one of those evanescent and 'transitive' facts of mind which introspection cannot turn round upon, and isolate and hold up for examination. . . . In the somewhat clumsy terminology I have used, it pertains to the 'fringe' of the subjective state, and is a 'feeling of tendency,' whose neural counterpart is undoubtedly a lot of dawning and dying processes too faint and complex to be traced" (*Principles*, 1:472). To be thinking, even when words are central, is to be aware of changes and transitions felt as a continuous backdrop to a sequence of discretely spaced words and images. James suggested other details—such as the felt affinity between words, which is a necessary condition for the fringe to function—to show how he contrasted thought, language, and images, and why he concluded with Berkeley that thought is a kind of algebra. In doing algebra we may race ahead without pausing to give values to the symbols or blank forms until we reach a terminal point; similarly, in thinking we do not interpret words one after the other but understand them collectively when a phrase or sentence is completed. There is a basic contrast between the stop-and-go character of particular words and images before the mind and the continuous process of thinking, which flows around and through those words and images. That James's characterizations are partly metaphorical is not objectionable, since ordinary language is being bent to a new job of description, an introspective report of the experience of thinking in which the literal facts are understood through a new or metaphorical use of established vocabulary. Nothing literally flows in consciousness, nor is consciousness itself something literally flowing; but in addition to the interrupted appearances of different words and images, there are meanings or feelings of direction and progression which, as barely introspectable features of our states, literally cause a feeling of continuity beyond the interruptions.[27]

James's distinction between thought and language was founded not only upon his own introspections but also upon the testimony of others; the experiences of others warranted his judgment that thought is possible without language. He came upon striking support in his work with deaf-mutes, whose general immunity to dizziness intrigued him. (One of his few experimental investigations was to determine whether the behavior of deaf-mutes supported the theory that the semicircular canals are unconnected with hearing and are simply organs of equilibrium.)[28] James quoted a deaf-mute named Melville Ballard to show that complex thinking can occur in the absence of verbal learning:

> I could convey my thoughts and feelings to my parents and brothers by natural signs or pantomime, and I could understand what they said to me by the same medium. . . . It was . . . some two or three years before my initiation into the rudiments of written language, that I began to ask the question: *How came the world into being?* . . . I set myself to thinking it over a long time. . . . What was the origin of human life in its first appearance upon the earth, and of vegetable life as well, and also the cause of the existence of the earth, sun, moon, and stars.[29]

This statement is only a fragment of Ballard's recollections of the range of thinking he experienced before learning to use words; taken together, they are a strong argument for the distinctness of language and thought. James also cited the testimony of Laura Bridgman, almost as famous as Helen Keller would become; her account is both moving and pathetic in its recall of her childhood, prior to being taught modes of communication, when she had longed to express to her family all of her thoughts.[30] The experiences of a deaf-mute can prove, James concluded, that tactile and visual images can be worked into a system of thought that rivals that of language. Such evidence backs up our introspections that thinking can occur more rapidly and elusively than even the internal or silent use of words, and that meaning, sense, or the feeling of movement and direction in thought are nonlinguistic.

One conclusion is that the mind-stuff in which thinking occurs can be of various sorts, including words and tactile, visual, or motile images. Words are the most convenient mental elements with which to think; not only "are they very *rapidly* revivable, but they are revivable as actual sensations more easily than any other items of our experience" (*Principles*, 1:266). James offers very little theory here, apparently satisfied with describing the data; he makes no effort, for instance, to specify the limits of thought's materials. It is uncertain whether he believed that all images and sensations, regardless of their character, are things in which thinking can occur, or whether olfactory images, for example, are as effective as words. (If asked what it means to say that we think in images, presumably he would refer to his account of intentionality and objective reference.) Nor is it clear that James was convinced that some mind-stuff or materials such as images are necessary for thinking, as Aristotle supposed. The relation between meaning and the materials of thinking is equally unclear. James suggested no theory of vehicular expression; one might guess that words or images are conceived as causing the occurrences in the fringe that constitute the sense or meaning as it is apprehended apart from verbal or imagelike materials. What the Würzburg psychologists during the first decade of this century called *Bewusstseinslagen* (layers of consciousness) are nonsensory, unanalyzable stretches of consciousness that can be introspected for their thought-content or meaning; they might be called naked thoughts, since they appear, upon careful introspection, unclothed in either words or images. The Würzburg experiments led to much debate in the 1920s and 1930s about imageless thought, provoking Wilhelm Wundt to criticize them for not meeting scientific standards and E. B. Titchener to rebut them on the grounds that their introspections were faulty, his own thesis being that all thinking is analyzable into sensory items like images and sensations.[31] Passages in *Principles* and elsewhere suggest that James was a believer in *Bewusstseinslagen* or imageless thought. In "On the Function of Cognition" he wrote:

> I . . . read the first sentence. . . . "Newton saw the handiwork of God in the heavens as plainly as Paley in the animal kingdom." I immediately look back and try to analyze the subjective state in which I rapidly apprehended this sentence as I read it. In the first place there was an obvious feeling that the sentence was intelligible and rational and related to the world of realities. There was also a sense of agreement or harmony between "Newton," "Paley," and

"God." There was no apparent image connected with the words "heavens," or "handiwork," or "God"; they were words merely. With "animal kingdom" I think there was the faintest consciousness (it may possibly have been an image of the steps) of the Museum of Zoology in the town of Cambridge where I write. With "Paley" there was an equally faint consciousness of a small dark leather book; and with "Newton" a pretty distinct vision of the right-hand corner of a curling periwig. This is all the mind-stuff I can discover in my first consciousness of the meaning of the sentence, and I am afraid that even not all of this would have been present had I . . . not pitched it out for an experiment. And yet my consciousness was truly cognitive. (*CER*, 33–34)

It is plausible to infer that James thought nonsensory states of mind or their nonsensory features deserved to be called thinkings or thoughts because of his references to "no apparent images," "feelings of" and "sense of." Such an interpretation seems to put the final seal on the distinction between thought and language (and images), justifying the judgment that James anticipated the Würzburgers' discovery of imageless thought. On the other hand, because these nonsensory mental items seem to be largely within the fringe of consciousness and are thus elusive, James had to be cautious about endorsing what his introspections hinted about their nature; moreover, declaring them to be purely nonsensory might imply a mentalism difficult to reconcile with either the physiological account of mental items that was emphasized in *Principles* or the abandonment of dualism and its rejection of mentalism in *Essays in Radical Empiricism*. James's reported introspections in *Principles* and elsewhere took him in opposite directions; some experiences led him to the belief that thinking is always physiological, while others indicated the presence of nonsensory, unanalyzable states of thought—resembling the *Bewusstseinslagen* of the Würzbergers—which defy description in sensory terms, much less in physiological ones. When stressing the differences between thinking and the use of language, James made no effort to fill in with physiological detail the gaps left in consciousness by the absence of imagery, sensations, and words; that is, he offered no physiological account of how meaning occurs in the fringe of consciousness. He acknowledged that his introspections might leave him uncertain, but not that they actually carried him in conflicting directions.[32]

Another apparent conflict in James's introspections is that on the one hand meanings are construed as transitional states of consciousness, carrying thought forward more rapidly than is possible when using words, but on the other hand meanings sometimes resemble static objects of awareness, especially the total idea or object of thought. James tended, from the earliest portions of *Principles* to his later pragmatism and radical empiricism, to understand the sense of meaning or the awareness of significance, which is a part of thinking, as a relational or transitional state of consciousness. This idea may have appealed to James because he entertained the vague notion that the meaning of anything is another thing; in any process of thinking, which necessarily involves a series of meanings, the mind moves or is led from one thing to another until the thinking stops. But this movement or being led is itself an important part of thinking, and when it occurs with a feeling of direction and progression, it is felt as an awareness of meaning. "The truth is that large tracts of human speech are nothing but *signs of direction* in thought, of which direction we nevertheless have an acutely discriminative sense, though no definite sensorial image plays any part in it whatsoever. Sensorial images are stable psychic facts. . . . These bare images of logical movement, on the contrary, are psychic transitions, always on the wing, so to speak, and not to be glimpsed except in flight."[33] James also wrote:

> It makes little or no difference in what sort of mind-stuff . . . his thinking goes on. The only images *intrinsically* important are the halting-places, the substantive conclusions, provisional or final, of the thought. Throughout all the rest of the stream, the feelings of relation are everything, and the terms related almost naught. These feelings of relation, these psychic overtones, halos, suffusions, or fringes about the terms, may be the same in very different systems of imagery. . . . It need only be added that as the Algebrist, though the sequence of his terms is fixed by their relations rather than by their several values, must give a real value to the *final* one he reaches; so the thinker in words must let his concluding word or phrase be translated into its full sensible-image-value, under penalty of the thought being left unrealized and pale. (*Principles,* 1:269, 271)

The purpose of a process of thinking, and perhaps even its retrospective identification, is stamped by the particular image or sensation ("halting-point") with which the thinking culminates. James clearly connected meaning with relational or transitional states of consciousness, so that meanings are somehow functions of a plurality of special events taking place in the dim fringes of consciousness.

On the other hand, he insisted that there can be only one object of thought before the mind, since the separate ideas of Locke are unacceptable; this point is underlined in James's relating thought to language.

> Now I believe that in all cases where the words are *understood,* the total idea may be and usually is present not only before and after the phrase has been spoken, but also whilst each separate word is uttered. It is the overtone, halo, or fringe of the word, *as spoken in that sentence.* It is never absent; no word in an understood sentence comes to consciousness as a mere noise. We feel its meaning as it passes; and although our object differs from one moment to another as to its verbal kernel or nucleus, yet it is *similar* throughout the entire segment of the stream. The same object is known everywhere, now from the point of view, if we may so call it, of this word, now from the point of view of that.[34]

James seems to have been expressing here the familiar claim that the individual words in a sentence are understood not singly but in context: "A good way to get the words and the sense separately is to inwardly articulate word for word the discourse of another. One then finds that the meaning will often come to the mind in pulses, after clauses or sentences are finished" (*Principles*, 1:281n). Another concept of meaning, different from the one understood in terms of relational and transitional states of mind, involves a single idea or object of thought that is apprehended continuously throughout a stretch of thinking. It is discretely apprehended, apart from feelings of movement and progression and other occurrences in the fringe of consciousness. The single object is actually identified with the fringe in the passage just quoted; thus the fringe is not only an area of consciousness in which the sense of meaning results from felt tendencies and transitions, it is also equated with a specific thought's single, enduring object. James never showed any awareness that his ideas might be interpreted to include two concepts of meaning, one defined in terms of a plurality of relations and another in terms of a unitary, static object, so he naturally did not attempt to show that the two concepts connect. A sensible mode of connection can no doubt be formulated, but it would be pure speculation to attribute any such connection to James. The identification of the object of thinking with the fringe is troubling because it raises the question of how to reconcile the picture of the object as an ideal or abstract complex of concepts, which is presumably not introspectable as are the concrete events in consciousness, with the picture of it as something introspectable, such as the fringe. That the concept of the fringe was given conflicting responsibilities is evident in another characterization of it: "Let us use the words *psychic overtone, suffusion,* or *fringe,* to designate the influence of a faint brain-process upon our thought, as it makes us aware of relations and objects but dimly perceived."[35] Even if we agree wholeheartedly with James that the experiences of both handicapped people and others amply testify to the need for distinguishing between language and thought, we may wish that his apparatus for explaining the distinction—meanings, sense of meanings, felt directions, images of logical movement, abstract objects, transitional states, and fringe—was more neatly designed. Nevertheless, genuine difficulties beset any attempt at accurate and lucid reporting of any experience of thinking, and James took many risks in making the attempt.

Those risks were certainly more than introspective adventuring. James's attempt to explicate thinking was mandated by the pragmatism that guided *Principles* and other writings even before he officially formulated the doctrine in 1898.[36] If words are meaningful, they have cash value; that is, if they are empirical and not purely formal, they can be connected with either introspective or perceptual experience. This pragmatic requirement applies to meaning too; James had to do some introspective scouting to locate the meaning of meaning, since he understood that the concept leads into heavily subjective territory. Having meaning or making sense is not inherent in words, images, or anything else, because it remains unmanifested unless some modification in awareness or subjectivity is realized. For example, one word can call up another in a sequence without their sense being called to mind. Consider a question that received much notice during the heyday of logical positivism: Is the expression "round square" meaningful? James answered: "The natural possibility or impossibility of the thing does not touch the question of its conceivability. . . . 'Round square,' 'black-white-thing,' are absolutely definite conceptions; it is a mere accident, as far as conception goes, that they happen to stand for things which nature never lets us sensibly perceive" (*Principles*, 1:463). There is an unfortunate confusion here between natural and logical impossibility; James was more on target when he wrote: "*Logically,* any one combination of qualities is to the field as *conceivable* as any other, and has as distinct a meaning for thought. What necessitates this remark is the confusion (e.g., Spencer, Psychology, 426–427) between the inconceivable and the not-distinctly-imaginable. How do we know *which* things we cannot imagine unless by first conceiving them, meaning *them* and not other things" (*Principles*, 1:464). Here James anticipated the arguments of later thinkers who have held that unless we understand what "round square" means, we cannot declare it an impossibility; as in the case of quantum physics, conceivable states of affairs are not always imaginable. But for James, conceivability had also to touch a subjective nerve if it was to be understood; meaning or sense, to be actual and not merely potential, must be felt, introspected, or intuited.

> The border line between objective sense and nonsense is hard to draw; that between subjective sense and nonsense, impossible. Subjectively, any collocation of words may make sense—even the wildest words in a dream—if one only does not doubt their belonging together. Take the obscurer passages in Hegel: it is a fair question whether the rationality included in them be anything more than the fact that the words all belong to a common vocabulary. . . . Yet there seems no reason to doubt that the subjective feeling of the rationality of these sentences was strong in the writer as he penned them, or even that some readers by straining may have reproduced it in themselves. (*Principles*, 1:264)

Sense, meaning, and conceivability can be realized only if feelings of understanding or rationality are present; beyond these feelings there is no sound test of meaningfulness. James joined his pragmatic and psychological concepts of meaning by declaring both that concepts have consequences and that those consequences can only be "designative."[37] When we understand words or grasp the concepts they express, we have some sense of their consequences, which we can designate or point to within our perceptual or introspectable experience. When we think of a concept without discovering an instance of its application, the relevant consequence is something designative that is inwardly felt rather than outwardly observed. Not only did James offer little explanation of how words and concepts relate, but when he said that the presence of meaning can be tested by the presence or absence of feelings, he ignored too many distinctions in applying the general label *feelings*. There are significant dissimilarities in our feelings, and James did not adequately identify the "logical sense" (feeling) on which his treatment of meaning is based.

THOUGHT AND MENTAL ACTS

We cannot theorize about acts of thinking without some analysis of the thinker. In "The Consciousness of Self" James sketched the self of the thinker phenomenalistically, in contrast with the traditional view of it as a substance. It is possible, he argued, to formulate a psychology of thinking on the minimal assumption that the thinker is a phase of the stream of consciousness, a phenomenon among the stream's phenomena, capable of being treated as a datum within experience and having the same basic nature as other data accessible to psychological inquiry. While this minimal assumption is consistent with the spirit of scientific psychology, however, James assumed that its truth or falsity cannot be assessed adequately without a full-scale philosophical investigation. For that reason I have deferred discussion of James's concept of the thinker, agent, or self until chapter 12.

From his earliest philosophizing, James was occupied with the question of how we make the distinction between subjectivity and objectivity. In a notebook he compared the realist view that the objective, physical world is presented in perception with the idealist position that the world is presented only mediately, through a subsequent reflective act of the mind.[38] James did not decide between the two views until he had worked out the metaphysics of radical empiricism in the last decade of his life, but we can detect even in his early ponderings and psychology the seeds of that decision. He wrote in the 1870 notebook:

> Be your reflection as agile as it may, you can never make it seize upon its very self, never make the instant of thinking become the thing thought of, any more than the man in Chamisso's [*Peter Schlemihl*] could overtake his pigtail by rotating. In other words, we never overtake the immediate in thought, the essence of whose form, consequently, is to posit an object distinct from itself. Thus the very form of thought implies a duality. While you think, you think of an object, be it thing or idea, not of your instant thinking. *This* the idealist must admit. (Quoted in RBP, 1:576)

This passage anticipates the one in "The Consciousness of Self" where James asserted that since all introspective knowledge is actually retrospective, the distinction between subject and object is never given immediately but is always drawn retrospectively.[39] The self or thinker is not simply given to introspection but is understood only after complex interpretation; James thus believed that laboratory psychology should concentrate on the experience of thinking and bypass philosophical questions about the role of the subjective term (thinker) in that experience. He sometimes expressed the same point by insisting that self-consciousness is not a primitive form of experience; an infant's experience does not include an elemental contrast between *me* and *not-me,* and the dichotomy of subject and object need not accompany every adult experience.

James claimed acquaintance with such acts as assenting, negating, and attending and identified them with bodily sensations; he agreed with Locke and others that through introspection we become aware of the mind's own activities. "In noticing the differences and resemblances of things, and their degrees, the mind feels its own activity, and has given the name of *comparison* thereto" (*Principles,* 2:643). The activity of comparing is particularly important in James's scheme. Strictly speaking, comparing involves analyzing points of difference and resemblance already noted, and it is not to be confused with the mere registering of likeness and dissimilarity which is a prerequisite for comparison. Our capacity to record in a preanalytic way the likenesses and differences presented to us is a brute, inexplicable fact; insofar as it occurs at a prereflective level of experience, it can be excluded from the category of thinking.[40] But the act of comparing is analytic, a kind of dissecting guided by thought, and is itself a species of thinking insofar as it considers the world in terms of ideas, images, and concepts. James believed that the world we perceive as a felt stream or flux becomes, when touched by thought and its concepts, a different world from the one originally felt. James gave an example of the difference that comparison makes: suppose two simple, different elements m and n happen in immediate succession such that their differences are felt. Instead of perceiving them as they are separately and intrinsically, we instinctively compare them, so that one is not experienced purely but as modified by the other. "As our brains and minds are actually made, it is impossible to get certain m's and n's in immediate sequence and to keep them *pure*. If kept pure, it would mean that they remain uncompared. With us, inevitably, by a mechanism which we as yet fail to understand, the shock of difference is felt between them, and the second object is not n pure, but n-as-different-from-m."[41]

James's reference to how "our brains and minds are made" is elaborated in "Necessary Truths and the Effects of Experience," the final chapter of *Principles*, where he makes the spectacular claim that the act of comparing exclusively underpins the pure science of logic and mathematics and results not from experience but from the brain's native or innate structure. (James's nativism included not only sensation and space, but mental activities and capacities as well.) James argued as follows: Comparison in terms of resemblance and difference is between characteristics that have been abstracted from things; these abstracted characteristics are ideal entities which can be compared independently of sense-perception. The relations discovered through this a priori comparison belong to the sciences of classification, logic, and mathematics; since such relations are the subject of these sciences, scientific knowledge is exclusively the result of comparison.[42] James's treatment of comparison, expressed in several chapters of *Principles*, is elaborate and often ingenious; it agrees substantially with much modern opinion about the a priori nature of logic and mathematics but is tedious in its unflagging effort to collect the relevant acts of thinking under the general category of *comparison*. James's discussion of the pure sciences includes little on concepts such as deduction, proof, set, number, identity, and contradiction; after introducing the idea of predication, he moved to a hypothesis not about the nature of predication but about the motive for employing it. Nevertheless, he touched upon an astonishing number of topics and issues and tried to lay the foundations of a systematic psychology that included a great variety of intellectual operations.

In "Discrimination and Comparison" James stated that the ability to arrange entire groups of differences in series (for example, the musical and color scales), to comprehend serial increases of differences in general, is a basic feature of intellectual life. He returned to this point in the final chapter, partly to illuminate another feature of human thought and partly to bolster the nativistic explanation of where that feature originates. The source of our comprehension of serial order is not sense-perception but rather the structure of the brain, particularly its innate capacity to perform the operation of comparing repeatedly on its own results. *"The mind thus becomes aware of sets of similar differences, and forms series of terms with the same kind and amount of difference between them, terms which, as they succeed each other, maintain a constant direction of serial increase"* (*Principles,* 2:645). A sense of constant direction, of the fact that terms constitute a series only when their differences run in the same direction, is required to perform any series of operations. When the mind understands the series as a whole, it sees that two terms remotely related differ more than two terms proximately related, that any given term differs more from a remote than from a proximate one, and that these rules hold whatever the terms or the kind of difference. If we have a series such that A is greater than B, B greater than C, and C is greater than D, we can eliminate the intermediaries B and C and transfer their relations to A and D by asserting that A is greater than D. James referred to the principle of transitivity here as the axiom of skipped intermediaries or of transferred relations, calling it the deepest law of man's thought. He recognized its limits; it does not hold for all series of homogeneously related terms, and it depends upon the kinds of relations in question. The series A is not B is not C is not D does not permit the relation to be transferred to remote terms, since no inference can be drawn from two negations. The fact that we understand how the relation is transferable in one sort of series but not in another cannot be explained as the effect of experience or of some learning process; it can be attributed only to something not yet understood in the nature of the brain. "Let it not be said that it is a mere matter of verbal association, due to the fact that language sometimes permits us to transfer the *name* of a relation over skipped intermediaries, and sometimes does not. . . . Nothing but the clear sight of the ideas themselves shows whether the axiom of skipped intermediaries applies to them or not. Their connections, immediate and remote, flow from their inward nature" (*Principles,* 2:660–61). Although James is known as a pragmatist and an empiricist, and his thought in this chapter is considered behavioristic with respect to the intentionality of thought, he followed the continental or rationalistic tradition in his explanation of how thinking occurs in mathematics, logic, and other subjects which require an innate intelligence. But he insisted in *Principles,* in appealing to the native structure of the brain to explain some features of how we think, that he did not want to reinstate the Kantian "machine-shop" or mind-body dualism in sanctioning innate ideas. He believed that the innate structure would eventually be understood as a part of the brain's physiology. James's attention to the peculiarities of serial ordering, and his argument that it can be explained only nativistically and not through verbal associations or conditioning, resemble some distinguished contemporary opinions and may therefore be relevant to current discussions.[43]

James's discussion of a priori knowledge in the pure sciences includes much talk about the abstract, ideal entities (meanings-as-objects) that our minds inspect and play with, recalling our question of how an account of meaning as something introspectable can connect with an account of meaning as something nonintrospectable. Following a tradition dating back to Plato, James tried to make plausible the idea that introspectable sense-experience is intimately related to abstract concepts, yet he also explained much of thinking not in the usual terms of introspection, but rather in terms of intuition or what F. H. Bradley called inspection. It is surprising that James did not pay more attention to the distinction between introspection and the awareness of objects that are eternal and unlike transitory states of consciousness. His failure to make this distinction may be partly responsible for the occasional insensitivities in his theorizing about thinking. In rejecting T. H. Huxley's proposal that abstract ideas can be equated with vague or generic images, James objected that a vague image does not itself represent anything. *"The use of either* [a vague or a distinct] *picture by the mind to symbolize a whole class of individuals is a new mental function,* requiring some other modification of consciousness than the mere perception that the picture is distinct or not" (*Principles,* 2:49). Instead of asking what it means to use an image for representing a whole class of things, he reverted without elaboration to the explanation that the meaning of an image is a function of the fringe of consciousness; he then remarked: "It is likely that the different degrees in which different men are able to make them sharp and complete has had something to do with keeping up such philosophic disputes as that of Berkeley with Locke over abstract ideas" (*Principles,* 2:49). Given the kind of difference represented by the very distinction between images and abstract ideas (ideal entities), it seems that James would have pointed not to variations in imaginative ability, but rather to the fact that introspection is simply not suited for either acquiring or inspecting abstract ideas. Another example is his contention—in opposing the Hegelian idea that concepts have the power to develop on their own and to generate other concepts—that it is false that the concept of 6 + 7 produces that of 13. "The conceptions 12, 13, and 14 are each and all generated by individual acts of the mind, playing with its materials" (*Principles,* 1:466). This picture of the mind generating, in act after act of thinking, each concept it has ever entertained suggests that it is a busy machine-shop indeed, even if not the Kantian one. James seems to have regarded concepts as bare nuggets which we can inspect, juxtapose, and play with, and in the process a new concept may appear in our awareness; they are thus portrayed as enumerable entities that can be correlated one-to-one with specific mental acts. That he did not consider this idea a mythology, as he did the doctrine of association of ideas, resulted from his uncritical modeling of a theory about how we think with concepts upon an account of how we introspect our own states of consciousness. Whatever the true philosophical analysis of conceptual thinking, it must eschew the idea that acts of thinking can be individually correlated with each concept that can be named.

James did occasionally make an effort to define "playing with" concepts. For instance, he distinguished between belief, which is a feeling and allied with emotion, and judgment, which is an act unlike sensation or feeling, sometimes described as merely thinking or conceiving a proposition. James generally avoided the term *proposition,* calling it an "unlucky" word in the writings of Bertrand Russell and G. E. Moore because it is ambiguous, sometimes meaning "belief" and sometimes "fact"; whereas some thinkers used *proposition* to designate an abstract entity, the object of one's thinking, others used it such that a true proposition is identical with a fact.[44] When James did use the term, he intended it to designate a complex, abstract object of thinking which includes a subject, a predicate, and their relation. These three elements are brought together by a mental act of thinking or judging that is a binding or knitting operation; the proposition as a complex object of thought is formed by these elements together with a judgment, that is, thinking the subject and predicate concepts in a certain relation to each other. "This sort of *bringing of things together into the object of a single judgment* is of course essential to all thinking. . . . The thinking them is *thinking* them together, even if only with the result that they do not *belong* together. This sort of *subjective synthesis,* essential to knowledge as such (whenever it has a complex object), must not be confounded with *objective synthesis* or union instead of difference or disconnection, known among the things."[45] When a proposition is formed, it can be an object of various attitudes—belief, disbelief, doubt, for example. Although James never undertook a study of the logic of propositions or judgments, he took sides on several issues that were debated during the development of modern analytic philosophy.

James objected to the manner in which some thinkers had distinguished between *existential* and *attributive* judgments, the first illustrated by "the candle exists," in which a claim of existence is made, the second by "the candle is large," in which a quality is attributed to the something. Based on his psychological analysis of belief as an emotional impulse to believe in something by the very fact of its being conceived, James argued that we cannot distinguish existential from attributive judgments by claiming that the latter excite our belief less than the former. The two judgments evoke our belief equally, simply by virtue of being conceived, and only if some ground for doubt is introduced will our tendency to believe them be inhibited. A second argument is that a synthesis occurs in both judgments; in other words, existence is no less predicated of the candle than largeness is.

> The syllable *ex* in the word Existence, *da* in the word Dasein, express it. "The candle exists" is equivalent to "the candle is *over there.*" And the "over there" means real space, space related to other reals. The proposition amounts to saying: "The candle is in the same space with other reals." It affirms of the candle a very concrete predicate—namely, this relation to other particular concrete things. *Their* real existence, as we shall later see, resolves itself into their peculiar relation to *ourselves.* Existence is thus no substantive quality when we predicate it of any object: it is a relation, ultimately terminating in ourselves, and at the moment when it terminates, becoming a *practical* relation. But of this more anon. I only wish now to indicate the superficial nature of the distinction between the existential and the attributive proposition. (*Principles,* 2:290n)

In the history of philosophical disputes about whether existence is a predicate and whether existential propositions should be considered akin to attributive ones,

James's reasoning is certainly a respectable contribution and may indeed be persuasive. More than just comparing existential and attributive propositions, James wanted ultimately to prove that the assertion of something's existence is the assertion of its having a practical relation to oneself, understood along the lines of pragmatism and radical empiricism. What does it mean to say that the candle exists, is over there? At the very least, if we move over there or look in that direction, we will see the candle. Further, we will act in certain ways with respect to the candle if we need it for light.

James's observations about negative and disjunctive propositions resemble those made later by Russell. In arguing for the innateness of mental acts, James urged that certain forms of judgment, including the disjunctive and hypothetical, are due to the brain's structure rather than to the impression of outward experience on the mind. Although he did not explicitly characterize these judgmental forms as he did negative judgments, his appraisal clearly applied to them, too; the form of such judgments—"not-p," "p or q," "if p, then q"—is not a duplicate of something in the natural world. The judgment "this road goes either to Boston or to Providence" may be true, but there is no state of affairs describable as "either this or that"; the road goes just one way, not two, and certainly not an "either-or" way. The use of either-or expresses hesitation or uncertainty, not the presence of a disjunctive property in a concrete situation. Although James did not offer this analysis, it is consistent not only with his mental nativism but also with his characterization of negative judgments, which was elicited by a Hegelian idea:

> Every negation, [Hegelian idealism] says, must be an intellectual act. Even the most *naïf* realism will hardly pretend that the non-table as such exists *in se* after the same fashion as the table does. . . . Try to make the position or the affirmation of the table as simple as you can, it is also the negation of the non-table; and thus positive being seems after all but a function of intelligence, like negation. Idealism is proved, realism is unthinkable. . . . I object. . . . The truth is that our affirmations and negations do not stand on the same footing at all. . . . An affirmation says something about an objective existence. A negation says something *about an affirmation*—namely, that it is false. There are no negative predicates or falsities in nature.[46]

Russell in effect quarreled with this view when he temporarily lobbied for the ontological status of negative facts. But James's argument is not only comparable to those used by others in directing philosophy from nineteenth-century idealism to contemporary analytic realism, it is also an important argument—anticipating one that Russell eventually urged himself—for the conclusion that logic is not a mirror of nature. Both James and Russell believed that the logical complexes symbolized by "not-p," "if p, then q," and "p or q" exist in thought but not in nature; as Russell once put it, the concepts of disjunction and negation may be needed for psychology but not for physics.[47]

James also sought a definition of reasoning. He was unimpressed by the answer of traditional associationism: *"Reasoning* is the perception that 'whatever has any mark has that which it is a mark of;' in the concrete case [the syllogism] the mark or middle term being always associated with each of the other terms and so serving as a link by which they are themselves indirectly associated together" (*Principles*, 1:599). He accepted most of associationistic psychology if its formulations were transferred from psychological to physiological or physicalistic language and if it were supplemented by an explanation that permits both voluntary (nonmechanical) activity and a greater variety of activities to qualify as reasonings. It is not obvious, he remarked, what reason is or what distinguishes reasoning from other thought sequences, especially those that lead to similar results. A revery or free flow of images, after all, can sometimes lead to sensible or rational outcomes. Animals as well as humans are presumably subject to onsets of imagery that may produce beneficial results. Both are capable of an elementary kind of inference, in a popular sense of the word, in anticipating what is signified (food) by the presentation of a sign (bell). Animals may also be able to abstract features of objects, to recognize "deerness" as well as a particular deer, and thus to acquire some of the generality that characterizes thought. *Recepts* or *generic ideas* were terms sometimes used to designate such primitive abstract objects, in contradistinction to concepts or general ideas that arise only at more sophisticated levels of thinking.

Thinking becomes reasoning when the mere association of images or signs is supplanted by a voluntary effort to find either the means to a certain end or one of the terms in an assumed causal relation; things inferred in the process need not be related associatively to whatever initiates the inference. The connections between terms or entities related through reasoning are general, abstract, and capable of being analyzed. In a typical case of reasoning, a person is confronted by a concrete fact or situation; he must not merely be fascinated by the fact in its entirety, he must also analyze it and abstract from it some essential attribute. This attribute has properties or consequences which were not understood to belong to the fact until the attribute and its properties were noticed. If the concrete fact is S, the essential attribute M, and the attribute's property P, then "the reasoned inference of P from S cannot be made without M's intermediation. The 'essence' M is thus that third or middle term in the reasoning . . . pronounced essential. *For his original or concrete S the reasoner substitutes its abstract property, M.* What is true of M, what is coupled with M, then holds true of S, is coupled with S. As M is properly one of the *parts* of the entire S, *reasoning may then be very well defined as the substitution of parts and their implications or consequences for wholes.*"[48] Agreeing with Mill, James asserted that the art of the reasoner calls for a sagacity or sharpness of mind to discover M in S, which one cannot accomplish merely going by the rules; there is no formula for recognizing that a lesion in certain nerve fibers is the cause of a person's illness. The reasoner must *learn*, must develop the ability to recall M's consequences or implications. In the syllogism "M is P, S is M, therefore S is P," the first or major premise requires the learning factor, and the second or minor premise requires sagacity for recognition and therefore represents a novel step in thought. "S is M" expresses a mode of conceiving S, and "M is P" expresses an abstract or general proposition. Agreeing with Locke, James argued that M, the attribute essential to S, is crucial only in relation to a special interest or purpose: "The only meaning of essence is teleological, and classification and conception are purely teleological weapons of the mind. The essence of a thing is that one of its properties which is so *important for my interests* that in comparison with it I may neglect the rest" (*Principles*, 2:335).

The key idea in James's psychology is that we are motivated to select and abstract from the world around us only those characteristics that respond to our interests or purposes. In his philosophy I call this idea subjective pragmatism; what we call real, true, or essential is so only and always to a biased, highly selective intelligence. Conception is abstraction, abstraction is selection from a larger totality, and selection is motivated by interest and purpose. "In looking back on the subject of reasoning, one feels how intimately connected it is with conception; and one realizes more than ever the deep reach of that principle of selection on which so much stress was laid towards the close of Chapter IX ["The Stream of Thought"]" (*Principles*, 2:369). The principle of selectivity, which is typical of conceiving (thinking), not only figures in the initiation of a process of thinking, it also affects the character of that process. James mentioned condensation, a feature of some thinking appreciated by Freud, Lev Vygotsky, and others, in which one word may do the work of a whole paragraph, or a momentary image seems to bear several thoughts at once.[49] James explained condensation in thinking as the result of an actual loss of mental content through progressive selectivity in thinking; gradually, through being ignored, items in consciousness simply disappear, allowing themselves to be represented if at all by the remaining condenser, an item which, by surviving through selection, has taken on several duties. (In Freud's scheme the thought of a house or a snake is a heavy worker.) Selectivity is a mark also of sagacity, which in some persons amounts to genius. Geniuses somehow shut out the irrelevant mass of distractions and discern the hidden analogies there.

> Beyond the analogies which their own minds suggest by breaking up the literal sequence of their experience, there is a whole world of analogies which they can appreciate when imparted to them by their betters, but which they could never excogitate alone. This answers the question why Darwin and Newton had to be waited for so long. The flash of similarity between an apple and the moon, between the rivalry for food in nature and the rivalry for man's selection, was too recondite to have occurred to any but exceptional minds. *Genius, then, . . . is identical with the possession of similar association to an extreme degree.*[50]

James closed the subject by throwing out hints that, as thinking becomes more sophisticated, the principle of selectivity is affected by aesthetic considerations such as harmony, elegance, and economy.

James made an enormous effort on behalf of the psychology and philosophy of thinking. He essayed an overview of a scattered field of topics, hunting for a systematic explanation of a rich variety of activities. He paid attention to a number of issues, including intentionality, the directedness of thinking, the distinction between act and object, and the relation of language to thought. Some of his contentions are still of lively interest, such as the argument that there are ways of thinking native to the brain itself, which cannot be explained as the effect of our environment. Perhaps the two most important legacies from James's theorizing about thought are his relentless insistence that interest is what motivates thinking and his demonstration of the scope and limits of introspective psychology in explaining how we think. We now have a conception of what introspection discloses about the phenomena connected with thinking, as well as what opportunities may exist for introspective inquiries of our own. Like James, we may have a better sense of how introspection both solves and creates the mysteries that are sometimes felt to be part of the experience of thinking. His enterprise shows how difficult it is to be sure whether such mysteries can be resolved introspectively, by laboratory experimentation, or by philosophical and conceptual analysis. This difficulty is especially true of the elusive questions that arise in trying to clarify the concepts of meaning and thought's object from the perspective of introspective psychology. James's work on thinking is a classic example of how introspective and philosophical inquiry both blend and separate. If we are to improve upon what he achieved, we must try to bring the two sorts of inquiry into clearer view, a task that may also be necessary to understand his theory of knowledge.

10 ❧ KNOWLEDGE

KNOWLEDGE AND BELIEF

James's pragmatism answered a question raised in *Principles*, one which he thought was unanswerable by empirical psychology and thus had to be delivered to philosophy: What is cognition, what is it to know something? This question may seem like a problem for empirical psychology if *knowing* designates a state of consciousness somehow related to the thing known, but James thought that for psychology "the *relation of knowing* is the most mysterious thing in the world."[1] This mystery results from the dualism between mind and body, between knower and known, espoused by psychologists; when subject and object are radically distinguished, any knowledge-relation between them is inexplicable and can be treated, like resemblance and difference, only as an ultimate or primitive relation, presumed rather than explained by the psychologist. Thus the anticipated inquiry can never occur.

That no psychological analysis of the cognitive relation will work is reiterated in *Principles;* any attempt at such analysis is an instance of the psychologist's fallacy of conceiving a person's cognitive state as identical with what he knows about that state.[2] Suppose that a psychologist knows that a subject's cognitive state resembles in certain respects what the subject knows, let us say a map he is looking at; the elements in the subject's perceptual experience of the map correspond to the elements on the map, leading to the conclusion that what is in his mind or experience resembles what he knows or perceives. At best, James argued, such resemblance is only one test of whether the subject knows the map; it certainly is not the knowledge-relation itself, and to confuse it with the relation of similarity is to exemplify the psychologist's fallacy.[3] The history of psychology shows another common instance of this fallacy: the doctrine that, assuming the basic materials of consciousness to be sensations, knowledge results when sensations are appropriately put together by the mind to represent objective reality adequately. But not only is such an analysis of cognition mythological and totally unsupported by evidence, James argued, it is not an analysis of the knowledge-relation at all; even if it were true and relevant, it would describe not the relation but only a condition or test for it. According to the dualism that characterizes both empirical psychology and common sense, there are states of consciousness and nonmental things known by those states, and "neither gets out of itself or into the other, neither in any way *is* the other, neither *makes* the other. They just stand face to face in a common world, and one simply knows, or is known unto its counterpart. This singular relation is not to be expressed in lower terms, or translated into any more intelligible name."[4]

Psychology is helpless to illuminate the epistemological problems of how subjects know objects and what that knowledge consists of, or the metaphysical problems of how mind and body are related and how brain processes cause conscious cognitive states in the first place.[5] A recurrent theme in *Principles* is that from the standpoint of psychology cognition is inevitably a mystery, partly because the cognitive relation is primitive or irreducible. This irreducibility results from epistemological dualism, which characterizes states of consciousness as staring knowingly at objects; but just as we can ask how, in face-to-face perception, the state of the percipient is related to the perceived object, we can also ask how the gulf between knower and known is bridged by the knowledge-relation. James and his contemporaries questioned the dualistic argument that a person's cognitive state is related to the thing known; he concluded that the dualists offered no explanation. Although he insisted in *Principles* upon the irreducible nature of the cognitive relation and upon the basic mystery of cognition itself, he nevertheless sought a revised account that would replace dualism with a combination of pragmatism and radical empiricism.

We might surmise that in his subsequent formulation of pragmatism James favored a purely dispositional analysis of knowing, such as Ryle's view today, but although James wanted to eliminate the mystery of the cognitive relation by explaining it along dispositional lines, he always assumed with psychology and common sense that some of our conscious states are unique knowings or cognizings. The idea that *knows* in "A knows B" designates only a disposition (to behave in various ways), but never an occurrent (a state of consciousness), seems not to have tempted him.[6] He did not trace the perplexity about cognition, as have Ryle and other modern thinkers, to an alleged error of talking as if there were episodes called knowings; rather, he thought it stemmed from the implications of metaphysical or epistemological dualism, which pictures knowledge as a sort of mental confrontation or vision of an object by a state of consciousness. James never addressed how we know that cognitive states occur, but if asked, I think he would have replied that we know that some states of consciousness are knowings simply because we often find ourselves claiming to know something that we subsequently discover is true. We know introspectively that such states of consciousness occur, states of belief or feelings of certainty, which prompt the claim of knowledge, but we cannot know introspectively that these states are actual knowings or that the claim is in fact true; that determination requires empirical testing and observation. When James argued that cognitive states occur and that the cognitive relation is primitive and irreducible, he did not mean that introspection can certify a state of consciousness to be a case of knowledge, or that the knowledge-relation is itself introspectable or otherwise inspectable. He meant simply that, given dualism, the relation of knowledge is unanalyzable into any other relation; we grasp this irreducibility not by any act of introspection or inspection, but by understanding the concepts involved.

When James appropriated John Grote's distinction between knowledge-by-acquaintance (*connaître, noscere, kennen*) and knowledge-about (*savoir, scire, wissen*), he did not mention the cognitive relation as an object of either type of knowledge.[7] It is significant that he omitted the cognitive relation from the things we are immediately acquainted with, and I think he would have asserted that we have knowledge only *about* it. This view would be more consistent with pragmatism than is the claim that there is a cognitive relation of which we are immediately aware; in his pragmatism, James eliminated the putative relation of intentionality or self-transcendency and thus the unique cognitive relation that the dualism in *Principles* seemed to mandate. But if this relation could be directly inspected, there would be no way to eliminate it when it so evidently existed. The proposed view is consistent also with James's rejection of the doctrine, which he attributed to Kant, that self-consciousness is essential to cognition and that to know something one must explicitly distinguish between it and oneself, a process that would presumably disclose the cognitive relation between them.[8] In insisting that we can know something without knowing that we know it, James allowed for the possibilities both that we can know something without being acquainted with a cognitive relation between it and ourselves and that we might never be acquainted with any such relation. He thus cleared the way for the elimination of a relation that, besides being primitive and irreducible, is sufficiently elusive and mysterious to make a pragmatist wonder whether it has any utility whatever. Like anything else, cognition must in a practical world serve a purpose.

Among the things we know by acquaintance, James listed secondary qualities, the passage of time, our own movement through space, the effort of attention, and the noticed differences between entities.

> *About* the inner nature of these facts or what makes them what they are, I can say nothing at all. I cannot impart acquaintance with them to any one who has not already made it himself. I cannot *describe* them, make a blind man guess what blue is like, define to a child a syllogism, or tell a philosopher in just what respect distance is just what it is, and differs from other forms of relation. . . . All the elementary natures of the world, its highest genera, the simple qualities of matter and mind, together with the kinds of relation that subsist between them, must either not be known at all, or known in this dumb way of acquaintance without *knowledge-about*. In minds able to speak at all there is, it is true, *some* knowledge about everything. Things can at least be classed, and the times of their appearance told. But, in general, the less we analyze a thing, and the fewer

of its relations we perceive, the less we know about it and the more our familiarity with it is of the acquaintance-type. The two kinds of knowledge are, therefore, as the human mind practically exerts them, relative terms. That is, the same thought of a thing may be called knowledge-about in comparison with a simpler thought, or acquaintance with it in comparison with a thought of it that is more articulate and explicit still. (*Principles*, 1:221–22)

Although the distinction between the two sorts of knowledge is often relative, as in the example of the child and the syllogism, in some cases the difference seems absolute. One person's acquaintance with a shade of blue and another's with a particular aroma can never be replaced by instances of knowledge-about, as James himself seems to have understood. Despite his reference to elementary natures and to the underpinning role of knowledge-by-acquaintance, he was willing to characterize the distinction as relative; he was diffident about hardening the distinction, as Russell and others were, into a foundational account of empirical knowledge. He rejected the doctrine that atomic sense-data, isolated sensations, or any such "simples" are the foundations of knowledge-about, arguing instead, despite the importance of sensations in his psychology, that our actual experiences begin and end with gestalten or wholes from which isolated sensations are, for theoretical reasons, sometimes abstracted.[9] Further, he was as reluctant to grant certitude to knowledge-by-acquaintance as he was to bestow it upon introspection; because his favorite examples of acquaintance were taken from sense-perception and because he judged observation to be fallible, it is not surprising that he rejected epistemologies that depend upon allegedly infallible cognitions.

James even hints that knowledge-by-acquaintance is a misnomer because acquaintance is contrasted with knowledge. "We can ascend to knowledge *about* it by rallying our wits and proceeding to notice and analyze and think. What we are only acquainted with is only *present* to our minds; we have it, or the idea of it. But when we know about it, we do more than merely have it; we seem, as we think over its relations, to subject it to a sort of *treatment* and to *operate* upon it with our thought" (*Principles*, 1:222). James then stated, with a distinctly Hegelian ring, that feelings are the vehicles of acquaintance and thoughts the vehicles of knowledge; feelings are the seeds of cognition and thoughts their fruition, an idea which further justified James's decision in *Principles* to use *feeling* and *thought* interchangeably to represent any state of consciousness. But did James really intend to assert that there is only knowledge-about, and that knowledge-by-acquaintance is only a figure of speech? In a trivial sense, he sometimes used the distinction between the two sorts of knowledge when comparing the knowledge of something present to the knowledge of something absent, calling the first acquaintance and the second knowledge-about. However, he did not believe in knowledge-by-acquaintance in the sense of a knowledge that occurs simply as a result of something's immediate presence to the awareness; he also denied incorrigibility to introspection. "If to *have* feelings or thoughts in their immediacy were enough, babies in the cradle would be psychologists, and infallible ones. But the psychologist must not only *have* his mental states in their absolute veritableness, he must report them and write about them, name them, classify and compare them and trace their relations to other things. . . . And as in the naming, classing, and knowing of things in general we are notoriously fallible, why not also here?"[10] Understanding this point is to understand the obverse side of James's declaration that knowledge always involves the participation of the knower; James denied that knowledge is ever simply impressed upon one who only passively feels things. The active participation of the knower is required in noticing, attending, naming, classifying, and predicating; without it there would be only feeling and acquaintance but no genuine knowledge. Active attending or noticing is equated with willing, which led Perry to say that the most important of James's insights in psychology was that knowledge depends ultimately upon will.[11] This idea, customarily associated with his later writings on pragmatism and religion, was already consolidated in *Principles*.

James never adopted a standard use of *knowledge* according to this interpretation; on the contrary, he continued occasionally to write as if acquaintance can be genuine knowing. His final explanation of how to characterize immediate perceptual acquaintance was his commentary in *The Meaning of Truth*, published a year before his death: "What now do we mean by 'knowing' such a sort of object as [one seen face to face]?" (47). Is direct perceptual acquaintance the same as knowledge-about, the sort of knowledge we sometimes have of things not immediately present, which must thus be verified to achieve actual knowledge? James's answer involves some subtleties. If we consider the page before us as something seen by someone else or possessing a molecular structure, then our alleged knowledge of it is tentative, conceptual, or representative, and we must take further steps to verify it. Knowledge-by-acquaintance is then really a form of knowledge-about.

> But if our own private vision of the paper can be considered in abstraction from every other event . . . then the paper seen and the seeing of it are only two names for one indivisible fact which, properly named, is *the datum, the phenomenon, or the experience*. . . . *To know immediately, then, or intuitively, is for mental content and object to be identical*. This is a very different definition from that which we gave of representative knowledge [knowledge-about]; but neither definition involves those mysterious notions of self-transcendency and presence in absence which are such essential parts of the ideas of knowledge, both of philosophers and of common men. (*The Meaning of Truth*, 49–50)

The notion that mental content and object can be identical, so that the dualism and the mystery of cognitive transcendency of *Principles* (and of common sense and empirical psychology) are discarded, is part of James's metaphysics of radical empiricism. This system presents an immediate problem of interpretation insofar as acquaintance seems to be regarded as a distinct kind of knowledge. This view can be consistent with our earlier formulation, however; merely because a coincidence of mental content and object occurs, it does not follow that the mind *knows* the object.

For that to happen, some activity of naming, noticing, or classifying must take place; if such an activity accurately reports the coincidence between mental content and object, there is no reason not to call it knowledge-by-acquaintance. This formulation supplies a type of knowledge in which the verification essential to all knowledge-about can terminate; knowledge-by-acquaintance is the verifying knowledge of the moment.[12] This knowledge is neither incorrigible nor infallible, since there is no guarantee that errors in noticing, naming, or predicating have been avoided; we can claim only that it is theoretically possible that the coincidence of mental content and object, and therefore knowledge-by-acquaintance, can occur. If in some situation we cannot be sure that we have not erred in noticing or classifying, we cannot truly know what we are acquainted with. In practice we must treat our claims of knowledge-by-acquaintance as we treat clear cases of knowledge-about; both need further testing. We may at some point become weary of testing, stop the process, and declare that we possess knowledge-by-acquaintance. Doing so proves nothing whatever. Other epistemologies have had the same fate, which is by no means a uniquely Jamesian problem. Perhaps the chief discomfiture that resulted for James's pragmatism is that, since in practice all claims to know are exactly like claims of knowledge-about, we have a distinction without any real difference.

James did not hesitate to speak of knowings as states of mind, whether the knowledge be direct acquaintance with or indirect knowledge about something; since no knowing carries with it a simultaneous knowledge of itself, it is not surprising that James concluded that the states of consciousness we call knowings are really states of belief. Like other philosophers, he defined knowing as a belief in something true, for which one has adequate evidence. James's only sustained account of belief is "The Perception of Reality," chapter 21 of *Principles,* which despite its title is more eloquent on the belief in reality than on the perception of it. The discussion of belief in this chapter was reprinted from "The Psychology of Belief," an essay published in 1889, a year before the appearance of *Principles.* Presumably belief was one of the last topics James pondered before his textbook went to press. This discussion explains James's psychology of belief-states and shows how his concepts of knowledge and reality depend upon a philosophy of belief.

In discerning the nature of belief, it is helpful to consider how believing contrasts with imagining and mere supposing; the difference, according to James, is that the object of belief, unlike those of the other attitudes, is "held to have reality. Belief is thus the mental state or function of cognizing reality. As used in the following pages, 'belief' will mean every degree of assurance, including the highest possible certainty and conviction" (*Principles,* 2:283). This formulation is critical to James's account of belief. If an object is imaginary but believed (or mentally entertained without grounds for disbelief), it still exists though not physically. Given James's reluctance to wield Occam's razor here, he held that any object of belief is real in one way or another.[13] Those philosophers accustomed to discussions such as Russell's and Quine's may judge, because James simply stated rather than argued his position, that he did not dispose of the problem confronting him. After all, we can have beliefs about things we do not hold to be real. Those who follow Russell and Quine will not be swayed by the point, on which James was enthusiastically in league with Spinoza and Bain, that *"any object which remains uncontradicted is ipso facto believed and posited as absolute reality."*[14] James was attracted to the idea, seemingly confirmed by anthropological studies, that there is a primitive impulse to assume that anything before the mind is real; unless some cause for doubt or contradiction occurs, the impulse will automatically manifest itself. James used this idea to reinforce his thesis that natural or primitive belief assumes its object to be real. However, we believe some things because we assume them to be true, though we need not believe also that they are real.

Although using *belief* to designate the whole range of assurance may be acceptable, James's identification of belief as the only mental state or function of cognizing reality is suspect. Not only do believing and cognizing (perceptually) differ prima facie, but we can believe what we *mis*cognize and disbelieve what we cognize correctly. If we take James less literally, however, his contention is that a cognizing state of consciousness normally involves belief in what is cognized; if belief is absent, cognition usually is as well. If we cannot simultaneously know something and know that we know it, then in any reflective moment we can at best characterize our reflected states as beliefs, no matter how much we are convinced that they are actual cognizings. Thus from any reflective or introspective perspective, cognizings are belief-states. What most interested James was the role of belief in knowledge; when he amplified his description of belief, its distinctness from knowledge quickly emerged. But this aspect of his account does not eclipse the controversy caused by his statement that belief and cognition overlap.

Above all, James wanted to establish kinship of belief to emotion; recalling Hume and anticipating Russell, he insisted that belief is a sui generis feeling, something with a distinct felt quality and which cannot be analyzed introspectively. One must experience belief to know what it is, so in one sense it is known by acquaintance. James gave many descriptions of belief in chapter 21 of *Principles;* it is said to resemble, for example, the feeling of consenting to something, the cessation of agitation and the resultant feeling of inward stability, and the feeling of nitrous oxide intoxication (with which James experimented) when "a man's very soul will sweat with conviction, and he be all the while unable to tell what he is convinced of at all."[15] James extracted from such comparisons a further one, crucial to his philosophy of belief. He compared believing to the experience of feeling vibrantly alive, the "sense of reality" which in pathological moments succumbs to *Grübelsucht* (brooding). During his depression in the 1870s, James knew well what such pathological experiences are like, and he learned to treasure the ability to believe and the emotional relief and stimulation it afforded. We can more fully appreciate James and his thought if we picture him as a picaresque philosopher, drawing his sword less in the presence of falsehood than when faced with a paralyzing doubt. In characterizing the emotional side of belief, he was rhapsodic, connecting belief with passion, Renouvier's notion of mental vertigo, the bodily commotion underlying all emotion, and the impulse to act explosively. When we wholeheartedly believe something, we are alive and well; James declared that an emotional reaction of the whole man signals the work of a healthy soul.

James agreed with Bain that an account such as J. S. Mill's makes belief too purely an intellectual state of mind. He agreed also with Franz Brentano, who distinguished belief from conception partly because belief is more emotional than conception but also because belief presupposes conception, judgment, or thought; we must already have thought or conceived a proposition before it can be believed. When a proposition is conceived, we can ask whether it is true, "and in the answer *Yes* to *this* question lies that new psychic act which . . . I prefer to call 'belief'" (*Principles*, 2:287). The proposition or object of belief has three elements—the subject, the predicate, and the relation between them—but the belief itself is simple and unanalyzable. Having identified belief as a sui generis state of mind, more akin to emotion than to thought and intimately connected with our sense of reality and healthy adjustment to our life and surroundings, James considered the conditions under which our belief or sense of reality is enlisted and preserved. In a display of Jamesian subjectivism, he declared that any world, whether that of sensations, mathematics and logic, aesthetics and morality, or fictions and fantasies, "*whilst it is attended to* is real after its own fashion; only the reality lapses with the attention" (*Principles*, 2:293). Things are not considered real until they are noticed, selected, or found interesting and important; the concept of reality does not come into play without active intervention on our part. That which excites our attention or will is deemed real, that which makes no impression upon it is unreal. "*In the relative sense,* then, the sense in which we contrast reality with simple *un*reality, and in which one thing is said to have *more* reality than another, and to be more believed, *reality means simply relation to our emotional and active life. This is the only sense which the word ever has in the mouths of practical men. In this sense, whatever excites and stimulates our interest is real*" (*Principles,* 2:295).

Although James characteristically held that psychological conclusions cannot be converted to philosophical ones without substantial argument, in the case of belief he did just that. Because psychology seems to show that we consider real only that which excites our attention or will, he declared:

> *The fons et origo of all reality, whether from the absolute or the practical point of view, is thus subjective, is ourselves.* As bare logical thinkers, without emotional reaction, we give reality to whatever objects we think of. . . . But, *as thinkers with emotional reaction, we give what seems to us a still higher degree of reality to whatever things we select and emphasize and then turn to* WITH A WILL. These are *living* realities. . . . A whole system may be real if it only hang to our Ego by one immediately *stinging* term. . . . *Our own reality, that sense of our own life which we at every moment possess, is the ultimate of ultimates for our belief.* "As sure as I exist!"—this is our uttermost warrant for the being of all other things. As Descartes made the indubitable reality of the *cogito* go bail for the reality of all that the *cogito* involved, so we all of us, feeling our present reality with absolutely coercive force, ascribe an all but equal degree of reality, first to whatever things

we lay hold on with a sense of personal need, and, second, to whatever farther things continously belong with these. . . . The world of living realities . . . is thus anchored in the Ego, considered as an active and emotional term.[16]

In his later years, while defending pragmatism against recurrent criticism, James lamented the need to reiterate his commonsense belief in realities independent of the ego; he might well have agreed that passages such as that quoted above contain enough hyperbole to mislead his readers into supposing that his subjectivism is more extreme than he intended. If this passage is qualified by what James averred elsewhere, a more judicious thesis results for his psychology, pragmatism, radical empiricism, pluralistic universe, and philosophy of religion. A study of the conditions which elicit belief and a sense of reality reveals that unless things possess the capacities to draw attention, arouse emotional interest, stimulate the will, and meet our aesthetic needs, they will never arouse our belief and thus never be included in what we call reality. For James it was only a short step from this psychological doctrine to the philosophical one that we can usually trust the demands and responses of our attention, our will, our emotions, and our moral and aesthetic needs; in short, we can justify beliefs by pointing to the demands and responses which elicited them. If this argument is challenged, the empirical reply is that experience overwhelmingly supports it because in most cases belief and reality do in fact coincide. James thought this empirical reply could itself be explained and understood at a deeper level: "I have now, I trust, shown sufficiently what the psychologic sources of the sense of reality are. Certain postulates are given in our nature; and whatever satisfies those postulates is treated as if real."[17] Because belief is part of our emotional nature, which is either genetic or evolved, we can, in a post-Darwinian climate, argue that our emotional, aesthetic, volitional, and cognitive demands are postulates of human nature which define reality. An evolved if not preestablished harmony exists between reality and ourselves such that, when we are subjectively touched to the point of active belief, we can generally be sure that genuine cognition is in process. James's subjective pragmatism is clearly formulated here: *"That theory will be most generally believed which, besides offering us objects able to account satisfactorily for our sensible experience, also offers those which are most interesting, those which appeal most urgently to our aesthetic, emotional, and active needs."*[18]

Each of us can probably provide a context or a mood in which the foregoing account of belief and its role in knowledge seems true, important, or profound. Few will quarrel with the statement that James's theory is highly interesting and stimulating and ingeniously combines a broad range of information and speculation. But problems arise with James's blurring of belief and a sense of reality. If this sense of reality is essentially only the condition of being normal, then it is at best a condition for acquiring sane beliefs; it is, however, identical neither with holding a belief nor with justifying one. Even if we accept the proposition that a preestablished harmony generally obtains between our emotional natures (including our beliefs) and a surrounding, independent reality, this idea is too vague and subject to too many exceptions to stand up in a heated moral, aesthetic, religious, or metaphysical debate. The more particular the issue, the more irrelevant the appeal to postulates of human nature.

A PRIORI AND EMPIRICAL KNOWLEDGE

Locke and Hume maintained that reasoning was either demonstrative (concerned with the relations of ideas) or empirical (concerned with existence and matters of fact). James followed suit, remarking in the chapter on conception in *Principles* that our knowledge accumulates "by rational and inward processes, as well as by empirical discoveries" and that some knowledge is a priori because it "merely comes from thinking" (*Principles,* 1:464). Empirical propositions are said to express time- and space-relations, and a priori or *rational* propositions to express the results of a comparison. The rational relations of logic and mathematics can be reduced to those of resemblance and difference, the knowledge of which is a priori or the result merely of thinking.[19] This knowledge of necessary relations between ideal or Platonic concepts is intuitive, innate, or a priori and is additional to the knowledges of acquaintance and description. It is intuitive because relations of comparison are directly inspectable (the relations between mental objects are "perceptually obvious at a glance, and no sense-verification is necessary"); a priori because "once true, always true, of those same mental objects"; and innate because it is due more to the native structure of the mind than to the effects of experience.[20]

Although James's distinction between a priori and empirical knowledge can be taken independently of his pragmatism, it was in fact developed as part of the package of ideas that culminated in the pragmatic philosophy. "Necessary Truths and the Effects of Experience" was written mostly in 1885 and contains James's only substantial comparison of a priori and empirical knowledge. He left the chapter intact, save for the addition of three pages, when *Principles* was published in 1890, and subsequent references to this chapter reaffirm its contents. It stems from his work on Spencer in the 1870s and from such essays as "Great Men, Great Thoughts, and the Environment" (1880) and "Reflex Action and Theism" (1881), and its argument thus represents a lifelong commitment. In particular, James denied in this chapter that all knowledge is the effect of sense-experience. He understood Spencer to claim that our minds merely mirror the external world as perceived through the senses and through habit and association. But, James objected, this claim is true only of such empirical generalizations as that glass refracts, fire burns, or heat melts snow; in these cases the mind acquires its information passively and, in a dualist theory, is an inner duplicate of an outer reality. In *Principles* James often remarked that he had tried in good faith to determine the limits of Spencer's doctrine, which makes the inner experience of cognition a rubber stamp of an external environment, and humans "mere offshoots and creatures of our environment" (*Principles,* 2:632–33). Two obstacles humble the grand vision of Spencer's "experience-philosophy." First, James disclosed again and again in *Principles* that psychology depends upon both the interest and volition of the subject and the contribution of the environment; this point has been reiterated in our own time by critics of behavioristic explanations that ascribe causality exclusively to the environment, critics who insist that the person makes his own contributions to cognition. Second, much of what occurs is inexplicable, but when the unknown factors become accessible, they will be found not in a straightforward relation between person and environment, but rather in the brain, physiology, idiosyncratic or idiopathic features, and Darwin's "accidental or spontaneous variations," which were neglected in Spencer's philosophy.[21]

The idea that most of our mental structure and much of our knowledge, especially the a priori or intuitive, cannot be explained as the product of experience but must rather be conceived as the result of "accidental" variations preserved by natural selection as relatively fixed features of the human species, is one of three general claims made in the final chapter of *Principles*. The second claim denies that the experience of the race can explain a priori knowledge any more than the experience of the individual can, and the third denies the Lamarckian hypothesis that a priori knowledge is an instinctive inheritance of traits acquired by our ancestors. No matter how much experience or how remote in time, it cannot account for the mind's immediate grasp of propositions that are necessarily true. James did not want to give the impression of defending an antinaturalistic theory; he emphasized that in his view the main source of a priori knowledge is an organic mental structure about which we know little. He gave an impressive list of features that are due to the mind's organic structure rather than to experience: elementary sensations, emotions, ideas of time, space, and number, ideas of difference and resemblance, ideas of causality, and various forms of judgment. For sensations to occur, the senses must be stimulated, but "cold, heat, pleasure, pain, red, blue, sound, silence, etc., are original, innate, or *a priori* properties of our subjective nature, even though they should require the touch of experience to waken them into actual consciousness" (*Principles*, 2:618). Sensations may owe their existence both to the brain and to sensory stimuli, but they owe their character more to the brain than to the things that stimulate it. Nothing in the environment matches the sensations of secondary qualities, a point particularly obvious in the case of subjective occurrences such as the judgments of affirmation, denial, or doubt. "All of these mental affections are ways of knowing objects. . . . Why may they not, in short, be pure *idiosyncrasies*, spontaneous variations, fitted by good luck (those of which have survived) to take cognizance of objects . . . without being in any intelligible sense immediate derivatives from them? I think we shall find this view gain more and more plausibility as we proceed."[22]

James's account of a priori knowledge (and of some empirical cognition) does not logically depend upon this genetic explanation, along Darwinian lines, of how human knowledge develops. Nevertheless he thought that such knowledge would seem less mysterious if its logical independence from space and time could be seen to correspond at least partially to its originating "accidentally" and independently of experience, within the organic structure underlying mental functioning. The idea that much of our knowledge is native to the mental structure itself consorts nicely with James's nativistic views of sensation, space, and time; the real significance of the idea, however, is its fortifying the comparative autonomy of the cognizing organism in its interaction with the environment. For much of its life the human organism actively gives to the environment more than it takes from it. James's argument that some knowledge is innate has a contemporary counterpart in Noam Chomsky's defense of innate mental functioning; James would have agreed with Chomsky that the human organism is not totally malleable by the environment, regardless of B. F. Skinner's philosophies.[23] Although the peculiarities of a priori knowledge do not literally demand its being explained nativistically, for many people such an explanation makes sense. The judgment that if a = b, and b = c, then a = c, appears innate in the internal, higher processes of the brain and not the result of exposure to external things; the occurrence of such judgments seems to confer upon those cerebral processes an autonomy that might otherwise go unsuspected.

The mental operation upon which a priori knowledge is founded, according to James, is the act of comparison, which is concluded to be innate because it cannot possibly be an effect of the order in which external stimuli are experienced. It is not plausible, for instance, that we compare black and white as we do because in our experience black and white have always been contrasted in the familiar way.[24]

> Why should we always have so found them? . . . There must have been either a subjective or an objective reason. The subjective reason can only be that our minds were so constructed that a sense of difference was the only sort of conscious transition possible between black and white; the objective reason can only be that difference was always there, with these colors, outside the mind as an objective fact. The subjective reason explains outer frequency by inward structure, not inward structure by outer frequency; and so surrenders the experience-theory. The objective reason simply says that if an outer difference is there the mind must needs know it—which is no explanation at all, but a mere appeal to the fact that somehow the mind does know what is there. (*Principles*, 2:643)

Here the argument becomes strained. James corrected the excesses of a philosophy, such as Spencer's, which ascribed all knowledge to the work of experience and the environment, but he may have erred in the opposite direction. It would seem that the act of comparison occurs as it does because of both the mind's structure and external stimuli; it is no more an explanation of our knowledge of the difference between black and white to say that we are structured to detect that difference than it is to assert that the contrast is already there to be noticed. In amplifying his own answer, James shows some uncertainty about the nature of the question and how to resolve it. Our knowledge of the contrast is said in one place to be due to the inward natures of the sensations, in another to the nature of the material themselves. The latter seems to veer toward the objective reason; sensations are objective and we might not be structured to notice them accurately, yet they—and not our innate cognitive capacities—are said to establish the a priori knowledge of the difference between black and white. "Difference and resemblance are thus relations between ideal objects, or conceptions as such. To learn whether black and white differ, I need not consult the world of experience at all; the mere ideas suffice. *What I mean* by black differs from *what I mean* by white, whether such colors exist *extra mentem meam* or not. If they ever do exist, they *will* differ" (*Principles*, 2:644). Even if we grant this point and ignore the problems of interpretation it presents, its appeal to objective ideal objects or abstract meanings rather than to the innate mental structure by which the relations between those meanings are recognized contradicts the thesis with which James began. If this thesis, which leans toward a subjectivist explanation, had taken into account the objective factors, the danger of conflict within James's own account could easily have been avoided.

What does the mental operation of comparison accomplish? Whether it be for mathematics, logic, or pure classification, James's answer was the same: it immediately and intuitively detects resemblances and differences between ideal objects (meanings or conceptions). The resultant knowledge is necessary and a priori because "the objects and their differences together form an immutable system. *The same objects, compared in the same way, always give the same results;* if the results be not the same, then the objects are not those originally meant" (*Principles*, 2:644). A judgment such as "7 + 5 = 12" is necessarily true because it is a logical consequence of the meanings we lay down, and eternally true as long as we adhere to our own legislated meanings. James took Mill to task for treating number as a physical property of things and arithmetical judgments as empirical generalizations: "*What we mean* by one plus one *is* two; we make *two* out of it; and it would mean two still even in a world where *physically* (according to a conceit of Mill's) a third thing was engendered every time one thing came together with another. We are masters of our meanings" (*Principles*, 2:655). In James's conception of logic and mathematics, the formulae of systems are guaranteed by prescribed meanings rather than by matters of fact, in contrast to empirical knowledge that is always testable by spatial and temporal occurrences. He thus corrected Mill and anticipated C. I. Lewis's view of the a priori.[25] Nevertheless, the final chapter in *Principles* does not offer much for students of logic and mathematics; James touched on those disciplines lightly without discussing the nature of implication, entailment, deduction, the logic of relations, formalism, intuitionism, sets, or paradoxes; he did not explore the work that led to Russell's and Whitehead's *Principia Mathematica*. Even though he argued against Mill for the logical independence of arithmetic from sense-experience, he may have betrayed his own position in writing, "*Number* seems to signify primarily the stroke of our attention in discriminating things" (*Principles*, 2:653). He always sought the cash value of terms used by psychologists and was never happy until he had discovered referents for them in experience; nor could he restrain himself from invading the domain of pure arithmetic, which is supposedly immune to such experiential analysis. Despite his references to abstract meanings and to the purely formal nature of mathematics, James did not succeed in eliminating "psychologism" entirely.

Instead of defining numbers as "the properties of predicates" such that "in our calculus *every number is represented as a predicate constant of second level,*"[26] he reported what he took to be the primary use of numbers in everyday experience. By making an act of comparison—presumably a form of observation by which resemblances and differences are discerned—the fundamental operation in logic and mathematics, he reduced these disciplines to a size that can be understood psychologically; yet, if they are truly formal and nonexperiential, this reduction ought not to be attempted.

James's concept of meaning is essential to his theory of a priori knowledge, and in this context it raises new questions. Not one but several accounts of meaning occur in *Principles* and elsewhere. Sometimes meaning is a matter of intention: we know our meanings because we know our intentions.[27] At other times, knowledge of what we mean is less direct and less connected with conscious intentions, the fringe of consciousness receiving the credit instead.[28] The notion of meaning as intentionality is reintroduced; also associated with James's pragmatism is the concept of meaning as the consequence, deduced or predicted, of a statement or belief.[29] In chapters 12 and 28 of *Principles*, James asserted that meanings are abstract entities whose likenesses and disparities we can directly inspect; this thesis figures most prominently in his explication of how some knowledge can be a priori. Since our meanings and their relations are fixed or eternal entities that we can immediately examine, our reports of them must be necessarily or eternally true, that is, knowable a priori. The important question is not whether these different concepts of meaning are consistent but rather whether the latter concept is a psychologism that leads to blind alleys.

Consider this thesis: "Difference and resemblance are thus relations between ideal objects, or conceptions as such. To learn whether black and white differ, I need not consult the world of experience at all; the mere ideas suffice. *What I mean* by black differs from *what I mean* by white" (*Principles,* 2:643–44). How do we know that black is necessarily different from white? According to James, we understand intuitively that their meanings differ; whenever the same meanings are involved, black necessarily differs from white. But this alleged comparison is difficult to envisage and seems to be an act invented to explain psychologically how we grasp our own meanings. As long as the examples focus on things like black and white, we may be seduced into assuming that the perceptual contrast between black and white things becomes an abstract and inspectable contrast between the meanings of *black* and *white*. This contrast cannot be one of imagery, because James explicitly rejected the proposal to equate images with meanings as abstract ideas.[30] Given his thesis, one might expect him to supply an idea of what it is like to inspect a single meaning as well as to compare two or more. No such attempt is made, not even for a basic concept like sameness. Essential to thought and knowledge is the ability to entertain the same meanings on different occasions and to know that they are the same; genuine sameness characterizes conceptions even though it may not be found in the perceptual world.[31] How do we ascertain that the constancy of meaning is in fact realized or that the same meaning is again before us? James never suggested an answer, at least not one comparable to his argument that the contrast between the meanings of *black* and *white* is registered psychologically by an explicit act of comparison.[32] If meanings are fixed, abstract entities that can be compared by the mind in the way that perceptions can, why is the confrontation of a single meaning not describable in similar fashion? The observational model, while seductive in some cases, breaks down even for James when meanings are defined as the discrete objects of psychological acts. "Even now, the world may be a place in which the same thing never did and never will come twice. . . . But in our meaning itself we are not deceived; our intention is to think of the same" (*Principles,* 1:460). How do we know that what we mean today is the same as what we meant yesterday? Perhaps we can reply only that it is our intention to know it; we can certainly know our intentions without observing and comparing discrete meanings.

James was uncertain about the formality of logic or mathematics, but he eventually concluded that to know how those disciplines work is to understand the psychological operations upon which they depend. This conclusion is hardly surprising given that the tension in his thinking between respecting the abstractness of logic and seeking the concreteness of psychological explanations was part of an ongoing philosophical struggle to balance the competing claims of rationalism and empiricism. Toward the end of his life, arguing against nominalism taken as the denial that sameness of meaning can occur twice, he wrote:

> What I am affirming here is the platonic doctrine that concepts are singular, that concept-stuff is inalterable, and that physical realities are constituted by the various concept-stuffs of which they "partake." It is known as "logical realism" in the history of philosophy; and has usually been more favored by rationalists than by empiricist minds. For rationalism, concept-stuff is primordial and perceptual things are secondary in nature. The present book, which treats concrete percepts as primordial and concepts as of secondary origin, may be regarded as somewhat eccentric in its attempt to combine logical realism with an otherwise empiricist mode of thought. (*SPP,* 106)

This eccentricity was not easy to make successful, but James consistently maintained that the core of the a priori is meanings (concepts, ideas, abstract or idealized objects, universals, mental entities). He wrote an enormous amount on the topic, and indeed the relation of concepts to percepts seems to have been his favorite interest. Concepts are formed as selections or abstractions from the perceptual world and are accordingly treated as secondary in origin to percepts. By association and other, presently unknown cerebral occurrences, the mind develops new conceptions in addition to those originating perceptually.[33] Once formed, concepts or meanings are described in Platonic terms as eternal and unchangeable abstracts. This formulation introduces a practical order into a constantly changing flux, permitting us to think and behave in a world of objects that are cut out of the flux; on the other hand, this picture tempts us to forget that concepts are only substitutes for the original flux-reality from which they have been abstracted. Because they are not the real thing, too much devotion to them and disregard for the perceptual and emotional worlds can lead to "vicious intellectualism."[34]

While pursuing these themes in James's writings, it is natural to wonder what is the status of meanings, abstract ideas, and idealized objects, and to what extent James was a logical realist or Platonist. In "On Some Omissions of Introspection" (1884), "On the Function of Cognition" (1885), and chapters 12 and 18 of *Principles*, he made copious references to concepts, abstract ideas, and general ideas, rejecting nominalistic efforts to make complex images perform the function of abstract notions. These references do not imply a commitment to Platonism. James declared that we can form abstract ideas only in the sense that we can make a concrete item of consciousness such as an image represent a whole class of things; it takes a special mental function (denied by the nominalists) to accomplish that representation, and James assigned that function to the fringe of consciousness. The function of using an item in consciousness to represent universally, he said, "is the mysterious *plus,* the understood meaning."[35] This functional analysis of meaning and abstract ideas anticipates pragmatism. Yet in the final chapter of *Principles,* on necessary truth, James stressed a nonfunctional account of meaning in which the function of making a single item represent a whole class is replaced by an intuitive inspection of meanings as abstract entities. In fact, this view is not confined to the final chapter but looms throughout *Principles*—even where the functional theory is expressed or implied—whenever abstract ideas are characterized as directly inspectable. The "eccentricity" of trying to accommodate an empiricistic psychology to abstract entities did not facilitate a consistent position.

If we put aside questions of textual interpretation and focus on James's expressed intentions, then logical realism was developed only after *Principles.* In 1909 he noted that whereas "On the Function of Cognition" recognized percepts as the only realm of reality, "I now treat concepts as a co-ordinate realm" (*The Meaning of Truth,* 42). The reference to percepts undoubtedly includes concrete particulars, and although in *Principles* and elsewhere he had sought a functional account of meaning that dispensed with abstract entities, in his later years he underwent a change of heart. Curiously, he never explained why.[36] We can only speculate that the explicit adoption of logical realism in such later works as *A Pluralistic Universe* and *Some Problems of Philosophy* was connected with James's rejection of the mind-body dualism in *Principles;* when he began to think from the perspective of a metaphysician rather than a psychologist, it was easier for him to countenance concepts or meanings as Platonic entities. The challenge of relating them to perceptual reality became more interesting than that in *Principles* of explaining them as functions within a stream of consciousness that confronted a world of physical things. Perhaps logical realism was there all along, and only in the later writings did James finally acknowledge it. As he argued for a "melting" of mind and body into pure experience in his later metaphysics, he approached the dualism of concepts and percepts: "I mean by [combining logical realism with empiricism] that [concepts and percepts] are made of the same kind of stuff, and melt into each other when we handle them together. . . . No one can tell, of the things he now holds in his hand . . . how much, from his . . . intellect, unites with that and makes of it this particular 'book'? The universal and the particular parts of the experience are literally immersed in each other, and both are indispensable."[37]

This reference to the universal parts of experience may surprise those readers who think of James as a nominalist. One source of this impression is the contention, formulated in *Principles* and conspicuous in his pragmatism, that *"the only meaning of essence is teleological; and that classification and conception are purely teleological weapons of the mind.* The essence of a thing is that one of its properties which is so *important for my interests* that in comparison with it I may neglect the rest."[38] This contention goes hand in hand with the claim that the choice of what is real or essential is ultimately founded in subjective reasons. But to say, as Wittgenstein later did, that the distinction between essential and inessential features is not always sharp, or that essentialness is relative to interest, was not in James's eyes tantamount to abandoning universals, which he always included among reality's constituents.[39] James broke with Berkeley on this issue, charging that Berkeley's nominalism precludes analysis or dissection of experience, which can be achieved only through a process of selection and abstraction.[40] In *Principles* James defended a conceptualist position and, in affirming our capacity to form general or abstract ideas and to entertain them thereafter, assigned to the fringe of consciousness the role of modifying sensibility in a way relevant to the apprehension of universals. He differed with traditional conceptualism (and with John Dewey) in denying that an abstract concept must in itself be a universal; it becomes either a particular or a universal only when we intend it to function as one or the other.[41] We may be tempted to suppose that James was a "closet" nominalist because of his tendency to characterize universals as man-made artifacts, not only dependent upon mental processes but also related to particular items in consciousness such as images. James's emphasis is actually the opposite; abstract concepts, whether particular or universal, are formed by the mind and then take on an eternal, unchangeable existence that is also occasionally "independent."[42] I interpret him to mean independent of percepts but not of mental or physical processes altogether; his conceptualism was closer to Aristotelianism than to Platonism: "Meanwhile, it is endlessly serviceable to be able to talk of properties abstractly and apart from their working, to find them the same in innumerable cases, to take them 'out of time,' and to treat of their relations to other similar abstractions. We thus form whole universes of platonic ideas *ante rem*, universes *in posse, tho none of them exists effectively except in rebus"* (*The Meaning of Truth*, 203; italics mine). Abstract ideas or concepts exist and are independent of the percepts from which they are originally formed; they are distinguishable from other aspects of particular, concrete processes, but they are not existentially separable from them. They are eternally the same, static and unchangeable nonhappenings, as long as they endure, but "they can cease to be, altogether" (*Principles*, 1:467).

In his psychology of cognition and in his metaphysics of knowledge, James drew upon the traditional materials of a priori knowledge—essences, general ideas, abstract concepts, and universals; our knowledge of them and their relations is in the form of necessary judgments that are independent of experience or the verifying processes upon which empirical knowledge is typically contingent. The qualification "typically" is required, because James did not acknowledge a clean division between the a priori truths of logic, mathematics, and metaphysics, on the one hand, and those of the empirical sciences on the other. The contrast between a logical truth and an empirical one (knowable only a posteriori) is not abrupt or clear-cut. In the final chapter of *Principles*, after emphasizing that the eternal verities of logic and mathematics do not necessarily correspond to the world of fact, James added: "Nor have [eternal verities], as Kant pretended later, a legislating character even for all possible experience. They are primarily interesting only as subjective facts. They stand waiting in the mind, forming a beautiful ideal network; and the most we can say is that we *hope* to discover realities over which the network may be flung so that ideal and real may coincide" (*Principles*, 2:664–65). Since the ideal and the real may coincide, the a priori may be incorporated into the body of scientific or empirical knowledge, which seems to contradict James's view.[43]

Did James believe that science can discover the objective realities in which the ideal and the real coincide, such that a priori judgments apply to them? He wrote:

> Science *thinks* she has discovered the objective realities in question. Atoms and ether, with no properties but masses and velocities expressible by numbers, and paths expressible by analytic formulas, these at last are things over which the mathematico-logical network may be flung, and by supposing which instead of sensible phenomena science becomes more able to manufacture for herself a world about which rational propositions may be framed. Sensible phenomena are pure delusions for the mechanical philosophy. The 'things' and qualities we believe in do not exist. The only realities are swarming solids in everlasting motion . . . whose expressionless and meaningless changes form the history of the world, and are deducible from initial collocations and habits of movement hypothetically assumed. (*Principles*, 2:665; italics mine)

In James's eyes, scientists talk as if they have discovered things in which the ideal and the real coincide, and they often act as if their laws and hypotheses are rational propositions, knowable a priori, about which only an imbecile could harbor doubts. But their knowledge applies to such a stripped-down world, describable in abstract, quantitative terms but lacking qualitative content—a consideration that seems to have engaged James more than whether the a priori creeps into the empirical knowledge of physics. He respected the role of deductive reasoning in scientific explanation, recognizing for example the increasingly prominent role of mathematics in theoretical physics. He may not have intended to endorse the rationalistic claim that some scientific formulations, such as laws in physics, are both discoveries about phenomena and universally and necessarily true. That he did endorse such a claim is suggested, however, by his comment about the stripped-down world of physics: "Of course it is a world with a very minimum of rational *stuff*" (*Principles*, 2:667). This view coincides with his explicit advocacy after *Principles* of logical realism, according to which concepts as well as percepts are the stuff of reality; it seems logical that some features of the factual world coincide with the ideal conceptions of physics, so that the formulations of their relationships are a priori, like the idealized ones. James's logical realism committed him to this position, and even in his most Bergsonian accusations that science falls short of reality, he called attention to the reality of concepts and the theoretical function of the intellect.[44] The combination of logical realism and the a priori character of some scientific knowledge represents a considerable strain of rationalism in James's otherwise empiricistic epistemology.[45]

The empiricistic bias generally dominated James's conception of science; he treated theories as instruments of prediction that, when well established, make it seem as if there is a constancy or conservation of energy, as if atoms with certain mathematically describable properties exist, and so on. No matter how successful, no knowledge—scientific or any other sort—can legislate for all possible experience. Were it not for his doctrine of logical realism—which, in his pluralistic universe, portrays concepts of reality waiting to coincide with the idealized concepts of physics—we might conclude that James found the scientific a priori only in if-then formulations and never in categorical reports about experience or phenomena of time and space. However, James wrote:

> Thus the world grows more orderly and rational to the mind, which passes from one feature of it to another by deductive necessity, as soon as it conceives it as made up of so few and so simple phenomena as bodies with no properties but number and movement. . . . But alongside of these ideal relations between terms which the world verifies, there are other ideal relations not as yet so verified. I refer to those propositions (no longer expressing mere results of comparison) which are formulated in such metaphysical and aesthetic axioms as "The Principle of things is one," "Nature is simple and invariable," . . . "*Ex nihilo nihil fit*" . . . "The world is throughout rationally intelligible," etc. (*Principles*, 2:669)

But for logical realism, we might suppose that James's meaning would be retained if *verified* were weakened to *confirmed* or *approximated*, thus eliminating the residue of rationalism in order to resemble contemporary, pragmatic concepts of science.

James insisted here that physics is a spectacular illustration that the human mind, by working with data supplied by the senses, can construct concepts and systematic relations between them; these concepts are invented by the mind and not merely impressed upon it through the senses, and in some cases they are applicable to the perceptual world. James stressed the disparity between ordinary perception and what physics postulates or constructs; the scientist must have imagination and creativity to elaborate upon what he perceives through the senses. Like logic and mathematics, physics originates within the mind or brain itself, but unlike them its hypotheses must be checked against experience. "The popular notion that 'Science' is forced on the mind *ab extra*, and that our interests have nothing to do with its constructions, is utterly absurd. The craving to believe that the things of the world belong to kinds which are related by inward rationality together, is the parent of Science as well as of sentimental philosophy."[46] James thus connected his lifelong conviction that even the most theoretical research is motivated by desires and interests, and that science is thus a response to subjective as well as objective pressures, with the notion that theoretical concepts are not passively received effects of external, objective stimuli but rather actively well up within us. What causes this welling up may be a combination of physiology, evolution, and personal experience; it is sufficiently "back-door" and obscure to label it a priori in contrast with the "front-door" a posteriori origins of our ideas of physical sensations.

James amplified his thoughts about science and metaphysics in this passage: "It cannot be too often repeated that the triumphant application of any one of our ideal systems of rational relations to the real world justifies our hope that other systems may be found also applicable. Metaphysics should take heart from the example of physics, simply confessing that hers is the longer task. Nature *may* be remodelled, nay, certainly will be remodelled, far beyond the point at present reached."[47] James recognized that nature and reality are simultaneously susceptible to different systems of thought; further, he believed that the success of physics, which radically reconceptualizes our prescientific ways of picturing the world, allows us to entertain other, more radical metaphysical interpretations, even though they are not scientifically testable. If as James assumed, reality is always changing shape partly because of human impact upon it, then the categories and schemes of explanation must keep pace; new explanations may alter or replace the old, for future experience may always upset the existing scientific a priori conceptions. Metaphysical axioms, such as "nothing can happen without a cause," are not expressions of knowledge, either a priori or a posteriori, but are rather ideals that incite us to strive for more order or understanding. With the possible exceptions of logic and mathematics, any claims to knowledge must work in actual practice, must test out pragmatically.

PRAGMATISM

The bibliography of James's writings and of those about him testifies to his enormous influence; although his thought was impressive for its variety in the field of psychology and he developed original insights in ethics, metaphysics, and religion, his only concept to start a movement was that of pragmatism. What he published about emotion, instinct, mind-body dualism, and pure experience provoked controversies, but nothing except his contentions about religion and freedom of the will created as much prolonged debate as his treatises on pragmatism. Indeed, his pragmatic writings are not entirely distinct from those on religion. The beginnings of pragmatism—which evolved into a school of thought with an exhilarating sense of mission, excited by slogans threatening a takeover, and spurred by its proponents' urgings for better teamwork—were actually quite modest. They consisted of two articles: "On the Function of Cognition," published in 1885, was clearly a philosophical excursion into the topic of knowledge while *Principles* was being written, and "Philosophical Conceptions and Practical Results," published in 1898, continued similar reflections on the nature and purpose of philosophy from twenty years earlier.[48] Jamesian pragmatism grew from two preoccupations, one with the technical concept of cognition that was left as a mystery in *Principles,* the other with the character of philosophy itself.

James believed that cognition is so resistant to psychological analysis—he himself left it in limbo in *Principles*—that only philosophers can approach it. Psychologists can explain the conditions without which knowledge cannot occur and the environmental causes of brain-states underlying a cognitive state of consciousness, but not *how* that consciousness knows something. James and others specified the problem in terms of spatial analogies; the knowing state of consciousness is here, the known fact is somewhere else, and there is an invisible cognitive connection between them, without which there would be only the consciousness and the fact, but no knowledge of the latter by the former. How knowledge spans the epistemological gulf between consciousness and fact is outside the domain of psychology; psychologists must assume the cognitive relation without explanation, treating it as ultimate, unmediated, mysterious; the puzzle of self-transcendency arises again, as it did with the concept of intentionality, because a state of mind, to be cognitive, must transcend itself in spanning the distance between it and what it knows. The problem was aggravated in *Principles* by the stress upon metaphysical dualism between mind and body, but the epistemological problem of how the knower and the known relate remained even after the dualism was replaced by a different metaphysics; as a result, James said that his pragmatic solution to the epistemological problem was independent of his metaphysics of pure experience.[49] "On the Function of Cognition" eliminated the epistemological gulf by recognizing that there is no connection between knower and known to be discovered by the mind; instead, the only relevant relation between the two is the process by which the knower verifies what he knows. When we know that the dog is on the log (we continue to speak of a cognitive relation between us and the dog), the actions that "lead" us to the dog and verify its presence on the log are the sole candidates for the cognitive relation between us. The mystery of cognition in *Principles* is not dispelled by factual discoveries of psychology or any other science; rather, it is dissolved by analyzing the concept of cognitive relation in practical terms. To ask how in practice a knower relates himself to what he knows will provide both a definition of knowledge and an illustration of pragmatic philosophizing. It is a pragmatic analysis of a concept central to pragmatism itself.

The seriousness with which James and his contemporaries regarded the mystery of the self-transcendent character of cognition is hard to appreciate without a sense of the philosophical atmosphere at the time. Neo-Hegelianism, idealism, and rationalism were powerful forces, reinforced by complicated abstract arguments that made Thought, Reality, and the Absolute seem accessible exclusively to pure intellect; what the intellect declared about such matters was much more crucial than what science and observation might appear to show. Such arguments often commanded respect, not only for the traditional philosophies they represented, but also for the societal and university values and beliefs, especially moral and religious, that they supported. For many, including James, the writings of such philosophers as T. H. Green, F. H. Bradley, and Josiah Royce afforded comfortable perspectives from which to assess a changing of the guard in philosophy at the end of the nineteenth century. Because idealism had run its course and the relevance of the developing sciences for philosophy was attracting younger thinkers' attention, the suspicion of abstract, a priori arguments created an allegiance to empiricism and common sense. G. E. Moore and Bertrand Russell took the lead in England, the positivists organized in Vienna, and James, Peirce, and Dewey launched pragmatism in America. But though James said "Damn the Absolute!" to Royce, he was close in spirit to Royce and Bradley, closer to their metaphysical reconceptualization of the world than to the laissez-faire conclusions of some positivistic or scientific thinking. Like Russell, James never carried his bent toward science and empiricism far enough to repudiate speculative philosophy; the more one studies his thought, the more one understands that he was at heart more a metaphysician than anything else. In "On the Function of Cognition," which takes a giant step toward pragmatism, James nevertheless noted that Royce's "powerful book," *The Religious Aspect of Philosophy*, contains an argument, a possible alternative to James's, that an absolute or all-inclusive mind can supply the connection that spans the epistemological gulf and thereby eliminate the mystery of cognition.[50] James rejected the argument but, as was his habit when responding to Bradley and Royce, only after careful consideration.

A link between "On the Function of Cognition" and "Philosophical Conceptions and Practical Results" is the emphasis on *function*. The rationalistic idea that there is a cognitive relation between knower and known that must be either postulated or believed to be "intellectually contemplatable" may result from filling one's head with abstractions and dialectical arguments and neglecting to ask what is the function of cognition. We may discover what knowledge is, and how the knower and the known are related, if we ask what knowledge does for us.[51] The answer, which he considered to be more effectively formulated after the 1885 essay, was this: the function of knowledge is to facilitate a satisfactory adaptation to the environment; in recognizing this function, we realize that to know something is to be able to go from here to there, in a context supplied by the natural environment and not by the idealist's absolute. Getting from the knowing-here to the known-there is generally beneficial, useful, or otherwise "satisfactory" from the knower's point of view.[52] This integral connection between cognitive consciousness and adaptation or action, which includes mental or theoretical adjustments, shows that solipsism is unfounded, that we know more than just the contents of our own consciousness. To say that we know an external object is to assert that we can move from here to there by way of an environment in which others also move. Clarifying the concept of knowledge pragmatically does not prove that other minds exist. According to James, an argument by analogy is needed: I reason that you are in pain when you scream because I know that I am in pain when I scream. Such an argument is not absolutely conclusive, so skepticism about other minds can be confronted only practically.[53] A pragmatic grasp of knowledge exhibits the pointlessness of supposing that we can know only what is in our own head, since what is in practice meant by knowledge presupposes an external environment in which other people's actions and cognitions intersect with our own. Solipsism, James believed, is one of many philosophical issues that can be appropriately treated when a pragmatic analysis of cognition has been made.

"Philosophical Conceptions and Practical Results," which is more commonly associated with the beginnings of pragmatism, makes no reference to "On the Function of Cognition" in tackling the concept of truth. (James only later acknowledged that the earlier essay was an earlier formulation of pragmatism.) "I will seek to define . . . what seems to be the most likely direction in which to start upon the trail of truth. Years ago this direction was given to me by an American philosopher. . . . I refer to Mr. Charles S. Peirce. . . . He is one of the most original of contemporary thinkers; and the principle of practicalism—or pragmatism, as he called it, when I first heard him enunciate it at Cambridge in the early '70's—is the clue or compass by following which I find myself more and more confirmed in believing we may keep our feet upon the proper trail."[54] Peirce was helpful, James said, in approaching the question, What is truth? and in asserting that the purpose of thought itself is to produce belief (an idea which harmonized neatly, for example, with "The Perception of Reality" in *Principles*); belief in turn exists for the sake of action (a point that supports an argument in "On the Function of Cognition"). To assert that we believe it will rain, for instance, is to imply that we are prepared to act appropriately if it rains and that our habits when rain is imminent (fetching coat and umbrella) are aroused and ready to discharge. This natural procession from thought to belief to action proves the inherently practical nature of thinking.

> If there were any part of a thought that made no difference in the thought's practical consequences, then that part would be no proper part of the thought's significance. Thus the same thought may be clad in different words; but if the different words suggest no different conduct, they are mere outer accretions, and have no part in the thought's meaning. If, however, they determine conduct differently, they are essential elements of the significance. . . . To attain perfect clearness in our thoughts of an object, then, we need only consider what effects of a conceivably practical kind the object may involve—what sensations we are to expect from it, and what reactions we must prepare. Our conception of these effects, then, is for us the whole of our conception of the object, so far as that conception has positive significance at all. This is the principle of Peirce, the principle of pragmatism. (*CER,* 411–12)

James supposed that this principle applies to truth and, without troubling to introduce it, directly asserted: "The ultimate test for us of what a *truth means* is indeed the conduct it dictates or inspires" (CER, 412; italics mine). Thus was born the celebrated theory of truth, commonly taken to be the core of pragmatism. The same pragmatic account seems to apply equally to meaning, intentionality, cognition, and truth; nevertheless, these concepts were not indistinguishable for James. Sometimes he ran intentionality and meaning together, but he also distinguished them, particularly when speaking of abstract meanings that are directly inspected. He indicated here, as elsewhere, that intentionality is distinguishable from cognition and truth. "But [truth] inspires that conduct because it first foretells some particular turn to our experience which shall call for just that conduct from us."[55] When we claim to know something or when what we believe is true, our state of consciousness points or refers to what is known or believed; this mysterious self-transcendency can be explained behavioristically as a tendency to undertake a sequence of actions leading to what is known or believed. There must be something in our state of consciousness (called either *idea* or *belief*) which blueprints the behavioral or verifying route followed; psychologists can identify to an extent what constitutes that tendency or intentionality, including various "motor and ideational" occurrences.[56] A belief is true if its verificatory route exists and we make good our claim to know it by running through its route. Cognition depends upon both intentionality and truth, while intentionality requires only that a belief be held, and truth is independent of both intentionality and cognition. In those places where James appeared to apply his pragmatic analysis to all three concepts in one flourish, he really meant, I think, to have such distinctions borne in mind.

James immediately moved from the remark about truth to the claim that "the effective meaning of any philosophic proposition can always be brought down to some particular consequence, in our future practical experience, whether active or passive" (CER, 412). From his earliest statements of pragmatism, he did not equate relevant consequences with conduct or overt behavior. Experiences (passive in contrast with overt actions) of perceiving, believing, or imagining are included, along with action and tendencies to act, among the consequences implied by a state of consciousness that is intentional and cognitive. James never settled for an extreme behaviorism in any of his analyses, although in places he temporarily appears to have done so (as in "The Tigers in India"). The single most important point in his version of pragmatism is that the meaning of a philosophical proposition resides in what it implies or predicts as a practical consequence.

> Suppose there are two different philosophical definitions, or propositions, or maxims, or what not, which seem to contradict each other, and about which men dispute. If, by supposing the truth of the one, you can foresee no conceivable practical consequence to anybody at any time or place, which is different from what you would foresee if you supposed the truth of the other, when then the difference between the two propositions is no difference,—it is only a specious and verbal difference, unworthy of further contention. . . . There can be no difference which doesn't make a difference. . . . The whole function of philosophy ought to be to find out what definite difference it will make to you

and me, at definite instants of our life, if this world-formula or that world-formula be the one which is true. (*CER*, 413–14)

Here, as in many of his pragmatic writings, James chose the controversy between materialism and religion to illustrate his point. In stressing the dependence of meaning upon the future, he concluded that if in the world's last moment the question of whether God or Matter initiated the universe were being considered as a retrospective issue, then the controversy would be an idle one. Brushing aside the purely intellectual problem that some might point to, and revealing his own preoccupation with the emotive meanings of the conflicting hypotheses, James clearly connected the meaning of a philosophical or religious proposition with what one might anticipate if it were true. He retained this connection in "Some Metaphysical Problems Pragmatically Considered," the third lecture of *Pragmatism*, which was published in 1907. Two years later in *The Meaning of Truth*, which was mainly a reply to critics, he observed that a flaw in the argument exaggerated the importance of the future.

> The flaw was evident when, as a case analogous to that of a godless universe, I thought of what I called an "automatic sweetheart," meaning a soulless body which should be absolutely indistinguishable from a spiritually animated maiden, laughing, talking, blushing, nursing us, and performing all feminine offices as tactfully and sweetly as if a soul were in her. Would any one regard her as a full equivalent? Certainly not, and why? Because, framed as we are, our egoism craves above all things inward sympathy and recognition, love and admiration. The outward treatment is valued mainly as an expression . . . of the accompanying consciousness believed in. Pragmatically, then, belief in the automatic sweetheart would not *work*. . . . The godless universe would be exactly similar. Even if matter could do every outward thing that God does, the idea of it would not work as satisfactorily, because the chief call for a God on modern man's part is for a being who will inwardly recognize them and judge them sympathetically. Matter disappoints this craving of our ego, so God remains for most men the truer hypothesis, and indeed remains so for definite pragmatic reasons. (*MT*, 189–90)

A curious twist occurred here in James's thinking, one of which he may never have been fully aware. He came to recognize, he said, that even if this were the final moment of the universe and there were nothing ahead for us to anticipate, the controversy between theism and materialism would still be meaningful because the hypothesis of a godless universe would not work pragmatically any more than that of an automatic sweetheart does; that is, it would not include the conceptual content needed to satisfy our subjective wants and desires. The assertion that meaning lies in the consequences had to be withdrawn or largely qualified, and as Perry observed, James decided that origins can make an emotional difference no matter what the consequences are.[57] The subsequent claim admits that an assertion is cognitively and emotionally meaningful, despite its lacking distinctive consequences, as long as its believed or known truth is subjectively satisfying. Unlike the thrust of the earlier essay to brush aside purely intellectual meaning and to focus instead on emotive significance, this claim implies that emotive significance may depend heavily upon the intellectual. As the fantasy of the automatic sweetheart illustrates, the truth of a hypothesis in which one wants to believe, upon which its emotional significance depends, may well be impractical or unusable insofar as it affords nothing to anticipate. Any satisfaction obtained from believing an impractical hypothesis cannot be attributed to its future derivative but must rather result simply from holding the belief itself. As James urged, there may always be a psychological craving or other motivation that inclines us toward one hypothesis rather than another, but the impractical truth of either hypothesis can be all-important in itself, even if it has no consequences. In his essay of 1898 and in *Pragmatism*, James always assumed some psychological motivation to believe theism rather than materialism; he argued that there must be some consequential difference between the two hypotheses, for if there were not, we would have no antecedent desire or will to believe one rather than the other. His emphasis on the consequences of competing hypotheses resulted from the assumption that consequences provide objective reasons for supporting an inclination to believe; the differences in the anticipated consequences will both justify and sustain a desire to believe one proposition instead of its rival. This theory was the crux of Jamesian pragmatism; it originated as a method for providing a basis for believing one philosophical proposition rather than another, in a field where it is easy to get lost in abstraction and end up either not knowing what to believe or not knowing how to supply objective reasons for an antecedent inclination to believe one thing rather than another. Pragmatism was originally a theory of meaning, cognition, intentionality, and truth, with the practical mission—always the most crucial one for James—of producing or sustaining belief.[58]

But if we are confronted by cases such as the "automatic sweetheart," where consequences are irrelevant and thus cannot affect the direction of our belief, then what will substitute for them in producing or sustaining belief? James answered that even if matter can do every outward thing that God does, nevertheless the "craving of our ego" is not satisfied by materialism, "so God remains for most men the truer hypothesis, and indeed remains so for *definite pragmatic reasons*" (MT, 190; italics mine). Here, I think, he misstated his case and confused his readers about what pragmatism meant. Belief that flows from the ego's craving and nothing more is subjectivism pure and simple, with nothing pragmatic about it. Why do I believe in God? According to James's pragmatism, a theory about the meaning of philosophical propositions as suggested originally by Peirce, it is no answer to declare: Because it makes me feel good. The correct pragmatic answer would be: Because I have traced the consequences of theism and of materialism, and after comparing them I have opted for theism because its consequences strike me as preferable to those of materialism. Whereas the first, purely subjective reply offers no reason beyond the mere gratification from a certain belief, the second, pragmatic response registers practical differences in the content of the rival hypotheses and offers those differences as reasons for moving toward one theory rather than another. They are objective differences or reasons even though the choice of one set over the other is admittedly subjective, leading us to label James's view *subjective pragmatism*. Reasons are first located in consequences, and for subjective reasons a choice is made between rival hypotheses because of a preference for one set of consequences. But to believe in God without even a comparison of the consequences of theism and those of materialism is to be merely subjective, exercising a so-called right to believe what we will but certainly not employing what James called the pragmatic method. He confused matters considerably when he wrote that, despite the absence of consequences to consult, the belief in God was based on definite pragmatic reasons; it is no wonder that many of his critics have judged his pragmatism to be nothing but subjectivism.[59]

My commentary here is not a reiteration of the criticism that Jamesian pragmatism outrageously identifies truth with utility or workability. Although he brought this objection upon himself by numerous statements in *Pragmatism* that imply that identification, he made it clear in *The Meaning of Truth* and elsewhere that he had not intended to do so.[60] By today's standards, pragmatism is not a genuinely technical theory of meaning or truth; it is rather a method of choosing what to believe from among philosophical and religious propositions, and in some cases of finding the motivation to believe anything at all. In the 1898 essay James approached the concept of truth by asking, as he did of cognition, what its meaning is in practical terms. He wanted not to define truth but to ascertain its role in producing and sustaining belief; most of his controversial statements about truth, which were commonly construed as his definitions or criteria of it, were intended instead to describe and dramatize its motivational role in making us believe. The curious twist in his thinking at times is that he allowed his pragmatic method to degenerate into pure subjectivism, as if he had temporarily forgotten that subjective pragmatism, as a way of making up our mind on philosophical issues, is an alternative not only to paralysis or bewilderment, but to extreme subjectivism as well. In this spirit, James asked: "Grant an idea or belief to be true, . . . what concrete difference will its being true make in any one's actual life? . . . What, in short, is the truth's cash-value in experiential terms?" (*Pragmatism*, 133). This question arose when James tried to make up his mind about philosophical hypotheses that could not be decided by observation and experimentation or when he wanted to resolve the impasse in contemporary philosophy between "tender-minded," traditional religious thinkers and "tough-minded," empiricistic and materialistic ones. His pragmatic answer: "True ideas are those that we can *assimilate, validate, corroborate and verify. False ideas are those that we can not.*"[61] This answer keeps pragmatism in line with science and does not permit extreme subjectivism, although his focus shifts to the unverifiable propositions of philosophy and to the motivational relevance of truth as something that we can assimilate to our lives, such that we optimistically believe any hypothesis that is harmonious and satisfactory to us. This type of pragmatism is subjective but not mere subjectivism; when James was faithful to his own method of making up his mind on philosophical issues, he had definite, pragmatic reasons for believing in addition to the fact that believing made him feel merry.

When James delivered "Philosophical Conceptions and Practical Results" at the University of California on 26 August 1898, officially announcing pragmatism, no one guessed that a movement or a whole controversial literature about cognition and truth was being launched; nor did James betray any awareness that he was moving toward something momentous. He told his audience that, employing an informal notion of meaning he credited to Peirce, they might discover pragmatic reasons for choosing a tender-minded religious hypothesis even in a tough-minded era. *The Will to Believe* had been published only a year before, and James's connection between pragmatism and religion was obvious enough. There was not much reaction to his paper until an altered version was published in 1904; but by 1906–07, his lectures in Boston and New York (which he published as *Pragmatism* in 1907) often attracted audiences of a thousand or more.[62] Added to the fact that James was America's foremost psychologist and the spokesman from Harvard of a new philosophy called pragmatism, he was an intriguing apologist for religion; the combination had an immediate attraction. Unquestionably, a movement was underway and was arousing popular curiosity. At the Universities of Michigan, Chicago, and Columbia, John Dewey gathered about him a group of students and colleagues known for their instrumentalism, an analysis of the cognitive process in teleological and pragmatic terms; James called this group the Chicago School.[63] F. S. C. Schiller, with whom James had established a philosophical relationship some years earlier, began a humanistic branch of pragmatism at Oxford, and many converts to pragmatism appeared later in Italy and Germany. Pragmatism was to its time what logical positivism and existentialism have been to the twentieth century, and James could take credit for having been a major force in making this philosophy effective by capturing the attention of professionals and amateurs alike.

James had always soft-pedaled the newness of the theory, subtitling *Pragmatism* "A New Name for Some Old Ways of Thinking" and citing Locke, Berkeley, Hume, and Kant as predecessors. By 1904 he had broadened the concept, introduced in his earlier essays, into something grander and more visionary, a novel way, he said, of conceiving the mind's relation to reality. Among the recent or contemporary influences he cited were Mill, Lotze, and Christoph Sigwart, whom he credited with having noticed the incongruence of our forms of thought with the order of experience. This issue was a major point in James's lifelong quarrel with Spencer; James believed that the mind, from its own interests and needs, uses its cognitions to transform the environment to its own ends. "Not only has the doctrine of Evolution weaned us from fixities and inflexibilities in general, and given us a world all plastic, but it has made us ready to imagine almost all our functions, even the intellectual ones, as 'adaptations,' and possibly transient adaptations, to practical human needs."[64] Finally, James wrote, the development of the sciences conclusively taught that in scientifically reading nature the mind does not have impressed upon it a series of eternal truths. There are no such truths, and science is satisfied to arrive at probabilities and approximations; the history of science strongly supports the pragmatist's view of the mind as an active, constructive agent in its intellectual and practical interactions with nature.

Given these influences, pragmatism was in the wind, James thought, and had been expressed independently by Karl Pearson in England, Ernst Mach in Austria, and "the somewhat more reluctant [Henri] Poincaré in France, all of whom say that our sciences are but *Denkemittel*—'true' in no other sense than that of yielding a conceptual shorthand, economical for our descriptions. Thus does [Georg] Simmel in Berlin suggest that no human conception whatever is more than an instrument of biological utility. . . . Bergson . . . and others in France have defended a very similar doctrine."[65] Conceived as an active, creative, striving, and purposeful relation with nature, and bolstered by illustrations and similar sentiments in many places, Jamesian pragmatism mushroomed from an analysis of cognition and a method for making up one's mind on philosophical questions into a visionary scheme that collected all the important themes of his psychology and philosophy. In his final years, James used pragmatism as a handy label for his collective philosophical convictions, most of which he smuggled in while reflecting on the concept of truth.

A traditional way of introducing James's theory of truth is to contrast it with the correspondence and coherence theories. He did not dwell on the hypothesis that truth is a coherence of beliefs or propositions, rejecting it for two main reasons: first, coherence and consistency can be achieved without having any application to the actual world, as in logic or mathematics, so empirical truth requires more than mere coherence between ideas; second, James repudiated the metaphysical picture of a universe whose parts are logically connected in a block, the picture which historically has belonged to the coherence theory of truth. James was always careful, however, to mention the importance of coherence as a practical test for truth; all seekers of empirical knowledge must be conservative and must not abandon theories and convictions formerly established as true if those theories can cohere with new and disruptive discoveries.[66] The more usual theory is that truth is an agreement or correspondence with reality; an idea or belief is true if it corresponds to fact, false if it does not. As early as 1878, James had criticized Spencer for the vagueness of his notion of correspondence (Spencer contended that the mind evolves through an inner correspondence with outward reality) and for having made the mind a passive respondent to the environment. James was thus ready to challenge the correspondence theory of truth.

Correspondence is not merely resemblance, for an idea can resemble or copy something without being true of it, just as a photograph is a likeness of but not a truth about its subject. Much of James's criticism of the correspondence theory was an argument against the "copy-theory" of knowledge or truth. He did not reject resemblance between an idea and its counterpart in reality as a pertinent psychological feature in the cognitive process, but he denied that resemblance alone can constitute either cognition or truth; without intentional reference, resemblance is cognitively irrelevant.[67] James was not the only thinker to question the idea of correspondence or to wonder what general or negative true propositions correspond to. What is the correspondent of "All men are mortal" or "Plato is not here"? In a preanalytic sense, we may consent to the statement that truth, as a property of an idea, belief, or state of consciousness, agrees with or corresponds to fact; when we proceed beyond this commonsense level to the meaning of truth, however, James thought the best explanation we can find is this:

> To "agree" in the widest sense with a reality *can only mean to be guided either straight up to it or into its surroundings, or to be put into such working touch with it as to handle either it or something connected with it better than if we disagreed.* . . . The essential thing is the process of being guided. Any idea that helps us to *deal*, whether practically or intellectually, with either the reality or its belongings, that doesn't entangle our progress in frustrations, that *fits*, in fact, and adapts our life to the reality's whole setting, will agree sufficiently to meet the requirement. It will hold true of that reality."[68]

James expressed a similar view in his discussion of intentionality and cognition; cognition and truth occur when a state of consciousness leads us through a verifying process to something that has been claimed as known. "Agreement [correspondence] thus turns out to be essentially an affair of leading—leading that is useful because it is into quarters that contain objects that are important. True ideas lead us into useful verbal and conceptual quarters as well as directly up to useful sensible termini. . . . All true processes must lead to the face of directly verifying sensible experiences *somewhere*" (*Pragmatism*, 141).

Pragmatism substitutes the verifying process for the "inert, static relation" between idea and reality in which some believe. According to his opponents, James said, truth is not something that changes but is rather a static, objective relation between beliefs and facts; when we know something it is because we somehow possess or realize it. James's characterization of his opponents' view is unclear, perhaps because he was himself unsure about how to understand his opposition. There is throughout *Pragmatism* and *The Meaning of Truth* a recurrent frustration in James's attempt to define the opposed theory of truth, as if he realized that his own formulations of it only confused matters further. His polemical and occasionally irritated tone in these books resulted from the exasperation he experienced in trying to define a clear issue; he realized that he might be only inventing what he called the opposition's position. He was not sure, in his talk about truth as a static, inert relation, whether he had identified the position implied by the idealistic, monistic metaphysics of such thinkers as Bradley and Royce. "What is it indeed? [Pragmatism's] critics make no explicit statements, Professor Royce being the only one so far who has formulated anything definite. . . . At present the lazy tradition that truth is *adaequatio intellectus et rei* seems all there is to contradict it with. Mr. Bradley's only suggestion is that true thought 'must correspond to a determinate being which it cannot be said to make,' and obviously that sheds no new light. What is the meaning of the word to 'correspond'? Where is the 'being'?" (*MT*, 66–67). In fact, there was no well-defined opposition; no one declared that truth is a static, inert relation, and James was often left fencing with his own image of the enemy. In a letter to James, Bradley protested that he had been misunderstood: "With regard to pragmatism, I do not seem to know exactly where we now are. I am beginning to wonder whether I have not always myself been a pragmatist."[69] When a leader of the opposition wanted to enlist as a pragmatist, and team members like Peirce and D. S. Miller offered their resignations, James was understandably frustrated. In no philosophical movement have the defenders and critics been more confused about each other's meaning than in American pragmatism in the first decade of the twentieth century.

Pragmatism was presented as an alternative to intellectualism, which James defined as "the belief that our mind comes upon a world complete in itself, and has the duty of ascertaining its contents; but it has no power for re-determining its character, for that is already given."[70] This belief was associated with traditional rationalism and idealism, which according to James was committed to the notion of a completed universe; if everything is part of an absolute already in place, then we are only catching up with truths already established. But pragmatism is a humanism, he declared, in maintaining that most truth is in the making. Reality that is wholly independent of human interpretation is rare, more often an ideal limit than an actual occurrence; Jamesian pragmatism claimed that the particular process by which knowledge is acquired contributes to our conception of reality. In explaining the notions of reality, truth, and knowledge, James stressed that "the trail of the human serpent is thus over everything"; the mind rarely if ever knows something totally untouched by its own influence.[71] In this respect James was closer to Kant than to Locke. If reality and truth are inevitably tainted by the mind's concepts and categories in the case of empirical science, it is even more likely to be so in everyday life. This argument reflects an increasing recognition that science is a construction placed upon reality rather than a transcript of it; by asserting that truth is unfinished, constantly being added to, and a human product, James made pragmatism coincide with and support his metaphysical vision of the universe as loosely knit, open to chance and novelty, a cosmos ever in the making. Whatever flaws his critics found, a large part of his readership plainly thought he was correct.

James invited most of the criticisms of his pragmatism by writing as if he were attempting what in fact he was not. In saying "*The true*, to put it very briefly, *is only the expedient in the way of our thinking, just as the right is only the expedient in the way of our behaving*," he seemed to be either defining truth or formulating its criteria.[72] Comparing what he wrote with what his critics rebutted, James's complaints about being badly misinterpreted hardly seem justified. His pragmatism asserted that the meaning of an idea or belief is its cash value, and its truth is its workability or utility; in light of what he said about utility, his critics naturally concluded that he actually meant to deny what they felt compelled to defend, that "the dog is on the log" is true if and only if the dog is actually on the log. Because James often equated utility with subjective satisfaction, his critics supposed that he had removed all external constraints on truth; because he connected this account of truth with the pure experience of radical empiricism, he had to reassert that he was a realist and that he believed that some truths exist before we uncover them. As he tried to make clear in *The Meaning of Truth* (especially in the preface and "Two English Critics"), he never intended to hold that utility, satisfaction, or anything but the dog's being on the log insures the truth of "the dog is on the log." As he wrote in a letter to C. A. Strong, the idea that truth conforms to an antecedent reality of some sort was a presupposition of the pragmatic debate about truth, not an assumption called into doubt during that debate.[73] Since he, like his critics, had always wanted the usual, commonsense constraints on truth, there is little doubt that the debate was largely over terminology.

Even if truth as conformity to fact is preserved, James felt to the end that his assertions *about* truth were genuinely interesting. As a psychologist, he wanted to understand why in everyday life people care at all about truth; among the reasons he offered were that truth makes us free, makes life easier, permits prediction and planning, satisfies curiosity, and makes for a saner, healthier mind. An ulterior motive underlies our concern for truth; we are moved to discover what is true because of some anticipated reward, and even when nothing more than curiosity is involved, locating the truth is satisfying and gives a sense of relief and achievement. James believed that there may be philosophical theories, possibly associated with traditional rationalism and monistic idealism, that contradict this psychological view, perhaps by arguing that truth exists for its own sake. James often wondered whether philosophers understand their own motives in caring about truth; he had always been intrigued by the fact that philosophy existed, asking what motivates us to philosophize. The standard answer, to attain a rational concept of things, does not explain how a philosopher concludes that he has found a rational conception. In "The Sentiment of Rationality" he wrote: "The only answer can be that he will recognize its rationality as he recognizes everything else, by certain subjective personal marks with which it affects him. . . . What then are the marks? A strong feeling of ease, peace, rest, is one of them. The transition from a state of puzzle and perplexity to rational comprehension is full of lively relief and pleasure" (*CER*, 83). The sentiment of rationality can be described further as active and dynamic. One philosophizes for the subjective reward, a satisfaction pursued either consciously or unconsciously.

James sympathized with the layman who cannot understand why some people actually devote their lives to philosophizing, which seems dull and abstract compared to such activities as sailing, hiking, making money, or pushing ahead in daily affairs. "This is why so few human beings truly care for Philosophy. The particular determinations which she ignores are the real matter exciting other aesthetic and practical needs, quite as potent and authoritative as hers." (*CER*, 122). James's motive in philosophizing was to create an inner sense of vitality and buoyancy by constructing a philosophical picture of the universe that is itself vivid, vital, and buoyant. He recognized the disapproval of his colleagues and was fully aware of their

charges that his manner of arguing had a pep-talk flavor, that too much temperament invaded the cool of his thought, and that excessive individuality complicated
any discussion of traditional problems. His response, wholly in character, was to
make temperament the springboard of all philosophizing. He thought and wrote
about truth in ways that dramatized its role in human existence. He sought reflections about truth that by their very nature added to the excitement of living and made
philosophy as innervating as sex, drink, music, or prayer, part of the texture of living.
His colleagues preferred to work more quietly, subordinating psychological to logical
concerns and enjoying the process of thinking abstractly without fear of tedium.
They occasionally pointed out what seemed to be flaws in James's reasoning, but he
replied that they were merely betraying their own temperaments. Technical details
and niceties tried James's patience. He disagreed with those who contended that his
pragmatic account of truth could not accommodate statements that refer to the
past—an apparent problem for pragmatists because of their emphasis upon future
consequences. Other critics were puzzled by his Protagorean relativism in seeming to
make the individual the measure of truth, complained that he never defined the
satisfaction in which he said truth resides, or argued that he could not know his own
theory of truth to be true. His responses to these criticisms, while certainly pertinent
and sometimes telling, tended to be perfunctory, ritualistic performances with little
enthusiasm. Often, he took a shortcut by playing the genial reconciler, proferring
pragmatism as the middle ground between absolutism and relativism, rationalism
and empiricism, or monism and pluralism. "With [pragmatism's] criterion of the
practical differences that theories make, we see that she must equally abjure absolute
monism and absolute pluralism. The world is One just so far as its parts hang together
by any definite connexion. It is many, just so far as any definite connexion fails to
obtain."[74] When he sought to connect the pragmatic notion of truth with a world
outlook, however, his enthusiasm was abundant.

James wrote in *Pragmatism*:

> Let me now say only this, that truth is *one species of good,* and not, as is usually
> supposed, a category distinct from good, and co-ordinate with it. *The true is the
> name of whatever proves itself to be good in the way of belief, and good, too, for definite,
> assignable reasons.* Surely you must admit this, that if there were no good for life
> in true ideas . . . then the current notion that truth is divine and precious, and
> its pursuit a duty, could never have grown up or become a dogma. . . . "What
> would be better for us to believe"! This sounds very like a definition of truth. It
> comes very near to saying "what we *ought* to believe"; and in *that* definition
> none of you would find any oddity. Ought we ever not to believe what it is *better
> for us* to believe? And can we then keep the notion of what is better for us, and
> what is true for us, permanently apart? Pragmatism says no, and I fully agree
> with her. (59–60)

There are intimate connections between the concepts of truth and goodness, reflecting both the practical and the moral utility that we associate with the pursuit of truth.

Pragmatism, more than nineteenth-century absolutism, gives a theoretical sense to the fact that in ordinary thinking we move naturally between truth and goodness. James perorated on this dimension of the pragmatic notion of truth, frequently advocating meliorism, the view that gradual improvement and progress throughout the cosmos is possible. Pragmatism, by conceiving that we ought to seek the benefits of truth in the making, "may naturally welcome free-will as a melioristic doctrine. It holds up improvement as at least possible, whereas determinism assures us that our whole notion of possibility is born of human ignorance, and that the necessity and impossibility between them rule the destinies of the world" (*Pragmatism*, 84). Pragmatism had motivated not only "The Dilemma of Determinism" in 1884 but also a review in 1875 entitled "German Pessimism," in which he wrote: "The world is thus absolutely good only in a potential or hypothetic sense, and the hypothetic form of the optimistic belief is the very signature of its consistency, and first condition of its probability. At the final integration of things, the world's goodness will be an accomplished fact and self-evident, but, till then, faith is the only legitimate attitude of mind it can claim from us" (*CER*, 19). In his own life James fought despair and pessimism, and philosophizing in the spirit of pragmatism lifted his morale almost to the heights of optimism. But meliorism is between the extremes of pessimism and optimism; anyone's notion of salvation is only a possibility which, to be attained, requires constant and strenuous striving. Pragmatism, because it shuns a fixed and certain universe, makes few promises; we must constantly exert our moral energies to make the universe a better place. Compared to absolute theologies and philosophies, pragmatism has one inferiority: "It has no saving message for incurably sick souls."[75] It is a moral struggle against sickness at heart, not allowing us to fall back upon the promises of a philosophy that claims to be certain and absolute. "Pragmatism can be called religious if you allow that religion can be pluralistic or merely melioristic in type" (*Pragmatism*, 193). Jamesian pragmatism was developed to make room for faith.

As a theory of knowledge, pragmatism dovetailed with the other parts of the Jamesian worldview. It resolved the mystery of cognition and its elusive self-transcendency described in *Principles* and gave further insight into the nature of knowledge-by-description or knowledge-about. This kind of knowledge, having as its object something either temporarily and perceptually absent or permanently so, was based on the empirical and scientific model of a claim or hypothesis followed by a verifying process that terminated in a perceptual observation. This analysis coincided with the idea of truth in the making, of a universe in process rather than the static universe to which James thought nineteenth-century absolute idealism was committed; he argued for the active participation of human consciousness, which uses concepts and true ideas as teleological weapons in the pursuit of further truth and goodness. A priori, nonempirical knowledge is not subject to pragmatic analysis; our knowledge that "$a = b$, and $b = c$, so $a = c$" is immediate and complete, the direct intuition of abstract concepts. But even in logical knowledge there is room for error, for we may misidentify or misname the concepts in question. Further, "In this realm of mental relations, truth again is an affair of leading. We relate one abstract idea with another, framing in the end great systems of logical and mathematical truth" (*Pragmatism*, 138). Since knowledge-about and its verifying process require a termination in perception at some point—so that "I claim to know" is often replaced by "Now I know"—it would appear that at that point we have knowledge-by-acquaintance. At the commonsense level, James had no doubts about this.

But he concluded one of his lectures in *Pragmatism* thus: "Retain, I pray you, this suspicion about common sense" (*Pragmatism*, 127). When we move beyond common sense into a metaphysics of perceptual experience, it becomes questionable whether seeing something is a simple case of knowledge, after all; we cannot be sure without considering the Jamesian reconceptualization of perceptual experience. It is tempting to suppose that we have knowledge-by-acquaintance when a perceptual object imprints its presence pristinely upon our attention, but James wrote in the final chapter of *Principles*: "We have no organ or faculty to appreciate the simply given order" (2:635). On the other hand, he insisted that his pragmatic theory of knowledge provided a "consummated acquaintance with reality" or a "total conflux of mind with reality. . . . If an idea should ever lead us not only *towards*, or *up to*, or *against*, a reality, but so close that we and the reality should *melt* together, it would be made absolutely true, according to me, by that performance."[76] This is picturesque language, but like Plato, James aimed the poetic word at a literal truth—literal, that is, if we accept the metaphysics of radical empiricism and pure experience, and their explanations of knowledge and reality.

Henry James, Sr., ca. 1865

Mary Walsh James, ca. 1865

Henry James, Sr., with grandchild

Alice Howe Gibbens
(future Mrs. William James), 1872

Alice James, 1870

Robertson James, ca. 1872

Garth Wilkinson James, ca. 1861

William James and wife, Alice, in Europe, 1900

Alice Gibbens James,
daughter Margaret,
William James,
and Henry James, Jr., 1905

William James and wife, Alice, in Farmington, Connecticut, ca. 1904

The James family home, 95 Irving Street, Cambridge, Massachusetts

William James's study in the house on Irving Street

William James and a friend at James's summer home in Chocorua, New Hampshire, ca. 1887

Charles Renouvier, 1893

William James and friends hiking in the Adirondacks, 1897

William James and Josiah Royce, 1903 (James to Royce: "Damn the Absolute!")

Caricature of William James by G. K. Chesterton, 1908

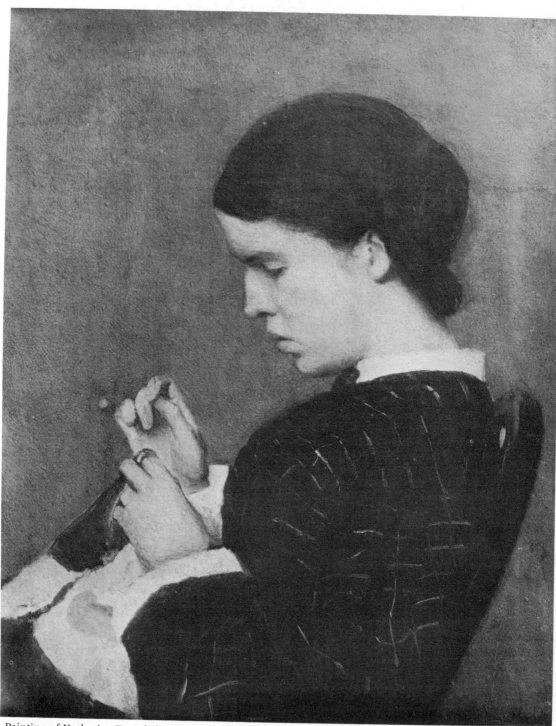
Painting of Katharine Temple by William James, ca. 1860

The lovely young Jewess looking up at the large end of the telescope

Drawing by William James

Drawing by William James, 1878

Supposed to be Billy when he is an old man. Cambr. Garden St. Dec 28. 1887

Drawing by William James, 1887

Drawing and script (opposite and overleaf), "The Foreboding Meeting; or, The Artist's Fate," in which James describes an encounter with Ralph Waldo Emerson. The script is transcribed in full on pages 420–21.

The Foreboding Meeting
or
The Artists' Fate.
Drama
Dram. Personae.
Sage of Concord
W. J.
Scene
Parker's boots blacking
establish
ment

Enter W. J.

W. J: I say, boy, just give my boots
a lick.
x   x   x   x
Enter. S of C.

S. of C.   Please to polish my
immortal boots.
                × × × ×
S. of C. + W. J. catch sight of
each other. ~~Meeting + tableau~~.
Heart-rending tableau, and usual
words of polite salutation. After
wh. —

S. of C. So I'm not to have my
boy at Concord on Saturday, — he
has given me the slip —

W. J. Oh! you mean J. B. Yes, he
expects to be busy moving all this week.
Great deal of furniture you know —
valuable paintings — carpets &c —
things collected in Europe — can't move
slowly.

S. of C. So! I had promised

myself on Saturday to hear what he had to say on the Relation of Art to Nature, I shd. like to become acquainted with
his theory, + to hear him criticise mr. Cabot's remarkable
articles — — —

W. J. Oh! yes! yes! nothing wd. please him more.
~~I suppos~~ S. of C. So I supposed — —
W. J. But between ourselves, he is rather weak as a metaphy-
sician.
S. of C. Want to know! Mrs. Tappan is my voucher
for his respectability — I have fm. her the very best account
of him.
W. J. Oh! yes! — S. of C. Well, we must have him

some other Saturday. You must do your best to send him along to
us.
W. J. I will do my possible. (They breathe a fond fare-
well + exeunt)   Finis.
The moral lesson of this Drama wh. actually happened on
Wednesday, Mch. 3rd is that you must read up on the
Physics + Esthetics. I will bring a lot of books on
Esthetics down with me for you. Show him that Cabot
is not original, but has plagiarised from the
Japanese poet what dyecallum, + he will
be delighted.

11 🎼 REALITY

RADICAL EMPIRICISM

The last decade of James's life was remarkably productive. In addition to *The Varieties of Religious Experience,* he wrote the essays that were published as *Pragmatism* and its sequel, *The Meaning of Truth,* as well as the articles on metaphysical subjects collected as *A Pluralistic Universe* and the posthumously published *Some Problems of Philosophy* and *Essays in Radical Empiricism.* The last three are the primary sources for a discussion of James's concepts of reality and pure experience; beginning in 1904 with "Does 'Consciousness' Exist?" (the first essay in the series on radical empiricism), he elaborated these ideas, moving toward a metaphysical replacement of the mind-body dualism that had been tentatively adopted in *Principles.*

Principles is sprinkled with doubts about mind-body dualism, but since these misgivings are metaphysical and consequently outside scientific psychology, James left psychology saddled with dualism until he could offer a metaphysical alternative, which he eventually developed in his philosophy of radical empiricism or pure experience. "Does 'Consciousness' Exist?" repeats more confidently the doubts about dualism suggested in *Principles.* In his earlier psychology James had stressed the difficulty of being sure that introspection reveals anything nonphysiological that can be called consciousness or awareness, but in 1904 he declared certainly that introspection discloses no such thing. Philosophers who believe that consciousness is something experiential must give it a positive description, sometimes claiming, as did G. E. Moore, that it is so diaphanous that we have difficulty seeing it rather than seeing through it.[1] Asserting that his own qualms about the existence of consciousness as a sui generis entity were at least twenty years old, James wrote: "I believe that 'consciousness,' when once it has evaporated to this state of pure diaphaneity, is on the point of disappearing altogether. It is the name of a nonentity. . . . Those who still cling to it are clinging to a mere echo, the faint rumor left behind by the disappearing 'soul' upon the air of philosophy. . . . It seems to me that the hour is ripe for it to be openly and universally discarded."[2] In James's final years, the suspicion that no uniquely psychical or nonphysiological consciousness is detectable by introspection, that everything accessible to introspection is a feature of some bodily process, had become a basic conviction. Most thinkers, if confident that their introspections revealed only physical processes, would argue for materialism, but James denied materialism even though he agreed that introspection finds only material (physiological) occurrences. This paradox was his most formidable challenge. When everything we perceive and introspect seems to be physical, how can we avoid conceiving the world materialistically? Radical empiricism was James's metaphysical answer. Although this theory resembled other revolts against Cartesian dualism in many respects, its aim was to establish an *anti*-materialistic metaphysics.

"Does 'Consciousness' Exist?" and the succeeding essays in radical empiricism argue that the distinction between the mental and the physical can be interpreted as falling within something more ultimate or primitive, that which James called *pure experience*. Instead of portraying the universe as consisting of two kinds of "stuff," one mental and the other physical, the metaphysics of radical empiricism viewed mind and body as different arrangements of one kind of stuff—pure experience— which in itself is neither mental nor physical. This formulation must be qualified, however, for James elaborated his concept thus: "Although for fluency's sake I myself spoke early in this article of a stuff of pure experience, I have now to say that there is no *general* stuff of which experience at large is made. There are as many stuffs as there are 'natures' in the things experienced. If you ask what any one bit of pure experience is made of, the answer is always the same: 'It is made of *that*, of just what appears, of space, of intensity, of flatness, brownness, heaviness, or what not.' "[3] The building blocks of the universe are pure experiences, which are interpreted either as sensations or as sensible objects. Reality is pluralistic and variety a primitive element in its constitution, a view that would have been contradicted had James proposed the monistic statement that pure experience is one stuff of which everything else is composed. The pluralistic character of his metaphysics required him to make pure experience*s* his fundamental concept. But what is meant by applying the label *pure* to such characteristics as intensity, brownness, and heaviness?

An experience is pure, James thought, when it occurs as it is innately, prior to being analyzed or conceptualized. "The instant field of the present is always experience in its 'pure' state, plain unqualified actuality, a simple *that*, as yet undifferentiated into thing and thought, and only virtually classifiable as objective fact or as someone's opinion about fact. . . . Only in the later experience that supersedes the present one is the *naïf* immediacy retrospectively split into two parts, a 'consciousness' and its 'content.' "[4] Repeated throughout the radical empiricism essays, the idea that the purity of an immediate experience can only be separated into a mind-body dichotomy by a retrospective experience was first suggested in "The Stream of Thought" and "The Consciousness of Self," where James had agreed with Mill that introspection is really retrospection and that the conceptualization of any experience, including its analysis into subjective and objective components, must therefore be the work of its successor.[5] As a radical empiricist he asserted that within the immediacy of an experience there is no room for mind-body or subject-object distinctions, which are the inventions of the subsequent experience of retrospection. But his theory never adequately answers the troublesome question of why, if these distinctions do not characterize initial experiences, we nevertheless find them there retrospectively. Consistent with his general principle that all conceptualization of experience is a fragmented selection for practical ends, James formulated this central thesis: "Subjectivity and objectivity are affairs not of what an experience is aboriginally made of, but of its classification. Classifications depend on our temporary purposes."[6] But we do not determine autonomously what is objective; rather, our purposes are determined by what antecedently is or seems to be objective fact. Despite James's attempts to maintain common sense within radical empiricism, there seems to be no commonsense ground for his claim that when we see something, we are entitled to judge it an objective fact merely because it serves our interests to do so. It is small wonder that his critics saw in this an excessive subjectivism, forcing him to insist repeatedly that he believed in extramental realities. On pragmatic grounds, he might have argued that if our purposes are served by analyzing an experience into certain subjective and objective components, that is the best reason to conclude that the experience actually consists of those components, that they are not merely the products of our analysis.

The doctrine of pure experience does not deny that minds and bodies exist; it denies only that the differences between them are ultimate and unanalyzable. According to James, minds and bodies are reducible to pure experiences, both made of the same kind of stuff. A real, objective pen is (metaphysically) a *that* or bit of pure experience, and our consciousness or perception of the pen is (metaphysically) the same *that* or bit of pure experience; the differences between the pen and our consciousness of it are not differences between two enduring things but are rather differences between successive contexts of the original *that*. In the context we call "using the pen," the *that* is an objective, physical pen; in the context of "imagining the pen," it is a subjective, mental consciousness of the pen. Pure experiences, in themselves actual complexes of sensations that are potentially physical or mental things, become mental or physical depending upon an individual's response to them. As James realized, it is difficult if not impossible to retain our commonsense notions within the framework of pure experience; he made strange contrasts, such as saying that "physical fire" will burn sticks while "mental fire" will not. He also wrote:

In the essay "Does 'Consciousness' Exist?" I have tried to show that when we call an experience "conscious," that does not mean that it is suffused throughout with a peculiar modality of being ('psychic' being) as stained glass may be suffused with light, but rather that it stands in certain determinate relations to other portions of experience extraneous to itself. These form one peculiar "context" for it; while, taken in another context of experiences, we class it as a fact in the physical world. This "pen," for example, is, in the first instance, a bald *that,* a datum, phenomenon, content or whatever other neutral or ambiguous name you may prefer to apply. I called it in that article a "pure experience." To get classed either as a physical pen or as some one's perception of a pen, it must assume a *function,* and that can only happen in a more complicated world. So far as in that world it is a stable feature, holds ink, marks paper and obeys the guidance of a hand, it is a physical pen. That is what we mean by being "physical" in a pen. So far as it is instable, on the contrary, coming and going with the movements of my eyes, altering with what I call my fancy, continuous with subsequent experiences of its "having been" (in the past tense), it is the percept of a pen in my mind. Those peculiarities are what we mean by being "conscious," in a pen.[7]

It was a frustrating project, James often acknowledged, to formulate the philosophy of pure experience to encompass rather than violate common sense. Here the attempt fails. The so-called "functional" analysis founders on the impossibility of identifying the undifferentiated *that* (bit of pure experience) which functions now as a pen, now as a consciousness of the pen. There is no way to point at a pure *that* and to assert that it may cease to function as a pen and begin to function as the consciousness of a pen. We can outwardly point at a pen or inwardly at our awareness of it, but we have no idea of the *it* that allegedly functions as both. One might reply that this is only a practical difficulty, but if the theoretical construct of pure experience can never in practice be contrasted with the pen or with our percept of it, then according to Jamesian pragmatism it is an inadmissible distinction because it makes no difference in practice. Further, we inevitably fall into contradictions by ascribing to the same bit of pure experience the incompatible properties of being both subjective and objective. So far as *it* is stable it is a physical pen, but so far as *it* is instable it is a mental one; a physical fire burns, a mental one does not. But this Jamesian contention only confuses us because we can never find an *it* that is sometimes a stable pen and at other times an instable awareness of a pen. It is disconcerting to be told that a mental fire differs from a physical one by virtue of not burning, when it is obvious that a so-called "mental" fire is no fire at all, any more than a physical fire is a burning consciousness of one. It is questionable whether a world in which mental and physical things abruptly exchange identities is intelligible, but such a world clearly cannot be used for explaining the world we experience.

Not only did James wrestle with making radical empiricism and common sense compatible, he also faced the obstacle of making it consistent with other of his theories, particularly the *esse est sentiri* doctrine of consciousness. A state of mind *is* what it is felt to be, unique and indivisible, a coincidence of appearance and reality not to be found in the physical world.[8] This concept was the centerpiece in his attack upon the atomistic ideas of the British empiricists, who postulated that simple ideas are associated in complex mental states; James contended, by contrast, that association is a cerebral process and that any mental effect of such a process is a unique state that is as it is felt to be. No such mental states can be part of another.

According to the doctrine of pure experience, however, we can designate the *that* or bit of pure experience as P which functions either as a pen or as a percept (consciousness) of the pen. If two people see the same pen and each has the same percept of it, then P is not a unique and indivisible state of consciousness but is a common part of both consciousnesses. If a mental state is allowed to become part of another, James thought, its identity owes something to the whole of which it is a part and thus can no longer reside simply in its being felt. This consequence of the doctrine of pure experience contradicted the *esse est sentiri* thesis of *Principles*. In November 1905 James mentioned this problem in the first entry of a notebook recording two and a half years of his agonizing over the difficulties of making radical empiricism or pure experience feasible:

> In my psychology I contended that each field of consciousness is entitatively a unit, and that its parts are only different cognitive relations which it may possess with different contexts. But in my doctrine that the same "pen" may be known by two knowers I seem to imply that an identical part can help to *constitute* two fields. . . . The fields are . . . decomposable into "parts," one of which, at least, is common to both; and my whole tirade against "composition" [of smaller mental states into larger ones] in the *Psychology* is belied by my own subsequent doctrine. How can I rescue the situation? Which doctrine must I stand by?⁹

If the same bit of pure experience can belong to two people whose consciousnesses differ by virtue of what else they include, it follows that *that* is the part in which both consciousnesses are identical—a contradiction of the doctrine in *Principles* that states of consciousness do not consist of parts at all. Despite all his agonizing, public and private, James never succeeded in eliminating these internal conflicts in his theory, which no one perceived better than he himself did; he finally joined Bergson and abandoned the whole logic of identity.

The great difficulty of making radical empiricism feasible was manifested by his response to the problem of how to justify ascribing both subjective and objective properties to the same pure experience. "'If it be the self-same piece of pure experience, taken twice over, that serves now as thought and now as thing'—so the objection runs—'how comes it that its attributes should differ so fundamentally in the two takings. As thing, it is red, hard, heavy; but who ever heard of a red, hard or heavy thought?'"¹⁰ The problem arises because of the apparent incompatibility between the two sorts of attributes; James simply denied the alleged incompatibility, arguing that the attributes are actually homogeneous; thoughts and objects have space and time in common, and—here James departed from the doctrine that thought cannot have parts—they are both complex and made of parts. Their homogeneity is further shown by the fact that in a given sense-perception, it is difficult if not impossible to tell at the moment of perception what is contributed by the object and what by the percipient. How we perceive something is due in some measure to subjective factors such as memories, expectations, and moods. James, unlike Descartes, held that thoughts as well as objects literally have extension, so his philosophy of pure experience takes his suspicion in *Principles*—that everything introspected in the stream of consciousness is physiological—to the verdict that all mental states are physical. Arguing for the homogeneity of mental and physical processes set the stage for contrasting physical fire with mental fire. Even if thoughts are physiological, it is not necessarily intelligible to suppose that a fire and our thought of it can be the same physical thing, as is required by the theory of pure experience.

James's fascination with unusual states of mind was in part motivated by a desire to find clues about the nature of pure experiences. In emphasizing his belief that the distinction between the subjective and the objective or between the mental and the physical is not sharp, he called attention to the historical uncertainties about secondary qualities, about whether heat, light, and sound are on one side of the distinction or the other. Sensations characteristically seem double-edged, as much subjective as objective; in dizzy spells, for instance, it is as if the outer world whirls as much as the inner one. In some experiences the subject-object and mind-body distinctions evaporate and we can glimpse momentarily a preconceptualized *that* or pure experience, unformulated yet rich in content.

> Pure experience is the name which I gave to the immediate flux of life which furnishes the material to our later reflection with its conceptual categories. Only newborn babes, or men in semi-coma from sleep, drugs, illnesses, or blows, may be assumed to have an experience pure in the literal sense of a *that* which is not yet any definite *what*, tho' ready to be all sorts of whats; full both of oneness and of manyness, but in respects that don't appear; changing throughout, yet so confusedly that its phases interpenetrate and no points, either of distinction or of identity, can be caught. Pure experience in this state is but another name for feeling or sensation. But the flux of it no sooner comes than it tends to fill itself with emphases, and these salient parts become identified and fixed and abstracted; so that experience now flows as if shot through with adjectives and nouns and prepositions and conjunctions. Its purity is only a relative term, meaning the proportional amount of unverbalized sensation which it still embodies.[11]

Pure experience is the stream of consciousness as it is before any conceptualization or distinction-making is applied to it. It is the experiential flux, which to the newborn babe is a "blooming, buzzing confusion," which gradually blooms or flowers, as it becomes conceptualized, from pure experience into the world of discretely organized objects and processes that we perceive in our maturity. Pure experience was for James like a dome under which favorite ideas could be collected. Relations are especially important for radical empiricism; the particular relations in which a given pure experience stands determine whether it is to be classified as physical or mental.[12] Whenever James stressed the role of relations, he criticized both traditional empiricism, with its atomic and independent ideas or impressions, for permitting too little metaphysical unity and connectedness, and traditional rationalism, with its doctrine of internal relations that makes it impossible for anything to change its relations without changing its identity, for permitting too little metaphysical independence and individuality. Unlike the empiricists, he found a relatedness between things that makes experience a flux rather than an atomic collection; unlike the absolutists, he found a relatedness that is given in experience and not imposed upon it by the mind, a relatedness that does not threaten, as Bradley supposed, to disrupt an absolute unity into irrational fragmentations.[13] Recognizing the reality and givenness of relations is also to recognize the relation between radical empiricism and pragmatism; although he had explicitly disavowed any relation in his preface to *Pragmatism*, he subsequently changed his mind:

> I am interested in another doctrine . . . radical empiricism, and it seems to me that the establishment of the pragmatist theory of truth is a step of first-rate importance in making radical empiricism prevail. Radical empiricism consists first of a postulate, next of a statement of fact, and finally of a generalized conclusion.
>
> The postulate is that the only things that shall be debatable among philosophers shall be things definable in terms drawn from experience. [Things of an unexperienceable nature may exist ad libitum, but they form no part of the material for philosophic debate.]
>
> The statement of fact is that the relations between things, conjunctive as well as disjunctive, are just as much matters of direct particular experience, neither more nor less so, than the things themselves.
>
> The generalized conclusion is that therefore the parts of experience hold together from next to next by relations that are themselves parts of experience. The directly apprehended universe needs, in short, no extraneous trans-empirical connective support, but possesses in its own right a concatenated or continuous structure. (*MT*, xii–xiii)

The movement of James's thinking from the psychology to the philosophy of intentionality and cognition, through such essays as "On the Function of Cognition," "The Knowing of Things Together," and "Philosophical Conceptions and Practical Results," reached its natural destination in the idea of pure experience. The seeming mysteries of intentionality's self-transcendency and of cognition could be explained within pure experience; whereas traditional philosophies left the truth-relation without experiential content, pragmatism insisted that everything in that relation can be experienced.

> The "workableness" which ideas must have, in order to be true, means particular workings, physical or intellectual, actual or possible, which they may set up from next to next inside of concrete experience. Were this pragmatic contention admitted, one great point in the history of radical empiricism would also be scored, for the relation between an object and the idea that truly knows it, is held by rationalists to be nothing of this describable sort, but to stand outside of all temporal experience; and on the relation, so interpreted, rationalism is wonted to make its last most obdurate rally. (*MT*, xiv)

Intentionality, cognition, meaning, and truth can all be interpreted as relations between pure experience, so that pragmatism and radical empiricism support each other.

There was virtually no service that the concept of pure experience could not perform for James's metaphysics, so it is not surprising that he wondered whether it might be as fertile a principle in philosophy as association had been in psychology.[14] Pure experience, the aboriginal stream of consciousness that occurs unbroken by conceptualization, is a catchall for space, time, conjunctive relations, change, activity—everything required for it to bloom into the structured world we learn to perceive. It contains concepts as well, but here we encounter a problem of interpretation. Experiences or acts of conceiving, imagining, and remembering are parts of pure experience, but are the concepts themselves? Again, James's uncertainty about the status of abstract objects shows. He wrote, for instance, that one dissection of the stream of pure experience "forms the inner history of a person, while the other [which includes concepts] acts as an impersonal 'objective' world, either spatial or temporal, or else merely logical or mathematical, or otherwise 'ideal.' "[15] But given his dedication to the thesis that concepts are discontinuous, how they can be part of a flux that is continuous throughout? He sensed the difficulty, writing in what was published posthumously as *Some Problems of Philosophy:* "The great difference between percepts and concepts is that percepts are continuous and concepts are discrete. Not discrete in their *being,* for conception as an *act* is part of the flux of feeling, but discrete from each other in their several *meanings*" (233). Yet he had included the "ideal world" (meanings) of logic and mathematics—and not only our psychological acts of conceiving that world—within the flux of pure experience. To challenge the interpreter even further, he wrote: "The world of common-sense 'things'; the world of material tasks to be done; the mathematical world of pure forms; the world of ethical propositions . . . of logic, of music, etc., all abstracted and generalized from long forgotten perceptual instances, from which they have as it were flowered out, return and merge themselves again in the particulars of our present and future perception. By those *whats* we apperceive all of our *thises.* Percepts and concepts interpenetrate and melt together, impregnate and fertilize each other."[16] Pure experience was intended to include concepts as well as percepts, but how this is possible remains a puzzle in the Jamesian metaphysics.

The concept of knowledge-by-acquaintance is also difficult to make consistent with radical empiricism, which might seem to allow that in a metaphysical manner beyond common sense knowledge-by-acquaintance occurs. At the commonsense level we can say that our perception of someone is a case of cognitive acquaintance, but if challenged by a skeptic demanding a check of our perception, where would we find proof in James's system? What sort of further experience terminates the claim to know? In "The Knowing of Things Together" James had asserted: "*To know* immediately, then, *or intuitively, is for mental content and object to be identical*" (McDermott, 157). Representative knowledge, on the other hand, involves a series of intermediary actions and experiences (*leadings*) to some terminus. Whatever the attendant difficulties, James was prepared in his radical empiricism to state that, since the same pure experience can be both subject and object, the identity of (mental) content and object required for knowledge-by-acquaintance is thoroughly satisfied. Once dualism is abolished, the act-content-object distinction in perceptual awareness—assumed by common sense and adopted in *Principles*—collapses into content alone, and the way is clear for radical empiricism to invoke knowledge-by-acquaintance.[17] So often the collapsing of this distinction is the thrust of radical empiricism in its references to the coalescence and confluence of ideas and things within a pure experience. "In this experience—full, concrete, undivided, such as it is, there, a *datum*—the objective physical world and the inner personal world of each one of us meet and fuse as do the lines at their intersection."[18] On the other hand, a contrary strain in James's thinking arises in his contention that no experience is reflexively conscious, that, as Shadworth Hodgson had argued, the minimum of consciousness demands two subfeelings, the second of which retrospects the first. "To be 'conscious' means not simply to be, but to be reported, known, to have awareness of one's being added to that being. . . . The pen-experience in its original immediacy is not aware of itself, it simply *is*, and the second experience is required for what we call awareness of it to occur."[19] The only consequence to be mentioned here is that consciousness (or knowledge-by-acquaintance) of anything is necessarily subsequent to what is known; the identity between knower and known required by James's own account of knowledge-by-acquaintance—precisely what the doctrine of pure experience ought to provide for—is thus impossible.

This difficulty can be eliminated by accepting a preconceptual awareness or consciousness, something not yet developed into explicit cognitive consciousness involving reports, verbalizations, and conceptualizations. In this way an experience could be self-aware but not so fully or explicitly as to qualify as self-*knowledge*. In fact, I think James may have made this distinction in his theory all along. It may be suggested as early as 1885 in "On the Function of Cognition," where he argued that a simple feeling, even though it cannot be cognitive without a retrospective experience, is nevertheless "no psychical zero" and is "a most positively and definitely qualified inner fact" (McDermott, 140). This may suggest the distinction that a feeling or experience can be self-aware but not yet at the level of knowledge. But this remains a conjecture on my part, and despite all that is customarily said about James's defense of immediate and intuitive knowledge, the problem of how to interpret his view here is inadequately appreciated.[20]

This is a minor consideration compared to the difficulties presented by the concept of pure experience itself. Neither James nor anyone else has justified the claim that the properties of physical objects or processes can be attributed to pure experiences which are sensations such as colors, tastes, and sounds. Unlike a physical pigment, the sensation of red cannot crack, erode, or harden in the can. Whenever James's radical empiricism is rediscovered as a revolutionary doctrine that anticipated twentieth-century thinking, attention is being directed toward one of his most implausible theses, though one that distinguished thinkers have supported.

Bertrand Russell began *The Analysis of Mind* with a tribute to James's essays in radical empiricism: "I believe this doctrine contains important new truth, and what I shall have to say will be in a considerable measure inspired by it."[21] But while Russell agreed with the rejection of consciousness as an entity and with the importance of seeking a neutral monism with which to replace Cartesian dualism, he recognized the lingering influence of idealism in the concept of pure experience and contended that experience, like consciousness, must be a product rather than a part of the primary stuff of the world.

A. J. Ayer has judged James's radical empiricism to be his "most original and fruitful contribution to philosophical theory" (*The Origins of Positivism,* 173). Logical positivism, which Ayer represents, advocates pragmatism's injunction to make philosophical propositions subject to criteria of meaning and truth similar to those found in science, and also resembles radical empiricism by seeking to reduce physical entities to sensations (or sense-data). Ayer's critique of James, however, more subverts than supports radical empiricism; the virtual abandonment today of positivism's claim to reduce physical things to sense-data, while not detracting from the originality of radical empiricism, does not enhance its plausibility. A critic must also remember that the revolt against dualism was led by others besides James, including Richard Avenarius, Ernst Mach, Henri Poincaré, and Charles Renouvier; views similar to radical empiricism are attributable to these thinkers as well.[22] Appreciating this naturally makes one hesitate before venturing a criticism as blunt as mine. It would be irresponsible to pass a critical judgment on unexamined theories, and doubtlessly each of these differs in certain respects from James's; I mean only to point out that the history of philosophy includes many "original and fruitful" ideas that are quite outrageous: Thales's notion that everything is water, Parmenides's idea of Being, Plato's Forms, Leibniz's monads, Hegel's Absolute, Schopenhauer's Will, Russell's logical atomism, the positivists' verifiability theory of meaning, Wittgenstein's picture-theory of meaning, and theories such as radical empiricism. Philosophers seem to have been motivated as much by the desire to forge a unique route to truth as by the desire to find truth itself, and have thus bequeathed to us many exciting but indefensible ideas. No positivist ever provided an actual example of a physical-object statement having been translated into a sense-datum statement; nor did James, even to his own satisfaction, ever adequately translate the commonsense statement "You and I see the same pen" into a pure-experience statement.

If we examine the eight essays that represent James's radical empiricism, we cannot detect any effort to work out in technical detail the vague blueprint of pure experience. Instead, we will find broad analogies and suggestions—that mental and physical things are not heterogeneous, that a given perceptual *that* may function now as a mental thing and now as a physical one, that radical empiricism may somehow be reconciled with the *esse est sentiri* doctrine of conscious states, that perhaps the concept of pure experience requires abandoning the notion that conscious states cannot have parts. There are outlines and suggestions, including worries about coherence and compatibility with common sense, but no methodological program. James made no serious attempt to show that the specific properties of a perceived thing can be more fundamentally expressed in terms of pure experiences. In fact, it would strike us as odd if James had essayed reductions of specific classes of things into specific classes of pure experiences, because to do so would violate the idea that pure experience is a metaphysical and not a scientific concept. It affords no predictions, nor is it defined by scientific properties from which the properties of common sense things can be deduced. How, then, does the metaphysical concept of pure experience function, what is its value, and why was James so attracted to it?

The beginning of an answer is provided by a remark repeated several times in his unpublished notes: "Philosophies are only *pictures* of the world which have grown up in the minds of different individuals."[23] James would have agreed with Wittgenstein that when we philosophize pictures grip our minds, and with Ayer that "the only point of having an ontology is to obtain a viable picture of the world."[24] For these three philosophers the metaphor of the picture is more than casual or offhand. In trying metaphysically to explain things to ourselves, whether through radical empiricism or some other scheme, we sometimes seem to make an idea intelligible or plausible by means of an image, analogy, or metaphor. Which kind of picture works depends upon the topic and the thinker. James invoked spatial, scenic imagery, and he often thought he had a grasp of a notion if he could imagine its application in a situation where seen things move relative to each other or one dynamic process occurs within the space of another. "Life is in the transitions as much as in the terms connected; often, indeed, it seems to be there more emphatically, as if our spirits and sallies forward were the real firing line of the battle, were like the thin line of flame advancing across the dry autumnal field which the farmer proceeds to burn."[25]

Readers of James are often struck by his pictorial language; the vividness of his imagery provokes various comparisons to the works of his brother Henry. The image is indispensable for the Jamesian metaphysics, much as it was for Plato's. It has often been asserted that what demarcates great from competent philosophers is the presence of *vision*, an idea to which James subscribed: "Let me repeat once more that a man's vision is the great fact about him. Who cares for Carlyle's reasons, or Schopenhauer's, or Spencer's? A philosophy is the expression of a man's intimate character, and all definitions of the universe are but the deliberately adopted reactions of human characters upon it."[26] Vision in philosophy often consists in associating or replacing abstract concepts with images, so that one can see, as it were, what one means or speaks of. Imagery represents more than the pleasant or decorative use of poetic and vibrant language; rather, it marks the mind's movement from a tentative grasp of an idea to a confident possession of it, exhibited by the ability to formulate it in an imagery that draws upon the concreteness of perceptual experience. This process was for James a test of whether he had made an idea truly his own, had taken full charge of an idea. A mind can initially soar with either abstractions or images, but it reaches an understanding of those abstractions or images when it can transform them into still further images, which are felt to be just what was needed to supply the meaning of the initial ones. The presence of imagery, coupled with this process of reformulation or referral, creates the experience of understanding.

This idea connects with James's calling his radical empiricism a mosaic philosophy, a philosophy of plural facts that are like mosaic pieces which cling together "by their edges, the transitions experienced between them forming their cement."[27] It is also a mosaic philosophy insofar as its doctrines—including the stream of consciousness, the nativistic concepts of space, time, and sensation, natural and logical realism, a pragmatic theory of meaning and truth, the externality of relations, the freedom of will and the will to believe, and pure experience—are pieces that James tried to *see* fitting together as in a jigsaw puzzle. I believe he mentally diagrammed pure experiences as an infinite variety of sensation-complexes occupying an indefinitely large spatial expanse; within that expanse the plurality of facts constituting the world could be pieced together and be mentally seen in their jigsaw relations. Minds and bodies and their interactions could be diagrammed as pure experiences in relation to one another, with each as an animated piece of space connected by an indefinitely large number of routes to other animated pieces of space in the same expanse. I have emphasized the pictorial, visionary character of James's concept of pure experience, for if it is appreciated, we can understand that, while the concept might have been shaken when he tried to preserve the *esse est sentiri* doctrine or the theory of unique and indivisible mental states, it would never be defeated by such technical problems, even if they were internal to the theory.

Although it may be difficult to explain how two minds can know the same thing, or how the same bit of pure experience can be both a mental and a physical thing, it will always seem possible to shift the mosaic pieces to create a coherent picture; something lurking in the picture may emerge to overcome the apparent obstacles, or perhaps the picture, to hang together, only demands a certain reconceptualization. Once a picture or vision has gripped the philosopher's mind—and heart—it endures regardless of arguments against it. Despite the perplexities and frustrations that James experienced in seeking to make pure experience cohere with other convictions and with common sense, he kept his metaphysical picture in its broad outlines until the end, shuffling the mosaic pieces in search of a breakthrough that never happened. He wrote: "For many years past my mind has been growing into a certain type of *Weltanschauung*. Rightly or wrongly, I have got to the point where I can hardly see things in any other pattern."[28] He was painting verbal pictures, not mounting methodological programs for reducing things to specific classes of pure experiences; we should not expect more than broad brush strokes, bold analogies, suggestive metaphors, and arresting imagery. However, I do not intend to retract my earlier charge of implausibility.

It is implausible to conceive of physical objects or processes in terms of pure experiences or sensation-complexes. (I say *sensation-complexes* because James clearly meant that the smallest bit of pure experience will contain not only an attribute but also a bit of space, time, sound, or smell—what he called *muchness-at-once*. By *pure* he meant preconceptual but not exclusively one kind of sensation.)[29] James came to the conclusion that physical things, while independently real, are analyzable into sensations or sense-data by the traditional route of the British empiricists. In *Principles* he had written:

Helmholtz says that we notice only those sensations which are signs to us of *things*. But what are things? Nothing, as we shall abundantly see, but special groups of sensible qualities, which happen practically or aesthetically to interest us, to which we therefore give substantial names, and which we exalt to this exclusive status of independence and dignity. . . .

And then, among the sensations we get from each separate thing, what happens? The mind selects again. It chooses certain of the sensations to represent the thing most *truly,* and considers the rest as its appearances. . . . But all these essential characteristics, which together form for us the genuine objectivity of the thing and are contrasted with what we call the subjective sensations it may yield us at a given moment, are mere sensations like the latter. The mind chooses to suit itself, and decides what particular sensation shall be held more real and valid than all the rest. (1:285–86)

This view that physical things are merely collections of sensations or sensible qualities (sometimes called phenomenalism, sometimes Berkeleyan idealism) might be hard to defend on the dualistic premise of *Principles,* but it fits neatly into the scheme of radical empiricism, where everything is made of sensations or sensible qualities. This thesis is emphasized in *Essays in Radical Empiricism:*

For common sense, two men see the same identical dog. Philosophy, noting actual differences in their perceptions, points out the duality of these latter, and interpolates something between them as a more real terminus—first, organs, viscera, etc.; next, cells; then, ultimate atoms; lastly, mind-stuff perhaps. The original sense-termini of the two men, instead of coalescing with each other and with the real dog-object, as at first supposed, are thus held by philosophers to be separated by invisible realities with which, at most, they are conterminous. . . .

The humanist sees all the time, however, that there is no absolute transcendency even about the more absolute realities thus conjectured or believed in. The viscera and cells are only possible percepts following upon that of the outer body. The atoms again, though we may never attain to human means of perceiving them, are still defined perceptually. The mind-stuff itself is conceived as a kind of experience; and it is possible to frame the hypothesis . . . of two knowers of a piece of mind-stuff and the mind-stuff itself becoming confluent at the moment at which our imperfect knowing might pass into knowing of a completed type.[30]

James evidently reasoned, with Berkeley, Hume, and Mill, that when a physical thing is identified exclusively with its perceptible properties, and its primary and secondary qualities are lumped together, physical things become simply bundles of sensations or sensible qualities. But this view is not plausible even as a vision or grand image, and the difficulty is more than a technicality. The properties of physical things cannot be borne by sensations, and there is no way of plausibly incorporating such a proposal within the vision of radical empiricism. Even if all properties of physical things were assumed to be perceptible, it would not follow that those properties are sensations or sensible qualities. Psychologists debate about the properties of sensations, but no one asserts that sensations have mass, charge, weight, or particle composition. Sensations do not flake, rust, corrode, fertilize, or explode. (The same is true of sensible qualities, if we take them to be exactly like sensations except that they exist independently of anyone's experience of them.) The tactile sensation of touching something porous is not a property of the object but a chemico-physical effect that it causes in the skin and nerve-receptors. There is no way of plausibly conceiving physical things as analyzable only into tactile sensations and the like. Since this conception is what radical empiricism proposes, it renders the vision of pure experience indefensible from the outset. Not only do James's philosophical visions encounter decisive objections, but his doctrine is a throwback to Berkeley's idealism. In fact, the adoption of something like Berkeley's view was precisely what saved James from materialism.

His relation to Berkeley was a curious one—another challenge for his interpreter—because he sometimes seemed close to Berkeleyan idealism and at other times opposed to it.

> Can we say that the psychical and the physical are absolutely heterogeneous? On the contrary . . . if . . . we take reality naively, as it is given, . . . this sensible reality and the sensation which we have of it are absolutely identical. . . . The words "the walls of this room" have only one meaning, and that is the fresh and sonorous whiteness which surrounds us. . . . The content of the physical is none other than the psychical. Subject and object confuse, as it were.
>
> It is Berkeley who first gave prestige to this truth. *Esse est percipi.* Our sensations are not small inner duplicates of things, they are the things themselves in so far as the things are presented to us. . . . This actuality, I say, is homogeneous—nay, more than homogeneous, but numerically one—with a certain part of our inner life.[31]

The concluding words of this passage indicate not only an agreement with Berkeley's concept of physical things as simple collections of sensible qualities, but also with his *esse est sentiri* principle that such qualities are mind-dependent, making the perceptible qualities of things akin to "our inner life." Despite his claim that radical empiricism is neutral and that pure experiences are neither mental nor physical until associated into larger contexts, James seems here to have tipped his hand. At stake for him, as for Berkeley, was whether physical things—which we normally consider utterly different from our sensations—are in fact nothing but the sensations at the core of our inner lives. Materialism, whatever its variations, has always maintained that everything, including sensations, is explicable by chemico-physical processes in which sensations have no part. Materialism allows no exceptions to the common belief that we live in a world where sensations depend wholly upon physical things; James and Berkeley believed exactly the opposite. If physical things are nothing but complexes of sensations, then the materialistic view—that everything begins and ends in physical processes which differ in character from the felt or noticed details of our sensations—begins to dissolve. All sorts of possibilities emerge: our conscious states may not depend totally upon our brains; our sensations and inner lives may coalesce in a larger context which cannot be conceived by analogy to the physical environment; and our own experiences may be part of a larger, godlike consciousness. A universe whose fundamental units are sensations (the pulses in the experienced stream of consciousness) rather than electrons, protons, and neutrons is compatible with such possibilities, James thought; that idea is the visionary crux of radical empiricism.

But James made negative judgments about Berkeley. For example:

Radical empiricism has, in fact, more affinities with natural realism than with the views of Berkeley or Mill. . . .

For the Berkeleyan school, ideas (the verbal equivalent of what I term experiences) are discontinuous. The content of each is wholly immanent, and there are no transitions with which they are consubstantial and through which their beings may unite. Your Memorial Hall and mine, even when both are percepts, are wholly out of connection with each other. Our lives are a congeries of solipsisms. . . . Never can our minds meet in the *same*.

The incredibility of such a philosophy is flagrant. It is "cold, strained and unnatural" in a supreme degree; and it may be doubted whether even Berkeley himself, who took it so religiously, really believed, when walking through the streets of London, that his spirit and the spirits of his fellow wayfarers had absolutely different towns in view.[32]

Our response to this criticism is complicated by the fact that Berkeley surely would have protested James's formulation of his theory; Berkeley went to great lengths to show that his position was compatible with common sense, that physical things are independent of finite minds (though dependent on God's), so that he and his fellow wayfarers indeed saw the same town. James certainly understood that Berkeley was an idealist with his *esse est percipi* doctrine but also a realist insofar as he held that the table we see is not in our minds but is "out there" in public space—despite the table's being only a complex of ideas—because it is preserved there by God's constant perception. We need to read James here as expressing dissatisfaction with Berkeley's theological explanation, not because his God is a deus ex machina but because his explanation construes our finite minds as parts of God's mind; this idea contradicts James's conviction, indelibly etched in *Principles*, that each mental state stands on its own, unique and indivisible, and that the compounding of such states is not possible.

While developing radical empiricism, James was troubled about having to abandon the *esse est sentiri* doctrine of mental states; in his criticism of Berkeley he still felt as he had in 1885: "I've just been lecturing on idealism . . . and found myself unable to come to a conclusion. The truth is, all these preliminaries lead one along very well to *immaterialism*. But when it comes to a *positive* construction of idealism, such questions as how many spirits there are, how the divine spirit sends us our representations if we are separate from him, and how if we are only bits of him we can have separate consciousness at all, and a host of others, start up and baffle *me*, at least, completely."[33] Idealism was attractive in that it was immaterialistic, which it achieved by envisaging individual experiences as parts of an absolute or all-encompassing experience. James wondered how a mind can be itself and also be part of another one. This was James's objection to Berkeley, and if this feature of the theory were removed, then Berkeley and his fellow wayfarers in London would never have seen the same town. But apart from refusing to invoke God as the omnipresent perceiver, James followed Berkeley to the letter in reducing physical things to sensations, considering them the stuff of our inner lives. Consequently, he faced the same problem that Berkeley had solved theologically: How, if physical things are pure experiences or sensations, can they exist, independently of anyone's experience as James's natural realism clearly required? I must concur with Perry that James left unanswered this and other questions, that his unfinished task included such issues as these: "Is it a neutral stream of 'pure' experience, or is it the mental series, which constitutes the metaphysical reality? . . . Does reality exist when no individual sentient being is consciously aware of it? And if so, in what sense, if any, can such existence be said to be 'experienced'? These questions are not answered."[34]

Another reason for James's criticism of Berkeley is important because it leads into one of the deeper and more elusive aspects of Jamesian metaphysics. He interpreted Berkeley as holding an entitative notion of things (the term *entitative* occurs throughout James's writings and unpublished notes); a Siberian tree, while nothing but a complex of ideas or sensations, is nevertheless an entity in God's mind and thus already exists in full detail in Siberia, awaiting our perception. It is a complete thing-in-itself, identified by a full assortment of properties, including a spatial configuration and boundaries that mark it as a discrete entity. In *Principles* one of the reasons for James's dislike of traditional ideas of the soul was that souls, as individual substances, must be discrete entities with boundaries (if only immaterial ones) that fundamentally separate them from each other and make them discontinuous.[35] For his vividly spatial imagination, boundaries meant chasms, breaks, and interruptions, barriers to cognition as well as to ultimate interactions between human psyches. When things are identified by boundaries, they are entities, objects, or substances that represent discontinuity. As I read James on Berkeley, there is a problem not only of how our minds and God's are related, but also of how continuity can occur in a universe that consists of boundaried entities discretely arranged in the public space that is actually God's all-encompassing experience. James accepted Berkeley's *esse est percipi* doctrine but not his entitative or commonsense view of things, which introduces a discontinuity that, for James, plagued both epistemology and metaphysics. James often wrote as if the atomism of British empiricism could be remedied only if relations and transitions between ideas and sensations were recognized; further, he demanded that the boundaries and entitative nature of things be abolished, because a relation or transition that runs into a boundary is a dead end.

The problem for radical empiricism was to retain the commonsense belief in ordinary realities (trees, human bodies) while metaphysically analyzing those realities such that their apparent boundaries disappear into a fluid continuity. (This problem was never solved by James, forcing him by his own admission to renounce the logic of identity.) A complex passage from James's notes conveys something of what he was after:

> My great trouble seems to lie in the diremption of real thing from sensation in the phenomenon of perception. Common sense dualism takes the same fact [twice] over—makes it figure first in the outer world say as that chair, then secondly as my mental copy of that chair. For phenomenism this is inadmissible. The one fact is my inner world and yet is entitatively the objective chair. . . .
>
> My point must be to show that *the beyond is part of the same continuum,* whereas for commonsense dualism, it is discontinuous, & separated by the epistemological chasm. . . . Your mind & mine might conceivably become continuous hereafter in directions made conceivable by such ideas as Janet's & such facts as those of mediumship. . . .
>
> Isn't the difficulty this?—*to get out of a solipsism without jumping a chasm?* So far, with my question about the more and my necessary "yes" in reply [to the question: Do objects and realities exist independently of my experience now?], I am solipsistic. For the "more" is continuous (being only a marginal object) with the focal "that" first posited absolutely; and the yes is a relation betw. the more on the one hand & the self & the whole field on the other. . . .
>
> For even assuming the Over-Soul as one's hypothesis, the passage from my present field to the rest of the Over-Soul is as much a chasm, as the passage to the "more," substantively taken. The Over-Soul seems indeed merely to be another name for the *continuity* betw. *the objective "truth"* and my "verification" thereof which commonsense dualism breaks up by its chasm. . . . The Oversoul theory says that nothing is verif*iable* by any finite which is not actually verif*ied* already by the Absolute [e.g., the tree in the Berkeleyan God's mind]. It denies *con*terminousness in plurality as an interpretation of knowledge, whilst such *conterminousness is the denkmittel which I am forced to make work, if I can.* . . .
>
> Arrived at the table in my field I say "more"—namely, that it is your table, too, or that molecules are in it . . . and so far as *my* verification goes I end there. . . . But the "truth" of my "more" consists in the fact that my "table plus more" which is my terminus is *con*terminous with you & with the molecules— there is no "chasm."
>
> *So the notion of conterminousness has to be defended.*[36]

James wanted to avoid the discontinuity of boundaried or entitative things, to dissolve such things into phases of the stream of consciousness, which can then be conceived as a continuum of sensations or pure experiences. To say that we perceive the tree is to say that our present stream of consciousness flows in a certain direction (described in commonsense terms as moving toward the tree) such that if two people see the same tree, their streams of consciousness literally flow together, become confluent or conterminous. These liquid metaphors were the best that James could manage in trying to picture our awarenesses of commonsense objects as pure experiences in which continuity and confluence replace the boundaried entities of common sense. We cannot comprehend James's literal use of these metaphors without first adopting something like Berkeley's *esse est percipi* doctrine, which implies that what are normally called physical things are really the stuff of which our inner lives are made, sensations in a constant flow. If we take that initial Berkeleyan step, James's philosophy of pure experience may assume an intelligible outline.

Principles is physiologically oriented and is the first of many works in which James declared that his introspections never revealed anything nonphysiological or purely mental. Readers naturally wonder how he preserved his antimaterialism, his idea that the brain may be only a transmitter of consciousness and not its condition, and his beliefs in free will and religion. I think he followed Berkeley by simply reinterpreting the physiological events disclosed to introspection and perception as mental, as sensations, feelings, and thoughts. Some thinkers suppose that introspection acquaints them directly with instances of the nonphysical, but James did not. Given his recognition that science—including evolutionary theory—was eroding mentalistic psychologies and religious faiths, he was never far from materialism. It is perhaps harmless to call him an introspective psychologist and a phenomenological philosopher, but experience and introspection never directly showed him an alternative to materialism. For that he needed an argument, and he adopted Berkeley's, which concludes that matter is mental. The philosophy of pure experience diverged from Berkeley insofar as it sought to explain things without depending upon a godly percipient, by replacing Berkeley's entitative ontology with one of ultimate flowings and confluences. I have expressed strong reservations about this line of thinking, but in the next chapter I am more favorable toward radical empiricism if it is taken not as a theory about the physical environment but as a set of suggestions about the nature of experience.[37]

James was an intense and prolific writer, often caught up in the mood and concentration of the moment, so that he was not always sensitive to the doubts or questions his reader might want him to address; this is surely not the case, however, with radical empiricism. He was always close to abandoning the attempt to make it work, so severe were his own frustrations, doubts, and self-criticisms. But characteristically trusting his own instincts, he persisted in trying to make the concept of pure experience credible, both in *A Pluralistic Universe* and the posthumous *Some Problems of Philosophy*.[38]

A PLURALISTIC UNIVERSE AND PHILOSOPHICAL PROBLEMS

Radical empiricism is the idea that the world's essentials are all found in the flux of intuited or perceived experience; this concept transmuted the stream of consciousness of James's psychology into the pure experience of his metaphysics. The flux, originally experienced as a "blooming, buzzing confusion," is from the outset a heterogeneous complex which blossoms, as we accumulate experience, into what we know as everyday reality. In his final writing effort, *Some Problems of Philosophy,* James retained his key notion that reality is revealed within the immediacy of perceptual or pure experience: "Here alone do we acquaint ourselves with continuity, or the immersion of one thing in another, here alone with self, with substance, with qualities, with activity in its various modes, with time, with cause, with change, with novelty, with tendency, and with freedom. Against all such features of reality the method of conceptual translation, when candidly and critically followed out, can only raise its *non possumus,* and brand them as unreal or absurd" (97). As Zeno's arguments against the reality of motion illustrate, philosophical conceptualizations often throw everything into doubt, leaving no recourse but to ignore such formulations and to strengthen our confidence in the realities of continuity, self, activity, and time by reacquainting ourselves with them as they occur in the stream of consciousness. But James continued to worry about four main issues: (1) Can the stream of consciousness, and hence pure experience, actually serve as a microcosm for all reality? (2) What is the effect of arguments, such as Georg Cantor's and Bertrand Russell's, on the belief that experience and reality are continuous? (3) What kind of continuity, if any, does experience disclose? (4) Does continuity require the compounding of consciousness?

The real question in (1) is this: Even if one's own stream of consciousness displays continuity, what does that tell us about the world-at-large?

> But, though the flux is continuous from next to next, non-adjacent portions of it are separated by parts that intervene, and such separation seems in a variety of cases to work a positive disconnection. The latter part, e.g., may contain no element surviving from the earlier part, may be unlike it, may forget it, may be shut off from it by physical barriers, or what not. Thus when we use our intellect for cutting up the flux and individualizing its members, we have (provisionally and practically at any rate) to treat an enormous number of these as if they were unrelated or related only remotely, to one another. We handle them piecemeal or distributively, and look at the entire flux as if it were their sum or collection. This encourages the empiricist notion, that the parts are distinct and that the whole is a resultant.
>
> This doctrine rationalism opposes, contending that the whole is fundamental . . . that the entire universe, instead of being a sum, is the only genuine unit in existence. . . .
>
> The alternative here is known as that between pluralism and monism. It is the most pregnant of all the dilemmas of philosophy. . . . Does reality exist distributively? or collectively?—in the shape of *eaches, everys, anys, eithers?* or only in the shape of an *all* or *whole?* . . . Pluralism stands for the distributive, monism for the collective form of being.[39]

James was always obsessed with the question of whether reality is distributive or collective. In *Principles* he had argued against the atomic ideas of the British empiricists on the grounds that such atoms cannot organize themselves into a coherent unity; on the other hand, he did not join the rationalists, who find unity through agents such as minds, souls, gods, or absolutes. Both the empiricists and the rationalists made continuity problematic by appealing to entitative ultimates. James preferred pluralism and recognized the problem of showing how a pluralistic theory can permit continuity and unity; most of his jousting with Bradley, Royce, and other monistic thinkers was over this issue. He never assumed as a matter of course that individual streams of consciousness can be taken as models upon which the whole of reality can be understood, but toward the end of his life—after pondering the pros and cons of monistic systems, different concepts of continuity, Bergson's *élan vital* and creative evolution, and his own radical empiricism—he decided that the stream of consciousness, if relieved of its former mind-body dualism and equated instead with pure experience, could be taken as reality in miniature. He wrote in an unpublished note:

> Apropos of my *reine erfahrung!* Isn't the difficulty of a simple smooth scheme uniting the subjective and the objective worlds due after all to the pluralistic constitution of things? Everything is many-directional, many dimensional, in its external relations; and after pursuing one line of direction from it, you have to go back, and start in a new dimension if you wish to bring in other objects related to it, different from those which lay in the original direction. No one point of view or attitude commands everything at once in a synthetic scheme. Yet all things are continuous through the mediation of the fact that each of them is contiguous to some other or others.
>
> To be more concrete, a sensible "experience" of mine, say this book written on by this pen, leads in one dimension into the world of matter, paper-mills, etc., in the other into that psychologic life of mine of which it is an affection. Both sets of associates are contiguous with it, yet one set must be dropped out of sight if the other is to be followed. They decline to make one universe in the absolute sense of something that can be embraced by one individual stroke of apprehension.[40]

This account supplies further details in James's picture of reality beyond any given stream of consciousness. Contiguity, adjacency, or what he often referred to as nextness is a datum for direct apprehension which can be assumed to exist throughout the universe such that any given experience or thing is connected by a series of contiguous intermediaries to any other experience or thing. The universe is not merely a disconnected assemblage of processes but is rather a concatenation or mosaic of pluralistic items. It has the continuity of nextness between things, which yields a degree of unity. Because of the metaphors that radical empiricism encourages, we can view the plural realities as accessible to each other by connecting paths, flowings of the sort that we know in our own streams of consciousness. Problems remained, but James felt he had made a significant step toward understanding how continuity can characterize a plural universe when the stream of consciousness is seen as a model of what things are really like.

(2) One reason for hesitating before adopting the stream of consciousness as a model of reality is that we need to know which concept of continuity is in question.[41] Despite what James had written about continuity in the stream of consciousness and the apparent contribution of space and time to such continuity (see chapter 5), he seems to have taken a different stance in *Some Problems of Philosophy*, advocating a discontinuity theory and remarking that space and time sunder as much as unite.[42] This change presents another interpretive problem, because the latter position appears to conflict with James's insistence that although concepts are static and discontinuous, reality is always changing and continuous. In working toward a solution, we need first to consider why he developed the later position.

He was persuaded by arguments, from Zeno to Kant, that pointed out the consequences of assuming infinitesimals and the completed infinite. These consequences pertain not to standing things such as space or past time, but to growing ones such as motion, change, and activity. According to Zeno's paradox, if we assume that motion is continuous and that what is continuous is actually divided ad infinitum, then since Achilles cannot occupy simultaneously all the points in any continuous amount of space, his motion is impossible. "The quickest way to avoid the contradiction would seem to be to give up that conception, and to treat real processes of change no longer as being continuous, but as taking place by finite not infinitesimal steps, like the successive drops by which a cask of water is filled, when whole drops fall into it at once or nothing. This is the radically pluralist, empiricist, or perceptualist position, which I characterized in speaking of Renouvier. . . . We shall have to end by adopting it in principle ourselves, qualifying it so as to fit it closely to perceptual experience" (*SPP*, 172). James concluded that if continuity is defined in terms of infinitesimals, then it cannot be instantiated experientially—a genial conclusion insofar as it illustrated his thesis that reality resists the concepts we try to impose upon it. He was therefore suspicious of those who claimed to have disproved the arguments of Zeno and Kant and who believed that "what in mathematics is called 'the new infinite' has quashed the old antinomies, and who treat anyone whom the notion of a completed infinite in any form still bothers, as a very *naif* person" (*SPP*, 173). In considering whether experience exhibits continuity, James consulted the work of Henri Poincaré, Louis Couturat, Edward Huntington, C. S. Peirce, Ernest Hobson, Georg Cantor, and Bertrand Russell.

He studied the innovative concepts of the number continuum and the new infinite. Philosophical mathematicians supposed that the number continuum was a conceptual equivalent for the quanta (amounts of space, intensity, etc.) that are the perceptual data of everyday experience. Any line in space can be divided infinitely by rational and irrational numbers which, because they are infinite, determine the line's continuity. According to Poincaré, the hallowed definition of continuity as unity in multiplicity should be abandoned because only the multiplicity remains. James commented, "The original intuition of the line's extent gets treated, from the mathematical point of view, as a 'mass of criticized prejudice' by Russell, or sneered at by Cantor as a 'kind of religious dogma' " (*SPP*, 174). According to the new concept of the infinite—which asserts that a one-to-one relation can be made in the number series between each element of a part and each element of its whole, such that part and whole belong to the same numerical class—paradoxical propositions (for example, that there are as many even numbers as there are odd *and* even numbers) are declared to be true. Instead of regarding these odd propositions, which are true of growing things such as the number series, as a reductio ad absurdum, mathematicians treat them as implications of the proper definition of infinity.

After a brief review of Cantor's theory of transfinite numbers, James described the upshot of the new infinite as the denial that the whole is greater than the part. Hence, as James read Russell, we solve Zeno's paradox by noting that for each point covered by the tortoise there is a corresponding point, at the corresponding point in time, covered by Achilles; such correspondence, according to the new theory, makes the set of points covered by Achilles as great as the set covered by the tortoise, so that there is no remainder represented by the tortoise's head start that allegedly cannot be made up by Achilles. Mathematically, the temporal termini of the tortoise's run, Achilles' run, and the race are identical; on James's reading of Russell, Zeno's paradox thus evaporates. James responded that if the mystery vanishes as soon as we understand that enumeration is not a part of the definition of whole and part, then Russell contradicted himself. "Whoso actually *traverses* a continuum, can do so by no process continuous in the mathematical sense. . . . Each point must be occupied in its due order of succession; and if the points are necessarily infinite, their end cannot be reached, for the 'remainder,' in [a growing] process, is just what one cannot 'neglect.' 'Enumeration' is, in short, the sole possible method of occupation of the series of positions implied in the famous race."[43]

Accordingly, James argued, when the process is one of growth, change, or motion, and the series in question is infinite, a "successive synthesis" cannot be accomplished.

> Either we must stomach logical contradiction, therefore, in these cases; or we must admit that the limit is reached in these successive cases by finite and perceptible units of approach—drops, buds, steps, or whatever we please to term them, of change, coming wholly when they do come, or coming not at all. Such seems to be the nature of concrete experience, which changes always by sensible amounts, or stays unchanged. The infinite character we find in it is woven into it by our later conception indefinitely repeating the act of subdividing any given amount supposed. The facts do not resist the subsequent conceptual treatment; but we need not believe that the treatment necessarily reproduces the operation by which they were originally brought into existence.

The antinomy of mathematically continuous growth is thus but one more of those many ways in which our conceptual transformation of perceptual experience makes it less comprehensible than ever. That being should immediately and by finite quantities add itself to being, may indeed be something which an onlooking intellect fails to understand; but that being should be identified with the consummation of an endless chain of units (such as "points"), no one of which contains any amount whatever of the being (such as "space") expected to result, this is something which our intellect not only fails to understand, but which it finds absurd. The substitution of "arithmetization" for intuition thus seems, if taken as a description of reality, to be only a partial success. Better accept, as Renouvier says, the opaquely given data of perception, than concepts inwardly absurd.[44]

What should we think of James's view here? Is it consistent with his insistence elsewhere that reality is continuous? It is difficult to assess the theory confidently because disputants of Zeno's paradoxes are often perplexed about whether they have understood his exact intent. James asserted that some processes of change are perceived to occur with abrupt alterations, sudden incremental additions or diminutions; calling the increments *drops, buds,* or *steps* conveys this idea. For other events these terms seem inappropriate; if we watch the smooth, continuous unfolding of a flower petal through time-lapse photography, no finite steps or pulsations in the process are necessarily observed. On the basis of perceptual experience alone, we cannot conclude, as James (and Whitehead) did, that reality comes only in chunks and drops or, as James declared in other places, only as an unbroken stream; the perceived environment seems plainly to display both sorts of processes. If the issue were whether mathematical concepts of infinity and continuity can be assimilated into theories of atomic physics, then we might decide for technical reasons whether things are really continuous, but that was not the issue James entertained. James argued that an infinite set cannot be run through in a finite time. He could not have perceived that everything changes in terms of finite phases or distinguishable increments, but he felt bound to assume that it does because it seemed to him intuitively contradictory that a change taking a finite length of time can run through an infinite series. It was just this sort of intuition that Cantor and Russell challenged, but James, rather than refuting their arguments, seems only to have reiterated his intuition.[45]

Equally troubling is James's idea that, whereas the new concepts of the number continuum and infinity do not apply to a process that is occurring, their retrospective application is workable. If a process is infinitely divisible in retrospect, it seems likely that it had the same feature while occurring. James thought that infinite divisibility does not imply that something is infinitely divided, but if a line that is already drawn is infinitely divisible into points, then while it was being drawn it must have covered an infinite number of points. This idea seems to have violated James's intuition, at least if points are construed as finite magnitudes, for it is contradictory to think that an infinite number of finite intervals can be covered in a finite length of time. However, Cantor and Russell did not construe points as finite. That the new infinite might be relevant to discussions of actual processes is compatible with James's commonsense conviction that whatever continuity characterizes mind-body processes cannot consist of an infinite series of finite magnitudes. James's polemic was designed to show the inadequacy of concepts in general, including the mathematical concept of continuity.

In answering (3) we must ask whether James contradicted his own conception of the continuity of the stream of consciousness by advancing the doctrine that reality comes in drops and steps. Perry asserted that had James lived to finish what he had set for himself in *Some Problems of Philosophy,* "he would not have left his 'abrupt increments of novelty' unrelieved."[46] James's discussions of the continuity of experience, from "On Some Omissions of Introspective Psychology" (1884) to *Some Problems of Philosophy* and *A Pluralistic Universe,* give us a good idea of how he would have reconciled this idea with what he claimed about discontinuity. We do not experience temporal passage simply from instant to instant but rather as a duration within which we can notice temporal succession (see chapter 5). These ephemeral specious presents are the basic units of our experience and can be thought of as phases or pulses that retain at least a momentary identity before being changed by the experiential flux of which they are a part. Continuity results if these minimal pulses of reality are considered the finite components of growing processes like motion and change, the finite drops, buds, or steps he mandated in his response to Zeno, Cantor, and Russell. If these specious presents are abrupt increments or interruptions in an otherwise unbroken flow, and therefore represent a kind of *discontinuity,* then James's pronouncements about the continuity of experience and reality are valid. "Novelty, as empirically found, doesn't arrive by jumps and jolts, it leaks in insensibly, for adjacents in experience are always interfused, the smallest real datum being both a coming and a going, and even numerical distinctness being realized effectively only after a concrete interval has passed."[47]

The continuity between one specious present and the next is felt even though it may be difficult to define. "No one elementary bit of reality is eclipsed from the next bit's point of view, if only we take reality sensibly and in small enough pulses. . . . Sensational experiences *are* their 'own others,' then, both internally and externally. Inwardly they are one with their parts, and outwardly they pass continuously into their next neighbors. . . . Their *names* . . . cut them into separate conceptual identities, but no cuts existed in the continuum in which they originally came."[48] If we dive back into the flux, as Bergson urges, we will find that "all *felt* times coexist and overlap or compenetrate each other thus vaguely, but the artifice of plotting them on a common scale helps us to reduce their aboriginal confusion. . . . Hasn't every bit of experience its quality, its duration, its intensity, its urgency, its clearness, and many aspects besides, no one of which can exist in the isolation in which our verbalized logic keeps it? They exist only *durcheinander.* Reality always is, in M. Bergson's phrase, an endosmosis or conflux of the same with the different: They compenetrate and telescope."[49] Even in *Some Problems of Philosophy,* where James advocated the discontinuity hypothesis, he wrote: "Rather does a whole subsequent field [specious present] grow *continuously* out of a whole antecedent field" (218, italics mine.

The picture of reality I attribute to James combines unbroken flow with comparatively abrupt changes—the pulses of specious presents, the experience of changing our focus of attention or of undergoing or noticing change. We can become aware that unbroken flow may occur within those specious presents as well as between them. In both his psychology and his radical empiricism he assumed that relations are responsible for the continuity flow. In *Principles* he had written: "There is not a conjunction or a preposition, and hardly an adverbial phrase, syntactic form, or inflection of voice, in human speech, that does not express some shading or other of relation which we at some moment actually feel to exist. . . . We ought to say a feeling of *and,* a feeling of *if,* a feeling of *but,* and a feeling of *by,* quite as readily as we say a feeling of *blue* or a feeling of *cold.*"[50] Since neo-idealism was still influential, James had to reconsider relations, which he categorized as internal or external. The idealists treated all relations as internal, so that if something changes any of its relations even only slightly, its identity necessarily changes. James stuck with common sense in holding that a change in spatial position, for example, is a change in an external relation and hence does not alter the thing's identity.[51] The relation of similarity between two things, on the other hand, is internal because their very natures enter into the relation. As long as external relations are admitted, the plurality of realities is assured, and the union of all things internally related in the one absolute of idealism is avoided. Another question, more difficult because it did not proceed from a purely abstract argument, was whether relations can separate as well as unify. Do they "stick out" as terms in the flux and thus, in an infinite regress, themselves demand to be related?

James recognized the problem, but his typical response was this:

Continuity can't mean mere absence of gap; for if two things are in immediate contact, at the contact how can they be two? If, on the other hand, you put a relation of transition between them, that itself is a third thing, and needs to be related or hitched to its terms. An infinite series is involved, and so on. The result is that from difficulty to difficulty, the plain conjunctive experience has been discredited by both schools, the empiricists leaving things permanently disjoined, and the rationalists remedying the looseness by their Absolutes and Substances, or whatever other fictitious agencies of union they may have employed. From all which artificiality we are saved by a couple of simple reflections: first, that conjunctions and separations are, at all events, co-ordinate phenomena which, if we take experiences at their face value, must be accounted equally real; and second, that if we insist on treating things as really separate when they are given as continuously joined, invoking, when union is required, transcendental principles to overcome the separateness we have assumed, then we ought to stand ready to perform the converse act. We ought to invoke higher principles of *dis*union, also, to make our merely experienced *dis*junctions more truly real. Failing thus, we ought to let the originally given continuities stand on their own bottom. We have no right to be lopsided or to blow capriciously hot and cold.[52]

If relations are immediate perceptual data, then they are distinct entities that need to be related as much as do blue and cold.[53] This consideration is not simply abstract or speculative; if we can literally see (hear, feel, touch) relations, as James claimed, then we must also be able to see those relations in relation to other things— making it impossible to avoid an infinite regress and to insure that relations supply continuity. If relations "stick out," they have an environment to which they are perceptually related. While James acknowledged that other philosophers discerned a problem here, his answer was simply to assert that the experiential facts resolve any philosophical perplexity. But it is those alleged experiential facts that puzzle us when we try to image our experiences as being cluttered with feelings of *and, but,* or *by,* which stick out for special attention yet are supposedly responsible for the flow and continuity of experience. James was not introspectively describing a merely subjective sense of *and* or *but,* as if they were sensed; when the stream of consciousness is equated with pure experience-as-reality, he argued, these relations are literally felt or perceived.

James believed that introspection uncovers more detail and richness of content than philosophers and psychologists had appreciated; he apparently also assumed that if key details are themselves relations, then the unity and continuity (absent in the ideas and impressions of the British sensationists) of an experience and of its perceptual object will be assured. However, those relations that stick out must also be related before continuity or unity can be secured. Generalizing from what I suggested in discussing James's theory of time, I think that relations are not perceptible items. Whenever we apprehend two things, we apprehend them in some relation to each other; we may wish to call that relation a kind of unity, but we should not conclude, as James did, that we are aware of such unity by perceiving the relation as a discrete item. If the British sensationists or the transcendentalists denied that things are given in their relations to each other, then James was right in opposing them, but not in suggesting that relations are given as discrete. Suppose, like James, we want to describe the continuity between one experience and the next, emphasizing that continuity is more than a gap; how do we describe the relation of continuity? We may find ourselves making negative characterizations: continuity is not a mere gap, is not intermittent, is not merely change. Attempting a positive account, we might say, as James did, that it is a flow, a coalescence, a compenetration, or an overlap and confluence of successive experiences. We may be tempted to think that *flow, coalescence,* and *overlap* are relational terms comparable to *red* and *cold,* meaningful only to one who has already experienced the relation; if these words did not designate noticeable items, what would warrant our confidence in using them to describe our experiences?

The answer, I believe, is that experience A can overlap experience B not because *overlap* describes a perceptible experiential item, but because we notice A and then B such that before A definitely terminates, we find that B has already begun. Relational terms are useful precisely because they do not designate experientially discriminable items; if they did, they would distract our attention from what they relate—and in so doing, from themselves. Paradoxically, if overlapping were like redness or loudness, we would fail to notice, in focusing on it, the experiences it relates. But without noticing those experiences, we cannot notice that one experience overlaps another. James's own examples of feelings of transition, anticipation, and tendency are cases in point, for they are not in fact relations between experiences but rather feelings in a present experience. We might think we feel related to an upcoming experience because our feeling of anticipation is exciting, but the anticipatory feeling is a property of the present experience, not something that dissolves the present experience into its successor. While I agree with James's view that successive experiences are continuous in overlapping or coalescing, I believe that that they appear so not because of relations but because we reflect upon our experiences and feel the continuity. If a discrete overlapping did appear between two events, we would have to witness its overlapping with other overlappings ad infinitum.

James held that every experience is fringed by a *more,* that every experience extends beyond what we can consciously focus upon. What is the nature of the *more?* This question suggests another, which is especially acute since James, while insisting that he was an epistemological realist, was also a Berkeleyan idealist in his analysis of physicality: What is the nature of the realities that exist beyond any experience? He was not prepared to follow Berkeley in preserving their existence through a godly percipient, nor was he satisfied to call them permanent possibilities of perception, as Mill did. If these external realities are part of the *more* (which is continuous with any conscious experience), they would appear to be Berkeleyan complexes of sensations. If so, panpsychism or the doctrine that the universe is psychical throughout, which his friend and fellow-philosopher C. A. Strong urged upon him repeatedly, would be an appropriate position. But though James was attracted to Strong's view, as their correspondence reveals, he did not accept it for fear of officially declaring that reality was mental or psychical. There were enough other problems with panpsychism to keep him from espousing it fully and decisively. At the conclusion of *Some Problems of Philosophy* he hinted that it might be his alternative, but he went no further.[54] On my reading of his metaphysics, panpsychism was the logical position to adopt (see chapter 12).

A Pluralistic Universe is filled with praise for Bergson and his view that the flow of reality is distorted in the attempt to conceptualize it. Connected with this idea is the emphatic abandonment (announced in 1895 in "The Knowing of Things Together") of the all-important doctrine in *Principles* that states of consciousness cannot be compounded. James now connected the belief in an ineffably continuous reality with the need to allow states of consciousness to compound themselves, though he believed that no coherent conceptual account of the compounding can be provided. Before proceeding with question (4), we need to review briefly the doctrine in *Principles.*

Although James had espoused mind-body dualism in *Principles* largely for strategic purposes, to keep his metaphysical doubts about dualism from occupying a book that was intended as a pioneering presentation of psychology as a natural science, dualism had its attractions. The *esse est sentiri* doctrine of mental states, the idea that the quality of such states is given to the awareness of their experiencers as it cannot be to anyone else, appealed to him. James referred to the attempt to replace the experiencer's description of his own mental state by an allegedly superior description as the psychologist's fallacy.[55] This fallacy occurs whenever an analysis of a mental state is proposed, as would occur if we sought to equate the perception of yellow with the joined perceptions of green and red, when in fact the perception of yellow is unique and indivisible. According to the argument in *Principles*, mental states, unlike physical objects and processes, do not have parts and are not divisible. The identity of a mental state is given in what it displays to our awareness; this identity can be a complex combination of characteristics, but the perceptual mental state is such a momentary unity that its characteristics are not parts, nor are they analyzable into more basic elements.

James assumed that no collection of things, whether mental or physical, can create its own unity. If unity is conceived as a set of emergent properties, then no collection of things can become a unity; it must remain a mere collection.

> In other words, no possible number of entities (call them as you like, whether forces, material particles, or mental elements) can sum *themselves* together. Each remains, in the sum, what it always was; and the sum itself exists only for a *bystander* who happens to overlook the units and to apprehend the sum as such; or else it exists in the shape of some other *effect* on an entity external to the sum itself. Let it not be objected that H_2 and O combine of themselves into "water," and thenceforward exhibit new properties. They do not. The "water" is just the old atoms in the new position, H-O-H; the "new properties" are just their combined *effects*, when in this position, upon external media, such as our sense-organs. (*Principles*, 1:158–59)

A unity or set of emergent properties is thus always a property of an effect produced in something else by the combined action of the parts of the collection; *synthetic unity*, *collective being*, and *systematic totally* always refer to the nature of an effect caused by a collection of things. If we accept this idea, as James did, then states of consciousness can not compound or organize themselves into complexes. A mental state has unity because it is an effect of a brain-state or something else. There are two main reasons behind James's doctrine in *Principles* that one state of consciousness cannot be a part of another: first, if they could, the *esse est sentiri* doctrine would be false, as would the theory that states of consciousness do not have parts, not even mental ones; second, each mental state can be explained as an effect, produced by the brain, which is responsible for the unity of the mental state. When James considered abolishing dualism, and with it the opportunity of treating mental states as the effects of physical ones, he had to find a new explanation for the unity of mental states. How can mere collections of mental states—collections of pure experiences, in the metaphysics of radical empiricism and a pluralistic universe—create the needed unity?

The force of this question led James to withdraw his opposition to the self-compounding of consciousness and the inclusion of one mental state within another; in effect he withdrew his objections in *Principles* to the mind-stuff theory and associationistic explanations of psychic processes. If the continuity of inner experience defines reality, as the pure experience hypothesis contends, then "all real units of experience *overlap*."[56] If each unit is a state of consciousness, then such states must overlap, which is to admit that part of one can be part of another. The continuity in James's universe features simultaneous as well as successive realities: "What is true here of successive states must also be true of simultaneous characters. They also overlap each other with their being. My present field of consciousness is a centre surrounded by a fringe that shades insensibly into a subconscious more."[57] The inclusion of one mental state within another in a successive series insures continuity in an individual's life, and the overlapping of simultaneous mental states guarantees continuity between the inner lives of different individuals; "privacy" of experience is not ultimately necessary. Since the Jamesian universe appears to contain only experiences—there is nothing comparable to the brain events that produce experiences as effects with the unity of emergent properties of states of consciousness—we need not require that experiences be effects. We can picture a world in which mental states can compound indefinitely; it is a world in which there is a continuity of selves, possibly constituting a continuum or hierarchy of personal states of consciousness.

James was attracted to the thoughts of G. T. Fechner, coauthor of the Weber-Fechner law that in a series of sensations the stimulus must increase geometrically if the increase is to be sensed. Indeed, a substantial part of *A Pluralistic Universe* is devoted to Fechner. James agreed with him that if some states of consciousness are more inclusive than others, they may exist in a hierarchy. In the dualistic world of everyday experience, consciousness may be attached in varying degrees to single cells, small organisms, plants, animals, and superhuman entities, in ways vaguely comparable to its attachment to the human brain. The recent speculations of Hannes Alven somewhat resemble the James-Fechner vision; Alven hypothesizes that the universe, like living organisms, has a cellular structure, and that the cosmos may be made of walls of electrical currents that divide space into cells similar to those in plants and animals; these cell walls in space may be what separate matter from antimatter. These cells might suffer leaks, resulting in a mixing of matter and antimatter and producing huge explosions that might explain such phenomena as quasars.[58] Whatever the merits of this hypothesis, it would surely have appealed to Fechner and James, who urged an analogy between humans and the rest of the universe; they would have enjoyed imagining what it would be like if each cosmic cell or group of cells had bits of consciousness.[59]

Coming to the decision that states of mind can compound was extraordinarily difficult for James; while he had announced his decision in 1895 in "The Knowing of Things Together," it was not until *A Pluralistic Universe* that he dramatized that decision by discussing its major costs and benefits. Had he emphasized the decision in the essays on radical empiricism, much of his public and private agonizing over making pure experience plausible might have been unnecessary. As he confessed, the years prior to *A Pluralistic Universe* were filled with self-doubts that endlessly compounded.

> Sincerely, and patiently as I could, I struggled with the problem for years, covering hundreds of sheets of paper with notes and memoranda and discussions with myself over the difficulty. How can many consciousnesses be at the same time one consciousness? How can one and the same identical fact experience itself so diversely? The struggle was vain. . . . I saw that I must either forswear that "psychology without a soul" to which my whole psychological and Kantian education had committed me,—I must, in short, bring back distinct spiritual agents to know the mental states, now singly and now in combination, in a word bring back scholasticism and common sense—or else I must squarely confess the solution of the problem impossible, and then either give up my intellectualistic logic, the logic of identity, and adopt some higher (or lower) form of rationality, or, finally, face the fact that life is logically irrational.[60]

The benefits of allowing states of consciousness to compound were metaphysical continuity and discernible possibilities describable as personal, ethical, and religious. The costs were the renunciation of the *esse est sentiri* doctrine and of the logic of identity, an idea which requires some interpretation. How, for example, should we understand this:

> Let us leave out the soul, then, and confront what I have just called the residual dilemma. Can we, on the one hand, give up the logic of identity?—can we, on the other, believe human experience to be fundamentally irrational? Neither is easy, yet it would seem that we must do one or the other. . . .
>
> For my own part, I have finally found myself compelled to *give up the logic*. . . . It has an imperishable use in human life, but that use is not to make us theoretically acquainted with the essential nature of reality. . . . Reality, life, experience, concreteness, immediacy, use what word you will, exceeds our logic, overflows and surrounds it. . . . I prefer to call reality if not irrational then at least non-rational in its constitution,—and by reality here I mean reality where things *happen*, all temporal reality without exceptions.[61]

James credited Bergson with showing him that abandoning the logic of identity was the only alternative, but he had already formulated his own scheme of an experiential flux that defies adequate conceptualization; it was not that Bergson convinced him but rather that he appreciated a colleague who was willing to endorse similar but unpopular contentions, and he was delighted to share responsibility for those contentions.[62] He cited Bergson as the decisive influence in demonstrating both the incongruity between intuition and intellectual logic and the advantage of repudiating the logic of identity in favor of intuition. The concept of identity had always intrigued him, both in connection with the notion of sameness in *Principles* and even earlier in its relevance for the ideas of explanation and rationality. He once wrote: "The insight that two coupled phenomena are at bottom one and the same phenomenon gives an explanation of the coupling that is rational in the ideal and ultimate sense of the word."[63] If both scientific and ordinary criteria for determining identity are scrapped, as was implied by the official renunciation of the logic of identity, then reality must be irrational.

Two of James's favorite ideas threatened to run afoul of some philosophers' theories about identity. First, because of the Heraclitean flux of experience, James believed that any momentary state is so fluid that it is as much past and future as it is present; when everything is reduced to a phase of the flux of pure experience, as in the Jamesian pluralistic universe, then things have a very slippery identity indeed. Sounding somewhat like Hegel, he remarked in *A Pluralistic Universe:* "It is that there is a sense in which real things are not merely their own selves, but they may vaguely be treated as also their own others, and that ordinary logic, since it denies this, must be overcome."[64] The second favorite idea was that no matter how small a momentary experience, it is a manyness-in-oneness, a collection of many heterogeneous things that simultaneously form a unity.

> We see that our old objection to the self-compounding of states of consciousness, our accusation that it was impossible for purely logical reasons, is unfounded in principle. Every smallest state of consciousness, concretely taken, overcomes its own definition. Only concepts are self-identical. . . . Nature is but a name for excess. . . . In the pulse of inner life immediately present now in each of us is a little past, a little future, a little awareness of our own body, of each other's persons, of these sublimities we are trying to talk about, of the earth's geography and the direction of history, of truth and error, of good and bad, and of who knows how much more? Feeling, however dimly and subconsciously, all these things, your pulse of inner life is continuous with them, belongs to them and they to it. You can't identify it with either one of them rather than with the others, for if you let it develop into no matter which of those directions, what it develops into will look back on it and say, "That was the original germ of me."[65]

James seems to have overstated the difficulty here; to allow states of consciousness to compound, he need not have concluded that logic and rationality were lost. Perry, trying to free James from an unnecessary commitment to irrationality, commented: "The outcome of James's thought is not so much to reject logic as to define its limits. What is needed to solve the problem of 'compounding' is to be able to say of a certain conscious state that it both is and is not the same as another: that, for example, your experience is the same as mine objectively, but not subjectively" (RBP, 2:590). This defense applies to some of James's formulations, but James did not find a solution in saying that two conscious states can be the same in one sense but different in another. It was impossible to follow Perry's recipe for dissolving the dilemma, because the pure experience concept did not permit clear distinction between the objective and subjective dimensions of a conscious state. Besides, it seemed apparent to James that the identity of a mental state consists not in the multiplicity of its contents or aspects but in its indivisible unity or in the unanalyzable awareness that distinguishes mental states.

Assuming that all mental states are indivisible and unrepeatable units whose identity is determined by those features rather than by their contents (which can be repeated indefinitely), then for one mental state to include another, for one indivisible unit to include another, would obviously be self-contradictory. A unit cannot be indivisible and at the same time include another unit, nor can it owe its identity simultaneously to being indivisible and to being part of a larger unit. These contradictions resulted from the admission that mental states can include each other, and James believed that nothing remained but to surrender any further attempts to talk coherently about the identity of the mental states that constitute the flow of pure experience. To abandon the original idea that mental states are units would have denied James the means of identifying any mental state. Without their nature as units, James thought, mental states are virtually indistinguishable, and we have lost the logic of identity. If we describe what we intuit or feel, we say not that two or more mental states may share something identical, but that they themselves may be identical. That formulation is clearly contradictory, however, for if they are identical they cannot be two. Yet, James held, that is what we want to assert but are prevented from asserting by logic. The only recourse is to return, with Bergson, to an intuitive acquaintance with the flow of reality and to stop attempting coherent reports of its details.[66]

James was not distressed by this result, even though he had striven for many years to avoid it and to cast the pure experience hypothesis into as rational a mold as possible. Even if he had preserved this rationality, he might have retained his conviction that what is intuitive defies adequate conceptualization—he believed, for instance, that the flow of experience cannot be captured in words—because this conviction does not require an irrational metaphysics. But his public renunciation of the logic of identity seems to have been accompanied by a feeling of liberation or exhilaration, as if a dramatic discovery had been made; not only are concepts no match for intuitions, but intuitions can defy the law of thought that a thing is what it is and not something else. James was by temperament a metaphysician, and if this response sounds odd in view of his antipathy for the abstract, we must remember that he couched his metaphysics in energetic, vibrant, and concrete expressions. His affinity for metaphysics is evident in the first version of "The Sentiment of Rationality" which both expounds human motives for philosophizing and touches on the concepts of being and nonbeing. The idea that seems to have revolted him most is that there will be a time when all mystery ends and perfect vision ensues.

> Whether for good or evil it is an empirical fact that the mind is so wedded to the process of seeing an *other* beside every item of its experience, that when the notion of an absolute datum which is all is presented to it, it goes through its usual procedure and remains *pointing* at the void beyond, as if in that lay further matter for contemplation. In short, it spins for itself the further positive consid-

eration of a Nonentity beyond the Being of its datum. . . . But there is no logical identity, no natural bridge between nonentity and this particular datum, and the thought stands oscillating to and fro, wondering "Why was there anything but nonentity? Why just this universal datum and not another? Why anything at all?" and finds no end, in wandering mazes left. . . . As Schopenhauer says, "The uneasiness which keeps the never-resting clock of metaphysics in motion, is the consciousness that the non-existence of this world is just as possible as its existence."

The notion of Nonentity may thus be called the parent of the philosophic craving in its subtlest and profoundest sense. Absolute existence is absolute mystery. . . . Nought remains but to confess that when all has been unified to its supreme degree . . . the notions of a Nonentity, or of a possible Other than the actual, may still haunt our imagination and prey upon the ultimate data of our system. The bottom of Being is left logically opaque to us, a *datum* in the strict sense of the word. . . . In this confession lies the lasting truth of Empiricism, and in it Empiricism and imaginative Faith join hands. The logical attitude of both is identical, they both say there is a *plus ultra* beyond all we know. . . . The mere ontologic emotion of wonder, of mystery, has in some minds such a tinge of the rapture of sublimity, that for this aesthetic reason alone, it will be difficult for any philosophic system completely to exorcise it. (*CER*, 127–28)

Years later, this discussion was echoed in *Some Problems of Philosophy*: "The question of being is the darkest in all philosophy. . . . Fact forms a datum, gift, or *Vorgefundenes*, which we cannot burrow under, explain or get behind. It makes itself somehow, and our business is far more with its *What* than with its Whence or Why" (46). To realize that there is something so inscrutable about the being of pure experience that a mystery which unsettles even the law of identity is permanently enshrined must have been an exciting moment for James. The difficulties of the theses in *Essays in Radical Empiricism* and *A Pluralistic Universe* raised anew various questions about the concept of *being*. Do successive experiences in the flux of pure experience have any being in common, so that more than mere succession or next-ness is present? Since existence is not a substantive quality, not something that sticks out and not an impression (as Hume had noted), how is the shared existence of overlapping experiences recognized?[67]

In pondering the question, which he never definitively answered, of how to interpret on radical empiricistic principles what lies beyond any present experience, James reflected about being in his notes, wondering if an outlying "cosmic omnibus of being" can be conceived as the "open possibility" of further experiences, which would fit strict pragmatism.

One *must* admit a cosmic omnibus of "being" for each "experience" in which what is true *of* it is realized, while *it* realizes only what it is immediately "of." (The question whether this being may not in the end consist wholly of other experiences may be left at present undiscussed; though it seems as if it might very well be so, provided one could admit that these others might be retro-spective, and all the facts true "about" an experience might only be "virtually" there before the retrospective experience came in.) This idea, worked along with my philosophy of possibility . . . may clear the way for a better discussion than with their lamentable groping the previous pages have shown.[68]

If he did not remain with Mill's permanent possibility of sensation, the realm of outlying being might have to be Strong's panpsychism; in another set of notes, he recorded: "The real existents are psychic facts which form a system of which we individuals only realize patches, the rest being conceptual filling in for those indi-viduals . . . but actual experiences for other real experients. . . . All this doesn't take me very far into the mystery!"[69]

The mystery of being was connected with another mystery, about the concepts of causality and activity. In *Principles* he said that causality is an enigma: "We have no definite idea of what we mean by cause, or of what causality consists in. But the principle expresses a demand for *some* deeper sort of inward connection between phenomena than their merely habitual time-sequence seems to us to be" (2:671). If at the commonsense level the philosophical problem of causality (a problem es-pecially acute since Hume and Kant) is admittedly enigmatic, it seems even more so in the metaphysics of pure experience, with its rejection of agents and forces in favor of pulses, phases, or fields of experiential flow as causes and effects. These pulses hardly seem capable of explaining causality.[70]

James tried both to improve upon Hume's concept of causation as constant conjunction, believing that a more intimate connection obtains between cause and effect, and to show that causality and activity are manageable by the pure experience hypothesis. We must first reject the old principle that the cause in some way already contains its effect, he said, because that idea implies that no effect can be genuinely novel, and if nothing new can be generated, then we are stuck with a static reality that can only be interpreted monistically, excluding the possibility of a plural uni-verse.[71] The solution is a return to the feel of immediate experience.

> If there *be* real activities in being, radical empiricism must say, somewhere they must be immediately lived. Somewhere the *that* of efficacious causing and the *what* of it must be experienced in one, just as the what and the that of "cold" are experienced in one. . . . It boots not to say that our sensations are fallible. They are indeed; but to see the thermometer contradict us when we say "it is cold" does not abolish cold. . . . To feel that our train is moving when the train beside our window moves . . . leaves motion, nearness, and solidity still in being. . . . And wherever the seat of real causality *is*, as ultimately known "for true" . . . a philosophy of pure experience can consider the real causation as no other *nature* of thing than that which even in our most erroneous experiences appears to be at work. Exactly what appears there is what we *mean* by working, though we may later come to learn that working was not exactly *there*. Sustaining, per-severing, striving, paying with effort as we go, hanging on, and finally achieving

our intention—this *is* action, this *is* effectuation in the only shape in which, by a pure experience-philosophy, the whereabouts of it anywhere can be discussed. Here is creation in its first intention, here is causality at work.[72]

Certain caveats must accompany this statement; there must be no implication of metaphysical forces, substances, or agents, or of causality as a perceptible link between cause and effect. "Rather does a whole subsequent field [of experience] grow continuously out of a whole antecedent field because it seems to yield new being of the nature called for, while the feeling of causality-at-work flavors the entire concrete sequence as salt flavors the water in which it is dissolved."[73] We *feel* what causality is in experiences such as striving or trying to overcome resistance, but what we *perceive* is the growth of a novel field of experience from a previous one; growth or emergence of one pure experience from another is thus the criterion for causality or activity. As "The Sentiment of Rationality" pointed out, however, not everything can be explained thus; the vision is not quite perfect yet. We may ask: "How is this feat performed? How does the pulling *pull?* How do I get my hold on words not yet existent, and when they come by what means have I *made* them come?"[74] James suggested that these questions are answered as well as possible simply by redescribing the experiences of activity, which reveal what causality and activity are like. In another sense, however, such queries remain unanswered: we must analyze the *how* of a causal transaction. In feeling ourselves perform an activity, we are not thereby enabled to describe how we do it. "Really it is the problem of creation; for in the end the question is: How do I make them *be?* Real activities are those that really make things be, without which the things are not, and with which they are there."[75] The problem of causality, in this form, is the question of *being.* When we cause something to happen, something *is* that before was not; causality is a movement to being from nonbeing, a movement whose inner nature remains permanently mysterious. The pure experience hypothesis can explain the fact and experience of causality and activity, but no philosophy can make a logical bridge between nonbeing and being.

According to what I call the subjective pragmatism of James, adopting a metaphysics of reality was an expression of preference for one kind of picture over others. If, after the theoretic and imaginative work has been responsibly executed, a particular picture satisfies our temperamental requirements better than others do, then it is rational for us to have faith in it. Despite the seemingly insurmountable problems confronting the philosophy of radical empiricism and a pluralistic universe, James continued to have faith in it; his intellectual labor had been responsibly carried out, and that philosophy afforded him more satisfaction than did its rivals. But why did a subjective pragmatist think his own preferences superior to others?

> How can I . . . justify the strong antithesis I constantly feel, namely, that certain philosophic constructions . . . are subjective caprices, redolent of individual taste, while other constructions, those which work with concrete elements, with change, with indeterminism, are more objective and cling closer to the temperament of nature itself. . . . What, on pragmatist terms, does "nature

itself" signify? To my mind it signifies the non-artificial; the artificial having certain definite aesthetic characteristics which I dislike, and can only apperceive in others as matters of personal taste,—to me bad taste. All neat schematisms with permanent and absolute distinctions, classifications with absolute pretensions, systems with pigeon-holes, etc., have this character. All "classic," clean, cut and dried, "noble," "fixed," "eternal" *Weltanschauungen* seem to me to violate the character with which life concretely comes and the expression which it bears of being, or at least of involving, a muddle and a struggle, with an "ever not quite" to all our formulas, and novelty and possibility forever leaking in. . . . It is obvious that such a difference as this, between me and Münsterberg, is a splendid expression of pragmatism. I want a world of anarchy, Münsterberg one of bureaucracy, and each appeals to "nature" to back him up. Nature partly helps and partly resists each of us.[76]

Each of us is on his own, having to discover the most plausible metaphysical picture that makes life worth living. To appreciate the satisfaction that James derived from his picture, we must consider his perception of the philosophical climate of his time. He saw a spirit of intellectualism as the major resistance to his own brand of thinking. Intellectualism, for him, was a belief that philosophizing has little practical bearing upon everyday living, begins and ends in abstract premises and conclusions in formal arguments, and has as its goal the establishment of propositions which are necessarily true or false. F. H. Bradley personified the intellectualist position; although he agreed with much of what James claimed about feeling, he thought that feeling has no real place in philosophy and discourse must proceed from a dialectical force. Whenever James asserted one of his favorite ideas, he found himself tripping over a dialectical argument of Bradley's (or Royce's), and while he sometimes attempted a dialectical rebuttal, to do so struck him as a tedious game calculated to preserve a view of philosophy that he meant to replace. When he adopted his own combination of pragmatism and radical empiricism, it was almost always on the premise that it was an embarrassment to intellectualism.

Among the putative advantages of pragmatism was humanism or the thesis that the real and the experienceable coincide. "*Pragmatic method* asserts that what a concept *means* is its consequences. Humanism says that when these are satisfactory, the concept is *true*."[77] Further, a metaphysics that emphasizes change, novelty, and indeterminism also highlights the fact that we can help to ameliorate the problems in our universe and that, as plural powers, we can each make a difference in promoting good and retarding evil.[78] In this connection, the pluralistic universe of pure experience is more consistent with the form of theism that posits a finite God who is not all-inclusive and thus is not responsible for the presence of evil, who is a member of the plurality and needs our strenuous assistance in making a better world.[79] Because James's metaphysics welcomes uncertainty, stresses probabilities rather than necessities, and waves mysteries in the face of those seeking certainties, it demands a role for faith and the justification of belief in the absence of compelling intellectual and theoretical reasons.[80] James was never more eloquent than when listing the assets of his metaphysical package.

James wrote:

> Experience in its immediacy seems perfectly fluent. The active sense of living which we all enjoy, before reflection shatters our instinctive world for us, is self-luminous and suggests no paradoxes. Its difficulties are disappointments and uncertainties. They are not intellectual contradictions.
>
> When the reflective intellect gets at work, however, it discovers in-comprehensibilities in the flowing process. Distinguishing its elements and parts, it gives them separate names, and what it thus disputes it can not easily put together. Pyrrhonism accepts the irrationality and revels in its dialectic elaboration. *Other philosophies try . . . to restore the fluent sense of life again,* and let redemption take the place of innocence.[81]

As many thinkers have testified, the value of philosophizing is as much in the process as in the product. It is an activity among activities, and like the others it can go well or badly. When it goes very well, it is as if thinking and living have merged into a single, harmonious, and vibrant process, as if thinking has found its goal in a newfound health of experiencing. James thought that a prolonged or chronic arrest or hesitation in thinking and living occurs at the onset of sickness or death; it is philosophy's mission to remove the blockage, to restore the fluency that is life itself. Composing his thoughts into linguistic pictures that imitate life's sensory flow was to seek the truth that paintings are said to have. It was also the only route to rationality, for "when subjectively considered rationality can only be defined as perfectly unim-peded mental function."[82] By making his own mental pictures reflect the unim-peded flow of pure experience, James felt a restoration, through thought itself, of a healthful fluency of thought that is the mark of rationality.

12 ❧ SELF

SELF-ACQUAINTANCE

If a topic interested James, he discussed it in essay upon essay; many of the chapters in *Principles*, for instance, are elaborations of earlier articles or are elaborated in later ones. But the concept of self, while a profound concern of his, is treated almost exclusively in "The Consciousness of Self."[1] The concept is implicit in his discussions of mind and body, consciousness, psychical research, and abnormal psychology, but we expect further studies of issues about the self. He may have judged that his ideas about the self beyond the context of the psychology of self-consciousness or of the mind-body relation were sufficiently personal to be confined to soliloquies and personal correspondence.[2] More important, he seems to have concluded that a philosophical account of the self gives way to a mystical one and that useful words on the subject are rapidly exhausted. In any event, he wrote prolifically about matters directly relevant to the concept of self, and we thus have adequate sources for reconstructing his own view of it.

While in Dresden in 1868, at the age of twenty-six, James read an article on children's mental development and commented on it in his diary.

> Use of "I" by child comes not fm. absence of concept but from his imitating literally what he hears others say. [The author's] child e.g. used to speak of himself with "*du*" as well as with "Arnold" and spoke of & to his Father with I. Quotes from Lazarus "das Kind wendet auch 'er' u. 'wir' nicht viel früher an als 'ich'." (The great discovery may be in the child that of other persons' possession of an I, similar to that wh. it itself has for a long time known. It is true that the child personifies everything. . . . At least I can remember, dimly, tho' strange to say the *scene* is forgotten, pondering and dwelling when a child on the thought that other people had just the same feelings in *all* respects as I, and were in fact each "cosmocentric," with a wonder that can only be explained by supposing it a new discovery).[3]

Almost twenty years later, in 1886, James discussed the philosophical significance of the first-person pronoun in "The Consciousness of Self"; when it appeared as chapter 10 of *Principles* in 1890, he wrote to his brother, Henry: "Most of [*Principles*] is quite unreadable, but you may find some pages in the second volume that will go. Also the earlier pages of the chapter on 'Consciousness of Self.' "[4] Those pages introduce the idea of self as combining the material self (one's body), the social self (one's reception by others), and—perhaps most important—the spiritual self (one's inner or subjective being). He claimed that our innermost or spiritual selves are introspectively found to coincide with our capacities to think, to observe, to be morally sensitive, and to exert willpower. In reflecting upon ourselves we also tend to become philosophical dualists, contrasting thought with physical things and identifying ourselves as mental or spiritual thinkers. Although James expressed doubts about such dualism and about a purely mental ego, his focus was the psychology rather than the metaphysics of self, so he moved without further argument to an analysis of the acquaintance with the self.

Each self can be identified with an entire stream of consciousness, but the self with which we are acquainted at any given time is some limited portion of that stream, since our past and future selves are only remembered or anticipated, not objects present to a momentary awareness. Each person identifies his innermost self with this limited bit of the stream of consciousness. James wrote some of his most sensitive introspective descriptions in describing the self. For example:

[Most] would call [the self] the *active* element in all consciousness; saying that whatever qualities a man's feeling may possess, or whatever content his thought may include, there is a spiritual something in him which seems to *go out* to meet these qualities and contents, whilst they seem to *come in* to be received by it. It is what welcomes or rejects. It presides over the perception of sensations, and by giving or withholding its assent it influences the movements they tend to arouse. It is the home of interest,—not the pleasant or the painful, not even pleasure or pain, as such, but that within us to which pleasure and pain, the pleasant and the painful, speak. It is the source of effort and attention, and the place from which appear to emanate the fiats of the will. A physiologist who should reflect upon it in his own person could hardly help, I should think, connecting it more or less vaguely with the process by which ideas or incoming sensations are "reflected" or pass over into outward acts. Not necessarily that it should *be* this process or the mere feeling of this process, but that it should be in some close way *related* to this process; for it plays a part analogous to it in the psychic life, being a sort of junction at which sensory ideas terminate and from which motor ideas proceed, and forming a link between the two. Being more incessantly there than any other single element of the mental life, the other elements end by seeming to accrete round it and to belong to it. It becomes opposed to them as the permanent is opposed to the changing and inconstant. (*Principles*, 2:298)

This introspective formulation of the experience of self is suggested by the feelings characteristic of that experience. Whatever the interpretation placed upon the referent of the first-person pronoun, it is surely not a mere abstraction; insofar as there occurs an experience or acquaintance with self, it exists as something felt. But James was not content with the foregoing account and tried to improve his introspective description:

> I am aware of a constant play of furtherances and hindrances in my thinking, of checks and releases, tendencies which run with desire, and tendencies which run the other way. Among the matters I think of, some range themselves on the side of the thought's interests, whilst others play an unfriendly part thereto. The mutual inconsistencies and agreements, reinforcements and obstructions, which obtain amongst these objective matters reverberate backwards and produce what seem to be incessant reactions of my spontaneity upon them, welcoming or opposing, appropriating or disowning, striving with or against, saying yes or no. This palpitating inward life is, in me, that central nucleus which I just tried to describe in terms that all men might use. (*Principles*, 2:299)

James's official announcement of pragmatism was not made until 1898, but long before then a pragmatic philosophy guided his approach to philosophical problems. Here he was seeking the pragmatic value of the first-person pronoun, of what philosophers call the self or what one means by *oneself*. If we are tempted to call James's introspections obscure, we should try to verbalize for ourselves the experience of self-introspection; no simple literal formulation is available, and thus the effort to describe it must be creative and metaphorical. We use language primarily to report the external environment, and only incidentally for introspective descriptions; consequently, few literal locutions apply to our introspections. What we attempt in setting out to introspect the self is hardly obvious, and James's introspections may confer meaning upon the very question of what it is like to be acquainted with the self. Whatever the philosophical worth of such introspections, there is no doubting the intensity of James's search for the experiential meaning of expressions like "experience of self," "feeling of self," and "self-acquaintance."

James believed that the self's activity consists of acts of attending, assenting, negating, and making an effort. His introspection disclosed that no purely spiritual or mental property is discernible in such activities; instead, they are experienced as physical movements in the head and sense organs. James's heroic introspections here are as arresting as they are amusing. "When I try to remember or reflect, the movements in question, instead of being directed towards the periphery, seem to come from the periphery inwards and feel like a sort of *withdrawal* from the outer world. As far as I can detect, these feelings are due to an actual rolling outwards and upwards of the eyeballs, such as I believe occurs in me in sleep, and is the exact opposite of their action in fixating a physical thing" (*Principles*, 2:300). The self's acts do not appear to our inner attention as nonphysical. But what else this introspection shows is uncertain. It is not evident, he said, whether acts such as attending or assenting are identical with bodily processes or are accompanied by such processes. Introspection is fallible, so something purely mental may be overlooked, especially on the fringe of consciousness, but for James the self seemed to be a collection of movements in the head; any feeling of spiritual or mental activity is probably a feeling of bodily processes we tend not to notice.

This passage in *Principles* provoked remarks that James's psychology was materialistic, despite his protestations to the contrary. Since the stream of consciousness in his psychology appears to be a stream of bodily processes, he had to interpret those processes metaphysically to avoid materialism; in his philosophy of pure experience he in effect adopted a form of Berkeleyan idealism. As a scientific psychologist, he was disposed to undercut Cartesian dualism by arguing that everything is bodily, but as a metaphysician he later interpreted all bodily processes as pure experiences, placing materialism on the defensive.

As "The Consciousness of Self" progresses, the bodily nature of the self is emphasized, suggesting a materialistic bias. In seeking to explain the motivation behind self-love or self-regard, we may conceive those feelings as so fundamental that we ought to describe them not psychologically but metaphysically; where self-concern exists, it is tempting to believe that its cause is an unconditional respect for the statement "I am I." James understood that one can suppose that some ontological loyalty to one's own "pure principle of individuation" underlies all manifestations of self-love, that interest in the body is a deflection of a more profound interest in the fact of one's own individuality. "But what is the abstract numerical principle of identity, this 'Number One' within me, for which, according to proverbial philosophy, I am supposed to keep so constant a 'lookout'?" (*Principles*, 1:318–19). The answer cannot be that the self we regard so highly is the spiritual one; rather, if we are to develop a self to care for, we must first find something so primitively and instinctively interesting that it stimulates the original attitude of self-concern on the part of the embryonic self. What is thus found is the body. The infant's self-love begins not in awe of some pure principle of individuality, but in fondness for his corporeal person; his body is the only self he can be inspired to love. The sense of self and the concern for self begin in the awareness of one's own body; the only self with which one is initially acquainted is bodily, and James suggested that the bodily self might be the only one we ever know.

A philosophical distinction accompanies the grammatical one between *I* and *me*, and what I have discussed thus far is what James called the *empirical me*. This concept includes the body (material self), which one learns about more through observation and experiment than through introspection, and the social self, which includes the ways in which one is received by others. But philosophers and laymen alike assume that the self is more than its overtly bodily and social aspects, is something that one must introspect for oneself; James thought he had succeeded in identifying the more subtle aspect of self as the spiritual self, characterized by mental acts that appear introspectively as bodily processes. Becoming acquainted with the spiritual self is the most intimate kind of self-acquaintance and is as far as one can proceed in introspecting the referent of the first-person pronoun.

Introspections of the sort that James himself offered give meaning to the expressions we use to report those profounder experiences or awarenesses of self. Yet whatever is introspected, like whatever is perceived, is something witnessed and therefore belongs to the *me* and not to the *I*. When the self is interpreted as the immediate referent of the *I*, it is debarred from being acquainted with itself, for an object of acquaintance is witnessed and therefore belongs to the *me* but not to the introspecting or witnessing *I*. The *I* is acquainted with various things, "including and contemplating its 'me' and its 'not-me' as objects which work out their drama together, but not yet including or contemplating its own subjective being" (*Principles*, 1:304). James thought this concept in itself did not constitute a psychological mystery, but his meaning is clearer in light of his notion of personal identity.

PERSONAL IDENTITY

James wrote only a couple of essays with "Self" in the title, perhaps because he thought the topic was in the end philosophically opaque.

> Ever since Hume's time, it has been justly regarded as the most puzzling puzzle with which psychology has to deal; and whatever view one may espouse, one has to hold his position against heavy odds. If, with the Spiritualists, one contend for a substantial soul, or transcendental principle of unity, one can give no positive account of what that may be. And if, with the Humians, one deny such a principle and say that the stream of passing thoughts is all, one runs against the entire common sense of mankind, of which the belief in a distinct principle of selfhood seems an integral part. Whatever solution be adopted in the pages to come, we may as well make up our minds in advance that it will fail to satisfy the majority of those to whom it is addressed. (*Principles*, 1:330)

If these remarks hint that James considered himself among the unsatisfied majority, he was nevertheless consistent in his public pronouncements about self-identity.

The starting point for psychology is that each of us seems to be aware of himself as identical through time. Psychologists must not only decide whether we are actually aware of an objective identity through time, they must also explain why it seems that we are. James located the sense of enduring as the same self or person in the continuity and resemblance between successive experiences and the resulting warmth, familiarity, and "mineness" we customarily feel in our experiences. If this continuity and resemblance of successive experiences is interrupted, as in pathological circumstances, the sense of being an identical person is disrupted; in such situations one feels dissociated, split, or fragmented. "*Resemblance among the parts of a continuum of feelings* (especially bodily feelings) experienced along with things widely different in all other regards, *thus constitutes the real and verifiable 'personal identity' which we feel.* There is no other identity than this in the 'stream' of subjective consciousness" (*Principles*, 1:336). James saw the origins of this explanation in traditional empiricism and associationist psychology; he praised Hume and Herbart for having found the cash-value significance of terms such as *self* and *personal identity*. But he also argued that the unity in the stream of consciousness had been destroyed by the empiricistic atomization of experience.

James saw his task as the reinstatement of unity into the experience of selfhood while retaining the Humian idea that the only verifiable *I* is a momentary section of the stream of consciousness. Whenever the dichotomy between *I* and *me* is experienced, the *I* can be identified as that part of the stream which momentarily contrasts itself with everything else in making judgments such as "I see" or "I do." This transient phase of the stream, sometimes called the passing thought, "collects,— 'owns' some of the past facts which it surveys, and disowns the rest,—and so makes a unity that is actualized and anchored and does not merely float in the blue air of possibility" (*Principles*, 1:338). But two questions immediately arise: Is the unity discovered rather than fashioned by the passing act of thinking? And does such unity require a substantial identity between past and present selves? James's answer to the first question relies heavily on peculiar analogies and presents interpretive problems. I believe he meant that when the relation between our present and past selves is construed as a relation between present and past momentary sections of the transient act of thinking, then the present self or act of thinking both finds and fashions the unity that causes us to think that we are the same person throughout successive experiences.

James used *appropriation* as the name for the act by which the present self recognizes its continuity with its former selves, and what he said about appropriation seems both to find and to fashion unity. The present self appropriates what it literally finds as warm and belonging to itself, yet since it has the unifying feature of any act of thought (collecting various items into a single act of attention or consciousness), it actively contributes to the judgment in terms of which the recognition of the continuity between past and present self is expressed.[5] James thought that he had thus regained the tie between past and present self which Hume and Mill had denied. "The knowledge the present feeling has of the past ones is a real tie between them, so is their resemblance; so is their continuity; so is the one's 'appropriation' of the other; all are real ties, realized in the judging thought of every moment" (*Principles*, 1:359–60). Whether he correctly characterized his position relative to his predecessors', his point of interest was this: the source of our assumption that we are continuous selves is introspectively discoverable in introspecting the ways in which any moment of the stream relates, particularly in the act of appropriation, to prior moments.

James's answer to the second question was negative, partly because no substantial self is verifiable and partly because to postulate one explains nothing.[6] Although Locke and Kant themselves believed in some kind of soul, he credited them with helping to undermine the hope that we can know anything about it. James understood the rationale behind traditional concepts of the soul, and in particular of the belief that the simplicity and substantiality of the soul assure immortality.

The Soul, however, when closely scrutinized, guarantees no immortality of a sort *we care for*. The enjoyment of the atom-like simplicity of their substance in *saecula saeculorum* would not to most people seem a consummation devoutly to be wished. The substance must give rise to a stream of consciousness continuous with the present stream, in order to arouse our hope, but of this the mere persistence of the substance *per se* offers no guarantee. Moreover, in the general advance of our moral ideas, there has come to be something ridiculous in the way our forefathers had of grounding their hopes of immortality on the simplicity of their substance. The demand for immortality is nowadays essentially teleological. We believe ourselves immortal because we believe ourselves *fit* for immortality. A "substance" ought surely to perish, we think, if not worthy to survive, and an insubstantial "stream" to prolong itself, provided it be worthy, if the nature of Things is organized in the rational way in which we trust it is. (*Principles,* 1:348–49)

Belief in a substantial soul goes hand-in-hand with the privacy of consciousness. "One great use of the Soul has always been to account for, and at the same time to guarantee, the closed individuality of each personal consciousness. The thoughts of one's soul must unite into one self, it was supposed, and must be eternally insulated from those of every other soul" (*Principles,* 1:349). Abnormal psychology shows, however, that there is nothing like a soul in some individuals to prevent the splitting of the unity of consciousness into separate groupings; as for insulation or privacy, "it would be rash, in view of the phenomena of thought-transference, mesmeric influence and spirit-control, which are being alleged on better authority than ever before, to be too sure about that point either. The definitively closed nature of our personal consciousness is probably an average statistical resultant of many conditions, but not an elementary force or fact. . . . And why is the *being*-an-individual in some inaccessible metaphysical way so much prouder an achievement?" (*Principles,* 1:349–50). A few pages earlier, in "The Consciousness of Self" chapter, James had said, "For my own part I confess that the moment I become metaphysical . . . I find the notion of some sort of *anima mundi* thinking in all of us to be a more promising hypothesis, in spite of all its difficulties, than that of a lot of absolutely individual souls" (*Principles,* 1:346). Thus he was intimating a conception of the self that agrees with his later religious and metaphysical speculations.

A world of individual and substantial selves, each private and irrevocably removed from its neighbor, was not an attractive idea for James. He preferred to believe in a world where continuity prevails, including that between individual streams of consciousness; to the extent that the concept of a substantial self encourages the belief in metaphysical discontinuity between individual selves, he opposed it. It is a common judgment that James's *Anschauung* was excessively individualistic and ignored the role of community; on the contrary, he sought notions of self and reality that permit communality of the profoundest sort—in the depths of the most intimate personal experience. He hoped that the metaphysics of radical empiricism and pluralistic universe would indicate that a genuine overlap of many individuals' experiences might occur at levels of consciousness we do not yet understand.

From the viewpoint of introspective psychology, there is no substance referred to by *I* that is identical through time; instead, the verifiable self is a combination of the *me* which is mainly the body and the *I* which is the passing, judging thought. James was anxious not to allow the distinction between the introspected *me* and the introspecting *I* to generate a philosophical mystery as superfluous as that which results from the assumption of a substantial self. Because he had explicitly asserted that the *I* cannot immediately introspect itself, that the ephemeral, judging thought cannot be acquainted with itself but can only be known by a subsequent passing thought, it might seem that the *I* is a mysterious, forever elusive je ne sais quoi.[7]

> The reply is that we take care not to be duped by words. The words *I* and *me* signify nothing mysterious and unexampled—they are at bottom only names of *emphasis;* and Thought is always emphasizing something. Within a tract of space which it cognizes, it contrasts a *here* with a *there.* . . . Of a pair of things it calls one *this,* the other *that.* I and *thou,* I and *it,* are distinctions exactly on a par with these,—distinctions possible in an exclusively *objective* field of knowledge, the "I" meaning for the thought nothing but the bodily life which it momentarily feels. The sense of my bodily existence, however obscurely recognized as such, *may* then be the absolute original of my conscious selfhood, the fundamental perception that *I am.* All appropriations *may* be made "*to*" it, *by* a thought not at the moment immediately cognized by itself. (*Principles,* 1:341)

We cannot affirm this statement on philosophical as well as psychological grounds, but there is nothing in its use which signals an inevitable mystery about the first-person pronoun.

We might expect James's later philosophy, which brought the notion of self closer to metaphysics and religion and to his own yearning for a survival of bodily death, to reintroduce mysteries into the self. Although he did mystify the issue, he nevertheless adhered in 1904 to what he had said in *Principles* about the first-person pronoun.

> The individualized self, which I believe to be the only thing properly called self, is a part of the content of the world experienced. The world experienced (otherwise called the "field of consciousness") comes at all times with our body as its centre, centre of vision, centre of action, centre of interest. Where the body is is "here"; when the body acts is "now"; what the body touches is "this"; all other things are "there" and "then" and "that." These words of emphasized position imply a systematization of things with reference to a focus of action and interest which lies in the body. . . . The body is the storm centre, the origin of co-ordinates, the constant place of stress in all that experience-train. Everything circles round it, and is felt from its point of view. The word "I", then, is primarily a noun of position, just like "this" and "here." . . . The word "my" designates the kind of emphasis. I see no inconsistency whatever in defending, on the one hand, "my" activities as unique and opposed to those of outer natures, and, on the other hand, in affirming, after introspection, that they consist in movements in the head. The "my" of them is the emphasis, the feeling of perspective-interest in which they are dyed.[8]

Given the religious and mystical overtones of his later metaphysics, it may seem surprising that he did not abandon the self of *Principles* for a nonbodily, spiritual, and mysterious referent for the first-person pronoun. In some respects he did refine the concept of the self developed in his psychology text, but he consistently adhered to his claims that the body is at the center of any experience of self, that nothing nonbodily shows itself definitely to introspection, and that nothing about using *I* makes a mystery of the self. A similarity is evident between the stream of consciousness of the earlier psychology and the pure experience of the later metaphysics; the former is recast in terms of the latter. Since the reformulation of bodily experience in terms of pure experience has Berkeleyan or idealistic connotations, it seems odd that James did not reformulate the self within the framework of pure experience; such a reformulation would in effect have de-emphasized the bodily features of the self in favor of characteristics that would equip the self for what is demanded not only by James's mystical metaphysics but also by his hopes for psychical research. If telepathy, clairvoyance, and precognition actually occur, our everyday equation of the self with bodily experience will surely require some revision. Yet instead of suggesting how his psychological concept of the self might have shifted during the progression from *Principles* to the metaphysics of pure experience, James wrote in his later period that this concept was a natural ally if not the original herald of that metaphysics. After declaring in "Does 'Consciousness' Exist?" that the relation of knowing can be taken as a part of pure experience, with one of its terms serving as the knower, he added in a footnote: "In my *Psychology* I have tried to show that we need no knower other than the 'passing thought.' "[9]

There is no mistaking the similarity between what he said about the self in his psychology and in his later metaphysics; although he was consistent in his explicit treatment of the self, an implicit vacillation seems to lurk here. In *A Pluralistic Universe* the soul or substantial self is as vigorously rejected as in *Principles;* in *Essays in Radical Empiricism* the knower is identified with part of a momentary field of consciousness."[10] "Forasmuch as experiences extend in time, enter into relations of physical influence, reciprocally split, warm, illuminate, etc. each other, we make of them a field apart which we call the physical world. On the other hand, forasmuch as they are transitory, physically inert, with a succession which does not follow a determined order but seems rather to obey emotive fancies, we make of them another field which we call the physical world."[11] The distinction between *I* and *me* falls within any given field of consciousness, the *I* being used to emphasize the point of view from which a judgment or perception is made. In his notes for a course given in 1895–96, James recorded the phenomenalistic thesis that the world contains only data and is itself only a complex datum containing an objective and a subjective part. There is neither pure ego nor material substance, but only "field-stuff, datum-stuff, experience-stuff. . . . Use the word 'field' here for 'datum'—it is conveniently ambiguous."[12] In the same notes he mentioned that his task would have been much easier had he been able to admit that the *I* is immediately given rather than a point of view within a field of consciousness or a stream of pure experience. The language changed somewhat—the stream of thought in *Principles* became a field of consciousness or a portion of pure experience, and the *I* as passing thought became a perspective within a field of pure experience—but basically the same doctrine of the self was retained in the later metaphysics.

James essentially retained the early concept of self as he moved from psychology to metaphysics because he vacillated between an idealistic and a nonidealistic theory of mind and self. In *Principles,* to the extent that he equated the self with bodily experience, he argued for a commonsense, nonidealistic conception, forcing him to explain why he was not a materialist. But to the extent that he equated the *I* with a passing thought or momentary act of judgment within an introspectable stream of consciousness, he conceived the self philosophically in concepts far removed from our everyday talk about our bodies. The stream of thought looms in Jamesian psychology as an idealistic framework—an alternative to that of the human body and its constitution—in terms of which the *I* is to be interpreted. When, as in the metaphysics of pure experience, he reconstructed the human body from sensations, feelings, and the fleeting items of the introspectable stream of consciousness, his view is so idealistic and Berkeleyan that commonsense ideas about the body and the bodily self seem threatened. James never reconciled his philosophy of pure experience with the very introspections that had suggested that philosophy. A partial reconciliation occurs insofar as the self is reconstructed as a portion of pure experience and is introspectively experienced as such.

Despite his idealistic leanings, James never reduced the human body to fleeting bits of pure experience at the level of introspection; such reduction occurs only at the level where a conceptual analysis of the body (and material substance in general) is provided. He was always careful about making assertions based on introspection, so despite the idealistic overtones of the concept of pure experience, he continued to insist that the body is the center of the experienced world. Perhaps the body can be philosophically interpreted in phenomenalistic or idealistic terms (as in *Essays in Radical Empiricism* and *A Pluralistic Universe*), but experientally it seems to have remained for him a constant and enduring piece of matter. Unlike the evanescent *I,* this matter, constantly at the center of the introspectable stream of consciousness, cannot be described introspectively as fleeting bits of pure experience. James felt the tension here and vacillated between the materialistic leanings of his introspections and the idealistic tendencies of his metaphysics as much in the later years as in the early ones, with the result that the concept of self was essentially unchanged as the stream of thought was developed into a stream of pure experience. James's introspective reports prevented what we might otherwise have anticipated: a dramatic shift from a bodily self to a more spiritual one in harmony with the idealistic metaphysics of radical empiricism and a pluralistic universe.

James's contemporaries appreciated the issue. The British philosopher James Ward wrote to him about the self: "I find it hard to believe that the same man has written such opposite and seemingly incompatible statements as some of yours on this topic are to me. . . . I shall some day perhaps play off James the psychologist against James the metaphysician, moralist, and humanist."[13] Ward's specific concern was that some provision had to be made for a common part throughout the successive states that identify a self; without any commonality, how can even the semblance of continuity occur? James replied:

> I don't wish *renovare dolorem* about the self, but . . . you say we need a part that is *common* in states *A* and *B,* to account for their identification as *my* states. I grant it; only whereas you give what seems to me the merely nominal definition of "ego" to the common something, I attempt to determine it more concretely and really, by saying that it is the *actually experienced relation* which these states have to state *M* which calls them "mine." That common relation *constitutes* practically what we *mean* by being part of an ego; and I say: "What need of reduplicating it by an abstract ego as its *ground?"* . . . So if *A* and *B* both know a common object *O,* there is again something common to them. But what? Why, what but the fact of that determinate relation to a third thing? No need of any *antecedent* commonness before the fact—no need, at any rate, for descriptive purposes.[14]

This response dissolves the ego or self into a set of relations that the passing thought bears to other states in the stream without any mention of the body as the substantial antecedent by virtue of which we find continuity in experience. His emphasis here is upon the relations between the comparatively fleeting phases of the stream of consciousness, which suggests a leaning toward the idealistic metaphysics of pure experience. Had he focused upon the introspective nature of an experience of self, the constancy of the body would have been stressed, leaving us with the problem of how to harmonize the idealistic conceptualization in terms of a flow of consciousness with the commonsense conceptualization of an enduring human body through which the stream can flow.

Just as Ward thought that the Jamesian self in *Principles* had drowned in the stream of consciousness, another acquaintance, the Polish philosopher Wincenty Lutoslawski, later judged that the self had vanished in the philosophy of radical empiricism. "I have the impression that your *Self,* whose pure experience you relate, disappears amidst its own productions; and I see not the slightest allusion to your eternal, substantial existence as a Being, a thing, a reality, a source of power. Thus I am afraid that you would deprive me of the certainty I enjoy that I shall meet you, yourself, your own soul, in a better life amidst new experiences."[15] Knowing that James wanted to believe in the continuation of our existence beyond death, Lutoslawski was perplexed about how a self, seemingly dissolved into momentary perspectives and relations in a flow of pure experience, can be capable of the sort of continuous existence associated with durability. James once wrote to Bergson: "I send you a little popular lecture of mine on immortality. . . . It may amuse you to see a formulation like your own that the brain is an organ of *filtration* for spiritual life."[16] If consciousness does not depend for its existence upon the brain, but is only filtered through the brain, how can it retain the bodily nature required by James's introspections? If a consciousness separated from the brain has no ego or substantial self to support it, how can it survive as an individual in a stream of pure experience? The Jamesian accounts of self, whether in *Principles* or in the subsequent metaphysics, ultimately did not answer these questions—and James knew it.

Why, after arguing in *Principles* that states of consciousness cannot compound, did James change his mind and defend the thesis that they can? In *Principles* he advanced the *esse est sentiri* doctrine: "The essence of feeling is to be felt, and as a psychic existent *feels*, so it must *be*. If the one feeling feels like no one of the thousand [from which it might be held to be compounded], in what sense can it be said to *be* the thousand?" (*Principles*, 1:163). How can we identify a headache with anything other than how it feels? One would be attempting such an oddity, James argued in *Principles*, if one located the identity of a state of consciousness in the identity of constituents that are themselves mental states. Because green and red light combine to create yellow light, it does not follow that perceiving yellow actually consists of perceiving green and perceiving red. Besides wondering how subfeelings can occur without being consciously felt, we must ask how one feeling (of yellow) can be identical with other, different feelings (the subfeelings of green and red). James thought that any such identity is impossible since it seems self-contradictory. However, we might question his generalization that all states of consciousness are defined by how they feel; some states, unlike headaches or sensations of yellow, may be peculiarly complex and thus owe their identity to their parts in combination. This possibility ought not to be ruled out a priori.

James believed his generalization was supported by the fact that a state of consciousness is a unique, indivisible unity, or at least appears to be to introspection. In *Principles* this unity is considered a feature that distinguishes mental from physical things, because physical entities are never more than parts in combination. James assumed that the unity is recognized by the feeling of experiencing it. In his later metaphysics, which rejected dualism, he understandably wanted to eliminate any feature—including unique and indivisible unity—which threatened to demarcate the mental. If the final authority for believing in such unity is introspection, which is fallible, he had the option of ceasing to believe in that unity on the grounds that a better authority than introspection demanded it. Although his change of heart about whether states of mind can have parts involves basic revisions in *Principles*, James did not, in committing himself to such revisions in his later years, perform a total about-face.

James followed a long, painful route to reach the point where he was prepared to abandon the *esse est sentiri* doctrine of mental states. Although the official renunciation is made most prominently in *A Pluralistic Universe*, which conveys the depths of his conflict over the issue, it had been announced much earlier, in the 1895 essay "The Knowing of Things Together," which illuminates the progression of his thinking on the problem. He had been led to the *esse est sentiri* principle partly as a consequence of presenting psychology in *Principles* as a natural science, free from epistemological and metaphysical complications. In deliberately not inquiring how we come to know things or whether psychophysical dualism is true, he had adopted the view that cognitive states of consciousness are named by identifying their objects.[17] Since this idea differs from asserting that a state of mind is identified by its simple feeling, it is not immediately apparent how he reconciled the two ideas.

He may have supposed that a cognitive state, insofar as it is held to be a unique unit, has its own unique feeling, but that for a fuller and more useful identification, we must refer to its objects. Cognitive states of consciousness, like all mental states, can accordingly be conceived as unique and indivisible, unaffected by the complexity of their objects. The only complexity that needs to be attributed to mental states is a functional one; by virtue of being cognitive they are externally related in multiple ways to the things they know. "Treat them all [mental states] as unique in entity, I said [in *Principles*]; let their complexity reside in their plural cognitive function; and you have a psychology which, if it doesn't ultimately explain the facts, also does not, in expressing them, make them self-contradictory (as the associationist psychology does when it calls them many ideas fused into one idea) or pretend to explain them (as the soul-theory so often does) by a barren verbal principle."[18]

But in 1895 he expressed his surprise and regret that his arguments in *Principles* against the compounding of consciousness and for the *esse est sentiri* doctrine had been "generally either misunderstood or despised. But do not fear that on this occasion I am either going to defend or re-explain. . . . I am going to make things more harmonious by simply *giving it up*. . . . I see, moreover, better now than then that my proposal to designate mental states merely by their cognitive function leads to a somewhat strained way of talking of dreams and reveries, and to quite an unnatural way of talking of some emotional states. I am willing, consequently, henceforward that mental contents should be called complex, just as their objects are, and this even in psychology."[19] This declaration is not elaborated, so one wonders what motivated James to change his mind. His explanation here is confusing, since in *Principles* the feeling of emotional states is emphasized, and some emotions are expressly exempted there from being intentional or cognitive; no "unnatural" way of talking about them occurs or is implied in *Principles*.[20] Perhaps he meant in 1895 that if we assume that a fuller identification of dreams, reveries, and emotions must refer to their objects, then, because it is not clear that feelings are always intentionally related to objects, we will be drawn into a strained way of speaking about them. How, then, are we to interpret the reasoning behind James's radical shift of position on the issue of whether states of mind have parts?

A clue is virtually hidden in one of the footnotes in "The Knowing of Things Together," where he discussed the tastes in lemonade. One can argue that the emphasis here is different from that in "The Mind-Stuff Theory," in which the *esse est sentiri* doctrine is endorsed. That chapter stresses the unique indivisibility of each mental state, whereas the 1895 essay acknowledges an inner and introspectable psychical complexity. In "The Mind-Stuff Theory" James wrote: "No more do musical sounds combine *per se* into concords or discords" (*Principles*, 1:159). In the 1895 article the complex character of a mental state is conceded to be the result of parts recognized as retaining some of their original identity, some of their original feel, even when altered by becoming a part of that mental complex. We can recognize the sour and the sweet in lemonade despite their being altered versions of the original sourness of lemon juice and sweetness of sugar. The point, perhaps inadequately appreciated in *Principles*, is that the mental state which is the *taste* of lemonade is not simply a unique, indivisible phenomenon; it is analyzable into simultaneously introspectable ingredients such as sourness and sweetness. Unlike *Principles*, which located the identity of a mental state in a simple and unanalyzable feeling, the 1895 essay locates it in a unity that can also be introspected as a diversity.[21] Here we come upon a favorite idea of James's, one that especially intrigued him during his later years: unity need not be simple, unanalyzable, or utterly homogenous. Our own experiences are unities that are also diversities. Our "knowledge of things together" is an instance; there are different things to see on the beach; of themselves they represent merely a multitude, but when we perceive them simultaneously we group them as the contents of a single state of perceptual consciousness. A state of mind such as this is not homogeneous but is rather a synthetic union of diverse elements. It is unlike anything in the physical world (James had not in 1895 eliminated psychophysical dualism) because in that world the parts of a so-called whole are separable; in a mental unity such as a state of perceptual awareness, on the other hand, the parts are distinguishable but not separable, for if any are detached, the unity which they help to constitute immediately collapses.[22]

To James, a state of awareness holds diverse elements together in a temporary union; when this phenomenon is noticed, we are faced with the question of how the whole is related to its parts. Is it constituted of them yet somehow different from them, or is it simply identical with them? In "The Knowing of Things Together" he agreed with the anti-associationists that the unity of the whole that forms a state of consciousness does not result from the association of mental parts, but must be made by something, such as an act of attention. To say this, however, gives little insight into how an act of attention or anything else produces unity with diversity. "The general *nature* of it we can probably never account for, or tell how such a unity in manyness can be, for it seems to be the ultimate essence of all experience, and anything less than it apparently cannot be at all."[23] No general causal account can explain how "unity in manyness" is produced. It remained for *A Pluralistic Universe* to decide that the unique whole of a state of consciousness is identical with the diversity of parts that in some sense compose it.

The three essays in *A Pluralistic Universe* which are directly relevant to the self are "Concerning Fechner," "Bergson and His Critique of Intellectualism," and "The Compounding of Consciousness." The last essay argues that the *esse est sentiri* doctrine of *Principles* makes each state of consciousness a unique entity that is neither a part of anything nor composed of parts. This doctrine, said James in 1909, is intolerable in a universe that enjoys continuity as its hallmark. In his psychology the unique psychic units or states of mind are insulated from each other—as were the substantial selves of traditional metaphysics—representing a basic discontinuity between experiences, which are the very stuff of reality. In "The Compounding of Consciousness," James developed the thesis that states of mind can be compounded from others beyond where he had left it in "The Knowing of Things Together."[24] He had now to deal directly with the questions of how the whole of an experience relates to its parts and whether it is identical with those parts. He realized that his decision that states of consciousness can be compounded did not in itself answer those questions. Indeed, the questions were severely aggravated by the assumption that a mental state can be compounded; that assumption led to the problem, with which James wrestled for many years, of trying to determine how a whole that consists of parts can be both itself and those parts simultaneously.

James's dilemma was this: either we accept discrete and discontinuous states of consciousness, thereby respecting traditional notions of identity and difference, or we accept the compounding of consciousness, thereby defying those notions. In opting for the compounding of consciousness, he thought he was compelled to abandon the logic of identity and intellectualistic logic and to surrender to a form of irrationalism.[25] He believed that wherever a whole-and-parts phenomenon exists it is possible to distinguish between the whole, granting that its identity is somehow contributed to by the parts, and each part. We can, for instance, distinguish between the unique taste (the whole) of lemonade and its different parts of dimensions, such as sourness and sweetness. If we must say that the whole is identical with its parts, we contradict the logic of identity because we are flatly affirming that two or more distinguishable things are a single thing.

The compounding of consciousness implies this conclusion because a whole must be in some sense the same as the parts of which it is composed. In the physical world one need not worry the issue, James thought.[26] In the experiential domain, however, the whole is experienced differently from the way its ingredients are experienced, indicating that they are different things; yet if the taste of lemonade is literally compounded of the tastes of its ingredients, then it must be equated with them, suggesting that we cannot separate and identify as the intellectualistic logic of identity demands. This way of putting the problem makes the dilemma result from contrasting what experience shows (difference between whole and part) with the claim that compounding occurs (identity between whole and part). On the other hand, if we think of the taste of the lemonade as a unity in diversity, a complex within which sourness and sweetness are distinguishable, then the alleged compounding confirms our experience; this was James's ultimate formulation of the problem. But even if such unity-in-diversity characterizes every state of consciousness and is experientially recognizable, no explication of how the unity of a conscious state is identical with its diversity seemed to James free of self-contradiction.

Those essays in *A Pluralistic Universe* which explain James's change of heart about the compounding of consciousness are preoccupied not with how unity and continuity in an individual life are possible, but rather with how unity and continuity between individual lives is possible. As the essay "Concerning Fechner" shows, James was fascinated by Gustav Fechner's vision of a hierarchy of inclusive systems of consciousness that culminates in the all-inclusive consciousness of God. In Fechner's speculative metaphysics the inclusion of one consciousness within another or the hierarchical compounding of consciousness had the effect of blurring boundaries that might isolate persons from one another. James was intrigued by Fechner because of ''his belief that the more inclusive forms of consciousness are in part *constituted* by the more limited forms.''[27] In this system, individuals represent limited forms of consciousness that are part of a more inclusive consciousness they help to constitute. By a liberal use of metaphors, Fechner and James tried to make this intelligible, but for James a problem remained: How can two people be who they are, have the identity they have, and yet somehow be each other and be parts of the identity of a more inclusive consciousness? Fechner fancied that we can somehow remain ourselves while merging into the identity of a larger self, and James remarked sympathetically: ''If you imagine that this entrance after the death of the body into a common life of higher type means a merging and loss of our distinct personality, Fechner asks you whether a visual sensation of our own exists in any sense *less for itself* or *less distinctly,* when it enters into our higher relational consciousness and is there distinguished and defined.''[28]

But James did not understand how metaphors could meet the difficulties presented by the compounding of consciousness and the inclusion of persons within persons. He himself gave up the attempt to make his position more rational by volunteering further Fechnerian analogies on its behalf, for he thought that the compounding of consciousness defies adequate conceptualization.[29] After citing such analogies and offering his own, he avoided interpreting personal identity in a sustained discussion that might allow us to see how two people and a larger self can both be and not be the same person. In the 1898 lecture ''Human Immortality,'' he remarked that our desire for immortality is a desire for the survival of our personal identities.

> What we all wish to keep is just these individual restrictions, these selfsame tendencies and peculiarities that define us to ourselves and others, and constitute our identity, so called. Our finitenesses and limitations seem to be our personal essences; and when the finiting organ [the body, particularly the brain] drops away, and our several spirits revert to their original source and resume their unrestricted condition, will they then be anything like those sweet streams of feeling which we know, and which even now our brains are sifting out from the great reservoir for our enjoyment here below? But into these higher and more transcendent matters I refuse to enter upon this occasion.[30]

In *A Pluralistic Universe,* where we might expect the concept of personal identity to be investigated again in light of James's change in position on the compounding of consciousness, he in effect makes the same refusal; any such investigation seems to have been disqualified once the logic of identity and intellectualistic logic had been explicitly abandoned.

The shift from the *esse est sentiri* doctrine to the idea that mental states can be compounded not only produced the insuperable problem of how to understand the identity of a mental state, it also made impossible any explanation of personal identity. James's adoption of the compounding of consciousness led to his silence about personal identity, for he was unable to disentangle the contradiction implied by the compounding of consciousness, that "a lot of separate consciousnesses can at the same time be one collective thing" or that "one and the same identical content of experience, of which . . . the *esse* is to be felt [*sentiri*], be felt so diversely if itself be the only feeler."[31] Insofar as he always assumed in *A Pluralistic Universe* an analogy between individual states of consciousness and individual persons, it may seem that he broke the silence to some extent, giving us a glimpse of what the union of persons in a larger consciousness is like. The unity in diversity that characterizes any moment of one's stream of consciousness baffles conceptualization, which cannot be attempted without artificially dissecting and distorting, but "in its sensational immediacy *everything is all at once whatever different things it is once at all. It is before C and after A, far from you and near to me* . . . *active and passive, physical and mental.*"[32]

In the stream of consciousness one literally experiences or encounters what seems self-contradictory at the level of conceptualization; as Hegel saw, things are both themselves and other things at once. This conclusion shows that the deeper features of reality are found in perception rather than in rational thought.[33] Even if we accept the blurring of identity and difference in the stream of consciousness, however, it is useless to claim by analogy that personal identities blur; there is no experience that indicates that we can literally experience ourselves being at once both ourselves and others. Essentially, then, James did not explain how selves can both retain and lose identity within a larger self.

The contradiction remained at the conceptual level, and no sort of experience could eliminate it at the experiential level, so only the silence of mystical faith was left. But James's mystical faith was such that he could not have been content with a straightforward analogy between a state of consciousness and a self, although he offered such an analogy in *A Pluralistic Universe* and identified the *I* in *Principles* with a passing thought or momentary state of consciousness. James did not think in his later years that he had formulated an adequate conception of the self in *Principles*, but despite the problems of that conception, he could hardly have envisaged a better formulation; all conceptualizations of personal identity were deficient, pointing to the need for mystical silence on the matter. I suspect that is why he did not write later essays specifically on the self.

One reason for thinking that he was not content with his account of the self in *Principles* is found in this remark from "The Compounding of Consciousness" in *A Pluralistic Universe:* "These fields of experience that replace each other so punctually [the successive phases of the stream of consciousness in *Principles*], each knowing the same matter, but in ever-widening contexts, from simplest feeling up to absolute knowledge, *can* they have no *being* in common when their cognitive function is so thoroughly common? The regular succession of them is on such terms an unintelligible miracle" (McDermott, 555). Behind this remark may have been the thought that the picture of one's inner life as nothing but a succession of ephemeral states of consciousness is not the direct report of introspection but is rather an elaborate theoretical construct imposed upon one's introspections and perhaps suggested by introspective findings; such a construct would be subject to revision, and James may have surmised that the requirement of greater continuity in his pluralistic universe than in his earlier psychology indicated that revisions were needed. One such revision was this: instead of conceiving the stream of consciousness as merely a series in which one momentary mental state succeeds another with minimal overlap, we must inquire into the possibility that the successive states share some *being*, which may have the capacity to endure through successive states. Although James did not elaborate, he may have been suggesting that what endures throughout successive states of consciousness is the self.

Why was James attracted to something resembling the substantial self which he had always publicly scorned? In *Principles* he had used the human body to anchor the successions in the stream, but the body was in effect "desubstantialized" by the doctrines of radical empiricism and a pluralistic universe. In the rarefied stream of consciousness of these doctrines, nothing remained to provide what substance had provided: the endurance of an entire system of things, which for humans includes feelings, memories, and activities. James surely appreciated the problem of trying to persuade the momentary *I*, whether the passing thought of *Principles* or the momentary perspective within a pure experience of the later metaphysics, to bear a burden that even a substantial self finds heavy. This difficulty was apparently in the forefront of his thinking, since in his notes of 1895–96 he wrote that his claim that the *I* is not immediately given is much harder to defend than is its converse. "The other alternative presupposes immediate self-consciousness of I. Everything easy on that basis except to define the I."[34]

The *I* here is the substantial *I*, and the difficulties that had beset traditional efforts to define it are outlined in "The Consciousness of Self." If James had been able to define something like a substantial self with a definition that had cash value and also allowed for continuity of experience between persons, he would gladly have opted for it, especially to fill the vacuum created by his desubstantialization of the human body in terms of pure experience. If he had defined something approaching a substantial self as an enduring system of properties rather than as the indivisible, bulletlike soul of traditional theorists, he might have found a *being* common to successive states of consciousness. In his thinking about personal identity, intimate human relationships, and immortality, he was drawn to the idea of a substantial self, but the problems he encountered led him to choose mystical silence about personal identity and the self instead.

In a memorable letter to his dying father, James wrote: "As for the other side, and Mother, and our all possibly meeting, I *can't* say anything. More than ever at this moment do I feel that if that *were* true, all would be solved and justified. And it comes strangely over me in bidding you good-bye how a life is but a day and expresses mainly but a single note. It is so much like the act of bidding an ordinary good-night.

Good-night, my sacred old Father! If I don't see you again—Farewell! a blessed farewell!"[35] James found many things mysterious—the nature of causality, the relation between mind and body, the concepts of continuity and infinity—but he encountered nothing more resistant to conceptualization than personal identity or the self. He must have said to himself what he said to his father: "I *can't* say." Nine years later, in 1891, he wrote an equally memorable letter to his dying sister, Alice:

> These inhibitions, these split-up selves, all these new facts that are gradually coming to light about our organization, these enlargements of the self in trance, etc., are bringing me to turn for light in the direction of all sorts of despised spiritualistic and unscientific ideas. Father would find in me today a much more receptive listener—all *that* philosophy has got to be brought in. And what a queer contradiction . . . the ordinary scientific argument against immortality (based on body being mind's condition and mind going *out* when body is gone), when one must believe . . . that some infernality in the body *prevents* really existing parts of the mind from coming to their effective rights at all, suppresses them . . . from participation in this world's experiences, although they are *there* all the time. When that which is *you* passes out of the body, I am sure that there will be an explosion of liberated force and life till then eclipsed and kept down. I can hardly imagine *your* transition without a great oscillation of both "worlds" as they regain their new equilibrium after the change! Everyone will feel the shock, but you yourself will be more surprised than anybody else.[36]

Although these words were an expression of intimate affection, I assume that James also meant them to be taken literally. In speaking of a *you* that is separable from the body, he expressed a conception different from that of *Principles,* where the *you* is a passing thought whose bodily qualities are distinctly felt. What James wanted to believe resembles a substantial soul more than it does a momentary state of consciousness, but he was not prepared to say what sort of personal identity would have satisfied him. When the concepts of self and personal identity were enmeshed in discussions of subliminal consciousness and the possibility of immortality, they ceased to be merely psychological notions and fused with the other features of James's mystical thought. He never presumed to understand what kind of personal identity fits most comfortably with the philosophy of pure experience or with a mystical faith in immortality, because in the end he saw it as part of that faith and thus unexaminable philosophically. In *A Pluralistic Universe* the effort to clarify personal identity by analogy to individual states of consciousness fails; even modest claims to explain where the identity of a given state of consciousness resides are surrendered along with the logic of identity and the ordinary rules of conceptualization. Despite James's reservations about the soul and the substantial self, his mystical faith finally dominated, with its belief in a self which is more enduring and substantial than any short-lived event that participates in the functions defined by the metaphysics of radical empiricism and a pluralistic universe.

SELF AND ACTIVITY

James, like Locke, linked personal identity with preservation of memory. This link is evident in "The Consciousness of Self," and James thought it an especially visible connection in abnormal psychology. Citing studies by Pierre Janet on the phenomenon of multiple personalities, James concluded that difference in memory is an important factor in differentiating one personality from another. An intact memory is a mark of an intact self, as was illustrated by the case of a man who had hallucinations in which his legs seemed no longer a part of him and his movements seemed to originate from external sources, as if "there was inside of me a new being. . . . I was never really a dupe of these illusions, but my mind grew often tired of incessantly correcting the new impressions. . . . I had an ardent desire to see my old world again, to get back to my old self. This desire kept me from killing myself. . . . I was another, and I hated, I despised this other. . . . It was certainly another who had taken my form and assumed my functions" (quoted in *Principles*, 1:378). In commenting on this case, James applied the terminology he had developed in the chapter on the consciousness of self: "In cases similar to this, it is as certain that the I is unaltered as that the *me* is changed. That is to say, the present Thought [momentary state of consciousness] of the patient is cognitive of both the old *me* and the new, so long as its memory holds good" (*Principles*, 1:378). The *I*, which in *Principles* is equated with a short-lived consciousness that fashions judgments in the first person, judges itself to be the same from day to day if the memory of *I* is essentially the same one day to the next.

James also remarked, "And yet turn we must, with the confession that our 'Thought'—a cognitive phenomenal event in time—is, if it exist at all, itself the only Thinker which the facts require" (*Principles*, 1:369). The self is thus a momentary phase in the stream of consciousness, the same as earlier ones not because they are numerically identical—they are not—but because essentially the same set of memories attaches to both. The Jamesian self in *Principles* is a series of short-lived processes in which memory is retained throughout, implying that the same self exists throughout the series. But how defensible is such a theory?

Even if we agree that the remembering self is only a brief moment in the stream of consciousness, we must ask how a momentary state of consciousness can be stocked with memories, connect such memories with the present, act upon them, or sort out the true from the false. Never has a momentary mental state been expected to be and do so much; indeed, such a state is, except in name, substantial. For this state to be so full, it must be considerably less momentary then alleged; the momentary state buckles under the burden James expected it to bear, which included all the functionings we normally ascribe to a person at any given time. We cannot conceive how the systematic collection of experiences and capacities that constitute a person can be attributed to an ephemeral phase of a stream of consciousness. How can a brief moment in the flow of consciousness create an autobiographical unity throughout the series to which it belongs? This view contradicts James's claims about the nature of the self's activity and thus introduces a serious problem for his interpreter.

How can we reconcile what he usually said about free will with what he asserted about it in the context of radical empiricism? In his psychology James bolstered the case for free will by insisting that consciousness is an agency that selects, attends, and fights for ends.[37] That consciousness displays these features is prima facie evidence for its being a free agent, though we can never prove whether it really is. If for pragmatic reasons we assume that as conscious creatures we choose freely, then our choices sometimes produce consequences which, from the viewpoint of a mechanistic metaphysics, are novel or unpredictable. In *Essays in Radical Empiricism* James wrote:

> I have found myself more than once accused in print of being the assertor of a metaphysical principle of activity. . . . I owe all my doctrines on this subject to Renouvier; and Renouvier, as I understand him, is . . . an out and out phenomenist, a denier of "forces" in the most strenuous sense. . . . Single clauses in my writing, or sentences read out of their connection, may possibly have been compatible with a transphenomenal principle of energy; but I defy anyone to show a single sentence which, taken with its context, should be naturally held to advocate that view. . . . "Free will" was supposed by my critics to involve a supernatural agent. As a matter of plain history the only "free will" I have ever thought of defending is the character of novelty in fresh activity-situations. If an activity-process is the form of a whole "field of consciousness," and if each field of consciousness is not only in its totality unique . . . but has its elements unique . . . then novelty is perpetually entering the world and what happens there is not pure *repetition*, as the dogma of the literal uniformity of nature requires. . . . A "principle" of free will, if there were one, would doubtless manifest itself in such phenomena, but I never saw, nor do I now see, what the principle could do except rehearse the phenomenon beforehand, or why it ever should be invoked.[38]

James had, as he claimed here, always striven for an experiential version of the will. As early as 1880, in "The Feeling of Effort," he had tried to describe our experiences of activity and effort, which cause us to believe we possess free will, without appealing to occult energies or forces.[39] He had always maintained that the sense of such expressions as "resolving to do," "causing an act," and "activating a series of" is gained through experiences with which all of us are familiar. We feel most active, he thought, in the face of physical or mental resistances which evoke responses exhibiting strain, will, and effort and which culminate as achievements or defeats. "Sustaining, persevering, striving, paying with effort as we go, hanging on, and finally achieving our intention—this *is* action, this *is* effectuation in the only shape in which, by a pure-experience philosophy, the whereabouts of it anywhere can be discussed. Here is creation in its first intention, here is causality at work."[40]

But we can interpret his claim for free will to mean merely this: if in one momentary experience we strive toward something and in a successive experience we find that our goal is achieved, and if the successive experience is new rather than a repetition or something predictable, then the first experience freely willed the second. The doctrine of free will may seem in "The Experience of Activity" to be reduced to the claim that sometimes an experience of striving is succeeded by an unpredictable experience in which one's purpose is realized. As far as the philosophy of pure experience is concerned, to talk about the manifestation of free will is only to refer to the fact that one experience, filled with effort and striving, is followed by another, a novelty that defies explanations, one in which a goal defined by the earlier experience is reached.

But then will is only the experience of strain, resistance, and mental and physical perseverance, and free will is only the unpredictable succession of one experience upon another. What is missing is "willing an act" in the sense of causing or doing an act, and willing it freely in the sense of being its origin. In "The Experience of Activity" James himself was confused and uncertain about whether this concept was missing. He had always been impressed by Hume's argument that although we say we will our arms to move, we do not experience what actually occurs in the nervous system between our willing and our movement. James thought that "causing one's arm to move" may not be a description of a special experience at all. This conclusion is reinforced by the argument that there are experiences in which, due to drugs or paralysis, we seem to be causing something that in fact we do not.[41] This argument in turn leads to the conclusion that the causal feature is not an introspectable aspect additional to the elements of strain and resistance within an experience. Unless we want to invoke a useless principle that we can only rehearse the phenomenon beforehand, the description of an experience of activity in terms of the phenomena of strain, perseverance, resistance, fatigue, and cessation of resistance, provides all we need to describe our experiences of *willing, making, creating*, or *initiating*. Anything else in the meaning of these terms applies not to the content of the experiences but to their connection with other experiences; to establish that connection requires more than introspective acquaintance with a single experience.

James had always been tempted by this line of thinking because the empiricist in him had trouble locating a special experiential sense for causal concepts such as willing and creating. Despite the difficulties, however, he had apparently succeeded, in the chapter on will in *Principles* (which owes much to "The Feeling of Effort"), in recognizing the sort of experience within which volition can be directly apprehended: volition is the attending to a difficult or painful idea and is thus "a psychic or moral fact pure and simple, and is absolutely completed when the stable state of the idea is there" (*Principles*, 2:560). The act of holding in mind the painful idea that we must arise on a cold morning—even if we do not arise—is something we do or cause to happen, and since it is a totally mental act, we can know that we do it. We do not merely infer from strains and resistances that we make an idea remain in our consciousness; on the contrary, we are directly aware of making it happen. This making, in experiential terms, is the difficult achievement of making recalcitrant ideas remain in the foreground of our minds. Although we may sometimes mistakenly claim to have made something happen, it hardly follows that such a claim can never be true.

James consistently held in *Principles* and elsewhere that the issue of whether holding an idea in mind is done freely or is determined by antecedent events is a metaphysical question. The causal or initiating nature of the act, on the other hand, seems in James's psychology to be establishable by experience. But in the context of radical empiricism, doubts about the experiential content of causal concepts returned, leading James to conceive of causality as a relation between pure experiences and to assert, without reference to initiating, making, producing, or causing, that "as a matter of plain history, the only 'free will' I have ever thought of defending is the character of novelty in fresh activity-situations." But a novelty not caused by someone is not a willed result, and in "The Experience of Activity" James settled for novelties that somehow emerge out of prior pure experiences without any direct awareness of our producing them. This focus conflicts with his typical commonsense defenses of free will. The reduction of active doing or causal activity to the experience of strains and stresses, to the introspective recording of resistances and feelings of effort, likewise conflicts with his usual insistence that we do as well as feel.

Another factor contributing to the uncertainty about the self's activity in "The Experience of Activity" and the philosophy of radical empiricism is James's hesitation to offer a definite opinion about what originates or initiates a willed act. Although he had officially renounced psychophysical dualism, he continued to formulate his ideas in the commonsense terms of that dualism, alternately emphasizing the body or consciousness as it suited his purposes. For example, in discussing whether our actions can be our own doing, he wrote: "So far as we are 'persons,' and contrasted and opposed to an 'environment,' movements in our body figure as our activities; and I am unable to find any other activities that are ours in this strictly personal sense. . . . The individual self, which I believe to be the only thing properly called self, is a part of the content of the world experienced. The world experienced (otherwise called the 'field of consciousness') comes at all times with our body as its centre."[42] Yet when focusing upon the feeling or experience of activity, he reverted to former descriptions of the stream of consciousness, implying that feelings and thoughts in the stream are experienced as "ours" due to special features that they and the stream possess. He realized that this account might seem to retain the formulation sometimes given in *Principles* that consciousness is a causal agency, and might thus seem to conflict with the metaphysics of pure experience and radical empiricism:

> Let me not be told that [mental activity describable as effort] contradicts "Does 'Consciousness' Exist?" in which it was said that while "thoughts" and "things" have the same natures, the natures work "energetically" on each other in the things (fire burns, water wets, etc.) but not in the thoughts. Mental activity-trains are composed of thoughts, yet their members do work on each other, they check, sustain, and introduce. They do so when the activity is merely

associational as well as when effort is there. But, and this is my reply, they do so by other parts of their nature than those that energize physically. One thought in every developed activity-series is a desire or thought of purpose, and all the other thoughts acquire a feeling tone from their relation of harmony or oppugnancy to this. The interplay of these secondary tones (among which "interest," "difficulty," and "effort" figure) runs the drama in the mental series. In what we term the physical drama these qualities play absolutely no part. The subject needs careful working out; but I can see no inconsistency. (McDermott, 289)

The philosophy of radical empiricism and a pluralistic universe, by alternating between the two poles of psychophysical dualism, never offered a definite answer to the question of where we should locate the source of human will and action. Nor did it offer a clear suggestion about the nature of the self as the place where initiative, willing, and causal activity are born. It did not because James believed it could not; he acknowledged the issue explicitly in "The Experience of Activity."

The metaphysical question opens here; and I think that the state of mind of one possessed by it is often something like this: "It is all very well," we may imagine him saying, "to talk about certain experience-series taking on the form of feelings of activity, just as they might take on musical or geometric forms. Suppose that they do so; suppose we feel a will to stand a strain. Does our feeling do more than *record* the fact that the strain is sustained? The *real* activity, meanwhile, is the *doing* of the fact; and what is the doing made of before the record is made? What in the will *enables* it to act thus? And these trains of experience themselves, in which activities appear, what makes them *go* at all? Does the activity in one bit of experience bring the next bit into being? As an empiricist you cannot say so, for you have just declared activity to be only a kind of synthetic object, or conjunctive relation experienced between bits of experience already made. But what made them at all? What propels experience *überhaupt* into being? *There* is the activity that *operates;* the activity *felt* is only its superficial sign. (McDermott, 284–85)

We might expect that in his radical empiricism James would have reduced psychophysical dualism to pure experience, endowed pure experience with all the causal and dynamic properties required, and then defined the self, taken as a causal agent, in terms of pure experience. But he did not apply the later metaphysics to the concept of self here because he found propositions in the form of "I do (cause, initiate) something" to be metaphysically problematic. First, there is a problem in deciding what the something is; we may think we are willfully dancing when in fact we are passively executing a hypnotist's command. In asking how an act is our act, there is no absolute or unambiguous way of specifying what the act is; its definition is always relative to our interests and perspective, and as that definition varies, so will the identification of whose act it is. Assuming that a definition can be determined, how is the personal origin of the act to be decided? In answering this question, James relied not upon radical empiricism but upon a combination of pragmatic and religious convictions. He observed that philosophers had proposed three answers to the question of the authorship of an action. The physiological answer is that nerve cells are the causal agents. Another answer, which recalls associationistic psychology, is that our action is the result of which competing idea, feeling, or impulse finally dominates. The third answer "takes a consciousness of wider time-span than ours to be the vehicle of the more real activity. Its will is the agent, and its purpose is the action done" (McDermott, 286).

At this point James claimed that neither science, common sense, nor philosophy can verify one of the answers. The question had to be approached in the spirit of subjective pragmatism. In the long-range view, he urged, the "more real activity" must be defined as the important or long-range consequences of our present behaviors. James was disturbed by the fact that the physiological and competing ideas theories are indifferent to the long-range results of present actions. Based on his assumption that an individual consciousness is part of a wider one, he stressed our desire for certain long-range results. If either nerve cells or struggling ideas were the sole causes of our deeds, there would be nothing about causality to allow our preferences to contribute to our future life.

> The question *Whose is the real* activity? is thus tantamount to the question *What will be the actual results?* Its interest is dramatic; how will things work out? If the agents are of one sort, one way; if another sort . . . differently. The pragmatic meaning of the various alternatives . . . is great. It makes no merely verbal difference which opinion we take up. You see it is the old dispute come back! Materialism and teleology; elementary short-span actions summing themselves "blindly," or far foreseen ideals coming with effort into act. (McDermott, 287)

James omitted a fourth possible answer to the question of what is the agency of human activity: perhaps the cause of some of that activity is a finite self. He seems to have refused to recognize this option. We cannot argue that he did so because his well-known "psychology without a soul" disallowed all philosophical uses of terms like *self* or *person* for he did not hesitate to refer to the wider consciousness with personal pronouns and such expressions. James evidently thought that his reflections on the experience of activity in the context of radical empiricism did not illuminate the nature of *I* in such propositions as "I did something" or "I caused something to happen," unless perhaps the unexplained dissolving of *I* into a wider consciousness counts as illumination. He did, however, contend that his descriptions of the experience of activity contained all that could be experienced, even if such words as *making, doing, creating,* or *initiating* were also applied to the experience. "I conclude, then, that real effectual causation as an ultimate nature . . . *is just what we feel it to be,* just that kind of conjunction which our own activity-series reveal" (McDermott, 290).

Despite his mention of persevering and sustaining, James thought that doing is experienced as the feelings of strains and resistances and should thus be analyzed in terms of particular sensations. We know that we are holding the anchor because of the sensations, including those of strain and resistance, felt throughout the body. But this account is mistaken; we do not know that we hold it because we correctly interpret the bodily sensations that occur. Equally erroneous is the claim that doing and making are nothing more than the awareness of special sensations. The state of mind that occurs when we are aware of ourselves doing or causing something is different from the state of mind that occurs when we focus upon sensations of strain and resistance. In raising the issue of whether they are different, James clearly appreciated my objection here, and his own lingering uncertainty is clear in this statement: "The healthy thing for philosophy is to leave off grubbing underground for what effects effectuation, or what makes action act, and try to solve the concrete questions of where effectuation is located, of which things are the true causal agents there. . . . If we could know what causation really and transcendentally is in itself, the only *use* of the knowledge would be to help us to recognize an actual cause when we had one." (McDermott, 290). This passage clearly suggests that there may be more to doing and making than is disclosed in the experience of activity, but that speculation about it is pragmatically profitless. For James to call such speculation "metaphysical grubbing" in the context of radical empiricism is odd, given his vulnerability to the same accusation in his pursuit of the metaphysical complexities of pure experience.

We might want to do some metaphysical grubbing ourselves in order to understand the relation between ourselves and our actions when propositions in the form of "I caused something" are true. As James's thinking became more metaphysical, he had less to say about the referent and the sense of the first-person pronoun. As long as he retained commonsense beliefs about the human body, he had commonsense explanations for human thought and behavior, and as long as he worked with psychophysical dualism, he was content with the theory of ideo-motor action to explain how we act deliberately. But if the human body is reconceived in terms of pure experiences, and the *I* or self is made part of an indefinitely large stream of consciousness or larger self, common sense seems not to survive at all. Because further speculation about the self and its role as agent became an exercise in "grubbing," nothing in the philosophy of pure experience and its account of activity could yield the secret of human selfhood. Who am I? What am I? Ultimately, James thought, we cannot answer such queries; if any state of mind could answer them, it would be a mystical state in which concepts and intellectualistic logic were no longer relevant. For James, then, the self was the ultimate mystery.

ABNORMAL PSYCHOLOGY AND PSYCHICAL RESEARCH

In 1909, a year before his death, James remarked to Ernest Jones (Freud's biographer and colleague) that "the future of psychology belongs to your work." In that same year he wrote, "Hardly, as yet, has the surface of the facts called 'psychic' begun to be scratched for scientific purposes. It is through following these facts, I am persuaded, that the greatest scientific conquests of the coming generation will be achieved."[43] These simultaneous testimonials to abnormal psychology, including psychoanalysis, and to psychical research were more than coincidental. James was mostly bored by ordinary laboratory work, expressing great relief when the direction of the Harvard psychology laboratory was transferred in 1892 to Hugo Münsterberg.

All the important research cited in *Principles* was performed by others and had been reported in the vast number of books and journals James consulted. His interest had always reached beyond the laboratory to such areas as abnormal psychology and psychical research. Concern for the former is more apparent in *Principles* than for the latter. He had become involved in the early 1880s with the English Society for Psychical Research and had been a founding member of the American Society in 1884, so the scant reference in *Principles* to psychical research (the topic is not even mentioned in the book's index) must have resulted from the fear that the topic, judged disreputable by most of his colleagues, would jeopardize his credibility in presenting psychology as a natural science. But his interest in psychical research was evident early in his career; in 1869, when he was a senior at Harvard Medical School, he wrote to his brother Henry: "I wrote a notice of a book on spiritualism (Planchette) for the [Boston Daily] Advertiser and got $10.00."[44]

The psychological research that James admired always promised to be useful for the layman as well as for the specialist, and his own investigations were no exception. In 1880 he reviewed experimental work on the physiology of the semicircular canals and their connection with dizziness, and two years later he published the results of his own studies, drawing on the cases of 519 deaf-mutes, which confirmed the relatively new theory that the semicircular canals are organs of equilibrium.[45] To locate the physiological source of dizziness is to gain information with potential practical applications, one of which, he hypothesized, might be the alleviation of seasickness. This malady might be due to an excitement of the semicircular canals, suggesting "the application of small blisters behind the ears as a possible counter-irritant to that excitement of the organs beneath, in which the most intolerable of all complaints *may* take its rise."[46]

James's homespun experiments that seemed to show that natural memory capacity cannot be improved through training were also undertaken for utilitarian reasons.[47] He conducted a nonexperimental study on the experience of amputees, who seem to be conscious of their missing limbs. Motivated by the fact that his father had lost a leg as a young man, James surveyed the reports given by 185 amputees. We might wonder whether any utility attaches to the introspective accounts given by such persons, but James thought that certain features of the illusion of sensation in lost limbs indicated the probable physiological cause of the phenomena. He considered the phenomena worthy of study because of their relevance to psychical research as well; some people claimed to have a clairvoyant or telepathic relation to their lost limbs, registering, for example, a feeling of pain if the lost limb is maltreated in a laboratory where it had been preserved. Assuming a physiological explanation for the illusion, James was skeptical about such claims, for "among all the pains which come and go in the first weeks of amputation, it would be strange if some did not coincide with events happening to the buried or 'pickled' limb."[48]

From the perspective of mainstream physiological psychology, James's most enthusiastic research interests were largely peripheral, and his study of hypnotism was no exception. In "General Conditions of Brain-Activity," chapter 3 of *Principles*, he described the effects of alcohol, caffeine, and morphine upon the time it takes to react to a signal. Citing his own investigations (and G. Stanley Hall's) of the hypnotic trance, he concluded that its effect upon reaction time to a signal is not constant.[49] The implications of hypnotic phenomena for theories about the human mind intrigued him, particularly in those respects that are unusual or occult. He argued that while the symptoms of the hypnotic state can be ascribed to our susceptibility to hypnotic suggestion, more than suggestibility is involved. Unlike other theorists, he judged the hypnotic condition to be a pathological state, and in citing such symptoms as catalepsy, lethargy, and somnambulism that had been described by Jean Charcot and Rudolph Heidenhain, he concluded that the efficacy of hypnotic suggestion depends upon the occurrence of a pathological or trancelike state. A symptom of the hypnotic trance that especially occupied James was the heightened perception or hyperesthesia of the senses: "One of the most extraordinary examples of visual hyperaesthesia is that reported by Bergson, in which a subject who seemed to be reading through the back of a book held and looked at by the operator, was really proved to be reading the image of the page reflected on the latter's cornea. The same subject was able to discriminate with the naked eye details in a microscopic preparation" (*Principles*, 2:609).

James surmised that hyperesthesia might help to explain the stranger manifestations of the hypnotic condition, such as the reputed effects of magnets and metals upon subjects. Often when a hypnotist secretly employed a magnet, the subject experienced paralyses, unilateral contractures, hallucinations, or movements. Even if suggestion by the hypnotist was a factor in producing these effects, James guessed that the subject's hyperesthetic perception of the magnet was involved, thus defeating the hypnotist's intention to keep its presence a secret.

> I myself verified many of the above effects of the magnet on a blindfolded subject on whom I was trying for the first time, and whom I believe to have never heard of them before. The moment, however, an opaque screen was added to the blindfolding, the effects ceased to coincide with the approximation of the magnet, so that it looks as if visual perception had been instrumental in producing them. The subject passed from my observation, so that I could never clear up the mystery. Of course I gave him consciously no hint of what I was looking for. (*Principles*, 2:611)

The most important hypnotic phenomenon, James thought, is the success of the posthypnotic command through which subjects often obey, after emerging from the trance but without any memory of it, a command given during the trance by the hypnotist. This tended to prove, James held, that the posthypnotic command is retained in consciousness but in such manner that the subject is unaware of it.

Among James's "peripheral" experiments were his adventures with nitrous oxide. Although he worried about drugs and alcohol (his brother Robertson suffered from alcoholism) he was interested in the feelings and insights allegedly provided by anesthetic revelation. In the 1882 essay "On Some Hegelisms," he included a remarkable footnote:

> Since the preceding article was written, some observations on the effects of nitrous-oxide-gas-intoxication which I was prompted to make by reading the pamphlet called *The Anaesthetic Revelation* and the *Gist of Philosophy*, by Benjamin Paul Blood, Amsterdam, N. Y., 1874, have made me understand better than ever before both the strength and the weakness of Hegel's philosophy. I strongly urge others to repeat the experiment, which with pure gas is short and harmless enough. . . . With me, as with every other person of whom I have heard, the keynote of the experience is the tremendously exciting sense of an intense metaphysical illumination. . . . The mind sees all the logical relations of being with an apparent subtlety and instantaneity to which its normal consciousness offers no parallel. . . . The effect upon me of the gas [was] the conviction that Hegelism was true after all. . . . It is impossible to convey an idea of the torrential character of the identification of opposites as it streams through the mind in this experience.[50]

But James's final verdict was that the intoxicating experience, instead of vindicating Hegel's identification of opposites, revealed that Hegel must have been unusually susceptible to such emotions of being wonder-struck by the curious togetherness of things; these emotions resulted in Hegel's "tolerably unscrupulous" method of philosophizing. Hegel aside, James preferred to believe that experiences of the sort induced by nitrous oxide are sometimes genuinely revelatory and afford firsthand acquaintance with a truly mystical occurrence. He wrote in *The Varieties of Religious Experience:* "Some years ago I myself made some observations on this aspect of nitrous oxide intoxication. . . . One conclusion was forced upon my mind . . . that our normal waking consciousness . . . is but one special type of consciousness, whilst all about it, parted from it by the filmiest of screens, there be potential forms of consciousness entirely different" (378). This belief constitutes the important connection between abnormal psychology and psychical research in James's thought.

After the mid-1880s James participated in seances, attended sessions designed to illustrate mediumship, clairvoyance, telepathy, and telekinesis, and experimented with automatic writing. He mentioned this latter topic in "The Consciousness of Self," feeling that its relevance to the concept of self needed no justification. He cited the case of Sidney Dean, a New Englander who had performed his own automatic writing experiments and who declared:

> The writing is in my own hand but the dictation not of my own mind and will, but that of another, upon subjects of which I can have no knowledge and hardly

a theory; and I, myself, consciously criticise the thought, fact, mode of expressing it, etc., while the hand is recording the subject-matter and even the words impressed to be written. If *I* refuse to write the sentence . . . the impression instantly ceases, and my willingness must be mentally expressed before the work is resumed. . . . Sentences are commenced without knowledge of mine as to their subject or ending. In fact, I have never known in advance the subject of disquisition. (*Principles*, 1:395)

In Dean's judgment it was an intelligent ego other than himself who did the automatic writing. James thus wondered who was the personality that initiated the writing and how it was related to Dean himself. Cases such as Dean's, James believed, complicate all notions of the self that assume each of us to be a single center of consciousness. It therefore seemed incumbent upon any student of the human mind to investigate phenomena such as automatic writing. Reporting on his own experiments with automatic writers invaded by alien but controlling intelligences, James wrote: "On the condition of the sensibility during these invasions, few observations have been made. I have found the hands of two automatic writers anaesthetic during the act. In two others I have found this not to be the case. Automatic writing is usually preceded by shooting pains along the arm-nerves and irregular contractions of the arm-muscles. I have found one medium's tongue and lips apparently insensible to pin-pricks during her (speaking) trance."[51] James urged others to conduct automatic writing experiments, and one of the people who did so was Gertrude Stein, then a Radcliffe undergraduate. She and a Harvard graduate student, Leon Solomons, tried to detect the precise moment when the writer's self "split" or was invaded by the secondary self that then directed the writing; they published the results of their studies in "Normal Motor Automatism" (*Psychological Review* 3 [September 1896]: 492–512). Stein had certain reservations about automatic writing experiments, and those who know her temperament will appreciate her complaint in an 1894 report that "this vehement individual is requested to make herself a perfect blank while someone practises on her as an automaton."[52]

James's forays into abnormal psychology and psychical research were partly motivated by the hope of discovering the causes and remedies of his own health problems. In experimenting in those areas he sought results that would be useful by pointing to ways of restoring physical and mental health. Suffering from nervous tension, anxiety, depression, backaches, eye-aches, and even a tendency to hallucination, he looked for a psychology—and a philosophy—that could explain and come to dominate such symptoms. Like others of his time, he took to mental healing and unorthodox procedures in mental hygiene, consistent with the attitude he had expressed at twenty-two: "A doctor does more by the moral effect of his presence on the patient and family than anything else."[53] It seemed to be James's fate to be disappointed more often than not by the far-out solutions that others pursued, yet until the end he held such pursuits to be worthwhile.

In 1894, James was a prominent opponent of bills entertained by the Massachusetts legislature to put mental healers out of business by requiring licenses based on medical examinations; he also assisted Clifford W. Beers, author of the famous *A Mind That Found Itself,* in organizing the National Committee for Mental Hygiene in 1909. In 1890, upon completing *Principles,* James published "The Hidden Self," in which he asserted that the "mystical style of philosophizing" is valuable because it is open to unusual experiences that bypass the academician; he urged his colleagues to give this style respectful attention because philosophy would profit by discovering how it could play a useful role in the struggles of mind over matter, thought over depression, and hope over despair. He praised the studies of Binet and Janet on hysteria and split personality and emphasized their possible applications, including the use of hypnotic suggestion, for the relief of human misery. Mental healing, abnormal psychology, and psychical research were brought together in James's account of the case of a young girl who had been cured of hysterical blindness by Janet.

Now for the cure! The thing needed was, of course, to get the sub-conscious personality to leave off having these senseless hallucinations. . . . Janet at last hit upon an artifice. . . . He carried the poor Marie back in imagination to the earlier dates. It proved as easy with her as with many others when entranced, to produce the hallucination that she was again a child. . . . Janet, replacing her in this wise at the age of six, made her go through the bedroom scene again, but gave it a different *dénouement.* He made her believe that the horrible child had no eruption and was charming; so that she was finally convinced, and caressed without fear this new object of her imagination. . . . The sub-conscious Marie, passive and docile as usual, adopted these new versions of the old tales. . . . All morbid symptoms ceased as if by magic. . . . She is no longer hypnotizable, as often happens in these cases when the health returns.

The mind-curers and Christian scientists, of whom we have lately heard so much, unquestionably get, by widely different methods, results, in certain cases, no less remarkable than this. The ordinary medical man, if he believes the facts at all, dismisses them from his attention with the cut-and-dried remark that they are "only effects of the imagination." It is the great merit of these French investigators, and of Messrs. Myers, Gurney, and the "psychical researchers," that they are for the first time trying to read some sort of a definite meaning into this vaguest of phrases. . . . It seems to me a very great step to have ascertained that the secondary self, or selves, coexist with the primary one, during the waking state. But just what these secondary selves may be, and what are their remoter relations and conditions of existence, are questions to which the answer is anything but clear. . . . The secondary and the primary consciousnesses added together can, on M. Janet's theory, never exceed the normally total consciousness of the individual. This theory certainly expresses pretty well the facts which have fallen under its author's own observation, though even here, if this were a critical article, I might have something to say. . . . I know a non-hysterical woman who, in her trances, knows facts which altogether transcend her *possible* normal consciousness. . . . My *own* impression is that the trance-condition is an immensely complex and fluctuating thing, into the understanding of which we have hardly begun to penetrate. . . . A *comparative study of trances and subconscious states* is meanwhile of the most urgent importance for the comprehension of our nature.[54]

Here James connects abnormal psychology, psychical research, and mental healing; he embraces the concept of the subconscious and the idea that at a subconscious level the waking personality may coexist with secondary, subliminal, or hidden selves. Students of abnormal psychology such as Janet discovered the existance of the subconscious and of secondary selves or personalities; psychical researchers such as Myers found evidence for the hypothesis that these hidden selves can function as mediums, displaying capacities for clairvoyance and telepathy. James thought that mind-curists might learn to tap the subconscious domain for healing purposes. This hope was sufficient to lure James out of the ordinary laboratory and to remark that Janet's *État mental des hystériques* was worth more than "all 'exact' laboratory measurements put together."[55] James believed that the new work in abnormal psychology and psychical research represented enormous strides in understanding the self beyond what traditional philosophy and psychology had accomplished.

In an encyclopedia article of 1895 which has been virtually forgotten, James briefly traced the history of theorizing about the self.[56] He noted that *person* was derived from *persona,* which originally meant "theater-mask" or an actor's "face"; the term is sometimes still used to denote physical appearance rather than imperceptible mental features. Then the notion developed of man in his social relations as a personage, and finally came the concept of man as an essentially spiritual being. In psychology, James observed, *personality* means individuality or personal identity, about which varying opinions have been held; Hindu philosophy embraces both the Sankhya system of independent finite souls and the Vedanta system of a single self, the supreme Brahman. In Jewish thought, "the spiritual principle of personality was the 'spirit' (*Ruach*) or warm breath of life which animated the dust, when breathed thereinto by Jehovah. This breath-spirit, which we find as the ruling conception in all primitive thought, maintains its place in both Greek and Christian philosophy, developing into the more physiological conception of 'animal spirits' on the one hand, and into the Pauline doctrine of the 'Spirit,' or *pneuma,* on the other."[57] Plato and Aristotle subordinated the idea of breath to the immaterial and rational psyche, leading eventually to Descartes's sharp distinction between mind and body and its attendant problems.

Locke's empiricistic revolution made personality or personal identity depend upon a recollecting consciousness; if the same remembering consciousness could migrate from one soul to another, it would constitute personal identity without identity of substance, and if one individual were the site of several incommunicable consciousnesses at different times, he would be successively different persons.

Locke's importance lies in his having eliminated substantial identity and his having made personal identity a verifiable phenomenon, a development that Hume carried even further in creating a psychology which depends upon associations but which works without a soul. "Since Kant's time the consciousness of subjection to moral law, and the autonomy and freedom implied by such a consciousness, have often been referred to as the specific marks of personality. On this view 'person' means a being with inner ideal ends, to which it freely acknowledges responsibility. Here the psychological notion passes over into the ethical and juridical conceptions of personality."[58] Recent psychology, James declared, mostly followed Locke, considering the empirical self a succession of associated ideas connected through memory.

James then discussed the idea of multiple personality as the innovative concept of future psychology, claiming that what Locke might have hypothesized about personality was now known to be a fact; in the same individual, different and incommunicable consciousnesses can exist. "In somnambulism, either natural or 'hypnotic,' the rule is for the subject to forget on waking all that he has done, but to remember it again on re-entering the somnambulist state. He may thus live two alternating personal lives with a distinct system of memory in each. It was first proved by Edmund Gurney that the memories of the hypnotic consciousness may coexist, after waking, with the normal consciousness of the subject, but be unknown to the latter."[59] One human body can be the site of many consciousnesses, personalities, or, in Locke's sense of the word, persons. How can we explain these secondary and alternating personalities, which Myers called subliminal selves? This is the urgent task, said James, for contemporary psychology. The temperaments of these accessory personalities seem inexplicable if we conceive them as only accidental improvisations born from certain groups of the patient's ideas that separate from the normal consciousness to assume a quasi-independent existence. "They have a generic similarity in many cases, as in automatic writing and trance-speaking, which suggests some common cause as yet imperfectly known, or at any rate a context which if explored might make the phenomena, with their peculiar regularity, appear more rational."[60] The connection of the primary self or personality with subsidiary ones remained a puzzle, but it certainly subverted traditional confidence in the concept of the self as unity of consciousness. "It is clear already that the margins and outskirts of what we take to be our personality extend into unknown regions. Cures and organic effects, such as blisters, produced by hypnotic suggestion show this as regards our bodily processes; while the utterances of mediums and automatic writers . . . though usually flimsy and incoherent . . . as the present writer believes, occasionally show a knowledge of facts not possessed by the primary person."[61]

The discovery of the subconscious by abnormal psychology, psychical research, and mind-healing excited James for its potential applications; it promised to revise traditional theories of mind and consciousness and possibly to explain the phenomenon that James often hailed, the sudden upsurge of energy or renewed vitality which seems sometimes to invade us from out of nowhere. Perhaps the "nowhere" is the subconscious, which may supply the re-energizing or be the conduit for it; who knows its capacities for mental healing? On the interpretation given by Janet, Myers, and James, the subconscious was not open to the objections that James himself had leveled against a type of unconscious in "The Mind-Stuff Theory" in *Principles*. That chapter had rejected the associationist doctrine that unconscious ideas can combine into a single conscious idea—an idea James abandoned insofar as he subsequently accepted the compounding of consciousness. The chapter had also denied an impersonal unconscious, a denial that James adhered to: "Every thought [feeling, mental event] tends to be part of a personal consciousness" (*Principles,* 1:225). In agreeing with Janet and Myers that the subconscious is personal, that its contents are accessible to subliminal or subsidiary consciousnesses while remaining inaccessible to the primary or waking self, James was unsympathetic to Freud's concept of the unconscious.[62]

Freud was acquainted with Janet's views (both men had been Charcot's pupils), and on several points he differed with those views, including that of the unconscious. Psychoanalytic theory troubles philosophers, Freud once observed, because it postulates an unconscious which deserves to be called mental (in the usual sense of the word) but which may be totally devoid of any consciousness. This notion of an "unconscious mental" seems a contradiction in terms to philosophers who assume that to be mental and to be conscious are the same. Such thinkers forget, Freud said, that with others we do not hesitate to infer the existence of mental processes of which we are not immediately aware. "But what held good for other people must be applicable to oneself. Anyone who tried to push the argument further and to conclude from it that one's own hidden processes belonged actually to a second *consciousness* would be faced with the concept a consciousness of which one knew nothing, of an 'unconscious consciousness'—and this would scarcely be preferable to the assumption of an 'unconscious mental.' "[63] The Freudian unconscious, being independent of consciousness, is not interpreted by analogy to consciousness but is more fruitfully understood as a set of impersonal functional systems that can clash as well as cooperate with each other; the results of such clashes are often registered as symptoms at the conscious level. The Janet-James contention that whatever exists unconsciously must exist for at least a subliminal consciousness, and that whatever is mental occurs in a personalized way, struck Freud as bordering on the unintelligible. Because the *esse est sentiri* doctrine had a strong hold upon James's thinking, he was one of the philosophers whom Freud criticized for assuming the concepts of *mental* and *consciousness* to be interchangeable.

James liked the concept of a personalized unconscious because it meant that if a primary self is somehow linked at the unconscious level with associated selves which together constitute a "multiple" personality, then the putative insularity of the self is dissolved and no self is ever entirely distinguishable from the community of selves or personalities into which its own identity blends; while he recognized that such a formulation was mysterious, James believed that it was confirmed by the work on multiple personality in abnormal psychology and by the study of mediumship in psychical research.[64] If something can exist in the unconscious but be conscious to a secondary or subliminal self, then whatever explanations of the relations between such selves are suggested must concede the absence of distinct boundaries between one self and another. Further, the formulation of a self's identity can be achieved only by including formulations of other selves' identities. If, as James believed, the data collected by abnormal psychology and psychical research are not fully explicable by those disciplines, then one is free to move to a religious or mystical pronouncement; the identity of the self defies adequate scientific conceptualization.[65]

We should not underestimate the perplexities presented by multiple-personality phenomena and the uncertainty that James felt about them. In fact, their explanation is yet to be found. In recent years psychologists and philosophers have revived Jamesian concerns about the unity of consciousness and self; interest in this issue has been stimulated by the "split-brain" phenomena which occur when connections between the cerebral hemispheres have been severed and which tempt observers to describe the patient as having been split into (at least) two minds, two selves, or two centers of consciousness. "The same patient, often at nearly the same time, will assert and deny a specific empirical claim or fact of memory. The left hand, as the expression goes, may not know what the right one is doing, or as today's commentator would say, the left brain doesn't know what the right one is saying, because the right one cannot speak."[66] Whether they be split-brain or other types of fissures in consciousness, these phenomena are variations of what had occupied James. Consider these examples:

> Now M. Janet found in several subjects like this [a hysteric] that if he came up behind them whilst they were plunged in conversation with a third party, and addressed them in a whisper, telling them to raise their hand or perform other simple acts, they would obey the order given, although their *talking* intelligence was quite unconscious of receiving it. . . . The primary consciousness meanwhile went on with the conversation, entirely unaware of these performances on the hand's part. The consciousness which presided over these latter appeared in its turn to be quite as little disturbed by the upper consciousness's concerns. (*Principles*, 1:204)

> Messrs. Bernheim and Pitres have also proved . . . that hysterical blindness is no real blindness at all. The eye of an hysteric which is totally blind when the other or seeing eye is shut, will do its share of vision perfectly well when *both* eyes are open together. But even where both eyes are semi-blind from hysterical disease . . . M. Binet has found the hand of his patients unconsciously writing down words which their eyes were vainly endeavoring to "see," i.e., to bring to the upper consciousness. Their submerged consciousness was of course seeing them, or the hand could not have written as it did. (*Principles*, 1:206)

> *In certain persons . . . the total consciousness may be split into parts which coexist but mutually ignore each other. . . .* More remarkable still, they are *complementary*. Give an object to one of the consciousnesses and by that fact you remove it from

the other or others. . . . M. Janet has proved this beautifully with his patient
Lucie. . . . In her trance he covered her lap with cards, each bearing a number.
He then told her that on waking she should not see any card whose number was
a multiple of three. . . . When she was awakened . . . she counted and said she
saw those only whose number was not a multiple of 3. To the 12, 18, 9, etc., she
was blind. But the *hand,* when the sub-conscious self was interrogated by the
usual method of engrossing the upper self in another conversation, wrote that
the only cards in Lucie's lap were those numbered 12, 18, 9, etc., and on being
asked to pick up all the cards which were there, picked up these and let the
others lie. . . . The anaesthesias, paralyses, contractions and other irregularities
from which hysterics suffer seem then to be due to the fact that their secondary
personage has enriched itself by robbing the primary one of a function which
the latter ought to have retained. The curative indication is evident: get at the
secondary personage, by hypnotization or in whatever other way, and make her
give up the eye, the skin, the arm, or whatever the affected part may be. The
normal self thereupon regains possession, sees, feels, or is able to move again.
(*Principles,* 1:206–07)

Such data (unlike the alleged ones of psychical research) are experimentally
established, and the phenomena of fragmented consciousness and multiple personality are generally accepted, so that James was on secure ground in using them for
conjecture about the self. Perhaps the self is not what we think of in only normal
cases. In abnormal situations, different groupings of consciousness, sometimes distinct enough to warrant calling them different personalities, are associated within
the same human body; perhaps that body's self is mainly one of those personalities,
or perhaps it should be conceived to be a mixture of all such personalities. In any
event, the fragmenting or assemblage of self seemed to James to be an affair of
consciousness, since the body remains intact, and the different groupings or personalities are defined not in terms of overtly physical attributes but in terms of memories,
feelings, and desires. At some level of consciousness something may connect the
different groupings, assuring an overlap of experiential content at the level between
them—an overlap that may extend even to other selves of other bodies. If literal
sharing of experiential content is denied, then the link may be described in the
language of psychical research, so that different centers of consciousness are aware of
each other telepathically or clairvoyantly.

We cannot ignore the hypothesis that our experience includes more than what
we consciously register in our perceptions, and that details can be felt and perceived
without being noticed consciously. The field of conscious experience would seem to
be continuous with the subconscious field by being a part of it. If the boundaries of
conscious experience blend into the subconscious, perhaps the same is true of the
boundaries of the subconscious; one's present experience may be part of an experience which, in terms of its conscious content, is also another's. We may need to
dispense with familiar notions of spatial and physical boundaries in thinking about

the scope and limits not only of experience and consciousness but of the self as well. One's own identity may not be fixed or isolated, and may not even be definable exclusively in terms of the consciousness associated with one's own body; the collapse of boundaries between experiences opens the possibility that one's identity may cross into experiences normally attributed to others, whether they be selves hidden in one's own subconscious or those associated with bodies other than one's own. If personal identity is a center of consciousness that radiates indefinitely into a dim periphery of experiential content, who knows where it terminates? James admired F. W. H. Myers, his friend and British colleague in psychical research, for trying to map a subconscious or subliminal realm.

> There are many first-hand investigators into the subliminal who, not having themselves met with anything supernormal, would probably not hesitate to call all the reports of it erroneous, and who would limit the subliminal to dissolutive phenomena of consciousness exclusively, to lapsed memories, subconscious sensations, impulses and *phobias,* and the like. Messrs. Janet and Binet, for aught I know, may hold some such position as this. Against it Myers's thesis would sharply stand out. Of the subliminal, he would say, we can give no ultra-simple account: there are discrete regions in it; levels separated by critical points of transition, and no one formula holds true of them all. . . . The problem of Myers still awaits us as the problem of far the deepest moment for our actual psychology, whether his own tentative solutions of certain parts of it be correct or not. . . .
>
> One cannot help admiring the great originality with which Myers wove such an extraordinarily detached and discontinuous series of phenomena together. Unconscious cerebration, dreams, hypnotism, hysteria, inspirations of genius, the willing game, planchette, crystal-gazing, hallucinatory voices, apparitions of the dying, medium-trances, demoniacal possession, clairvoyance, thought-transference—even ghosts and other facts more doubtful—these things form a chaos at first sight most discouraging. . . . Yet Myers has made a system of them . . . verified in some cases and extended to others by analogy.[67]

We can of course be intrigued by the possibilities of the subliminal without following James, Myers, and Gurney into the arcane realm of psychical research. But what did James actually think about the claims of such research? As usual, he was of two minds; he was impressed by the data and fascinated by the occult hypotheses Myers and others offered to explain them, and he clearly wanted to believe in occult speculations, but he could not entirely desert his scientific self and accordingly had to remain skeptical. He reserved the right to indulge his own guesses about psychic phenomena, which took him in a more religious direction than others might have wanted to go. In 1886, while in the earlier phases of his psychical research, he complained of "wasting" time on it, but in 1909 he referred to Henry Sidgwick, philosopher and founding member of the British Society for Psychical Research, as follows:

Like all founders, Sidgwick hoped for a certain promptitude of result; and I heard him say, the year before his death, that if anyone had told him at the outset that after twenty years he would be in the same identical state of doubt and balance that he started with, he would have deemed the prophecy incredible. It appeared impossible that that amount of handling evidence should bring so little finality of decision.

My own experience has been similar to Sidgwick's. For twenty-five years I have been in touch with the literature of psychical research, and have had acquaintance with numerous "researchers." I have also spent a good many hours (though far fewer than I ought to have spent) in witnessing (or trying to witness) phenomena. Yet I am theoretically no "further" than I was at the beginning; and I confess at times that I have been tempted to believe that the Creator has eternally intended this department of nature to remain *baffling,* to prompt our curiosities and hopes and suspicions all in equal measure, so that, although ghosts and clairvoyances, and raps and messages from spirits, are always seeming to exist and can never be fully explained away, they also can never be susceptible of full corroboration.[68]

Much of James's study of psychic phenomena focused upon Mrs. William J. Piper, the celebrated Boston medium whom he met in 1885 and with whom he worked until his death. In 1890 he declared his belief in her supernormal powers while confessing his inability to explain her trance phenomena, which purported to be under the control of departed spirits. "The *prima facie* theory, which is that of spirit-control, is hard to reconcile with the extreme triviality of most of the communications. What real spirit, at last able to revisit his wife on this earth, but would find something better to say than that she had changed the place of his photograph? And yet that is the sort of remark to which the spirits introduced . . . are apt to confine themselves."[69] Despite the challenges to credulity that even James acknowledged, he continued to believe in Mrs. Piper's extraordinary abilities.

But it is a miserable thing for a question of truth to be confined to mere presumption and counter-presumption, with no decisive thunderbolt of fact to clear the baffling. For me the thunderbolt *has* fallen. . . . If you wish to upset the law that all crows are black, you must not to seek to show that no crows are; it is enough if you prove one simple crow to be white. My own white crow is Mrs. Piper. In the trances of this medium, I cannot resist the conviction that knowledge appears which she has never gained by the ordinary waking use of her eyes and ears and wits. . . . So when I turn to the rest of the evidence, ghosts and all, I cannot carry with me the irreversibly negative bias of the "rigorously scientific" mind, with its presumption as to what the true order of nature ought to be. . . . As a matter of fact, the trances I speak of have broken down for my own mind the limits of the admitted order of nature. Science, so far as science denies such exceptional occurrences, lies prostrate in the dust for me; and the most urgent intellectual need which I feel at present is that science be built up again in a form in which such things may have a positive place.[70]

In 1906, exhibiting typical ambivalence toward any self-enthusiasm, James wrote that his friend and coworker in psychical research, Richard Hodgson (who had just died), had become too obsessed with Mrs. Piper and had ignored other avenues of inquiry, and that for lack of a competent executive secretary to succeed Hodgson the American branch of the Society for Psychical Research might have to close down. "To tell the truth, I'm rather glad of the prospect of the Branch ending, for the Piper-investigation—and nothing else—had begun to bore me to extinction."[71] Although James had wearied of sittings with Mrs. Piper and yearned for fresh evidence, he had by no means rejected her claims to mediumship. In reporting later sittings with Mrs. Piper, in which messages from the deceased Hodgson were allegedly received through her, he hypothesized that these might be the result of her "will-to-personate" in conjunction with another's (possibly Hodgson's) "will-to-communicate." James's conclusion mixed belief with skepticism. *"I myself feel as if an external will to communicate were probably there,* that is, I find myself doubting, in consequence of my whole acquaintance with that sphere of phenomena, that Mrs. Piper's dream-life, even equipped with 'telepathic' powers, accounts for all the results found. But if asked whether the will to communicate is Hodgson's, or be some mere spirit-counterfeit of Hodgson, I remain uncertain and await more facts, facts which may not point clearly to a conclusion for fifty or a hundred years."[72]

If James could see what has happened since he made these remarks, he would be severely disappointed. Psychical research has won over neither the scientific community nor the the popular mind. Today's discoveries are all in other disciplines, and the investigative directions pioneered by Myers and others seem to have led nowhere. Furthermore, the subliminal realm, while more respectable than in James's day and still intriguing on a theoretical level, has not yielded much if anything practical. Contemporary controversies about Freudian theory sometimes illustrate that the concept of the unconscious is more interesting as a theoretical construct than as an instrument for achieving practical results. However one evaluates James's conjecture about the nature of the subliminal, of its interpretation by psychical research, and of its relevance to the self, one must conclude that his hopes for its illumination by an enlightened science of the future have not been realized.

James's speculations on the subliminal also create tensions within his own views. Something like a substantial self results from the hypothesis that each of us is part of a larger consciousness or experience, that our own centers of consciousness extend at the subliminal level into a coexisting consciousness (whose nature, plural or monistic, can only be guessed at). The picture of the self in this subliminal interpretation differs from the self described as passing thought in *Principles*. In James's psychology, the introspecting self had been desubstantialized into an ephemeral phase of the stream of consciousness; the "psychology without a soul" had liquefied the self into a momentary current of the stream, something that presented itself for a moment and then dissolved into its next brief presentation. The self is a series of momentary durations in a flow of time and consciousness, and the *forward* direction of the flow dominates. But a sideways movement occurs in connecting our present conscious experience through the subliminal with a coexisting consciousness or coexisting centers of consciousness. To make the self part of a simultaneous, larger consciousness is to rescue it from its fleeting appearance in the stream and to absorb it into a kind of standing pool of consciousness. A standing pool, while perhaps less substantial than a standing condominium, is considerably more substantial than a passing moment in a stream; it endures, consists of parts and relations, and can be represented as a system of sorts. If we link the evanescent self with a larger, sturdier, and more durable consciousness, as James did, then to the extent that it enjoys some of the properties that characterize the larger consciousness, it becomes quite a substantial self.

A more vivid tension within the Jamesian scheme arises with the subliminal interpretation: the scheme appears to contradict the thrust of "Does 'Consciousness' Exist?" and radical empiricism in general. For the reader who has adjusted to James's denial of consciousness as an entity, many of his formulations before and after "Does 'Consciousness' Exist?" demand interpretation because they explicitly exploit the noun *consciousness*. Whether writing on immortality, the self, mind-body dualism, or a pluralistic universe, James repeatedly appealed to consciousness as a kind of reservoir, mother-sea, cosmic environment, and supraliminal life. It would have been dogmatic to assert the impossibility of translating these expressions into the language demanded by radical empiricism or pure experience, but James never attempted such a translation; any such effort would appear doomed to failure. He described pure experience thus: "It is made of *that,* of just what appears, of space, of intensity, of flatness, brownness, heaviness, or what not"—sensible natures or sensations.[73]

Is pure experience the only thing we are connected with at the subliminal level? Are not will, activity, intention, attitude, reflection, and introspection also features of the larger, mother-sea consciousness into which our finite selves subliminally blend, according to James? In commenting on Myers's studies of psychic phenomena, he asked, *"What is the precise constitution of the subliminal?"*[74] Interestingly, he himself did not volunteer an answer in terms of sensible natures or sensations. In proferring his own hypothesis that the brain only filters or transmits consciousness and is not a necessary condition of its existence, James wrote: "Consciousness in this process does not have to be generated *de novo* in a vast number of places. It exists already, behind the scenes, coeval with the world."[75] Instead of simply identifying consciousness with pure experience, defined as the range of sensations, James delivered its character over to religious speculations. The same is true of this: "If, then, there be a wider world of being than that of our every-day consciousness, if in it there be forces whose effects on us are intermittent, if one facilitating condition of the effects be the openness of the 'subliminal' door, we have the elements of a theory to which the phenomena of religious life lend plausibility" (*VRE,* 513). The subliminal links us with a larger consciousness, but the nature of this link is metaphysically and theologically uncertain—and so, in radical empiricism, is the nature of the relation of the subliminal realm to the consciousness (or its replacement).

James's psychology conceives of the self largely in terms of the body, but in the later writings on metaphysics, psychical research, and religion, the emphasis is predominantly upon the self as defined by consciousness and its subliminal extensions. This raises again the question of how a self, understood commonsensically and with appropriate deference to the role of the body, can retain its character when interpreted as a bodiless and free-floating sea of consciousness:

> There is a continuum of cosmic consciousness, against which our individuality builds but accidental fences, and into which our several minds plunge as into a mother-sea or reservoir. . . . Not only psychic research, but metaphysical philosophy, and speculative biology are led in their own ways to look with favor on some such "panpsychic" view of the universe as this. Assuming this common reservoir of consciousness to exist, this bank upon which we all draw, and in which so many of earth's memories must in some way be stored, or mediums would not get at them as they do, the question is, What is its own structure?[76]

James seems to be wondering here what in the cosmic consciousness, and thereby in the selfhood of each of us, contributes the durability, organization, and dynamics of the human body that helps to constitute a self or person. After posing questions of whether individuation can be secured in the cosmic consciousness, whether there are hierarchic orders, and if so, whether they are permanent or transient, he inquired: "What, again, are the relations between the cosmic consciousness and matter? Are there subtler forms of matter which upon occasion may enter into functional connection with the individuations in the psychic sea, and then only, show themselves?—so that our ordinary human experience, on its material as well as its mental side, would appear to be only an extract from the larger psychophysical world?"[77] Although he did not specifically ask whether matter or some physical refinement of the human body is required for its normal systematic organization, it is evident that he at least entertained the idea that the subliminal realm has a physical dimension. The same idea is entertained elsewhere in his writings.

Even Myers, who construed the subliminal world largely as a spiritual world, an actual "world of spirits," was forced "to abandon purely mental territory" and purely psychic entities, and to refer to the spatial aspects of such entities in order to explain telekinesis, mediumship, and the like.[78] Fechner's influence repeatedly showed itself, indicating that James, despite the official pronouncements of radical empiricism, never closed the door firmly on metaphysical or psychophysical dualism. One of the Fechnerian ideas that James adopted was this:

> The vaster orders of mind go with the vaster orders of body. The entire earth on which we live must have, according to Fechner, its own collective consciousness. So must each sun, moon, and planet; so must the whole solar system have its own wider consciousness, in which the consciousness of our earth plays one part. So has the entire starry system as such its consciousness; and if that starry sum be not all that *is,* materially considered then that whole system, along with whatever else may be, is the body of that absolutely totalized consciousness of the universe to which men give the name of God.[79]

It is difficult to determine how literally James was prepared to understand this idea, but without doubt he found it fascinating. Consider this:

> Fechner in his *Zend-Avesta* and elsewhere assumes that mental and physical life run parallel, all memory-processes being, according to him, coordinated with material processes. If an act of yours is to be consciously remembered hereafter, it must leave traces on the material universe such that when the *traced parts of the said universe systematically enter into activity together* the act is consciously recalled. During your life the traces are mainly in your brain; but after your death, since your brain is gone, they exist in the shape of all the records of your actions which the outer world stores up as the effects, immediate or remote, thereof, the cosmos being in some degree, however slight, made structurally different by every act of ours that takes place in it. Now, just as the air of the same room can be simultaneously used by many different voices for communicating with different pairs of ears, or as the ether of space can carry many simultaneous messages to and from mutually attuned Marconi-stations, so the great continuum of material nature can have certain tracts within it thrown into emphasized activity whenever activity begins in any part . . . in which the potentiality of such systematic activity inheres. The bodies (including of course the brains) of Hodgson's friends who come as sitters, are naturally parts of the material universe which carry some of the traces of his ancient acts. They function as receiving stations. . . . If, now, the *rest* of the system of physical traces left behind by Hodgson's acts were, by some sort of mutual induction throughout its extent, thrown into gear and made to vibrate all at once, by the presence of such human bodies to the medium, we should have a Hodgson-system active in the cosmos again, and the "conscious aspect" of this vibrating system might be Hodgson's spirit redivivus, and recollecting and willing in a certain momentary way.[80]

The influence of Fechner reveals James's willingness to retain a place for the body or at least for some form of matter in a scheme of hierarchical and evolutionary psychophysical parallelism (which includes the subliminal realm), despite his having startled the world some years earlier by rejecting any such dualism. The change of heart indicates the difficulties he met in trying to discard all connections with the physical bases of selfhood as he incorporated subliminal into a cosmic consciousness. But we must not exaggerate the Fechnerian psychophysical dualism in his thinking, since the concept of matter James entertained is somewhat incidental or intermediary; we must assume that if James could respond now, he would reassert his radical empiricistic abandonment of dualism, metaphysically reinterpreting the matter of the subliminal in a Berkeleyan manner.

The physical thus dissolves into pure experience, into sensations and sensible natures, into the stuff of which mind is made. Nothing in James's metaphysics of the subliminal resembles the human body or its role in his psychology, for the important sources of structure, organization, and dynamics are almost always at least implicitly assigned to consciousness.[81] The brain becomes a transmitter, but what it transmits, consciousness itself, contains its own full nature independently of the brain or any other physical thing. How a self or finite portion of the subliminal realm or cosmic consciousness can assume a full character without the contributions of the body must remain, despite the analogies of Fechner and others, a mystery fit for the contemplation of a mystic.

James wrote in his final days:

> One need only shut oneself in a closet and begin to think of the fact of one's being there, of one's queer bodily shape in the darkness (a thing to make children scream at, as Stevenson says), of one's fantastic character and all, to have the wonder steal over the detail as much as over the general fact of being, and to see that it is only familiarity that blunts it. Not only that *anything* should be, but that *this* very thing should be, is mysterious. Philosophy stares, but brings no reasoned solution, for from nothing to being there is no logical bridge. (*SPP*, 39–40)

The metaphysical dimensions of the self surmount the understanding. These are not the only dimensions of selfhood, however; there are moral dimensions as well, and in some respects both kinds work with and for each other. Perhaps the self, in a Jamesian universe, can never know its own ultimate nature, but it can strive for the moral goals that mirror, if not the metaphysical self, at least the kind of fulfilment proper to it.

13 ❧ MORALITY

MORAL PHILOSOPHY AND MORAL LIFE

In his first philosophical statement, the letter written at age sixteen to Edgar Van Winkle, James pondered possible careers; he felt strongly that his eventual vocation must be morally defensible. "What ought to be everyone's object in life? To be as much use as possible."[1] James's moral earnestness as a teenager, revealed in the correspondence with Van Winkle, may be traceable to his family's Calvinistic heritage and to his father's habit of daily subjecting the cosmos to an idiosyncratic moral assessment. Henry James, Sr., was a literary Zeus hurling moral thunderbolts that kept the family atmosphere in a steady state of excitement. When he renounced his own Calvinistic inheritance in a letter to a former colleague at Princeton Theological Seminary, his tone was scarcely offhand: "You, I imagine, can hardly conceive the completeness of my contempt, on the one hand, for all those monstrous and odious caricatures of the Divine name which make our Calvinistic literature a sickening abomination to the heart, more even than a falsity to the intellect."[2] When he declared that the "moral atmosphere of Colleges was very debasing" and that the collegiate curse was idleness, his son William understandably saw himself and his future through somewhat anxious eyes.[3] Whereas some of us reach adulthood before our moral sensitivites are shaken into working order, James was at sixteen already involved with the perplexities of moral issues.

Trained from boyhood to discuss religion and morality, James would have betrayed everything he had been taught if he had not eulogized the dutiful nature of human existence. By upbringing and temperament he was prepared to define life in moral terms. But for reasons that were both personal and philosophical, his confidence in the worth of moral commitment sometimes faltered, and he called such occasions, marked by depression and anxiety, moral crises. A diary entry dated 22 May 1868, written while he was in Dresden, reiterated what he had expressed to Van Winkle ten years earlier: the need to lead a morally useful life.

Tonight while listening to Miss H's magic playing and the Dr. and the Italian lady sing my feelings came to a sort of crisis. The intuition of something here in a measure absolute gave me such an unspeakable disgust for the dead drifting of my own life for some time past. I can revive the feeling perhaps hereafter by thinking of men of genius. It ought to have a practical effect on my own will—a horror of waste life, since life can be *such*—and Oh God! an end to the idle, idiotic sinking into *Vorstellungen* disproportionate to the object. Every good experience ought to be interpreted in practice. Perhaps actually we can not always trace the effect, but we won't lose if we *try* to drop all in which this is not possible. Keep sinewy all the while—and work at present with a mystical belief in the reality interpreted somehow of humanity.[4]

When he felt his will weakening and his zest for life ebbing, even while seeking cures through baths, travel, medication, and mental healers, James saw his predicament as a moral one. A person constituted of proper stuff could summon the requisite willpower, he thought. Years later, in the aftermath of a marital tiff, he wrote in a letter of 3 October 1890 to his wife Alice: "I have achieved a moral victory over my low spirits and tendency to complain. . . . I have actually by steady force of will kept it down and at last got it under for a while and mean to fight it out on that line for the rest of my life, for I see that is my particular mission in the world." In 1907, while seeking help from a Boston mental healer identified only as Mrs. Newman, he noted in his diary on May 20: "Remarkable improvement in moral and physical 'tone'— and what was unlooked for in my power to walk without angina."[5] James's emotional crisis of 1870 was also recorded in his diary. He wrote on 1 February: "Today I about touched bottom, and perceive plainly that I must face the choice with open eyes: shall I *frankly* throw the moral business overboard, as one unsuited to my innate aptitudes, or shall I follow it, and it alone, making everything else merely stuff for it? I will give the latter alternative a fair trial. Who knows but the moral interest may become developed. . . . Hitherto I have tried to fire myself with the moral interest, as an aid in the accomplishing of certain utilitarian ends" (quoted in RBP, 1:322).

James later rejected traditional utilitarianism, but this diary entry shows that as early as 1870 he found it self-defeating to use moral interest in the service of utilitarian goals. To keep the moral impulse inwardly alive seemed to require thinking of it as autonomous, serving only itself. He connected his occasional sense of hopelessness with an obsessive doubt as to whether true freedom exists, whether decision and action ever originate in ourselves rather than in antecedent circumstances. At this period of James's life, his reading and reflections seemed only to aggravate the obsession. Then on 30 April 1870 he confided in his diary:

I think that yesterday was a crisis in my life. I finished the first part of Renouvier's second *Essais* and see no reason why his definition of free will—"the sustaining of a thought *because I choose to* when I might have other thoughts"— need be the definition of an illusion. At any rate, I will assume for the present—

until next year—that it is no illusion. My first act of free will shall be to believe in free will. . . .

Hitherto, when I have felt like taking a free initiative, like daring to act originally without carefully waiting for contemplation of the external world to determine all for me, Suicide seemed the most manly form to put my daring into; Now, I will go a step further with my will, not only act with it, but believe as well; believe in my individual reality and creative power. My belief to be sure *can't* be optimistic—but I will posit life (the real, the good) in the self governing *resistance* of the ego to the world . . . [the remainder of the page is torn out].[6]

This diary entry, revealing James's intention to follow the suggestion of Renouvier, is the key to his ethics. In declaring that his first free act would be to choose to believe in free will, he expressed the existentialist thesis that ethics rest finally upon choice and commitment; there is a clear resemblance between James and Kierkegaard, Nietzsche, and Sartre. Questions such as whether to believe in free will, whether to be moral, and even whether to live rather than commit suicide tend, when asked in moments of despair and hopelessness, to elicit the response, "Only if I choose to, it's all up to me." In facing such questions it dawns upon us that the answer lies within ourselves; we either have or do not have the inner resources to give a positive response, and the struggle of groping for those resources is felt more as a crisis of will than as one of intellect. There comes that moment when we realize that we must stop pondering and decide.

If, as James believed, such questions as "Why be moral?" and "Why go on living?" must be confronted before an ethical standpoint can be developed, then the whole structure of ethics depends upon resolution or commitment. The decision to be moral or to see life as having moral dimensions is better described as a decision that makes morality possible than as one that is itself moral; once a moral framework is thereby established, one's decision to save an innocent person from the hangman, for example, is indisputably moral. James did not contend that the questions "Why be moral?" and "Why go on living?" are inherently unanswerable; he realized that some persons might answer, "Because it will make life easier" or "Because it will please my family." During crises like that of 1870, James found such answers inadequate and perhaps even frivolous, but he still wanted to find a motive for being moral and for living. Even if certain reasons worked for some individuals, those reasons lacked solid justification if challenged by other individuals or if suddenly doubted by those for whom they had hitherto served as reasons. James wanted to see life in moral terms and to live longer, but a compelling reason could not be found.

His response was to assert that his need could be satisfied; he trusted that this bold assertion would supply the motivation for being moral and for continuing to live, a motivation that could not be obtained from any theoretical explanation. This response is in part what existentialists mean in claiming that one must find the meaning in life within oneself or that one must *give* life the required meaning; what is mandated is not the discovery of a missing reason but the decision to treat one's want as being satisfiable. The crisis is one of motivation, and one thus decides to generate the wanted motivation through an act of one's own; the act undertaken will depend upon the circumstances and upon one's general temperament, but in James's case it was a speech act or an act of thought, a declaration to himself that he would henceforth avow that he had freedom of will, that he would behave and think in ways that would solidify his belief that avowal, trusting that he would thereby eventually avoid suicide and yet be able to apply moral distinctions to human existence.

James never intended to denigrate the difficulties of choosing between the moral and social options that confront us in our daily lives, but he paid special tribute to those occasions when the whole meaning and worth of existence teeter wildly in our minds. On such occasions one seems to be thrown back upon one's own resources. "The most characteristically and peculiarly moral judgments that a man is ever called on to make are in unprecedented cases and lonely emergencies, where no popular rhetorical maxims can avail, and the hidden oracle alone can speak; and it speaks often in favor of conduct quite unusual, and suicidal as far as gaining popular approbation goes."[7] Moral judgments are distinctly least confined in the range of their effects and are disposed instead to affect the heart and soul of one's entire life. The kind of choice that is particularly moral is "between one of several equally possible future Characters. What he shall *become* is fixed by the conduct of this moment. Schopenhauer, who enforces his determinism by the argument that with a given fixed character only one reaction is possible under given circumstances, forgets that, in these critical ethical moments, what consciously *seems* to be in question is the complexion of the character itself. The problem with the man is less what act he shall now choose to do, than what being he shall now resolve to become."[8]

James emphasized that an appreciation of the significance of moral consciousness depends very much upon having experiences in which the very point of morality is temporarily suspect, and in which we must decide irrevocably the kind of person or character we will become. An easygoing morality was not morality at all for James; his view, sometimes associated with the tradition in German philosophy of opposing inclination and duty, was that the moral life, while often boasting exhilaration, is nevertheless a life of sweat and tears. It seemed self-evident to him that the sweat and tears are worthwhile only if we have the freedom to choose between alternatives. James yearned to think of himself as the origin of events which would not have occurred without his influence. He wanted to do what he ought to do, but one sensibly wants to do what is obligatory only if one is free to do it. James's mental crisis of 1870, according to his own testimony, was connected with his obsession that perhaps we are never free in our choices and actions, that our choices are merely links in a causal chain and are never originating causes. James never confidently located the source of his worry, which was the sort of concern that often infects the philosophically inclined; the philosophical temperament is as responsible as anything else for plunging an individual into depression once he is seized by the idea that his choices are simply the effects of antecedent events.[9]

Whatever its cause, James resolved his crisis of 1870 not through discovery but through a self-reinforcing decision. The lesson learned in that experience was the single most important factor in his thinking on ethics and metaphysics; he gained the conviction that when ethical questions puzzle the intellect and paralyze the will, the only recourse is to make a decision and to fortify that decision with persuasive reasoning. Even when a decision comes easily, we must not forget that the decision was first and its reasons secondary. In ethics and metaphysics, as James conceived them, the issues are eternally debatable and can never be resolved either argumentatively or experimentally; it is by a decision, which then gathers reasons around itself, that we are motivated to choose one belief instead of another. When we understand that competing reasons are at a standoff, we realize that no reason activates a choice; our decision must be hoisted under its own strength. As we mature through the repetition of such situations, we absorb the effects of past choices, and rather than having to exercise our will laboriously in each new dilemma, we allow past experience to determine the solution with relative ease. According to the Jamesian perspective, arguments and theories in ethics and metaphysics serve personalities and their choices rather than vice versa.

Do we ever choose freely? Determinism replies no, indeterminism yes; James always agreed with the indeterminists. To say that we choose freely is to say that we choose what we want and that we could choose differently; indeed, if the same situation were duplicated, we might well choose differently. On James's definition, determinists declare this option impossible, holding that if a situation were replicated, we could choose only as we originally did. Indeterminists maintain, to the contrary, that our making a variety of decisions is compatible with the same set of antecedent circumstances. The controversy between determinism and indeterminism was to James a metaphysical one; if the validity of ethics depends upon its resolution in favor of indeterminism, he thought, then a metaphysical solution must occur before ethical inquiry can begin. But ''The Dilemma of Determinism'' and James's later treatment of the problem in the chapter on the will in *Principles* reveal that he actually followed a different procedure (see chapter 7).

In ''The Dilemma of Determinism'' James argued that the issue between determinism and indeterminism is metaphysical and depends on untestable speculations about what is possible; simply pointing to facts to support one view or the other is therefore irrelevant.

> And the truth is that facts practically have hardly anything to do with making us either determinists or indeterminists. Sure enough, we make a flourish of quoting facts this way or that. . . . But who does not see the wretched insufficiency of this so-called objective testimony on both sides? . . . What divides us into possibility men [indeterminists] and anti-possibility men [determinists] is different faiths or postulates—postulates of rationality. To this man the world seems more rational with possibilities in it,—to that man more rational with possibilities excluded; and talk as we will about having to yield to evidence, what makes us monists or pluralists, determinists or indeterminists, is at bottom always some sentiment like this.[10]

The very possibility of ethics depends upon freedom of choice, but we can never prove or refute such freedom by factual evidence. There is even a touch of insincerity in our claims for evidence, James suggested, because what motivates us toward determinism or indeterminism is whatever we want to be the case, whatever conforms to our prejudiced canons of rationality. If we acknowledge that our appeal to evidence is used to bolster whatever view we want to be true, then the concern about insincerity can be dropped.

In *Principles* James remarked on the inability of psychologists, in their study of how the will operates, to decide between determinism and indeterminism. Commenting that his own reasons for believing in indeterminism were ethical rather than psychological, he referred his reader to "The Dilemma of Determinism," alluding to his crisis of 1870, when he had taken his cue from Renouvier: "If, meanwhile, the will is undetermined, it would seem only fitting that the belief in its indetermination should be voluntarily chosen from amongst other possible beliefs. Freedom's first deed should be to affirm itself" (*Principles,* 2:573–79). For James, the procedure was not to clear the path for ethics by first resolving the problem of free will through metaphysical argument; instead, it was to choose indeterminism and then to offer ethical reasons in support of that choice; he wanted to make ethics bear upon a metaphysical dilemma rather than the other way around.

James's argument for indeterminism in "The Dilemma of Determinism" is that we initially want to judge certain classes of actions as bad or good. One aspect of wanting to condemn certain actions is that we regret their occurrence, but if determinism were true and only one choice could have occurred in a specific context, then the sentiment of remorse or regret is pointless. "I cannot understand regret without the admission of real, genuine possibilities in the world."[11] Like Aristotle, James believed that the existence of a thing proves that it has a function—nature abhors a purposeless existent—so the very occurrence of a remorseful feeling about an action is prima facie evidence that the act need not have been chosen. Merely because we regret a certain action is no guarantee that a different choice was psychologically or physiologically possible in the context. Besides suggesting that a different choice *generally* could have been made, the feeling of regret serves a purpose even in those situations where no other choice was available; it keeps alive the sense of moral outrage over certain deeds. Perhaps some murderers should be hospitalized rather than executed, yet the regret we feel over their crimes is not wasted if it contributes to the amoring of human sentiment against murder and the consitions that encourage it.

The strategy of James's argument, characteristic of his pragmatic approach to philosophical issues, was to describe the consequences of rival hypotheses, to compare the effects of those consequences upon what we want to be the case, and—when the factual evidence is mostly tentative—to choose the hypothesis (indeterminism) whose consequences are compatible with what we want. This strategy is certainly limited, James assumed, because it fails to move many thinkers, but its main force is to motivate the belief of the person using it by offering reasons which make the belief more than merely arbitrary and show it to be compatible with the person's wants. Such a strategy is a personal method of working through a philosophical dilemma. "This personal method of appeal seems to be among the very conditions of the problem; and the most any one can do is to confess as candidly as he can the grounds for the faith that is in him, and leave his example to work on others as it may."[12]

James entered treacherous territory in openly embracing the personal approach and saying in effect that we should not be too concerned about particular arguments because we are already either determinists or indeterminists by temperament. Throughout his career, as in "The Dilemma of Determinism," he was convinced that philosophies are essentially the expressions of temperament and that the arguments used by philosophers are largely rationalizations of the conclusions already sanctioned by their personalities. This rationale buckles under the charge that James's advocacy of indeterminism was merely the expression of his own temperament, that even he did not freely choose his arguments since they were determined by the kind of person he was. In seeking to be tolerant of his opponents' positions, James relied further on this rationale. He imagined that his opponents were like himself, ensconced in their libraries, bringing forth the philosophy lying within themselves. When the philosophers left their libraries to compare notes, they discovered their differences in temperament and returned to their libraries to determine how those differences could be even more sharply drawn philosophically. James found this an adequate state of affairs, for philosophy was to him mainly an exercise in self-discovery which involved comparing himself to others.

James underestimated the alterability of the philosophical nerves in one's temperament through dialogue and debate. We need to remind ourselves, when entranced by the Jamesian mood, that we are rational creatures who are swayed by arguments and are capable of directing our personalities in accordance with new insights and the changes of heart that these arguments produce. Our task is more than a personal one, more than being sincere and undogmatic; we must also be receptive to the voice of reason, whether in others or in ourselves, even if that voice offends a temperamental sensitivity. We must avoid the notion that as philosophers we are trapped within the biases of our temperaments, that we will reject unfriendly arguments regardless of their soundness. James does not seem to have recognized fully that an argument or insight can have the force that he reserved for temperament or personality alone; the force of an argument by itself may not activate a decision, but it can liberate us from our prejudices so that we can make more enlightened (and therefore freer) choices about the beliefs and norms by which to guide our lives. Whatever James may have said at times, he did not believe that arguments could have sufficient force to modify one's philosophical prejudices or preconceptions; this resistance to the arguments of others is often overlooked by readers charmed by the sincerity and graciousness of James's "personal method."

James's analysis is vulnerable also to the objection that he too quickly classified the problem of free will as a metaphysical one. Insisting that it was a philosophical and not a scientific issue—and consequently an untestable controversy—he treated it in the spirit of subjective pragmatism. Is it obvious that the statement that humans sometimes choose and act freely is wholly untestable and must be taken on faith? James acknowledged that what can be called *soft* determinism is a testable hypothesis; this thesis removes the harshness of the doctrine by holding that determinism and freedom are actually compatible. A soft determinist may assert that a person chooses freely if the choice is self-determined, that is, determined simply by his own character, in the absence of external constraint. In this sense, James agreed, determinism presents no problem of freedom. "No matter what the soft determinist mean by it,—whether he mean the acting without external constraint; whether he mean the acting rightly, or whether he mean the acquiescing in the law of the whole,—who cannot answer him that sometimes we are free and sometimes we are not?"[13]

What has divided philosophical opinion throughout history, he urged, is not soft but *hard* determinism, the belief that because all choices and deeds are caused by what has preceded, we can never choose or act other than as we do. In this version of determinism, the hypothesis that all our choices are determined by antecedent events is incompatible with freedom, and given its untestability James wrote that "the utmost that a believer in free-will can *ever* do will be to show that the deterministic arguments are not coercive. That they are seductive, I am the last to deny; nor do I deny that effort may be needed to keep the faith in freedom, when they press upon it, upright in the mind" (*Principles*, 2:573–74). James believed this not only because he knew he was powerless to convert convinced determinists but also, I suspect, because he could never totally subdue in his own mind the thought that they might be right. We can indeed sympathize with him, for it is a human inclination, when an issue is judged to be forever debatable, to debate it forever.

James was surely correct in thinking that soft determinism does not go to the heart of the problem; even if a choice is self-determined and not externally constrained, that fact is no guarantee that the choice was free or that another could have been made in its place. A person can be the prisoner of his own character traits, as in the cases of alcoholics and compulsive gamblers; although their choices in critical situations may be entirely their own, such individuals are seemingly unable to make other choices instead. In this sense they do not choose freely in those situations. But if there are times when people do not freely choose or act, it would seem that there are other times when they do, yet this possibility is denied by hard determinism. If the question is theoretically unresolvable, James's approach to it can hardly be surpassed. But despite our inability to convert the hard determinist or to demonstrate in borderline cases whether a choice was freely made, we should not jettison the methods we use in daily life to sort out free from unfree choices and actions. We suppose in our routine existence that hard determinism is not only testable but is also false; we should not scrap the evidence to which we commonly appeal in calling a choice free merely because someone suggests, without relevant evidence, that perhaps no choice is ever free. I suspect that James was not entirely clear about the source of his own nagging doubts, which survived even the pressure of our usual commonsense evidence. It is not clear why James, as a pragmatist, did not insist upon viewing the issue of determinism as testable; had he done so, he might have eliminated his own doubts by forcing the philosophical imagination to return to the facts of our daily lives.

In 1879, when James first taught philosophy after five years of teaching anatomy, physiology, and psychology at Harvard, he published "The Sentiment of Rationality," in which he wrote: "This is why so few human beings truly care for Philosophy. The particular determinations which she ignores are the real matter exciting other aesthetic and practical needs, quite as potent and authoritative as hers. What does the moral enthusiast care for philosophical ethics?" (CER, 122). In the same year, in a laudatory review of essays by W. K. Clifford, he wrote: "Why do these lectures seem to the reader almost funny in the inadequacy with which they shadow forth anything fit to form a 'creed' for modern life?"[14] The difficulty of focusing the chaotic scene of human values for ethical theorizing was also described in another review of the same year: "We can never on evolutionist principles altogether bar out personal bias, or the subjective method, from the construction of the ethical standard of right."[15] That year he also wrote in a letter to his wife that he had come to recognize something in himself which pointed up the clash between feeling and theory:

> This characteristic attitude [of feeling intensely active and alive] in me always involves an element of active tension, of holding my own . . . but without any *guaranty*. . . . Make it a guaranty—and the attitude immediately becomes to my consciousness stagnant and stingless. Take away the guaranty, and I feel . . . a sort of deep enthusiastic bliss. . . . Although it is a mere mood or emotion to which I can give no form in words, [it] authenticates itself to me as the deepest principle of all active and theoretic determination which I possess. (LWJ, 1:199–200)

How can such emotions and feelings, which are virtually incapable of adequate formulation and yet which strike us as the authenticating sources of moral energy, be tamed and branded by some ethical theory?

Pondering the role of moral philosophy, James was perplexed about what a theory of ethics should resemble. How can one enter "that jumbling together of different questions and different points of view which constitutes most ethical discussion" without merely adding to the babble?[16] Faced with the myriad concepts of good and bad, right and wrong, and virtue and vice, what is a philosopher to do? James's temperament might have led him to dismiss ethics as he did aesthetics (see below), but he hinted as early as 1879 that such was not his inclination. Answering his own query about why Clifford's moralizing represented less than the desired achievement, he became positively rhapsodic:

> The miraculous achievement, the achievement upon which we are all waiting for our faculties to burst into movement like mill-wheels at the touch of a torrent, must be a metaphysical achievement, the greatest of all time—the

demonstration, namely, that all our different motives, rightly interpreted, pull one way. . . . Can the synthesis and reconciliation come? It would be as rash to despair of it as to swear to it in advance. But when it does come, whatever its specific character may be, it will necessarily have to be of the theoretic order, a result of deeper philosophic analysis and discrimination than has yet been made.[17]

No philosopher has exceeded James's enthusiasm in contrasting experience favorably with theory; odd as it may seem, he was a Hegelian at heart, excited by the vision of an impending theoretical insight in which apparent opposites are reconciled in an overarching unity. Just when we might expect James to have surrendered theory to experience, he announced the possibility of a theoretic triumph, permitting us to see how the apparent war of different human motives is actually a complex version of everyone pulling in one direction.

Making this idea credible was a dominant motive in "The Moral Philosopher and the Moral Life," commonly described as James's only systematic essay in ethics. He intended the essay to show the impossibility of constructing an ethical philosophy in advance of the entire experience of the human race, for ethics, like science, consists of hypotheses that require experimental testing, and the moral experience of every individual must be included as evidence. A moral philosophy is constructed of everyone's concrete experiences, partly because, given the moral worth of each individual, ethical theorizing must take account of the wants and feelings of each individual in relation to those of all others, and partly because of what a moral philosophy must look like. On this point James in effect returned to the rhapsodic hint of 1879. The good of ethics as a theoretical discipline is "to find an account of the moral relations that obtain among things, which will weave them into the unity of a stable system, and make of the world what one may call a genuine universe from the ethical point of view."[18] Not as a partisan proselytizing for his own ideals, but as an objective systematizer of the variety of human ideals into a unity which satisfies as many people and disappoints as few people as possible, does the moral philosopher have a defensible function. By studying the evolution of conventional moralities and appreciating how certain ethical principles have taken precedence over others through generations of moral behavior, so that in its vast experiment the human race has already shown its collective ability to make some ideals more inclusive than others, the philosopher is encouraged, as Plato was, to seek the unifying moral system indicated by the existence of a conventional though incomplete order of values. James thought that he had fashioned a good essay in "The Moral Philosopher and the Moral Life"; besides supposing that he had offered a rich discussion, he was especially pleased to have defined the role of the moral philosopher.[19]

The philosopher's first job is to distinguish three kinds of ethical inquiries: the *psychological* question of how our moral ideas originate; the *metaphysical* question of how moral terms such as *good* and *right* are to be understood (discussed below); and the *casuistic* question of how the immense variety of values are to be sorted and measured. This last inquiry is essential if the moral philosopher is to play a neutral, unifying role in identifying "the true order of human obligations."[20] (The ethical philosopher, so defined, treats moral skepticism as James and Renouvier treated hard determinism—he chooses to reject it simply by pronouncing it irrelevant to his task of reconciling the array of moral judgments made by nonskeptics.)

In his response to the psychological question about the origin of moral ideas, James emphasized what he had asserted in the final chapter of *Principles,* that the origin is in fact obscure. Both associationism and evolutionism ultimately fail in their claims to explain moral beginnings. Although associationists such as Bentham, Mill, and Bain were correct in saying that many ethical ideals arose from their association with acts producing pleasure or relief from pain, James stressed that not all ethical ideas have such origins. Comparing them to Darwin's spontaneous variations, he contended that some moral concepts originate not from pleasure or utility, nor from the external environment or our experience of it, but rather as mutations within our cerebral or mental structures. Hedonism and utilitarianism are therefore mistaken theories about the origins of moral beliefs, as is Spencerian evolutionism, which holds that such beliefs are "stamped into" us by the sheer force of the environment. It seemed to James that many sentiments and preferences, including the enjoyment of intoxication, shyness, gregariousness, fear of high places, and the love of intellectual pursuits, are innate. The evidence, he argued, points in that direction and against the notion that sentiments are somehow the effects of experience. Shyness, for instance, seems to occur not because it is useful, learned, or associated with pleasure, but because it is inborn.

> A vast number of our moral perceptions also are certainly of this secondary and brain-born kind. They deal with directly felt fitnesses between things, and often fly in the teeth of all the prepossessions of habit and presumptions of utility. . . . The sense for abstract justice . . . is as excentric a variation, from the natural-history point of view, as is the passion for music. . . . The feeling of the inward dignity of certain spiritual attitudes, as peace, serenity, simplicity, veracity . . . are quite inexplicable except by an innate preference of the more ideal attitude for its own sake. The nobler thing *tastes* better and that is all we can say.[21]

Ethical theory, in explaining the psychological sources of morality, must make room for intuitionism, the doctrine that some moral judgments are based on intuition grounded in cerebral rather than environmental structures. Those readers accustomed to hearing that James's pragmatic philosophy is a testimonial to the guiding role of consequences may be surprised to come upon this: " 'Experience' of consequences may truly teach us what things are *wicked,* but what have consequences to do with what is *mean* and *vulgar?*"[22] If a person exults in another's misfortune we do not need to await the consequences to judge this attitude to be mean and vulgar; it is a behavior which we simply intuit to deserve those epithets. Our notions of vulgarity may change, but in James's view such changes are themselves intuitively based. Intuition was as sufficient to disprove utilitarianism for

James as it was for Alyosha in *The Brothers Karamazov*. If we could implement a utopia on the condition that a single innocent individual must live a life of torture, the consequent and almost universal happiness could not, James felt, justify such implementation. No future consequences can overthrow one's intuition of the injustice of a general happiness being bought at such a price.

There seems to be a tension between James's moral intuitionism and what he proposed in treating the casuistic ethical question of how the moral philosopher is to arrange the variety of actual ethical judgments in an ordered system, eliminating ethical chaos as well as skepticism without at the same time imposing his own ethical prejudice. Defending the thesis that the history of the human race is a mammoth ethical experiment directed toward determining the kind of ethical system most inclusive of what people have come to value, James thought that conventional morality must be presumed obligatory until proved otherwise.

> The course of history is nothing but the story of men's struggles from generation to generation to find the more and more inclusive order. *Invent some manner* of realizing your own ideals which will also satisfy the alien demands,—that and that only is the path of peace! Following this path, society has shaken itself into one sort of relative equilibrium after another by a series of social discoveries quite analogous to those of science. . . . Though some one's ideals are unquestionably the worse off for each improvement, yet a vastly greater total number of them find shelter in our civilized society than in the older savage ways. . . . Up to date, the casuistic scale is made for the philosopher already far better than he can ever make it for himself. An experiment of the most searching kind has proved that the laws and usages of the land are what yield the maximum of satisfaction to the thinkers taken all together. The presumption in cases of conflict must always be in favor of the conventionally recognized good. The philosopher must be a conservative, and in the construction of the casuistic scale must put the things most in accordance with the customs of the community on top.[23]

An apparent problem for James's ethics is illustrated by what he said about retributive justice; although sanctioned by conventional morality, it had recently been disputed, he noted, by such thinkers as Leo Tolstoy and Edward Bellamy. Their dissent could not be attributed in a Spencerian manner to the effects of experience, but must rather have been born from within their moral sensibility. "Purely inward forces are certainly at work here. All the higher, more penetrating ideals are *revolutionary*. They present themselves far less in the guise of effects of past experience than in that of probable causes of future experience."[24] In one breath, James claimed a conservative obedience both to the ethical laws established by the great experiment of past generations and to the revolutionary intuitions of outstanding individuals, intuitions which sometimes directly confront tradition and the great experiment. Can he have it both ways?

He seems to have meant that individual intuitions can sometimes catch on, become adopted, and thereby alter tradition, in the long run belonging to the great experiment rather than permanently challenging it; if a fundamental conflict occurs between intuition and the lessons of the great experiment, however, then intuition must yield. James took as a major theme the idea that we must seek the moral order which includes the greatest number of moral claims, though we will necessarily exclude some intuitions in the process. In drawing the analogy between ethics and science, he believed that such a moral order would be revealed through the great experiment rather than through a single person's intuitions. There is thus no conflict in upholding both intuition and the great experiment, but another serious problem arises in James's formulation.

How do we ascertain the goal of the great experiment? Scientific experiments have predefined aims, determined as part of the initial conception of the undertaking. James described the goal of the great experiment as a world in which the greatest possible number of people are morally satisfied.[25] (This utilitarian goal is superior to the hedonistic one which defines satisfaction in terms of pleasure or happiness. If our aim is to characterize the best moral universe, then the first requirement should be the maximum satisfaction of moral sensibilities; it is of secondary importance whether those moral sensibilities involve pleasure or happiness.) But what secured James's confidence in this goal? Nothing purely factual, including the mores that civilization has gradually adopted, is capable of justifying such a goal, for James appears to have assumed that *ought* is not derivable from *is*. The following occurs in one of his notebooks on ethics: "To *prove* a thing good, we must conceive it as belonging to a genus already admitted good. Every ethical proof therefore involves as its major premise an ethical proposition; every argument must end in some such proposition, admitted without proof."[26] James's confidence in the great experiment's goal as he described it must be based solely on his own intuition that that goal is what ought to be.

But if James's idea of the moral goal is the fruit of his intuition, and if this is true of anyone's idea of it as well, then the alleged sciencelike progress of the great experiment cannot be a final, objective check on individual intuitions. On the contrary, the nature and direction of the human race's ethical experiment throughout history is always subject to evaluation according to every individual's intuition of whether it is moving toward the proper goal. Not only does a logical impasse occur when different intuitions about the moral goal collide, but moral intuitions, rather than being absorbed within the process of the great experiment, will always be independent potential checks on that experiment. This inevitable reliance upon intuition by the objective philosopher as well as the partisan moralist undermines James's exhortation that the "entire undertaking of the philosopher obliges him to seek an impartial test" and thereby to delineate the character of a "stable and systematic moral universe."[27] There is thus no possibility of the "miraculous achievement" of which he spoke in his 1879 review of Clifford's lectures, whereby an objective, moral universe would be philosophically sketched in which we could see how "all our different motives [and intuitions], rightly interpreted, pull one way."[28] Despite James's hopes, the achievement eludes even the most tolerant and objective of philosophers because no one can be a subject in the great experiment and evaluate it at the same time.

A further difficulty with the concept of moral intuition, and one that is particularly embarrassing for James's ethics, is that he rejected traditional utilitarianism on the grounds that the general happiness (a life of pleasure) is unacceptable if it requires the suffering of a single individual, and yet his own intuition, which he believed was nonpartisan and incumbent upon every objective moral philosopher, claimed that everyone's supreme obligation is to maximize the good, to satisfy or accommodate the maximum number of moral ideals. This view seems to be a variant of utilitarianism, except that it substitutes moral ideals for pleasure or happiness; more important than an inconsistency in labels, however, is the logical split within James's ethical thinking.[29] How can an intuition which rejects the general happiness on behalf of the solitary sufferer dwell in the same breast with an intuition which accepts the general accommodation of moral beliefs on the condition that some individual's moral beliefs be unaccommodated: "Some part of the ideal must be butchered, and [the moral philosopher] needs to know which part. It is a tragic situation, and no mere speculative conundrum, with which he has to deal."[30] Because of his own moral earnestness, James may have supposed that butchering an individual's morality is more tragic than destroying his pleasure, but in renouncing the principle of general happiness while adopting the ideal of general morality, he seems to have concluded otherwise. Why did he reject the intuition that would save the dissenting individual's moral ideals, when in confronting traditional utilitarianism he had not rejected the intuition that would preserve the happiness of the individual who was marked for torture in order to secure the general happiness? If one reason for James's high estimation of "The Moral Philosopher and the Moral Life" was his delight at having defined the role of the moral philosopher, his audience's tepid response to it (according to his own account) may have resulted from his failure to provide even a hint of how the moral philosopher ought to select which part of the ideal to save and which to butcher.

James never tried to be the kind of moral philosopher he described in his essay. Nor did he cite anyone who demonstrated that the role actually could be played. He saw an intimate connection between ethics and religion (see chapter 14), and although he took care to insure that ethics is logically independent of theology (see sections 2 and 5 of "The Moral Philosopher and the Moral Life"), he always stressed in his life and writings the incentive that religion gives to morality. "The capacity of the strenuous mood lies so deep down among our natural human possibilities that even if there were no metaphysical or traditional grounds for believing in a God, men would postulate one simply as a pretext for living hard, and getting out of the game of existence its keenest possibilities of zest."[31] When the complexities of moral life are referred to the ultimate answers of religion, which for James were shrouded in mysticism, then the goal of the moral philosopher—the formulation of a systematic hierarchy of values—is theoretically but no longer actually available. The formulation of a stable moral universe in which all our wills pull in one direction becomes such a "miraculous achievement" that anyone less than God is incapable of it.

> It would seem, too,—and this is my final conclusion,—that the stable and systematic moral universe for which the ethical philosopher asks is fully possible only in a world where there is a divine thinker with all-enveloping demands. If such a thinker existed, his way of subordinating the demands to one another would be the finally valid casuistic scale; his claims would be the most appealing; his ideal universe would be the most inclusive realizable whole. If he now exist, then actualized in his thought already must be that ethical philosophy which we seek as the pattern which our own must evermore approach. . . . We, as would-be philosophers, must postulate a divine thinker. . . . Meanwhile, exactly what the thought of the infinite thinker may be is hidden from us . . . so that our postulation of him after all serves only to let loose in us the strenuous mood. . . . If we invoke any so-called philosophy, our choice and use of that also are but revelations of our personal aptitude or incapacity for moral life. . . . The solving word, for the learned and the unlearned man alike, lies in the last resort in the dumb willingnesses and unwillingnesses of their interior characters, and nowhere else.[32]

James may have been delighted that the moral philosopher's job implies a theological equation, but many readers were disappointed to discover that the job is virtually an illusion, that the search for moral objectivity is doomed to defeat since each individual must fall back upon the willingnesses and unwillingnesses of his own interior character. It is odd that James never appreciated how much of what he had promised for the moral philosopher is retracted in the conclusion, quoted above, of "The Moral Philosopher and the Moral Life." His real message is that in our personal struggles to inject more objectivity and inclusiveness (tolerance) into our own ethical opinions, we must incorporate such struggles into an appropriate religious faith. The same appeal to a religious solution was responsible for James's famous remark in characterizing the pragmatic concept of truth: " 'The true' . . . is only the expedient in the way of our thinking, just as 'the right' is only the expedient in the way of our behaving. Expedient in almost any fashion; and expedient in the long run and on the whole of course; for what meets expediently all the experience in sight won't necessarily meet all farther experiences equally satisfactorily."[33]

This statement has caused some readers to see a distinct element of cynicism and to wonder whether cynicism is necessarily implied by a pragmatic ethics. Why, given the heralded integrity of James's character and intentions, did he permit himself such a startling utterance?[34] James would have vigorously denied any tendency toward cynicism and to disprove it would eventually have invoked religious reasons. What is expedient (advantageous as well as morally convenient) in the long run is what will receive divine approval and therefore similar approval from the best of us. James went to great lengths to associate his pragmatism with religion, for he meant the truly expedient act to be identical with what, from the strictest religious and moral perspective, is judged to be the right act. As a moral thinker, James felt that through the ultimate religious solution he had prevented his ethical philosophy from being cynical. But the tendency to move ethics into religion is also the tendency to be impatient with what James called concrete ethics. Although James had a highly sensitive social conscience, he directed it toward specific issues without attempting to arrange them into a systematic hierarchy of social and moral values. He constructed nothing resembling a structural social philosophy or a moral system in which the solutions to concrete issues are correlated and some are subordinated to others. He was indifferent to the complex relations between law and morality, something that is all the more surprising when one remembers that Justice Oliver Wendell Holmes, Jr., was his lifelong friend.[35] The religious dimensions of morality so occupied James that a field such as the philosophy of law struck him as all too human.[36]

Before leaving "The Moral Philosopher and the Moral Life," we must consider the second or metaphysical question about the meaning of moral terms such as *good, right,* and *obligation.* James argued that value terms have no meaning apart from feelings or desires. Values are not part of a purely physical universe, nor are they of a purely abstract order, despite the temptation of some philosophers to suppose that only an a priori abstract system of values can arbitrate human differences. "The moment one sentient being, however, is made a part of the universe, there is a chance for goods and evils really to exist. Moral relations now have their *status,* in that being's consciousness. So far as he feels anything to be good, he *makes* it good. It *is* good, for him; and being good for him, is absolutely good, for he is the sole creator of values in that universe, and outside of his opinion things have no moral character at all."[37] James was surely right in holding that consciousness is in some sense a condition for the existence of moral values, but his argument leaves the main question unanswered.

His inquiry concerned the meaning of moral terms, but he seems to have thought that the meaning of *good* is determined simply by recognizing that our feeling something to be good makes it good. But the proposition that a feeling or intuition of goodness is sufficient for justifiably calling something good is hardly an explication of *good.* We are left with the question of what one feels in feeling that something is good. James nowhere proposed straightforward definitions of *good, right,* or *ought.* After somewhat misleadingly declaring that "we have learned what the words 'good,' 'bad,' and 'obligation' severally mean," he said that he really meant this: "They mean no absolute natures, independent of personal support. They are objects of feeling and desire, which have no foothold or anchorage in Being, apart from the existence of actually living minds."[38] By itself this statement scarcely represents an answer to the essay's second question about the meaning of moral terms; if we are already puzzled by what *good* means, James's remark that it refers to an object of desire is not very helpful, leaving us to ponder which object of desire he meant.

The key to interpreting the position that James sought to formulate is in his concept of demand. "Take any demand, however slight, which any creature, however weak, may make. Ought it not, for its own sole sake, to be satisfied? If not, prove why not. The only possible kind of proof you could adduce would be the exhibition of another creature who should make a demand that ran the other way."[39] He used *demand* interchangeably with *claim*, clearly connecting both terms with the concepts of feeling and desiring; this connection is especially interesting. It is in the nature of a desire to build itself into a claim or demand; we can thus give a psychological explanation of how obligation originates from feeling or desire and how *ought* is derived from *is*. (I bypass the problem of whether this can be made consistent with James's idea that to prove that something is good, one must use a premise already employing the concept of goodness; I believe the two views can be made consistent if we distinguish properly between finding something to be good and proving it to be good.) Some desires thus intensify into imperatives, a view which led James to write: "The only possible reason there can be why any phenomenon ought to exist is that such a phenomenon actually is desired. Any desire is imperative to the extent of its amount; it *makes* itself valid by the fact that it exists at all."[40] This argument may seem vulnerable to the objections cited above to J. S. Mill's similar formulation, but James wanted only to explain the psychological source of moral concepts, not to prove a particular applicability of any one of them.[41]

James was drawn to the conclusion (though he never explicitly stated it) that *good* and *ought* are indefinable; they cannot be better expressed in other words and thus deserve to be called primitive terms in the language of morals. The fact that he never offered simple definitions of either term suggests the conviction that one can understand such words only through experiencing the requisite desires or imperatives; moral terms are in this respect like sensory terms such as *red, hot,* and *shrill.* James was uninterested in formally relating the different moral terms, but I think he might have agreed that *right action* is definable as "what one ought to do." He continued to hold that the meanings of *good* and *ought* are available only within the experience of the appropriate desire or demand. In the interest of economy, we might define *good* as "what ought to be," retaining obligation as the only primitive concept; *ought* is thus the only term that defies definition, that must be experienced to be understood.

There remains the question of how James thought moral judgments are determined to be true or false. In rejecting moral skepticism, he was bound to hold that moral judgments are true or false, that our universe is actually a moral one. Subjectivism or the doctrine that moral utterances are merely expressions of feelings, and thus neither true nor false, was always anathema to James.[42] If Adam were the only living person, James argued, then whatever he experienced as a desire or demand would be self-validating, for the question of its truth would not arise. If we introduce other persons with conflicting ideals, however, the question of truth becomes practically as well as theoretically important, for Adam's simple feeling that something is good is no longer sufficient to make it good.

Since nothing is obligatory or good, according to James, except as it is claimed to be so by someone, moral judgments can be true or false only on the condition that some persons's judgments are true and therefore superior to the false ones of others. How are true and false moral judgments to be separated? True judgments are those that can be included within the objective, impartial philosopher's most inclusive moral system, while false ones are rejected. Even if the moral philosopher's ideal of an objective, inclusive ethical system were realized, James saw that the grounds of its authority were open to question.

His recognition of this problem is evident in his assertion that if there were a divine thinker whose moral system attracted us, we would still need to ask about the ground of the declared obligation to adopt his system. No a priori rationale can be claimed.

> Do we, perhaps, think that we cover God and protect him and make his impotence over us less ultimate, when we back him up with this *a priori* blanket from which he may draw some warmth of further appeal? But the only force of appeal to *us,* which either a living God or an abstract ideal order can wield, is found in the "everlasting ruby vaults" of our own human hearts, as they happen to beat responsive and not irresponsive to the claim. So far as they do feel it when made by a living consciousness, it is life answering to life. A claim thus livingly acknowledged is acknowledged with a solidity and fulness which no thought of an "ideal" backing can render more complete.[43]

A moral system has no authority and an ethical judgment no truth unless we acknowledge them sharing in the desires and imperatives which are their sources. The respect James paid to ethical tradition and conventional morality indicates that he did not see the entire life of morality as one of feeling and desire; much of it is habitual behavior or an understanding of means to ends and of why some ethical proposals cohere and others do not. But he believed that the only moral authority that is binding upon us is what we willingly accept as authoritative; if our acceptance can survive putting that alleged authority to the test, then it is morally justified because it is the result not of a vacant assent but rather of a sharing in the feeling-source of the authority itself.[44]

THE ETHICS OF OPTIMISM

The theme of optimism versus pessimism occupied James throughout his life, and although he searched for every possible argument for an ethics of optimism, he has been characterized as "Melancholy William."[45] But there is nothing paradoxical in these characteristics; like the self-sufficient individual who courts pessimism to keep his ambitions from appearing boundless, the chronically melancholy person understandably pursues the escape promised by a philosophy of optimism. It would be paradoxical if the profession of optimism yielded only further depression; in James's case it contributed to his humor, curiosity, enthusiasm, productivity, and, as his sister Alice put it, his seeming "to be born afresh every morning" (RBP, 2:686).

His life was not all melancholy, and his determination to see things optimistically was largely responsible for his better spirits.

Extreme pessimism leads to the conclusion that existence is nothing more than the familiar and dreary facts of routine experience, and that consequently life is not worth living; when the suicidal person asks for a good reason not to end his life, he seeks what is unavailable. What ultimately saved James from such pessimism was his conviction that the cosmos was essentially what he wanted it to be. This was the idea behind his claim that our desires determine what is rational and that we are justifiably motivated to rethink the facts of routine existence according to our emotional preferences, in a language suggesting the presence of hidden meanings.[46] Among the attitudes that led James to this conclusion was one expressed in a letter written in 1868 to a troubled friend, Thomas W. Ward, after a winter "when I was on the continual verge of suicide"—the attitude of sympathy.

> All I can tell you is the thought that with me outlasts all others, and onto which, like a rock, I find myself washed up when the waves of doubt are weltering over all the rest of the world; and that is the thought of my having a will, and of my belonging to a brotherhood of men. . . . We can, by our will, make the enjoyment of our brothers stand us in the stead of a final cause; and through a knowledge of the fact that that enjoyment on the whole depends on what individuals accomplish, lead a life so active, and so sustained by a clean conscience as not to need to fret much. . . . We long for sympathy, for a purely *personal* communication. . . . A sympathy with men as such, and a desire to contribute to the weal of the species . . . contains All that we acknowledge as good . . . sufficient to keep one's moral pot boiling in a very lively manner to a good old age. (*LWJ*, 1:127–33)

For James, a practical ethics is partly a product of what German philosophers emphasized—the perceived conflict between duty and inclination—and he thought the moral impetus was to perform the duties involved in making life worth living and to fight off inclinations toward pessimism. Doing one's duty is aided by psychological insights, whether from the laboratory or from everyday experience; Jamesian psychology is unique in its attention to the practical hints for living that emerge from both technical research and reflections on common experience. In his psychological writings, James hypothesized about what might accelerate motivation, improve the quality of existence, and foster optimism. Cultivating the attitude of sympathy helps in these respects and thus deserves ethical recognition. If we view an optimistic faith in the future as a moral desideratum, we can then list sympathy for our fellows as something we ought to achieve. James countered any suspicion that his positive reaction to the sentiment of sympathy was idiosyncratic, or that sympathetic feelings are merely disguises of egoistic feelings:

> If the zoological and evolutionary point of view is the true one, there is no reason why any object whatever *might* not arouse passion and interest as primitively and instinctively as any other, whether connected or not with the interests

of the me. . . . I might conceivably be as much fascinated, and as primitively so, by the care of my neighbor's body as by the care of my own. The only check to such exuberant altruistic interests is natural selection, which would weed out such as were very harmful to the individual or to his tribe. . . . The sympathetic instincts and the egoistic ones are thus co-ordinate. They arise, so far as we can tell, on the same psychologic level. (*Principles*, 1:325)

Ethics demands a place for altruistic feelings, and psychology shows that the ethical demand is wholly sensible; here, as elsewhere, James the psychologist and James the ethicist thought in tandem.

Sympathy is the main subject of "On a Certain Blindness in Human Beings," an essay James especially valued, describing it as more than the sentimental piece that it might seem to some readers; he considered it his expression of a "definite view of the world and of our moral relations to it,"[47] the germ of his pluralistic and individualistic philosophy, which insists that truths are arrived at only through the perspectives of many individuals and that an adequate ethics must democratically respect the sacredness of individuality. The essay argues that each of us is blind to the inner lives of others. We are too self-absorbed to appreciate those experiences that make life significant for others. James cited his own former blindness to the lives of settlers in the mountains of North Carolina, remarking that his eyes had been opened to the fact that where they lived was radiant rather than desolate. Among the writers who have achieved a similar appreciation of others, he mentioned Stevenson, Whitman, Wordsworth, Shelley, Tolstoy, Emerson, W. H. Hudson, Richard Jeffries, and Josiah Royce.[48] He applauded Tolstoy for depicting Peter in *War and Peace*, once the richest man in the Russian empire, as undergoing a revolution in values as a result of the cold, hunger, vermin, and other miseries he experiences as a prisoner. In the companion essay "What Makes A Life Significant," James praised Tolstoy again for perceiving the special virtues of peasants. Calling the famous Chautauqua Assembly, in which he had once participated, a "middle-class paradise" and a "community so refined that ice-cream soda water is the utmost offering it can make to the brute animal in man," he confessed:

Many years ago, when in Vienna, I had a similar feeling of awe and reverence in looking at the peasant-women, in from the country on their business at the market for the day. Old hags many of them were, dried and brown and wrinkled, kerchiefed and short-petticoated, with thick wool stockings on their bony shanks, stumping through the glittering thoroughfares, looking neither to the right nor to the left, bent on duty, envying nothing, humble-hearted, remote;—and yet at bottom, when you came to think of it, bearing the whole fabric of the splendors and corruptions of that city on their laborious backs. For where would any of it have been without their unremitting, unrewarded labor in the fields? And so with us: not to our generals and poets, I thought, but to the Italian and Hungarian laborers in the Subway, rather, ought the monuments of gratitude and reverence of a city like Boston to be reared.[49]

This passage is easily misread if its context in the pair of essays is ignored; by such a misreading, many readers have denounced it as sentimental, sexist, and patronizing. Before interpreting this passage, however, we must ask two larger questions: What was James's main intention in these essays, and why was he so enthusiastic in composing them? We are apt to feel upon a first reading that something in James's message has eluded our attention. We understand his concern that we should not be blind to the values of others, whether they are subway workers or Boston Brahmins, and we realize that this concern is essential to a philosophy that demands respect for each individual. But given the tone of the essays, James seems to have been after something more. A clue lies in James's response to a challenge made by his friend Chauncey Wright when they were young men. Wright had defended the naturalistic view that physical nature is just what it seems to be; he called it "mere *weather* . . . a doing and undoing without ends," because it contains no hidden meanings and points to nothing transcendental or divine, but only to itself.[50] There is no metaphysical problem of appearance and reality, because appearance and reality in the natural order of things actually coincide. James interpreted Wright to mean that everything that is occurs in full view and is nothing but the familiar thing that it appears to be.

Essays such as "Is Life Worth Living?" represent James's responses to Wright's challenge, and his excited tone results from his having identified what he took to be the decisive point, that the inner lives of other people are hidden from our sensory observations. Those lives are like meanings suggested by gestures, words, and other forms of behavior, which differ from the inner experiences they are used to express. Realities differ from appearances; they lie behind the appearances, which to the resourceful person serve as clues to the realities. The gestures and words of another person are more than mere weather, as are any perceptible things when perceived with the meanings that the perceiver assigns to them. Reporting his experience in North Carolina and comparing his visitor's perception of the natural setting with that of the natives, he noted: "But when *they* looked on the hideous stumps, what they thought of was personal victory. The chips, the girdled trees and the vile split rails spoke of honest sweat, persistent toil and final reward. . . . In short, the clearing, which to me was a mere ugly picture on the retina, was to them a symbol redolent with moral memories and sang a very paean of duty, struggle, and success."[51] This appreciation involves a dawning of the fact that, because there is a "vast world of inner life beyond us, so different from that of outer seeming," a genuinely "mystic sense of hidden meaning" can now be admitted, bringing "authentic tidings of indivisible things."[52] The idea that the familiar and routine is not everything—an idea proved in the case of the hidden lives of other persons—motivated James as he wrote these essays.

Sympathy for others means not only being sensitive, considerate, tolerant, and responsive, but also being aware of the many ways in which existence can be exhilarating; it is therefore a source of optimism. What James found important in appreciating the experience of others was not only what he could give to others by being responsive but also what he could gain by learning how others find joy in their lives. "Even prisons and sick-rooms have their special revelations."[53] Identifying with someone else's perspective can be an epiphany in which an event, object, or individual is transformed from something uninteresting into something with exciting new meanings. "This higher vision of an inner significance in what, until then, we had realized only in the dead external way, often comes over a person suddenly; and when it does so, it makes an epoch in his history. As Emerson says, there is a depth in those moments that constrains us to ascribe more reality to them than to all other experiences."[54] Experiences of sudden revelation are exciting, interrupt the dull routine, and make the future look more interesting.

To subvert the criticism that James's encomium to laborers and subway-workers is condescending and sentimental insincerity, and that his study of the lives of North Carolinians and others is a sort of masturbatory indulgence, we need only consider certain remarks in "What Makes a Life Significant." For example: "If it is idiotic in romanticism to recognize the heroic only when it sees it labelled and dressed-up in books, it is really just as idiotic to see it only in the dirty boots and sweaty shirt of someone in the fields. . . . But, instinctively, we make a combination of two things in judging the total significance of a human being. We feel it to be some sort of a product . . . of his inner virtue *and* his outer place—neither singly taken, but both conjoined."[55] We can admire another's life, however alien in vocation, garb, or setting, provided there is evidence that within that life is an animated center from which the world is interpreted or evaluated spiritedly and optimistically. "The barrenness and ignobleness of the more usual laborer's life consist in the fact that it is moved by no such ideal inner springs."[56] There is no nobility in merely being a laborer or serving any other role, but nobility may reside in the inner, animated recesses of the most ignoble-looking peasant or professor. "And your college professor, with a starched shirt and spectacles, would, if a stock of ideals were all alone by itself enough to render a life significant, be the most absolutely and deeply significant of men. Tolstoi would be completely blind in despising him for a prig."[57]

But James's main point was that the values and ideals embodied in a single individual are insufficient for an ethics of optimism, for making a life worth living. Referring again to Tolstoy and to any concept of what is ideally valuable, he claimed that no single ideal can rescue life from pessimism and insignificance. "Culture and refinement all alone are not enough to do so. Ideal aspirations are not enough, when uncombined with pluck and will. But neither are pluck and will, dogged endurance and insensibility to danger enough, when taken all alone. There must be *some sort of fusion, some chemical combination* among these principles, for a life objectively and thoroughly significant to result."[58] In his characterizations of sensations, the stream of consciousness, and the pure experience of radical empiricism, James always called them "muchness-at-once" or "unity-in-manyness"; every reality is a combination of multiple aspects, and we must not, when analyzing single components, overlook the indefinable mixture that constitutes the whole thing. The same rule holds for ideals and values. The peculiar mixture of ideals and values that gives life meaning and hope can be be analyzed in terms of its parts, but its particular fusion remains permanently indefinable. Why do we find someone lovable? What set of values makes us enthusiastic about life? We can respond intelligently to these questions to an extent, but beyond a certain point we are unable to comprehend how the factors we have isolated fuse into the dynamic mixture of the lovable person or the motivating ideal.

James believed that there is little danger of our sentimentalizing the peasant compared to the risk we run of simply banishing him from view and thus failing to appreciate that his perspective, if spirited, must be taken into account in our own process of finding values that make life worth living. Furthermore, he was genuinely sympathetic with the concerns of the underprivileged. About what was then called the labor question he wrote: "Society . . . has undoubtedly got to pass towards some newer and better equilibrium, and the distribution of wealth has doubtlessly got to change." He regretted that "one-half of our fellow-countrymen remain entirely blind to the internal significance of the lives of the other half." But he volunteered that social reform can never make "any *genuine vital difference,* on a large scale, to the lives of our descendants," because "the solid meaning of life is always the same eternal thing—the marriage, namely, of some unhabitual ideal, however special, with some fidelity, courage, and endurance; with some man's or woman's pains.—And whatever or wherever life may be, there will always be the chance for that marriage to take place."[59] That James was insensitive here to the genuine and vital differences effected on a large scale by economic and social reforms is undeniable, but his point is that even with economic and material improvements, it is not clear whether life is worth living. He saw it as an eternal challenge to find values that make it so.

Although James never asserted, as Albert Camus would, that suicide is the only important philosophical issue, he understood from personal experience that suicidal fantasies bring forth questions about the meaning of life. Such questions fuel the search for a philosophy of life, and in that context the question arises whether we are justified in incorporating optimism into a factual description of the universe.[60] When this process is set in motion, many things assume an air of temporary or permanent relevance, and for James the theory of evolution demanded assessment before he could confidently decide between Emerson's and Schopenhauer's universes.[61] Darwinian theory, or its variation in Spencer and others, was never threatening to James; indeed, he put the notion of natural evolution to his own uses. He could accept apes as ancestors, but he could not abide dogmatic extensions of Darwinism which denied free will, the efficacy of consciousness, or the value of the individual. One could extract a philosophy of pessimism from Darwinism, claiming that individual efforts count for nothing since they are merely the helpless effects of the ruthless process of natural selection. James's defense against such formulations had been firmly established ever since he had first followed Renouvier's lead, and in 1875 he wrote:

Nothing is more certain than this, that no one need assent to . . . pessimism unless he freely prefer to do so. . . . Now if [a moral] order in the world is possibly true, and if, supposing it to be true, it may afford the basis for an ultimate optimism . . . there is no reason which should deter a person bent on having some commanding theory of life from adopting it as his hypothesis or working faith. He may of course prefer pessimism, but only at the price of a certain internal inconsistency. . . . For pessimism is really only consistent with a strictly dogmatic attitude. It is fatalistic in the thorough Oriental sense, being by its very definition a theory from which one is bound to escape, *if he can*. Its account of things is confessedly abhorrent, and nothing but coercive outward evidence should make one stay within its pale. Now, a hypothetical door like that offered by the notion of a ransoming moral order "behind the veil" is better than no loophole of escape; and to refuse to give one's self the benefit of its presence argues either a perfectly morbid appetite for dogmatic forms of thought, or an astounding lack of genuine sense for the tragic, which sense undoubtedly varied, like every other, from man to man.[62]

James's charge that pessimism is internally inconsistent because it refuses to allow the possibility of an escape from itself is suspect, since pessimism holds not only that misery prevails but also that there is no escape from it. If such an assertion is dogmatic, the ethics of optimism is no less dogmatic in contradicting it. James's defense is merely the Renouvierian assault against pessimism that is simply a choice to reject it; given such an attitude, neither Darwinism nor any other doctrine was likely to dissuade James. Nevertheless, evolutionism was a lively topic at the time and therefore had to be addressed, and in sometimes supporting and sometimes opposing it, James found that he could score points of his own.

James liked to remark that "Tweedledum is not after all Tweedledee." He also quoted the Irishman who, when asked, "Is not one man as good as another?" replied: "Yes, and a great deal better, too!" and an "unlearned carpenter" friend who said: "There is very little difference between one man and another; but what little there is, *is very important.*"[63] For James, respect for one's own individuality as well as for that of others was intertwined with respect for life itself. If one turns against oneself, finding one's own character to be a cause of indifference or chagrin, it is as if the life has gone out of life itself. James is often criticized for stressing the individual at the expense of the community, but he thought the two entities are dialectically related, each needing the other. In that vein he declared, "The community stagnates without the impulse of the individual. The impulse dies away without the sympathy of the community."[64] Is Darwinism incompatible with individuality or individual initiative?

James, like Plato, sometimes tried to answer that question by looking at things through a magnifier, in this case the concept of great men. Willing to be called a hero-worshipper, James held that large-scale social changes are caused by a few leaders; he thus opposed Spencerian evolutionism, which claimed that such changes occur not because of key individuals but because of the environment. In "Great Men and Their Environment" and "The Importance of Individuals," he argued against Spencer's position, seeing the issue as that of free will versus determinism. Darwin had drawn an important distinction, allegedly ignored by Spencer and other evolutionists, between the causes that produce something and those that maintain it; this distinction, James said, must be respected in determining how much credit for social change can be attributed to world leaders. In Darwin's scheme the individuality of a genius or a great person is explained as a physiological spontaneous variation rather than as a result of environmental pressures.

Since biological causes of change were even less known to Darwin than they are today, Darwin turned his attention to the causes that maintain or preserve things "under the names of natural selection and sexual selection studied . . . exclusively as functions of the . . . environment." Some evolutionists mistakenly argue, for example, that the tall trees in the giraffe's environment cause it to reach high for leaves and thus over time cause the long neck. These theorists argue: "The exercise of the forge makes the right arm strong, the palm grows callous to the oar, the mountain air distends the chest, the chased fox grows cunning and the chased bird shy, the arctic cold stimulates the animal combustion, and so forth."[65] But Darwin himself realized that few actual changes are produced by direct adaptation, since the evidence shows that the peculiarities of individuals, such as the necks of giraffes, are at best *preserved* by the environment, not originally produced by it. Instead, changes result from accidental variations, biological changes within a creature that we do not yet fully comprehend. The evolutionist can investigate only whether the environment is likely to preserve or eliminate a creature because of the peculiarities with which it was born. James appreciated Darwin's conviction that such accidental or spontaneous variations follow a natural law that would one day be understood, yet despite sometimes allowing for this possibility, he seems to have believed that the secrets of individuality, greatness, and genius were unsolvable no matter how successful future biology might be. The very term *spontaneous variation* suggested to him phenomena beyond scientific explanation. In notes made when first reading Darwin, he wrote: "Find 'laws' wh[ich] are violated by individual idiosyncracies! Collate examples of the latter!"[66] This remark suggests agreement with Aristotle's idea that individuality eludes definition and explanation, including whatever the evolutionist might offer.

> The causes of production of great men lie in a sphere wholly inaccessible to the social philosopher. He must simply accept geniuses as data, just as Darwin accepts his spontaneous variations. For him, as for Darwin, the only problem is, these data being given, How does the environment affect them, and how do they affect the environment? Now, I affirm that the relation of the visible environment to the great man is in the main exactly what it is to the "variation" in the Darwinian philosophy. It chiefly adopts or rejects, preserves or destroys, in short *selects* him. And whenever it adopts and preserves the great man, it becomes modified by his influence in an entirely original and peculiar way. He acts as a ferment, and changes its constitution, just as the advent of a new zoological

species changes the faunal and floral equilibrium of the region in which it appears.[67]

James's contribution was not simply a defense of the common belief that great persons influence history or that the origins of great persons defy the explanations of social scientists borrowing from Darwinism; he was in effect questioning the picture of the great person versus the environment, replacing it with the transactionist theory that both person and environment are mutually transformed by their transactions with each other. It makes no sense to use static features of a static environment to explain the initiative of individuals, he argued, because the static environment is a myth; the environment changes in response to the individual's influence, just as the individual responds to it. An evolutionary theory of history that scorns the significance of heroic initiative is therefore utterly vague and unscientific, and in "Great Men and Their Environment," often called James's contribution to the philosophy of history, anything like Marxist theories are totally rejected. James never mentioned Marx in his writings, but his opposition to a scientific interpretation of history is clear. "It is folly, then, to speak of the 'laws of history,' as of something inevitable, which science has only to discover, and whose consequences any one can then foretell but do nothing to alter or avert. Why, the very laws of physics are conditional, and deal with *ifs.*"[68] Despite some evolutionists' readings of history, James said, the evidence shows that the accidental traits of great persons sometimes *originate* great historical changes. To the extent that these persons show "in the large" what is true of each of us, and that individual initiative is what it seems to be and not merely a passive response to the environment, the ethics of optimism is valid. "I . . . cannot but consider the talk of the contemporary sociological school about averages and general laws and predetermined tendencies, with its obligatory undervaluing of individual differences, as the most pernicious and immoral of fatalisms."[69]

James's response to evolutionistic determinism was connected to one of his favorite themes, that we are in a moral battle to improve an imperfect world. According to his ethics of optimism, the world can be improved and we can hope to improve it. He sometimes used the theory of evolution to support the idea that we are evolving, through increasingly civilized choices, toward a better condition. The concept of progress, often associated with James's thought, has been called an indispensable aspect of his Americanism. But when he focused upon the psychological or inner struggle to be optimistic about one's existence, he seems to have felt that our condition is always the same; in any life and in any age, the dynamics of the efforts to give one's life meaning do not change. In this respect, he seems to have believed that successive generations can neither create nor witness progress.

> In this solid and tridimensional sense, so to call it, those philosophers are right to contend that the world is a standing thing, with no progress, no real history. The changing conditions of history only touch the surface of the show. The altered equilibriums and redistributions only diversify our opportunities and open chances to us for new ideals. But with each new ideal that comes into life, the chance for a life based on some old ideal will vanish; and he would needs be a

presumptuous calculator who should with confidence say that the total sum of significance is positively and absolutely greater at any one epoch than at any other of the world.[70]

When James focused upon the arguments for and against optimism, especially after 1898 as he developed pragmatism as a part of the argument, he began to assert the notion of meliorism more confidently. He preferred the term *meliorism* to *optimism* in *Pragmatism,* where he introduced optimism as the doctrine that progress or improvement is inevitable. Meliorism is midway between optimism and pessimism, because it maintains only that moral and social improvement is possible and that any improvement is up to us. "It is clear that pragmatism must incline towards meliorism."[71] Combined with the claim in "The Moral Philosopher and the Moral Life" that the experience of the human race has been a vast experiment in which progress has been made in the installation of values, this view confirms that in professing pragmatism James saw opportunities for real progress in human history.[72]

Philosophizing was therapeutic for James, and the developing and reiterating of favorite themes afforded him considerable rewards, but philosophy also offered practical lessons. The ethics of optimism or meliorism had a practical side in its strategies for implementing its own recommendations. It drew upon empirical psychology, abnormal psychology, psychical research, mind-healing, and positive thinking. James searched for the kind of mind-body condition that would best allow him to meet the next day optimistically. A strain in his thought emphasizes vitality, the need to be useful, to strive for improvement, to be morally strenuous, and to anticipate the future, but there is an opposite strain; he also cautioned against being overly strenuous, tense, or anxious. He saw excessive ambition, hyperbolic ideals, and allowing oneself to be battered by the superego as an overactive conscience, particularly prevalent in New Englanders.[73]

How can you be optimistic if "you never wholly give yourself to the chair you sit in, but always keep your leg- and body-muscles half contracted for a vise; if you breathe eighteen or nineteen instead of sixteen times a minute, and never quite breathe out at that,—what mental mood *can* you be in but one of inner panting and expectancy, and how can the future and its worries possibly forsake your mind?"[74] Besides stressing what in the world of ideas can help us to relax, James advised a program of behavior, of physical exercise, which he saw as more effective in removing "bad feelings" than is wrestling with them introspectively, which tends only to fix them more firmly in our minds. Yet the proper mental and physical condition is not so relaxed that nothing wants to stir. "To relax, to say to ourselves (with the "new thoughters") 'Peace! be still!' is sometimes a great achievement . . . [but] how to keep [energy] at an appreciable maximum? How not to let the level lapse? That is the great problem."[75] To be healthy-minded or optimistic requires the ability both to relax and to remain energized. Because an ethics of optimism demands great energy, to energize below one's normal maximum is to fail morally. James was also concerned with the moments of faltering when one is tempted to see life as too challenging for one's energies. He remarked that vitality can be lost because of repression:

"One part of our mind dams up—even *damns* up!—the other parts," which can be the work of the superego. "Conscience makes cowards of us all."[76]

In his psychology James held that all stimulus responses, including ideas and feelings, react through the efferent nervous system and discharge through some action or behavior. If that process of discharge is blocked (the similarity here to Freudianism is obvious), the result at the experiential level is morbidity. One of the most useful ways to unblock the path of energy is to act deliberately in order to give the obstructed energy some outlet, so that it can eventually find its normal routes of escape. The healthy-minded or optimistic person, James thought, exhibits fluency, a good part of which is the free flow of ideas, feelings, and inner stimulations into appropriate discharges through action.

To the extent that pragmatism is a philosophy of action and includes such claims as that theories are instruments, that concepts are guides to action, and that truth lies in verifying behaviors, it connects neatly with Jamesian psychology. His ethics of optimism dovetails with both his psychology and his pragmatism, becoming a philosophy of action.[77] The question arose with James, as it did with Nietzsche, of the danger of the ethic. Do ominous implications lurk in his pragmatic morality? Does it implicitly sanction action for its own sake or any means to a desired end?

These questions were answered in 1926, when Benito Mussolini stated in an interview that his Fascism was indebted to James:

> Nietzsche enchanted me when I was twenty, and reinforced the anti-democratic elements in my nature. The pragmatism of William James was of great use to me in my political career. James taught me that an action should be judged rather by its results than by its doctrinary basis. I learnt of James that faith in action, that ardent will to live and fight, to which Fascism owes a great part of its success. . . . For me the essential was to act. But . . . it is to Georges Sorel that I owe the greatest debt. . . . His rugged theories on revolutionary tactics contributed most decisively to the forming of the discipline, the energy and the power of the Fascist cohorts.[78]

In commenting on this interview, Perry argued that Mussolini's statement should not be taken literally, since Mussolini also included among the influences on his philosophy Machiavelli, Schopenhauer, and Strindberg, and could easily have located almost anywhere what he claimed to have discovered in James.[79] While minimizing Mussolini's claim on James, Perry concluded that "there is no good reason for doubting that the young Mussolini knew at least fragments of Jamesian doctrine and found them to his liking. He remembers also to have made James's personal acquaintance" (RBP, 2:575).

Even this influence was denied by Horace M. Kallen in his contribution to a discussion that went on for at least a decade after Mussolini's statement. Kallen, who had studied with James and later helped to keep his reputation alive, wrote:

> The opportunity . . . came in the fall of 1926 when I had a chance to ask Mussolini directly what he had read of William James's. His only answer was a show of irritation; it was apparent that whatever Mussolini meant by "prag-

matism" was not based on anything he had gotten from James. . . . If Mussolini owes anything to William James, he owes it to a William James he had never met and not a word of whose works he had ever read, except the word "pragmatism." His claim of a pragmatist ancestry to his fascist philosophy was an effort to legitimize it in American eyes.[80]

No one was concerned about James's intentions, but only about the unintended but possibly dangerous implications of his pragmatic ethic. I am content with Kallen's assessment of the issue:

> It was good publicity, worth headlines in the American press, where I learned of the new ducial debt to the American spirit. The story sounded unlikely. I was fairly familiar with the philosophy of William James [a deliberate understatement], and I could not reconcile the great pragmatist's individualism, pluralism, radical empiricism with fascist totalitarianism, organicism, and dogmatic rationalism. I could not see how Mussolini could derive his militarism and étatism from James's pacifism, democratism, and anti-imperialism. I could not see how James's tolerance, his scrupulous concern that alternatives should have an equal freedom to make good their claims, could spawn the authoritarian intolerance, the coercion and destruction of alternatives integral to fascism. ("Mussolini, William James, and the Rationalists," 256)

It would indeed be paradoxical and extremely distressing if James's ethics of optimism were found to be inherently totalitarian, for he not only ruled out success at any price but worried about the dangers of overestimating worldly success. He complained to H. G. Wells about "the moral flabbiness born of the exclusive worship of the bitch-goddess SUCCESS."[81] James never allowed his meliorism to get out of control, for he believed that restraint must be exercised in the pursuit of any goal. An extravagant claim was almost always acknowledged as such and immediately qualified. He professed a cautious moral optimism as wary of excess as of pessimism.

Whether an ethics leans toward optimism or pessimism need not incline it toward liberalism or conservatism, anarchism or authoritarianism. The glaring vulnerability of James's version of optimism is its premise that the universe is ultimately what he wants it to be. We may be inclined to commend him for his bravado in declaring this premise for all the skeptical world to hear. It is sometimes tempting to follow suit, to construct the most attractive conceptual world possible. Arranging such a world metaphysically and ethically is a creative exercise and a welcome challenge to the artistic imagination. Indeed, James the psychologist and James the philosopher slip often into James the artist, leaving his critic to follow a chameleonic trail.

ETHICS AND AESTHETICS

The relation between art and philosophy defines a discourse that stretches from Plato and Aristotle through Aquinas, Shaftesbury, Kant, Hegel, Schopenhauer,

Kierkegaard, and Nietzsche to such philosophers as James and Dewey. James never proposed a systematic aesthetics, for he cared even less for aesthetic than for ethical debating. Given that he had once entertained painting as a possible career, that the arts were for him a constant source of personal delight, that artistic sensitivity was a family trait evidenced in his brother Henry, and that he thought talking about art compromised its marvels, it is not surprising that he wrote: "One's first impulse is to shy away from any book with the word 'Aesthetics' in its title, with the confident expectation that, if read, it could only emphasize once more the gaping contrast between the richness of life and the poverty of all possible formulas."[82] In reacting to Bernard Berenson's claim that the Florentine painters were successful because their pictures suggested tactile values and, more important, displayed "life-communicating values," James wrote: "Mr. Berenson himself has to add 'spiritual significance' to his other terms of 'life-enhancing value.' But until we can define just what the superior 'significances' are, in the better of two good pictures—and surely we hardly ever can—the explanation of all merit by significance remains somewhat unsatisfying. The better picture remains simply the better picture, and its ultimate superiority might, in the end, be a matter of immediate optical feeling and not a matter of extraneous suggestion or significance at all."[83]

James thought useful talk about art is rare not because he held that the arts are too noble or spiritual to be analyzed but because their effect upon us is so immediate that subsequent discussion, the aim of which is to recapture that immediacy, tends instead to distance us from it. Talking about art is often self-defeating, just as, in James's metaphysics, talking about reality (the attempt to conceptualize pure experience or the stream of consciousness) is ineluctably distorting. James occasionally saw an exception to this rule; for example, he praised Santayana's *Sense of Beauty* and Marshall's *Pain, Pleasure, and Aesthetics:* "The great merit of both works is the concreteness and reality with which their authors grasp the subject. An artist reading them will not find the deepest instincts of his Being violated as it is by so much of the grotesque stuff called Aesthetics in the systems of Baumgarten and Kant downwards. These American writers, he will say, have been there, and know how I and those like me feel about our work." In his review of Marshall's book, however, he retracted some of this praise, reprimanding Marshall for attempting to explain the many feelings of pleasure and displeasure with a single formula.[84]

In the preface to *Principles*, James said that he regretted not having treated the subjects of pleasure and pain and of moral and aesthetic feelings; in the preface to the abridged version (in which about "two fifths of the volume is either new or rewritten, the rest is 'scissors and paste'") he repeated that sentiment: "I regret to have been unable to supply chapters on pleasure and pain, aesthetics, and the moral sense" (*Psychology*, iii). It is significant that he mentioned moral sense with the other topics. He seems to have discovered these topics to be so complex that an adequate discussion would have expanded *Principles* into a three-volume work. The particulars of pain and pleasure and of the aesthetic and moral senses are so varied that all authors (especially Spencer) stumble in trying to offer a unified explanation. In an

1877 review, James scolded Grant Allen for trying to accomplish this. "[His] omission of tickling, of the comical, of the bliss of anaesthesia, of various intoxicants, of the pleasures of a slow crescendo simply as such, and of mere distinctness; of the intensely disagreeable shock of suddenly interrupting any sensation, or any voluntary or habitual tendency to motion; his neglect to consider the effects of habituation in blunting some enjoyments and in increasing others, of acquired tastes, etc., are all grave shortcomings in a book of such pretensions."[85] James himself never tried to systematize this field of phenomena.

This attitude reveals James's enduring doubt that feelings could be incorporated into his physiological account of emotions. All emotions are bodily commotions, and the uncertainty he expressed in "The Physical Basis of Emotion" about the relation of feelings to emotions was never resolved; he refused to endorse any formula by which to explain the range of feelings and yet refrained from dogmatically asserting that their scientific classification and explanation are impossible. Nothing resists scientific or philosophical neatness, he thought, more than the feelings of pleasure and pain and our moral and aesthetic sensibilities. James seems to have made the same link between moral and aesthetic feelings that many others have assumed in discussing the sentiments underlying morality and aesthetics. In the late 1890s he wrote on the flyleaf of Kant's *Critique of Judgment:* "The last standard of 'beauty' is in *someone's feeling*. . . ." Since he had said the same thing about morality, the link was evident to him. Perry understood this connection and devoted a short chapter to it, titled "Ethics Versus Aesthetics."[86] Ethics and aesthetics were so intimately connected in James's life and thought that he had to decide which took priority; Perry was confident that in James's struggle with the Kierkegaardian "either-or," ethics won out.

James certainly supposed that executing one's moral duty is superior to listening to music or looking at pictures. He explicitly warned against excessive reading and theatergoing; while he also warned against an overly strenuous conscience, he never saw any danger in performing one's moral duties to excess. He respected the inherent value of aesthetic experience and regarded it as a major element in the good life, but he saw it as less important than one's ethical duty; in a conflict with a moral duty, aesthetic concerns were almost self-indulgent.[87] To be or not to be an aesthete was never James's question, although it is hardly evident what he *would* have included as part of the life of the moralist. He did not condemn an artistic career, including that of his brother's, as morally inferior to being a professor of ethics, so the choice between ethics and aesthetics was not a vocational one.

Art or aesthetic experience was for Kant a reconciliation of pure and practical reason and for Schopenhauer an escape from the maniacal will; for these two philosophers, at least, aesthetics was thus an indispensable element in a philosophical system. The same emphasis occurs in the thought of Peirce, who fused ethics and aesthetics by identifying the good with the beautiful and by calling aesthetics the science of what is intrinsically desirable. Wittgenstein wrote: "It is clear that ethics cannot be expressed. Ethics are transcendental. (Ethics and aesthetics are one.)"[88]

Perry's reading of James—that aesthetics was subordinated to ethics, and that ethics, despite having its origins in feeling, developed a role for the moral will to which feelings were subordinated—suggests that Peirce's and Wittgenstein's formulations of the relation between ethics and aesthetics would have run afoul of James. For James the meaning of moral terms differed from that of aesthetic ones, and the differences did not totally blur at the experiential level.

Yet James's deep involvement in the aesthetic dimensions of experience makes us question the success of his attempt to subordinate aesthetics to ethics. His writings, including reviews and notices, lead us to think of him as a critic-at-large, responding to literature and painting, and less frequently to sculpture, music, and dance. Criticism seems to have been an inseparable part of his life and thought.[89] He cited Bacon as having captured the German spirit by declaring that beauty must have "some strangeness in the proportion," whereas the classical muse had always endeavored to avoid strangeness; James added that he saw the lovability of artistic works as part of their uniqueness: "Love, when once kindled, feeds on every point of peculiarity which its object offers. The Germanic genius loves unique objects, rich in curves and quirks, and points of peculiarity."[90] His interest in genius was not limited to its ethnic origins and associations, although at the close of the nineteenth century the identification of what is uniquely Italian, French, Spanish, or German in art was a favorite intellectual pastime to which both he and his brother Henry were drawn. James was also interested in the psychology of artistic creation, and considered the question of whether artistic genius demands an abnormal psyche. His notes for the 1896 Lowell Lectures contain the following: "In the artistic life the excessive sensibility of the psychopath . . . Everywhere the haunting . . . Search for what is lost/Metaphysics/Moral intensity/Belief in mission . . . who shall absolutely say that the morbid has no revelation about the meaning of life? That the healthy-minded view so called is *all?*"[91] In the aftermath of *Principles* in the 1890s, James intensified his interest in the cognitive and therapeutic potential of the subconscious and of abnormal states of consciousness. The possible overlap of artistic sensibility and pathological forms of consciousness, he thought, might contribute greatly to human existence, might also be the exclusive source of truths or insights without which *ethics* would be impoverished. If such were the case, ethics and aesthetics might have a common origin.

There are two even more important respects in which James's thinking, despite Perry's reading, tended to blend rather than to separate ethics and aesthetics. First, he asserted throughout his life that aesthetic principles play a cognitive role. "After the emotional and active needs come the intellectual and aesthetic ones. The two great aesthetic principles, of richness and of ease, dominate our intellectual as well as our sensuous life."[92] Such domination, James contended in the spirit of subjective pragmatism, is justifiable. He sometimes characterized philosophy (as Wittgenstein and Ayer did later) as a kind of picture painting or putting visions into words (see chapters 10–11). In a notebook he wrote: "What, on pragmatist terms, does 'nature itself' signify? To my mind it signifies the non-artificial; the artificial having certain definite aesthetic characteristics which I dislike, and can only apperceive in others as matters of personal taste,—to me bad taste" (quoted in RBP, 2:700). This statement is echoed in *Pragmatism,* where the debate between materialism and spiritualism is taken up. "Treated as it often is, this question becomes little more than a conflict between aesthetic preferences. Matter is gross, coarse, crass, muddy; spirit is pure, elevated, noble. . . . I remember a worthy spiritualist professor who always referred to materialism as the 'mud-philosophy,' and deemed it thereby refuted" (*Pragmatism,* 70). The second way in which James blended ethics and aesthetics was his use of the aesthetic device of *le bon mot* in extolling ethics. Just as the painter's content requires a certain form, the moralist's formulation uses an aesthetically guided mode of expression. James seems to have supposed (perhaps through his role as his brother's critic) that style is decisively a part of the idea being expressed, that indeed the style of a thought's expression defines the thought as much as does its content. The aesthetic dimension, the required mode of expression, is an original and inseparable aspect of any form of moral consciousness.

I think that James was prepared to assert that the relation between ethics and aesthetics is sufficiently intimate that what is morally ugly will almost always be aesthetically reprehensible, that moral intuitions are not always easy to separate from aesthetic ones, and that moral and aesthetic premises in arguments are sometimes almost indistinguishable.[93] But if that was indeed the case, what remains of Perry's interpretation that James subordinated aesthetics to ethics? My interpretation comes close to asserting that James's ethical values were grounded in intuitions and visions that he preferred because of their aesthetic characteristics. Were such ethical notions as pluralism, individualism, freedom, tolerance, and optimism selected because they fit intuitions or pictures that James thought were inherently delightful to behold? Aesthetic experience begins to look like the court of last appeal.

Aesthetics permeates James's ethics so completely that I believe he would have accepted most of what I have just outlined. But his response to such a formulation would, I think, have emphasized two considerations important enough to reinstate one aspect of the priority of ethics over aesthetics. First, although moral reasoning may contain both aesthetic and ethical intuitions that are difficult to disentangle, it is always more than an intuition, picture, vision, or momentary experience. It also involves arguments with premises and a conclusion that something ought to be done or is the right thing to do. Intuitions alone may provide clues about oughtness, rightness, and goodness, but they must be supplemented by arguments. They must cohere with logical considerations, or their attractiveness can badly mislead us. They are comparable both to the perchings in the stream of consciousness, which must be supplemented by flights or transitions, to the single introspections that must be checked by experiment and observation, and to the claims for "knowledge-by-acquaintance" (see chapters 10–11) that demand further verification.

One of the most interesting yet overlooked items in the James Collection is a small holograph titled "The Foreboding Meeting, or the Artist's fate." (This document is reproduced in the illustrations section.) It was inspired by an actual encounter with Ralph Waldo Emerson, and judging from the drawing with which the manuscript begins, it was done when James was in his twenties.[94] The drawing, one of James's funniest caricatures, portrays Emerson on the left in familiar garb and smiling benignly, and James himself on the right in the guise of a young dandy staring smartly at Emerson. Between them are two shoeshine boys, one with his rump toward us and wearing patched pants; Emerson and James each have a foot on a shoe-rest. The accompanying text is as follows:

The Foreboding Meeting

or

The Artist's Fate.

———

Drama

———

Dram[atis] Personae.

———

Sage of Concord

W[illiam] J[ames]

———

Scene

Parker's boot blacking

establish

ment

Enter W. J.

W. J. I say, boy, just give my boots
    a lick.

      X X X X

Enter. S. of C.

S. of C. Please to polish my
    immortal boots.

        X X X X

S. of C. and *W. J.* catch sight of
each other. Meeting & tableau [phrase struck out]
Heart-rending tableau, and usual
words of polite salutation. After
wh[ich]—

S. of C. So I'm not to have my
boy at Concord on Saturday,—he
has given me the slip—

W. J. Oh! you mean J. B. Yes, he
expects to be busy moving all this week.
Great deal of furniture you know—
valuable paintings—carpets to[o]—
things collected in Europe—can't move

slowly.

S. of C. So! I had promised
myself on Saturday to hear what he had to say on the Relation of Art to Nature, I sh[oul]d like to become acquainted with
his theory, & to hear him criticise mr. Cabot's remarkable
articles———

W. J. Oh! Yes! yes! nothing w[oul]d please him more.
I supp [struck out] *S. of C.* So I supposed———

W. J. But between ourselves, he is rather weak as a metaphy=
sician.

S. of C. Want to know! Mrs. Tappan is my voucher of ["of" struck out]
for his respectability—I have f[ro]m her the very best accounts
of him.

W. J. Oh! yes!———*S. of C.* Well, we must have him
some other Saturday. You must do your best to send him along to
us.

W. J. I will do my possible. (They breathe a fond farewell & exeunt)   Finis
The moral lesson of this Drama wh[ich] actually happened on
Wednesday, M[ar]ch 3rd is that you must read up on Metaphysics & Esthetics. I will bring a lot of books on
Esthetics down with me for you. Show him that Cabot
is not original, but has plagiarised from the
Japanese poet whatdyecallum, & he will
be delighted.[95]

The moral is that a sage's intuition is not enough; reading, reasoning, and argument are also obligatory. James characterized Santayana's *Life of Reason* thus: "[Santayana] is a paragon of Emersonianism—declare your intuitions, though no other man share them; and the integrity with which he does it is as fine as it is rare" (quoted in RBP, 2:399). The artist's fate is to be judged by such intuitions. But it is never sufficient simply to declare those intuitions, no matter how sincere or arresting they may be. Moral and aesthetic intuitions are key elements in determining values, but they must always be woven into a larger fabric that includes reasoning and behavior as well.

The second point that James wanted to make was that while intuition figures in both moral and aesthetic thinking, morality involves a choice that aesthetics does not. To be moral, one must move beyond intuition or insight and choose to act in order to make the world better. But the burden of proof will always rest upon the person who argues that this requirement is equally true of artistic endeavor. The artist (or the philosophical visionary) may be obliged to do his best, such that a kind of morality supervises his activity, but he does not necessarily have an obligation to improve the universe. (This idea is contemptuously dismissed by artists and visionaries themselves.) That *Guernica* exists may have added to the general good, but whatever Picasso's intentions, such a result is extrinsic to its being an aesthetic achievement; to assert that because a work of art is an aesthetic achievement it must also be a moral achievement is like arguing that what is good for General Motors is good for America.

James took our moral obligation to be the amelioration of an obviously deficient world; what makes that obligation especially onerous is not only the objective obstacles to it but also our inward susceptibility to feeling that what we do ourselves has little chance of altering the big picture. To live with the self-imposed injunction that we must help to improve a deficient world is not an easy task. Too many menacing questions arise. Are we really free? Is the world actually alterable? Do our small deeds really matter? Can we fashion a worldview that replies to these questions and restores our moral confidence? In following Renouvier, James responded to such threats by beginning with the choice of adopting a belief in freedom in order to make his self-imposed injunction sensible. This course in itself demonstrated a connection between morality and action that is missing in aesthetics. The choices and actions that are the foundations for one's morality cannot be supported merely by unassailable intuitions. Momentary intuitions such as Emerson's are essential in fighting off moral diffidence, but so are the arguments and elaborations into which they develop. The subjective precariousness of our basic moral beliefs led James to return to them repeatedly, using fresh words and new twists in old arguments to bolster not an aesthetic vision but rather the moral will to act as if the world will be the better for that action.

SOCIAL VIEWS

Temperamentally, and therefore philosophically, James was concerned with the individual struggling to hold his own. His ethical thought included a duty to intervene whenever justice and respect for the individual failed. His thought gravitated toward social commentary and criticism, and as a result he has been described as a fin de siècle liberal and reformer. Although he was essentially a conformist in his personal affairs and supported ordinary morality in his ethics, he dwelt less upon conventional wisdom than upon the potential insights within the individual, no matter how eccentric that person might appear. Whenever an isolated person was victimized by society's machinery, James reacted with moral outrage, as in 1899 when Captain Alfred Dreyfus, a French army officer and a Jew, was condemned in a court of appeal as a traitor. "The incredible has happened, and Dreyfus, without one may say a single particle of *positive* evidence that he was guilty, has been condemned again. The French Republic, which seemed about to turn the most dangerous corner in her career and enter on the line of political health, laying down the finest set of political precedents in her history to serve as standards for future imitation and habit, has slipped Hell-ward and all the forces of Hell in the country will proceed to fresh excesses of insolence."[96] In another letter he wrote: "This verdict proves that the

spirit of caste is the strongest force in society. I am glad I belong to a republic"
(quoted in RBP, 2:195–96).

James's tendency to sympathize with the underdog or the outsider sometimes
caused him to declare that he was an anarchist;[97] to chide him for undervaluing the
community has become almost a standard criticism. But he never meant such declarations literally, and in essays such as "Great Men and Their Environment" a non-
anarchistic respect for the community is clear. Nor did he intend to commend
individuality in all cases. Unlike the Social Darwinists, he did not admire the American business tycoon.

> John D. Rockefeller, the richest man in America, and possibly in the world
> (rumor places his fortune at 1,000,000,000 of dollars made by the most abom-
> inable practical methods, but all *business*, no stock speculations or finance) is
> staying with us, and is a curious psychological study. The most powerful human
> organism I have ever seen, cunning, flexible, a volcano of passion under abso-
> lute self-control, a devout Christian of the narrowest sectarian type, not an
> interest in the world except *business*, and the endowment of universities, which
> he has taken up as a fad or hobby in middle life.[98]

James objected to Rockefeller's business methods but not to his financial success.
(The grandson of an immensely wealthy entrepreneur, James did not want to scorn
the career of business; he said of himself that after inquiring about a stranger's
vocation, he liked to ask next about his income.) Rockefeller also disappointed
James by being insufficiently individualistic in his moral and religious thinking,
settling for something of the "narrowest sectarian type." The strong, solo figure that
strode unchallenged through the corridors of petroleum corporations, as James saw
it, sank docilely into the pew that afforded an external comfort that ought to be
achieved from within.

To be publicly concerned with the plight of minority and disadvantaged groups,
including American blacks, was part of the Jamesian ethic. In 1897 he said:

> Since the 'thirties the slavery question had been the only question, and by the
> end of the 'fifties our land lay sick and shaking with it. . . . "Only muzzle the
> Abolition fanatics," said the South, "and all will be well again!" But the Aboli-
> tionists would not be muzzled,—they were the voice of the world's conscience,
> they were a part of destiny. Weak as they were, they drove the South to mad-
> ness. . . . And when South Carolina took the final step in battering down Fort
> Sumter, it was the fanatics of slavery themselves who called upon their idolized
> institution ruin swift and complete. What law and reason were unable to ac-
> complish, had now to be done by that uncertain and dreadful dispenser of God's
> judgments, War. . . .
>
> Our great western republic had from its origins been a singular anomaly. A
> land of freedom, boastfully so-called, with human slavery enthroned at the

heart of it . . . what was it but a thing of falsehood and horrible self-contradiction? . . . But at the last that republic was torn in two; and truth was to be
possible under the flag. Truth, thank God, truth! even though for the moment it
must be truth written in hell-fire.[99]

James was not given to climbing onto soapboxes, but his moral thought was
activistic, as is clear from his lectures, teaching, writing, friendships, and activities
supporting social change. For a Harvard professor, he was singularly ahead of his
time in his attitude toward blacks, foreigners, Jews, exceptional individuals, and
spokesmen for unpopular aspirations.[100] Much of the literature about James is a
monument to the fairness with which he treated others, including those who were
society's outsiders. Walter Lippmann spoke for many in asserting, "It is an encouraging thought that America should have produced perhaps the most tolerant man of
our generation."[101] James's tolerance, generosity, and goodwill were recognized
and appreciated universally, but his moral consciousness may have stopped there;
for instance, was he only tolerant toward women, or did his thought assume further
dimensions?

James wrote only one short review article about women, so his thoughts on the
topic must be pieced together from family data, correspondence, and occasional
remarks. Since he was often influenced by his father's opinions, we cannot ignore
the fact that Henry James, Sr., frowned upon the education of women; this attitude
was connected with his belief that women are spiritually superior to men. He and his
wife were both against the movement for women's rights that developed in the
United States during the second half of the nineteenth century; he assumed that
woman's goal is to be a first-rate wife and mother.[102] Sentiments expressed in
William's letters to his wife suggest that he followed his father's opinions here.
Occasional remarks such as the one in the chapter on instinct in *Principles* about an
antisexual instinct deepen the suspicion.[103] Did James's ethics, democratic and individualistic, falter in its application to women?

In 1869, when James was twenty-seven and nine years before he was married,
he wrote one of his first articles, a combined review of Horace Bushnell's *Women's
Suffrage: The Reform Against Nature* and J. S. Mill's *Subjection of Women*.[104] Because
Bushnell's sentiments resemble those of Henry James, Sr., the review is particularly
interesting. While prepared to allow women access to some educational and vocational opportunities, Bushnell was especially opposed to women participating in
governmental or administrative posts. Women, he held, are not naturally suited for
the conflict and turmoil that such occupations involve; they are by nature meant to
be subordinate, inclined to yield to rather than to combat evil and violence. Left in
that form, James said, Bushnell's book might be regarded as another statement of the
"inexplicable sentiment" that dominated public opinion at the time. But Bushnell
employed arguments that damaged his entire position.

If we invoke the idea of Henry James, Sr., that the subordination of women
actually attests to their moral superiority, as illustrated by their gentleness and

patience, it follows that women should not join the competitive male world with its "coarse forbidding masculinities." James replied that this argument was nothing but the old Catholic doctrine that to suffer is better than to act; whereas that belief may have consoled some, "there has probably not been an unjust usage in Christendom which has not at some time sought shelter under its wing. No well man or free man ever adopted it for his own use. . . . Modern civilization, rightly or wrongly, is bent on developing itself along the line of justice, and any defence of woman's position on ascetic principles will fall with little weight on the public ear" (558). In fact, James continued, to deny women access to politics is to impose a restricted moral development upon them, and this conclusion implied the harshest verdict he could have pronounced upon Bushnell. In James's eyes, nothing was more unjust than a policy that would stunt a person's capacity for moral growth. The remainder of the Bushnell review is highly sarcastic; James commented that the author's portraits of how women would appear twenty-five years after gaining suffrage are "almost too harrowing to quote." The claim that women would degenerate, becoming "sharp-featured, lank, and dry," elicited this remark from James: "We cannot help noticing . . . how common this two-stool line of argument is in the school to which Dr. Bushnell belongs,—first, a vociferous proclamation of the utter and radical peculiarity of the womanly nature; then a nervous terror of its being altered from its foundations by a few outward changes. Mr. Mill's belief in the power of education is timid in comparison with this" (559). James obviously enjoyed confronting the reader with Bushnell's remedy for much of "the present dissatisfaction"; to relax women's modesty, because most bachelors were allegedly single out of timidity; women should be allowed to assist these timid males by making matrimonial advances themselves.

The review becomes more serious when treating *The Subjection of Women.* James was disappointed by Mill's emotional involvement with the subject and by his superfluous argument, for instance, in his trying to prove that, while we do not yet know the true mental nature of women, there is no reason to suppose that they are less musically gifted than men. While lamenting Mill's "nervous anxiety" about his subject, James acknowledged that Mill posed some interesting (if curious) questions. Previously, James observed, the "woman question" had been mainly a practical one. "The etiolated and stunted condition of single women on the one hand, and the interests of order in the family on the other, have been the chief points of attack by the reformers, and retort by the conservatives. On purely sentimental grounds no well-organized warfare has as yet been waged, since both parties have not seemed unwilling on the whole to recognize the same standard. . . . The most noteworthy feature of this . . . noteworthy book is its thorough hostility to the accepted sentimental ideal of the personal intercourse of man and wife" (561). James then suggested that what troubled Mill was not so visible in America; legal abuses of women were mainly obsolete, the brutality in the sense of masculine superiority was foreign, and American husbands were less sensitive than Englishmen about their wives occupying "a position of independent publicity." National differences apart, however, Mill had a point of view to reckon with; his view perturbed James, for it was an "intense contempt" for the usual familial and marital arrangement. Mill had gone beyond the practical "woman question" and had, in a uniquely disturbing way, attacked the sentimental basis upon which conventional morality between the sexes rested.

Mill charged men with indulging a kind of self-worship in the way they cared for their wives and children, and said that the family structure was designed to serve primarily the man's interests. It was time, he argued, to move beyond the morality of submission, of chivalry and generosity, to a morality of justice by which human beings are equals. After examining Mill's concept of equality between spouses, James concluded that it made marital love and friendship indistinguishable. But "the representative American" (which clearly described James himself) was certainly opposed to such an equation.

> However he might shrink from expressing it in naked words, the wife his heart more or less subtly craves is at bottom a dependent being. In the outer world he can only hold good his position by dint of reconquering it afresh every day: life is a struggle where success is only relative, and all sanctity is torn off of him; where failure and humiliation, the exposure of weaknesses, and the unmasking of pretense are assured incidents: and he accordingly longs for one tranquil spot where he shall be valid absolutely and once for all; where, having been accepted, he is secure from further criticism, and where his good aspirations may be respected no less than if they were accomplished realities. In a word, the elements of security and repose are essential to his ideal; and the question is, Are they easily attainable without some feeling of dependence on the woman's side,—without her relying on him to be her mediator with the external world,—without his activity overlapping hers and surrounding it on almost every side, so that he makes as it were the atmosphere in which she lives?[105]

But James separated himself from the typical American in thinking that a man could be happily married without having to be his wife's "mediator with the external world." He foresaw the day when women would function importantly outside the home while preserving the mutual dependence in love that takes marriage beyond friendship. James was not hiding behind the references to the representative American; rather, he was for the first time in this review articulating the thesis which years later would be central to "The Moral Philosopher and the Moral Life": that conventional morality is the most recent result of the human race's moral experiments, and that we must proceed cautiously before replacing it. Conventional morality is a community achievement that has been long in the making, and in its presence we must curb any arrogance of self-assertion we may feel to be identified with our view of what is morally right. It was Mill's failure, James thought, not to have tried to discern what was responsible for the way that the institution of marriage had developed. Had he made that effort, he might have come upon the forces behind the popular ideal of marriage which, when understood, reveal it to be less contemptible than Mill judged it.

James tried to identify what in the popular mind resisted the equation of love with friendship. It was in part the sentiment that mutual respect, sympathy, and interest alone are a weak bond compared with "that flattering interplay of instincts,—egotism, since you prefer to call it so, on the one hand, and self-sacrifice on the other" (563). Mill had ignored the instinctive basis of the love relationship and its consequent differences from mere friendship. He argued that when two persons "both care for great objects," they are more likely to endure together. James caricatured this idea, saying that it implied that the most important feature in an astronomer's wife is her being passionate about astronomy; if this is ever true, he said, it is the exception that proves its converse. He did not mean that an alteration in women's positions was neither inevitable nor desirable, but only that reformers should fully understand the nature of what they wanted to change. One argument against such change (an argument James found pointless) was that it would cause the final disappearance of gallantry and chivalry. James's reason for dismissing this argument is curious: "This leaves altogether out of sight the mere animal potency of sex. An individual man, however his interests may clash with those of an individual woman, will always shrink from appearing personally like a brute in her presence" (564). To see the world from such a perspective is odd indeed, but it reveals James's belief that the gender confrontation is instinctive from the first meeting.

In responding to Mill, James preferred neutral ground; he left it to the future to decide whether Mill was right, whether a revolution in sexual relations and in the position of women was about to occur. But even in 1869, when James was not only a neophyte writer but also a bachelor and most likely sexually inexperienced, he understood that the status quo deserved to be changed. Mill might have failed to deal with the difficult corollaries of his position—such as divorce at will and its implications for the family—yet James detected in his book the "ultimate tendencies of the democratic flood which is sweeping us along" (565). The merits of Mill's case for the new woman (and man) had to be recognized. The question was largely how the forces for change, based on concepts of equality and justice, could most effectively modify the forces for tradition, based on habit and (to an extent) on instinct. Even in 1869, when James himself longed for a woman who would make him "valid absolutely and once for all," his ethics of individualism did not falter in its application to women.

In a review written in 1887, James treated the subject of romantic love and personal beauty with a light, relaxed touch. The author, Henry Finck, had eulogized adolescent love or prematrimonial infatuation, treating it as the romantic sentiment from which all health and beauty stem. He declared that the French married for social convenience and money and then had ugly children, whereas Americans married for love and had beautiful offspring. James rebutted the contention that romantic love is a late product of evolution. To Finck's complex argument that modern, cultivated love was unknown in earlier periods, James replied, "It is incredible that individual women should not at all times have had the power to fill individual manly breasts with enchanted respect; and Mr. Finck's literary quotations prove it, though meant to prove the opposite. So powerful and instinctive an emotion can never have been recently evolved."[106] In this regard James's thought had not changed since 1869.

In prior eras, James suggested, a stoic ideal of being free from passion had been pursued, and although men had doubtless been slaves to feminine charms even then, they had not celebrated such servitude. In his own day, James said, sensibility was considered not a weakness but a strength, and lovesickness had become something admirable. Finck had mistakenly inferred that the emotion of romantic love had recently evolved, James argued, because he gave a faulty interpretation to traditional literature, confusing life and literature through an irresponsible borrowing from Darwin. (At this time James was especially sensitive to theories inspired by Darwin, since he was only three years from completing *Principles,* the final chapter of which would expressly exempt instinctive emotions from being the fruits of an evolutionary process.) All he could assert in favor of Finck's book was that it was a readable celebration of the ideal of American young people, a pleasant tribute to Cupid's arrow. James concluded the review thus: "Our author is no believer in the incurability of Cupid's wounds. Second love may be better than first. *'For his size,* a boy may love as ardently as a man; but the man is bigger' " (238).

James was prepared to follow the recommendations made by intelligent women for changes in women's roles, although he was not of a temperament to pretend to head their cause. He had no problem in deferring to women's judgments and assumed that he could depend upon women to define their own best interests. He was not put off by women who were active suffragettes; indeed, he felt great esteem for Jane Addams, a cofounder of Chicago's Hull House, who eventually won the Nobel Peace Prize in 1931. In 1907 he sent her book *New Ideals of Peace* to George Bernard Shaw, telling him that it dealt with American problems of immigration.

> You will notice the extraordinary absence of rancor in her temper, and the big holes her criticisms make in the official and orthodox opinions that prevail in the U.S. about the way in which our immigrants ought to be handled. I think you will agree that the little woman . . . is a real genius for perceiving the truth in things human. . . . I send the book to *you,* because while reading it and having all kinds of scales fall from my eyes, I kept chortling to myself "How Bernard Shaw would relish this, or that, passage!" It seems a book eminently calculated to nourish your own peculiar genius, both by its ungrained benignity, and by its new array of examples of conventional stupidity.[107]

James's friend Pauline Goldmark was a social activist involved in running the Consumers' League, and James wrote to her on 20 February 1909: "I am also in the philanthropic business, having come [to New York City] to help launch a national committee on insanity, after the pattern of your league. Welcome me into the fold."

Edith Franklin Wyatt testified to James's enlightened attitude toward women. She recalled in 1928 that James, on a hiking trip in the Adirondacks accompanied by a group that included Wyatt and other Bryn Mawr students, was amused by their wearing knickerbockers. He commented on their impudence in the Victorian era, but "I remember especially that he made us all feel in the van of progress . . . by saying of the convenience of our clothes for climbing—'I'm glad it's come. I'm glad I've lived to see it'—and how grateful to him I was."[108]

Such anecdotes hardly identify James as a committed activist, and the protest that his biographers have exaggerated his role as a social reformer is well heeded.[109] Admittedly, most of his causes were served through lecturing and publishing, but for a college professor he had an unusually pronounced social conscience that prompted him to speak out on many issues. His doing so is all the more remarkable given that he began his career rather late, that he was intensely engaged in both psychology and philosophy, that he was a prolific writer, and that he often had incapacitating bouts of ill health. That he had the energy to be concerned with the position of blacks, women, immigrants, minorities in other countries, the care of the insane, vivisection, medical legislation, educational policy, the temperance movement, the imperialism and militarism of the Spanish-American War, the annexation of the Philippines, and the Monroe Doctrine is a remarkable feature of his life and thought. It is all the more striking when we compare him in this regard to the average college professor then and now.

In looking at James's social views, we must ask whether they emerge naturally from his ethics; in doing so, we need to consult biographical particulars. Perry is an invaluable source of information and insight, yet he made one odd assertion: "The root of James's politics is to be found not in his ethics and philosophy, but in the fact that he belonged to the educated class, and accepted on that account a peculiar role and a peculiar responsibility. . . . Neither his democracy nor his gospel of action implied a leveling of differences. He did not believe either that one man was as good as another, or that all causes were equally worthy. His politics was governed by the principle of discrimination. The educated man was the man who knew how to criticize."[110] Perry's apparent assumption, that James saw ethical philosophy and social or political philosophy (with educational and class distinctions built in) as two different things, would have offended James, I think. He supposed that his social and political convictions were rooted in his ethical beliefs, which require for their recognition and implementation a capacity for discrimination that one person may display better than another. Like Plato, James assumed a connection between morals and intelligence, and he undoubtedly also assumed that as the social and political issues became thornier, more brainpower was needed. But this view does not imply that morality ought to develop from a democratic source, whereas social or political positions ought to emerge from elitist origins. James believed that morality, politics, and normative sociology are interrelated and that it is a constant moral imperative to make education serve democracy and a constant democratic imperative to make morality serve public policy. He acknowledged that those who are better educated are also better prepared to cope with the complexities of moral and social problems; however, this belief showed not that ethics and politics differ in their origins, but rather that if the educated constitute an elite, then democracy is distinctly deficient. A major goal of education in a Jamesian democratic society is the elimination of the educated as a privileged class.

James corresponded and lectured about lynching, mob psychology, militarism, the tyranny of the majority, international conflicts, alcoholism, responsibilities of Harvard undergraduates, curriculum reform, and the effects of the Ph.D. degree in America. He could not possibly have been a card-carrying member of every organization relevant to his causes, nor could he have presumed that, beyond speaking out and sometimes making generous donations, he might somehow be more effective.[111] One may fault him for not being more explicitly and aggressively against American racism, for not sympathizing more with his sister Alice's siding with the Irish against England, or for betraying vacillation on some positions, but overall he made good his claim that one who upholds an ethic of democratic individualism is obligated to take part in social or political change. To be ethically sincere yet socially unconcerned was for James a moral contradiction, and however we may quarrel with his social criticism there is no doubt that he extended his ethics, sometimes jeopardizing his reputation, to the public controversies of his time.

One area of public contentiousness was medicine. James suffered both from neurasthenia and from the inability of doctors to remedy it. Long before he resorted to baths, medicine, and psychic healers, he had been intrigued by how the mind may affect the body; in 1868 he had reviewed a book on "moral medication." This term was used for the alleged process of achieving medicinal effects through the power of thought or suggestion rather than through drugs or other physical means. James was reserved and critical of the author's claims, but after citing evidence that the pulse of somnambulists can be diminished by the experimenter's suggestion and that a congestion on their cutaneous surface can thus be produced, he agreed with the author that if the mind can yield such effects, then it might also produce therapeutic results. Relishing the idea that there should no more be "an aristocracy of remedies than of physicians," James urged educated medical men to look seriously into the misty territory of mental or moral healing.[112] It seemed evident that this technique promised some help and that established medicine ought not to ignore it altogether.

Thirty years later the same conviction led him to testify at the Massachusetts State House against a proposed medical license bill which, by requiring the examination and licensing of medical practitioners, was aimed at abolishing faith-healers and Christian Scientists. James had protested a similar bill in 1894, because to eliminate the mind-curists would halt experiments in moral medication, which he saw as important for both science and therapy. While claiming not to support mind-healers, he argued that "they are proving by the most brilliant new results that the therapeutic relation may be what we can at present describe only as a relation of one person to another person," and that they were therefore justified in resisting legislation that "would make 'examinable' information the root of medical virtue, and hamper the free play of personal force and affinity by mechanically imposed conditions" (*LWJ*, 2:69–70). In his address at the second hearing before the Committee on Public Health at the State House in Boston in March 1898, he added that mind-healing had become a religious or quasi-religious movement in which personality seemed to be one condition of success and in which impressions and intuitions may accomplish more than chemical or anatomical information. He also emphasized the imperfect state of medical knowledge and its susceptibility to conflicts of opinion. "The Commonwealth of Massachusetts is not a medical body, has no right to a medical opinion, and should not dare to take sides in medical controversies. . . . Above all things, Mr. Chairman, let us not be infected with the Gallic spirit of regulation and resignation for their own abstract sakes." In so testifying, he acknowledged that his task was an unpleasant one: "I count some of the medical advocates of this proposed law among my dearest friends; and well do I know how I shall stand in their eyes hereafter for standing to-day in my present position."[113] James's side won, and the bill did not pass.

Whether James was on the right side of the issue is certainly debatable, but I agree with him that there are ways short of adding to the legal machinery to insure that persons understand the risks of patronizing practitioners on the periphery of the medical profession. The extraordinary development in America of the therapeutic movement, much of it lying outside of mainstream medicine, indicates that a vaguer kind of treatment than the medical doctor likes to tolerate seems to help some people; it would be a pity to abort that option through impulsive legislation. James's position on the issue was part and parcel of his ethics, which advocated freedom, toleration, individualism, and an open mind, and also required one to act upon his ethical beliefs, to take a public stand in their defense.

This continuity between James's ethics and his social commitments is exhibited also by what he did on behalf of the insane. As a psychologist and himself a victim of neurosis, James was concerned about the care of the insane. In 1880 there were more than 40,000 mental patients confined to hospitals, and he would not have been surprised to learn that by 1922 the number would be 267,000, and by 1932 more than 300,000. He wondered about the causes and possible cures of mental illness, the continuity between normality and abnormality, the diagnoses of psychosis, and the treatment of the insane. He was suspicious of the standard psychosis in terms of which patients were diagnosed, agreeing with Enrico Morselli that "many forms of insanity which the nosographs distinguish and circumscribe within sharp limits are, despite their apparent divergence, only *clinical varieties or different stages of a probably unique malady which is modified diversely according to the personality of the individual whom it affects.*"[114] In the interest of fairness, James thought, it should be remembered that even mental patients are individuals and should not be pigeonholed. Early in his career he had spoken of "responsibility in mental disease," taking a harder line than might be expected. He disagreed with the idea that the criminally insane should be protected from punishment. "We hold that the punishment of the insane is after all a matter of public *policy*, to be decided by many other considerations than the psychological one . . . namely, whether the subject have flexibility of choice enough to make him properly 'accountable' to us for his deeds."[115] He said nothing further on this score, and presumably he meant only that society must be protected from the criminally insane, who should therefore be incarcerated. It is odd that he did not explicitly stipulate that the punishment of the insane should be a humane form of hospitalization, but he more than adequately addressed that issue in later writings.

In his final years James became associated with Clifford W. Beers, author of the classic *A Mind That Found Itself: An Autobiography*. A former mental patient, Beers described the onset of his illness, incarceration, and eventual recovery. Pleading that mental patients are sick people who can be rehabilitated, he worked hard to found the National Committee for Mental Hygiene to improve the conditions of the mentally ill in America, especially those in asylums. He regarded James's help, both in finding a publisher for his book and in being a founding member of the committee, as a significant boost to his efforts. James, in bad health and with only three years to live, was disinclined to be responsible to another organization; he could not ignore Beers's cause, however, and in 1907 he helped to plan the committee, which was founded two years later. The year before, when Beers first came to him with his manuscript, James had written that it was the most effective case of its kind. He was impressed by Beers's account of how he had gone mad, of the suddenness with which he had moved from delusion to mania; never before had James heard of so rapid a change in a person's mental system. Remembering what he had written years earlier about responsibility in mental disease, he commented that in that condition Beers must have been imperious. Convinced of the need to improve the lot of the insane and to revamp the asylums, James wrote: "I have long thought that if I were a millionaire, with money to leave for public purposes, I should endow 'Insanity' exclusively."[116] In 1908 he sent Beers a thousand dollars for his national committee and unsuccessfully approached John D. Rockefeller for funds on Beers's behalf. Given James's circumstances, he devoted a remarkable amount of time and effort to this cause during the last four years of his life.

James also took on the medical profession over the issue of animal vivisection, still a lively issue in philosophy. He felt affection for animals and enjoyed observing them; some of his most winning drawings are of dogs and monkeys seen during his travels. He said that he felt qualms whenever he heard the shrieking of experimental animals in the laboratories of physiologists and psychologists.[117] Whether vivisection is moral was a question that brought his personal feelings into conflict with his sense of scientific obligation to experiment in the interest of the larger good. He never examined the problem systematically, but he said in "The Moral Philosopher and the Moral Life" that the moment one sentient being exists good and evil can also exist; it would thus seem that animals make their own moral demands of us. In an article that challenged the reader to distinguish between brute and human intellect, James noted the intelligence of which dogs are capable: "Dogs thus discern, at any rate so far as to be able to act, this partial character of *being valuable*, which lies hidden in certain things."[118] Some years ago, Benjamin A. G. Fuller wrote an essay called "The Messes Animals Make in Metaphysics"; to the extent that they show kinship with humans, they make the untidy philosophy of morals untidier still.[119] Sensitive to the issue, James wrote his first piece on vivisection in 1875; he continued to write on the subject throughout his life, his last article on it appearing in 1909, and he was disputing the issue just a few months before his death in 1910.

The first article was prompted by controversies over the issue in France, England, and America, and James was unimpressed by the arguments of both sides. The antivivisectionists were ignorant of the facts, not considering that a dog might rather have an artery tied than be etherized, and the vivisectionists were unresponsive to charges of cruelty. "We have heard that a distinguished toxicologist of Berlin, when he wishes to exhibit the effect of corrosive substances on the alimentary canal, simply thrusts a funnel down the throat of a living rabbit, and pours sulphuric acid into it. These are plainly revolting excesses, and it is pleasant to think that no physiologist of Anglo-Saxon blood is likely to be guilty of them."[120] James warned that nothing more deadens the moral sensibility of medical students than to become accustomed to bloodshed for trifling ends. But, he concluded, the remedy is not in legislation that would interfere with the acquisition of biological information that might help animals as well as humans, especially since laboratory investigators would clandestinely defy such laws anyway. Instead, vivisectionists must be willing to monitor themselves and seek to eliminate needless cruelty.

The *New York Evening Post* on 22 May 1909 reprinted a letter from James to the secretary of the Vivisection Reform Society:

I am made of too unorganizable stuff to be a vice president of the Vivisection Reform Society, and moreover I make it a principle not to let my name appear anywhere where I am not doing practical work. But I am glad to send you . . . a statement of my views. . . .

Much of the talk against vivisection is, in my opinion, as idiotic as the talk in defence of it is uncandid, but your society (if I rightly understand its policy) aims not at abolishing vivisection, but at regulating it ethically. *Against any regulation whatever* I understand the various medical and scientific defenders of vivisection to protest. Their invariable contention, implied or expressed, is that it is *no one's business* what happens to an animal, so long as the individual who is handling it can plead that to increase *science* is his aim.

This contention seems to me to flatly contradict the best conscience of our time. The rights of the helpless, even though they be brutes, must be protected by those who have superior power. . . .

But the public demand for regulation rests on a perfectly sound ethical principle, the denial of which by the scientists speaks ill for either their moral sense or their political ability. So long as the physiologists disclaim corporate responsibility, formulate no code of vivisectional ethics for laboratories to post up and enforce, appoint no censors, pass no votes of condemnation or exclusion, propose of themselves no law, so long must the anti-vivisectionist agitation, with all its expansiveness, idiocy, bad temper, untruth, and vexatiousness continue as the only possible means of bringing home to the . . . experimenter the fact that the sufferings of his animals *are* somebody else's business as well as his own, and that there is "a God in Israel" to whom he owes account.

One of those distressed by James's criticism of the medical profession for not monitoring itself was his colleague, W. B. Cannon, at the Harvard Medical School, who was to become a distinguished critic of the James-Lange theory of emotion. On 4 June 1909 Cannon wrote to James, on stationery that connected him with the medical school, the American Medical Association, and the AMA's Council on Defense of Medical Research, that although James pained his friends with his charges, he did so in "such a tolerable manner" that they could forgive him; Cannon insisted that most researchers were responsible toward their animals. Observing that about twelve thousand cats and six thousand dogs were killed annually in Boston merely to get rid of the excess, whereas perhaps two dozen cats were used annually for medical demonstrations, he asked James: "Can you have the will to believe that your vivisectionist friend is capable of burning with moral indignation at cruelty to animals?" He later wrote to James that perhaps the self-monitoring plan was the most efficacious way of assuring uniformly humane treatment of animals, and promised to use his influence within the medical profession to bring about that goal. This reply was more congenial than one Cannon had made in reaction to James's letter to the Vivisection Reform Society, where Cannon declared that "our house is in order" and "we are not callous creatures, rejoicing in pain"; with this letter (10 May 1909) he sent his association's "Rules Regarding Animals." Then, in a letter of 11 February 1910, he charged James with making public statements that betrayed a misunderstanding of the AMA's position. "You will perhaps be interested to know that in an antivivisection 'chamber of horrors' in New York City, your name is posted with others in large letters as having expressed opposition to vivisection. . . . I get very much discouraged at times about this fight. We are all too prone to misinterpretation. . . . Surely I should turn quietly to my investigations if I did not feel that grave problems of human welfare were dependent for their solution on freedom of medical research." James surely agreed with this last sentiment, though he took some satisfaction in knowing that he had largely helped to formulate the controversial issue for both popular and professional attention.[121]

Politics had also figured in James's application of ethics to the practical world. In 1884, in addition to publishing a number of important works, he worked on the campaign that led to Democrat Grover Cleveland's defeat of Republican James G. Blaine. Deserting the Republicans with the mugwumps, he saw himself supporting the cause of clean government, reforms, and high ideals in Washington. He hoped that the Democrats would be ousted in another four years, replaced by "a new national party with something of an intellectual character in purposes, which will devote itself to civil service and economic reform, and perhaps ultimately to certain constitutional changes of which we are in pressing need."[122] Joining the political fray at this time did not represent a sudden new interest in American politics on James's part. His father had held strong social views, and because of his family's European travels he had grown up with relatives and friends whose conversation included comparative assessments of society and politics in America and Europe. In the 1870s he and his family had been closely acquainted with E. L. Godkin, who had founded the *Nation,* to which William and Henry both contributed prolifically, and later became editor of the *New York Evening Post.* Godkin, who attacked the carpet-baggers, the corruption under President Grant, free silver, and high tariffs, was considered by Perry to have been the most powerful influence in forming James's liberal social and political convictions. James certainly had like-minded colleagues at Harvard and elsewhere who contributed to those convictions.

Between 1884 and the completion of *Principles* six years later, James intensified his social concerns. He wrote letters to the *Harvard Daily Crimson,* urging undergraduates to govern themselves and to assume various responsibilities; he also penned articles on the importance of individuals and, in 1891, his major essay in ethics, "The Moral Philosopher and the Moral Life." All of this writing was sandwiched between articles and reviews in psychology and notices and reports on psychical research. In 1895 he wrote a brief letter (one of fourteen publications that year) to his Congressman, Samuel W. McCall, protesting the actions of President Cleveland and Congress in the Venezuelan incident. The longstanding dispute between Venezuela and Great Britain over the boundary between Venezuela and British Guiana had flared up, largely due to the discovery of gold in the region, and succeeding events led to diplomatic tensions between England and the United States. The British responded hostilely to a broader than usual interpretation of the Monroe Doctrine by the Cleveland administration, and on 17 December 1895 the president delivered a message to Congress saying that the United States had a duty to assist in the determination of the boundary, and if necessary to resist British aggression. Congress agreed, and some talk of war followed. Four days later James wrote to McCall:

> My Dear Sir:
> As one of your constituents I urge you to use your influence to mitigate the further results of the calamity which President Cleveland and Congress together have sprung upon the country.
> The good fame that one hundred years have won for us, and that has made the rest of the world view us with an indulgence accorded to no other great power, the character, namely, of being safe, and always to be counted on as throwing our vast weight into the scale that stands for humanity and civilization, has in three days of delirium been flung so far away over the roof tops that fifty years of sane conduct will doubtfully buy it back. We have written ourselves squarely down as a people dangerous to the peace of the world, more dangerous than anything since France under Napoleon. The grotesque logic of the Cleveland-Olney [Secretary of State] communications is only matched by their gratuitously insulting form. Was there anything more infernally cynical than to make of an incident where we pretend to urge upon others the humaner international methods the pretext and vehicle of a wanton and blustering provocation to war?
> The President's fearful blunder was in coupling his direct threat of war with

his demand for a commission. It is the passions aroused by that that so fatally complicate the situation. . . . The threat compels England to disregard the commission's decision. It compels us to declare war if she disregards it. Compels, that is, under penalty of flagrant cowardice on the one hand, under penalty of confessing to a buffoon government on the other. It is monstrous that so sharp and calamitous an issue should be abruptly sprung on two friendly countries by the very first public utterance of our Executive. It has made retreat with honor impossible to either side. . . . Congress must do what it can to minimize your full share in all that may occur.[123]

Although James was relieved by the fact that war was avoided (Britain yielded to the broad interpretation of the Monroe Doctrine, and the border dispute was settled in 1899, mostly in her favor), he was thenceforth keenly concerned about colonialism, imperialism, international relations, militarism, and America's role in the world scene. America had been at peace for almost thirty years when Cleveland made his Venezuelan address in 1895, and James feared that the administration might decide on its own to end that peace. Samuel Eliot Morison, once a student of James's, wrote that Harvard students, who were not generally concerned with public affairs, were stirred by the war scare into debates for and against the Cleveland administration; during this period the *Crimson* carried an exchange between Theodore Roosevelt (also a former student of James's) and James. Roosevelt scolded Cleveland's critics for their "stock-jobbing timidity" and "colonial dependence on England," and James replied ("in the true Harvard tradition"): "May I express a hope that in this University, if no where else on the continent, we shall be patriotic enough *not* to remain passive whilst the destinies of our country are being settled by surprise. . . . Let us refuse to be bound over night by proclamation, or hypnotized by sacramental phrases through the day. Let us consult our reason as to what is best, and then exert ourselves as citizens with all our might."[124]

As 1900 approached, it was clear to James and others that political forces were at work for the first time to make America a great world power. The traditional idea that America's destiny lay in its own continental opportunities rather than in foreign exploits would soon be discarded, and among those who urged a new national aggressiveness were Theodore Roosevelt, Henry Cabot Lodge, Alfred Thayer Mahan, and Josiah Strong.

In many respects the times were auspicious for the young agitators' designs on America and the world. European powers, with Great Britain at the head, were then going into imperialism on a vaster scale than ever. They were building bigger navies, raising bigger armies, seizing territories in Asia, Africa, and the islands of the seas, forming secret alliances, carrying on undercover maneuvers, and preparing for the climax—the World War which opened in 1914. The sight of this "grand strategy" in Europe filled the American world-power politicians with envy and a burning desire to get into it.[125]

It was a sight that filled James with foreboding. The world, and the United States in particular, seemed at the time of the Spanish-American War on the verge of violating James's deepest social convictions. He feared that small countries would be dominated by large ones and that militarism would replace democratic, rational attempts at negotiations.

Tensions between Spain and the United States had been intensifying for a long time over the struggle of Cuba to secure independence from Spain; when the U.S. battleship *Maine* was sunk in Havana harbor on 15 February 1898 with a heavy loss of life, anger at home understandably was inflamed. President McKinley addressed Congress and requested authority to intervene in Cuba, which led to Spain's declaration of war against the United States on 24 April 1898; Congress replied the next day that a state of war had existed prior to the Spanish declaration. By June, James was writing to friends about his own reactions. The most important feature of this outbreak of war, he thought, was that it illustrates how history is made, how "a nation's ideals can be changed in the twinkling of an eye, by a succession of outward events partly accidental."[126] The sinking of the *Maine* was such an event, and like a Darwinian mutation or spontaneous variation, it was the accidental spark that caused the dynamite magazine to explode. The American people prior to that event had supposed themselves to be a nation morally superior to most by being safe at home, unburdened by savage ambitions, determined to exert international influence through moral force rather than by arms. The sentiments of the American people had been unquestionably noble, James wrote, and their hostility toward Spain had resulted not from imperialistic motives but from sympathy for the oppressed Cubans.

James was struck by the fact that once a state of national belligerency had been established, all that was required for a rapid chain of events to occur was an accidental incident such as the sinking of the *Maine*. What ensued, he said, exemplified the psychology of the crowd and could be understood only as a phenomemon of group psychology. Like Freud, James had read the single notable work in group psychology, *The Crowd: A Study of the Popular Mind*, by Gustave Le Bon. James reviewed it in 1897, recommending it not for its wisdom but for its being the first scientific exploration of group psychology. "With public opinion ruling more and more the world, the psychology of public opinion, the sources of its strength and weakness, its pathology and hygiene, and the causes of its stability and of its alterations, ought to be studied with ever-increasing care by those interested in the welfare of mankind."[127] Le Bon was much too materialistic, pessimistic, and misanthropic for James's taste; James considered his work valuable only in that it proved the need for better beginnings in group psychology. In any event, James thought, the reactions of the American public as well as the actions of Congress were examples of group hysteria. He regretted in this instance that Congress rather than the executive branch had the power to declare war, for he considered McKinley's behavior restrained and calculated to avoid armed conflict. But individual efforts at negotiation were trampled in the stampede of a people toward war; they had been readied for war, and in accordance with the psychological principle of the summation of stimuli that James had articulated in *Principles,* the sinking of the U.S. battleship was but the final stimulus required for Congress and the people to convert their readiness for war into overt action. The spirit of excitement, sport, and adventure took over as the nation flexed its muscles. Although at the outset James neither severely condemned his own country nor condoned Spain's behavior, he was clearly vexed by the massive display of animal aggression transformed into a kind of sport. "Civilization, properly so called, might well be termed the organization of all those functions that resist the mere excitement of sport."[128]

When Admiral Dewey defeated the Spanish fleet in Manila harbor, a victory greeted with wild acclaim by Americans, James saw the sudden rise of an imperialist party in America that would command "all the crude and barbaric patriotism of the country."[129] By the end of 1898 the Spanish Empire was virtually eroded, and the ownership of Puerto Rico, Guam, and the Philippines had been transferred to the United States. Why did all this happen? Why did the United States move against the Philippines only days after the outbreak of war with Spain? According to George F. Kennan, "The fact of the matter is that down to the present day we do not know the full answer to this question."[130] As James watched the United States wrest control of the Philippines from the Spanish and then crush the bid of Filipinos led by Emile Aguinaldo for independence from all foreign powers, he attributed both actions to the new imperialism that was sweeping America. From 1899 to 1904 he was preoccupied with the Philippine issue, as is revealed in his correspondence, in his letters to the *Boston Evening Transcript,* the *Springfield Daily Republican,* and the *New York Evening Post,* and in his activities as a vice president of the Anti-Imperialist League. He was concerned also about the fate of local autonomy in the Boer War and later in the Russo-Japanese conflict; he deplored what he called the insolence of the white race in Asia. But the Philippine question over the years elicited most of his thoughts on oppression, imperialism, wealth and poverty, international relations, and militarism. The military occupation of the Philippines by the United States, which had been described by McKinley as "benevolent assimilation," was denounced by James as signaling a loss of moral prestige that could not be regained by the "cold pot-grease of McKinley's eloquence" (*LWJ,* 2:94).

In the autumn of 1898 James was, according to Santayana, "terribly distressed" by the events of the Spanish-American War. Five years later, on 6 December 1903, James wrote to Josephine Lowell: "I am glad you still have the gift of tears about our national soul. I cried, *hard,* when the hostilities broke out and General Otis refused Aquinaldo's demand for a conference,—the only time I've cried in many a long year, and I know one other person who did likewise, a man of 60." In the same letter he lamented the "great disease" overtaking the country, an increasing unwillingness to do anything that had little chance of succeeding. The discovery of our age, he wrote, is the organization of great machines for "slick" success, leaving the individual to acquiesce in silence. Eventually acquiescence itself becomes organized, and against this "the only remedy is that every little donkey like your correspondent should keep making a vow. We want people who are willing to espouse failure as their vocation. I wish that *that* could be organized—it would soon 'pass into its opposite.'" James associated the military annexation of the Philippines with the new tendency of the corporate voice to drown out the individual's, the tendency of organizational bigness to grow ever bigger. James's father had been attracted to Fourier's version of socialism, and James, questioning the economic motives behind the actions that followed the brief war with Spain, echoed his father's declaration of forty years earlier that international trade was based on unlimited competition and was a system of "rapacity and robbery." Writing in this vein to his brother Henry, he expressed hope that the competitive era was winding down, to be superseded by a socialistic equilibrium.[131]

But why was James so upset about the Philippines? One might even speculate that his intense sentiments on the matter were connected with his ill health after 1898. A remarkable letter from James was published in the *Springfield Republican* on 4 June 1900 and included interpretive comments upon his own translation of the diary of "A Lieutenant X of the French navy" who had witnessed the actions of the United States military in Manilia and was critical of them. James referred to the French officer's diary to support his own argument that America had failed to treat the Filipinos as political and moral beings. "Decidedly, American party politics and clever business manipulations are not the school in which to learn how to extend an empire!" It was not ill health that made James focus on the Philippines, but rather his perception of injustice and stupidity in American foreign policy. In 1899 he acknowledged that the American administration and people felt goodwill for the Filipinos. "But what worse enemy to a situation of need can there be than dim, foggy, abstract good will, backed by energetic officiousness and unillumined by any accurate perception of the concrete wants and possibilities of the case? Cynical indifference . . . would work less irreparable harm."[132] In 1903 he acknowledged that nothing immediate could be done to effect Philippine independence but urged his fellow anti-Imperialists to work patiently toward inducing Congress to return the islands to the Filipinos.[133] A year later he called for similar efforts, declaring that "the real obstacle to a promise of independence by our Congress is the old human aversion to abdicating any power once held. When the love of power and the desire to do good run to double harness the team is indeed a difficult one to stop. . . . Let [Filipinos] work out their own issues. We Americans surely do not monopolize all the possible forms of goodness."[134] Again, armed aggression in the service of a well-intended but stupid attitude, as he perceived it, caused James great frustration over American politics.

Why did James become so upset over the effects of the war with Spain? Santayana answered:

Because he held a false moralistic view of history, attributing events to the conscious ideals and free will of individuals: whereas individuals, especially in governments, are creatures of circumstance and slaves to vested interests. . . . He cried disconsolately that he had lost his country, when his country, just beginning to play its part in the history of the world, appeared to ignore an ideal that he had innocently expected would always guide it, because this ideal had been eloquently expressed in the Declaration of Independence. But the Declaration of Independence was a piece of literature, a salad of illusion.[135]

Santayana added that the Declaration had been the American Colonies' rehearsal of independence and that in 1898 the United States was rehearsing domination over South America; given the commercial and military interests and the "imaginative passions" involved, the move toward such domination was inevitable. James had not lost his country, Santayana insisted, for the country was in good health and approaching its puberty; James had "merely lost his way in its physiological history," a curious case of a physiological psychologist misreading physiological history.[136]

Santayana was not alone in judging that the anti-imperialists were sentimental, unrealistic, and even elitist. They were a minority which was neither the voice of America nor the voice of college campuses.

> If students had been indoctrinated at all, it appears more likely that it was to support expansion, if the wildly enthusiastic receptions that Roosevelt received on college campuses, including the University of Chicago, in 1900 is any gauge. Addressing a gathering of Harvard alumni and students, Professor Charles Eliot Norton was rudely hissed at when he criticized the government's handling of the Philippines. For every Professor James at Harvard, there was a Professor Giddings at Columbia who countered academic criticism of the war with intellectual justification of American conquest.[137]

But even those who were not anti-imperialists sided with James against Santayana's deterministic concept of history; like James, most people took a moralistic view of history and assumed that great individuals affect the course of events. On this point James understood better than Santayana that a nation must prize its inspirational myths.[138] At the same time, Santayana's sardonic reaction to James's feeling of tragic loss over the Philippines is understandable and to an extent justified. In making the Philippines his crusade, James did exaggerate the lessons he claimed were revealed by the issue; he thus showed less sophistication about the nation's history than Santayana did. As Beisner has argued,

> James's error lay in supposing that it had taken imperialism to reveal that Americans had their quota of human frailty. . . . To think that war and the suppression of insurrection in the Philippines had revealed for the first time that the American people shared the universal human condition was to overlook a history which included religious conflict and witch-hangings, slavery and lynchings, corruption and industrial warfare, and the near-extermination of the American Indian. More to the point, it was to ignore a long history of battles for expansion and control.[139]

The significance James ascribed to the new imperialism was arguably the result of his looking too blindly at the nation's past.

Whether or not Santayana was correct in his view of history, he understood why James took the Philippine issue so much to heart. James felt that he had lost his country, that the ideals with which he had identified had perhaps been lost forever. He had believed, partly because of his international travels, that America was different and, because of its geography and resources, could remain so. It could encourage the rest of world to be free, magnanimous, democratic, individualistic, and essentially pacifistic. There can be great nations just as there can be great individuals, and one aspect of America's greatness was its ability to develop without war. Unlike nations with few options other than to be belligerent, America, James assumed, could in its isolation and independence be a model of how progress and prosperity can be achieved through peaceful negotiation. But with the Spanish-American War and the subsequent events, America had "deliberately pushed itself into the circle of international hatreds and joined the common pack of wolves."[140] As a psychologist James had wondered about the degree to which instinctive aggressiveness is civilizable, and as an ethical and social activist he had hoped that America would demonstrate that pugnacity can be sublimated. As he moved into his final years, he became increasingly preoccupied with the question of militarism. America had betrayed him, and the only remaining hope for global peace lay in an international linking of anti-imperialist forces. D. B. Schirmer has observed that James came to see liberal intellectuals as the embodiment of anti-imperialism, for they successfully used reason to curb instinctive aggressiveness. "These, the forces of reason, were the antidote to imperialism. It is just here that James struck a new note, a note of internationalism, which he felt to be in keeping with the times. This was a note which the more typical anti-imperialists, in their subliminal longing for a return to the past, did not give forth. . . . Men of reason in America now face the same problems as have their counterparts in imperial Europe. Therefore, those Americans must make common cause with their allies the world over; that is the only way out."[141] Schirmer's point here is an important one, helping us to understand James's anti-imperialist motivation and the respect in which it was distinctive.

For anti-imperialism to have any chance of success, however, the psychology of aggression and militarism had to be understood and put to work so that reason could dominate our pugnacious instincts. From the aftermath of the Spanish-American War until his death in 1910, James thought a great deal about the origins of warlike feelings and behavior and about their ramifications in the rituals and institutions that constitute the militaristic way of life. He studied the history of war, the development of armies and navies, the soldier's training and discipline, the claims made about martial virtues, military biographies, life in the barracks, and the extension of military attitudes into the fabric of societies.[142] Given the evidence he thus assembled, he could not see the issue as a clearcut one, even though he abhorred war and feared warlike instincts. History amply showed that militarism had contributed to the development of civilization and to some of our finer character traits, and James thus could not make a simplistic indictment of war. He never doubted that warlike instincts are an inescapable part of human nature; indeed, he stressed those instincts when in the company of fellow pacifists in order to insure a realistic view of the obstacles confronting the peacemaker. Although he embraced the irrational and the mystical in his metaphysics, he sought in his social philosophy a rational solution; like Plato and Freud—neither of whom can be described as an optimist about human nature—he hoped that reason could bridle instincts and passions, including the martial ones.

Despite the biological bellicosity of human nature, he argued in 1904 that rationality might sublimate warlike feelings:

> We do ill, I think, therefore, to talk much of universal peace or of a general disarmament. We must go in for preventive medicine, not for radical cure. We must cheat our foe, circumvent him in detail, not try to change his nature. . . . Let the general possibility of war be left open, in Heaven's name, for the imagination to dally with. Let the soldiers dream of killing, as the old maids dream of marrying.
>
> But organize in every conceivable way the practical machinery for making each successive chance of war abortive. Put peace men in power; educate the editors and statesmen to responsibility. How beautifully did their trained responsibility in England make the Venezuela incident abortive! Seize every pretext, however small, for arbitration methods, and multiply the precedents; foster rival excitements, and invent new outlets for heroic energy; and from one generation to another the chances are that irritation will grow less acute and states of strain less dangerous among the nations. . . .
>
> The last weak runnings of the war spirit will be "primitive expeditions." A country that turns its arms only against uncivilized foes is, I think, wrongly taunted as degenerate. Of course it has ceased to be heroic in the old grand style. But I believe that this is because it now sees something better. It has a conscience. It will still perpetuate peccadillos. But it is afraid, afraid in the good sense, to engage in absolute crimes against civilization.[143]

James continued this line of reasoning in "The Moral Equivalent of War," which appeared the year of his death. The essay reflects his deep study of the subject, beginning with a brief history of Greek and Roman conquests, whose cruelty James called incredible. There is no evading the truth that we have inherited this trait and that "for most of the capacities of heroism that the human race is full of we have to thank this cruel history."[144] It is thus understandable that thoughtful persons, especially military personnel, should be fatalistic about the prospects for eliminating war in the future. Nevertheless, James held (displaying his belief in evolutionary social progress), the civilization that has developed since the Fall of Rome is different from what prevailed then. Warlike instincts and ideals still exist, James said, but they are confronted by reflective criticism which severely restricts their former freedom. The world is more aware of the bestial side of military service, and the ancient motives of loot and enslavement, no longer acceptable in the United States, must be attributed to enemies such as Germany and Japan. We talk of arming ourselves only for peace while our enemies aim at riches and glory. "It may even reasonably be said that the intensely sharp competitive *preparation* for war by the nations *is the real war*, permanent, unceasing; and that the battles are only a sort of public verification of the mastery gained during the 'peace'-interval."[145]

The danger in our civilized era comes less from open warfare than from the preparations for it, James argued; we are duped by the idea that peaceful intervals are movements away from hostility, when in fact, as the Spanish-American conflict abundantly demonstrated, such intervals can be merely the rehearsals of war itself. If war results from this gradual preparation, what can be done to prevent it? James's essay argues that it cannot be prevented by the pious utterances of pacifists and anti-imperialists. He took the argumentative position that he had always liked, striking an Aristotelian mean between extremes: "I see how desperately hard it is to bring the peace-party and the war-party together, and I believe that the difficulty is due to certain deficiencies in the program of pacifism which set the militarist imagination strongly, and to a certain extent justifiably, against it."[146] In not quite belonging to either party, James envisaged himself as a catalyst for compromise. Pacifists needed to hear not only that aggression is an ineradicable part of human nature but also that it is responsible for some of the nobler features of civilized society. Trying to preach it out of existence on the grounds that it is all bad is to offend the intelligence of most listeners, and in the forum of practical politics it is a ridiculous gesture.

> Militarism is the great preserver of our ideals of hardihood, and human life with no use for hardihood would be contemptible. Without risks or prizes for the darer, history would be insipid indeed; and there is a type of military character which every one feels that the race should never cease to breed, for every one is sensitive to its superiority. The duty is incumbent on mankind, of keeping military characters in stock—of keeping them, if not for use, then as ends in themselves and as pure pieces of perfection,—so that Roosevelt's weaklings and molly-coddles may not end by making everything else disappear from the face of nature.[147]

Pacifists failed to comprehend the horror with which their opponents pictured a world without martial virtues. He attributed the opponents' revulsion to a blend of aesthetic and ethical sentiments. They were unwilling to accept on aesthetic grounds a worldview dulled by the absence of handsome army uniforms and by nations fulfilling their destinies not through the drama of war but through the insipid process of evolution. Morally, they resisted seeing "the supreme theatre of human strenuousness closed" and the "splendid military aptitudes" of men forever suppressed. James cautioned against making light of these sentiments, for they reflect popular thinking. As much as anything else, eternal peace presents a dreary picture that makes the average person reject it in his heart even if assenting to it publicly. "So long as anti-militarists propose no substitute for war's disciplinary function, no *moral equivalent* of war, analogous, as one might say, to the mechanical equivalent of heat, so long they fail to realize the full inwardness of the situation. And as a rule they do fail. The duties, penalties, and sanctions pictured in the utopias they present are all too weak and tame to touch the military-minded." This shortcoming was true, he said, not only of pacifists but of socialists such as G. Lowes Dickinson and H. G. Wells, with whom he sometimes aligned himself.[148] Can a state of constant peace be more than a stew of mediocrity and inferiority? Can more than a meek yes be offered by utopians to the shout of Frederick the Great: "Dogs, would you live forever?" James set out in "The Moral Equivalent of War" to locate that something more.

He found it in his moral equivalent for war, a nonmilitary conscription which would achieve several ends at once: it would help to avoid war by sublimating the warlike instincts through alternative outlets of release; it would serve justice by placing a similar responsibility on poor and rich alike; and it would preserve the discipline and manly virtues formerly found in the military. James's moral equivalent of war was "a conscription of the whole youthful population to form for a certain number of years a part of the army enlisted against *Nature.*" It seems ironic that such language could be used by a friend of Emerson's (and himself a hiker and lover of nature). "To coal and iron mines, to freight trains, to fishing fleets in December, to dishwashing, clothes-washing, and window-washing, to road-building and tunnel-making, to foundries and stoke-holes, and to the frames of skyscrapers, would our gilded youths be drafted off, according to their choice, to get the childishness knocked out of them, and to come back into society with healthier sympathies and soberer ideas. They would have paid their blood-tax, done their part in the immemorial human warfare against nature."[149] It has been pointed out that the Civilian Conservation Corps of Franklin Roosevelt's era resembled James's moral equivalent of war, and to the extent that such projects have been successful, James's suggestion has some merit.[150] As a social program intended for national utilization, it was certainly naive, and it could never function as the panacea that James claimed it to be. What survives is the notion that there may be a moral equivalent for the pugnacious impulse, and others have probably been stimulated by it to search for what works for them as such an equivalent. For those who continue to hope that wars can be avoided, James's conviction that there are ways of sublimating aggressive emotions is supportive. We must believe that something of the sort is possible if reason and self-restraint are to govern international efforts to maintain peace. James knew that innovative diplomatic and other forms of international machinery are required for the avoidance of war, but he also knew that basic psychological transformations such as finding moral equivalents are equally essential.

James's approach to social issues, illustrated by "The Moral Equivalent of War," was innovative and infectious in its belief that new methods can be made to work. He did not recommend routine solutions for nonroutine problems. Instead, he conveyed a lively hope that we are not doomed to repeat the past. Creativity is demanded of the sensitive, curious, and alert moral and social consciousness. The pacifist must overcome any initial blindness to the feelings of the military-minded. He must grasp the merits of his opponent's position in order to learn how to negotiate with him. He must understand the psychology of aggression and militarism before he can conceive ways to rechannel aggressive instincts. James's social ethic is distinguished by a fresh attack and an absence of stereotyped suggestions. Far from delivering a fully developed solution, he was thinking through the problem as he wrote. The sense of a need for creative approaches is contagious, and readers are thus stimulated and encouraged.[151]

Given his lifelong religious commitments, it is striking that James did not ultimately define the moral equivalent in religious terms. It would have been in character for him to have argued that only global religious belief would bring enduring peace, but it was also in character for him to separate some moral and social decision-making from religion. That separation was not always easy to achieve, however, for religion was for James more important than anything else.

14 ✣ RELIGION

FAITH AND RATIONALITY

Because ethics is logically independent of religion, James believed that one can be moral without being religious. Morality is not only a matter of deed, he thought, but also one of mood and motivation; it can be easygoing (an evasion of present ills) or strenuous (a concern for ideals that transcend the present and its problems). Strenuous morality is rarer and requires "wilder passions," "big fears, loves, and indignations," and a strong commitment to some issue of justice or freedom.[1] It is a mood in which one conceives ordinary morality as all too human and rejects, for instance, the suggestion that our moral job is to assist in the evolution of superior human beings. That finite role is not enough, for "we see too well the vacuum beyond"; strenuous morality involves infinitude and mystery.[2] Making a religion of humanity itself will not shake us out of genial, easygoing attitudes.

In "The Moral Philosopher and The Moral Life," James concluded that the strenuous mood demands the presence of a God. Theism carries us beyond a morality of prudence and of the satisfaction of daily needs into an "ethics of infinite and mysterious obligation from on high." Our moral mood intensifies when we cease to suppose that "there are none but finite demanders" and believe instead that we live also "for an infinite demander's sake."[3] Believing in a superior power brings a surge of energy, perseverance, and courage. Morally strenuous people continue to prevail over the easygoing type, and religion continues to triumph over irreligion; the balance of energy is on the side of theism.

> The stable and systematic moral universe for which the ethical philosopher asks is fully possible only in a world where there is a divine thinker with all-enveloping demands. If such a thinker existed, his way of subordinating the demands to one another would be the finally valid casuistic scale; his claims would be the most appealing; his ideal universe would be the most inclusive realizable whole. . . . Meanwhile, exactly what the thought of the infinite thinker may be

446

is hidden from us even were we sure of his existence; so that our postulation of him after all serves only to let loose in us the strenuous mood.[4]

The connections James made between ethics and religion were deliberately vague because he saw religion as a vague response to a vague human need. Trying to spell out religious details means disregarding the sense of mystery that is part of the desire to see the universe as religious. (On the other hand, being so vague as to be merely platitudinous is also to be eschewed; the vagueness should be invested with hints of specificity.) James adapted traditional religious concepts such as salvation, regeneration, and evil to his own purposes, but, having extracted them from their theological contexts, he tended to leave their meanings obscure and haunting—like the religious impulse itself. Evil, for instance, is a recurrent topic in his moral and religious discussions. Unlike his father, who had considered it an inevitable part of God's plan, James viewed evil as our constant enemy. Its existence makes for a moral drama that is never wholly scrutable. In a letter to F. H. Bradley, he remarked that the question of how chance or nonchance action connects with responsibility and merit was uninteresting. "The *deep* questions which the moral life suggest are metaphysical: 1) Is evil *real?* 2) Is it *essential* to the universe? If these questions are to be answered with a yes I care not who is responsible, or may be called so; and I wish indeed that you would elaborate and analyze a little more the position you hold that with a determinate self given, 'freedom' and 'responsibility' begin and end with its reactions. Isn't that a terribly subjective view, narrow as that which makes ethics relate wholly to 'merit' and 'demerit'?"[5] Ethics becomes significant only if it is incorporated into metaphysics, metaphysics takes on depth only if it becomes religious, and religion runs deep because it represents a permanent mystery.

James's approach here was Socratic; he was convinced that about deep matters we are really ignorant. He repeatedly declared that human experience may not be the highest form of experience, that we may stand in relation to the cosmos as our cats and dogs stand to us. They share only a part of our lives and do not know the larger significance of the world in which they participate; likewise, we are probably conscious of only a small part of the cosmos.[6] (The Jamesian spirit survives in today's speculations that higher forms of life may exist somewhere in the universe.) James used this claim as a rebuttal to his two major adversaries on religion, the rationalistic defenders of the Absolute and the scientific proponents of materialism. Both held that reason, whether aided by observation and experiment or not, can ascertain the main features of reality; James countered that reality would always be a mystery to human understanding.

James was disturbed that religion was being increasingly disowned by his fellow intellectuals. He was embarrassed by being viewed as an eccentric product of Protestantism, and he said that he wrote as he did about religion because his audience was composed of intellectual skeptics.[7] He was not satisfied by the kind of piety exhibited by neo-Hegelians and transcendental idealists.

Whoever claims *absolute* teleological unity, saying that there is one purpose that every detail of the universe subserves, dogmatizes at his own risk. Theologians who dogmatize thus find it more and more impossible, as our acquaintance with the warring interests of the world's parts grows more concrete, to imagine what the one climacteric purpose may possibly be like. We see indeed that certain evils minister to ulterior goods. . . . But the scale of the evil actually in sight defies all human tolerance; and transcendental idealism, in the pages of a Bradley or a Royce, brings us no farther than the book of Job did—God's ways are not our ways, so let us put our hands upon our mouth. A God who can relish such superfluities of horror is no God for human beings to appeal to. . . . In other words, the 'Absolute' with his one purpose, is not the man-like God of common people.[8]

The concluding sentiment here, even more than the problem of evil, brings us closer to James's reason for resisting the idealists' attenuation of God into an absolute or an oversoul.

Hegel's system dominated the transition from eighteenth- to nineteenth-century philosophy and foreshadowed Nietzsche's verdict that Christianity was dead. The appeal of Hegel's idealism could be attributed, James believed, to its language, which retains the flavor of Christianity while seeking to replace it. This, he suspected, was what neo-Hegelians like Royce and Bradley were still doing. Like Hegel, they were creating God and other religious ideas from nothing but other ideas; they had intellectualized religion, concocting it through cerebral exercises rather than discovering it through actual experience. In effect, they were trying to achieve, through high-minded philosophical talk about the Absolute and cosmic unity, the sort of emotional response that had formerly been yielded only through Judeo-Christian concepts. In Western academia, transcendental idealism and neo-Hegelianism threatened to be the sole representatives of anything like traditional religion. James sought to prevent the revision of traditional, popular religion by academic philosophy, to halt the movement that would if unchecked produce the appearance of piety by artfully articulating abstract concepts such as Unity, Oneness, and the Absolute. The danger was that people would pray to and worship concepts of their own making, when the heart of popular or non-academic religion was a conception of God, evil, obligation, and salvation generated from experiential data rather than as an abstract construct.[9] If the roots of genuine religion are in experience, however, then their nature and source may be mysterious, and we therefore cannot assume, as rationalistic idealists do, that all of reality is accessible to reason. If we have reason to believe that we are not aware of all that the cosmos includes, then there may be religious aspects in its unseen order.

James's motive in opposing scientific materialism was different, for the materialists threatened not merely to disguise religion but rather to eliminate it entirely. In his reaction to scientific materialists, James connected ethics and religion, though it is sometimes difficult for his readers to formulate that connection. Consider, he suggested, the claims of mechanical evolutionism, one variety of materialism. According to this theory, the energies of the universe will decay and the world as we know it will end. "This utter final wreck and tragedy is of the essence of scientific materialism as at present understood. . . . Materialism means simply the denial that the moral order is eternal, and the cutting off of ultimate hopes; spiritualism means the affirmation of an eternal moral order and the letting loose of hope. Surely here is an issue genuine enough, for any one who feels it; and, as long as men are men, it will yield matter for a serious philosophical debate."[10] We should not underestimate, he added, the pragmatic significance of this issue for the religious person.

For James, then, the basic connection between ethics and religion rests in the idea of eternity. Just as a desire tends to develop into a demand, so do moral demands tend to develop into the religious demand that there be an eternal moral order. This was James's demand, one that he believed was also made by other representatives of strenuous morality. He did not demand personal immortality but rather a continuous moral order. If the universe is destined to end millions or billions of years in the future, he argued, then our present moral efforts are really in vain. Although he insisted on the importance of this point, he did not illuminate the extent of his feeling in this regard. Many of us may have shared his sentiment, feeling a sudden depression at the thought that the world we have come to cherish will inevitably cease to exist. But failing to locate any utility in that feeling, we tend to outlive it. Though we may wish that the physical universe peopled with moral agents could be eternal, we probably do not feel the kind of moral urgency that James did over the issue. We need not and ought not conclude that our present moral endeavors are in vain simply because nothing is eternal; if there were no morality in the present, there could be none in the eternal.

But we should interpret James less stringently. He seems to have meant that even if the laws of nature require the physical world's demise, we should hope that a moral or spiritual system will survive in which our endeavors continue to have an effect. It is human nature to hope that long after we are gone, our contributions will continue to be effective. But this hope usually assumes that things will endure much as they are now; the picture becomes immediately hazy when we try to imagine a disembodied moral or spiritual order eternally modifiable by the moral exertions of countless past individuals. Such haziness pleased James, who considered it a mark not of confusion but of depth; if challenged, he based his claim on what his religious feelings intimated but which concepts could never clarify. Something in his subjective experience strongly suggested the existence of an unseen order; the idea of it was not concocted from other ideas but was experientially stimulated. Once installed, the idea could be pondered and defended, its haziness made acceptable. We can make sense of the notion that our present ideals are continuous with higher ideals in that unseen order by considering the dog on the vivisectionist's table; it cannot grasp the fact that its suffering serves a higher purpose.[11] Our efforts and sufferings may likewise help to realize goals and ideals in an unseen order that is only hazily suggested by what we feel.

Morality was clearly based on levels for James: the lowest level is the automatic conformity to rule and convention, the highest is the performance of religious duties. Except for the degree of energy, strenuousness, and perseverance involved, the actual behavior of the ordinary moralist and the religious one may be distinguishable only experientially, by feeling, mood, and intention. The religious moralist believes that his actions produce consequences in an unseen system whose full significance can be understood only from that system's perspective. That system, if we could view it, would seem superior to the one we know, richer psychologically and morally, more inspiring and rewarding. Insofar as our moral deeds extend into its domain, we can judge them to be more significant than those confined to the here and now. Whether we realize it or not, James suggested, we may, when striving to improve the world and ourselves morally, assist a finite god or gods to vanquish evil with good in a dimension of existence that has no termination.

If the religious belief or demand is thus rendered meaningful, if it makes a difference whether it is true or false, and if the moral and psychological impetus behind the desire to believe makes sense, we must then ask whether believing is justified. It is one thing to assert the mere possibility of an unseen moral and godly world, but quite another to assert its actuality. James's correspondence and writings demonstrate that he was anxious to prove to himself—let alone to others—that his religious faith was rational. He had stressed the scope of human ignorance in arguing against both the idealistic absolutists and the scientific materialists. If the religious hypothesis cannot be confirmed by enough relevant evidence, can we assert its truth and still be rational? Or is such an assertion only wishful thinking, self-deception, a disregard for the conditions of truth that is downright immoral? His ponderings on such questions came together in "The Will to Believe," an essay that argued for the rationality of religious faith even in the absence of adequate evidence.

James was fully aware that there was no evidence for his own religious belief and was plainly nervous about statements such as those made by T. H. Huxley and W. K. Clifford. He quoted Huxley: "My only consolation lies in the reflection that, however bad our posterity may become, so far as they hold by the plain rule of not pretending to believe what they have no reason to believe, because it may be to their advantage so to pretend, they will not have reached the lowest depth of immorality." And Clifford: "Belief is desecrated when given to unproved and unquestioned statements for the solace and private pleasure of the believer. . . . It is wrong always, everywhere, and for every one, to believe anything upon insufficient evidence."[12]

James cited two types of cases to disprove these claims. The first includes what he called truths dependent on personal action. It is not wrong for me to believe the statement "I will get well" without evidence, James said, because my believing it may help to make it true. Faith, as he put it, can create its own verification, and such cases are a counterexample to Huxley's and Clifford's generalization. The second type includes the varieties of religious beliefs. In this discussion James knew that he was confronting his opponents more in the spirit of their generalization than he had done with the first type. Suppose we consider the statement "God exists"; suppose also that we view this hypothesis as *living* (interesting), *forced* (unavoidable in that we must choose for or against it), and *momentous* (important to the point of urgency).

Under these circumstances the statement describes a genuine option for us, and if we choose to believe it, even though the evidence and argumentation for and against it are entirely inconclusive, we are being rational. If there is no significant evidence or good argument against the statement, then the only thing to prevent our believing it is the absence of evidence for it. But if we choose to believe it because we benefit from doing so, this benefit outweighs the mere absence of evidence. It would be *ir*rational to rid oneself of a rewarding belief merely because evidence is wanting.

James's readers are often puzzled by his insistence that the option of believing that God exists is forced, that skepticism is not an alternative. The choice of "God does not exist" is from the religious believer's standpoint a bad one, but what of "God may or may not exist"? It is an unsatisfying belief for the religious person, but should this be outweighed by the fact that there is no evidence? In other words, is the religious person obliged to adopt the irritating belief of skepticism? Herein lies the issue not only between James and his opponents but also between James and himself. When there is no evidence for or against a statement, are we morally obliged to be noncommittal about that statement? Since James thought that one is morally bound to believe what the evidence points to, he felt pressured to conclude that the absence of evidence for or against "God exists" is itself evidence for "God may or may not exist" and that accordingly one is obliged to assert agnosticism.

In "The Will to Believe" James chose not to study the logical intricacies of this dilemma, settling the matter instead by rejecting the skeptic's assertion that it is always wrong to believe upon insufficient evidence. He objected to this argument because it is emotionally based, itself formed from passion rather than intellect. It is hardly clear that the absence of evidence for or against p is itself evidence that p may or may not be true, or that this is what the skeptic is obliged to believe; perhaps nothing more than suspending belief is required of him. Why must one who has noticed that evidence is absent exchange a satisfying belief for a skeptical, dissatisfying one? One may prefer the agnostic position, but by what right can one impose it upon another, or upon oneself?

If, as James believed, one's relation to truth is a moral matter, is there not a prima facie duty to withhold belief in the absence of evidence, just as one is bound to follow where the evidence points? If the evidence points nowhere then one ought to go nowhere. James consented to this reasoning in some cases but refused it when vital religious beliefs were at stake. He might have helped his cause by simply admitting what he himself must have felt, that there *is* a moral pressure to be agnostic when there is no evidence, that to be other than agnostic in such circumstances can make one feel and perhaps be morally inconsistent. Instead, he attacked religious skepticism as unacceptable and unwarranted, implying that one has a duty to avoid it.[13]

We cannot escape the issue by remaining sceptical and waiting for more light, because, although we do avoid error in that way *if religion be untrue,* we lose the good, *if it be true,* just as certainly as if we positively chose to disbelieve. It is as if a man should hesitate indefinitely to ask a certain woman to marry him because he was not perfectly sure that she would prove an angel after he brought her home. Would he not cut himself off from that particular angel-possibility as decisively as if he went and married someone else? Scepticism, then, is not avoidance of option; it is option of a certain particular kind of risk. *Better risk loss of truth than chance of error*—that is your faith-vetoer's exact position.[14]

This passage tends to confuse rather than to illuminate because it is vague about what is gained if one's beliefs turn out to be true, and because it reads like an endorsement of "Pascal's wager" without acknowledgment of the long line of criticism that this wager has received.[15] In addition, James's reasoning seems to confuse the beneficial implications if p (that God exists) is actually true with those derived merely from believing p to be true.[16] Consequently, it is obscure what is gained if p is true, over and above what is gained from believing it even if it is false. By drawing the analogy with the maritally hesitant man, James came close to treating religious hypotheses as if they were truths dependent on personal action or instances where faith creates its own verification; this emphasis misleadingly suggests that faith in a god will somehow help to create that god.

If we focus on James's notion of risk in his rejection of skepticism, we may succeed in identifying his real intent. Although he clearly meant to include the risk that lies in disdaining religious propositions that turn out to be true, he never defined the nature of that risk; what we would lose by not believing a true proposition is obscure. What is not obscure, however, is the risk James thought we run here and now if we desert belief for skepticism. "The Will to Believe" asserts that if religion is true then "the best things are the more eternal things," but it also implies that "we are better off even now" if we believe in those eternal things that we are "supposed to gain, even now, by our belief, and to lose by our non-belief, a certain vital good."[17] The present risk was supremely important in James's resistance to skepticism, and that risk could be specifically described. James had a multifaceted need to believe, a need so strong that his belief made the difference between finding life worthwhile and not. In responding to a questionnaire in 1904, he answered "Emphatically, no" to the question of whether he believed in God because of some argument; when asked whether he believed because he had experienced God's presence, he replied, "No, but rather because I need it so that it 'must' be true."[18] The nature of James's need to believe, as well as of the risk involved if he were to lose his religious faith, is indicated by this: "By being faithful in my poor measure to this [religious] over-belief, I seem to myself to keep more sane and true" (*VRE*, 519). We know from James's writings that he attributed his regenerative experiences—the sudden, surprising recoveries of energy and cheerfulness—to his religious beliefs. He believed that the new energy was supplied by a wider consciousness with which his was conterminous. To flirt with skepticism would be to risk losing this experience.

It is almost certain that James was tempted by the moral arguments for religious skepticism, that an inner voice suggested to him that one is obliged to withhold belief when there is no evidence. But pulling from the other side was an intense need to believe, and to deny that need by being skeptical was to run an enormous psychological risk. James described the risk as a moral one as well, intimating that he felt a duty to believe because one has a moral obligation to preserve one's own inner integrity. To resolve this seemingly insoluble moral conflict, James responded as he had in 1870 in following Renouvier, by making a decision that was misleadingly conveyed as a stubborn willing of a belief into existence. The so-called will-to-believe was not the creation of a belief or the decision to believe; it was rather the deliberate choice to endorse a religious belief already in place. The will-to-believe was a judgment that the moral obligation to preserve one's own integrity outweighed the moral obligation to be skeptical and withhold belief in the absence of supportive evidence. It was called a will rather than a wish not because James's belief needed something stronger than a wish in order to survive, but because a mere wish could not accomplish what was needed—the firm decision that his moral debt to himself was heavier than the obligation to espouse skepticism.[19] If we have the right to make such a decision—and that we do was the main point of "The Will to Believe"—then believing a religious hypothesis without evidence can be legitimate and rational. James later responded to his critics that he should have titled the essay "The Right to Believe."[20]

A risk is involved even in belief. We may later conclude that we have erred in assessing the moral obligation to our own integrity as being more important than that to skepticism, just as one might err in believing a hypothesis that turns out to be false. It is up to each person to decide which risk to run; in asserting the right to make that decision independently, James seems to have been appealing to a spirit of tolerance on the part of his critics. Tolerance was an important concern, especially in an area as sensitive as religion, but more than tolerance was at issue. A more important point, and one around which all James's philosophizing revolved, was the claim that we have the right to decide between competing hypotheses in the absence of evidence when there is a strong subjective inclination to one theory rather than another. If this right is valid, then religious faith can no longer be called irrational or immoral. *"Our passional nature not only lawfully may, but must, decide an option between propositions, whenever it is a genuine option that cannot by its nature be decided on intellectual grounds; for to say, under such circumstances, 'Do not decide, but leave the question open,' is itself a passional decision."*[21] The point is not that we should literally will to believe something, which James agreed is a silly notion. He meant only that many of our beliefs originate nonrationally from what he called our willing nature, which includes not only deliberate volitions but also fear, hope, prejudice, passion, and imitation.[22] If a belief originated in this way remains vital to our passional or willing nature, and if there is no evidence either for or against it, then the choice between the two risks is up to us. James wrote to Dickinson Miller, "When an hypothesis *is* once a live one, one *risks* something in one's practical [including moral] relations towards truth and error, *whichever* of the three positions (affirmation, doubt, or negation) one may take up towards it. *The individual himself is the only rightful chooser of his risk.* Hence respectful toleration, as the only law that logic can lay down."[23] Insofar as the risk is felt as a moral conflict, James seems to have meant that the inner voice which speaks with the greatest need and intensity has the right to decide which risk to take.

James's notion of risk gets at the heart of the issue, as a believer understands it, especially if its moral dimension is not forgotten. There comes a point when the choice of a risk is called for, when our subjective preferences or willing nature must determine our decisions. It borders on the irrational, James felt, to require that such preferences be ignored or deliberately rejected. Yet readers of "The Will to Believe" may be subject to a nagging doubt about James's view. That dissatisfaction may issue from the suspicion that James has fabricated an artificial situation in which the will or right to believe applies. Perhaps fewer of us than he appreciated assume that we hold or reject religious beliefs in a complete vacuum of evidence.

Both believers and atheists usually believe that their convictions are supported by something taken as evidence. What the devout person counts as evidence (alleged historical episodes, sacred writings, and authoritative institutions) is supposedly independent of how he may feel or of his subjective preferences. He thinks that certain events are part of a religious scheme, and since that feeling provokes his belief, there is no need to invoke a will-to-believe. The atheist, on the other hand, concludes that whatever is taken as religious evidence can be explained otherwise; he therefore judges that exercising the will-to-believe is either a deliberate or an unwitting misinterpretation of where the evidence actually points. James's scenario, in which the right-to-believe applies, can thus appear contrived; it assumes a total absence of objective evidence, with only internal feelings to go by.

Yet this scenario was where James found himself, alone with his own feelings and no objective evidence—an ideal situation for faith. If we reduce knowledge, inflate ignorance, and summon feelings to center stage, everything is set for faith's appearance. James did make room for a "science of religions," saying that the study of God could proceed from the study of his creation; he also averred that future discoveries about the subconscious might confirm some religious hypotheses.[24] Objective evidence was not absolutely excluded in the Jamesian philosophy of religion, but whatever evidence might be offered, James could not have abandoned his position in "The Will to Believe": "But practically one's conviction that the evidence one goes by is of the real objective brand, is only one more subjective opinion added to the lot."[25] He never believed that objective religious evidence might some day obviate the right-to-believe. His faith seemed to leap such a lack of evidence that some friends wondered whether that faith actually existed. Santayana wrote: "All faiths were what they were experienced as being, in their capacity of faiths; these faiths, not their objects, were the hard facts we must respect. We cannot pass, except under the illusion of the moment, to anything firmer or on a deeper level. There was accordingly no sense of security, no joy, in James's apology for personal religion. He did not really believe; he merely believed in the right of believing that you might be right if you believed."[26]

James asserted in his correspondence that his faith was robust enough, although more often he confessed his need to believe; he seems to have had no interest in separating faith from the need to believe, especially since the latter was based on the conviction that religion was in some way true, even if it was not part of James's faith to be confident about interpretive details. While he offered no clearcut religious interpretations of it, he was frank about the need to believe, and it would not be fair to say that he himself did not really believe. Noting that he had wholly outgrown the Christianity of his infancy, he wrote that his faith lay in his "mystical *germ*. It is a very common germ. It creates the rank and file of believers. As it withstands in my case, so it will withstand in most cases, all purely atheistic criticism."[27] His need to believe was tantamount to having faith. "I mean that the fear was so invasive and powerful that if I had not clung to scripture-texts like 'The eternal God is my refuge,' etc., 'Come unto me, all ye that labor and are heavy-laden,' etc., 'I am the resurrection and the life,' etc., I think I should have grown really insane."[28]

The nature and intensity of this need was essential to James's concept of the risk involved in turning to skepticism and thus to his defense of the right-to-believe. Underlying his argument that faith is rational was the existence and character of that need. The argument moves elusively from the premise that defines the need-to-believe to the conclusion that faith is rational, but it is never clear that need necessarily makes for rationality. Although James did not move from need to rationality without any connection, his texts sometimes make readers wonder whether he supposed that there is some rationality built into need itself. If that were the case, not only would the decision to indulge the need be rational, but the need-to-believe would be *inherently* rational. That James did think this way is borne out by the notion that the subjective method in philosophy is justifiable because there is a presumed harmony between our subjective interests and the objective world. Our feelings and emotions, including those of remorse and regret, exist for a purpose; although they do not correspond exactly with the extramental world, they are clues to its nature. "They [scientists, artists, and James himself] all postulate in the interests of their volitional nature a harmony between the latter and the nature of things," and it is more than probable "that to the end of our time our power of moral and volitional response to the nature of things will be the deepest organ of communication therewith we shall ever possess."[29] James's trust that subjectivity is obliquely cognitive, a blurry apprehension of objective realities, was the constant underpinning of his mysticism and his pragmatic equation of truth with what is satisfactory.

This view can make the need-to-believe seem warranted by its very character, because it is taken as a natural, symptomatic response to the nature of things. The decision to indulge this need rather than to adopt skepticism is thus seen as rational. But there is a danger that in calling the need-to-believe rational we will forfeit the option of criticizing it. Even if we grant the rationality of the Jamesian right to fulfill the need, we may have doubts about the need itself. We may consider a strong need-to-believe pathological. (James himself worried about this possibility but dismissed it by trusting in a connection between subjectivity and reality.) It may be rational for a person to decide to indulge a pathological need rather than to resist it, but that decision does not reduce the pathological character of the need.

Biographers have conjectured about the source of James's need. It may have resulted from the strict Presbyterianism of his powerful and wealthy grandfather, the elder William James, or from his father's rebellious, freethinking bouts with Calvinism; other influences may have been the piety of his mother, his early reading of Jonathan Edwards, and his study of the Great Awakening in American history. James may have had a sense of mission to revive religion in an increasingly secular era, to make it popular, contagious, and concrete, to safeguard it against the criticisms of academic philosophy, and to connect it with the mind-healers and the New Thought movement. Josiah Royce showed how such a case can be made:

> Our nation since the civil war has largely lost touch with the older forms of its own religious life. It has been seeking for new embodiments of the religious consciousness, for creeds that shall not be in conflict with the modern man's view of life. It was James's office, as psychologist and philosopher, to give a novel expression to this our own national variety of the spirit of religious unrest. . . . Some men preach new ways of salvation. James simply portrayed [in *The Varieties of Religious Experience*] the meaning that the old ways of salvation . . . still do possess, in the inner and personal experiences of those individuals whom he called the religious genuises. . . .
>
> But James's own robust faith was that the very caprices of the spirit are the opportunity for the building up of the highest forms of the spiritual life; that the unconventional and the individual in religious experience are the means whereby the truth of a superhuman world may become more manifest. And this robust faith . . . is as American in type as it has already proved effective in the expression which James gave to it. It is the spirit of the frontiersman, of the gold seeker, or the home-builder, transferred to the metaphysical and to the religious realm. . . . Above all, let not your abstract conceptions . . . pretend to set any limits to the richness of spiritual grace . . . that, in case you are duly favored, your personal experience may reveal to you. . . .
>
> [*The Varieties of Religious Experience*] is full of the spirit that, in our country, has long been effective in the formation of new religious sects; and this volume expresses . . . the recent efforts of this spirit to come to an understanding with modern naturalism, and with the new psychology.[30]

Whether or not James wanted to lead his own religious revival, he definitely believed that to keep his sanity he required religious sustenance. James urged that the need-to-believe is rational, but the critic may just as easily consider it irrational. But this is to misidentify the dispute about rationality, since needs in themselves are neither rational nor irrational. Thirst, hunger, and libido do not resemble opinions and judgments; we may or may not choose to indulge such needs, but to debate their rationality is pointless. A critic may grant James's plea for religious tolerance and thus respect his right-to-believe without granting any rationality to the need-to-believe. The critic may also feel that such a need is pathological or unfortunate. The Jamesian philosophy of religion sometimes appears to accept the separation of paths between believers and nonbelievers, and at other times insists upon having the last word. James seems to have held that the need-to-believe is mystically inherent in the world and therefore is inherently rational. Just when the critic thinks that the impasse has been mutually recognized and that further dialogue is useless, he must challenge the Jamesian again to protest the parting shot. His sympathy may have been elicited for the genuine need-to-believe, but having granted that its causes and effects warrant investigating, he cannot in good conscience agree that it is a rational need.

Such a critic may not realize that the Jamesian philosophy links certain psychological phenomena with rationality by construing rationality itself as a psychological phenomenon. The need-to-believe is not a physiological one, and James argued that no established discipline can give a straightforward explanation of it. We must first develop a psychology and a philosophy of belief, knowledge, truth, meaning, reality, and rationality. Throughout his career James sought to analyze these concepts such that rationality would ultimately be a satisfaction of our deepest need-to-believe. No reader of *Pragmatism* can fail to notice James's exuberance in making room for faith, but it is easy to overlook the assertion that faith is rational.

Philosophers reputed to be irrationalists usually reveal considerable rationality upon inspection, and James was no exception. He subscribed neither to Tertullian's assertion that certainty arises from impossibility nor to Kierkegaard's notion of faith as a floating upon seventy thousand fathoms of water, but he did believe that some sensible questions resist rational solutions, that actions must sometimes be undertaken without any guarantee of their rationality, and that justifiable motives for action are not always the results of reasoning. Such irrationalism seems more harmless than one might have feared.

In 1879 James expressed his idea of rationality, which had been jelling for years. The philosopher, he wrote, will recognize

> rationality as he recognizes everything else, by certain subjective marks with which it affects him. When he gets the marks he may know that he has got the rationality. What then are the marks? A strong feeling of ease, peace, rest, is one of them. The transition from a state of puzzle and perplexity to rational comprehension is full of lively relief and pleasure. . . . This feeling of the sufficiency of the present moment . . . this absence of all need to explain it, account for it or justify it—is what I call the Sentiment of Rationality. As soon, in short, as we are enabled from any cause whatever to think of a thing with perfect fluency, that thing seems to us rational.[31]

James was not defining rationality psychologically; he meant only to note the psychological marks of the rational and to describe the experience of finding something to be rational. What is puzzling is his assertion that we always recognize rationality by certain subjective symptoms; this argument conflicts with the requirement that rationality must be independently recognizable, such that the correlation between it and its psychological earmarks occurs subsequently. James seems to have been uncertain as to whether psychological features merely correlate with the fact of thinking rationally or whether they are actually the decisive criterion of thinking rationally. In either case, his treatment of rationality veers toward the psychological.

James employed this subjectivistic concept of rationality to legitimize the religious impulse. Since only those ideas which produce specific psychological effects are considered rational, it follows that religious ideas are rational if they can produce emotional and intellectual ease or satisfaction. (James did not seriously consider the obvious counterexample of a person who is disturbed by being shown that a belief he had accepted as unreasonable is actually reasonable. If the feeling of disturbance dominates the discovery that the belief is actually rational, it is not valid to argue that the disturbance is caused by something other than the discovery of rationality.) In the early 1880s, James made a case for the rationality of religious belief in such essays as "Rationality, Activity, and Faith" and "Reflex Action and Theism," essays stating what would later appear in *Principles*, "The Will to Believe," and other writings.

James developed the idea that a rational belief not only rests the mind but promises it permanent peace; believing in God, perfection, love, or reason is attractive because it produces such peace with a completeness and finality that defy future contradiction. As long as we connect our theorizing to practical interests, we will not admit as rational any belief that fails to serve that function—a repetition of the pragmatic thesis that adequate theories must be satisfactory in practice, which includes having the psychological marks of rationality. James worried about the tendency of academics to become lost in a maze of abstractions, to lose touch with reality, and to succumb temporarily to intellectualistic definitions of rationality. Without idolizing common sense, he was anxious to enlist the support of the practical-minded, who believe in the practical payoff of holding a rational belief. A pragmatic definition of rationality was especially important in the case of religion. James was democratic in his religious thinking, largely because he trusted the judgment of practical people more than he did that of his fellow professors. For a philosophy to be as rational as possible, to produce the maximum practical payoff, it must have the subjective marks of rationality or "define the future *congruously with our spontaneous powers*," for "the inmost nature of the reality is congenial to *powers* which you possess."[32]

James asserted the connection between his definition of rationality and his philosophy of religion in "Reflex Action and Theism," where he argued that an analysis of the physiology of reflex action which shows that thinking is the mediator between sensation and action is not inconsistent with religion, but can actually support it. Materialistic physiologists fail to apprehend, he claimed, that the so-called reflex theory of mind commits them to treating the mind as a teleological mechanism. The argument was a tour de force, as James later acknowledged; it was overly clever in the way it purported to find God in physiology, and as a result he did not consider it one of his favorite essays.[33] Nevertheless, he advanced basic themes there, notably the contention that thought ultimately functions in the service of action or reaction upon the outer world. Rational thought will produce a satisfying response to the environment, a response congruous with the environment's reality. God is the most rational object for our minds to entertain because He most adequately serves as the objective reality to which our thoughts can react with satisfaction. As usual, James's own view is presented as the middle ground between polar opposites; here his theism mediates between materialism and agnosticism. "Now, theism stands ready with the most practically rational solution it is possible to conceive. Not an energy of our active nature to which it does not authoritatively appeal, not an emotion of which it does not normally and naturally release the springs. At a single stroke, it changes the dead blank *it* of the world into a living *thou,* with whom the whole man may have dealings."[34]

Any conception less than God is irrational, measured by the strictest standard of rationality, because it is less richly satisfying; the same is true of any conception that pretends to transcend theism. "The attempts to fly beyond theism . . . are attempts to get over this ultimate duality of God and his believer, and to transform it into some sort or other of identity."[35] In this essay James stressed that God as a personality most effectively fits our emotional needs and is thus the most rational idea; he used this argument against the philosophical Absolute and all forms of pantheism, which are attempts to fly beyond theism. (He did not see how we could literally share an overlapping identity with God, although his metaphysics of pure experience would later permit a theism that has been described as both pluralistic and pantheistic.)[36] Religion is argued to be rational because there is an alleged congruity or harmony between our subjective needs and an objective reality. *"The perfect [most rational] object of belief would be a God or 'Soul of the World,' represented both optimistically and moralistically (if such a combination could be), and withal so definitely conceived as to show us why our phenomenal experiences should be sent to us by Him in just the very way in which they come"* (*Principles,* 2:317). If religion is so thoroughly rational, is there any need for faith? If so, what kind of faith?

We associate faith and irrationalism in James because of statements like this: "In the end it is our faith and not our logic that decides [religious and metaphysical] questions, and I deny the right of any pretended logic to veto my own faith."[37] There comes a point in confronting an intellectually unresolvable issue when one must decide one way or the other, and the decision can be called an act of faith. In this sense *faith* need have no religious connotations, any more than it does when we say that scientists often proceed on faith, or that we sometimes act on faith in attempting something difficult. Faith may in such a case create its own verification; it is simply a belief without adequate evidence, and we cannot maneuver through our daily lives without some show of faith. The exercise of faith in this sense is rational, even necessary on occasion if one is to be rational.

James often did his utmost to make religious faith as rational as possible, although in many passages he seems to have been determined to be an irrationalist. When he contrasted reason and faith, he knew that there was a danger of slipping into purely verbal games; much of what he suggested reflects his ongoing debates with absolute idealists and scientific materialists. When asked to compare reason and faith, he tried to sharpen the distinction thus: "Faith's form of argument is something like this: Considering a view of the world: 'It is *fit* to be true,' she feels; 'it would be well if it *were* true; it *might* be true; it *ought* to be true,' she says; 'it *must* be true,' she continues; 'it *shall* be true,' she concludes, '*for* me; that is, I will treat it as if it *were* true so far as my advocacy and actions are concerned."[38] James acknowledged that this argument is not an intellectual chain of inferences like the sorites in logic textbooks; he suggested that it be called the "faith-ladder" or "the sort of slope on which we all live." To call it an argument is misleading; it is more like a pep talk in preparation for a gamble. James realized that even if it were construed as an argument, it could also be called an exercise of reason, thus blurring the alleged distinction between reason and faith.

Without doubt, James endorsed irrationalism in his discussion of the compounding of consciousness and the nature of experience in *A Pluralistic Universe* (see chapter 11). To the extent that his philosophy of religion depends upon the metaphysics developed there, it is tinged with the irrationalism involved in abandoning the logic of identity. But faith itself never seems to be irrational in James's view. In unpublished notes titled "Faith" he wrote: "One *can't* convert a genuine disbeliever in religion any more than one can convert a protestant to Catholicism, etc. Take Santayana!"[39] By resisting all argument, faith, whether the believer's or the atheist's, is insensitive to reason and thus irrational. For James, however, dogmatic faith was as repugnant as dogmatic rationalism; he always advocated a faith sensitive to reason, experimental in nature, and therefore susceptible to revision. While faith is "one of the inalienable birth-rights of our mind . . . it must remain a practical, and not a dogmatic attitude. It must go with toleration of other faiths, with the search for the most probable, and with the full consciousness of responsibilities and risks" (*SPP*, 225).

James's public advocacy of faith was remarkable at a time when skepticism was spreading on college campuses; indeed, many of his friends needled him for his faith. After reading papers he had received from James, Henry Adams wrote back on 27 July 1882: "My wife is quite converted by [your writing about faith]. . . . Since she read it she has talked of giving five dollars to Russell Sturgis's church for napkins. As the impression fades, she says less of the napkins."[40] James enjoyed such humor and responded in kind, at the same time trying to make his case more persuasive. Faith was for him a way of life, and no one succeeded in disturbing it. It is essentially a rational response by a sensitive human being to something in reality that evokes it. In the unpublished notes on faith, James wrote that "a man's religion is the deepest and wisest thing in his life. I must frankly establish the breach between the life of articulate reason, and the push of the subconscious, the irrational instinctive part, which is more vital. . . . In religion the vital needs, the mystical overbeliefs . . . proceed from an ultrarational religion. They are *gifts*. It is a question of *life*, of living in these gifts or not living" (quoted in RBP, 2:328). The source of faith is an impulse which is nonrational in that it is produced by feeling rather than by intellectual argument, and religion is "wise" in doing justice to that impulse. "No philosophy will permanently be deemed rational by all men which does not . . . make a direct appeal to all those powers of our nature which we hold in highest esteem. Faith, being one of those powers, will always remain a factor not to be banished from philosophic constructions."[41]

James's philosophy of religion respected canons of rationality, echoing the reasonableness of its author. The fundamental premise upon which his philosophy of religion rested was that our subjective natures, feelings, emotions, and propensities exist as they do because something in reality harmonizes with them; insofar as they are yearnings and longings, reality will ultimately fulfill them. No philosopher has ever proposed a more outrageous premise for faith than this. Because we want the world to be a certain way, our desire actually makes it so. If the premise were true, it would lend rationality to faith, but is the premise itself defensible? Another Jamesian premise was that something in our feelings and experience tells us that an objective reality will fulfill our deepest yearnings. Can this premise be defended any more than the first? Certainly not by argument, since all its force is derived from the character of an experience. The faith that this premise is true is the mystic's faith, a faith in the deliverances of emotional experiences. If a faith of this sort is irrational, then James's philosophy of religion is without doubt irrational. But before making that judgment, we need to examine James's mysticism.

MYSTICISM AND REALITY

James focused on religious experience and mysticism in *The Varieties of Religious Experience,* undoubtedly his most popular book, which has been called the "most famous of all American treatises on religion."[42] Among those influenced by it were Bertrand Russell and Ludwig Wittgenstein. After a meeting with Wittgenstein in 1919, Russell wrote to a friend: "I had felt in [Wittgenstein's *Tractatus Logico-Philosophicus*] a flavour of mysticism, but was astonished when I found that he has become a complete mystic. He reads people like Kierkegaard and Angelus Silesius, and he seriously contemplates becoming a monk. It all started from William James's *Varieties of Religious Experience.*" Russell himself had written upon the publication of the book, "We have all been reading with great pleasure James on Religious Experience—everything good about the book except the conclusions."[43] Russell applauded its survey of religious experience, achieved largely through the testimony of mystics and religious leaders or *geniuses* (James's term), but balked at James's construction of the outlines of a religion from the materials of personal experience.

Santayana's verdict on *Varieties* was predictably harsh. He saw James as a religious outsider (a judgment with which James agreed in this case, where mystical experience rather than faith was the subject), but he objected mainly to the book's concentration upon "religious disease," upon accounts by the sick and morbid rather than by dignified, pious folk who enjoy a simple faith in their religious traditions. James was ever uncomfortable with conventional philosophizing, said Santayana, and paid his respects to the religions that had grown overnight in America: "communistic, hysterical, spiritistic, or medicinal—[which] were despised by select and superior people. You might inquire into them, as you might go slumming, but they remained suspect and distasteful."[44] Miller, a close friend of both men, recorded an exchange between James and Santayana about *Varieties:* "Seeing James one day after his 'Varieties of Religious Experience' had come out, Mr. Santayana crossed the street and said to him with a friendly smile, 'You have done the religious slumming for all time.' 'Really?' answered James genially; 'That is all slumming, is it?' 'Yes,' was the answer, 'all.' In repeating this James chuckled to himself: 'Santayana's white marble mind.'"[45]

Charles Peirce praised the book: "His *Varieties of Religious Experience* I think the best of books. His penetration into the hearts of people was most wonderful; and he was not one of those who chiefly sees the evil things in hearts."[46] As Peirce recognized in the subtitle "A Study In Human Nature," something good and appealing seemed to characterize human nature in James's treatment of religious experience. His "religious slumming" had revived an old message, that refreshing and profound visions into the purpose of living can emerge from bouts of suffering and morbidity, or so the testimony of the religious individuals cited in *Varieties* seemed to prove. Many readers have felt the powerful effect produced by confession upon confession, such that even the most staunch atheist may begin to wonder whether a religious dimension might exist whose threshold he has never crossed.

Varieties comprises the twenty Gifford Lectures delivered at the University of Edinburgh in 1901–02. James originally planned for the first ten lectures to provide data (accounts about the character of religious experience) and for the second ten to offer philosophical interpretation. A notebook titled "Memoranda for Gifford Lectures" gave the following titles for the two projected volumes: *The Varieties of Religious Experience* and *The Tasks of Religious Philosophy*. In the book's preface, James wrote that he had considered calling the first part "Man's Religious Appetites" and the second "Their Satisfaction Through Philosophy"; he believed that there is within the religious need a propensity to seek satisfaction through philosophical interpretation of itself. While in the early stages of writing the lectures, James wrote to a friend that his first aim was to defend "against all the prejudices of my 'class,'" for the role of experience, unlike that of philosophy, is the "real backbone of the world's religious life"; his second aim was to make his reader understand that religion, despite its many absurdities, is still "mankind's most important function." Conceding that it would be almost impossible to fulfill both aims, he described his attempt as *"my* religious act."[47] As it turned out, psychological discussion monopolized the lectures, and James was forced to squeeze his philosophical conclusions into a single lecture.

Perry claimed that James wrote the lectures that became *Varieties* either out of filial piety or to fulfill a pledge made to his wife twenty years earlier.[48] Given that James mentioned his father nowhere in *Varieties,* Perry admitted that a direct link was unlikely but credited the father's influence in James's use of personal experiences as the chief source of his religious beliefs. James described the impetus for *Varieties* in the first sentence: "This book would never have been written had I not been honored with an appointment as Gifford Lecturer on Natural Religion at the University of Edinburgh." This honor, rather than filial piety, seems to have been the reason for taking on a difficult assignment which was made even more taxing because of the cardiac problems he suffered during its preparation. What he meant in calling the writing of *Varieties* his religious act is a matter for conjecture. It was certainly a project undertaken on behalf of religion, but I think he had a more specific mission: to defend experience against the prejudices of his fellow academics.

In 1868, at age twenty-six, James had written a long, pensive letter to Oliver Wendell Holmes, Jr., which included these thoughts:

> I am tending strongly to an empiristic view of life. . . . Already I see an on-tological cloud of absolute idealism waiting for me far off on the horizon, but I have no passion for the fray. . . . One thing makes me uneasy. If the end of all is to be that we must take our sensations as simply given or as preserved by natural selection for us, and interpret this rich and delicate overgrowth of ideas, moral, artistic, religious and social, as a mere mask, a tissue spun in happy hours by creative individuals and adopted by other men in the interests of their sensa-tions,—how long is it going to be well for us not to "let on" all we know to the public? How long are we to indulge the "people" in their theological and other vagaries so long as such vagaries seem to us more beneficial on the whole than otherwise? . . . I know that no mind can trace the far ramifications of an idea in the mind of the public; and that any idea is at a disadvantage which cannot enlist in its favor the thirst for conquest, the love of absoluteness, that have helped to found religions; and which cannot open a *definite* channel for human sympathies and affections to flow in. It seems exceedingly improbable that any new *religious* genius [the term used in *Varieties* thirty-four years later] should arise in these days to open a fresh highway for the masses who have outgrown the old beliefs. How ought not we . . . to begin to smite the old, hip and thigh, and get, if possible, a little enthusiasm associated with our doctrines? If God is dead or at least irrelevant, ditto everything pertaining to the "Beyond." If happiness is our Good, ought we not to try to foment a passionate and bold will to attain that happiness among the multitudes? . . . The sentiment of phi-lanthropy is now so firmly established and apparently its permanence so guar-anteed by its beneficent nature, that it would be bold to say it could not take its place as an ultimate motive for human action. I feel no *confidence* . . . that society is as yet ripe for it as a popular philosophy and religion combined. . . . And certainly there is something disheartening in the position of an esoteric philosopher.[49]

James wrote this letter a year before finishing medical school, four years before he was appointed an anatomy instructor at Harvard, ten years before undertaking *Principles,* and eleven years before teaching his first philosophy course. It shows his early conviction that those who keep the philosophical flame have an obligation to the people. Moral and religious ideas ought to be disseminated, and, as James would explicitly urge years later, people's reactions to them over time are tests of their validity. Creators of such ideas are potential leaders who are obliged to demonstrate the worth of their creations to the public and "to foment a passionate and bold will" among the multitudes to adopt them; whatever specific character the ideas may take, they should have the lively appeal of "a popular religion and philosophy combined." Whether it be Utilitarianism or Unitarianism, James argued in 1868, the philosopher's role includes not only crystallizing the doctrine but also presenting it in the most persuasive light to the populace. Despite the regret that some felt when James deserted the seminar for popular philosophizing (James himself sometimes shared their regret), the evidence indicates that from the beginning he was convinced that the philosopher ought to take his ideas to market, that the public needs those ideas as values by which to live, and that the ideas themselves are tested and refined by public response. James admired the inventor of ideas, but he trusted the public's appraisal of their practicality.

What he called his religious act in writing *Varieties* was the attempt to fashion a fresh blend of religion and philosophy that would have popular and not merely academic appeal. He went "slumming" in order to get firsthand accounts of religious experience from mystics, cranks, eccentrics, and inspired but lowly people, partly to dramatize by their excesses the power of religious experience, but partly also to insure that he would, by using concrete examples and allowing the faithful to testify on their own behalf, remain close in spirit and language to the multitudes he hoped to inspire. In 1868 he had already adopted the posture that would become his philosophical trademark—the middle term in a Hegelian triad, in this instance between academia and the populace; in *Varieties* he took religious experience to academics and philosophical interpretations of that experience to the people. His philosophy of religion was not delivered directly to the public from pulpits or soapboxes, for his actual audience was obviously academic, but he hoped that the influence of *Varieties* would spread far beyond college campuses. His hope was in some measure realized, judging from the popular success of the book and from its reputation as a source of inspiration.

We must not underestimate James's suspicion that the academic life, with its dedication to esoteric ideas, too often involves a withdrawal from body, feeling, and sensation; its intellectual preoccupation is so persistent that its interruptions may be experienced as a return to reality; further, a great deal of intellectual labor fails to yield practical results. Compared to the believers quoted in *Varieties*, the academic is more likely to be out of touch with his feelings and what they suggest. James was not only presenting the testimony of saints and mystics as data for philosophical interpretation; he was also suggesting to his agnostically inclined colleagues that there was an unfamiliar world of feeling and vivid experience in which they should participate. The act of writing *Varieties* was religious in its attempt to convert the skeptics in academe by convincing them to surrender experimentally to experiences that suggested the existence of a religious order. The deep, irrational roots of belief, he remarked, "are familiar to evangelical Christianity and to what is nowadays becoming known as 'mind-cure' religion or 'new thought.' " He once urged "some of the younger members of this learned audience to take this hint to heart," because "the current of thought in academic circles runs against me, and I feel like a man who must set his back against an open door quickly if he does not wish to see it closed and locked."[50] Writing *Varieties* was a religious act less because it was a venture into the philosophy of religion than because it was a genuine effort to spark a resurgence of popular religiousness.

Since *Varieties* includes countless first-hand reports of religious experiences that are rhapsodic in the extreme and thus are easily dismissed by skeptics as pathological, James had to face the argument that such experiences can be explained scientifically and are not a valid basis for religious belief. One such report is a sufficient example: "Looking up, I thought I saw that same light . . . though it appeared different; and as soon as I saw it, the design was opened to me, according to his promise, and I was obliged to cry out: Enough, enough, O blessed God! The work of conversion, the change, and the manifestations of it are no more disputable than the light which I see, or anything that ever I saw" (*VRE,* 215). It seems likely that such an extreme account can be explained as a manifestation of psychological or physiological imbalance. James gave a threefold reply to this objection, since he recognized that it was "quite common nowadays among certain writers, of criticizing the religious emotions by showing a connection between them and the sexual life. Conversion is a crisis of puberty and adolescence. The macerations of saints, and the devotion of missionaries, are only instances of the parental instinct of self-sacrifice gone astray. For the hysterical nun, starving for natural life, Christ is but an imaginary substitute for a more earthly object of affection. And the like" (*VRE,* 11–12). James replied, first, that even pathological genius cannot be explained away by science; second, that the value of religious reports can be tested pragmatically; and third, that the mystical basis of such reports must be respected.

Not all religious reports border on the pathological, and even when they do, James observed, that feature in itself does not disqualify them; his studies of genuis in nonreligious areas suggested that extreme neurosis can be a condition of genius. But this only proves the need for medical materialists to proceed cautiously before labeling a person's beliefs false or irrational simply because of his personality. A positive appraisal of such beliefs must await pragmatic testing, regardless of the self-certification or immediate luminousness that mystics find in their experiences. Assuming that the believer's reports are coherent, their value can be determined by the kind of moral or psychological succor they provide. Repeatedly calling his approach to religion empiricistic and pragmatic, and emphasizing its openness to experimental work in abnormal psychology and psychical research, James agreed with Jonathan Edwards, in assessing religious beliefs, that "by their fruits ye shall know them," that it is not their origin but their consequences which indicate their worth.[51] James's was supposedly a pragmatic religion.

But the significance of such a characterization seems questionable. Demanding that religious beliefs relate to behavior and character may have been distinctive when idealistic absolutism held sway; certainly one will favor religious experiences that inspire or console over those which bear no fruit whatever. But the proposal that "you must all be ready now to judge the religious life by its results exclusively, and I shall assume that the bugaboo of morbid origin will scandalize your piety no more" was not one that James could sustain, something he in effect acknowledged in *The Meaning of Truth.*[52] Throughout the survey of religious experience in *Varieties,* one is interested in origins as well as consequences. The moral and psychological consequences are important in themselves, but since they are considered evidence of a divine or supernatural agent, they are important also for speculations about origins. James did not simply defer the question of origins until the final chapter, where he subjected religious experience to philosophical interpretation. By that point he wanted to convey his own "over-belief" and thus to invalidate the claim that science can explain religious phenomena. His declaration at the beginning of *Varieties* that his approach was pragmatic, his focus on consequences, succeeded only in putting aside the question of how science might outdo philosophy in clarifying the sources of religious feelings. His own mystical interpretation was hardly pragmatic, for it ran not from phenomenon to consequences but from phenomenon to inferred origins, such that there was no way for such an interpretation to be tested. His philosophy of religion is indeed intriguing, but it is certainly not pragmatic.

Origins rather than consequences are especially important in theorizing about emotion in religious experience, although James was not as explicit on this topic as we might expect. Emotion is emphasized throughout *Varieties,* and the premise behind the book's organization and content is that "feeling is the deeper source of religion, and that philosophic and theological formulas are secondary products, like translations of texts into another tongue" (*VRE,* 422). The vast number of individuals' reports of religious experiences in the book focus on joy, hope, despair, peace, conflict, tenderness, sacrifice, union, and ecstasy. Differences in character result from differences in susceptibility to emotional arousal, James thought; some persons seem emotionally indifferent to religion, but that characteristic might be only a temporary condition, changeable through some releasing experience. Given the intensity of James's own need to believe, as well as his assumption that the majority of people shared that need, it was difficult for him not to suppose that emotional indifference is a deficiency in sensibility. He did not, however, believe in a single, elementary religious emotion common to all religious experiences. To the contrary, he held that religious awe, fear, joy, and love are the usual emotions associated with these words; the term *religious* means only that they are connected with religious beliefs or objects. An emotion of love is religious if it is directed toward a religious object; there is no sui generis religious emotion in addition to the familiar emotions. This view is consistent, he remarked, with the fact that "as concrete states of mind, made up of a feeling *plus* a specific sort of object, religious emotions of course are psychic entities distinguishable from other concrete emotions" (*VRE,* 29). The entire religious emotional experience, consisting of emotion, attendant feelings, and specific beliefs, can be distinguished from nonreligious experiences, but the emotional component need not be uniquely religious. The complexity of the experience is illustrated by what Saint Teresa of Avila once reported: "Our lord made me comprehend in what way it is that one God can be in three persons. He made me see it so clearly that I remained as extremely surprised as I was comforted . . . and now, when I think of the holy Trinity, or hear it spoken of, I understand how the three adorable Persons form only one God and I experience an unspeakable happiness."[53]

Saint Teresa located the origin of emotion in God, and James liked to think that she was right in doing so. But he showed no interest in exploring the relation of such religious emotions to the James-Lange theory of emotion and its implications. He commented that Saint Teresa's ecstatic states of consciousness obviously differed from ordinary ones, in part by the intensity of her organic sensibilities which verged on bodily pain and were almost too extreme to endure. Without commenting on it, James noted that she had discriminated between pain in which the body has a part and pain that is purely spiritual; he pointed out that some doctors had debated whether in the condition known as *raptus* or ravishment, during which breathing and circulation are suppressed, the soul is temporarily separated from the body. A few pages later he praised this sort of consciousness as antinaturalistic, but he never explained how it connects with the naturalistic thrust of the James-Lange theory and its exclusion of nonbodily emotions. According to the James-Lange concept, the origin of emotions is always the afferent system within one's own body—a theory that is decidedly not antinaturalistic.

It is surprising, in view of the conspicuous role of emotion in *Varieties,* that he did not mention the James-Lange theory. In *Principles* he had expressly declared that the theory is not materialistic or naturalistic. "Let not this view be called materialistic. It is neither more nor less materialistic than any other view which says that our emotions are conditioned by nervous processes. . . . If [emotions] are deep, pure, worthy, spiritual facts on any conceivable theory of their physiological source, they remain no less deep, pure, spiritual, and worthy of regard on this present sensational theory."[54] As far as James's introspection could determine, every emotion is physiologically saturated. If any emotion is to be regarded as spiritual and as evidence for an antinaturalistic hypothesis, it must be so regarded on the basis not of introspection but rather of some philosophical interpretation of the origin of the emotional experience. If there is a more remote and spiritual cause of the changes in one's body—which according to the James-Lange theory are the proximate causes as well as the constituents of the emotional experience—then the emotional experience is the spiritual and bodily effect of that cause. As far as James was concerned, Saint Teresa did not need to prove that any part of her mystical experience was exclusively noncorporeal in order to render antinaturalism plausible. It was sufficient to claim that there was a good reason for holding that her experience owed its spirituality neither to its consequences nor to an inherent noncorporeality but instead to its divine origin. The crucial line of reasoning, in ascertaining the spiritual character of an experience, is not from phenomenon to consequences but from phenomenon to origin. An experience, whether mental or bodily in its introspective content, is spiritual solely because it is the effect of a spiritual cause. This argument hardly resembles pragmatic reasoning.

James objected to irreligious moralities because they lack emotional depth. Had he not been religious, he might have chosen Stoicism or Epicureanism, but Stoic insensibility and Epicurean resignation are too pessimistic, he thought; compared to the enthusiasm that religions have historically provided, these surviving Greek moralities offer only a sort of dignity in despair. "If religion is to mean anything definite for us, it seems to me that we ought to take it as meaning this added dimension of emotion, this enthusiastic temper of espousal, in regions where morality strictly so called can at best but bow its head and acquiesce" (*VRE,* 48). Irreligious moralities are too simplistic and thus fall short of the rich, heterogeneous blend of ideas and sentiments that James always demanded in his own ideals. Such moralities characterize the *once-born* attitude, a term borrowed from Francis W. Newman, who described the once-born religious person as happy and childlike, comfortable in his religious consciousness. He exemplifies what James called the religion of healthy-mindedness, whereas the twice-born are sick souls and divided selves who must be born twice to be happy in their religiousness.[55]

A famous passage in *Varieties* describes the sick soul, and although James presented it as a first-hand account by a French correspondent, it actually described an experience of his own as a young man. In a moment of panic and temporary hallucination, he identified with "an epileptic patient whom I had seen in the asylum, a black-haired youth with greenish skin, entirely idiotic. . . . He sat there like a sort of sculptured Egyptian cat or Peruvian mummy, moving nothing but his black eyes and looking absolutely non-human. . . . *That shape am I,* I felt, potentially. . . . There was such a horror of him, and such a perception of my own merely momentary discrepancy from him, that it was as if something hitherto solid within my breast gave way entirely, and I became a mass of quivering fear." James then described how the need-to-believe is born from harsh experience: "I mean the fear was so invasive and powerful that if I had not clung to scripture-texts like 'The eternal God is my refuge,' etc., 'Come unto me, all ye that labor and are heavy-laden,' etc., 'I am the resurrection and the life,' etc., I think I should have grown really insane."[56]

Religion is not the only safety net for the panic-stricken, but James believed its superiority lies in the richer balance of attitudes it produces in the believer. Furthermore, the kind of religion for which one reaches from the midst of anxiety produces a richer mixture of attitudes. The twice-born, whose religious consciousness is born again out of suffering and desperation, appreciates the bitter side of existence which the once-born or natural optimist ignores. The twice-born develops the proper blend of pessimism and optimism; he understands that wrongness (evil, sin, imperfection) infects the natural world and thus justifies the inclination toward pessimism, but he keeps his pessimism in check. "The mood of a Schopenhauer or a Nietzsche—and in a less degree . . . of our own sad Carlyle—though often an ennobling sadness, is almost as often only peevishness running away with the bit between its teeth. The sallies of the two German authors remind one, half the time, of the sick shriekings of two dying rats. They lack the purgatorial note which religious sadness gives forth" (*VRE*, 38). The person whose religion is born partly from his anxiety about the presence of evil and the evident vanity of mortal things cannot afford the optimism of the healthy-minded; nor can he tolerate the morbidity of hellfire theology or the extreme pessimism of former philosophies.

James embarked in *Varieties* upon a search for that mixture of emotions and attitudes which is the richest product of religious experience. Sorting the great variety of experiences about which he had read or heard, he assembled a kind of recipe for the right blend of attitudes.[57] He examined reports of religious conversion, regeneration, saintliness, mystical communion, prayer, and revelation, and from all of this he distilled a heterogeneous yet harmonized personality that he admired most. The mixture included solemnity blended with joy, pessimism with optimism, exertion with relaxation, assurance with faith, egotism with humility, saintliness with worldliness, and mysticism with thoughtfulness. These attributes are only a sampling of what James sketched, with the help of graphic reports by individuals seized with faith, in his lectures on conversion, saintliness, and mysticism. Even such an incomplete list demonstrates his conservatism in evaluating attitudes and emotional propensities, including religious ones. Any single trait might domineer or become fanatical, but none was valuable enough to be allowed to flourish except in a balanced and rich combination with others. He praised the enthusiastic temperament only if it knew when to be depressed; indeed, irrevocable emotional commitment in any direction was foreign to his thought.

If religious experiences and beliefs can produce the ingredients of the ideal personality, then we can call the defense of religion a pragmatic argument. Religion is valuable because it shapes the believer's spirit more nobly. In both *Varieties* and *Pragmatism*, James satisfied those like Bertrand Russell, who once wrote to him: "The pragmatic difference that pragmatism makes to me is that it encourages religious belief, and that I consider religious belief precious. I dare say this is a prejudice, but it has been fed by reflection on history and current politics. However, my reason for saying this is merely that I do not wish to pretend to be solely influenced by intellectual considerations in this matter."[58] James selected his case histories with care because he meant *Varieties* to be a massive testimonial, from celebrated saints as well as unknown cranks and eccentrics, to the good that religious belief can accomplish in people's lives. He rested his case for religion upon that good rather than upon any creed or authority. We may call this approach pragmatic, though it is surely part of every religion to claim that it works wonders for those who believe. James's philosophy of religion is distinctive not in its pragmatism, but rather in its special interpretation of the range of religious experiences presented in *Varieties*.[59]

James was cautious about extracting a philosophy of religion from the vast amount of experiential and confessional data he had collected. He was so cautious throughout *Varieties*, in fact, that his qualifications tend to erode distinctions that would otherwise be sharp. Perhaps the most prominent contrast, that between the once- and twice-born, was deliberately blurred when James wrote that "the final consciousness which each type reaches of union with the divine has the same practical significance for the individual" (*VRE*, 477–78n). In presenting examples of mystical literature, with its self-contradictory phrases such as "whispering silence," "teeming desert," and "dazzling obscurity," and in suggesting that mystical writings are really musical compositions which best express mystical truth, he commented on an obscure quotation from H. P. Blavatsky thus: "These words, if they do not awaken laughter as you receive them, probably stir chords within you which music and language touch in common. Music gives us ontological messages which non-musical criticism is unable to contradict, though it may laugh at our foolishness in minding them" (*VRE*, 412). James knew he was treading a fine line between the sublime and the ridiculous; although he pressed the analogy between music and mystical writings, he wanted his audience to realize that he was moving with caution.

This caution is evident in that James settled for vague and tentatively expressed ideas; in summarizing the main religious beliefs described in *Varieties*, he was content to say only that they included the conviction that "the visible world is part of a more spiritual universe from which it draws its chief significance" and that "union or harmonious relation with that higher universe is our true end" (*VRE*, 475). There was one critical point upon which he took a defiant stand, without apology or hesitation: that we have the right to believe in any reality which will satisfy our deepest longings. Not surprisingly, he found this claim to be a feature of all religions. "The pivot round which the religious life, as we have traced it, revolves, is the interest of the individual in his private personal destiny. Religion, in short, is a monumental chapter in the history of human egotism" (*VRE*, 480). James wanted to protect the individual's right to believe that his egotistic interests were founded, however obliquely, in the nature of things; he thought it absurd to declare in the name of science or rationality that such catering to self-interest is indefensible. At this point he and his critics reached an impasse.

But apart from his unquestioning assertion of the right to believe, James also approached belief with caution. Although he ventured a religious hypothesis of sorts, he thought that the religious impulse is itself vague and thus demands no specific object. Traditional arguments for the existence of God left him cold. The only one he considered at all valid was the argument from design, but the idea that the world is the product of a grand designer, he observed, had been exploded by Darwinism. "Conceived as we now conceive them, as so many fortunate escapes from almost limitless processes of destruction, the benevolent adaptations which we find in Nature suggest a deity very different from the one who figured in the earlier versions of the argument. The fact is that these arguments do but follow the combined suggestions of the facts and of our feeling. They prove nothing rigorously. They only corroborate our preexistent partialities" (*VRE*, 428–29). About analyses of God's possible metaphysical attributes James wrote: "From the point of view of practical religion, the metaphysical monster which they offer to our worship is an absolutely worthless invention of the scholarly mind."[60] James distanced himself from specific religions, including Christianity (although there were occasions when he spoke of "us Christians"); when Miller was ordained in the Episcopal Church, James wrote to a friend that Miller had taken an unheroic step and that to be entangled with Church Christianity is to be infected with sophistry.[61]

James's aloofness from organized religion and his disdain for theology caused Weber to object that "the content of ideas of a religion is, as Calvinism shows, far more important than William James [in *Varieties*] is inclined to admit. . . . If the God of the Puritans has influenced history as hardly another before or since, it is principally due to the attributes which the power of thought has given him."[62] While James evidently disliked theological discussion and was convinced that the appeal of popular religions is more emotional than intellectual, he was not wholly inattentive to the influence of dogma. He appreciated Weber's concern, as well as James Leuba's contentions that as long as people can use their God they care little about theology and that the value of religious belief is generally felt as a stimulant or anesthetic rather than as an intellectual satisfaction.[63] James was closer to the viewpoint of Weber than to that of Leuba in writing: "When, however, a positive intellectual content is associated with a faith-state, it gets invincibly stamped in upon belief, and this explains the passionate loyalty of religious persons everywhere to the minutest details of their so widely differing creeds. Taking creeds and faith-state together, as forming 'religions' . . . we are obliged, on account of their extraordinary influence upon action and endurance, to class them amongst the most important biological functions of mankind" (*VRE*, 496). James realized that he needed to include *some* intellectual content in the need-to-believe.

In formulating what he believed on the basis of his own need as well as upon the accounts in *Varieties*, James identified a vital connection between mystical experience, abnormal psychology, the mind-cure movement, and psychical research. The connection lay in the psychological concept of the subconscious, which he theorized is susceptible to a nonnaturalistic, religious interpretation. Psychologists and religious mystics alike understand that any experience, when we reflect upon it, has no definite boundary but radiates from its center into a surrounding *more*. (The word *more* was a favorite of James's, for it expressed his belief that we should never cease our moral striving.) Experiences and consciousness do not have boundaries as do physical objects; even where there are limits on how much one can take in, as in vision, such limits are vague at best, and there is always a *more* which we can apprehend simply by adjusting our perspective. The continuity of what is distinctly within the range of consciousness with a *more* that lies beyond is taken for granted.

The nature of this *more* must be determined, James said, by a combination of abnormal psychology, psychical research, and mind-cure. To the extent that these experimental disciplines shed light on the question, religion may obtain scientific support, although James did not expect the scientific establishment to be impressed by such so-called support. Nevertheless, he hoped to make mystical experience seem more reasonable by showing that it resembled what mind-curists, psychical researchers, and abnormal psychologists were attempting to study under controlled conditions. He declared 1892 a significant year because it was then that F. W. H. Myers reported his work on the subconscious self, stating: "Each of us is in reality an abiding psychical entity far more extensive than he knows—an individuality which can never express itself completely through any corporeal manifestation."[64] James favored Myers's treatment of the subconscious because, unlike other well-known researchers, Myers thought that the study of subconscious motivation led into psychical research and religion. James said that Binet, Janet, Freud, Joseph Breuer, and Morton Prince had conducted "wonderful explorations" into the subliminal consciousness of hysterics and had accomplished successful treatment by altering or abolishing through suggestion the malevolent subconscious ideas and memories causing the hysteria. James was impressed by their work even though they did not take it in the direction that he and Myers desired.[65]

The "age of the subconscious/unconscious" had arrived and James knew it; he anticipated its influence in science and society, foreseeing and lamenting the anti-religious development in Freudian theory. With Myers, Gurney, Sidgwick, and other members of the British Society for Psychical Research, he saw that the subconscious or the psychical *more* could be used in the name of religion, as did some of the mind-curists who attributed the relief of mental or spiritual suffering to divine intervention operating through a person's subconscious. James was drawn to the notion of the subconscious not only because it gave a rationale to his own religious need but also because it fitted neatly with important events in his life, regenerative experiences in which a sudden, surprising resurgence of energy occurred in the midst of a pathological apathy or *anhedonia* so pervasive that he felt that life was worthless. To regain one's energy in such circumstances is like a gift from heaven, James felt. "To have its level raised is the most important thing that can happen to a man, yet in all my reading I know of no single page or paragraph of a scientific psychology book in which it receives mention—the psychologists have left it to be treated by the moralists and mind-curers and doctors exclusively."[66] Psychologists could illuminate the subconscious realm, he thought, by uncovering its properties, locating its physiological connections, and discovering how much control we might have over it. Mind-curists and individuals like James himself, who experimented with meditation and exercise for modifying consciousness by modifying the subconscious, hoped to benefit from such psychological findings. Through resolute exertions of will and displays of moral strength, one might discover that some control over the subconscious—and thus over the contents of consciousness—is possible.

What often marks the religious experience, James concluded in *Varieties,* is a regeneration achieved not through moral exertion but through a kind of self-surrender or relaxation of the will. He explained this phenomenon as do religious mystics who speak of opening themselves to the divine presence or to the surrounding spiritual universe and of receiving in return the gift of regeneration. James was struck by the fact that his own recoveries from depression sometimes seemed to result from unknown forces rather than from his conscious willpower. He conceived of the subconscious *more* as a spiritual universe in which we are somehow joined both with each other and with superior (divine) powers.

James's "over-belief," the religious speculation he based on the data gathered in *Varieties*, was this:

> The individual, so far as he suffers from his wrongness and criticises it, is to that extent consciously beyond it, and is in at least possible touch with something higher, if anything higher exist. Along with the wrong part there is thus a better part of him, even though it may be but a most helpless germ. With which part he should identify his real being is by no means obvious at this stage; but when stage 2 (the stage of solution or salvation) arrives, the man identifies his real being with the germinal higher part of himself; and does so in the following way. *He becomes conscious that this higher part is conterminous and continuous with a MORE of the same quality, which is operative in the universe outside of him, and which he can keep in working touch with, and in a fashion get on board of and save himself when all his lower being has gone to pieces in the wreck.*[67]

The next step was to identify this *more* with God; in "The Moral Philosopher and The Moral Life," James emphasized that making such an equation involves staking one's belief in a permanent moral order. He claimed that this act in itself saves theism from being merely subjective, transforms it into a genuinely pragmatic hypothesis; but the confusion between what follows from the proposition that God exists and what follows from the belief in that proposition arises again. Given the deliberate vagueness of James's notion of faith, it seems questionable whether his theism can be considered at all pragmatic. His occasional talk of a science of religions and of verification of religious hypotheses was mainly a gesture to the scientific establishment—as well as to his own pragmatic conscience. I do not mean to imply that his religious formulations are unintelligible because they are not pragmatic; indeed, one gets the flavor of what he meant and can attach at least a vague sense to his expressions of his faith. For instance, James made frequent efforts in his writings to sketch the differences implied by certain religious and metaphysical propositions. The problem remains, however, of how to relate what is intelligible in James's writings to specific consequences or predictions, such that his religious propositions can be considered genuinely pragmatic hypotheses.[68]

James's theistic interpretation of the *more* that surrounds each experience was connected not only to the subconscious but also to the concept of pure experience as presented in *A Pluralistic Universe*. James used pure experience to blur the distinctions between mind and body, one person and another, and God and humanity. The subconscious and the *more* of any consciousness are the boundary-free parts of a vast system of pure experiences. When contemplated religiously, the *more* can be called God to emphasize that it is personal and is a source of causation. It can also be called a mother-sea to emphasize that we are neither distinct from nor identical with God (or gods), but are somehow "co-conscious." Just as the microcosmic sensations in terms of which James defined pure experience are always heterogeneous unities, so the macrocosmic world of pure experience is a manyness-in-oneness, and we and God are together as boundary-free parts of it.[69] This belief defies explanation since it requires abandoning the logic of identity. James believed it despite its irrationalism because he thought that individuals and deities can somehow be both themselves and others. In *Principles* he had declared that experiences do not have parts, but in the metaphysics of pure experience he changed his mind and said that consciousness and experiences can compound without total loss of identity. Finally, in his writings on religion, he stated that the paradox is unresolvable; at the end of his career he called the belief in the unity of us all with its compounding of consciousness a matter of faith or mystical intuition. In considering whether experiences have parts, James moved from being a psychologist to being a philosopher, and finally to being a mystic.

Although he did not specify further details, James felt obliged to beef up his account of how our true selves may be related—through the extension of our experiences beyond what we are conscious of at any moment—to divine selves, just as narrow experiences are related to wider ones. He was assisted by Fechner's speculations that "vaster orders of mind go with the vaster orders of body" in a hierarchy of consciousness, so that there may be souls of the earth, the solar system, and so on.[70] James praised Fechner's analogy between humanity and "sense-organs of the earth's soul"; like Plato's imagery, this analogy vivified James's own religious conceptions. Moreover, Fechner's hierarchy of consciousness suggested that we might be related to superior beings through a series of levels of consciousness. As for God, Fechner "provides us with a very definite gate of approach to him in the shape of the earth-soul, through which in the nature of things, we must first make connexion with all the more enveloping superhuman realms, and with which our more immediate religious commerce at any rate has to be carried on."[71]

Fechner's ideas also supported a pluralistic religion, encouraging a departure from absolutism and transcendental idealism—and even from theism if it is too inflexible—because their attractiveness is consistent with either a polytheistic or a monotheistic interpretation. "Fechner, with his distinct earth-soul functioning as our guardian angel, seems to me clearly polytheistic; but the word 'polytheism' usually gives offense, so perhaps it is better not to use it."[72] James was largely indifferent about whether his philosophy of religion was monotheistically or polytheistically inclined. What is important is the existence of plural forces, including humanity and God or gods, who together can work to ameliorate a universe still in the process of development. In notes made while preparing a course in 1905, he wrote: "So far I have been *atheistic*. But if evolution—Gods may be one of the results," suggesting that in some such way religion might accommodate Darwinism.[73] In a universe that is still evolving and that may be improved by human as well as divine action, the divinity—whether singular or plural—must have finite capabilities.

The line of least resistance, then, as it seems to me, both in theology and in philosophy, is to accept, along with the superhuman consciousness, the notion that it is not all-embracing—the notion . . . that there *is* a God, but that he is finite, either in power or knowledge, or in both at once. These . . . are the terms in which common men have usually carried on their active commerce with God; and the monistic perfections that make the notion of him so paradoxical practically and morally are the colder addition of remote professorial minds operating *in distans* upon conceptual substitutes for him alone. . . .

Thus does foreignness get banished from our world, and far more so when we take the system pluralistically than when we take it monistically. We are indeed internal parts of God and not external creations, on any possible reading of the panpsychic system. Yet because God is not the absolute, but is himself a part when the system is conceived pluralistically, his functions can be taken as not wholly dissimilar to those of the other smaller parts—as similar to our functions consequently.

Having an environment, being in time, and working out a history just like ourselves, he escapes from the foreignness from all that is human, of the static timeless perfect absolute.[74]

In his postscript to *Varieties* James said that he had been silent about immortality partly because it was for him a secondary matter; he usually made this observation when the subject came up, although he was more interested in the possibility of immortality in his final years.[75] While he might have scorned certain notions of immortality, it seems impossible, given his yearning that there always be a *more,* that he never harbored any hope of life after death. He preferred to leave its form unspecified, for if such a life were in the offing, it would be a surprise.

An obvious difficulty for the hope that personal consciousness can survive after death is the apparent dependence of consciousness upon the brain. This is a difficulty, however, only if we presume that the brain *produces* consciousness; if, on the contrary, the brain merely transmits a consciousness already existent, then consciousness need not depend upon the brain for survival. Some forms of consciousness may be like signals that are not originated in but only transmitted by our brains. James did not press the hypothesis that the brain is merely an organ that manifests consciousness; he asserted only that the complete dependence of consciousness upon the brain had not been proved. He cited an analogy from Fechner to support the hypothesis that individual consciousness is related to an eternal, cosmic consciousness, such that the brain is only a partial and temporary transmitter between the two. According to the analogy, consciousness has a threshold that rises or falls; when it falls (as when we are especially alert), we become conscious of things that were concealed from us, and when it rises (as in cases of drowsiness), consciousness shrinks and we become unconscious of what was there to apprehend. "This rising and lowering of a psycho-physical threshold exactly conforms to our notion of a permanent obstruction to the transmission of consciousness, which obstruction may, in our brains, grow alternately greater or less."[76]

The conception of personal immortality as a relation between an individual consciousness and a cosmic one (a reservoir or mother-sea of consciousness) defies the logic of identity and depends upon an intuition which cannot be conceptualized and is thus mystical. But if an analogy can rescue an idea from unintelligibility, James reasoned, then Fechner's speculations may help.

> Now, according to Fechner, our bodies are just wavelets on the surface of the earth. We grow upon the earth as leaves grow upon a tree, and our consciousness arises out of the whole earth-consciousness,—which it forgets to thank,—just as within our consciousness an emphatic experience arises, and makes us forget the whole background of experience without which it could not have come. But as it sinks again into that background it is not forgotten. On the contrary, it is remembered and, as remembered, leads a freer life, for it now combines, itself a conscious idea, with the innumerable, equally conscious ideas of other remembered things. Even so is it, when we die, with the whole system of our outlived experiences. During the life of our body, although they were always elements in the more enveloping earth-consciousness, yet they themselves were unmindful of the fact. Now, impressed on the whole earth-mind as memories, they lead the life of ideas there, and realize themselves no longer in isolation, but along with all the similar vestiges left by other human lives, entering with these into new combinations, affected anew by experiences of the living, and affecting the living.[77]

A second objection to immortality is that it is absurd to imagine countless individuals living forever; overpopulation would be too staggering to contemplate. James realized that he verged on the comic in taking this objection seriously and that he appeared like a theological novitiate who has not yet learned how the world's religions have handled that objection. He thought it troubled people and therefore ought to be treated publicly. The notion of selective salvation deeply offended him, for he felt that immortality must be democratic and that aristocratic visions of it were archaic. To judge that others do not deserve eternal life is to be blind to their inner lives and to see the world selfishly; it is also to "project our own incapacity into the vast cosmos, and measure the wants of the Absolute by our own puny needs."[78] Laboratory animals, which James called heroic for their sacrifices for humans, ought not to be excluded from the eternal; indeed, James could not determine what would warrant such exclusion. But what sort of realm could possibly contain countless individuals in a simultaneous and eternal society?

In *Principles* James remarked on the difficulty of conceiving consciousness in relation to space. "The truth is that if the thinking principle (consciousness) is extended we neither know its form nor its seat; whilst if unextended, it is absurd to speak of its having any space-relation at all" (*Principles*, 1:215). Images, thoughts, and feelings cannot be located in public space; a surgeon operating on a patient's brain does not find the patient's conscious images there. It is a philosophical challenge to explain how consciousness relates to space; what is called public space may be an intellectual construct from the private or subjective spatial experiences of individuals. The space of eternity may be like private rather than public space. "Each new mind brings its own edition of the universe of space along with it, its own room to inhabit; and these spaces never crowd each other,—the space of my imagination, for example, in no way interferes with yours. The amount of possible consciousness seems to be governed by no law analogous to that of the so-called conservation of energy in the material world. . . . Professor Wundt, in fact . . . has formulated a law of the universe which he calls the law of increase of spiritual energy, and which he expressly opposes to the law of conservation of energy in physical things."[79] The nagging image of an overcrowded room must not interfere with the desire to believe in an eternal spiritual space, one more akin to the space of dreams and imagination than to that of science or common sense.

As James was the first to acknowledge, his religious notions were vulnerable to many objections. How, for instance, is the concept of consciousness as something preexistent or eternal, as a reservoir or mother-sea with which individual con- sciousnesses are somehow mingled, consistent with James's denial of consciousness as an entity in his metaphysics of radical empiricism? Is his religion inconsistent with his metaphysics? He did not think answers to such queries were possible; when he had attempted answers, he had found he could not adequately formulate what he wanted to believe in metaphysics and religion. He had a sense of what he believed, but no matter how he said it, it fell short of how he sensed it ought to be said. He attempted statements such as this: "Just so there is a continuum of cosmic con- sciousness against which our individuality builds but accidental fences, and into which our several minds plunge as into a mother-sea or reservoir."[80] Even if such a passage approached what he believed, he knew that when the words were ques- tioned their sense would dissolve. Rather than admit that this situation meant that he did not really understand his own words, he held that he did know at least minimally what he meant, even if it could be conveyed only through analogy and metaphor. Something in his experience encouraged him to believe that what he sensed to be true actually was. This attitude led him to defend mysticism over philosophy when metaphysical and religious "over-beliefs" were at stake.

James regretted that he had never had a genuinely mystical experience and that he had to defer to the accounts of others in his writing about the subject; he did, however, recall experiences that resembled mystical events. A feature of those epi- sodes, he said, was "the sense of a tremendous *muchness* suddenly revealed."[81] To have a sense of something is to feel on the verge of something. James's experiences of the sense of *more* and *muchness* were harbingers whose content was exciting less for its intrinsic detail than for its unknown possibilities. The sense of something might not entail a specific belief, as James testified in describing an echo of a mystical experience:

What happened each time was that I seemed all at once to be reminded of a past experience; and this reminiscence, ere I could conceive or name it distinctly, developed into something further still, and so on, until the process faded out, leaving me amazed at the sudden vision of increasing ranges of distant fact of which I could give no articulate account. The mode of consciousness was per- ceptual, not conceptual—the field expanding so fast that there seemed no time

for conception or identification to get in its work. . . . The *content* was thus
entirely lost to retrospection—it sank into the limbo into which dreams vanish
as we gradually awake. The feeling—I won't call it belief—that I had had a
sudden *opening*, had seen through a window, as it were, distant realities that
incomprehensibly belonged with my own life, was so acute that I cannot shake
it off to-day.[82]

James's echoes of mystical experience were not the starting point of his religious
belief but entered later in the formation of belief. His beginning point was almost
always something noticed in everyday experience; for example, he said that we find
the idea of manyness-in-oneness in every sensation; every color, taste, and sound is
a heterogeneous unity, an indivisible oneness that somehow blends several qualities
at once. This idea suggested an analogous question: can individual creatures be
related in a deeper and more unified way than ordinary existence permits? The
analogy between the relations of individual creatures and the manyness-in-oneness
of sensations impressed James because it supported his faith in spirituality; if the
manyness-in-oneness of everyday sensations is a unity that we take for granted but
that can never be adequately conceptualized, then the fact that we cannot conceptualize a collective human spirituality that is a muchness-at-once does not rule out
belief in it. But if the analogy provides an intuitive intelligibility for the belief, it
scarcely provides any reason for holding it. The motive for holding the belief is the
very desire to hold it. Is such a desire justified?

It might appear that James, rather than seeking to justify his wanting to believe a
certain metaphysical or religious proposition, merely supported such propositions
upon the desire to believe, even though he admitted that this reason is not justified.
But in defending the subjective method throughout his career, he meant to give his
need the added weight of a more basic conviction, that the universe will satisfy our
deepest yearnings.[83] Our yearnings are justified insofar as they will be in part satisfied by a universe that has evolved to create and fulfill them. Our inner lives are in
essential harmony with an objective reality. Can any evidence be offered for such a
theory? Is not its falsity starkly apparent when we witness the daily disappointment
and frustration of many human needs and desires? How can we hope that our world
will ultimately satisfy religious longings?

The daily frustration of human wants and needs seems to have been irrelevant
to James's thinking, for he did not use pedestrian wants to defend metaphysical or
religious hypotheses. His own deepest yearnings were so vague that their status was
unaffected by ordinary subjectivity. James did not build a metaphysics or religion
from a list of needs and wants that ought in a rightful world to be fulfilled. To bolster
his faith that amorphously expressed religious sentiments might in some more specific respects be true, he appealed less to the facts of daily life than to the state of
human ignorance. He indicted the scientist or academic who claimed to know more
than he really did. James hoped to make religion more attractive by portraying its
opponents as arrogant and dogmatic. If the expanse of human ignorance was accept-

ed, James could induce a mood of wonderment, one of susceptibility to metaphysical and religious lyrics. To profess Socratic ignorance means admitting that anything might be true, including the claim that the universe is responsive to our deepest desires.

What can be said for this claim? For James to have accepted it simply as an intellectual claim or a rational demand would have been out of character, given his lifelong commitment to the empiricistic injunction that rational demands have experiential roots. His confidence in this claim depended upon allegedly experiential evidence, the evidence of mystical experience. He relied on the testimony of mystics and upon his own experiences which resembled mystical ones. Something in those experiences, he felt, strongly suggested that the universe is mysterious and yet inclined to satisfy our deepest yearnings, even to make us more fully aware of those yearnings. Something indescribable yet compelling about the experience caused James to trust the claims which it suggested. It disposed him, despite flashes of skepticism, to surrender to its suggestions and to feel the relief of letting go. If we cannot know its charms unless we experience it, if we cannot appreciate the source of the trust that it instills in its own suggestions as claims without having lived through a mystical event ourselves, then we must either choose not to believe or wait, as James did, for such an experience to descend upon us.

In 1882 James wrote from London to his dying father in Boston: "As for the other side, and Mother, and our all possibly meeting, I *can't* say anything. More than ever at this moment do I feel that if that *were* true, all would be solved and justified. And it comes strangely over me in bidding you good-bye how a life is but a day and expresses mainly but a single note. It is so much like the act of bidding an ordinary good-night. Good-night, my sacred old Father! If I don't see you again—Farewell! A blessed farewell!" (*LWJ*, 1:220). Writing to his dying sister Alice in 1891, he alluded to the study of the subconscious in abnormal psychology and psychical research; sounding more convinced than he had nine years earlier about the chances of life after death, he wrote: "Farewell until I write again!" (*LWJ*, 1:311). Both letters are strangely matter-of-fact and emotionally distant, as well as devoid of any mention of religion. Not long before his own death in 1910, he wrote his last item for publication, a piece about his friend B. P. Blood titled "A Pluralistic Mystic." A farewell occurred here too, presumably one to himself. For James the imminence of death seems not to have been an occasion for excitement, anticipation, fear, grief, not even an occasion to be regarded as the acid test of one's faith. It was as if he felt, as death approached, that the work of faith was finished, that all of the suggestions of mystical experiences had been collected, and that it was a time to suspend all expectations. Whether such an attitude was appropriate in a man who claimed the benefits of religious faith and of experiences resembling the mystic's is perhaps suggested by James's concluding words in "A Pluralistic Mystic":

> The "inexplicable," the "mystery" . . . remains; but it remains as something to
> be met and dealt with by faculties more akin to our activities and heroisms and

willingnesses, than to our logical powers. . . . Let *my* last word, then, speaking in the name of intellectual philosophy, be *his* [Blood's] word:—''There is no conclusion. What has concluded, that we might conclude in regard to it? There are no fortunes to be told, and there is no advice to be given.—Farewell!''[84]

ABBREVIATIONS

All references to documents such as diaries, unpublished manuscripts, and correspondence are, unless otherwise noted, to items in the James Collection in Harvard's Houghton Library. References to items in the Harvard Archives are separately noted. Because the Harvard editions of James's works were not all available while this book was being written, I have in most cases referred to more readily available editions. Unless otherwise noted, I refer to the editions listed below.

APU *A Pluralistic Universe* (Cambridge: Harvard University Press, 1977)

CER *Collected Essays and Reviews* (New York: Russell and Russell, 1969)

ERE *Essays in Radical Empiricism* (Cambridge: Harvard University Press, 1976)

LWJ *The Letters of William James,* ed. Henry James III, 2 vols. (New York: Kraus Reprint Co., 1969)

McDermott *The Writings of William James,* ed. John J. McDermott (Chicago: University of Chicago Press, 1977)

MS *Memories and Studies* (London: Longmans, Green, & Co., 1911)

MT *The Meaning of Truth* (London: Longmans, Green, & Co., 1909)

Principles *The Principles of Psychology,* 2 vols. (New York: Dover, 1950)

RBP Ralph Barton Perry, *The Thought and Character of William James,* 2 vols. (Boston: Little, Brown, 1935)

SPP *Some Problems of Philosophy* (London: Longmans, Green, & Co., 1911)

Talks *Talks to Teachers* (New York: Norton, 1958)

TCWJ Ralph Barton Perry, *The Thought and Character of William James* (New York: Braziller, 1954)

VRE *The Varieties of Religious Experience* (New York: Modern Library, n.d.)

WTB *The Will to Believe, and Other Essays in Popular Philosophy* (New York: Dover, 1956)

NOTES

1. LIFE AND CAREER

1. "William James," *Journal of Philosophy, Psychology, and Scientific Methods* 7, no. 19 (15 September 1910): 506.

2. Quoted in Gay Wilson Allen, *William James: A Biography* (New York: Viking, 1967), 493–94.

3. Morris R. Cohen, for instance, wrote that in

> William James . . . we meet a personality of such large proportions and of such powerful appeal to contemporaneous sentiment that we may well doubt whether the time has yet come when his work can be adequately estimated. . . . The width and depth of his sympathies and the irresistible magic of his words have undoubtedly transformed the tone and manner of American philosophic writing. . . . Yet despite the enormous influence which James has exercised, he has left behind him no school of technical philosophers with a definite core of unified doctrines. (*American Thought: A Critical Sketch* [New York: Collier, 1969], 356)

Ernest Nagel wrote:

> It is true that not all the positions for which [James] fought in psychology and philosophy have become widely accepted; nor did he leave behind him a sizable following of disciples who subscribed to the essential details of his thought. But the larger features of his work—its voluntaristic naturalism and empiricism, its distrust of dogmatic claims to final truth, whether in science, philosophy or religion, and its emphasis upon the novelties and contingencies which characterize the operations of nature—have been intimately absorbed into our own modes of thought; we can appreciate the innovations they represented only by contrasting the quality of our own intellectual atmosphere with that of James's generation. . . . Because he communicated the freshness which comes from sailing courageously on the unfathomable ocean of experience, he brought relief from the stiff dogmatisms of less-traveled folk and helped introduce new standards of intellectual forthrightness and honesty. Of James, it may be said what he said of [Thomas Davidson]: he was the knight-errant of the intellectual life. ("The Progress of Science: William James, 1842–1910," *Scientific Monthly* 55 [October 1942]: 379, 381)

The idea that James had few disciples may have originated with a piece written by Sidney Hook, which included these remarks:

> It is significant that not until capitalism had run its natural course was the attempt made

by a few American philosophers to bring the pragmatic test to bear upon the whole framework of social ideals within which great technical advances had been made.

William James was not among these. His viewpoint remained that of a sensitive European become pioneer. His primary concern was with his own soul. ("Our Philoso- phers," *Current History* 41 [March 1935]: 700)

This self-concern partly explains, said Hook, why James allegedly had no disciples and exerted little lasting influence. This claim is wrong, as is the charge that James lacked a sociohistorical sense. The vast amount of literature on James since 1935, much of it focusing on his moral and social views, certainly makes its own case. In the same article, however, Hook called James's *Principles of Psychology* "the greatest and most influential treatise on psychology in modern times" (700).

C. I. Lewis once wrote about Henri Bergson that "with the possible exception of William James, no philosopher of our time has issued so vigorous a challenge to his contemporaries or given a new direction to the thinking of so many people." Many readers of James, while challenged and even occasionally inspired by his writings, did not consider themselves James- ians, perhaps for the same reason that Lewis did not: "Of my teachers at Harvard, Royce impressed me most. His ponderous cogency kept my steady attention, even though I never followed to his metaphysical conclusions. James, I thought, had a swift way of being right, but how he reached his conclusions was his own secret" (*Collected Papers*, ed. John D. Goheen and John L. Motherhead, Jr. [Stanford: Stanford University Press, 1970], 4, 42).

4. *Pragmatism* (Cambridge: Harvard University Press, 1975), 125. Subsequent references to this work, unless otherwise noted, are to this edition.

5. "Transatlantic 'Truth'" (a review of James's *Pragmatism*), *Albany Review* 2 (January 1908): 393. For a full presentation of exchanges between James and Russell on this issue, see *MT* (Cambridge: Harvard University Press, 1975), appendix 4. William Barrett gives a favor- able evaluation of James's personal style and refers to Russell in "Our Contemporary, William James," *Commentary* 60, no. 6 (December 1975): 55–62.

James's continuing popular appeal was confirmed in 1928 by Charles H. Compton, a librarian at the Saint Louis Public Library who took a survey of a hundred readers of William James, Carl Sandburg, Homer, Sophocles, and Euripides. The readers of these authors in- cluded few academics and consisted mainly of the following: a lawyer, a few doctors, several ministers, a trunk maker, a machinist, some stenographers, a saleswoman, a laundry worker, a black salesman, and a Jewish student who said that reading *The Letters of William James* was "to indulge in a real pleasure . . . to introduce oneself to the greatest of personalities" ("The Outlook for Adult Education in the Library," *Adult Education and the Library* 3, no. 3 [July 1928]: 2). Compton later compiled references to James by distinguished people, under the title *William James: Philosopher and Man* (New York: Scarecrow, 1957).

6. Russell's comment occurred in an obituary notice for James in *Nation*, 3 September 1910, 793. A. J. Ayer has written: "[*Principles*], which uniquely combines a physiological with a philosophical approach to the traditional problems of psychology, remains a classic, and is probably the best general review of the subject that has yet been written" (*The Origins of Pragmatism* [San Francisco: Freeman, Cooper, 1968], 173).

Joseph Adelson has recently written: "*Principles*, first published in 1890, is the single great- est work in American psychology. Among books written by psychologists, its only rival is Freud's *The Interpretation of Dreams*. It was James's first major work, and at the same time his last significant contribution to psychology, thus the same book stands as both his debut and swan song" ("Still Vital after All These Years," *Psychology Today* 16, no. 4 [April 1982]: 52). Adelson's article was a review of the Harvard edition of *Principles*. For other evaluations of James's book, see my introduction to that edition of *Principles* (Cambridge: Harvard University Press, 1981, xi–xl).

The psychologists C. W. Bray, E. G. Boring, R. B. MacLeod, and R. L. Solomon have said: "James's *Principles* is without question the most literate, the most provocative, and at the same time the most intelligible book on psychology that has ever appeared in English or in any other language" (*William James: Unfinished Business*, ed. Robert B. MacLeod [Washington: American Psychological Association, 1969], iii).

7. *LWJ*, 1:333. Where practical, subsequent references to this work are given parenthetically in the text.

8. Letter of 1 March 1858. A longer excerpt is reproduced in Ralph Barton Perry, *The Thought and Character of William James: Briefer Version* (New York: Braziller, 1954), 52–53. Several letters from James to Van Winkle, written between 1857 and 1859, were donated to the James Collection at the Houghton Library too late for Perry to use them in his original two-volume study of James. Perry quotes briefly from two other letters (*Briefer Version*, 54–55).

Van Winkle was a student at Union College and was considering a career in engineering (he subsequently became Chief Engineer of the Department of Public Parks of New York); knowing Van Winkle's interest in the field, James had written to him from Boulogne on 4 September 1857 and 4 January 1858 that he, too, might consider engineering as a career. But in the letter cited here he concluded that he was probably not suited for the field. He nevertheless praised Van Winkle's choice and seems to have felt wistfulness and a touch of envy in acknowledging his uncertainty about his friend's intentions.

I have quoted this letter at some length to emphasize that James was already disposed, by temperament and upbringing, to a career that traded in words rather than deeds. Taking a microscope into the woods or becoming a farmer were romantic notions at best. In 1865, when he made an expedition to Brazil with the Harvard naturalist Louis Agassiz, he tended to philosophize more than to use a microscope, writing to his mother: "I thoroughly *hate* collecting, and long to be back to books, studies, etc., after this elementary existence" (RBP, 1:225).

The letter also shows James's concern about the fact that his father had never worked because of an inheritance and was free to read, write, and travel. The James children were sometimes at a loss about what their father did. Though he was neither doctor nor lawyer nor engineer, the elder Henry James's life had been useful, and in this letter William may for the first time have been exploring the justification of philosophizing his way through life as his father had done. In his letter of 4 January 1858, he had written to Van Winkle that he "detested trade" and that, despite the value of medicine, he was incapable of doing dissections and operations. After receiving his M.D., he chose not to practice, which suggests that he had narrowed his options to psychology and philosophy.

9. RBP, 1:216. See also Perry's chapters 10–11 for more on James's decision to study science and to pursue a medical degree.

10. Hans Von Kaltenborn, "William James at Harvard," *The Harvard Illustrated Magazine* 8 (February 1907): 94. James's medical diploma in the Houghton Library bears the signatures of Oliver Wendell Holmes, Sr., a professor at Harvard Medical School and a friend of the James family, and of Charles William Eliot.

11. I follow Robert S. Harper's dating of appointments, which agrees with that of the Harvard Archives, rather than Perry's (and McDermott's, which repeats Perry's). Perry dated James's first appointment in anatomy and physiology as 1873, but Harper wrote:

> James became, on August 3, 1872, an instructor in physiology, and he worked at first in the Museum of Comparative Anatomy, at that time on the first floor in Boylston Hall. In the academic year 1872–73, he taught Natural History 3, a course described as Comparative Anatomy and Physiology. . . . James refused President Eliot's offer of reappointment as an instructor in physiology for 1873 [because of ill health], but he returned to the post in 1874." ("The Laboratory of William James," *Harvard Alumni Bulletin* 52 [5 November 1948], 169–70)

James's personal history card (incomplete) in the Harvard Archives lists his appointments as follows: instructor in physiology, 1 September 1872; instructor in anatomy and physiology, 1 September 1873; assistant professor of physiology, 14 February 1876; assistant professor of philosophy, 25 April 1881; professor of psychology, 11 November 1889; professor of philosophy, 4 October 1897; Ingersoll lecturer, 15 February 1897; and professor emeritus of philosophy, 1 September 1907. His first position paid a salary of three hundred dollars, and his top salary was five thousand dollars for 1897–98. On a reduced teaching load in his final years he received two thousand dollars annually.

12. Again, I follow Harper, who wrote:

> The history of the migration of experimental psychology at Harvard is now clear. James first gave instruction in Boylston Hall in 1872–73 and 1874–75. He established what may be called his first laboratory in Lawrence Hall in 1875 and it was continued there until 1891. This is really the world's first laboratory. Certainly it is ahead of Leipzig's, founded in 1879. James also had additional laboratory space in the period 1877–81 in the Museum of Comparative Zoology and had students doing physiological experiments there as early as 1875. In 1891, James, with a few thousand dollars he had collected, formally "founded" the Psychological Laboratory in Dane Hall, and it stayed there until 1905, when Emerson Hall was ready. Emerson Hall was actually planned by the architects to contain a psychological laboratory on its third floor, and the laboratory remained there from 1906 to 1946, forty years altogether, with adjuncts in Boylston Hall, in the Biological Laboratories, and at the Psychological Clinic during the latter twenty of the forty years. Since 1946 the Laboratory has been in its newly-outfitted quarters in the basement of Memorial Hall. (173)

The claim that James set up the first psychological laboratory was challenged, as early as 1894, by Hall, who had been a student of James's and had received his Ph.D. from Harvard. The relationship between the two was always edgy, and James was disconcerted when his former student claimed to have created the first American laboratory in experimental psychology at Johns Hopkins in 1881. James wrote a letter to the editor of *Science* in which he disputed Hall's claim, saying that he had been truly surprised "at the statement [by Hall]. . . . A statement the more remarkable in that [Hall] . . . studied experimental psychology himself at Harvard from 1877 to 1879" ("Experimental Psychology in America," *Science* n.s. 11, no. 45 [1895]: 626).

The claim that James was America's first experimental psychologist has been challenged by Thomas C. Cadwallader and Joyce V. Cadwallader on the grounds that Charles Peirce deserves the distinction instead. They list five categories—earliest recognition of German psychophysiology, book reviews, theoretical papers, experimental papers, and teaching—and conclude: "In the above five categories, Peirce has priority over James in all save teaching. Had Peirce only half the charm of James (and/or perhaps somewhat less of his own genius) he probably would have been offered a position during the late 1860s and even possibly have been earlier than James in teaching" ("America's First Modern Psychologist: William James or Charles S. Peirce?" *Proceedings of the American Psychological Association*, 1972, 7:774). As evidence for the priority for Peirce, Thomas Cadwallader cites Peirce's "Note on the Sensation of Color" in the April 1877 issue of the *American Journal of Science*. See Cadwallader's summary of this paper in "Charles S. Peirce (1839–1914): The First American Experimental Psychologist," *Journal of the History of the Behavioral Sciences* 10 (1974): 293–96.

Even if Peirce's or someone else's experiments were more important or earlier than James's, it seems clear that James founded the first laboratory and the one that most effectively determined the course of American psychology.

For more on James as a psychologist, see William R. Woodward's informative introduction to James's *Essays in Psychology* (Cambridge, Harvard University Press, 1983), xi–xxxix.

13. Harper, 171.

14. Black was one of many of James's former students who wrote to Perry about their recollections of James's courses as Perry prepared his book. This part of Black's letter is reproduced in Harper, 171.

That James's personality left an indelible impression on his students is indicated by many such correspondents of Perry's, whose letters are in the Harvard Archives. Some of the letters are critical, one referring to the "loquacity, vagueness, and obscurity" of James's lecturing. Others mentioned that there were times when James would say, "I can't think today. We had better not go on with the class." As one student put it, "He would dismiss us then. He was unwilling to give anything but his best." Another former student recalled that James would say, "When I am angry I have this sensation in this portion of my body: What do you have?" The students then proceeded to consider their own sensations, but this correspondent recalled having felt that the value of this discussion as lab work was questionable. The same student wrote:

> James came once to lecture at Vassar. He had come directly from Cambridge; his train was late; he had been unable to get lunch, was given a heavy dinner and rushed at once to the lecture. He started off well, but presently indigestion made him grow slower and slower until finally he stopped short, put his hand to his mouth and gave a prodigious yawn. Then much refreshed he went on. And the subject of his lecture, afterwards printed as an essay, was The Gospel of Relaxation! There should have been added "with an illustration." Could anything be more like James?

There is some evidence from students' letters that James's impact as a teacher of anatomy and physiology was less powerful than when he turned to psychology and philosophy. Theodore Roosevelt, a member of the Harvard class of 1880, was a student in James's course in comparative zoology in 1879 and apparently liked to argue with his professor more than to imbibe his wisdom.

15. These included "Remarks on Spencer's *Definition of Mind as Correspondence*, "Quelques considérations sur la méthode subjective," and "Brute and Human Intellect."

16. "Chauncey Wright," in *CER*, 24.

17. Ibid.

18. "Lewes's 'Problems of Life and Mind,'" in *CER*, 11.

19. "The Sentiment of Rationality," in *CER*, 85.

20. "Remarks on Spencer's *Definition of Mind as Correspondence*," in *CER*, 67. The same convictions occur in "Quelques considérations sur la méthode subjective," where James wrote: "Croyant à mes forces, je m'élance; le résultat donne raison à ma croyance, la vérifie. . . . Il y a donc des cas ou *une croyance crée sa propre vérification*" (*CER*, 71).

21. "The Mind and the Brain," *Nation* 24 (1877): 356. This is an unsigned review by James of books by David Ferrier, Henry Maudsley, and Jules Luys.

Ian Hacking is among those who have noted that Ludwig Wittgenstein was intrigued by James's observations about introspection and subjected them to considerable criticism. "Philosophical psychology is not introspection, whose noblest practitioner was William James. James is the only psychologist (besides some of the Gestalt people) to whom Wittgenstein regularly alludes. The vigor of James's writing is used to make plain the bizarre paths into which we are led by the very idea of a faculty of introspective knowledge. The danger here lies in postulating that there is an exclusively subjective means of gaining self-knowledge" ("Wittgenstein the Psychologist," *The New York Review*, (1 April 1982, 43).

22. See, for example, "The Energies of Men" in McDermott, 671–83.

In a remarkable account of his own self-help program (combined with orthodox medical treatment), which led to successful recovery from an illness that had been diagnosed as incurable, Norman Cousins writes: "I have learned never to underestimate the capacity of the human mind and body to regenerate—even when the prospects seem most wretched. The life-force may be the least understood force on earth. William James said that human beings tend to live too far within self-imposed limits. It is possible that these limits will recede when we respect more fully the natural drive of the human mind and body toward perfectibility and regeneration" (*Anatomy of an Illness as Perceived by the Patient* [New York: Bantam, 1981], 48. After a heart attack, Cousins reiterated the message of the first book in *The Healing Heart* (New York: W. W. Norton, 1983). For an assessment of James's role in the mind-cure movement in America, see Donald Meyer, *The Positive Thinkers* (Garden City, N.Y.: Doubleday, 1965), especially chapter 1 and postscript 1.

Aldous Huxley, an admirer of James, wrote:

> Nor are changes in the knower's physiological or intellectual being the only ones to affect his knowledge. What we know depends also on what, as moral beings, we choose to make ourselves. "Practice," in the words of William James, "may change our theoretical horizon, and this in a two-fold way: it may lead into new worlds and secure new powers. Knowledge we could never attain, remaining what we are, may be attainable in consequence of higher powers and a higher life, which we may morally achieve." (*The Perennial Philosophy* [New York: Harper & Row, 1945], viii)

23. *MS*, 198. See Gardner Murphy and Robert O. Ballou, eds., *William James on Psychical Research* (New York: Viking, 1960). See also chapter 61 of RBP and chapter 12 below.

James was sometimes severe toward critics of psychical research, accusing them of having closed minds. In correspondence with E. B. Titchener, a psychologist at Cornell, James expressed distress over the critics' "unfair" reactions to the Boston medium Mrs. William J. Piper. In a letter of 28 May 1899, Titchener granted that scientists are often closed-minded about psychical research but charged that James was equally so. Titchener spoke for many academics and scientists in writing to James:

> I rather resent the airs of martyrdom that psychical researchers put on. You are perfectly free to work. . . . Your society is very flourishing. . . . We are supposed to have freedom of thought here. But is there any single university in the States where a young instructor could avow himself, even quietly and not blatantly, as a Huxleian agnostic, without suffering for it? . . . Can one avow oneself an atheist as openly as one can avow oneself a Baptist or Congregationalist? There, it seems to me, there is martyrdom. But you do not lose caste, or lose position, because you take up psychical research.

In the same letter Titchener defended Royce and Münsterberg against James's charges of unfairness, remarking that the researcher needs to be in the laboratory and not at medium-sittings: "It may be, too, that R. and M. are annoyed, as I have been, by your reiteration of the thesis that science is now orthodoxy, and that University societies are ruled by the scientific spirit. Surely, surely, this is miles from the actual fact." Part of this letter is reproduced by Daniel W. Bjork, *The Compromised Scientist: William James in the Development of American Psychology* (New York: Columbia University Press, 1983), 94. Chapter 4 of Bjork's book discusses Titchener, whose relationship with James was always uneasy. See also W. B. Pillsbury, "Titchener and James," *Psychological Review* 50 (1943): 71–73.

James conducted experiments in automatic writing with several of his students, including Gertrude Stein. Another student, E. L. Thorndike, who became a distinguished psychologist in his own right, wrote to James on 28 September 1904 and referred to one of his own books, which included curves, figures, and formulas that "would drive you mad." Thorndike compared the book to "the examples of automatic scribbling which you used to show us in a course on abnormal psychology."

Not all established scientists were horrified by James's psychical research. In a letter of 19 March 1908 Jerome D. Greene asked James's advice about a Shinto priest named Suga, who had applied to Greene for the chance to demonstrate before a body of scientific men that he could "walk barefoot over a bed of live coals, or up a ladder, each step of which consists of the up-turned edge of a keen sword-blade. . . . I wonder whether you have heard about him and consider him genuine. . . . Suga's object is to raise money for a temple, and he hopes that after his genuineness is vouched for by a few scientific men he can give public performances for hire. To me, this money-making object is the most suspicious feature of the case." James replied the next day:

> Dear Greene—I can neither investigate Suga, nor advise you. The subject is too complex, and the *physiologists* ought first of all to tackle him. He has been already in communication with some of them at the medical school. I will see Cannon and find out whether they have simply shirked the challenge or found any good positive reason for not accepting it. The bed of embers has to be of *pine* wood (I think) and prepared in certain ways, all which suggests a natural rather than a supernatural type of performance.

Greene's letter and James's response are among the papers of Harvard's President Charles W. Eliot in the Harvard Archives.

24. Bird T. Baldwin, "William James's Contributions to Education," *Journal of Educational Psychology* (2 September 1911): 373–74. See also my introduction to *Talks to Teachers* (Cambridge: Harvard University Press, 1983), xi–xxvii, and Erwin V. Johanningmeier, "Ruminations on the Beginnings of Educational Psychology: William James and the Foundations of a Profession," *Educational Theory* 28 (Spring 1978): 111–19.

25. Letter of 2 May 1932 to Perry, Perry Papers, Harvard Archives.

26. *Talks* (Harvard edition), 114. Where practical, subsequent references to this work are given parenthetically in the text.

27. "The Proposed Shortening of the College Course," *The Harvard Monthly* 11 (January 1891): 132–33.

28. "The True Harvard," *MS*, 352–54. In another essay, "The Ph.D. Octopus," James lamented the trend toward regimentation and "bigness" represented by increasing the requirements for examinations and degrees. "It is indeed odd to see this love of titles—and such titles—growing up in a country of which the recognition of individuality and bare manhood have so long been supposed to be the very soul" (*MS*, 346). See Jack Lindeman, "William James and the Octopus of Education," *School and Society* 98 (October 1970): 365–67.

Bruce Kuklick remarks: "James's critique of the Ph.D. mill is appealing. But the 'manufacture' of new doctorates, their placement in an expanding university system, their movement through the ranks on the basis of technical publications, and the accompanying growth of an academic bureaucracy and its politics did not develop in the steady, planned way that his frequent use of 'machine' suggested. Institutionalized scholarship almost surprised Harvard" (*The Rise of American Philosophy* [New Haven: Yale University Press, 1977], 251–52). See especially Kuklick's sections on James and all of part 5, "Philosophy as a Profession."

29. Quoted in Hans von Kaltenborn, "William James at Harvard," *The Harvard Illustrated Magazine* 8 (February 1907): 94. James wrote in 1906: "But the first thing is to get out of the treadmill of teaching, which I hate and shall resign from next year" (*The Selected Letters of William James*, ed. Elizabeth Hardwick [New York: Farrar, Straus and Cudahy, 1961], 226).

30. William Allan Neilson, "William James as Lecturer and Writer," *The Harvard Illustrated Magazine* 8 (February 1907): 99. See also *LWJ*, 2:11–17.

Samuel Eliot Morison's notes from James's introductory philosophy course in 1906–07 indicate the informality of James's relationship with his students: "This automatism [the doctrine that humans are only automata and that the mind does not interact with the body] was never thought of till this century. Huxley took it up. Willie clings to interaction."

It was not mere informality but James's downright generosity that his students often remembered. In a letter of 7 December 1911 to Henry James III, Thorndike wrote:

> When I was experimenting with chickens and had been denied space in the Agassiz

Museum, and threatened with eviction by my landlady, Prof. James took me and my chicks in; the cellar of his home being given up to my experiments for several months. On another occasion he tried to lend or give me money, I don't remember which. Yet at the time he hardly knew more of me than my name and that I had some devotion as a student.

31. Letter of 24 August 1917 from Dickinson S. Miller to Henry James III. The notes of Clarence Alfred Bunker for James's Philosophy 2 course in 1887–88, dated 4 January 1888, bear this out. James urged that early marriage is more healthful and that the disinclination to it is an unwholesome result of luxury. (Bunker gave no indication that James was making a reference to the fact that he himself was thirty-six when he married.) This view was connected in the lecture with Darwin's elaboration of the idea that the "congress of two persons" is better for the offspring than what would issue from one sex alone. This theory led to a discussion of why the marriage of cousins is ill advised, although James cited a study concluding that Peru had a superior race despite fifty generations of brothers and sisters intermarrying. In England, the lecture continued, no signs of deterioration were evident. But in insane asylums and homes for the deaf and dumb (both of which James had visited for his own studies), the percentage of children of cousins was higher than that in the general population. James recommended various readings and was clearly willing to discuss topics which some professors might have avoided.

32. "The Teaching of Philosophy in Our Colleges" (unsigned), *Nation* 23, no. 586 (1876): 178.

33. W. E. B. DuBois, *Dusk of Dawn: An Essay Toward an Autobiography of a Race Concept* (New York: Harcourt, Brace & Co., 1940), 33, 38. For more on DuBois and Harvard, see idem, *The Education of Black People*, ed. Herbert Aptheker (Amherst: University of Massachusetts Press, 1973), 89; Francis L. Broderick, *W. E. B. DuBois: Negro Leader in a Time of Crisis* (Stanford: Stanford University Press, 1959), especially 30–31; and Elliott M. Rudwick, *W. E. B. DuBois* (Philadelphia: University of Pennsylvania Press, 1960), especially 23, 120–50.

In *Dusk of Dawn*, DuBois noted that it was James who encouraged him to turn from philosophy to history and social science. James had said to him: "If you must study philosophy you will; but if you can turn aside into something else, do so. It is hard to earn a living with philosophy" (39). (DuBois did not indicate whether James said that it had been hard for him to support a family by teaching philosophy.) DuBois also credited James, who was mainly a pre-Freudian, with having prepared him for a Freudian understanding of the irrational and unconscious roots of racial prejudice. When DuBois planned in 1909 to do an "Encyclopaedia Afrikana," he enlisted James and Franz Boas, among others, to serve on his board of advisors. DuBois maintained his friendship with James until James's death.

34. Letter of 3 August 1920 from Horace M. Kallen to Perry, Perry Papers, Harvard Archives.

35. Wilder Penfield, *The Mystery of the Mind* (Princeton: Princeton University Press, 1975), 49n.

Philosophical phenomenologists have played an important part in reviving interest in James. See, for example, James M. Edie, "William James and Phenomenology," *Review of Metaphysics* 23, no. 3 (March 1970): 481–526. Edmund Husserl, a leading figure in the phenomenological movement, admired James; see Herbert Spiegelberg, "What William James Knew About Edmund Husserl: On the Credibility of Pitkin's Testimony," *Life-World and Consciousness: Essays for Aron Gurwitsch*, ed. Lester C. Embree (Evanston: Northwestern University Press, 1972), 407–22.

On James's influence upon Niels Bohr's thinking in physics, see Max Jammer, *The Conceptual Development of Quantum Mechanics* (New York: McGraw-Hill, 1966), 176–79, 349.

36. Letter of 5 November 1906 to Perry, Perry Papers, Harvard Archives. It is odd that James and Santayana considered themselves opposed in their philosophies; in the following passage

from a letter of 18 December 1887 to James, Santayana expressed a view that could easily have been written by James:

> If philosophy were the attempt to solve a given problem, I should see reasons to be discouraged about its success: but it strikes me that it is rather an attempt to express a half-discovered reality, just as art is, and that two different renderings, if they are expressive, far from cancelling each other add to each other's values. The great bane of philosophy is the theological animus which hurries a man towards final and intolerant truths as towards his salvation. . . . Philosophy seems to me to be its own reward, and its justification lies in the delight and dignity of the act itself.

Sidney Hook has speculated that Santayana's attitude toward James was cordial until "Santayana learned about James's judgment of him in 1919 when William James's son (Henry, III) published some of his father's letters. James's phrase 'the perfection of rottenness,' characterizing the standpoint of Santayana's *Life of Reason*, went to the quick of his *amour propre*. From that time on Santayana realized, and expressed it in different ways, that even apart from temperamental differences he and William James were separated by a philosophical abyss" ("William James and George Santayana," *I Carb S.*, 1, no. 1 [Carbondale: Southern Illinois University, Fall–Winter 1973], 39). Nevertheless, the 1906 letter from Santayana to Perry shows that the strain between him and James existed long before 1919.

37. Alfred North Whitehead, *Modes of Thought* (New York: Free Press, 1938), 2. John Jay Chapman described being at Oxford when James gave his lectures for *A Pluralistic Universe* there in 1908:

> It was remarkable to see the reverence which that very unrevering class of men—the University dons—evinced towards James, largely on account of his appearance and personality. The fame of him went abroad, and the Sanhedrin attended. A quite distinguished and very fussy scholar, a member of the old guard of Nil-admirari Cultivation,—who would have sniffed nervously if he had met Moses—told me that he had gone to a lecture of James's "though the place was so crowded, and stank so that he had to come away immediately."—"But," he added, "he certainly has the face of a sage" (*The Selected Writings of John Jay Chapman*, ed. Jacques Barzun [New York: Farrar, Straus and Cudahy, 1957], 206)

Roland Hall has listed Jamesian words such as *feltness, healthy-minded, Hegelism, time-line, pluralism, withness, excusation, pragmatistic,* and *purpurine,* saying: "[These] items have appeared [in James's books], antedating the earliest quotations for these words in the main body of the *Dictionary.* . . . [They] need permanent record so long as no revision of the main body of the O.E.D. is in sight" ("O.E.D. Antedatings from William James," *Notes and Queries* 208 [September 1963]: 341).

William J. Gavin has written several articles on James's linguistic style, including "Vagueness and Empathy: A Jamesian View," *Journal of Medicine and Philosophy* 6 (1981): 45–65; "James's Metaphysics: Language as the House of 'Pure Experience,'" *Man and World* 12 (1979): 142–59; and "William James and the Indeterminacy of Language and 'The Really Real,'" *Proceedings of the Catholic Philosophical Association* 50 (1976): 208–18.

38. F. S. C. Schiller, James's British colleague in pragmatism, wrote seventeen years after James's death: "James, I think, realized when it was too late, what a bad name 'pragmatism' was." In support of his contention, Schiller quoted a letter he had received from James's wife, dated 16 August 1921, in response to his review of *The Letters of William James* in the *Quarterly Review*:

> I have read three times over your beautiful review of the Letters, and cannot tell you how it touches me. You are so much nearer to William than to anyone else, and you speak for

492 NOTES TO PAGE 17

him as he could not for himself. . . . You are right in what you say of confessing to
obligations which he never owed. It used to puzzle me in so strictly truthful a nature. Even
Charles Peirce said to me "I never thought, much less taught, the views William says I did.
I have very different opinions." For years poor C.S.P. had appealed to William for help
until at last he acquired the habit of tugging that poor derelict through troubled wa-
ters. . . . When William was a student in the chemical laboratory, and absorbed in philosophy, he found Charles Peirce a stimulating acquaintance; so when years after William
sought to give a name to the faith he had long held, he glanced backwards and said to
himself, "I must have owed Pragmatism to Peirce." I protested and begged him not to
handicap a cherished belief with so wanton a name. He was sorry afterwards, and preferred Humanism. (Quoted in Schiller's "William James and the Making of Pragmatism,"
The Personalist 8 [April 1927]: 90–91)

The copy of Schiller's article from which I have taken this is in the Houghton Library and was
annotated as follows by Schiller: "She also assured me in it that I was quite right in being
sceptical about the extent of J.'s indebtedness to Peirce. We may take it then that J. *always*
overstated his intellectual debts." Schiller had proposed that James use the term *humanism*
and was thus pleased to have Alice James confirm that his influence was more important than
Peirce's.

Henry James III, in a memo left in the Houghton Library, noted that his father's dedication
of *Principles* to François Pillon was gratuitous, as were most of his expressions of indebtedness
to Chauncey Wright and C. S. Peirce. He noted in the memo that he considered saying as much
in his 1920 edition of his father's letters. "But I was ultimately deterred by the feeling that
there would be a certain disloyalty in my exploding the compliments which my Dad took great
pleasure in paying these friends."

39. Henry James, Sr., "Autobiography," in F. O. Matthiessen, *The James Family: Including
Selections from the Writings of Henry James, Senior, William, Henry, and Alice James* (New York:
Vintage Books, 1980), 17–18. (I owe my appreciation of this quotation and its use here to Saul
Rosenzweig's essay, "William James and The Stream of Thought," in Benjamin B. Wolman,
ed., *Historical Roots of Contemporary Psychology* [New York: Harper & Row, 1968], 163–77).
Sources of relevant biographical information to which I am indebted are Matthiessen, RBP
and Allen.

See also Frederic Harold Young, *The Philosophy of Henry James, Sr.* (New Haven: College and
University Press, 1951): C. H. Grattan, *The Three Jameses: A Family of Minds* (New York:
Longmans, Green, 1932); Henry James, *A Small Boy and Others* (New York: Scribner's, 1913),
and *Notes of a Son and Brother* (New York: Scribner's, 1914); Leon Edel, *Henry James*, 5 vols.
(1953–72; reprint, New York: Avon, 1978); with Intro., *The Diary of Alice James*, ed. Leon Edel
(1964; reprint, New York: Penguin, 1982); Jean Strouse, *Alice James: A Biography* (Boston:
Houghton Mifflin, 1980); Jacques Barzun, *A Stroll With William James* (New York: Harper &
Row, 1983); and, finally, *A William James Renaissance: Four Essays By Young Scholars* (special
issue of the *Harvard Library Bulletin* 30, no. 4 [October 1982]).

40. *The Literary Remains of Henry James* (Boston: J. R. Osgood, 1885), 296–97. This passage
is quoted in Cushing Strout, "The Pluralistic Identity of William James: A Psycho-historical
Reading of *The Varieties of Religious Experience*," *American Quarterly* 23 (May 1971): 145. Strout
has written perceptively and sympathetically in various articles about the life and thought of
William James, and although I question the confidence with which psychohistorians tend to
present their hypotheses, I consider his writings to be invaluable for an understanding of
James's personality. Whereas Allen's biography suggests that James's neuroticism resulted
from typical Victorian sexual repressions, Strout employs neo-Freudian ideas (primarily Erik
Erikson's) to demonstrate the dynamics he infers in the interaction between William James
and his father. See also by Strout: "Ego Psychology and the Historian," *History and Theory* 7
(1968); "William James and the Twice-Born Sick Soul," *Daedalus* 97 (Summer 1968); and

"Pragmatism In Retrospect: The Legacy of James and Dewey," *The Virginia Quarterly Review* 43 (Winter 1968).

41. Young, 65.

42. Allen, 27. See also Henry James, *A Small Boy and Others* and *Notes of a Son and Brother.*

43. Harold D. Lasswell, "Approaches to Human Personality: William James and Sigmund Freud," *Psychoanalysis and the Psychoanalytic Review* 47 (Fall 1960): 65.

44. Letter of 29 July 1889 to his sister, Alice; quoted in RBP, 1:412. Unless otherwise indicated, the biographical data in this section are readily available in Matthiessen, Allen, and RBP.

45. Quoted in RBP, 1:513. Where practical, subsequent references to this work are given parenthetically in the text.

46. *VRE*, 166. Where practical, subsequent references to this work are given parenthetically in the text.

47. Marian C. Madden and Edward H. Madden, "The Psychosomatic Illnesses of William James," *Thought* 54, no. 215 (December 1979): 376–92. The Maddens argue: "James's neuroses were not deep enough to require many of the psychoanalytic explanations given and were too deep to be explained on rational grounds. These inadequacies suggest that environmental and learning factors have been unduly neglected and need to be taken into account along with unconscious suppressions and rational considerations" (377). They also propose that "the most damaging, pervasive lesson that William learned during his rootless and accidental childhood was to make short-term decisions, never long-term ones, to solve problems by changing the scene, and to keep his options open at all costs" (382).

48. This is Elizabeth Hardwick's assessment also. See *The Selected Letters of William James* (New York: Farrar, Straus and Cudahy, 1961), 3. For ample confirmation, see the letters in Perry's chapter "Shall He Become a Painter?" (RBP 1:190–201).

For a different point of view, see Howard M. Feinstein, *Becoming William James* (Ithaca: Cornell University Press, 1984). For anyone interested in the James family and William's place in it, this exercise in psychobiography is essential reading. There is much to recommend in Feinstein's book, which contains considerable information, some of it fresh, about the Jameses. Although the book's subject is ostensibly William, its real topic is the line of influence that Feinstein thinks extended from the grandfather William, through the father, to the younger William, who enters and exits on the stage of Feinstein's study depending upon which members of the extended family occupy the author's attention. The early chapters on the conflict between the grandfather and the father and the later chapters which focus on the Civil War and the younger brothers, Robertson and Garth Wilkinson, are especially valuable. Feinstein includes several reproductions of drawings by William James, which he uses as evidence that the father's influence in steering William toward science rather than painting was largely responsible for the conflicts in William's personality and his successive mental crises.

Feinstein repeats this theory throughout the book, as in this passage: "Though William complied with his father's efforts to cut him off from [William Morris] Hunt and the lure of painting, he was torn by angry feelings that threatened to overwhelm his lighthearted facade. The conflict that was germinating beneath the surface bursts through his drawings" (124). Despite their apparent playfulness, the drawings, according to Feinstein, betray a preoccupation with violence and rage, revealing William's "real feelings" toward his meddling father.

Despite the resourcefulness of Feinstein's case, I am far from convinced. He seems heavy-handed in his interpretations of the drawings and in his attempt to locate the psychological origins of William's ill health in the grandfather's lingering influence and the father's preference that he pursue science rather than art. The reader who is skeptical about the psychoanalytical hypotheses employed and by the fragmentary evidence will certainly be unconvinced. Nevertheless, it can be fascinating to consider James from Feinstein's perspective, even if one wishes the view were advanced more guardedly, for it adds intriguing dimensions to all the other speculations that continue to accumulate.

Feinstein's book focuses primarily on the James family and upon William's development into his twenties. The scholarship is rewarding though not comprehensive; one must still rely on Perry, Allen, and others, and there is no mention, for instance, of the Van Winkle correspondence. Approximately the final fifty pages of Feinstein's book offer a quick but unsatisfactory look at James in his maturity. Feinstein would doubtlessly have found it helpful to have been able to examine William's correspondence with his wife. Nevertheless, Feinstein's book is an important and perceptive work.

49. This point is made by Allen, 21. See also Allen's chapters 3–5.

50. See RBP, 1:200–01.

51. For example, in a letter of 4 September 1857.

52. "But to William this whole episode [school in Paris] in his life was farcical. He thought he was learning nothing of value to him, and he looked upon most of his associates as zanies" (Allen, 43).

53. Rebecca West, *Henry James* (New York: Holt, 1916), 11. For a recent comparison of the thought of the brothers, see Richard A. Hocks, *Henry James and Pragmatistic Thought: A Study in the Relationship between the Philosophy of William James and the Literary Art of Henry James* (Chapel Hill: University of North Carolina Press, 1974). See also note 59 below.

54. Leon Edel, *Henry James*, 5 vols. (New York: Avon, 1978), 1:241. Where practical, subsequent references to this work are given parenthetically in the text.

55. For instance, Edel, 2:154–56.

56. In this letter to Van Winkle, William described Henry (calling him Harry, as was the family habit) as taller and more broad-shouldered and raw-boned than himself. He did not engage in his usual fraternal bantering, however—perhaps because he was thinking seriously about his career.

In the snippet which Henry added to William's letter, something of the Jamesian manner is already apparent.

57. Edel, 5:298. The dates of William's and Henry's arrivals are in Allen, 444. Since Henry was visiting William's Cambridge home on 17 June, when William wrote the letter which allegedly showed his hostility for Henry, Barzun's quarrel with Edel here is not without merit; for instance, Barzun asserts: "When one knows the two men as persons, not cases, it is beyond the bounds of imagination that the day after their reunion William vented his secret spleen behind Henry's visible back in two derogatory adjectives. . . . The likelihood is that William showed or read the letter to [Henry] as they discussed, inevitably, the instant decision not to accept the empty title of academician" (*A Stroll With William James*, 226).

58. Jacques Barzun, who was then president of the National Institute of Arts and Letters, published the letter in full in *The New York Times Book Review* (16 April 1972, 36), in making a case against Edel's interpretation of it. (Edel cited portions of the letter, which he had also seen in the Institute's files, but did not present the full text.) In the same issue of the *Book Review*, Edel argued that the full letter only strengthened his own interpretation (37).

59. *The New York Times Book Review*, 16 April 1972, 37. See also Edel, 5:299. Barzun contends in the *Book Review* that James's letter was playful and ironic. In the same issue, Hilton Kramer sides with Edel, saying that James was "patently dishonest" in writing that the election to the Academy was "the very first call" to vanity that he had entertained (37). Kramer's reading here seems unnecessarily strained.

The Times Literary Supplement also served as a forum for the dispute over this letter. Barzun rejected Edel's interpretation in the issue of 15 September 1972. Edel replied in the October 13 issue, and Lionel Trilling, in the October 20 issue, sided with Barzun: "Leon Edel has radically misinterpreted the letter in which William James refused election to the American Academy of Arts and Letters and has in consequence misrepresented what that document implies of William's feeling for his brother Henry" (1257).

Harry T. Moore refers to William's letter and the controversy surrounding it in *Henry James* (New York: Viking, 1974), 110–11. Philip M. Weinstein is favorably disposed to Edel's Jacob-Esau comparison (although he does not focus on the letter of resignation) and refers to its manifestations in Henry's writings; see his *Henry James and the Requirements of the Imagination* (Cambridge: Harvard University Press, 1971), 110–11. D. W. Jefferson is more skeptical about Edel's depiction of the fraternal relationship; see his *Henry James* (New York: Capricorn, 1971), 101–02.

Louis Auchincloss echoes both Edel's reading of the resignation letter and the Jacob-Esau theme. See his *Reading Henry James* (Minneapolis: University of Minnesota Press, 1975), 82. Richard Hocks begins *Henry James and Pragmatistic Thought* with Edel's interpretation of the letter. Hocks is less interested in the personality problem than in advancing the thesis that the brothers shared a genuine intellectual affinity. Jean Strouse refers to the resignation letter, and her characterization of William leans toward Edel's; see Strouse, 29.

The controversy about the relationship between William and Henry has been heightened by the fact that previous scholars such as Perry and Matthiessen, whose interpretations became more or less the standard view, depicted the relationship in a positive light. Given that view, the Freudian analyses offered by Leon Edel and others were as shocking as they were surprising.

60. Henry knew Johnson, an editor and poet, as their considerable correspondence in the Houghton Library establishes; Johnson edited *Century*, a magazine which published some of Henry's writings.

61. William's unsent letter, which is in the Houghton Library, reads as follows:

Cambridge, June 17, 1905

Dear Mr. Underwood,

Just back from three months in Europe, I find your letter of May 16th., announcing the very flattering news of my election into the Academy of Arts and Letters. I own that my reply gives me terrible searchings of the heart. On the one hand the lust of distinction, and the desire to be yoked in one social bond with so many illustrious names tempt me to say "yes." On the other hand, bidding me say "no," there is my life-long practice of never letting my name figure where there is not definite work to be done for which I am ready to be responsible, and my life long preaching against "the world and its vanities."

I am unable to understand what practical work this "Academy" is to exist for. It suggests *tout soit peu* the notion of an organization for the bare purpose of distinguishing certain individuals, with their own connivance and cooperation, and enabling them to say to the world at large "we are in and you are out." Ought a preacher against vanities to plunge in at the first call? Ought he not rather to "refrain, renounce, abstain," even though it seem a sour and ungenial act? On the whole it seems to me that for a person of my pretensions to philosophy and righteousness the only consistent course is to give up this honour, and treat myself as unworthy, which I assuredly am. And I am the more encouraged to this heroic course by the fact that my younger and vainer brother is already in the Academy, and that the other families represented there might think the James influence too rank and strong.

"Let me go," therefore, I beg you, "return me to the ground." If you knew how much à contre-coeur I pen these duty-inspired lines, you would not deem me unfriendly or ungenial, but only a little cracked.

By the same token, I think that I ought to resign from the Institute, which act I herewith also perform.

Believe me, with longing and regret, heroically yours,

William James

I must credit Mary Chiffriller for helping me to identify this letter and its variations from the one sent. Her contributions to my thinking about the relationship between William James and his family permeate this chapter's discussion.

62. I am grateful to Nancy Johnson, of the American Academy and Institute of Arts and Letters, for permission to see this letter and quote from it, as well as from the resignation letter from James to Johnson. These letters are in the Archives of the American Academy and Institute of Arts and Letters.

63. Letter of 20 April 1902, in *LWJ*, 2:165. William's wife often remarked on his lack of interest in honors, writing on 4 February 1898 to Henry, Jr., about William's election to the Gifford Lectureship: "William takes this with his usual incredible modesty, but he knows in his heart that it really is a great honor. I am delighted beyond measure. I dream of it—o'nights."

64. Resignation was often on James's mind during the final decade of his life. Because of fatigue and illness, he repeatedly said in letters, conversations, and diary entries that he would resign from various responsibilities and decline various honors. He first offered to resign from Harvard in 1903. In January 1905 he received a letter from President Eliot requesting him not to do so. His diary entries during late 1905 indicate his frame of mind: "Oct. 26, 'Resign!' Oct. 28, 'Resign!!!' Nov. 4, 'Resign?' Nov. 7, 'Resign!' Nov. 8, 'Don't resign.' Nov. 9, 'Resign!' Nov. 16, '*Don't* resign!' Nov. 23, 'Resign.' Dec. 7, 'Don't resign.' Dec. 9. 'Teach here next year'" (quoted in RBP, 1:144). Finally, in 1907 he did resign from Harvard.

65. This letter of 1 February 1905, which is in the Massachusetts Historical Society, is quoted in George Monteiro, *Henry James and John Hay: The Record of a Friendship* (Providence: Brown University Press, 1965), 42–43. I am indebted to Monteiro's discussion of the National Institute of Arts and Letters and its membership (40–45), especially because it made me aware of Henry's less than enthusiastic response to his invitation of membership. My observation about Henry's probable attitude toward John Hay and Theodore Roosevelt is taken from Monteiro (42–43).

66. William was a fan of Henry, hardly his constant critic. Early in their careers they seem to have collaborated on "'The Manners of the Day' in Paris" (a review of Ernest Feydeau's *La Comtesse de Chalis*), *Nation* 6 (1868): 73–74. Perry did not list this review in his original bibliography of William's writings. Having discovered it later, Perry wrote on 17 March 1931 to LeRoy Phillips, Henry James's bibliographer, that it had been written by William "although edited by his brother before transmitting it to the Nation. . . . I am interested in knowing the evidence on which you assigned it to Henry James. In a sense I suppose it is a case of joint authorship, but William James was certainly the original author" (Perry Papers, Harvard Archives). Assuming that Perry is correct, we can conclude that William respected Henry's literary style enough to lean upon him editorially. The review is included in Perry's updated bibliography of William's works; see McDermott, 813.

That William's thought may have influenced Henry's writings is argued in Hocks, *Henry James and Pragmatistic Thought;* see notes 53 and 59 above.

There is a widespread view that William James's psychology, especially his concept of the stream of consciousness, influenced literary style, including Henry James's. Daniel Bell assumes this influence on the works of James Joyce, Virginia Woolf, and Gertrude Stein but does not mention Henry James. See Bell's *Cultural Contradictions of Capitalism* (New York: Basic Books, 1976), 113–14. Saul Rosenzweig also refers to the alleged influence of James's stream of thought on Joyce; see his "William James and The Stream of Thought," in *Historical Roots of Contemporary Psychology*, ed. Benjamin B. Wolman (New York: Harper & Row, 1968), 162–77.

For a discussion of the influence of James's psychology on modern American literature, see Ellwood Johnson, "William James and the Art of Fiction," *The Journal of Aesthetics and Art Criticism* 30 (Spring 1972): 285–96. Johnson writes, for example, that "James's psychology marked a turning point in American literary history" (285), and that because of James's psychology there developed "a tendency for American writers to present fictional characters as kinds of experience" (292). Johnson uses William Faulkner as an illustration of his thesis.

Matthiessen thought that there was no connection between Henry's style and William's concept of the stream of consciousness.

> There is a vast difference between James's method and that of the novels of "the stream of consciousness." That phrase was used by William James in his *The Principles of Psychology*, but in his brother's novels there is none of the welling up of the darkly subconscious life that has characterized the novel since Freud. James's novels are strictly novels of intelligence rather than of full consciousness; and in commenting on the focus of attention that he had achieved through Strether, he warned against the "terrible fluidity of self-revelation." ("The Ambassadors," in *The Question of Henry James: A Collection of Critical Essays*, ed. F. W. Dupee [New York: Holt, 1945], 221)

Matthiessen's view provoked a dissenting reply from Maxwell Geismar, who called Matthiessen one of the first antipsychological critics; like Edel, Geismar argued that an unconscious realm of emotion and motivation was indeed revealed by Henry James's fiction. See Geismar, *Henry James and the Jacobites* (Boston: Houghton Mifflin, 1963), 270–71.

Other relevant studies include: Edel, *The Psychological Novel, 1900–1930* (New York: Lippincott, 1955); Melvin Friedman, *Stream of Consciousness: A Study in Literary Method* (New Haven: Yale University Press, 1955); and Erwin R. Steinberg, *The Stream-of-Consciousness Technique in the Modern Novel* (Port Washington, N.Y.: Kennikat Press, 1979).

67. See *Talks*, Harvard edition, 244–66.

68. James Jackson Putnam, "William James," *Atlantic Monthly* 106 (December 1910): 837.

69. Letter of 1883 to Grace Norton, in Leon Edel, ed. *Henry James Letters*, 4 vols. (Cambridge: Harvard University Press, Belknap Press, 1975), 424–25; quoted in Munro Beattie, "Henry James: 'The Voice of Stoicism,'" in *The Stoic Strain in American Literature: Essays in Honour of Marston La France*, ed. Duane J. MacMillan (Toronto: University of Toronto Press, 1979), 63. I am indebted to Beattie's essay for the idea of contrasting Henry and William in this way.

70. I do not presume to assess the possible complexities of Henry's side of the relationship, though I am generally skeptical of Freudian interpretations of the brothers' relationship. Henry certainly retained a remarkable affection for William till the end, whatever may have been its darker aspects. See notes 59 and 66 above.

71. Robertson's paintings in the Concord, Massachusetts, Public Library, are creditable achievements. I wish to thank Marcia E. Moss, curator at that library, for showing me the paintings.

Henry James, Jr., commented on the talent for painting throughout generations of Jameses: "It was an odd enough circumstance, in respect to the attested blood in our veins, that no less than three of our father's children, with two of his grandsons to add to these, and with a collateral addendum representing seven, in all, of our grandfather's, William James's, descendants in three generations, should have found the artistic career in general and the painter's trade in particular irresistibly solicit them" (*Notes of a Son and Brother*, 45). The artistic talent of the Jameses, even today, is being researched by Dr. Roberta Sheehan, who is interested in documenting the Boston art world, including the contributions of several generations of Jameses.

72. Letter of 16 May 1878, written on stationery of the North Chicago Rolling Mill Company in Milwaukee, Wisconsin, where Wilky was employed. Wilky's dying was a pathetic family process; see Allen, 270.

73. Letter of 2 February 1897, written on stationery of the Sanatorium, which was described thus: "The Jackson Sanatorium: Health By Right Living."

74. In addition to the more authoritative and standard biographies, see *Alice James: Her Brothers, Her Journal*, ed. Alice Robeson Burr (New York: Dodd, Mead, 1934), which includes discussions of Robertson and Wilky.

75. These remarks about Jean Strouse's *Alice James: A Biography* (Boston: Houghton

Mifflin, 1980) occur in Linda Blanken, "The Jamesian Genius: Alice James," *Humanities* 4 (August 1983): 18. Where practical, subsequent references to Strouse's work are given parenthetically in the text. See also Edel, ed., *The Diary of Alice James* (New York: Penguin, 1982), and Ruth Bernard Yeazell, ed., *The Death and Letters of Alice James* (Berkeley and Los Angeles: University of California Press, 1981).

76. *LWJ*, 1:311. For more on the relation between William and his sister Alice, see RBP, 1:411–22; and for a different view of William's response to Alice's dying, see RBP, 2:280.

77. Letter of 17 January 1900 to Elizabeth Glendower Evans. This letter is in the Schlesinger Library, Radcliffe College.

78. In a letter of 6 November 1911 to Henry James III, Sarah Harney Porter reminisced about William, referring to a summer night in Keene Valley, New York, when William had talked about his wife and all that she meant to him. There are numerous examples of such praise for Alice in James's correspondence.

79. The letters are dated 11 June 1888 and 24 May 1889. This praise of Santayana may surprise readers acquainted with James's description in 1900 of Santayana's philosophy as the "perfection of rottenness" (*LWJ*, 2:122). On 22 April 1888, William wrote to Alice: "This A.M. came an essay from Santayana. . . . The whole thing quite characteristic. Very exquisite, but too much like a poem."

80. The second quote is from a letter of 25 January 1883, the first from a postcard dated July 3, the year of which has been lost. It may have been 1880.

81. These letters were written 29 and 30 September 1887; the second was occasioned by Hall's not sharing James's enthusiasm for investigating the alleged mediumistic abilities of Piper.

82. James frequently visited his affluent friend George Dorr, of Bar Harbor, Maine. Dorr was interested in psychical research and sometimes hosted James, Richard Hodgson, and others. I am grateful to the Bar Harbor Public Library for showing me newspaper articles which announced the visits of James, treating him like a celebrity.

83. Letter of 2 September 1898 from Berkeley, California. This letter is in the Schlesinger Library, Radcliffe College.

Two years later both William and Alice were writing from France to Evans. Once, they both wrote on the same day, 17 January 1900, and Alice's message was that William had suffered a "complete nervous break-down which naturally has aggravated all the cardiac symptoms."
William's letter of the same day included this:

> My sense of your value was so much greater than almost anybody else's—though I wouldn't have anything in this construed prejudicial to Fanny Morse. Bowed as I am by the heaviest matrimonial chains, ever dependent for expression on Alice here, how can my spirit move with perfect spontaneity, or "voice itself" with the careless freedom it would wish for in the channels of its choice? I am sure you understand, and under present conditions of communication anything more explicit might be imprudent. She has told you correctly all the outward facts. I feel within a week past as if I might really be taking a turn for the better, and I know you will be glad. (*LWJ*, 113)

Henry III included this in his edition of his father's letters, because he thought it was simply a discrete letter in which William did not want to reveal to Evans how sick he had been, for fear of such a message being reported back to Alice and upsetting her. He probably thought William had spared Alice some knowledge of what he had endured during this part of 1900, although her letter to Evans shows that she was not spared much of anything.

The reference to Fanny Morse, another friend of William's and Alice's, would seem to eliminate any suspicion that this is a love letter. On the other hand, given his earlier letter to Evans, one wonders just what led Williams to say that because of Alice's presence he could not write freely. Whatever may have been the nature of Evans's attractiveness to James, I continue to think that they shared a warm friendship and no more.

84. The description of Alice Gibbens James's "hysterical" behavior occurs in the diary of Theodora Bosanquet, the secretary of Henry, Jr. See H. Montgomery Hyde, "Henry James and Theodora Bosanquet," *Encounter* 39, no. 4 (October 1972): 6–12.

85. This advice was appended to a letter of 25 November 1899, begun by William, in which both he and Alice persuaded Henry III not to take a certain job in Cuba.

Alice may have been sympathetic with nineteenth-century feminists, since she first met her father-in-law at the Radical Club and seems to have held her own entrenched opinions, as this letter shows. There is no evidence, however, that she ever belonged to anything like the Cambridge Cooperative Housekeeping Society, the members of which "charged their husbands for clean laundry and for cooking and serving food. Some of the husbands included famous literary figures of the day—including Charles Sanders Peirce, the philosopher, and William Dean Howells, the novelist. The experiment lasted three years" (Suzanne Slesin, "Household Planning By Early Feminists," *The New York Times*, 19 March 1981, C10).

I have not suggested that Alice James had a special intellectual influence upon her husband, beyond her shared interest in religion and psychical research. But Horace M. Kallen, who took his Ph.D. with James and knew him perhaps as well as anyone ever did, wrote in his review of Perry's *TCWJ*:

> [Alice] was not only the exemplary wife and mother that Perry properly appreciates (Chapter XXI, 375–76); she exercised a very positive intellectual influence on her husband's life. I am inclined to believe that the unconscious redirection of William's thought toward that of Henry the Elder's [William's father] would scarcely have gone as far as it did without the conscious as well as continuous reaction upon it of Alice James; that her role in the mutations of William's thought was far greater than that of many correspondents to whom Perry gives chapters" ("Remarks on R. B. Perry's Portrait of William James," *Philosophical Review* 46 [January 1937]: 78).

Kallen may be right, especially in the last sentence quoted here, but there is no evidence for his claim that Alice influenced James's philosophy and psychology. James never expressly credited his wife with any of his intellectual insights, and he was unusually generous toward those whom he credited with influence.

Taking Kallen's line more recently are Marian C. Madden and Edward H. Madden, "The Psychosomatic Illnesses of William James," *Thought* 54, no. 215 (December 1979): 391; and Mark R. Schwenn, "Making the World: William James and the Life of the Mind," *Harvard Literary Bulletin* 30, no. 4 (October 1982): 442–43.

86. Dorothy Rieber Joralemon (the painter's daughter), "Too Many Philosophers," *American Heritage* 31, no. 6 (October/November 1980): 17. This briefly recounted episode gives an entertaining insight into this group of Harvard philosophers.

87. Samuel Delano described James thus in a letter of 3 October 1929 to Perry (Perry Papers, Harvard Archives).

88. Barzun calls James a gentleman in *A Stroll With William James*, 272–76. The note is from James's scrapbook, labeled "J," in the Houghton Library; "God is no gentleman" occurs in *Pragmatism*, 40.

Barzun's book, which has been described as a "worshipful" tribute to James, is helpful not only in portraying James as a personality but also in showing him vividly against the backdrop of his times. See Alfred Kazin's review in *The New York Review*, 10 November 1983, 3–6.

89. This story was told by H. G. Wells in his *Experiment in Autobiography* and is quoted in Charles Compton, *William James: Philosopher and Man* (New York: Scarecrow Press, 1957), 194–95; for another amusing episode of James as a nongentleman, see the description quoted from Logan Pearsall Smith in Compton, 182–83. Where practical, subsequent references to Compton's work are given parenthetically in the text.

90. W. R. Sorley wrote to Perry on 1 February 1935 that Bradley was unknown personally to few people outside Oxford, and that even at Oxford he lived a "retired" existence; it was

thus not likely that a photo of Bradley could be secured for inclusion in *TCWJ*. "I remember William James telling me with much surprise how Schiller took him along to the door of Bradley's room in Merton (not New College) and when James said 'Won't you come in' he got the reply 'I don't know him'" (Perry Papers, Harvard Archives).

91. I base these remarks on entries in James's diaries from 1907–10. President Eliot's response of "preposterous" is recorded on 18 February 1907.

92. Unsigned manuscript in the Houghton Library. This review of Thomas Huxley's *Lectures on the Elements of Comparative Anatomy* was published in an 1865 issue of the *North American Review*, as was James's review of Alfred Wallace's *Origin of Human Races*. These two items should be added to McDermott's bibliography, which begins with 1867.

93. Letter of 14 February 1907, in *LWJ*, 2:264. For a classic example of William's style, see a letter to his brother Henry in which he criticizes Henry's "third manner" of fictional writing (*LWJ*, 2:277–79).

94. Henry James III, "Remarks on the Occasion of the Centenary of William James," *In Commemoration of William James (1842–1942)* (New York: Columbia University Press, 1942), 4.

95. William Allan Neilson, "William James as Lecturer and Writer," *The Harvard Illustrated Magazine*, VIII (February 1907), p. 99.

On William James as literary stylist, see Van Wyck Brooks, *Sketches in Criticism* (New York: Dutton, 1932).

96. *Principles*, 1:628; "A Word More About Truth," *The Journal of Philosophy, Psychology and Scientific Methods*, 18 July 1907, 404.

97. Letter of 18 April 1928 to Perry (Perry Papers, Harvard Archives). An example of James's larking is the partly tongue-in-cheek essay "On Some Hegelisms," which some of his contemporaries regarded as being not only frivolous but in bad taste.

98. Morton White, for example, mentions this in his review of Allen's biography; see "The Lives of Philosophers," *Perspectives in American History* 3 (1969): 491. White reacts negatively to Allen's attempt to write a biography without drawing upon philosophy or psychology. White has tended to be dissatisfied over the years with Jamesian scholarship; in another instance, he complained that A. J. Ayer's *Origins of Pragmatism* was written with almost no reference to the voluminous literature about James.

99. "The Energies of Men," *The Philosophical Review* 16 (January 1907): 3–4. See also chapter 14.

100. Quoted in RBP, 1:323. See also Perry's chapter 19.

101. See Madden and Madden.

102. *Principles*, 1:655; see RBP, chapters 41–43. A stronger and more effective exposition of James's indebtedness to Renouvier is Wilbur Harry Long, "The Philosophy of Charles Renouvier and Its Influence on William James (Ph.D. diss., Harvard University, 1925). Apparently the only copy available is in the Hoose Library of Philosophy at the University of Southern California, to which I am grateful for being permitted to see that copy. Long points out that James was impressed by Renouvier's "moral heroism," his indifference to prevailing opinion, and his refusal to accept the increasingly popular materialistic philosophy (22). I mention this because it supports my line of argument in the text. It was also characteristic of James to find his chief influence in a continental figure mostly unknown to his colleagues.

103. Quoted in RBP, 1:514; italics mine. James William Anderson also notes this, although he offers his own interpretation of James's personality, "'The Worst Kind of Melancholy': William James in 1869," *Harvard Library Bulletin* 30, no. 4 (October 1982): 378. Anderson is concerned with James's low period in 1869, preceding the 1870 depression. See also the essays by Robert J. Richards, Mark R. Schwenn, and Eugene Taylor in this issue of the *Harvard Library Bulletin*.

104. I am indebted to Carleton Sprague Smith's presentation of this account; see his "William James in Brazil," in *Four Papers Presented in the Institute for Brazilian Studies* (Nashville: Vanderbilt University Press, 1951), 137.

105. We must keep in mind the physiological aspects of James's illnesses in assessing James William Anderson's statement that James's medical records are in the McLean Hospital in Belmont, Massachusetts, formerly the McLean Asylum in Boston. Because the authorities there will not release those records, Anderson cannot determine when or under what circumstances they got there. He assumes that James was a patient at the asylum, but because James was a member of the Boston medical community, I believe that he might well have had tests or treatments there, provided by friends on an outpatient basis. Other than Anderson's claim, I know of no reference to James's involvement with the McLean Asylum. See Anderson, 386. This kind of speculation is encouraged by what Nathan G. Hale, Jr., has written about McLean Hospital in *Freud and the Americans* (New York: Oxford University Press, 1971), 152–53. Hale notes that McLean was called the "richest and most elegant" mental hospital in the world. Moreover, its director, Edward Cowles, had been influenced by William James's ideas, including the notion that forms of insanity may have a psychosomatic rather than a hereditary or organic basis. Cowles tried to show in his laboratory that stress and fatigue can cause autointoxication of the nervous system. He was also interested in James's idea that obsessions may result from a deficiency in the capacity for attentiveness. Cowles, as Hale puts it, was a historical link between the "moral treatment" of mental illness and later psychiatry and psychoanalysis. For a historical account of the McLean Hospital and its relation to its parent institution, Massachusetts General Hospital, see Francis R. Packard, *History of Medicine in the United States*, 2 vols. (New York: Paul B. Hoeber, 1931), 1:265–69.

106. The manuscript of these lectures is in the Houghton Library; see pt. 5, p. 42. See also Eugene Taylor, "William James on Psychopathology: The 1896 Lowell Lectures on 'Exceptional Mental States,'" *Harvard Library Bulletin* 30 (October 1982): 455–79.

Taylor has made a remarkable reconstruction of James's 1896 Lowell Lectures in *William James on Exceptional Mental States* (New York: Charles Scribner's Sons, 1982, 1983). James's lecture notes are so fragmentary that an enormous amount of painstaking research was required to fill in the content. Taylor's reconstruction is especially valuable in adding to our knowledge of what James said on genius and mental degeneration and such recherche topics as witchcraft and demonic possession. Taylor comes to interesting conclusions in his reconstruction. For example, "James was inexorably drawn to the conclusion that it was 'not the witches, but the victim's accusers who were insane, possessed persons'" (125). Especially provocative is this: "The degenerate now injects a 'metaphysics' into his mental operations, James tells his audience, an 'infinite *Grübelsucht'*—the metaphysical tendency to brood on subtleties, which James himself admitted he had suffered from in the late 1860s" (139). (If we broaden this idea so that pathology and degeneration are not involved, it resembles Wittgenstein's notion that certain metaphysical preoccupations are obsessive and constitute deep "cramps" within the psyche.) In interpreting one of James's notes on genius, Taylor writes: "James's meaning here is clear: that inner events in any form are denigrated to the level of pathology by the normal, externally oriented, predominantly verbal attitude of medical science" (151).

Taylor's reconstruction is also valuable for what it reveals about James's readings in abnormal psychology. Much of what Taylor has done is to show what James recounted to his audience from the various sources he had been reading. In Taylor's version, James added very little to what he had already written earlier, particularly in *Principles*. The concept of the unconscious or subliminal, for instance, was not developed beyond the speculations offered in *Principles*, and nothing like Freud's ambitious formulation of it was attempted. Hence Taylor's reconstruction does not supply a link between *Principles* and such later works as *The Varieties of Religious Experience*, despite his claim that it does. As popular lectures, they are interesting in revealing James's attitude in greater depth towards the history of witchcraft, for example, but, for theoretical content, they tend simply to repeat earlier publications.

107. See, for example, Erikson, Strouse, and Rosenzweig.

108. *A Small Boy and Others*, 68; quoted in Matthiessen, 72.

109. James added this in the margin of the original page of notes about optimism and pessimism; the page was included in a letter of 7 June 1877.

110. Letter of 31 July 1896(?). See also Allen, 165.

111. The "heroism" of James has been noted by Perry (RBP, 2:270–74), Hardwick, xiv, and Barzun, 268–76.

2. CONSCIOUSNESS

1. *Principles,* 1:1. In the abridged version of *Principles,* James was more explicit that his own writing was confined to the study of human mental life: "Let it also be added that the *human mind is all that can be touched upon* in this book. Although the mental life of lower creatures has been examined into of late years with some success, we have no space for its consideration here, and can only allude to its manifestations incidentally when they throw light upon our own" (*Psychology: Briefer Course* [New York, Holt, 1913], 3). Where practical, subsequent references to this work are given parenthetically in the text.

2. *Psychology,* 6.

3. See, for instance, *Human Immortality: Two Supposed Objections to the Doctrine* (Boston: Houghton Mifflin, 1898).

4. See "Does 'Consciousness' Exist?" in *ERE.*

5. "[Psychology] gains absolutely nothing by a breach with common-sense in this matter, and she loses, to say the least, all naturalness of speech" (*Principles,* 1:137).

6. James cited Shadworth H. Hodgson as having declared in 1870 that feelings have no causal efficacy whatever. Hodgson compared feelings to "colors laid on the surface of a mosaic, of which the events in the nervous system are represented by the stones. Obviously the stones are held in place by each other and not by the several colors which they support" (*Principles,* 1:130). Besides Hodgson, James cited T. H. Huxley and W. K. Clifford as being advocates of the epiphenomenalistic or "conscious automata" theory of mental states. Much the same view is proposed today by B. F. Skinner in *About Behaviorism* (New York: Random House, 1974).

7. *Principles,* 1:141. This view of consciousness as a source of selectivity and interests was formulated by James prior to writing *Principles.* It is either explicitly or implicitly present in a number of reviews published in 1875 and 1876, as well as "Remarks on Spencer's *Definition of Mind as Correspondence," Journal of Speculative Philosophy* 12 (1878): 1–18; "Quelques considérations sur la méthode subjective," *Critique philosophique* 2 (1878): 407–13; and especially "Are We Automata?" *Mind* 4 (1879): 1–22.

8. "Human Immortality: Two Supposed Objections to the Doctrine," in *WTB,* 17–18.

9. "For twenty years past I have mistrusted 'consciousness' as an entity; for seven or eight years past I have suggested its nonexistence to my students, and tried to give them its pragmatic equivalent in realities of experience. It seems to me that the hour is ripe for it to be openly and universally discarded" ("Does 'Consciousness' Exist?" in *ERE,* 4). This essay originally appeared in 1904, so 1884 would seem to be when his serious doubts about Cartesian dualism originated. The year 1884 saw the publication of two essays, "What Is an Emotion?" and "On Some Omissions of Introspective Psychology," both of which bring into question the alleged irreducibility of mental and physical processes. It can be argued that these two essays are the key ones directing James toward the metaphysics of radical empiricism. For a helpful discussion, see Andrew J. Reck, "Dualisms in William James's 'Principles of Psychology,'" *Tulane Studies in Psychology* 21 (1972): 23–38.

10. "Remarks on Spencer's *Definition of Mind as Correspondence,"* in *CER,* 64.

11. Throughout his life James wrote about consciousness in a way that invites the interpretation that it is an entity or process of some sort. For example, he wrote in "A Suggestion About Mysticism":

Transmarginal or subliminal, the terms are synonymous. Some psychologists deny the existence of such consciousness altogether (A. H. Pierce, for example, and Münsterberg apparently). Others, e.g., Bergson, make it exist and carry the whole freight of our past. Others again (as Myers) would have it extend (in the "telepathic" mode of communication) from one person's mind into another's. For the purpose of my hypothesis I have to postulate its existence; and once postulating it, I prefer not to set any definite bounds to its extent. (*CER*, 502–03)

12. *Principles*, 1:201. See also 1:455–58.

13. Sigmund Freud, *An Autobiographical Study* (New York: Norton, 1963), 59. See also Freud's *Five Lectures on Psycho-Analysis* (New York: Norton, 1977), 21–22, 25–26.

14. "The Knowing of Things Together," in *CER*, 372. This passage recalls the discussion in *Principles*, 1:158–62.

15. *Principles*, 1:301–02. This passage occurs in chapter 10, "The Consciousness of Self," written in 1886, two years after "On Some Omissions of Introspective Psychology." The latter essay is the basis for chapter 9, "The Stream of Thought," so the apparent change in emphasis from the nonphysiological stream in chapter 9 to the physiological one in chapter 10 indicates a change in viewpoint between 1884 and 1886. Once he had called attention to what introspective psychology had overlooked—relations, intentions, nonlinguistic states of understanding—James returned to the main idea of "What Is an Emotion?" and concluded that nothing in emotional experience is decisively nonphysiological. It is as if the psychological nature of the stream of consciousness is retained in chapter 9 from "On Some Omissions of Introspective Psychology," whereas the physiological character of the stream is retained in chapter 10 from "What Is an Emotion?" Thus a shift in viewpoint can be seen between 1884 and 1886 only if one of the two essays is assumed to be more important than the other.

16. See, for instance, "Does 'Consciousness' Exist?" in McDermott, 180.

17. "The Knowing of Things Together," in *CER*, 372. Since I stress the change of position from *Principles* to this essay, I must mention that the footnote in *Principles* 1:158 concludes thus: "The entirely new taste [of lemonade] which is present *resembles*, it is true, both these tastes [sour and sweet]; but . . . resemblance can not always be held to involve partial identity." Since he said virtually the same thing in the 1895 essay, it may appear that I am inventing a change of position. He says there: "The sour and sweet in lemonade are extremely unlike the sour and sweet of lemon juice and sugar, singly taken, *yet like enough for us to 'recognize' these 'objects' in the compound taste*" (*CER*, 398; italics mine). The change of position is contained in the italicized phrase; the new idea is that the state of consciousness that is the taste of lemonade is a complex compound whose elements include smaller units of consciousness such as the taste of sweet and the taste of sour.

James invited the quarrel that he later had with F. H. Bradley by arguing that resemblance between things does not presuppose the existence of something identical in them. To have allowed in *Principles* that resemblance presupposes identity would have required, in the case of conscious states, an adoption of the mind-stuff theory that he explicitly rejected in chapter 6. On the other hand, since he continued to hold this view on the nature of resemblance even after abandoning his opposition to the mind-stuff theory, he obviously thought it worth defending on other grounds as well (see chapter 3).

18. "Does Consciousness Exist?" in McDermott, 172.

19. "The Notion of Consciousness," in McDermott, 189.

20. Bertrand Russell, *The Analysis of Mind* (London: Allen & Unwin, 1949), 24.

21. "*Human Immortality: Two Supposed Objections to the Doctrine*," in *WTB*, 23.

22. *Principles*, 1:185. As early as 1873, in a diary entry dated 10 April, James wrote: "You can't divorce psychology from introspection, and immense as is the work demanded by its purely objective physiological part, yet it is the other part rather for which a professor thereof is expected to make himself publicly responsible."

23. John Locke, *An Essay Concerning Human Understanding*, bk. 2, chap. 2.

24. I argue this in "Introspection and Self-Knowledge," in a forthcoming issue of *The American Philosophical Quarterly*.

25. *Principles*, 1:189–90. This is a virtual reproduction of what James wrote in "On Some Omissions of Introspective Psychology," *Mind* 33 (1884): 1–2. Gilbert Ryle also drew a distinction between merely having a feeling and introspecting it; see his *The Concept of Mind* (London: Hutchinson & Co., 1949), chapter 6.

26. *Principles*, 1:190. James's grounds for identifying introspection-as-observation with retrospection differ from Ryle's. Whereas James thought a time lapse separated observed and observing, Ryle argued that there are no mental states to serve as the inner objects of introspection.

27. *Principles*, 1:195. James added in a note: "In English we have not even the generic distinction between the thing-thought-of and the-thought-thinking-it, which in German is expressed by the opposition between *Gedachtes* and *Gedanke*, in Latin by that between *cogitatum* and *cogitatio*."

28. See *Principles*, 1:234.

29. To attempt such an explanation here would be tangential, but I have sketched a plausible approach to the topic in "Feelings Into Words," *The Journal of Philosophy*, 19 December 1963, 801–11.

30. When phenomenologists point out a phenomenological strain in James, they sometimes argue that his reliance upon introspection must be modified if genuine phenomenology is to be achieved. See, for instance, James M. Edie, "The Genesis of a Phenomenological Theory of the Experience of Personal Identity: William James on Consciousness and the Self," *Man and World* 6 (September 1973): 322–40.

Other writings that connect James to phenomenology include: Herbert Spiegelberg, *The Phenomenological Movement* (The Hague: Nijhoff, 1960); Johannes Linschoten, *On the Way Toward a Phenomenological Analysis: The Psychology of William James*, ed. Amedeo Giorgi (Pittsburgh: Duquesne University Press, 1968); Bruce Wilshire, *William James and Phenomenology* (Bloomington: Indiana University Press, 1968); John Wild, *The Radical Empiricism of William James* (Garden City, N.Y.: Doubleday, 1969); Ash Gobar, "The Phenomenology of William James," *Proceedings of the American Philosophical Society* 114 (August 1970): 294–309; D. C. Mathur, *Naturalistic Philosophies of Experience: Studies in James, Dewey, and Farber Against the Background of Husserl's Phenomenology* (Saint Louis: Warren H. Green, 1971); and Richard Stevens, *James and Husserl: The Foundations of Meaning* (The Hague: Nijhoff, 1974). See also Lester Embree, "The Phenomenology of Speech in the Early William James," *Journal of the British Society for Phenomenology* 10, no. 2 (May 1979): 101–09. This essay focuses on James's concept of speech from a phenomenological perspective. Embree's references to phenomenological literature about James are also helpful.

31. For example: "The whole mind-stuff controversy would stop if we could decide conclusively by introspection that what seem to us elementary feelings are really elementary and not compound" (*Principles*, 1:191). Whether James was always consistent in refusing to declare his philosophical position on introspection is controversial. At times his defense of the *esse est sentiri* doctrine relies almost exclusively on introspection. But he later abandoned the *esse est sentiri* doctrine, deciding that mental states can compound. The earlier introspective evidence for the doctrine was overruled by subsequent arguments.

32. See *Principles*, 1:225.

33. *Principles*, 1:271. The preceding pages of *Principles* give textual details of what I have been describing here. Certain ideas that are introduced here are discussed later; for instance, thought and language and the concept of the fringe are taken up in chapter 9, and the topic of relations is considered in chapter 11.

34. James appreciated that he might be accused of seeming to say both that consciousness can sometimes feel discontinuous and that it must by nature feel continuous. "If the words

'chain' and 'train' had no natural fitness in them [for describing how consciousness seems to feel], how came such words to be used at all?" (*Principles*, 1:139). His answer was that this objection is based partly on a confusion between consciousness and its objects and partly on superficial or sloppy introspections (*Principles*, 1:140).

James realized that his distinction between preintrospective experiencing and the introspective observation of that experiencing was not always understood. In a letter of 30 September 1884 to Renouvier, for instance, he had to make a special point of it.

> But before it is reflected on [introspected], consciousness is *felt*, and as such is continuous, that is, it potentially allows us to make sections anywhere in it, and treat the included portion as a unit. It is continuous as space and time are. And I am willing to admit that it is not a *chose en soi*, for this reason, if you like, any more than they. But as we divide *them* arbitrarily, so I say our divisions of consciousness are arbitrary results of conceptual handlings of it on our part. The ordinary psychology, on the contrary, insists that it is naturally discrete and that the divisions *belong* in certain places. This seems to me like saying that space exists in cubes or pyramids, apart from our construction.

This letter was written in the same year as "On Some Omissions of Introspective Psychology"—the essay that formed the basis of "The Stream of Thought" chapter in *Principles*—indicating that the distinction between preintrospective feeling and introspective observation was crucial to James's initial treatment of introspection.

The reference in this letter to the "arbitrary results of conceptual handlings" brings up a special problem: James held in his later metaphysics that conceptualization of the stream of events is necessarily an arbitrary dissection, such that a distortion occurs in the conceptualization. Since James saw introspection as a process of observation and reporting that clearly involves classification and conceptualization, it is not clear whether he thought introspection necessarily dissects and distorts the stream of consciousness, whether it fails to record adequately what the stream is like. Is accurate introspective observation really possible?

35. Quoted in *Principles*, 1:245.

36. This is the thirty-ninth of forty-four questions, criticisms, and comments that Peirce wrote in a bluebook as he read the first volume of *Principles;* the bluebook is in the Peirce Collection at Harvard. I am indebted to Max Fisch for allowing me to consult it some years ago. Query 39 is included in RBP, 2:108.

George S. Brett made a point similar to Peirce's, although it is intended to apply to James's philosophy more generally. He noted James's tendency to discuss one's sense of reality instead of reality itself, while tending to infer the latter from the former. See Brett, "The Psychology of William James in Relation to Philosophy," in *In Commemoration of William James* (New York: Columbia University Press, 1942), 83–84.

37. "The Refutation of Idealism," *Mind* n.s. 12 (1903): 450.

3. SENSATION AND PERCEPTION

1. *Principles*, 2:9–10. James quotes book 3, chapter 2 of Ralph Cudworth's *Treatise Concerning Eternal and Immutable Morality*.

2. *Principles*, 1:254. His unpublished notes include the statement:

> Pure sensation is the vague. It has to be discriminated or analyzed into different qualities. For this *attention* seems necessary. . . . And a discriminatory attention does not seem possible without some *discriminating* interest on the subject's part; i.e., some quality strikes him more than others as pleasant or unpleasant. Thus for any distinct sensation to occur there must be discriminating reaction on the subject's part, and apperception involving the use of concepts.

This note bears no date but has been placed, perhaps by Perry, in folder #4465 alongside notes for "The Sentiment of Rationality." Since that article originally appeared in 1879, this note may indicate that this key doctrine in Jamesian psychology was formulated before *Principles*. James consistently held that perception and distinct sensation "bloom" out of a "buzzing confusion" or conglomeration of vague sensations.

3. *Principles*, 2:5–6. In a review of George T. Ladd's *Physiological Psychology* (*Nation* 44 [1887]: 473), James first claimed that sensations are cognitive. This review may have been written at the time he was formulating his ideas on sensation for *Principles*. See chapters 10 and 11 for a critical discussion of this claim and of James's concept of knowledge by acquaintance.

4. *Principles*, 2:33n and 2:31. The quotation of Schopenhauer is from *Satz vom Grunde*, that of Ladd from *Physiological Psychology*.

5. See, for example, Edwin G. Boring, *Sensation and Perception in the History of Experimental Psychology* (New York: Appleton-Century-Crofts, 1942). See also Boring's *History, Psychology, and Science*, ed. Donald Campbell and Robert Watson (New York: John Wiley, 1963), 103–04. For Perry's discussion of Jamesian nativism, see RBP, 2:80–87.

6. See, for example, *Principles*, 1:487 and 2:3. This conviction led James to begin *Principles* not with a discussion of sensations, which come only after the analysis of experiences, but instead with an account of experiences (stream of consciousness, consciousness of self, etc.) as they occur before philosophical and psychological analysis.

7. See ibid., 2:7–9. This discussion of the purity of sensations clearly anticipates the notion of pure experience that will become the centerpiece of James's radical empiricism (see chapter 11). The later metaphysics retains both the special idea of purity and the tendency to equate experiences primarily with sensations.

8. This point is elaborated in chapter 11.

9. *Principles*, 1:554. See also, for example, 2:103. Interestingly, this idea is not explicit in the earlier version of the chapter on association in *Principles*, which appeared as "The Association of Ideas," *The Popular Science Monthly*, March 1880, 577–93.

10. *Principles*, 1:488. In addition to his view that sensory experience contains all the "categories of the understanding," James also claimed that the coalescence of sensory data provided for both the "oneness" of space and the "segregation" of objects within space. He presumably believed that his theory of sensations anticipated the kind of objection that Wolfgang Köhler, for example, expressed: "James . . . though attacking atomism in the treatment of experience, clearly fails to recognize natural segregations in the sensory field" (*Gestalt Psychology* [New York: Liveright, 1929], 369). Köhler's remark also qualifies the claim that Gestalt psychology essentially resembles James's.

See also Anthony V. Corello, "Some Structural Parallels in Phenomenology and Pragmatism," in *Life-World and Consciousness: Essays for Aron Gurwitsch*, ed. Lester Embree (Evanston: Northwestern University Press, 1972), 367–88. Corello contends, I believe correctly, that James explicitly provides for field-organizational principles, including those of perceptual organization. James clearly supposed sensory fields to be inherently organizable:

> If a lot of dots on a piece of paper be exhibited for a moment to a person in *normal* condition, with the request that he say how many are there, he will find that they break into groups in his mind's eye, and that whilst he is analyzing and counting one group in his memory the others dissolve. In short, the impression made by the dots changes rapidly into something else. In the *trance-subject*, on the contrary, it seems to *stick;* I find that persons in the hypnotic state easily count the dots in the mind's eye so long as they do not much exceed twenty in number. (*Principles*, 1:407n)

Since a sensory field is always conceived as being for a percipient, the condition of the percipient is one of the conditions considered in predicting how a sensory field will be organized. But to admit this is wholly consistent with the claim that sensory fields are inherently organizable—a claim that Köhler may not have recognized to be as strenuous as it actually is in James's philosophy. For example, James also discussed *"all brain-processes such as give rise to what we may call* FIGURED *consciousness"* (*Principles*, 2:82).

11. See "The Perception of 'Things' " and "The Perception of Reality," chapters 19 and 21 of *Principles*, and "Pragmatism and Humanism," lecture 7 in *Pragmatism*.

12. For more on this view, see chapter 11.

13. *Principles*, 2:80. Roderick Firth has credited this statement with summarizing the percept theory "as concisely as it has ever been stated." See "Sense-Data and the Percept Theory," *Mind*, 1949, 1950. Reprinted in *Perceiving, Sensing, and Knowing*, ed. Robert J. Swartz (Berkeley: University of California Press, 1965), 204–69.

14. Evidence that James had considerable difficulty writing "The Perception of Reality" is found in letters to his wife Alice. On 15 February 1888 (just over two years before the book was finished) he wrote that he was beginning work on that chapter, and three days later he commented: "The chapter I am on has some intellectual substance in it, so I am at home again. What I can't stand is those chapters of mere compilation." The chapter eventually focused on the concept of belief, as well as one of his favorite ideas, that "the *fons et origo of all reality, whether from the absolute or the practical point of view, is thus subjective, is ourselves,"* so it is understandable that he approached it with a special joy. It is thus surprising—especially since the completed chapter is just forty-one pages long, including many quoted passages—that he wrote to Alice on 25 March that he was rewriting the chapter. He complained that after two months of work at least 150 pages had been discarded. Then on 16 April he wrote: "Completion (!!!) of the chapter . . . tis one of the freshest and most interesting chapters in the book. I begin to feel as if there was more life in the world. The truth is, I have had a fearful sense of impossibility and discouragement and finding the inexplicable slowness with which (so contrary to expectation) the Psychology went on this year."

Because it seemed that of all chapters this should have been an easy one for him to write, I considered briefly the idea that he was referring not to "The Perception of Reality" but to "The Perception of 'Things.' " (Although he used the former name in his letters, he sometimes changed titles or made careless errors.) The latter chapter, almost seventy pages long, with seemingly more complex material, might easily have been frustrating to write. But the problematic chapter was indeed "The Perception of Reality," for it was published under the title "The Psychology of Belief" in *Mind* in 1889, and James explicitly states in *Principles* that this article was the basis of "The Perception of Reality." (Indeed, the essay title seems more appropriate than the chapter title for the revised version that appears in *Principles*.)

The editors of the Harvard edition of *Principles* observe that James mailed the essay "The Psychology of Belief" to *Mind* in November 1888; they, too, discovered his reference to beginning the essay in his letter to his wife on 15 February 1888. They then remark: "When the chapter was completed has apparently not been recorded; however, the normal inference would be that it need not have taken more than a month or two" (*The Principles of Psychology*, 3 vols. [Cambridge: Harvard University Press, 1981], 3:1554). We now know that on 16 April 1888, two months after beginning the chapter, he wrote to his wife that he had at last completed it.

This and many similar facts of dating give a reasonably good picture of when and how James wrote the twenty-eight chapters of *Principles* between 1878 and 1890. It is well known that James felt the pressure of producing a book that had been twelve years in the making; his correspondence with his wife alone testifies to that pressure. His letters in 1888, while he was composing "The Perception of Reality," exhibit restlessness and edginess. For example, on 4 March 1888, when Alice was on an extended stay in South Carolina, he wrote to her that he had spent most of a night reading his old letters to her. Clearly reliving the uncertainties, confusions, and anxieties recalled by the contents of those letters, he wrote: "Oh! The reality of the moral life—that is what all those poor pages with their writhings, and turnings back, and homages to you, *confess.*"

Many such examples of tension appear in James's correspondence at this time; such distractions, coupled with the need to finish *Principles*, hardly allowed him a calm frame of mind. In addition, he and his family were moving into a new, not yet completed house on Irving Street in Cambridge in the autumn of 1889 (see Allen, 311–12).

Consequently, the following account in "The Perception of 'Things'" seems significant:

> High authorities have doubted the power of imagination to falsify present impressions of sense. Yet it unquestionably exists. Within the past fortnight I have been annoyed by a smell, faint but unpleasant, in my library. My annoyance began by an escape of gas from the furnace below stairs. This seemed to get lodged in my imagination as a sort of standard of perception; for, several days before the furnace had been rectified, I perceived the "same smell" again. It was traced this time to a new pair of India rubber shoes. . . . It persisted in coming to me for several days, however, in spite of the fact that no other member of the family or visitor noticed anything unpleasant. My impression during part of this time was one of uncertainty whether the smell was imaginary or real; and at last it faded out. (*Principles*, 2:98–99)

What interests us in this autobiographical report of how imagination can affect perception and sensation is the reference to his library; we can assume this to be the impressive room, often described by visitors, in the new home on Irving Street. Since he did not move into the house until August 1899, he may have been writing "The Perception of 'Things'" as late as a month or two before completing the entire manuscript in May 1890. If so, it is likely that he was composing it under great pressure and as quickly as possible; indeed, it may have been the unidentified chapter that, according to a letter he wrote in March 1890, remained to be written (see the Harvard edition of *Principles*, 3:1558). The footnote reference at the end of the chapter (to an article by F. W. H. Myers, published in 1889) was thus probably included at the time of writing. The somewhat impatient frame of mind in which James may have written about the philosophy of perception in *Principles* was apparently resolved when the book was finished; on 31 July 1890 he wrote to his wife: "Last night at half past eleven under the jaundiced moon-hued sky, I ran out under the apple tree in a state of nature, (after playing the hose on the grass as long as I could) and Coggeshall and Royce played them over me. Very jolly and free—a thing you can't do in term time!—I arose at four and something, read Rudyard Kipling till seven and have been at proofs hammer and tongs all day long with no nap."

James's letters thus support the judgment that he did not work out thoroughly the philosophy (as distinguished from the psychology) of sense-perception in *Principles* or any other writings prior to 1890. Perhaps his most extensive wrestling with the epistemological issues of perception is recorded in the "Miller-Bode" notes (see RBP, appendix 10). But even here the epistemological issues tended to become metaphysical ones. In later discussions of sense-perception, used to defend pragmatism and radical empiricism, he was less concerned with specific epistemological problems than with how sense-perception leads to speculation about the nature of consciousness and of experience in general. In the posthumously published *Some Problems of Philosophy* (1911), the metaphysical relation between concepts and percepts likewise dominates the discussion to the exclusion of epistemological concerns. That we cannot cite *Some Problems of Philosophy* as the final version of James's philosophy of sense-perception is indicated by a letter of 7 April 1911 from Horace M. Kallen—who helped to prepare the manuscript, which James characterized as his "unfinished book," for publication—to Henry James III, William's eldest son, who edited it and added a prefatory note. Kallen wrote:

> I cannot agree with you about the condition of the book. The chapter on Percept and Concept certainly would have had much revision and some complete changes—that I know from conversations your Father and I had just before he left for Europe. . . . I have the feeling that each chapter would have been subjected to considerable revision, in the end. He had a great plan in mind, touching subjects on which he was himself not al-

together certain, and he was experimenting—if our conversations are anything to go by—a good deal by the way. . . . It is a hard way to steer between mis-interpretation and over-literalness, isn't it?

The James collection in the Houghton Library contains a memo by Henry III which shows that Perry was called in to settle a dispute between Kallen and Henry about how best to put the unfinished manuscript into book form. For many reasons, then, *Some Problems of Philosophy* is a hazardous source from which to make definitive interpretations. For more on *Some Problems of Philosophy*, see Peter H. Hare's introduction to the work, vol. 7 of the Harvard edition (Cambridge: Harvard University Press, 1979), xiii–xli. See also the editors' section on the history of its text, 198–207.

15. For a similar statement, see G. J. Warnock, *The Philosophy of Perception* (London: Oxford Press, 1967), 35. Warnock refers to James's position in "The Perception of 'Things'" and to Firth's critical discussion of the percept theory, of which James's position is cited as an example (see note 13 above).

16. See *Principles*, 2:3, 44–48, 103–07, 114–22.

17. Because of the condensed text and more explicit statement of the thesis, the identification of *sensation* with the sensing experience (the act of sensing) and *sensible quality* with the object of sensation is clearer in *Psychology* (13).

18. *Pragmatism*, 68. For my interpretation of the relation between James and Berkeley on perception, see chapter 11. James seemed occasionally to say conflicting things about Berkeley's position. For instance, in the same context in *Pragmatism* he wrote: "So far from denying the external world which we know, Berkeley corroborated it. It was the scholastic notion of a material substance . . . *behind* the external world . . . which Berkeley maintained to be the most effective of all reducers of the external world to unreality" (67). Yet in this book's sequel, *The Meaning of Truth*, he said: "In spite of all berkeleyan criticism, we do not doubt that [external physical realities] are really there" (88). Of course, he may have meant by "berkeleyan" those critics who thought they were following Berkeley's lead but who did not really understand their leader.

Although James always adhered to Berkeley's and Hume's conception of perceptual objects, the difficulties of making that conception consistent caused him at times to confess uncertainty and faltering confidence. Consider, for instance:

There is no *ringing* conclusion possible when we compare these types of thinking [common sense and physical science] with a view to telling which is the more absolutely true. . . . Common sense is *better* for one sphere of life, science for another, philosophic criticism for a third; but whether either be *truer* absolutely, Heaven only knows. . . . We are witnessing a curious reversion to the common sense way of looking at physical nature, in the philosophy of science favored by such men as [Ernest] Mach, [Wilhelm] Ostwald and [Pierre] Duhem. According to these teachers no hypothesis is truer than any other in the sense of being a more literal copy of reality. They are all but ways of talking . . . to be compared solely from the point of view of their *use*. The only literally true thing is *reality;* and the only reality we know is, for these logicians, sensible reality, the flux of our sensations and emotions as they pass. "Energy" is the collective name (according to Ostwald) for the sensations just as they present themselves . . . when they are measured in certain ways. . . . No one can fail to admire the "energetic" philosophy. But the hypersensible entities, the corpuscles and vibrations, hold their own with most physicists and chemists, in spite of its appeal. Profusion, not economy, may after all be reality's keynote. (*Pragmatism*, 125–26)

19. *Principles*, 1:285; see also 2:237–40 and "The Perception of Reality." James thought the distinction between primary and secondary qualities was also, as Berkeley had helped him

to grasp, ultimately an arbitrary one which could not be used to define an absolutely "real" object of perception. See, for instance, *Principles,* 2:305–06.

20. This concept is clear in "The Perception of Reality," one of the last chapters written before the book's publication (see note 14 above). Despite its title, the chapter actually focuses on the psychological sources of one's sense of reality, and for that reason I refer to it more in chapter 10 than here. It connects more integrally with James's pragmatism and theory of knowledge than with the particulars of sense-perception.

George S. Brett described "The Perception of Reality" as "revolutionary." See "The Psychology of William James in Relation to Philosophy," in *In Commemoration of William James* (New York: Columbia University Press, 1942), 90.

21. *Principles,* 2:630–31. The suggestion that the nature of sensations is due more to the brain and physiology than to the character of external objects not only cast doubt upon a simpleminded epistemological dualism, it also set the stage in James's thinking for abolishing dualism altogether and replacing it with radical empiricism (see chapter 11). This view of sensations, while perhaps helping James to move toward radical empiricism, actually presents a problem for the later metaphysics. Mach, for example, defined the subject matter of psychology as everything dependent on the central nervous system, namely, sensations. But James wrote "Decidedly *not*" in the margin of his copy of Mach's *Analyse der Empfindungen.* In James's radical empiricism the key concept of pure experience, explicated in terms of sensations, was the basic, primitive concept, yet the concept fails if sensations are dependent on physiological stimuli. James argued for such dependence in *Principles,* and there is no satisfactory explanation in the later philosophy of why he changed his mind (see RBP, 2:389–90, for the reference to Mach and for Perry's interpretation).

The passage discussed here occurs in the last chapter of *Principles,* "Necessary Truths and the Effects of Experience" (629–88). Later in the same chapter, two pages from the end, James wrote: "I leave my text practically just as it was written in 1885." Save possibly for three pages, then, this chapter was written before such chapters as "The Perception of 'Things' " and "The Perception of Reality," and probably before "Sensation" and "Imagination"—all the chapters in volume two, except the one on the perception of space, that specifically treat sense-perception. The fact that James did not bring his chapters on sensation and perception in volume two explicitly into line with the rejection of epistemological dualism in chapter 28 (written several years earlier) is perhaps further evidence that these chapters were composed hurriedly, under pressure to complete the manuscript.

James's skeptical attitude toward an epistemological dualism—of the kind that conceives veridical perceivings as mental duplicates of the perceived, or the kind that conceives perception as an inner structure resulting from and corresponding to the external world—is a return to a viewpoint James had expressed before undertaking *Principles,* in his "Remarks on Spencer's *Definition of Mind as Correspondence,*" *Journal of Speculative Philosophy* 12 (1878): 1–18.

22. See *Psychology,* 13.

23. Ibid., 13–14.

24. Gilbert Ryle, *Dilemmas* (Cambridge: Cambridge University Press, 1954), 92. For an account of the influences upon James's thinking about sensation and perception as well as of James's different ideas about the subject during his career, see RBP, chapters 33–36, 55–57, 72–74, and 84. A more recent assessment of James on sensation and perception, by a philosopher sympathetic to the phenomenalistic emphasis of James's theories, is found in A. J. Ayer, *The Origins of Pragmatism* (San Francisco: Freeman, Cooper & Co., 1968), 215–24. For a critical response to Ayer's assessment, see Edward H. Madden, "James's 'Pure Experience' versus Ayer's 'Weak Phenomenalism,'" *Transactions of the Charles S. Peirce Society* 12 (1976): 3–17. Finally, for a discussion of James's "natural realism," see Robert G. Meyers, "Natural

Realism and Illusion in James's Radical Empiricism," *Transactions of the Charles S. Peirce Society* 5 (1969): 211–23.

25. The topic of images, while not stressed as much as others in James's writings, was important for him. For example:

> All the medical authors speak of mental blindness as if it must consist in the loss of visual images from the memory. . . . This is a psychological misapprehension. A man whose power of visual imagination has decayed . . . is not mentally blind in the least, for he recognizes perfectly all that he sees. On the other hand, he *may* be mentally blind, with his optical imagination well preserved. In the . . . interesting case of mental blindness . . . the patient made the most ludicrous mistakes, calling for instance a clothes-brush a pair of spectacles, an umbrella a plant with flowers. . . . It is in fact the momentary loss of our non-optical images which makes us mentally blind, just as it is that of our *non*-auditory images which makes us mentally deaf. I am mentally deaf if, *hearing* a bell, I can't recall how it looks; and mentally blind if, *seeing* it, I can't recall its *sound* or its *name*. As a matter of fact, I should have to be not merely mentally blind, but stone-blind, if all my visual images were lost. (*Principles,* 1:50)

And this: "all the different mental operations may be concerned to consist of images of sensation associated together" (ibid., 1:598).

26. Ibid., 2:44.

27. Ibid.

28. Ibid., 2:65–68, 70–71.

29. Ibid., 2:72. This conclusion is interesting because of its bearing upon what was reported to Henry James III by W. B. Cannon (William's colleague at Harvard Medical School and a famous critic of the James-Lange theory of emotions) in a letter of 22 November 1911:

> The law of forward conduction is referred to by [Sir Charles S.] Sherrington in his chapter on the spinal cord, Schaefer's Text-book of Physiology, Vol. 2, p. 785. It is an important conception of nervous action which emphasizes the fact that nerve impulses enter the central nervous system by sensory pathways, go out by motor pathways, and cannot be reversed in direction. This valve-like function in the nerve centres your father called attention to in 1880 in a publication of the Boston Society of Natural History ["The Feeling of Effort"]. Sherrington refers also to Scribner's Magazine, 1888 ["What the Will Effects," of which James wrote to his wife on 29 February 1888: "It certainly seems to have more success than all my literary performances put together"], and the Text-Book of Psychology, 1890, vol. 2, p. 580 [where James wrote: "I submit as my first hypothesis that *these paths all run one way,* that is from 'sensory' cells into 'motor' cells into muscles, without ever taking the reverse direction. . . . Let this direction be called the 'forward' direction. I call the law an hypothesis, but really it is an indubitable truth." Dover edition, 581]. . . . As you probably know, your father made use of this conception in emphasizing the importance of the central nervous complexes in modifying the motor expressions of a sensory stimulus.

Since James concluded in his discussion of imagination (an earlier chapter in *Principles,* but written later than the one on the Will, where the "forward" hypothesis is said to be indubitable) that the currents can flow backwards, he may have forgotten to include the physiology of imagination as an exception, or he may have assumed that in the chapter on Will he was understood to be referring to strictly sensory-motor pathways only.

30. *Treatise on Human Nature,* parts 1, 4; quoted by James in *Principles,* 2:46.

31. *Principles,* 2:291–93.

32. Ibid., 2:63. James reported that he was "a very poor visualizer, and find that I can

seldom call to mind even a single letter of the alphabet in purely retinal terms. I must trace the letter by running my mental eye over its contour in order that the image of it shall have any distinctness at all" (ibid., 2:61). He considered himself a "*motor*-type," meaning that he used, in memory, reasoning, and all intellectual activities, images derived from movement.

Gordon Allport wrote an interesting letter about this bit of Jamesian autobiography to Perry (13 June 1933), when the latter was preparing *The Thought and Character of William James*. (This letter is in the Perry Papers, Harvard Archives.) Allport noted that Binet, Ribot, and Galton had popularized the "type" theory of imagery, dividing people into visual, auditory, motor, and tactile types. James, according to Allport, helped to develop the notion that the sensory type is slower and more patient than the quicker, more impulsive or less patient motor type. (There is some basis for distinguishing William from his brother Henry in these terms; see chapter 1.) Allport calls attention to James's "famous" discussion of the explosive will, instantiated in the swift, impulsive personality. But Allport concludes that there is insufficient evidence that so-called motor types are more impulsive; he calls the idea "one of James's brilliant, unsupported sallies into the mysterious realm of personality." James once discussed why Laura Bridgman (a deaf-mute who was the subject of a popular book published in 1903) was intellectually superior to other deaf-mutes, and why Helen Keller was superior to Bridgman:

> Touch-images and motor-images are the only terms that subjects 'congenitally' blind and deaf can think in. It may be that Laura and Helen were . . . more 'tactile' and 'mobile' than their less successful rivals in the race for education, and that Helen, being more exclusively motor-minded than any subject yet met with, is the one least crippled by the loss of her other senses. . . . What is not conjecture, but fact, is the philosophical conclusion. . . . Their thinking goes on in tactile and motor symbols. . . . What clearer proof could we ask of the fact that the relations among things, far more than the things themselves, are what is intellectually interesting, and that it makes little difference what terms we think in, so long as the relations maintain their character. All sorts of terms can transport the mind with equal delight, provided they be woven into equally massive and far-reaching schemes and systems of relationship. ("Laura Bridgman," *CER*, 456–57)

33. Ludwig Wittgenstein, *Philosophical Investigations*, 3d ed. (New York: Macmillan, 1958), 202. See also Ryle's chapter on imagination in *The Concept of Mind* for an influential discussion of how we go wrong in thinking of images as special entities. Bertrand Russell offers an opposing view in *The Analysis of Mind*. The alleged existence of images makes Russell think that the doctrine of neutral monism is true only in a qualified way; if images were identical with sensations, then the doctrine would be true without qualification. Closer to Ryle's view was that of America's early behaviorist, John B. Watson, who occasioned vehement opposition when he denied the existence of mental images.

34. *Principles*, 1:438.

35. Helmholtz's position has been revived in our own time by U. T. Place. See "The Concept of Heed," *British Journal of Psychology* 45 (1954): 243–55.

36. See *Principles*, 1:439, where James refers to his descriptions elsewhere in the book of such abnormal experiences (1:341, 373, and 377).

37. See Mary Warnock, *Imagination* (Berkeley and Los Angeles: University of California Press, 1976). This book is especially valuable for its historical treatment of such figures as Hume, Kant, Coleridge, and Wordsworth. See especially part 4, which discusses the nature of the mental image, including the views of Sartre and Wittgenstein.

38. *Principles*, 2:10–11. Some students of James, as a result of being overly impressed by his concern with relations (which he claims are "external" and are "given" to introspection as well as to sensation and perception), seem to resemble neo-Hegelians insofar as they interpret him as absorbing the terms of a relationship into the relationship itself.

39. See ibid., 2:13–27, a section written, as James tells the reader, by "my friend and pupil Mr. E. B. Delabarre." James indicates his agreement with Delabarre's conclusions on the Helmholtz-Hering issue, then further develops the position of Hering.

40. Ibid., 2:86–87. In asserting that "the one thing which now touches them, therefore, seems in two places, i.e. seems two things," the Robertson-James hypothesis anticipated an objection raised by H. H. Price: "Is it ever sense to say that from a certain place something is *doubled?* I think it is not. For 'doubleness' is not a quality at all. *A is doubled* really means *there are two A's. . . .*" *Perception,* 2d ed. (London: Methuen, 1950), 57.

41. See *Principles,* 2:111–12.

42. Ibid., 1:548. For an interesting article on Fechner (with a helpful bibliography), see Helmut E. Adler, "The Vicissitudes of Fechnerian Psychophysics in America," in *The Roots of American Psychology: Historical Influences and Implications for the Future,* ed. Robert Rieber, Annals of the New York Academy of Sciences, vol. 291 (New York: The Academy, 1977), 11–23.

43. For James's discussion of hysterical blindness, see *Principles,* 1:206–10. For his account of nitrous oxide use, see "Consciousness under Nitrous Oxide," *Psychological Review* 5 (1898): 194–96. (See Allen, 161–62, for a discussion of James's interest in nitrous oxide.) Disruptions in sense of self are described in *Principles,* 1:373–400. All of chapter 27 of *Principles* is devoted to hypnotism. James discusses mediums in *Principles.* 1:393–401; see also Gardner Murphy and Robert O. Ballou, eds., *William James on Psychical Research* (New York: Viking, 1960). James was interested in lost limbs largely because his father had had a leg amputated early in life; see "The Consciousness of Lost Limbs," *CER,* 285–303. On the experiences of deaf-mutes, see "The Sense of Dizziness in Deaf-Mutes," *CER,* 220–44. James discusses the sensation of movement under anesthesia in *Principles,* 2:105. One of his accounts of melancholy and depression occurs in *Principles,* 2:298.

44. Bradley's argument is contained in three articles, all entitled "On Professor James's Doctrine of Simple Resemblance" and reprinted in his *Collected Essays,* 2 vols. (Oxford: Clarendon Press, 1969), 1:287–302. On James's side of the dispute, see "Mr. Bradley on Immediate Resemblance" and "Immediate Resemblance," *CER,* 333–38. See also Richard Wollheim, *F. H. Bradley* (London: Penguin, 1959), 35–36.

45. *Principles,* 2:300.

46. James makes an interesting observation in connection with his discussion of resemblance and difference in "Discrimination and Comparison":

> I have noticed a curious enlargement of certain "distances" of difference under the influence of chloroform. The jingling of the bells on the horses of a horse-car passing the door, for example, and the rumbling of the vehicle itself, which to our ordinary hearing merge together very readily into a *quasi*-continuous body of sound, have seemed so far apart as to require a sort of mental facing in opposite directions to get from one to the other, as if they belonged in different worlds. I am inclined to suspect, from certain data, that the ultimate philosophy of difference and likeness will have to be built upon experiences of intoxication, especially by nitrous oxide, which lets us into intuitions the subtlety whereof is denied to the waking state. (*Principles,* 1:531n)

This illustrates James's interest in sensations connected with unusual experiences and also confirms his views about the contrast between sensations and the intellect and how, for apprehending sensory resemblances and differences, the intellect's influence needs to be diminished by something like nitrous oxide. Incidentally, James here referred his readers to *The Anaesthetic Revelation, and the Gist of Philosophy,* by his mystically inclined friend B. P. Blood. (For his relation with Blood, see chapter 83 of RBP.)

A more thorough treatment of James on sensations would make more of his belief that sensory resemblance is not a transitive relation (*Principles,* 1:310–11). If we exclude his later radical empiricism, James's position coincides with remarks by Wittgenstein in *Lectures and Conversations*, ed. Cyril Barrett (Berkeley and Los Angeles: University of California Press, 1967), 42:

> When we are studying psychology we may feel there is something unsatisfactory, some difficulty about the whole subject or study—because we are taking physics as our ideal science. We think of formulating laws as in physics. And then we find we cannot use the same sort of "metric," the same ideas of measurement as in physics. This is especially clear when we try to describe appearances: the least noticeable differences of colours; the least noticeable differences of length, and so on. Here it seems that we cannot say: "If A = B, and B = C, then A = C," for instance. And this sort of trouble goes all through the subject.

Another important aspect of James on sensations is his criticism of Mill and Hume. "At bottom [Mill] makes the same blunder as Hume: the sensations *per se*, he thinks, have no 'tie.'" But, James countered, "The knowledge the present feeling [or sensation] has of the past ones is a real tie between them, so is their resemblance; so is their continuity" (*Principles*, 1:358, 360). James's assessment of Mill and Hume is something of a puzzle; there may be more to his criticism than that Mill and Hume believed sensory resemblance is not a "real tie" supplying unity to experience, whereas James believed that it is.

47. *Principles*, 2:40.

48. Ibid., 1:215.

4. SPACE

1. The James Collection in the Houghton Library at Harvard includes a notebook dated 1863 which contains, in addition to notes on Schopenhauer and Spencer, a penciled discussion entitled "Theory of Space." (Henry James III asserts in a note on the document that James made this entry years after the other notes.) In any event, space-perception was among the first topics in philosophical psychology to intrigue him. In this notebook entry he compared the spatial quale yielded by the retina and the skin with properties supplied by the other senses. He said also that spaces differ by their positions and discussed the need to distinguish "real space, and the felt or perspective space which artists get by study to notice." (We should recall that James studied painting with William Morris Hunt in 1860–61).

2. Royce's letter, dated 8 January 1880, is reprinted in RBP, 1:783–84. James apparently agreed, since he wrote in 1880 to Royce that he had come to despise his own article on space.

3. Each of these questions is the subject of one section in the chapter on space in *Psychology*.

4. *Principles*, 2:271. James here quotes Bain's *Senses and Intellect*.

5. *Principles*, 2:272.

6. Ibid., 2:273–75. The quotation of Schopenhauer is from *Über Vierfache Wurzel des Satzes vom zureichenden Grunde*.

7. See John D. Pettigrew, "The Neurophysiology of Binocular Vision," *Scientific American* 227 (August 1972): 84–95.

8. Ibid., 84.

9. Ibid., 86–87. James, like Pettigrew, refers to Wheatstone's contributions to the topic in *Psychology*, 351.

10. Pettigrew's and James's accounts are opposed to Berkeley's theory that depth is not given in sensation but is learned through associating data of sight with those of touch.

11. *Principles*, 2:273n.

12. Ibid., 2:150. In a footnote James added: "The whole science of geometry may be said to owe its being to the exorbitant interest which the human mind takes in *lines*. We cut space up in every direction in order to manufacture them." James held that all disciplines are traceable to an interest rooted in sensations. This was perhaps the controlling idea in all his thinking.

13. Ibid., 2:171–76.

14. Ibid., 2:178.

15. Ibid., 2:179–80.

16. Ibid., 2:180. James here quotes from Joseph Jastrow and Frederick Whitton, "The Perception of Space by Disparate Senses," *American Journal of Psychology* 3 (January 1890), 49–54.

17. *Principles*, 2:182–83.

18. Ibid., 2:275. Relevant discussions of issues raised here occur in: A. M. Quinton, "Spaces and Times," *Philosophy* 37 (1962): 141–44; Richard Swinburne, *Space and Time* (New York: St. Martin's Press, 1968), 31–49; and J. R. Lucas, *A Treatise on Time and Space* (London: Methuen, 1973), 124–28.

19. This account in "The Perception of Space" neatly anticipates radical empiricism.

20. *Principles*, 2:185.

21. Ibid., 2:184. For James's discussion of "coalescing" and "fusing" sensations, see, for example, 2:145–46, 181, 184, 186–87, 227, and 269.

22. Compare ibid., 2:183–85 and 2:275. For more on the fusion of sensations, see chapter 3.

23. Among the passages which are inexplicit where one might expect a pronouncement on the reality of a spatial continuum are *Principles*, 2:166, 183, 185, 265, and 275.

24. See ibid., 2:134–44 and 153–66, the most important passages where James gives evidence for the claim that all sensations have spatial properties.

25. Ibid., 2:181–82; see also 187–88.

26. It is odd that James was tempted into the "little world" concept of sensations in his chapter on space, since one of his main doctrines was that sensation is a cognitive acquaintance from the outset with the one real world.

27. *Principles*, 2:154. This example essentially represents James's view of space. He once wrote: "I well remember the sudden relief it gave me to perceive one day that *space* relations at any rate were homogeneous with the terms between which they mediated. The terms were spaces, and the relations were only other intervening spaces. For the Greenites space relations had been saltatory, for me they were thenceforward ambulatory" ("A Word More About Truth," *The Journal of Philosophy, Psychology, and Scientific Methods*, 18 July 1907, 398).

28. James's doctrine of sensation (see *Principles*, chapter 17), that sensations acquaint us with the real world, seems difficult to reconcile with his theory of initially separate spatial worlds of sensations.

29. Ibid., 2:145.

30. Ibid., 2:155–66.

31. Ibid., 2:270–82.

32. See, for instance, 1:196, 278, and 153; and 2:281.

33. See chapter 13 of *Principles*.

34. See, for example, *Principles*, 2:270–82.

35. *SPP* (Harvard edition), 54.

36. For textual support for this interpretation, see *Principles*, 2:145–47.

37. See "Bergson and His Critique of Intellectualism," in *APU*.

38. *Principles*, 2:185.

39. "The Knowing of Things Together," in McDermott, 157.

40. "The Types of Philosophic Thinking," in McDermott, 485. For amplification of the same idea and use of the expression "carve out," see also "Pragmatism and Humanism," lecture 7 in *Pragmatism*.

Interpreting James to mean that we carve out an ordered space from an initially indeterminate immensity or vastness, somewhat as a sculptor carves a figure out of a marble block, yields an interesting parallel between James's theories of space-perception and time-perception. Temporal order is apprehended only within an initially apprehended *block* (or *whole*) of time. Although hostile to the notion of a block universe, James held that blocks of time and space must be apprehended before we can grasp such relations as up-and-down and before-and-after. These relations, he argued, are really discriminated as parts of wholes. There are brief statements of this claim in relation to space in *Principles*, 1:619–22 and 2:146–47.

Support for this interpretation comes from the consideration that if *ordered* space is not carved out of space-as-vastness, what else could it be out of? This is the Jamesian query, I think.

41. "A World of Pure Experience," in McDermott, 212.

42. "The One and the Many," in McDermott, 416. In "Pragmatism and Common Sense," space is said to be a "less vague notion" than time, perhaps even than "thing" (McDermott, 424–25). Contrast this with the time and space given to the topic of space, and what James said, for example, in his letter to Stumpf about the difficulty of understanding space (see RBP, 2:70).

43. Florian Cajori, ed. *Sir Isaac Newton's Mathematical Principles of Natural Philosophy and His System of the World: A Revision of Mott's Translation* (Berkeley and Los Angeles: University of California Press, 1934), 6. Quoted by Max Jammer, *Concepts of Space* (Cambridge: Harvard University Press, 1954), 97. See Jammer's chapter 4 for a helpful discussion of the distinction between relative and absolute space in Newton.

44. Bertrand Russell, *The Analysis of Matter* (1927; reprint, New York: Dover, 1954), 122, 270–71.

45. William Kingdon Clifford, "On the Space-Theory of Matter," in *The Common Sense of the Exact Sciences*, ed. J. R. Newman (New York: Knopf, 1946), 202; quoted by Jammer, 161. Jammer's interesting discussion of Clifford on space includes this comment: "The only one who allied himself firmly to Riemann was the translator of his works into English, William Kingdon Clifford" (161). There is no evidence that James, whose ethics of belief originated as a response to Clifford's views on what counts as rational belief, was influenced by Clifford's thoughts on space.

46. *SPP*, chapters 10–11. Space is so little discussed here that Horace Kallen did not list the subject in the index.

47. In "The Perception of Reality," which immediately follows "The Perception of Space" in *Principles*, James does not discuss what sort of space is *real* but focuses instead on the subjective method of determining what is real; in effect the chapter is an essay on the psychology of belief.

48. Robert Ackermann, *The Philosophy of Science* (New York: Pegasus, 1970), 102.

49. James J. Gibson, *The Perception of the Visual World* (Boston: Houghton Mifflin, 1950), 5. Gibson discusses many interesting features of what it would be like to be suspended in a sphere of pure air that resembles James's vastness.

50. James makes this point explicitly in the chapter on time (*Principles*, 1:619–27), but not in "The Perception of Space." The requirement of change for perception is mentioned in several places.

51. Albert Einstein, Foreword to Jammer's *Concepts of Space*, xiv.

52. See, for example, his use of the term in "The Continuity of Experience," in McDermott, 292–301.

53. Such references occur in various writings, including *A Pluralistic Universe* and *The Varieties of Religious Experience*.

54. *Principles*, 2:154. The reader may wonder whether this passage is consistent with some things James wrote in "Sensation." There he seems to have suggested that an infant apprehends place as part of its first sensations without realizing it. "The places thus first sensibly known are elements of the child's space-world which remain with him all his life; and by memory and later experiences he learns a vast number of things *about* those places which at

first he did not know. But to the end of time certain places of the world remain defined for him as the places *where those sensations were*" (*Principles*, 2:35).

A. J. Ayer, recapitulating this passage, writes: "In fact, [James] maintains that even though a newborn child knows nothing about the ways in which his sensations are spatially related either to each other or to anything else in the world, he nevertheless feels them as being at a place" (*The Origins of Pragmatism*, 224). Ayer's interpretation is misleading, however, and seems inconsistent with the passage from *Principles*, 2:154. What the infant senses is at a place, but according to James the infant is unaware of the place of sensations and has no experience of "feeling them at a place." This locution posits a kind of place-awareness that James denied to infants.

55. For the history of this topic, see E. G. Boring, *A History of Experimental Psychology* (New York: The Century Co., 1929) and his *Sensation and Perception in the History of Experimental Psychology* (New York: Appleton-Century-Crofts, 1942). Interesting discussions of the local sign theory also occur in J. J. Gibson, *The Perception of the Visual World* (Boston: Houghton Mifflin, 1950).

See also G. N. A. Vesey, *The Embodied Mind* (London: Allen and Unwin, 1965). Vesey refers to James's account in a chapter entitled "The Local Sign Theory" (49–57) and argues that contemporary philosophers such as C. A. Campbell and Gilbert Ryle have returned to something like the local sign theory associated originally with the philosopher and psychologist Rudolph Lotze. In a later chapter (63–70) Vesey presents an interesting alternative theory.

Another useful study is George S. Brett's *History of Psychology*, 3 vols. (New York: Macmillan, 1921), 3:112–19. See also William N. Dember, ed., *Visual Perception: The Nineteenth Century* (New York: John Wiley, 1964), especially chapter 4 and the selection from Rudolph Lotze and surrounding editorial comments (129–42).

56. An additional detail in James's treatment of position-perception is his use of the notion of *body-image*. After describing how certain localized parts of the body are felt in relation to each other, he says: "A point can only be cognized in its relation to the entire body at once by awakening a *visual* image of the whole body" (*Principles*, 2:161).

57. James himself appreciated the difficulty of making the local sign theory defensible, as shown by a long footnote in *Principles*, 2:163–66. On James and the local sign theory, see Vesey, 49–50. For contemporary studies of issues involved here, see Ian P. Howard and William B. Templeton, *Human Spatial Orientation* (New York: John Wiley, 1966) and Jacques Paillard and Michèle Brouchon, "Active and Passive Movements in the Calibration of Position Sense," in *The Neuropsychology of Spatially Oriented Behavior*, ed. Sanford J. Freedman (Homewood, Ill.: The Dorsey Press, 1968), 37–57.

58. *Principles*, 2:180.

59. See G. J. Warnock's remarks on Marius von Senden's studies of space-perception by the congenitally blind in the appendix to von Senden, *Space and Sight: The Perception of Space and Shape in the Congenitally Blind Before and After Operation* (London: Methuen, 1960), 319–26. Warnock observes that whereas Berkeley believed touch to be the source of spatial concepts, von Senden argues the opposite, that the congenitally blind lack real awareness of space and that vision is therefore the source of spatial awareness. James wrote: "The blind man's space is very different from our space, yet a deep analogy remains between the two" (*Principles*, 2:209–10). Von Senden's view, as interpreted by Warnock, is a revival of William Hamilton and John Stuart Mill; see *Principles*, 2:208.

60. "A World of Pure Experience," in McDermott, 210.

61. G. E. Moore, " 'Percepts' and 'Places'," in *Commonplace Book (1919–1953)*, ed. Casimir Lewy (New York: Macmillan, 1962), 156–57. Moore's thoughts are brief notes or questions referring to a few pages of James's "World of Pure Experience." See also chapter 3 of Ayer's *Origins of Pragmatism*. Ayer's discussion, helpful in understanding James, is a sympathetic but critical study of James's theory of space-perception, referring both to *Principles* and to *ERE*.

62. "A World of Pure Experience," in McDermott, 211–12.

63. Moore, 157.

64. See Ayer's discussion for a fuller critical examination of James's assumption of a common space based on the alleged identity of place for different persons' perceptions.

For more examples of puzzles that arise about space and place-perception with respect to sense-data, see C. D. Broad, "Hume's Doctrine of Space," *Proceedings of the British Academy* 47 (London: Oxford University Press, 1962), 161–76. Hume asserted the existence of "punctiform elements," or sense-data having sensible qualities but lacking extension—a fundamental difference from the Jamesian doctrine that all sensations have extensity.

65. Quoted by G. J. Warnock, *Berkeley* (London: Penguin, 1953). For a helpful discussion of Berkeley's view, see Warnock, 21–43.

66. *Principles*, 2:214. James elaborates this explanation in the text which follows it.

67. Ayer sides with James here: "James argues, to my mind convincingly, that depth is no less an intrinsic property of our visual sense-fields than length and breadth" (230). But Gibson writes: "William James, for example, although he did not actually assert that a form was a sensation, did believe that a visual line was a simple datum rather than a row of point sensations. As a last possibility, it might have been assumed that *all* constituents of space were sensed. But actually no one ever supposed that depth and distance were simple sensations, and the visual third dimension was and remained a phenomenon which only perception could explain" (15–16). Gibson seems unaware that James, in opposition to Berkeley, Wundt, Helmholtz, and others, considered distance a simple sensation. I agree with Gibson that James seems nowhere to have argued explicitly that form is a sensation, although his insistence that all space-relations are sensations of particular lines (see *Principles*, 2:152) and his comments about shape (2:238–39) certainly imply that conclusion.

Also interesting is James's response to what in psychological literature is called Molyneux's query. William Molyneux wrote to John Locke: "Suppose a man born blind, and now adult, and taught by his touch to distinguish between a cube and a sphere . . . so as to tell, when he felt one and the other, which is the cube, which is the sphere. Suppose then the cube and sphere placed on a table and the blind man to be made to see; query, whether by his sight, before he touched them, he could now distinguish and tell which is the globe, which the cube?" (Locke, *Essay Concerning Human Understanding*, bk. 2, chap. 9; quoted in *Principles*, 2:210).

Locke replied: "I agree with this thinking gentleman whom I am proud to call my friend, and am of the opinion that the blind man at first sight would not be able to say which was the globe, which the cube, whilst he only saw them; though he could unerringly name them by his touch and certainly distinguish them by the difference of their figures felt" (*Essay Concerning Human Understanding*, bk. 2, chap. 9; quoted in *Principles*, 2:210). James observed: "This opinion has not lacked experimental confirmation. From Chesselden's case downwards, patients operated for congenital cataract have been unable to name at first the thing they saw. 'So, Puss, I shall know you another time,' said Chesselden's patient, after catching the cat, looking at her steadfastly, and setting her down" (*Principles*, 2:210).

But James believed that this postoperative incapacity resulted partly from the general mental confusion of the patient, partly from the unfavorable conditions of perception of a postoperative eye. He then made this revealing remark: "That the analogy of inner nature between the retinal and tactile sensations goes beyond mere extensity is proved by the cases where the patients were the most intelligent, as in the young man operated on by Dr. Franz, who named circular, triangular, and quadrangular figures at first sight" (2:210–11). James was reluctant to accept usual interpretations of the few known experiments on congenital cataracts, which concluded that form is learned, not sensed; he evidently thought that experiments and arguments pointed the other way. See his reference to Thomas Nunnely's cataract patient who was said to have postoperatively recognized the difference between a cube and a sphere at once (2:148).

For a more recent essay on the nature-versus-nurture controversy in relation to form-perception, see Robert L. Fantz, "The Origin of Form Perception," *Scientific American* 204 (May 1961): 2–8. Further from Gibson and closer to James, Fantz tentatively decides that "results to date do require the rejection of the view that the newborn infant or animal must start from scratch to learn to see and to organize patterned stimulation" (8).

68. Helmholtz, *Handbuch der physiologischen Optik* (Leipzig: Voss, 1867), 438; quoted in *Principles,* 2:218.

69. *Principles,* 2:216. This definition was first given in chapter 17, "Sensation."

70. Ibid., 2:219–20 and chapter 21, "The Perception of Reality."

71. RBP, 2:70. For more on the experiments relevant to this topic, see Harvey A. Carr, *An Introduction to Space Perception* (New York: Longmans, Green & Co., 1935).

72. *Principles,* 2:170.

73. In *Psychology* this topic has a brief chapter of its own, "Sensations of Motion," 70–77.

74. *Principles,* 2:171.

75. D. M. Armstrong, *Perception and the Physical World* (New York: Humanities Press, 1961), 185–86.

76. *Principles,* 2:248–52.

77. Ibid., 2:144. Compare this discussion with Sir W. Russell Brain's in *Mind, Perception and Science* (Oxford: Blackwell, 1951), 3–22, and his *Nature of Experience* (London: Oxford University Press, 1959), 25–47.

78. See Boring, *Sensation and Perception in the History of Experimental Psychology,* 529–35.

79. See Howard and Templeton, 66–67. Howard and Templeton refer not to James's chapter on space-perception, but to the chapter on will. They interpret correctly what James wrote about Helmholtz on this issue, but their reference to kinesthesis in James's theory must be qualified by what I have said in the text.

80. *Principles,* 2:205–06. James reviewed writings on the physiology of the semicircular canals in 1880 and did some experimenting of his own, as reported in 1881, on their role in the feeling of dizziness. References to James's work on this phenomenon are occasionally found in today's literature.

81. James's philosophy of space-perception has caused controversy recently. Nicholas Pastore argues that contradictions are involved in the theory; see his *Selective History of Theories of Visual Perception* (New York: Oxford University Press, 1971). Richard High argues against Pastore, holding that James's views can be made consistent; see his "Shadworth Hodgson and William James's Formulation of Space Perception: Phenomenology and Perceptual Realism," *Journal of the History of the Behavioral Sciences* 17 (1981): 466–85. Pastore replies to this criticism in the same issue of *Journal of the History of the Behavioral Sciences,* 486–89, and High responds in *Journal of the History of the Behavioral Sciences* 18 (1982): 176–80.

5. TIME

1. James borrowed this term from an obscure Irish-American writer, E. R. Clay, who coined it in his book *The Alternative* (1882). See RBP, 2:87.

2. See, for example, *Principles,* 1:606, 622. There is an obvious similarity here between James and Gestaltists, although the resemblance has not attracted much notice.

3. This concept agrees with the later account of pure experience, which is defined as an apprehended *muchness* all at once. See *ERE,* for example.

4. *Principles,* 1:628–30.

5. Hermann von Helmholtz, *Physiological Optics;* quoted in *Principles,* 1:628. Bertrand Russell made a similar claim in *The Problems of Philosophy.*

6. Wilhelm Volkmann, *Lehrbuch der Psychologie;* quoted in *Principles,* 1:629.

7. The concept of a single act of attention needs clarification of a sort that James did not give it, but without which the idea of the specious present remains unwarrantably vague. Perry comments: "But though others had preceded James in his general conception [of the specious present], he claimed originality for fixing the amount of temporal duration clearly intuited, and for developing (characteristically) a neural hypothesis to account for it" (RBP, 2:87).

8. See, for example, *Principles,* 1:611, 613, 618, 622, 630, 631, 635, and *Psychology,* 280–86.

9. *Principles,* 1:1–9. See also "On the Function of Cognition," in McDermott, 140.

10. For criticism of this theory, see my "William James on Time Perception," *Philosophy of Science* 38 no. 3 (September 1971): 353–60.

11. *Principles,* 1:619.

12. Compare this position with Nelson Goodman's in "Time and Language, and the Passage of Time," in *Problems of Space and Time,* ed. J. J. C. Smart (New York: Collier-Macmillan, 1964), 365–68. See also Bertrand P. Helm, "William James on the Nature of Time," *Tulane Studies in Philosophy* 24 (1975): 33–47.

13. *Principles,* 2:613–14.

14. Ibid., 1:605.

15. This is a main contention in my article cited in note 10 above.

16. Ernst Mach, *Beitrage zur Analyse der Empfindungen,* 103–06; quoted in *Principles,* 2:635.

17. See Edwin B. Newman, "Perception," in *The Foundations of Psychology,* ed. E. G. Boring, H. S. Langfeld, and H. P. Wald (New York: John Wiley, 1948), 215–49. Newman writes: "James's discussion of space and time and of the stream of consciousness . . . has been modified by many new facts, but the breadth of his account is still without peer" (249). His discussion of the perception of time (242–49) often resembles James's; Newman, too, asks: "Do we have some kind of a time sense which, acting by itself, tells us of the passage of time? Psychologists agree that the answer to this last question is pretty obviously *no.* Time cannot be apprehended directly, nakedly, as such; it can only be known through some process which goes on in time" (243). But it is unclear whether, like James, they believe that time, as an accompaniment of some such process, is *sensed.*

The same uncertainty exists in William T. Powers's discussion in *Behavior: The Control of Perception* (Chicago: Aldine, 1973): "One does not however experience time by itself, but only in terms of the duration of transitions—only in connection with other perceptions." Royce's account of time-perception, which resembles James's, leaves the question equally uncertain. See Bruce Kuklick, *Josiah Royce: An Intellectual Biography* (Indianapolis: Bobbs-Merrill, 1972), 113–15.

What Richard Swinburne argues in *Space and Time* seems correct. He thinks it confusing to talk of two kinds of time, physical and psychological. " 'Physical time' describes the true time interval between two events. 'Psychological time' is not a measure of an equally correct interval between the events. It is a measure, which may or may not be correct, of how observers not using clocks, *judge,* as well as they can, what is the interval of 'physical time' between the events" (246, italics mine). *Judging* here is a matter of guesstimating rather than sensing or intuiting.

J. R. Lucas makes an interesting defense of the specious present as a conceptual necessity:

> It is difficult to be clear about the phenomenon of the specious present, partly because it is inherently indeterminate. As Whitehead says, "The temporal breadths of the immediate durations of sense-awareness are very indeterminate and dependent on the individual

percipient. . . . What we perceive as the present is the vivid fringe of memory tinged with anticipation" (*The Concept of Nature,* Cambridge, 1920, pp. 72 ff.); but fringes, if uncertain intervals, are certainly not instants. And therefore an instantaneous "now" is empirically inadequate. It remains, however, theoretically indispensable. For [there is] the mathematical fact that an infinite set of nested intervals defines a present instant. (*Treatise on Time and Space,* 24)

18. See Richard Stevens, *James and Husserl: The Foundation of Meaning* (The Hague: Martinus Nijhoff, 1974), especially 53–57 and 58–65.

19. *Principles,* 1:623.

20. Ibid., 1:622. He also wrote: "Awareness of change is thus the condition on which our perception of time's flow depends" (1:620).

21. "The Knowing of Things Together," in McDermott, 157–58. This passage (and one from "The Continuity of Experience," in McDermott, 294), with its use of *reflection,* reveals the influence of Shadworth Hodgson, whose views on time-perception are cited, in this essay and elsewhere, as more relevant than those of E. R. Clay to James's theory of the specious present.

Concerning the elementary memory, James wrote: "The number of these direct experiences which the specious present and immediately intuited past may embrace, measures the extent of our 'primary,' as Professor Exner calls it, or, as Professor Richet calls it, of our 'elementary,' memory" (*Principles,* 1:638; James quotes his own article, "The Perception of Time," in *The Journal of Speculative Philosophy* 20, no. 4 (October 1886): 403.

22. Classified under Loose Notes [A] 10 in the James Papers, Houghton Library.

23. For more on "mere succession," see "The One and the Many," in McDermott, 415. James evidently appreciated the force of the argument that Lucas has recently formulated thus: "The notion of denseness and continuity is incompatible with the notion of *nextness,* and hence, there cannot be a next instant after this one; because for any instant after this one there is, by the definition of denseness, *another* instant between it and this one; so that it could not have been the next one" (*Treatise on Time and Space,* 29).

24. "Bergson," in McDermott, 564. James does refer in this essay to the "stream of time" (565), but the reference to "real time" is rare, and it is not clear whether he meant real time or only each experience of it.

25. Ibid., 565. "The flow of real time" is an expression James quotes from Bergson's *Creative Evolution.* James seems to belong to what George Schlesinger calls the "anti-passage-of-time philosophers," thinkers who refuse to refer to "time as if it were something flowing, advancing or moving." See his essay "The Passage of Time," *Contemporary Philosophy in Australia,* ed. Robert Brown and C. D. Rollins (New York: Humanities Press, 1969), 204–13.

26. See "Pragmatism and Common Sense," in McDermott, 422, where James comments on real time.

27. James subscribed to the following: "What I do feel simply when a later moment of my experience succeeds an earlier one is that though they are two moments, the transition from the one to the other is *continuous.* Continuity here is a definite sort of experience" ("A World of Pure Experience," in McDermott, 198). But given James's analysis of time-perception, the problem is to show how such continuity is possible, wherein it consists, and that time, like experience, is continuous.

28. James's problem here results in part from the analysis of time-perception as a "fine-grained" or "granular" experience. Swinburne argues that time is both continuous and granular, calling it "a minimum length of period" (*Space and Time,* 208). Lucas counters: "But that is not to say that time is granular. If time were granular, moments or 'epochs' or 'chronons' would succeed one another the same for all systems" (*Treatise on Time and Space,* 32). See also Swinburne's discussion (33–46) of Anthony Quinton's "Spaces and Times," *Philosophy* 37 (1962): 130–47.

29. References to time are scattered but brief in *ERE* and *APU* and seem incidental to other points about the continuity of experience. In his index for *SPP*, Horace Kallen includes *continuity* but not *time*.

30. A short, semipoetic passage in "The Continuity of Experience" (McDermott, 294) touches on this issue, but James never discusses what B. C. Van Frassen calls the "very important, but elusive concept of *direction*." See Van Frassen's essay "The Anisotropy of Time" in *An Introduction to the Philosophy of Space and Time* (New York: Random House, 1970), 81–95.

31. The following entry occurs in James's notes for his Philosophy 9 course in 1904–05: "Every sensation passing away leaves what we call a memory of itself, in which it figures as the 'same.' The sameness means no break, no discontinuity. These are not given. Time-continuity is. The self, which is part of every experience, is similarly given as unbroken." The problem is to see how time could be given as continuous, in light of James's theory of time-perception.

In arguing that time is not a psychological datum, my reservations about Jamesian theory apply also to C. D. Broad's claim that he hears temporal boundaries, and that such boundaries are thus psychological data. See Broad's *Examination of McTaggart's Philosophy*, reprinted in Smart, 328.

32. RBP, 1:698. The correspondence with Renouvier in the early 1890s discloses that James's psychology course at Harvard seems to have reflected the popularity of his psychology text, the condensed version of which was then available. He wrote in February 1892 that he had eighty laboratory students (RBP, 2:708). He may have wanted Renouvier to appreciate his reputation as a psychologist, since as early as 1878 James was known abroad as a philosopher before he was known as a psychologist.

33. See James's footnote, *Principles*, 1:632–34.

34. *Principles*, 2:632. This view persisted at least until 1895 in "The Knowing of Things Together"; see the note in McDermott, 161–62. James's speculations about cerebral processes are not only about the causes of sensations, but sometimes represent analogies between mind and brain, using the latter as a model for describing the former.

35. James's explicit argument was that we *cannot* know this correspondence to be true, that in a dualistic metaphysics, which separates known objects from knowing states of consciousness, cognition is a miracle (*Principles*, 1:216–23). If he had been meticulous, he would have said in this passage from the final chapter that we believe or postulate the temporal relation in sensation to be duplicated in the world of objects, but that we do not know it. The dualistic premise that cognition is a miracle is, after all, what motivated James to abandon dualism for radical empiricism. If James's remarks in the final chapter are a definite statement of his belief, he apparently viewed time-sensation as objective, in that its object resembles something in the external world.

36. "The World of Pure Experience," in McDermott, 210. This is to misinterpret Berkeley, who was, like James, a natural realist in his views on human perception.

37. "The One and the Many," in McDermott, 416. This statement leads to further reflections on how to relate, if possible, private spaces and times with a unified spatial-temporal system in a Jamesian metaphysics. It shows also the intimate connection between James's psychology and pragmatism.

38. "Bergson," in McDermott, 565.

39. Ibid., 564. This comment applies to motion but what precedes it explicitly applies to time and other concepts. In context, this remark strengthens the case against any conceptualization of time as matching our temporal intuitions.

40. Ibid.

41. "Pragmatism and Common Sense," in McDermott, 424–25. See also 422–23.

42. This interpretation is perhaps supported by "The One and the Many," in McDermott, 415–16.

43. Syllabus for Philosophy 3, "The Philosophy of Nature," taught in 1902–03. The entire

syllabus is reprinted in RBP, 2:745–49. The seminar seems to have been introduced by Dickinson S. Miller, whose lectures on traditional issues, especially the mind-body problem, were followed by James's on materialism, idealism, and pragmatism. Students' notes for this course are in the James Collection, Houghton Library; the notes of J. S. Moore were acquired in 1939, those of Edwin De T. Bechtel in 1958, and those of E. L. Porter in 1960.

44. RBP, 2:373.

45. E. L. Porter recorded in his notes that James, in discussing Kant, Renouvier, and Zeno, said that "the *inanity* of infinite time and space disinclines the mind to their acceptance, and panpsychistic idealism, for which infinity no longer forms a problem, seems the most satisfactory theory to adopt." See also RBP, 2:373, especially James's letter to Pillon.

46. *Principles,* 1:151. The sui generis, relatively indistinct sensation of *more* is the same for different sense-modalities but becomes a spatial or temporal sensation when distinctness of perception and measurement are introduced. The concept of *more* is important for all of James's thought, ranging from his psychology to his religious views as expressed in the concluding sections of *The Varieties of Religious Experience,* reproduced in McDermott, 774–75.

47. "Bergson," in McDermott, 564.

48. *SPP,* 155. See also Alfred North Whitehead, *Process and Reality* (New York: Macmillan, 1929), 105. James made similar remarks in "Bergson" (McDermott, 563) and in a 1907 letter to Bergson (RBP, 2:618–21).

49. *SPP,* 164–65.

50. See, for instance, "Bergson," in McDermott, 580.

51. "The Thing and Its Relations," in McDermott, 215.

52. "The Dilemma of Determinism," in McDermott, 609n.

53. "The Varieties of Religious Experience," in McDermott, 770. There are points of resemblance between John Dewey and James here. Dewey writes: "Genuine time, if it exists as anything else except the measure of motions in space, is all one with the existence of individuals as individuals, with the creative, with the occurrence of unpredictable novelties" ("Time and Individuality," in *Time and Its Mysteries* [New York: Collier, 1962], 157).

54. "The Varieties of Religious Experience," in McDermott, 768.

55. Ibid., 775.

6. MEMORY

1. *Principles,* 1:643–48. A. J. Ayer writes: "What James presumably had in mind was that there must be an interval between the experiencing of an event and its revival in memory, but this is inconsistent with his own theory that the constituents of the specious present fade gradually out of the reach of sensation and into the domain of memory" (*Origins of Pragmatism,* 245). But there is no such inconsistency, as we have just interpreted James. There must be an interval between an event and the memory of it, and that interval must be greater than the time between the moment of recall and the earliest moment of the specious present within which the recall occurs. This theory may be problematic, but it is not inconsistent in the way Ayer alleges.

2. See Ayer, 245–46, for a similar criticism. Ayer argues persuasively that James's definition results in serious inconsistencies with another thesis he wants to defend. See also Robert Reiff and Martin Scheerer, *Memory and Hypnotic Age Regression* (New York: International University Press, 1959) 24–25.

3. I discuss this capacity in "Memory and Consciousness," *Proceedings of the Seventh Inter-American Congress of Philosophy* (Laval University, 1968), 78–82.

4. *Principles,* 1:649.

5. Fechner called these experiences "memory-after-images" (quoted in *Principles,* 1:645). James presumably did not call them memory images because they occur together with the

remembered event within the same specious present. See Ayer, 243, for criticism of James's belief that images are a necessary condition of memory.

6. Gilbert Ryle, *The Concept of Mind*, 245–79.

7. *Principles*, 1:650. This is certainly a controversial thesis. It has been affected by recent research, but its commonsense basis seems to have been preserved. Alan D. Baddeley writes: "It appears then that the *recall* of visual material is relatively poor, shows rapid forgetting . . . and tends to rely on verbal coding, whereas visual *recognition* shows relatively little forgetting after the first few seconds and is not apparently affected by verbal factors" (*The Psychology of Memory* [New York: Basic, 1976], 216–17).

8. The explanation of verbal meaning in terms of fringes is given in *Principles*, 1:249–58. Wittgenstein discusses the idea that thought is surrounded by a fringe or halo in *Philosophical Investigations*, #97. See also the passages from Christian Wolff and James Mill that James quoted to support this contention (*Principles*, 1:651–52).

9. *Principles*, 1:652. James's views fit into the Hume-Russell tradition of treating belief as an emotion or feeling.

10. See, for example, ibid., 1:335–36.

11. The Jamesian ingredients of memory can all be present but still be insufficient for remembering. "It is quite possible to believe truly that a certain event occurred, to locate it correctly in one's past experience, to imagine it vividly, but still not to remember it" (Ayer, 246). I have emphasized that these ingredients are not to be found in the first place, as James claimed.

12. See *Principles*, 1:163. Here James seems to be denying strenuously the existence of unconscious mental states, but he meant only to deny the existence of mental states of which no one is conscious. In fact, he regarded the ideas of Janet, Binet, Freud, and others on the unconscious as a discovery of revolutionary importance. See my discussion in chapters 2 and 12.

13. Again, chapters 2 and 12.

14. See Sigmund Freud, *The Interpretation of Dreams*, ed. A. A. Brill (New York: Modern Library, 1938), 489–90. For more on Freud here, see David Rapapport, *Emotions and Memory* (New York: Science Editions, 1961), especially chapter 5. Whereas Rapapport is much concerned with James's theory of emotion, he says nothing about James's theory of memory. There is some similarity between Freud and James in what both said on the role of words in remembering. See, for example, Freud, *The Ego and the Id* (New York: Norton, 1962), 10–14.

James allows for unconscious memories in *VRE*; the concept apparently figured in his mysticism while receiving little or no notice in his psychology.

15. *Principles*, 1:654. James considered this point to have been established earlier in *Principles*, when he discussed the concept of association; see 1:550–604.

16. Henri Bergson, *Matter and Memory* (1896; reprint, Garden City N.Y.: Doubleday, 1959), 232.

17. Wilder Penfield, *The Mystery of the Mind* (Princeton: Princeton University Press, 1975), 31.

18. Ibid., 32. Penfield discusses the role of the hippocampus in memory on page 35.

19. Ibid., 49. Penfield was especially impressed by the difficulties James noted in trying to compose a coherent picture of mind-body relationships. Penfield writes: "As an undergraduate, majoring in philosophy at Princeton, I was much impressed by my reading of William James's *The Principles of Psychology*. That was, I suppose, the beginning of my curiosity about the brain and the mind of man" (49n).

Charles Hendel quotes from one of his own letters to Penfield in his foreword to Penfield's book:

Your mention of James' *Psychology* touches me closely. I have never forgotten James' *Principles* and the role of the mind in purpose, attention, interest, and decision. Again and again in my own experience, and study of others, I have found these ideas fruitful, and indeed quite "proven," to my own satisfaction. They have been confirmed as being as nearly true as anything can be in regard to the nature of the mind. (xx)

20. Heinz Von Foerster, "Memory Without Record," *The Anatomy of Memory* (Palo Alto: Science and Behavior Books, 1967), 410. The other articles in this volume, originally part of a conference in 1963 on the anatomy of memory, discuss the current state of research on the material basis of memory at that time.

21. James does seem committed to a form of record or trace theory when he writes: "The persistence or permanence of the paths is a physiological property of the brain-tissue of the individual" (*Principles*, 1:659).

22. Ibid., 1:628–29. See W. Von Leyden's discussion of this passage in *Remembering: A Philosophical Problem* (London: Duckworth, 1961), 37.

23. See Irvin Rock, "A Neglected Aspect of the Problem of Recall: The Höffding Function," in *Theories of the Mind*, ed. Jordan Scher (New York: Free Press of Glencoe, 1962), 645–61. In his discussion of association, Rock criticizes James's speculations about the brain. He points to some puzzles about James's concept of brain-paths and discusses whether it differs from the concept of memory traces in the brain (648–49).

Those who might argue that James wanted only to explain retention, but not conscious recall itself, by association should consider this statement: "We have to distinguish between [memory's] potential aspect as a magazine or storehouse and its actual aspect as recollection now of a particular event. . . . Both the general retention and the special recall are explained by association" (*Talks to Teachers* [New York: Norton, 1958], 88–89).

24. An unidentified correspondent quoted in *Principles*, 1:668.

25. *Principles*, 1:659.

26. Carl Hovland, "Retention and Transfer of Learning," in *The Foundations of Psychology*, ed. E. G. Boring, H. S. Langfeld, and H. P. Weld (New York: Wiley, 1948), 178.

27. *Principles*, 1:667.

28. Hovland, 178. For a moderate claim on behalf of transfer of training, similar to James's claim about memory, see Ernest R. Hilgard, *Introduction to Psychology* (New York: Harcourt, 1962), 319.

Another assessment was made by Robert S. Woodworth, *Experimental Psychology* (New York: Holt, 1928), 189–90. Woodworth does not contradict James's claim that training is ineffective in improving the general power of memory retention, but he does comment: "James did not state how much his Os gained in the practice series itself, but from other experiments in the learning of poems it is certain that great improvement can occur. Ebert and Meumann (1905) conducted a practice experiment in memorizing nonsense syllables and found great improvement, which consisted largely in better technique" (190). But the discussion of this experiment in the light of later ones yielded little if any evidence for the anti-Jamesian thesis that transfer of training actually occurred.

29. *Principles*, 1:662. Norman L. Munn cites this passage approvingly in his once widely used psychology textbook, *Psychology: The Fundamentals of Human Adjustment* (Boston: Houghton Mifflin, 1946), 165.

30. Woodworth, 190.

31. *Principles*, 1:673. James's reference is to Spencer's *Principles of Psychology*.

32. Hermann Ebbinghaus, *Über das Gedächtnis*, translated as *Memory* by Henry Ruyer and Clare E. Bussenius (New York: Teachers College Press, 1913).

33. See *Talks*, 100, and *Principles*, 1:677.

34. Irvin Rock, "Repetition and Learning," in *Frontiers of Psychological Research*, ed. Stanley Coopersmith (San Francisco: W. H. Freeman, 1966), 143.

35. Benton J. Underwood, "Forgetting," in Coopersmith, 157. Underwood continues: "This interpretation is borne out by the fact that in trying to recall the associations in the first

list the subject often gives a word or two from the second list and vice versa. It is as if the two learning batches had been poured into a single beater and became mixed together by diffusion as time passes."

36. *Principles*, 1:667.
37. Ibid., 1:673.
38. George A. Miller, "Information and Memory," in Coopersmith, 164.
39. *Talks*, 93–94.
40. *Principles*, 1:685.
41. *Talks*, 96.
42. *Principles*, 1:684; James repeated this statement verbatim in *Talks*, 91.

7. ATTENTION AND WILL

1. For James's view, see especially *Principles*, 1:402–58. For a modern view, see Donald E. Broadbent, "Attention and the Perception of Speech," *Scientific American* 207 (April 1962):

Paying attention—and not paying attention—are surely two of the most important abilities of human beings. Yet in spite of their crucial role in learning, and in a host of other intelligent activities, psychologists for many years did not consider them proper topics for study. . . . In the past ten years, however, the concept of attention has begun to force itself on the attention of psychologists in various ways (143)

See also Jane F. Mackworth, *Vigilance and Attention* (London: Penguin, 1970): "The concept of attention has recently returned to favour in psychological and physiological research. It is acquiring not only a qualitative but even a quantitative aspect, with the borrowing of the idea of capacity from information theory, biology and physics" (13)

Other useful discussions are Paul Bakan, ed., *Attention* (New York: Van Nostrand, 1966) and Andrew McGhie, *Pathology of Attention* (London: Penguin, 1969).

2. Donald E. Broadbent, ed., *Perception and Communication* (New York: Pergamon, 1958), 58, 301.

3. See, for example, Ryle, *The Concept of Mind*, 136–53, and U. T. Place, "The Concept of Heed," *The British Journal of Psychology* 45, no. 4 (1954): 243–55.

4. See, for example, "Remarks on Spencer's *Definition of Mind as Correspondence*," *Journal of Speculative Philosophy* 12 (1878): 1–18, and "Quelques considérations sur la méthode subjective," *Critique philosophique* 6, no. 2 (1878): 407–13.

5. James often expressed his regret that this vagueness was typical in psychology. In a letter to James Sully, acknowledging his receipt of Sully's paper on attention, he wrote: "It seems to me that psychology is like physics before Galileo's time—not a single *elementary* law yet caught a glimpse of. A great chance for some future psychologue to make a greater name than Newton's, but who then will read the book of this generation?" In a letter to his brother Henry about his own book on psychology, he wrote: "As 'Psychologies' go, it is a good one, but psychology is in such an ante-scientific condition that the whole present generation of them is predestined to become unreadable old medieval lumber, as soon as the first genuine tracks of insights are made. The sooner the better, for me!" (Both letters are quoted in RBP, 2:113–14.) For more on James's attitude about the future of scientific psychology, see RBP, 2:112–24.

6. Sigmund Exner, Pflüger's *Archiv*, 11:4293–4431; quoted in *Principles*, 1:410.

7. *Principles*, 1:410. Ernst Mach argued that time is a sensation, on the grounds that we cannot distinguish in memory the first stroke of a clock from the second unless we attach to each a special time-sensation which is also remembered. See *Principles*, 1:635.

8. Wundt, *Grundzüge der physiologischen Psychologie*, 2d ed., 2:238–40; quoted in *Principles*,

1:411. Uncharacteristically, James's gloss of Wundt does not help the reader nearly enough. He does not do justice to Wundt's claim that we find it hard to divide attention because of a tendency to blend things into one composite object of consciousness.

9. Wundt, 262; quoted in *Principles*, 1:411.

10. Wundt, 264–66; quoted in *Principles*, 1:413.

11. See note 5 above.

12. E. B. Titchener, *Experimental Psychology*, 2 vols. (New York: Macmillan, 1902), 1:108–25.

13. *Principles*, 1:416. This sentence is repeated verbatim in *Psychology* (221), suggesting that it was an important conviction. The extensive cutting and revising of *Principles* for the condensed version did not permit repetition of anything James considered dull or trivial.

14. I discuss James's aesthetics in chapter 13, but it is important to ask here whether James was prepared to defend the proposition that all aesthetic interest is passive and involuntary. It is possible that in the present context he was not thinking of aesthetics at all, but by making effort a necessary part of voluntary attention, he seems committed, if only unwittingly, to such a proposition about aesthetic attending. For further insight into James's views on this point, see *Principles*, 1:451.

15. James noted in his chapter on attention that some of the basic effects of attending are discussed in the chapters on association and time-perception. In the latter chapter he discussed the dissection of originally presented wholes in perception. He believed that the isolated sensation, idea, or impression discussed in Locke or Hume was a mythological abstraction, something at best arrived at by analysis, cetainly not a *datum* of experience.

James noted also the special role attention plays in the association of ideas: it emphasizes certain elements such that only their associates are evoked subsequently (see *Principles*, 1:594). For specific connections between the chapters on attention and time, compare 1:409–10 and 1:611, 621, and 632–42.

16. *Principles*, 1:450. See also 1:594.

17. Some of James's ideas on this point occur in chapter 13, "Discrimination and Comparison." James's notion here is that clearness and distinction, even in the case of sensations, are the result of intellectual discrimination, not mere heeding. See, for example, *Principles*, 1:426.

18. For a concise discussion of Herbart, his concept of apperception, and its influence in psychology, especially upon theories of educational development, see E. G. Boring, *A History of Experimental Psychology* (New York: Century, 1929), 238–50.

19. J. F. Herbart, *Psychologie als Wissenschaft*, 128; quoted in *Principles*, 1:418.

20. *Principles*, 1:417–18.

21. *Principles*, 1:421.

22. James recounted Helmholtz's experiments in *Principles*, 1:423.

23. For example, James wrote:

> The faculty of voluntarily bringing back a wandering attention, over and over again, is the very root of judgment, character, and will. No one is *compos sui* if he have it not. An education which should improve this faculty would be *the* education *par excellence*. But it is easier to define this ideal than to give practical directions for bringing it about. The only general pedagogic maxim bearing on attention is that the more interest the child has in advance in the subject, the better he will attend. (*Principles*, 1:424)

For practical application, see also the chapters on attention and apperception in *Talks*.

James discussed briefly the relation between genius and attentiveness, suggesting that what distinguishes genius is the richness of associations and apperceptive processes. Geniuses can sustain attention on a given topic because they have many intellectual associations leading to it; their attentiveness is largely passive, and *"it is their genius making them attentive, not their attention making geniuses of them.* . . . It is probable that genius tends actually to prevent a man from acquiring habits of voluntary attention, and that moderate intellectual endowments are the soil in which we may best expect, here as elsewhere, the virtues of the will, strictly so called, to thrive" (*Principles*, 1:423–24).

24. Andrew McGhie, *Pathology of Attention* (Baltimore: Penguin, 1969), 51–56.

25. Cameron's studies are recounted in ibid., 52.

26. *Principles*, 1:439. There is a tendency in today's psychological literature to use the term *vigilance* to cover what James meant by *anticipatory attention* and *expectant attentiveness.*

27. *Principles*, 1:433–34. James repeatedly referred to the law or principle of the summation of stimuli: *"A stimulus which would be inadequate by itself to excite a nerve-centre to effective discharge may, by acting with one or more other stimuli (equally ineffectual by themselves alone) bring the discharge about.* The natural way to consider this is as a summation of tensions which at last overcome a resistance" (*Principles*, 1:82).

28. Ibid., 1:232.

29. See ibid., 1:435 and 450. Given today's philosophical debates about whether attention is a disposition or an occurrence, it is important to understand that James was certain that it is an occurrence. This was one issue that divided Gilbert Ryle and U. T. Place (see note 3 above).

30. *Principles*, 1:435. For a fuller phenomenological description of this kind of experience, James referred the reader to 1:302, in the chapter "The Consciousness of Self."

31. G. T. Fechner, *Revision der Psychophysik*, 271; quoted in *Principles*, 1:426. James commented on this passage: "Were it otherwise we should not be able to note *intensities* by attending to them. Weak impressions would, as Stumpf says, become stronger by the very fact of being observed" (1:426). He then quoted from Stumpf: "I should not be able to observe faint sounds at all, but only such as appeared to me of maximal strength, or at least of a strength that increased with the amount of my observation. In reality, however, I can, with steadily increasing attention, follow a diminuendo perfectly well" (Carl Stumpf, *Tonpsychologie*, 2:71; quoted, 1:426).

32. *Principles*, 1:435.

33. Ibid., 1:436. The reference is to Fechner's *Elemente der Psychophysik*, 2:475–76.

34. In presenting his theory of emotion, James cited experimental evidence as being relevant to the question of whether emotions have a purely mental element. Nevertheless, his final stance regarding attention was that the issue is nonexperimental.

35. Hermann Helmholtz, *Physiol. Optik*, 741; quoted in *Principles*, 1:438.

36. Ewald Hering, *Hermann's Handbuch*, 3:548; quoted in *Principles*, 1:438.

37. *Principles*, 1:447.

38. Ibid., 1:452.

39. These problems are apparent to any reader of the biographical studies mentioned in chapter 1. Always cited in this connection is the extreme depression James suffered in 1870 at the age of twenty-eight, from which he recovered, he said, only by exercising a "vigor of will." See, for instance, Perry's chapters, "Depression and Recovery" (1:320–32) and "Morbid Traits" (2:670–81).

40. "Decisions with effort merge so gradually into those without it that it is not easy to say where the limit lies. Decisions without effort merge again into ideo-motor, and these into reflex acts; so that the temptation is almost irresistible to throw the formula which covers so many cases over absolutely all" (*Principles*, 2:575). James also wrote:

> The only conception at the same time renovating and fundamental with which Biology has enriched Psychology, the only *essential* point in which "the new Psychology" is an advance upon the old, is, it seems to me, the very general, and by this time very familiar notion, that all our activity belongs at bottom to the type of reflex action, and that all our consciousness accompanies a chain of events of which the first was an incoming current

in some sensory nerve, and of which the last will be a discharge into some muscle, blood-vessel, or gland. This chain of events may be simple and rapid, as when we wink at a blow; or it may be intricate and prolonged, as when we hear a momentous bit of news and deliberate before deciding what to do. But its normal end is always some activity. ("What the Will Effects," *Scribner's Magazine* 3, no. 2 [February 1888]: 240)

(Only a brief portion of this article appears in the chapter on will in *Principles;* this passage, for instance, is unduplicated there.)

When James's son Henry was considering the publication of a volume of his father's essays to be titled *Counsels for Courage,* he suggested including "What the Will Effects." But Perry advised that the article was largely unimportant because the theory of ideo-motor action presented in the article was out of fashion. The essay adds little to the discussion of will in *Principles,* but it does contain a few passages which help us to appreciate James's view of the new psychology, to which he was introducing his readers.

41. Hughlings Jackson, "Clinical and Physiological Researches on the Nervous System," reprinted from the *Lancet,* 1873; quoted by James in "The Feeling of Effort," *Anniversary Memoirs of the Boston Society of Natural History* (Boston, 1880), 4. Perry said of this essay that "it constitutes the author's earliest discussions of the will, the 'feeling of innervation,' ideo-motor action, and the psychology of free will" (*CER,* 151n). Perry observed that several pages of the essay were duplicated in the chapter on will in *Principles;* in fact, the 106 pages of this chapter are a rewriting rather than a reprinting of the earlier piece.

Perry noted also that "The Feeling of Effort" appeared in 1880 in *Critique philosophique* under the title "Le Sentiment de l'effort," marking the beginning of James's great popularity among French psychologists. See Perry's "William James," *Harvard Graduates' Magazine* 19, no. 74 (December 1910): 212–25.

42. Wundt, 316.

43. Perry wrote: "As regards the feeling of effort James reversed a judgment which he had himself formerly held, that the feeling of effort accompanies the efferent (outgoing) current which innervates the muscle" (RBP, 2:88). Perry's conclusion is borne out by an endorsement of "feelings of innervation" in James's notebook of 1878. In later discussions of such feelings, James always argued intensely against them; he was apparently discomfited by the failure of Wundt and others to note more carefully and publicly his arguments on the matter. In an 1894 review, "Professor Wundt and Feelings of Innervation" (*Psychological Review* 1:70–73), he returned to the issue, expressing approval that Wundt had at last abandoned the so-called feelings of innervation; he also remarked that Wundt could have saved himself fourteen years of error by reading "The Feeling of Effort" in 1880. In the same review, James took issue with Wundt's reference to him in the fourth edition of *Physiologische Psychologie.* James summarized his own earlier explanation of this phenomenon: when the "external rectus-muscle of a man's eye (say the left eye) is wholly or partly paralyzed, objects lying in the left half of the field of view appear to that left eye to lie farther to the left than they really are" (70). Wundt had explained this phenomenon by postulating an excessive leftward feeling of innervation when the man turns his afflicted eye toward the object; James had located the cause in the inward squinting of the right or sound eye. Although he had abandoned feelings of innervation, Wundt still questioned James's solution; James's reply in the review indicated his discomfiture:

The point is a minute one, certainly in itself not worthy of notice; and the existence or non-existence of feelings of innervation is an alternative on which, so far as I can see at present, no general theoretic consequences seem to hinge. I should consequently not have been stirred to write this note were it not that Professor Wundt's peculiar manner of revising his opinions is objectionable from the point of view of literary ethics, and is beginning, I fancy, to arouse in other readers besides myself an irritation to which it is but just that some expression should be given. (72)

The remark here that "no general theoretic consequences" hinge on the issue of whether innervation feelings exist might have been sincere if the consequences in question had been confined strictly to experimental psychology. But given James's repeated attacks on such alleged feelings, there is no doubt that he considered the issue of real significance for the philosophy of psychology; we must view the remark with a grain of salt, or possibly as a gesture to indicate his refusal to debate the matter again with Wundt.

James covered innervation feelings in his courses as well. When he was an assistant professor of philosophy, the readings for his Philosophy 5 in 1880–81 (while he was still in the early stages of preparation for *Principles*) included Alexander Bain's *Body and Mind,* Henry Maudsley's *Body and Mind* and *Physiology of Mind,* Henry Calderwood's *Brain and the Mind,* and Henry Bastian's *Relations of Brain and Mind.* The lectures often dwelled on whether feelings of innervation exist, as well as on how to explain the phenomenon of perceptual displacement in the case of a paralyzed eye. James's emphasis on these topics is clear from the notebook of George Albert Burdett, a student in James's course; the notebook is in the Houghton Library.

44. In both "The Feeling of Effort" and *Principles,* James first presented actual or speculative biological information and then developed a detailed physiological model in terms of which volition can be explained.

45. In a letter dated 22 November 1911 Cannon wrote to James's son Henry that Sherrington was acquainted with "The Feeling of Effort," "What the Will Effects," and the chapter on will in *Principles.*

A modern scientist who draws on James's physiological speculations is Karl Pribram; see note 47 to chapter 8.

The physiological information in the chapter on the will is to a great extent speculative; more established physiological facts are found in chapter 22, "The Production of Movement." This short chapter has little psychological or philosophical interest, although historians of science may be intrigued by James's discussion of Bain's law of diffusion, which says that "as an impression is accompanied with feeling, the aroused currents diffuse themselves over the brain, leading to a general agitation of the moving organs, as well as affecting the visceral" (*Principles,* 2:372).

46. Carpenter and Bain, who were friends and two of the most influential authors in physiological psychology in the nineteenth century, were obvious models for James to follow in *Principles.* They wrote on both the physiological and introspectable aspects of such topics as sensation, emotion, attention, and will (see E. G. Boring, *A History of Experimental Psychology,* 228–29). As much as any of his predecessors, Carpenter and Bain inclined James to the habit of writing in back-and-forth terms—now introspectively, now physiologically—as if with a double-aspect view of mind and body.

47. In arranging James's literary estate, Perry noted that James was reading the 1852 edition of Lotze's *Medicinische Psychologie* during 1867–68; James wrote on the flyleaf of his copy of the book, now in the Houghton Library, "Emotions due to bodily reverbations," which suggests that Lotze was also a source of his theory of emotions (see RBP, 2:89). In the chapter on the will in *Principles,* he credited Lotze with being one of the first to see that muscular exertion is an afferent and not an efferent feeling (2:523).

Renouvier's influence began as early as 1868, since a letter dated 5 October 1868 shows that James was apparently first reading Renouvier then (*LWJ,* 1:138).

48. Rudolph Lotze, quoted in *Principles,* 2:523.

49. *Principles,* 1:599.

50. "The Consciousness of Lost Limbs," 1887; reprinted in *CER,* 286. See also *Principles,* 2:546, especially the quotation from Joseph Guislain.

51. *Principles*, 2:561. James often made statements of this kind, italicized or otherwise highlighted, testifying to the intimate connection he saw between volition and attention; see especially 2:559–79.

52. The following passage, an example of the mentalistic or dualistic flavor of the chapter on will, further illuminates the significance of the controversy about afferent and efferent sensations:

> Let all our thoughts of movements be of sensational constitution; still in the emphasizing, choosing, and espousing of one of them rather than another, in the saying to it, "be thou the reality for me," there is ample scope for our inward initiative to be shown. Here, it seems to me, the true line between the passive materials and the activity of the spirit should be drawn. It is certainly false strategy to draw it between such ideas as are connected with the outgoing and such as are connected with the incoming neural wave. (*Principles*, 2:518)

53. Ibid., 2:564. It is interesting to compare James's views on the power of ideas with Freud's. See, for instance, Richard Wollheim, *Sigmund Freud* (New York: Viking, 1971), especially 51–58, 175–99.

54. Perry wrote: "That Renouvier was the greatest individual influence upon the development of James's thought cannot be doubted. Renouvier's phenomenalism, his pluralism, his fideism, his moralism, and his theism were all congenial to James's mind, and in them James found support and confirmation" (RBP, 1:655). Perry discusses at great length the relationship between Renouvier and James, which I summarized briefly in chapter 1.

See James's "Bain and Renouvier" (originally a review in *Nation*), *CER*, 26–35, and his "Réponse aux remarques de M. Renouvier, sur sa théorie de la volonté" (1888; reprinted in *CER*, 303–09).

The notebook of Edwin De T. Bechtel, a student in James's Philosophy 3 course in 1902–03, is now in the Houghton Library. The following entry is dated 11 February 1902: "Determinism and Indeterminism. It is not a thrashed out question. At first the youth is a Determinist, i.e. on reflection, reinforced by scientific ideas for uniformity. As James was a Determinist till he read Renouvier, and today J. will follow the mode induced by Renouvier."

55. *LWJ*, 1:147. Renouvier's definition is from his *Deuxième Essai*, secs. 9, 11. See RBP, 1:654–93, for a description of James's depression or crisis of 1870, which was brought on partly by his continuing to think, as he had said the year before, "that we are Nature through and through, that we are wholly conditioned, that not a wiggle of our will happens save as the result of physical laws" (RBP, 1:654). Perry also asserts that Renouvier's concept of free will helped James to survive that period of depression. James wrote in his diary on 30 April 1870:

> Hitherto, when I have felt like taking a free initiative, like daring to act originally, without carefully waiting for contemplation of the external world to determine all for me, Suicide seemed the most manly form to put my daring into; Now, I will go a step further with my will, not only act with it, but believe as well; believe in my individual reality and creative power. My belief to be sure *can't* be optimistic—but I will posit life, (the real, the good) in the self governing *resistance* of the ego to the world [the rest of the page is torn out].

See chapters 1, 13, and 14.

56. *Principles*, 2:573–74. We must keep this passage in mind in assessing Perry's remark that "in the long run the proof that carried most weight with James was the moral argument developed in his 'Dilemma of Determinism'" (1:658). Perry did not underestimate Renouvier's influence here, yet he suggested that it was superseded by the "moral argument" in the "Dilemma" essay of 1884, fourteen years after the crisis when James credited Renouvier's argument with saving his faith in free will. That James developed other reasons for his defense

of free will is plain enough, but when the debate got tough, Renouvier's reasoning still worked its magic. Nothing, in fact, could ever have replaced its priority for James.

57. "The Dilemma of Determinism," in McDermott, 607.

58. Since James was a moralist throughout his life, his call to meet the moral challenge that living represented is evident everywhere in his writings.

For more on the topic of activity, a significant concept in James's philosophy of psychology, see "The Experience of Activity," in McDermott, 277–91. He noted in that essay that the activity of attending (and of consenting or deciding), far from being transphenomenal, is a phenomenon that can be experienced and introspected. See also RBP, 2:663–64.

On another point, James referred to C. S. Peirce in "The Dilemma of Determinism" because he thought that Peirce's doctrine of tychism supported his own belief that chance events sometimes happen. Years later, when James was developing the concept into his later metaphysics, he received a letter from Peirce, dated 18 March 1897:

> There are some things in your *Dilemma of Determinism* that I cannot assent to. I cannot admit that the will is free, for reasons that may be found in my *Man's Glassy Essence*. Namely, chance can only amount to much in a state of things closely approximating to unstable equilibrium. Now in the act of willing there is no such state of things, the freedom lies in the *choice* which long antecedes the will. *There* a state of nearly unstable equilibrium is found. But this makes a great difference in your doctrine.

The letter is in the Houghton Library. Perry reprinted portions (RBP, 2:223) but did not include this passage.

The correspondence between Peirce and James reveals a contrast between the lives of these two lifelong friends; James was successful and famous, Peirce a struggling recluse. James was a constant source of support, financially and psychologically, for Peirce, and he benefited in turn from the stimulation of Peirce's ideas. Both men wove philosophy into their personal lives, and that Peirce shared James's interest in the will is indicated, for example, in a letter dated 12 June 1902:

> There is a point of psychology which has been interesting me. . . . The question is what passes in consciousness . . . in the course of forming a new belief. . . . My duty, as I see it, will be to treat my life just as I would an aching truth that there was no hope of making useful. I will have it out. I am not going to act hastily; but it looks as if it were coming to that, and when it does, I wish my friends to know that what I do I do from long deliberated conviction.

As early as 1872 James wrote that the experience of activity has a generic quale of consciousness that introspectively distinguishes it from merely passive sensations. See his unsigned review of Taine's *On Intelligence* (*Nation* 15 [1872]: 140).

59. James wrote: "But what can good maxims do, when even good resolutions, as we know, are no equivalent for those *acts* of volition on whose constant repetition the formation of character depends?" (Unsigned review of W. B. Carpenter's *Principles of Mental Physiology* in *Atlantic Monthly* 34 [1874]: 495).

60. I have been glib in endorsing James's claim that acts of attending and willing are introspectively distinguishable. Since James's time the behaviorist outlook has dominated academic psychology and philosophy, and belief in mental acts has become increasingly suspect and unfashionable. Today the writings of philosophers such as Gilbert Ryle and psychologists such as D. O. Hebb are influential examples of that outlook, but the movement away from introspective psychology and discussions of mental acts began much earlier.

For instance, John Dewey asked James in a letter of 6 May 1891: "Would you have needed any 'special' activity of attention, any 'special' act of will?" Dewey's continued objections are clear in his treatment of attention in "Does Reality Possess Practical Character?" in *Essays*

Philosophical and Psychological in Honor of William James (New York: Longmans, Green, and Co., 1908), 53–80. E. L. Thorndike offers an interesting criticism in "The Mental Antecedents of Voluntary Movements," *Journal of Philosophy, Psychology, and Scientific Method* 4 (1907): 40–42. Thorndike made special reference to the fiat of the will.

A. A. Roback, whose work on James is still valuable to scholars, wrote: "A few of his cherished notions have been discarded by his contemporaries in America. Among these are the *'fiat* of the will' and the organic view of the emotions" (*William James: His Marginalia, Personality and Contribution* [Cambridge: Sci-Art Publishers, 1942], 310–11). George Humphrey, commenting on the advent of behaviorism with John Watson about the time of the First World War, wrote: "Watson was to direct an attack on the whole introspective method, using the concept of attention as an example of the untrustworthy nature of introspective evidence in general" (*Thinking: An Introduction to Its Experimental Psychology* [New York: John Wiley, 1951], 113).

61. *Principles*, 2:529–30.

62. See, for instance, ibid., 1:427 and 1:455–58.

63. Roback wrote: "It may well be conceded that had James then the time to examine the issues, he might have accepted the chief tenets of psychoanalysis, as did Stanley Hall and James Putnam, but what argues against this change is James's inability to see the microcosm playing its part through symbols. Freud's mysticism originated in Cabbala (theoretical); James's in Celtic phantom seeking (physical)" (88).

Because of his *esse est sentiri* doctrine of mental states, James was forced to reject Freud's depersonalized unconscious; he held that if a mental state exists of which we are unconscious, it must be conscious to another "subpersonality." This interpretation followed Janet's explanation of multiple personalities.

For Freud's rejection of the Janet-James view in favor of his own depersonalized system of the unconscious, see, for instance, his *Autobiographical Study* (New York: Norton, 1963), 52–60.

64. The hypnotic or trance state displays many intriguing symptoms, one of which is sometimes an apparent suspension of the critical reasoning capacities. But, James reported, "It ought to be said, that in trying to verify in other ways this hypothesis of the trance subjects' non-analytic state of mind, we have met with exceptions which invite further study. Certain it is that, when expressly stimulated thereto, trance-subjects will reason and analyze acutely" ("Report of the Committee on Hypnotism," *Proceedings of the American Society for Psychical Research* 1 [1886]: 99).

65. *Principles*, 1:316. James's thesis in "The Moral Equivalent of War" is that a program conscripting youth for manual labor might sublimate their innate aggressive and military impulses.

66. See *Principles*, chapters 26 and 28.

67. Ibid., 1:409. Although most children outgrow this behavior, some do not; according to Bruno Bettelheim, some autistic children cannot or will not use first personal pronouns. They refer to themselves not as "I" or by name, but as if to something or someone else. See Bettelheim, *The Empty Fortress: Infantile Autism and the Birth of the Self* (New York: Free Press, 1967). See also chapter 12, note 3.

68. Biographical studies such as Allen's and Strouse's certainly give this impression. James's reference to "what might be called the *anti-sexual instinct*, the instinct of personal isolation, the actual repulsiveness to us of the idea of intimate contact with most of the persons we meet, especially those of our own sex" (*Principles*, 2:437–38) is sometimes cited to support this impression. James was certainly reserved about the topic of sex, but that reserve was not unusual for a man in his position and in his times; see chapters 1 and 13.

Havelock Ellis said of James: "A partial contribution to the analysis of modesty has been made by Professor James, who, with his usual insight and lucidity, has set forth certain of its characteristics, especially the element due 'the application to ourselves of judgments primarily passed upon our mates' " (*The Psychology of Sex* [London: F. A. Davis, 1901], 1).

69. *Principles,* 2:439. For other remarks about sex, see 2:412 and 2:437–38.

70. David Hume, *An Inquiry Concerning Human Understanding,* sec. 1; quoted in ibid., 2:558n.

71. "The Energies of Men," in McDermott, 680.

72. "The Varieties of Religious Experience," in McDermott, 759.

73. *Principles,* 2:688. In this context James discussed heredity, evolution of instinct, and the passage of traits from one generation to another; he favored Darwin's theory to that of Jean Lamarck, which asserts that traits acquired by one generation are transmitted to the next (*Principles,* 2:686–88).

8. EMOTION

1. "What Is an Emotion?" *Mind* 9 (1884): 188–205. "The Physical Basis of Emotion," *Psychological Review* 1 (1894): 516–29. A fourth source, "The Gospel of Relaxation" (*Scribners Magazine* 25 [1899], 499–507), is concerned with possible applications of James's theory of emotion in everyday living. He retained this title for the chapter in *Talks to Teachers* instead of using a short title, as he did for the chapters called "Attention," "Memory," and "The Will." He may have feared that a one-word title would evoke the theoretical issues associated with the three earlier discussions of emotion, when his aim in *Talks* was to examine practical applications.

2. RBP, 1:702.

3. See chapter 7 for a discussion of afferent versus efferent processes. One argument in "The Feeling of Effort" is that voluntary movements are like the movements that accompany emotions, and that neither involve feelings of innervation. Since it is generally admitted, James wrote, that emotional movements are caused by the mere presence of an exciting idea, he needed only to show that voluntary movements have a similar etiology in order to validate his theory of ideo-motor action. Emotions are peculiar, he urged, not because they result from a physiological condition different from those of volition and perception, but rather because they display a

> peculiar congenital connection of certain forms of ideas with certain very specially combined movements, largely of the "involuntary" muscles, but also of the others—as in fear, anger, etc.—such connection being non-congenital in voluntary action. . . . That one set of ideas should compel the vascular, respiratory, and gesticulatory symptoms of shame, another those of anger, a third those of grief, a fourth those of laughter, and a fifth those of sexual excitement, is a most singular fact of our organization, which the labors of a Darwin have hardly even begun to throw light upon. ("The Feeling of Effort," 18–19)

4. "What Is an Emotion?" *CER,* 246.

5. *Principles,* 2:472–73. References today to James's speculative physiology, when they occur at all, are almost always for historical reasons. A recent exception is Karl H. Pribram's criticism of James's brain theory; Pribram argues, however, that with modifications the theory is more sophisticated than is generally assumed and contains insights for today's neurophysiologist. In elaborating upon James's contention that emotional reactions usually terminate in the body while instinctive or motivational reactions usually extend into the environment, Pribram says: "The proposal derived directly from Jamesian theory states simply that emotion is essentially based on closed-loop feedbacks, while motivations go beyond these and 'enter into practical relations' by way of information-processing, open-loop, feedforward mechanisms" ("Self-Consciousness and Intentionality: A Model Based on an Experimental Analysis of the Brain Mechanisms Involved in the Jamesian Theory of Motivation and Emo-

tion," *Consciousness and Self-Regulation: Advances in Research,* 2 vols. ed. Gary E. Schwartz and David Shapiro (New York: Plenum, 1976), 1:84. See also note 47 below.

6. *Principles,* 2:448–49. James's complaint about the inability of psychology to formulate an adequate theory of emotion has been echoed indefinitely. D. O. Hebb wrote: "The discussion of emotion has been about as confused as that of any topic in psychology, partly because the terminology is often equivocal and partly because tradition carried great weight in this part of the field and it is hard to keep a modern point of view consistently" (*The Organization of Behavior* [New York: John Wiley, 1959], 235).

7. See, for example, the essays in Amelie O. Rorty, ed., *Explaining Emotions* (Berkeley and Los Angeles: University of California Press, 1980), and in K. D. Irani and Gerald E. Myers, eds., *Emotion: Philosophical Studies* (New York: Haven, 1984).

8. *Principles,* 2:479. John Dewey wrote two articles in 1894 and 1895 on the theory of emotion, in which he sought to unite Darwin's idea that emotional behavior is reminiscent of ancestral behavior with James's theory of emotions. He wrote:

> [Consider] the *shrug* of impotence and the raising of hands in astonishment. I feel certain that the rational hypothesis is to suppose that *these are survivals of certain acts, and not symbolic indications of certain emotions.* . . . I suggest the possibility that the throwing up of the arms in attention is partly the survival of a movement of warding off the approaching hostile object, and partly a reinforcement of the holding of the chest full of air characteristic of expectancy and of astonishment—a movement whose analogue is found in the raising and drawing back of the arms in yawning. The shrug of impotence seems to be complex; the union of survivals of three or four distinct acts. The raising of the brows is the act of retrospect, of surveying the ground to see if anything else could have been done; the pursing of the lips, the element of tentative rejection (doubt); the raising of the shoulders, the act of throwing a burden off. . . . Summing up, we may say that all so-called expressions of emotions are, in reality, the reduction of movements and stimulations originally useful into attitudes. ("The Theory of Emotion: [I] Emotional Attitudes," *Psychological Review* 1, no. 6 [1894]: 568–69; italics indicate James's underlining)

James's added emphasis in his copy of Dewey's article (now in the Houghton Library) indicates agreement that behaviors ordinarily described as expressive of emotion are in reality survivals of former patterns of action that can be interpreted along the lines of Darwin's and Spencer's explanations. Dewey's point, in the spirit both of evolutionary theory and of James's theory of emotions, was that emotional attitudes can be explained by reference to useful behavior, either as survivals or disruptions of purposeful actions, and not the other way around. "In every case the idea of expression of emotion does not enter in only to confuse" (556; James underlined these words as well). James approved of Dewey's formulation because it was essential to his own theory that the everyday bodily movements said to be expressive of emotion are, to the contrary, either the causes of the emotion or the actual stuff of which the emotion consists; they are not, Dewey and James argued, mere symptoms or indicators of emotion.

Dewey occasionally amends James and Darwin. For example: "While Darwin's explanation of shutting the eyes—to protect blood-vessels from gorging on account of the violent screaming—undoubtedly accounts for the selection of this attitude, it can hardly account for its origin. I think originally it had the same end as screaming—to shut out or off some threatening object, as the ostrich, etc., or as one shuts his eyes on firing a gun for the first time" (560). Dewey's thoughts are similar to what Jean-Paul Sartre said about the intentional character of emotions in *Esquisse d'une théorie des émotions* (1939).

In his second essay on emotion, Dewey both criticized and defended the James-Lange theory of emotion (described below in the text) within the Darwinian framework developed in his first essay. He praised the theory for going beyond "arbitrary and subjective schemes" and giving a definition of emotion. "Emotion in its entirety is a mode of behavior which is purposive, or has an intellectual content, and which also reflects itself into feeling or Affects, as the subjective valuation of that which is objectively expressed in the idea or purpose" ("The Theory of Emotion: [II] The Significance of Emotions" *Psychological Review* 2 [1895], 13). Other than indicating with a check the title of this essay, James made no markings on his copy of Dewey's second article.

Dewey's second essay also discusses history and personal influence:

> In my *Psychology, e.g.,* p. 19 and pp. 246–49, it is laid down, quite schematically, that feeling is the internalizing of activity or will. There is nothing novel in this doctrine; in a way it goes back to Plato and Aristotle. But what first fixed my especial attention, I believe, upon James's doctrine of emotion was that it furnishes this old idealistic conception of feeling, hitherto blank and unmediated, with a medium of translation into the terms of concrete phenomena. I mention this bit of personal history simply as an offset to those writers who have found Mr. James's conception so tainted with materialism. On the historical side, it may be worth noting that a crude anticipation of James's theory is found in Hegel's *Philosophie des Geistes,* 401. (15)

In addition, Dewey applied James's theory of emotion to his theory of attention.

> It seems to me that the application of James's theory of emotion to his theory of attention would give some very interesting results. As it now stands, the theory "in attention" of preferential selection on the *basis* of interest seems to contradict the theory of emotional value as the *outcome* of preferential selection (that is, specific reaction). But the contradiction is most flagrant in the case of effort, considered, first, as emotion and then as an operation of will. (19–20)

James's account is vulnerable to Dewey's criticism here, and it was perceptive of Dewey to see that James treated emotion with an attitude different from that with which he treated will and attention.

James seems to have accepted uncritically the Darwinian and Spencerian statements on emotion, endorsing the genetic explanation of emotional behavior as a scientific step forward. He stopped short of the enthusiasm with which Dewey applied evolution to emotion. James's discussion of the genetic explanation is brief compared to the account of his own theory; the genesis that impressed him was related more to what he called physiological mechanics than to the natural history of the evolutionists (see, for example, *Principles,* 2:454). Dewey was aware of this possible difference between him and James (see Dewey's first essay, 563).

9. *Principles,* 2:403–41, 2:678–86.

10. McDermott, 662. See also ibid., 2:410–11.

11. *Principles,* 2:418–19.

12. Ibid., 2:478, 483. For a recent discussion of facial expression of emotion, see Paul Ekman, Wallace Friesen, and Phoebe Ellsworth, *Emotion in the Human Face: Guidelines for Research and an Integration of Findings* (New York: Pergamon, 1972). The authors conclude: *"There is one fundamental aspect of the relationship between facial behavior and emotion which is unusual for man: the association between the movements of specific facial muscles and specific emotions. This has been found true for the facial appearance associated with anger, sadness, happiness, and disgust, and perhaps also for surprise and fear"* (179). James was prepared to accept this sort of judgment, given its limited claim and the numerous questions which the authors leave open for future studies. He might also have agreed with George Mandler's statement: "It is rather surprising that facial expression has rarely been used in controlled studies of emotion, that is as a dependent variable in conjunction with some of the other emotional variables. . . . If people can make such reliable judgments, then psychologists also should be able to do so to use expressive behavior more consistently in the laboratory. We might then have a reliable and

useful dependent variable for the study of the whole emotional complex" ("Emotion," *New Directions in Psychology* [New York: Holt, Rinehart & Winston, 1962], 307; quoted in Ekman et al., 180).

James would have stressed, however, that just because we can obtain emotional information from a person's face, we should not assume that each facial muscle and its movement are uniquely related to a specific emotion. The conclusion in Ekman et al. is consistent with that point of view.

13. In stressing James's reservations about evolutionary or teleological explanations, I do not mean to underestimate the influence of Darwin and Spencer upon his thought. For an authoritative account of Spencer's influence, see RBP, 1:474–93.

Perry also remarks that Darwin's influence was an early and profound one in James's career and that James considered Darwin a model scientist and respected him for his careful experimentalism and his modesty.

> James's conception of the *a priori* factors in human knowledge was an application of the Darwinian notion of spontaneous or accidental variation; Darwinian, too, was his tendency to view life as a hazardous experiment, with all of its instrumentalities on trial. James did not follow the Darwinian emphasis on continuity. That nature never makes leaps—*natura non facit saltum*—was no part of his vision of things. On the contrary, he felt the individual to be a locus of abrupt differences. The essence of Darwinism, for James as for [T. H.] Huxley, lay in the idea that whether individual variations are great or slight, they prove and disprove themselves—survive and disappear—as their environment dictates. The individual nominates, the environment elects. (RBP, 1:470)

See Robert J. Richards, "The Personal Equation in Science: William James's Psychological and Moral Uses of Darwinian Theory," in *A William James Renaissance*, Harvard Library Bulletin 30, no. 4 (October 1982), 387–426.

James's ideas about instinct have by no means been completely forgotten. The editors of a recent anthology, which includes part of the *Principles* chapter, write in their introduction: "We begin with William James because his treatment of the subject gives the first hint that empirical studies were to become increasingly important as a means of resolving issues, while his theoretical treatment sets the question as one of learning *vs.* heredity—the form it was to have for half a century" (R. C. Birney and R. C. Teevan [eds.], *Instinct: An Enduring Problem in Psychology* [New York: Van Nostrand, 1961], vii).

See Ronald Fletcher, *Instinct in Man: In the Light of Recent Work in Comparative Psychology* (New York: Schocken, 1966) for a summary of James's contributions to the psychology of instinct. Fletcher asserts that James's inclusion of a cognitive element within instinctive experience, such that we instinctively recognize the significance of a certain perception or object, is still appreciated by many psychologists, who label the idea *instinct-meaning* or *instinct-interest* (31). Given such a cognitive element, Fletcher says that learning can occur in the first performance of an instinct, as James suggested. Moreover, certain instincts are transitory and gradually disappear, another point in James's favor (34). Fletcher also applauds James for noticing that developmental "periods of importance" for learning are connected with periods when the instincts are still present. The idea that learning thus occurs more quickly and effectively at certain stages in maturation is called by some the Critical Period Hypothesis, which Fletcher says was "supported by both Psycho-Analysis and Comparative Ethology [and] was put forward quite clearly and explicitly by William James" (287).

Compare these recent assessments with remarks by America's first noted behaviorist, John B. Watson: "James was right when he said most people do not learn after 30, but there is no reason for it except that most people after 30 have explored the mysteries of sex and get their food and water without speeding up or having to do anything unusual in order to obtain it" (*Behaviorism* [New York: The People's Institute, 1924, 1925], 172). Watson attacked James's list of instincts as well as the whole theory of instincts, concluding that the only scientific procedure is "to single out for study whatever act is in question and to watch and record its life history" (104). However, in *Behavior: An Introduction to Comparative Psychology* (New York: Holt, 1914) he argued with James differently, especially on the claim that instincts wane through age and disuse. James had described in *Principles* (2:399) his observations of a Scotch terrier puppy which played at burying an object by scratching the carpet with his front feet, dropping the object, scratching all around it, and finally leaving it. The behavior was clearly useless, and the dog, after performing the act four or five times, was never seen to repeat it. The instinct, unfulfilled, had faded away.

Watson commented:

> The case of the Scotch terrier attempting to bury food in the carpet and then finally giving over the attempt on all subsequent occasions has often been cited. . . . The observation, so far as it goes, is unquestionably true, but there is no evidence that the instinct is lost. Given the proper environment and the proper conditions of hunger, and we should expect to see the instinct reappear in all its pristine vigor. . . . That instincts are overlapped and obscured by later habits is unquestionable. Whether this process of obscuration results finally in the complete elimination of the instinct is certainly not proven by any observation we have in the field at the present time. (*Behavior,* 146)

See also Watson's *Psychology: From the Standpoint of a Behaviorist* (Philadelphia: Lippincott, 1919), 253–56.

On the other hand, a modern psychologist, while cautioning us not to "build too much on the limited observations and theorizing" of James, recognizes that the Jamesian hypothesis of the "transitoriness" of instincts is still a lively one. That instinct and learning can combine is an interesting feature of animal and human development. "This type of behaviour has excited great interest in recent times: Thorpe (1956, 1963) in his book *Learning and Instinct in Animals* . . . judged this behaviour to be of 'rather exceptional interest'; the study of it, in Thorpe's view, promised to shed a good deal of light on the relationship of instinct to 'plastic processes in general'" (Wladyslaw Sluckin, *Imprinting and Early Learning* [Chicago: Aldine, 1967], 3).

14. *Principles,* 2:449. The dating of Lange's essay is somewhat confusing. In *Principles* (2:443) James referred to a German translation of 1887, but in "The Physical Basis of Emotion" he dated it 1884, the same year as "What Is an Emotion?" Perry's dating in *The Thought and Character of William James* (2:89) is 1887, which obviously follows James's reference in *Principles,* but he gives 1895 (probably a typographical error) in his *Annotated Bibliography of The Writings of William James* (New York: Longmans, Green & Co., 1920). According to Boring, Lange's paper *On Sindsbevoegelser* appeared in 1885, then in a German translation, *Ueber Gemütsbewegungen,* in 1887. Lange's monograph is reprinted in *The Emotions,* ed. Knight Dunlap, *Psychology Classics* 1 (Baltimore: Williams and Wilkins, 1922). See Boring, *A History of Experimental Psychology* (New York: Century, 1929), 532–33.

15. "The Physical Basis of Emotion," in *CER,* 346. James's idea that emotions are bodily commotions seems to have originated as early as 1867–68, when he was reading Lotze. See RBP, 2:89.

16. Some commentators have concluded that "The Physical Basis of Emotion" retracted what was striking and controversial in "What Is an Emotion?" and in the chapter on emotion in *Principles*. For example, J. Mark Baldwin wrote: "In my opinion, he now states a theory so different from that in his book that it is fair to say either that criticism has driven him out of his old position or that what he has himself called his 'slap-dash' treatment—I call it above (written before his paper appeared) 'naive' treatment—misled us all. At any rate, no one should now read, much less teach, his book without practically substituting this article for his chapter on 'Emotion' " ("The Origin of Emotional Expression," *Psychological Review* 1 [1894]:

621). Nevertheless, I believe that James preserves in the 1894 essay the essentials of his theory as previously articulated.

E. B. Titchener questioned the originality of the James-Lange theory in 1884, recounting what he took to be its earlier formulations (see his "Historical Note on the James-Lange Theory of Emotion," *American Journal of Psychology* 25 [1914]). The professional relationship between James and Titchener seems to have been fairly tense, although they did not meet until 1909, at a famous meeting at Clark University, which included Freud and Jung. See RBP, 2:123.

Boring comments on historical antecedents: "Many other French physiologists of this period held similar views, and because of their tendency to localize the emotions in the viscera they are the logical and perhaps actual progenitors of the James-Lange theory of emotion. All in all, the point of view about the body and the mind was not so very different from that of Descartes, whose influence is shown in this manner. Thus the relation of the mind is to the whole body, not merely to the brain" (*A History of Experimental Psychology*, 58).

17. "What Is an Emotion?" in *CER*, 247–48.

18. Ibid., 253–55; the same passage appears in *Principles*, 2:452–53.

19. James was aware of this criticism, as he noted in "The Physical Basis of Emotion," in *CER*, 349–52.

20. See *Principles*, 2:444–49.

21. "The Physical Basis of Emotion," in *CER*, 351–52. James explained the last sentence in a footnote: "When the running has actually commenced, it gives rise to *exhilaration* by its effects on breathing and pulse, etc., in this case, and not to *fear*."

22. "What Is an Emotion?" in *CER*, 252; the same passage appears in *Principles*, 2:450.

23. "What Is an Emotion?" in *CER*, 252. It may seem plausible to say that James down-graded the value of emotions considering them, in the Victorian spirit, as nuisances. Such an interpretation might be based not only on biographical data and on James's characteristically moral if not puritanical statements, but also on his provocative introspective account of the "central self," an account which ignores emotion and emphasizes cognitive and moral activity (*Principles*, 1:298–305). Indeed, James may seem to have had less enthusiasm for introspecting emotion than volition, and to concede the physiological makeup of emotion more readily than that of volition or attention.

Such an interpretation may cause uncertainty about the importance of emotion in James's psychological writings, but parts of his texts strongly suggest the opposite interpretation. "The Consciousness of Self" chapter in *Principles* does not in fact ignore emotion. James discusses "self-feeling" and the emotions of self-satisfaction and abasement, which are described as "a primitive emotional species as are, for example, rage or pain. Each has its own peculiar physiognomical expression" (1:307). In view of this remark, it is clearly possible to link the concepts of self and emotion in James's psychology.

> It would be perhaps too much to expect [a subject] to arrest the tide of any strong gust of passion for the sake of any such curious analysis as this; but he can observe more tranquil states, and that may be assumed here to be true of the greater which is shown to be true of the less. Our whole cubic capacity is sensibly alive; and each morsel of it contributes its pulsations of feeling, dim or sharp, pleasant, painful, or dubious, to that sense of personality that every one of us unfailingly carries with him. It is surprising what little items give accent to those complexes of sensibility. When worried by any slight trouble, one may find that the form of one's bodily consciousness is the contraction, often quite inconsiderable, of the eyes and brows. ("What Is an Emotion?" in *CER*, 252–53)

This introspectively sensitive passage clearly links emotions and their physiological details to an inner sense of personality.

Consider another passage: "[A merely cognitive] existence, although it seems to have been the ideal of ancient sages, is too apathetic to be keenly sought after by those born after the revival of the worship of sensibility, a few generations ago'' ("What Is an Emotion?" in CER, 255–56). Together with James's wry statements about emotionless Chautauqua in "What Makes a Life Significant" (McDermott, 648–60) and his discussion of emotionless stoicism in "The Varieties of Religious Experience" (McDermott, 752), this passage contradicts the impression that James considered a life without intense emotion superior to our emotional life.

Nevertheless, it is difficult to be sure of James's real feelings about the value of emotion in human life. Consider the following passages: "The peace of rationality may be sought through ecstasy when logic fails. To religious persons of every shade of doctrine moments come when the world, as it is, seems so divinely orderly, and the acceptance of it by the heart so rapturously complete, that intellectual questions vanish. . . . *Ontological emotion* so fills the soul that ontological speculation can no longer overlap it and put her girdle of interrogation marks round existence" ("The Sentiment of Rationality," in McDermott, 324; italics mine). "There is no ground for assuming a simple abstract 'religious emotion' to exist as a distinct elementary mental affection by itself, present in every religious experience without exception. As there thus seems to be no one elementary religious emotion, but only a common storehouse of emotions upon which religious objects may draw, so there might conceivably also prove to be no one specific and essential kind of religious object, and no one specific and essential kind of religious act" ("The Varieties of Religious Experience," in McDermott, 742).

24. "What Is an Emotion?" in CER, 250–52.

25. "The Physical Basis of Emotion," in CER, 358.

26. Ibid., 355–56.

27. Ibid., 350.

28. Ibid. James discusses the criticisms by Wundt and others in the pages preceding this passage.

29. Ibid., 352.

30. Ibid., 353.

31. Ibid., 353–54.

32. See, for example, Robert C. Solomon, *The Passions: The Myth and Nature of Human Emotion* (Garden City: N.Y.: Anchor, 1977), 141–46. Solomon argues that James reduced emotions to mere epiphenomena, an understandable interpretation but one which should be qualified substantially.

33. "The Gospel of Relaxation," in *Talks*, 132. Published in 1899, five years after "The Physical Basis of Emotion" and nine years after *Principles*, this essay suggests everyday applications of James's theory of emotion. He referred here to his "paradoxical formula," that we are sad because we weep or afraid because we run, as a possible exaggeration, but he doubted that the exaggeration was very great. As in "The Physical Basis of Emotion," if *cry* and *run* do not refer to overt acts but rather to "invisible visceral" changes in the body that precede and perhaps accompany the acts, then the apparent paradox or exaggeration is minimized. There is no shift of position in the James-Lange theory in "The Gospel of Relaxation."

34. "The Gospel of Relaxation," in *Talks*, 133. Here James seems to have wandered into a possible inconsistency. Given his allegiance to the theory of ideo-motor action, it seems odd that he did not suppose our emotions, taken as states of consciousness and thus comparable to ideas, to be within the direct control of the will. If emotions, like ideas, are somehow mental, his account of emotion seems to conflict with his theory of the will.

But if emotions are, as the James-Lange theory declares, bodily commotions rather than mental states, there is no inconsistency at all. Yet James said explicitly in *Principles* that his theory of emotion is not materialistic, suggesting that something in an emotion is not bodily but mental, in which case the inconsistency reappears. Much will depend, therefore, on how we interpret his repudiation of a materialistic theory of emotion.

35. *Talks*, 133. There is a decidedly existentialist sound to this statement. The idea that we

are what we choose or that we are the sum of our deeds echoes Aristotle and looks ahead to Sartre.

36. Hannah Whitall Smith, *The Christian's Secret of a Happy Life,* quoted in *Talks,* 134, where it is described as an "admirable and widely successful little book."

James's suggestion that emotion is not high in the hierarchy of human experience accords with his omission of emotion in his definition of the self in *Principles,* which in turn echoes "The Feeling of Effort":

> There *is* a feeling of mental spontaneity, opposed in nature to all afferent feelings; but it does not, like the pretended feeling of muscular innervation, sit among them as among its peers. It is something which dominates them all, by simply choosing from their midst. . . . All our mind's contents are alike empirical. What is *a priori* is only their accentuation and emphasis. This greeting of the spirit, this acquiescence, connivance, partiality, call it what you will, which seems the inward gift of our selfhood, and no essential part of the feelings, to either of which in turn it may be given,—this psychic effort pure and simple, is the fact which *a priori* psychologists really have in mind when they indignantly deny that the whole intellect is derived from sense. (*CER,* 204)

Emotion is not as important to selfhood as will and attention, which are considered as acts of "acquiescence" and "greetings of the spirit." Compared to will and attention, and perhaps also to thought and other mental faculties, emotion was not a significant part of the self in James's thinking. He perpetuated a long tradition in philosophy and psychology of viewing emotions as belonging to the body rather than to the allegedly nobler and more etherial regions of the mind, and even as being alien to the mind's natural and worthy interests. He may have thought that emotions are worrisome and that an ideal life would not need them. Though he may have thought most emotions are problematic, he entertained other ideas about feelings.

37. *Talks,* 134.

38. On James's attitude toward Freudian symbolism and dream interpretation, see RBP, 2:122–23. James does not specifically refer to psychoanalytic clinical practice, but his criticism of it seems implicit in "The Gospel of Relaxation."

39. *Principles,* 2:458–59.

40. The central theme in "The Gospel of Relaxation" was not always couched in terms of physical education. References to mind-cures and medicine also occur, but James's emphasis is upon the physical attack we can launch against the physiological causes of burdensome emotions.

James wanted to correct the growing neurasthenia in America (something he was aware of in himself and in his family), and one of the causes in his estimation was what Freud called the superego, the domineering conscience that we inherit from parental and other influences.

> The need of feeling responsible all the livelong day has been preached long enough in our New England. Long enough exclusively, at any rate,—and long enough to the female sex. . . . Even now I fear that some one of my fair hearers may be making an undying resolve to become strenuously relaxed, cost what it will, for the remainder of her life. It is needless to say that this is not the way to do it. The way to do it, paradoxical as it may seem, is genuinely not to care whether you are doing it or not. (*Talks,* 148)

41. "What Is an Emotion?" in *CER,* 263; this passage occurs also in *Principles,* 2:466–47.

42. "The Sentiment of Rationality," in McDermott, 332. This essay is devoted to the idea that there is a sentiment which psychologically underlies our desire for rationality, a feeling that some things are sufficient and require no explanation. The fact that this sentiment is a feeling or an emotion rather than a mere cognition is important, James thought, in justifying the subjectivism of his own pragmatic method.

43. See, for example, McDermott, 605.

44. *Principles*, 2:473.

45. Ibid., 2:473–74; the same passage occurs in "What Is an Emotion?" in *CER*, 270–71.

46. "The Physical Basis of Emotion," in *CER*, 369.

47. W. B. Cannon's work was originally brought together in his *Bodily Changes in Pain, Hunger, Fear and Rage* (New York: Appleton-Century-Crofts, 1915). For his later views, see the second edition (1929); "The James-Lange Theory of Emotions: A Critical Examination and an Alternative Theory," *American Journal of Psychology* 39 (1927): 106–24; and M. L. Reymert, ed., *Feelings and Emotions: Wittenberg Symposium* (Worcester, Mass.: Clark University, 1928), 257–68. For a criticism of Cannon, see J. R. Angell, "A Reconsideration of James's Theory of Emotion in the Light of Recent Criticisms," *Psychological Review* 23 (1916): 251–61 and E. G. Boring, *A History of Experimental Psychology*, 533. See also Cannon's "Again the James-Lange and Thalamic Theories of Emotion," *Psychological Review* 43 (1931): 281–95. Boring's references to Cannon's work are particularly helpful to the reader interested in the history of the debate about the physiology of emotion. Cannon's work is often associated with that of Charles Sherrington, Henry Head, and Philip Bard; in fact, his theory is sometimes referred to as the Cannon-Bard hypothesis.

An unusually critical response is this: "The James-Lange thesis was proven to be incorrect on physiological grounds, primarily by W. B. Cannon, who argued conclusively that the same visceral and neurological changes accompanied very different emotional states and that artificial induction of these changes did not produce the appropriate emotion" (Robert C. Solomon, *The Passions* [Garden City, N.Y.: Anchor, 1977], 152–53.) Solomon overlooks both James's explicit response to this objection and the complexity of determining what is at issue physiologically in deciding in favor of James or Cannon. A more typical verdict is this:

> We must conclude, therefore, that neither the James-Lange theory nor the thalamic theory is completely satisfactory as an explanation of the relation between emotional experience and emotional behavior. That we are often aware of bodily changes in emotion . . . shows that visceral and skeletal components play their part. We cannot therefore throw out the James-Lange theory altogether, nor can the thalamic theory be ignored, for the thalamus, whether or not it is the center for emotion, contributes a great deal to emotional behavior. (N. L. Munn, *Psychology* [Boston: Houghton Mifflin, 1946], 280)

Or this: "The theories of James and Cannon are not fundamentally incompatible, and each was aimed primarily at explaining different phenomena, with one pertaining primarily to feeling [James] and the other to 'emotional' reactions [Cannon], or expressions. Thus, the protest against James's theory by proponents of the thalamic theory has usually been directed against 'a straw man'" (R. E. Mason, *Internal Perception and Bodily Functioning* [New York: International Universities Press, 1961], 124). A recurrent criticism of Cannon has been that he could not be sure that experimental animals, in *behaving* as if they were angry in the absence of visceral impact, were actually *experiencing* the emotion of anger. Mason provides an excellent bibliography. For an extremely valuable study of this topic, including detailed criticism of the Cannon-Bard hypothesis, see Edmund Fantino, "Emotion," in *The Study of Behavior*, ed. J. A. Nevin (Glenview, Ill.: Scott, Foresman & Co., 1973), 281–320. Fantino also includes an excellent bibliography. His essay focuses upon recent investigations of emotion that ought to be evaluated in assessing the James-Lange theory in the light of twentieth-century psychology. For an essay that combines current research with a look at the James-Cannon debate, see William Kessen and George Mandler, "Anxiety, Pain, and the Inhibition of Distress," in *Theory and Research in Abnormal Psychology*, ed. David Rosenhan and Perry London (New York: Holt, Rinehart and Winston, 1969), 67–75. A standard reaction to the controversy was expressed by the psychologist Ernest R. Hilgard: "Psychologists and physiologists have tried unsuccessfully for many years to differentiate among human emotional states according to characteristics of the bodily indicators of emotion" (*Introduction to Psychology*, 3d ed. [New York: Harcourt, Brace, and World, 1962], 163). He listed four main reasons: (1) specific emotional responses do not specify a particular emotion; (2) a person can express any emotion in a variety of ways; (3) the name of an emotion usually depends on supplementary information about its stimuli and circumstances; and (4) the introspective or conscious identification of an emotion is ordinarily influenced by the surrounding circumstances (163). Hilgard concluded that the effort to locate a physiological basis for emotions has not proved fruitful, with the result that the James-Cannon controversy has become less interesting to contemporary psychology (167).

On the other hand, Karl Pribram has tried to develop a "model based on an experimental analysis of the brain mechanisms involved in the Jamesian theory of motivation and emotion"; see his "Self-Consciousness and Intentionality," in Schwartz and Shapiro, 51–100. See note 5 above. Pribram observes:

> We have a considerable amount of evidence which demands a modification of the James-Lange position that "bodily changes follow directly the perception of the exciting fact and our feeling of these same changes in the emotion." *Feelings* of familiarity, of elation and depression, of assertion and aggression, and of sleepiness and alertness have been shown to depend on *brain* processes. . . . Bodily changes are *initiated* by these brain processes, but not, as James thought, by the processes that directly perceive. . . . We note, therefore, that the contemporary view of the theory of motivation and emotion proposed by William James is in one respect grossly misleading. While James wrote that emotional feeling was based on visceral sensations, he also wrote that such feeling was coordinate with a brain process resulting from the visceral sensation. This central aspect of Jamesian theory becomes even more clearly stated with respect to motivation and has been little appreciated by James's critics. (74, 82)

James's own correlation of emotion with cerebral processes further complicates any comparison of his theory with Cannon's. The complexity of the issue is indicated by this description of the Cannon-Bard view:

> Afferent impulses from peripheral receptors may evoke patterned efferent "emotional" responses directly through reflex pathways at the thalamic level, and/or indirectly through arousal of "conditioned responses" at the cortical level, which in turn release diencephalically integrated patterns of emotional response from cortical inhibition. At the same time, upward discharges from the activated diencephalon reach the cortex, thus adding a patterned "quale" to the sensory experience and transforming the "object-simply-apprehended" to the "object-emotionally-felt." (L. E. Hinsie and R. J. Campbell, eds., *Psychiatric Dictionary*, 3d ed. [London: Oxford University Press, 1960], 108)

Pribram adds, however: "James was in error in suggesting that emotion depended on immediate visceral sensation. . . . Cannon's classic experimental demonstrations that an organism is capable of emotional responses despite visceral deafferation have been the source of the major rebuttal to James's position, although exceptions to the validity of Cannon's claims have also been voiced (e.g., Beebe-Center, 1971; Schachter, 1967; Mandler, 1967)" (83). The interested reader should consult Pribram's bibliography for these articles and others by Pribram himself on the biology of emotion.

In reviving interest in James's physiology of emotion and motivation, Pribram seizes upon James's point that emotions tend to terminate within the organism while motivations connect with the external, exciting event; Pribram's proposal "derived directly from Jamesian theory states simply that emotion is essentially based on closed-loop feedbacks, while motivations go beyond these and 'enter into practical relations' by way of information-processing, open-loop, feedforward mechanisms'' (84).

See James Olds's famous paper, "Pleasure Centers in the Brain," *Scientific American* 195 (1956): 105–16. Rats with electrodes in their brains were found to ignore food in favor of stimulation to pleasure centers in their brains, at a rate of more than two thousand times per hour for twenty-four successive hours. Pleasure is not a complex emotion, but if, as Olds tentatively concluded, emotional and motivational mechanisms analogous to pleasure centers can also be localized in the brain, James's view that the brain has no special centers for the emotions would be undermined.

See Fred S. Fehr and John A. Stern, "Peripheral Physiological Variables and Emotion: The James-Lange Theory Revisited," *Psychological Bulletin* 74 (December 1970): 411–24. See also note 56 below.

Perhaps the most elegant summation of the visceral versus centralized dispute was made by George Santayana in his review of *Principles*.

> The question between Prof. James and other modern psychologists is not, then, one of principle; it can only be one of detail. Prof. James thinks that the cerebral condition that produces violent passion involves the excitement of the sensory centres; unless we feel the agitation of the body we cannot be greatly stirred by emotion. Others might say that the excitement of ideational centres would suffice. . . . The hypothesis that all the emotional elements come from below the brain, and that the internal excitement of that organ would produce mainly cold and intellectual perception, has certainly the charm of clearness and the merit of originality. It is so simple and luminous that one cannot help wishing it may be true. At the same time, what shall assure us that it does not abstract too much, or that the most limpid of the images of our fancy could ever have the tincture of emotion quite washed out of it? (*Atlantic Monthly* 67 (1891):556)

Santayana must have had in mind a passage such as this: "Emotion and cognition seem then parted even in this last retreat; and cerebral processes are almost feelingless, so far as we can judge, until they summon help from parts below" (*Principles*, 2:472).

48. "What Is an Emotion?" in *CER*, 271.

49. Ibid., 274–75.

50. Paul Sollier, "Recherches sur les rapports de la sensibilité et de l'émotion," *Revue philosophique* (March 1894), 241; quoted in "The Physical Basis of Emotion," in *CER*, 368.

51. "The Physical Basis of Emotion," in *CER*, 370.

52. George Santayana, review in *Atlantic Monthly* 67 (1891): 555.

53. See, for example, *Principles*, 2:452.

54. Ibid., 2:453. On the apparent conflict between James's spiritualism and his theory of emotions, see Howard M. Feinstein, "William James on the Emotions," *Journal of the History of Ideas* 31 (January–March 1970); 133–42.

55. *Principles*, 1:296–305.

56. James declared his resolve to use the word *feeling* in both senses in chapter 7, "The Methods and Snares of Psychology." After complaining about the difficulty of finding a convenient word for all states of consciousness, he wrote: "*My own partiality is for either Feeling or Thought. I shall probably often use both words in a wider sense than usual, and alternately startle two classes of readers by their unusual sound; but if the connection makes it clear that mental states at large, irrespective of their kind, are meant, this will do no harm, and may even do some good*" (*Principles*, 1:186–87).

57. "The Physical Basis of Emotion," in *CER*, 358.

58. For more on this interpretation, see my "William James's Theory of Emotion," *Transactions of the Charles S. Peirce Society* 2 (1969): 67–89. Textual evidence for thinking that James may have been drawn to this conception includes his use of the distinction between knowl-

edge-by-description and knowledge-by-acquaintance (*Principles,* 1:221–23); his reference to the "intrinsic feeling-tone of the object" ("The Physical Basis of Emotion," in *CER,* 364), with which he apparently identified an emotional feeling; and his emphasis that the quality of an emotional feeling seems to be due entirely to the character of the felt bodily events.

B. F. Skinner, like James, writes: "What is felt or introspectively observed is not some nonphysical world of consciousness, mind, or mental life but the observer's own body. This does not mean . . . that introspection is a kind of physiological research, nor does it mean (and this is the heart of the argument) that what are felt or introspectively observed are the causes of behavior" *About Behaviorism* (New York: Vintage, 1976), 18–19. Unlike some behaviorists, Skinner has long been willing to accept private events and the process of introspections. See, for example, his *Science and Human Behavior* (New York: Free Press, 1965), 257–82. James would have rejected Skinner's epiphenomenalistic view that private events are never causes, but unlike Skinner, James was not alert to the question of whether, if introspection or feeling acquaints us with events in our bodies, it is a kind of internal, physiological research. See Skinner, 237–39.

59. RBP, 1:697–98. That the concept of emotion—and not only James's manner of writing about it—can confuse and surprise us is clear in a letter to James from Carl Stumpf, a philosopher and psychologist who published a criticism of the James-Lange thesis: "Between [Franz] Brentano and me things have taken a curious turn. I thought I was rather in agreement with him in respect of the emotions, and now I receive a letter from him, seven pages long, in which he definitely declares himself for your views and against mine. A rather humiliating effect of my arguments!" (RBP, 2:193–94).

60. *Principles,* 2:468–72.

61. See, for example, ibid., 2:451, 455.

62. In an early letter (1866–67?) to Oliver Wendell Holmes, Jr., James wrote: "But as a man's happiness depends on his feeling, I think materialism inconsistent with a high degree thereof, and in this sense maintained that a materialist should not be an optimist, using the latter word to signify one whose philosophy authenticates, by guaranteeing the objective significance of, his most pleasurable feelings" (*LWJ,* 1:82–83). This passage indicates the other side of that ambivalence which may have characterized James's attitude toward emotion. He sometimes implied that emotions, while admittedly essential to the human condition, are nevertheless nuisances in his eyes—perhaps in ours, too, if there is ambivalence. On the other hand, he based large-scale philosophies or outlooks upon *feeling.* The conviction that philosophies are temperamentally rooted in and finally justified by their appeal to sentiment, feeling, and emotion was formulated early in his life and adhered to until the end. In one sense he was the quintessential emotional philosopher or philosopher-for-emotion.

A suggestion in the letter to Holmes was echoed years later: "Ontological emotion, however stumbled on, has something authoritative for the individual who feels it" (Review of B. P. Blood's *Anaesthetic Revelations, Atlantic Monthly* 34 (1824): 628). References to ontological emotion do not occur in James's major discussions of emotion but appear elsewhere from time to time, without much elaboration. He was probably referring to emotional experiences which we are tempted to describe in metaphysical terms or to consider, whether literally or poetically, as having some unusual connection with the cosmos.

Another example of what James said about emotion outside the context of discussing the James-Lange theory is this: "Within religion, emotion is apt to be tyrannical; but philosophy must favor the emotion that allies itself with the whole body and drift of all the truths in sight. I conceive this to be the more strenuous type of emotion; but I have to admit that its inability to let loose quietistic raptures is a serious deficiency in the pluralistic philosophy which I profess" ("The Absolute and the Strenuous Life," *The Journal of Philosophy, Psychology, and Scientific Methods* 4 [1907]: 548).

63. "What Is an Emotion?" in *CER,* 256. Nicholas Rescher notes that James once wrote

that humans can never hope to *sympathize* with elephants and tigers (see *TCWJ*, 224). Rescher comments: "James seems to be mistaken here in exaggerating the extent to which the feelings at issue in 'sympathy' must be capable of reciprocation. But he is no doubt right that sympathy has its limits—one cannot sympathize with a statue" (*Unselfishness* [Pittsburgh: University of Pittsburgh Press, 1975], 14).

64. Although James sometimes said that bodily changes only cause emotion, at other times he seemed to contradict himself. "Whatever moods, affections, and passions I have are in very truth constituted by, and made up of, those bodily changes which we ordinarily call their expression or consequence" (*Principles*, 2:452). Such passages indicate that when he equated emotion with the feeling of bodily changes, he conceived the feeling as a complex having these changes as its elements. This idea appears to conflict with the doctrine, defended in *Principles*, that a feeling is sui generis, unique, and partless.

9. THOUGHT

1. This statement occurs in the manuscript titled "Phenomenalism," [A]J9K of "Loose Notes" in the James Collection at the Houghton Library. Perry (RBP, 2:580) tentatively dates this manuscript 1884 and includes part of the passage quoted here (RBP, 2:582).

2. Destutt de Tracy, *Elémens d'idéologie*, 3d ed. (Paris: Courcier, 1817); quoted in *Principles*, 1:247n. To appreciate the Hegelian flavor of James's thinking here, compare his statement that "feelings are the germ and starting point of cognition, thoughts the developed tree" with what F. H. Bradley said in *Appearance and Reality*, 2d edition (London: Allen & Unwin, 1916), 459, and in *Essays on Truth and Reality* (Oxford: Clarendon, 1914), 174, 197. See also J. N. Findlay, *Hegel* (New York: Collier, 1962), 347–48. I respond to Findlay in "Emotion and Attitude: Findlay on Emotion," in K. D. Irani and Gerald E. Myers, eds., *Emotion: Philosophical Studies* (New York: Haven, 1984), 119–41. Findlay replies in the same volume: "Reply to Gerald Myers," 141–44.

James's decision to solve a linguistic problem by using *thought* and *feeling* to refer to any state of consciousness is announced in *Principles*, 1:186.

3. See Gilbert Ryle, "Adverbial Verbs and Verbs of Thinking," *On Thinking*, ed. Konstantin Kolenda (Totowa, N.J.: Rowman and Littlefield, 1979), 17–31.

4. Whereas separate chapters in *Principles* are devoted to sensation, emotion, memory, instinct, attention, and habit, there is no chapter reserved for thinking or thought as a specific mental activity. "The Stream of Thought" is certainly essential, but it concerns thought in the broad sense of any mental or conscious state. The short chapter on conception is also essential, but it focuses upon abstract concepts, ideas, and universals. To formulate James's notion of thought we must draw from many of his writings.

5. George Humphrey, *Thinking: An Introduction to Its Experimental Psychology* (London: Methuen, 1951), 13.

6. See the discussion of will and attention in chapter 7; see also *Principles*, 1:454 and 2:569–79.

7. Kurt Lewin, quoted in Humphrey, 21.

8. See *Principles*, 1:196, 278, 353, and 2:281.

9. Ibid., 1:278. This statement supports Perry's account: "There are mental units of a sort in James's view, but they are total pulses or waves, each having an indivisible unity, a transitory existence, and a unique identity. And these units are neither simple themselves, nor analyzable into simple constituents. In short, James rejected the fundamental presupposition of associationism, namely, its psychic atomism or 'elementarism'" (RBP, 2:77). Although James's discussion clearly applies to thought as any state of consciousness whatever, we are concerned here with its application to thinking in the narrower sense.

10. *Principles*, 1:278.

11. See ibid., 1:478–79n.

12. *Principles,* 1:300.

13. "The Consciousness of Self," which immediately succeeds "The Stream of Thought" in *Principles,* may seem to contradict some of the distinctive introspective reports offered in the earlier chapter. In "The Stream of Thought" James used his introspections to make a case for mind-body dualism, but his emphatic assertions in "The Consciousness of Self" that everything disclosed to introspection is physical do not square with those truly unusual introspective descriptions. James must have thought that the two chapters could be harmonized, intending "The Consciousness of Self" as a deliberate clarification of the preceding chapter. "The Stream of Thought" dates essentially to 1883 (much of it first appeared in January 1884), and "The Consciousness of Self" appears to have been written in late 1886. See James's letter of 4 October 1886 to Croom Robertson (RBP, 2:41).

Compare James's statement that "the feeling of the movement of this air [through throat and nose] is, in me, one strong ingredient of the feeling of assent" with one by E. B. Titchener: "I was not at all astonished to observe that the recognition of a gray might consist of a quiver in the stomach" (*Lectures on the Experimental Psychology of the Thought Processes;* quoted in Humphrey, 127). Both statements are examples of the attempt through introspective psychology to discover the physiological aspects of mental acts.

14. The same skepticism is evident in *Principles,* 1:296–97 and 1:401. The unkept promise is made at 1:305. In "Necessary Truths and the Effects of Experience," the final chapter of *Principles,* James states: "I leave my text practically just as it was written in 1885" (2:686). The conclusion was thus composed about the same time as "The Consciousness of Self," in which he promised to return to the topic. He may have intended to develop what he had written in 1885 into a clarification of his discussion of thought and its object, but this clarification never happened.

15. *Principles,* 1:279. From 1895 on, this contrast between thought and its object had to be modified, for in "The Knowing of Things Together" (*Psychological Review* 2 [1895]:105–24) he abandoned the doctrine that each state of consciousness is an indivisible unity, though he retained the introspectable distinction between the felt undividedness of the experience and the felt divisibility of the object.

16. To avoid making the discussion more difficult to follow, I have not mentioned some textual evidence that further supports my interpretation. For evidence that James considered introspection a form of retrospection, see *Principles,* 1:190. For his argument that consciousness or knowledge of an object does not carry with it an immediate awareness of that knowledge, see 1:272–75. In his notebook for a seminar in psychology in 1895–96, which contains the beginnings of the later philosophy of pure experience, he wrote: "Retrospectively, then, we find every past datum dividing into two parts, things cognized and the cognizing thereof." Compare this statement with *Principles,* 1:304.

In developing radical empiricism, James later said that introspection fails to show a mind-body distinction within experience and that consciousness cannot be distinguished as a different kind of entity from the things we are conscious of. The concept of radical empiricism was very much on his mind even while he was composing "The Consciousness of Self"; see *Principles,* 1:305n.

The following passage may clarify James's distinction between thinking and its object, and explain why the object is not better conceived as the content, an integral part of the act of thinking itself: "The mental state is aware of itself only from within; it grasps what we call its own *content,* and nothing more. The psychologist, on the contrary, is aware of it from without, and knows its relations with all sorts of other things. What the thought sees is only its own *object;* what the psychologist sees is the thought's object, plus the thought itself" (*Principles,* 1:197; italics mine). I emphasize *content* and *object* to indicate that James was not averse to using them interchangeably; being committed to distinguishing thinking from its object, however, he did not abandon his commitment merely by switching to *content*. What might be called the content of thinking is still distinguishable from the act of thinking.

17. *Principles*, 2:528n; see also 2:569–70. "The brain-processes may be agents, and the thought as such may be an agent. But what the ordinary psychologies call 'ideas' are nothing but parts of the total *object* of representation. All that is before the mind at once, no matter how complex a system of things and relations it may be, is one object for the thought" (2:569).

18. "The Sentiment of Rationality"; quoted in *Principles*, 2:335–36. James discussed concepts elsewhere in *Principles*, particularly in "Conception," "Discrimination and Comparison," and "Necessary Truths and the Effects of Experience." See also chapters 1, 2, and 4 of *MT*, chapters 4–6 of *SPP*, chapter 2 in *ERE*, and lectures 3, 5, 6, and 7 in *APU*.

19. Passages here and there in *Principles* show that James was already working toward the behavioristic solution formulated in *The Meaning of Truth*, but they are generally cryptic, vague, and virtually forgotten after being mentioned. For example: "All that a state of mind need do, in order to take cognizance of a reality, intend it, or be 'about' it, is to lead to a remoter state of mind which either acts upon the reality or resembles it" (1:471). The reference to a remote state of mind has a distinctly mentalistic flavor and does not suggest the subsequent behavioral and physiological analysis of intentionality in "The Knowing of Things Together." Whereas the later view analyzes intentionality into dispositions (tendencies to behave) which are describable only from without, from a nonintrospective point of view, James expressly stated in *Principles*: " 'Tendencies' are not only descriptions from without, . . . they are among the *objects* of the stream, which is thus aware of them from within" (1:254).

20. Review of Josiah Royce's "Religious Aspect of Philosophy," in *Atlantic Monthly* (1885); reprinted in *CER*, 278. This review was written about a year later than "On Some Omissions of Introspective Psychology," which figures in chapters 7, 9, 10, and 12 in *Principles*. Another significant essay, "On the Function of Cognition," also appeared in 1885, in *Mind*. This essay adumbrates the development of pragmatism, in part by examining objective reference.

This period was fruitful for James. "Absolutism and Empiricism," "The Dilemma of Determinism," and "What Is an Emotion?" all appeared in 1884, as did *The Literary Remains of the Late Henry James*, in which he contributed an introduction and other editorial work on his father's writings.

In his review, James credited Royce not only with specifying the problem of intentionality and objective reference (the way a thought refers to something objective), but also with formulating a plausible idealistic or transcendentalist solution. In a note added in the 1909 version of the original "The Function of Cognition" (1885), however, he said that he had found an alternative to Royce's that fitted in better with his own radical empiricism and pragmatism. See *MT*, 22n.

21. Compare James's statement with Wittgenstein's: "What makes my image of him into an image of *him*? Not its looking like him. . . . What makes this utterance into an utterance about *him*?—Nothing in it or simultaneous with it ('behind it'). If you want to know whom he meant, ask him" (*Philosophical Investigations* [Oxford: Blackwell, 1953], 177). Wittgenstein read James with enjoyment and often responded questioningly or negatively as he developed his own philosophical psychology in *Philosophical Investigations* and elsewhere.

22. "The Knowing of Things Together," *The Psychological Review* 2 (1895):107–08.

23. Ibid., 108–09. James credited a colleague and former student, Dickinson S. Miller, with having shown him the way to this view in "Meaning of Truth and Error," *Philosophical Review* 2 (1893):408–25.

I had the good fortune to become acquainted with Miller a few years before his death in 1963. He talked about discussions he had with James on this topic and showed me a letter from James which praises Miller as the single person who actually led him to pragmatism. If this seems to contradict the traditional notion that C. S. Peirce inspired James's pragmatism, we should remember that James's wife, and to a lesser extent Perry, objected to his frequently attributing to others the origin of his own ideas. They considered his generosity highly exaggerated and concluded that, if he had not been able to find a predecessor for any given doctrine, he would have invented one (see chapter 1).

Miller's philosophical contributions have been compiled by Loyd D. Easton in *Philosophical Analysis and Human Welfare* (Boston: Reidel, 1975); some of the papers included focus specifically on James. My review of this volume contains some personal observations about Miller; see *Transactions of the C. S. Peirce Society* 12 (Fall 1976):402–07.

24. Much of the 1895 essay "The Knowing of Things Together" is retained verbatim in "The Tigers in India," chapter 2 of *MT* (1909). There is, however, one significant difference. The later work substitutes "phenomenal fact" for "physical fact": "In all this there is no self-transcendency in our mental images *taken by themselves.* They are one phenomenal fact; the tigers are another" (*MT,* 45). This change indicates a further effort to abolish dualism altogether. The same doctrine appears in "A Word More About Truth," chapter 3 of the same book, and is discussed explicitly in an essay on radical empiricism, "A World of Pure Experience," in McDermott, 205–08. See also "The Existence of Julius Caesar," chapter 10 of *MT.*

25. James's reference to F. H. Bradley may indicate a commitment to such acts of intuition and inspection, which differ from introspection by being awareness of abstract objects, though his remark is in a different context. See *Principles,* 2:648n..

26. See the discussion of images in chapter 3.

27. The flow of consciousness that James thought is integral to the process of thinking may be compatible with the activity of Rodin's *Thinker.* The statuesque ponderer looks quite static, but with strong imagination we may possibly picture his mind as absolutely lightninglike behind the stony quiet. But a more definite impression is given by Rodin's *Thought* at the Rodin Museum in Philadelphia. Created around 1886, this bronze likeness of a woman's head exudes weight and heaviness. The head is anchored to a heavy, slanted, rectangular base which dwarfs the head itself. The woman wears a Shakerlike bonnet, and her eyes are tilted contemplatively toward the ground. Thought seems in this blocklike representation to exclude all suggestion of flow, being a frozen stream at best. Did Rodin understand something about thought that James did not?

28. See "The Sense of Dizziness in Deaf-Mutes," *American Journal of Otology* 4 (1882):239–54; reprinted in *CER,* 220–43. (James referred to this article in *Principles,* 2:89n.) The article was preceded by a short summary, "Notes on the Sense of Dizziness in Deaf-Mutes," *Harvard University Bulletin* 2 (1881):173. James's interest in the topic was evident also in his review of Karl Spämer's *Experimental and Critical Contribution to the Physiology of the Semicircular Canals, American Journal of Otology* 2 (1880):341–43. He wrote in the 1882 article:

> It occurred to me that deaf-mute asylums ought to offer some corroboration of the theory in question, if a true one. Among their inmates must certainly be a considerable number in whom either the labyrinths or the auditory nerves in their totality have been destroyed by the same causes that produced the deafness. We ought therefore to expect, if the semicircular canals be really the starting-points of the sensation of dizziness, to find, on examining a large number of deaf-mutes, a certain proportion of them who are completely insusceptible of that affection, and others who enjoy immunity in a less complete degree. (*CER,* 221)

After presenting his evidence he declared: "The surmise with which I started is thus proved, and the theory that the semicircular canals are organs of equilibrium receives renewed corroboration" (*CER,* 222). The evidence came from the National College in Washington, the Hartford School, the Boston School, and the deaf-mute institutions in Northampton, Massachusetts. J. J. Putnam, James's colleague at Harvard and one of the psychologists instrumental in bringing Freud to America in 1909, assisted James in his investigation, especially with galvanic observations.

29. *Principles,* 1:266–67. Ballard was an instructor at the National College in Washington. Wittgenstein responded to this passage in *Principles:*

> William James, in order to shew that thought is possible without speech, quotes the recollection of a deaf-mute, Mr. Ballard, who wrote that in his early youth, even before he could speak, he had had thoughts about God and the world.—What can he have meant?—Ballard writes ". . . I began to ask myself . . . how came the world into being?"—Are you sure—one would like to ask—that this is the correct translation of your wordless thought into words? . . . Do I want to say that the writer's memory deceives him?—I don't even know if I should say *that.* These recollections are a queer memory phenomenon,—and I do not know what conclusions one can draw from them about the past of the man who recounts them. (*Philosophical Investigations,* 109–110)

If one finds it difficult to conceive how such thinking can occur independently of language, then one will sympathize with Wittgenstein's hesitation in accepting Ballard's testimony. But James saw no reason to be skeptical.

In the same work Wittgenstein wrote: "When I think in language, there aren't 'meanings' going through my mind in addition to the verbal expressions: the language is itself the vehicle of thought" (107). James's only rebuttal to such an argument would have been to charge that Wittgenstein did not know how to connect his words with his introspections, or that he was looking in the wrong place or not looking at all.

30. See *Principles,* 2:62, 358, and 420; see also "Laura Bridgman," *Atlantic Monthly* 93 (January 1904):95–98; reprinted in *CER,* 453–58, and "Thought Before Language: A Deaf-Mute's Recollections," *Philosophical Review* 1 (1892):613–24.

31. For a definitive treatment of the Würzburg school and its critics, see Humphrey, especially chapters 2–4.

32. Among James's unpublished papers in the Houghton Library are his notes for a seminar on cognition in 1903–04. He had been reading Bernhard Natorp and G. E. Moore, and one entry reads: "*Bewusstheit* does not exist at all on my view. The *beziehung auf ein Subject* by which N. explains it, is a perfectly assignable phenomenal relation." Although this statement is not tantamount to denying *Bewusstseinslagen,* it may be in line with his rejection of Moore's diaphanous consciousness in "Does 'Consciousness' Exist?" The conviction expressed can be understood to conflict with the notion of imageless thought, which is ghostly and diaphanous in its own way.

33. *Principles,* 1:252–53. James believed that thinking, like knowledge as described by C. I. Lewis, transcends the immediate moment. See Lewis, *Mind and the World-Order* (New York: Charles Scribner's Sons, 1929), 132–36.

34. *Principles,* 1:281. Something like this idea is expressed in *Some Problems of Philosophy:* "Concepts are notes, views taken on reality, not pieces of it, as bricks are of a house" (200). But the similarity may be illusory, because it is not clear how words and concepts compare. The passage from *Principles* continues: "The consciousness of the 'Idea' and that of the words are thus consubstantial. They are made of the same 'mind-stuff,' and form an unbroken stream" (1:281–82). Words are apparently pieces of the reality that is the stream of consciousness, as well as views of the total idea or object which is also part of that reality. This is a further indication of the introspectable complications which for James surrounded the relation of words to thoughts. See note 17 above.

35. *Principles,* 1:258; see also 1:568. In a note James tried to clarify what he meant by *fringe,* commenting on a criticism of his use of the term in an earlier publication, presumably "On Some Omissions in Introspection" (1884). Parts of this essay reappeared in "The Stream of Thought" and other chapters of *Principles.* In another context James wrote: "The word 'real' itself is, in short, a fringe" (*Principles,* 2:320). See Stephen H. Daniel, "Fringes and Transitive

States in William James' Concept of the Stream of Thought," *Auslegung* 3 (March 1976):64–80.

36. See "Philosophical Conceptions and Practical Results," *University of California Chronicle* (1898):24. This essay was James's announcement of pragmatism and, with C. S. Peirce's "How to Make Our Ideas Clear," is the original document of the pragmatic movement.

37. The first or pragmatic claim is found throughout James's writings on pragmatism; see, for example, "Two English Critics," in *The Meaning of Truth*, 275. The second or psychological claim occurs in "The Stream of Thought" and perhaps even more forcefully in *SPP*, 111.

38. This notebook, titled "Idealism, etc.," is dated 1870. It contains thirty pages of discussion, much of it obscure. A problem that was foremost in James's mind at the time (relevant to the distinction between subjectivity and objectivity) was whether "consciousness differentiates itself into a me and not-me," or whether the contrast between me and not-me is given. The notebook also includes discussions of related matters, including the question of whether John Stuart Mill's idealism can allow for an explanation of how we know that other minds exist. See RBP, 1:575–80, for helpful comments on this notebook.

39. *Principles*, 1:304. If the thinker is a construct rather than a given, we might suppose that psychology's starting point, the experience of thinking, must at least contain a diremption between the act of thinking and the object thought of. But in some unpublished notes which Perry dated 1880–84, James doubted, apparently in the early stages of writing *Principles*, that even such a separation is always a given.

> I should say the *rudiment* of thought was always of an object in the logical sense of something in which the discrimination of sub[ject] and ob[ject] had not yet been affected, a neutral experience, a phenomenon, or as Hume says an impression, originally vague, but gradually elaborating itself by separation and accretion until *inter alia* the notions of inward and outward or subject and object materially considered, had been evolved. Now, exactly *how*, granted this primitive logical objectivity (which I take it is all that Spencer can legitimately claim for himself) the evolution of thought and its complicated [upshot?] of which the consciousness is one of the incidents occurs is one of the fundamental problems of philosophy. ("Idealism," Loose Notes [A]J2K in the Houghton Library)

Even at this date James doubted both the self-transcendency of thought as an introspectable property and the distinction between act and object as a given in primitive or preanalytic experience. He was also thinking that consciousness, with its complications of act, object, and subject, might be an evolution from something neutral (the pure experience of radical empiricism), in itself neither subjective nor objective, and aware of an object only logically or potentially but not actually or materially.

40. *Principles*, 1:528–29. James's views on comparison prompted criticism from F. H. Bradley who maintained that perceived resemblance between things is never in itself ultimate but is always analyzable into the presence of qualitatively identical elements in things that are similar. Both men exchanged criticisms in print. See James's "Mr. Bradley on Immediate Resemblance" and "Immediate Resemblance," both reprinted in *CER*. See also Richard Wollheim, *F. H. Bradley* (Harmondsworth: Penguin, 1959), 35–36.

James considered the issue of comparison to be of primary importance, mentioning it in "Monistic Idealism," in McDermott, 506. He was troubled by the fact that if Bradley were right, then resemblance would be an illegitimate category because it admits of degrees, and comparisons would be relegated to "absolute identity" and "absolute noncomparability." The result, James thought, would be the ultimate bifurcation of the conceptual and the perceptual worlds, since comparisons could not be applied to the degrees of difference and resemblance in the perceived world. See chapter 3.

41. *Principles*, 1:498. This passage is one of many that pose a problem of interpretation.

James contrasted feeling something and thinking or interpreting it; he claimed that whereas feeling conveys the object purely, thinking always causes some distortion and impurity. But here even the feeling of difference between *m* and *n* contains an impurity. It thus appears that he did not adhere to his own distinction between merely noticing a difference and comparing (analyzing) it, unless his formulation needs only to be tidied up slightly. He may have meant that in practice it is difficult if not impossible—because of "a mechanism we as yet fail to understand"—to keep comparison from instinctively coloring the merest noticing (feeling) of a likeness or difference. In general, if feeling is not always a feature of experience contrasted in its purity with the "contamination" of thought, if indeed it is sometimes infected by thought, then can we ever tell when feeling gives us something not as it seems but as it actually is? James had difficulty both in keeping this question in mind and, when he did, in always giving it the same answer.

42. Ibid., 2:641; see also 1:496 and 501. In "Humanism and Truth" James wrote:

> Relations between invariant objects will themselves be invariant. Such relations cannot be happenings, for by hypothesis nothing shall happen to the objects. I have tried to show in the last chapter of my *Principles of Psychology* that they can only be relations of comparison. No one so far seems to have noticed my suggestion, and I am too ignorant of the development of mathematics to feel very confident of my own view. But if it were correct it would solve the difficulty [of how certain properties and relations can be eternal] perfectly. Relations of comparison are matters of direct inspection. As soon as mental objects are mentally compared, they are perceived to be either like or unlike. But once the same, always the same, once different, always different, under these timeless conditions. Which is as much as to say that truths concerning these man-made objects are necessary and eternal. (*MT*, 83–84)

James's heavy reliance on comparison may have seemed to most of his contemporaries to be too vague and diffuse to help explain the a priori character of mathematics and logic. For more on James's analysis of comparing, see chapters 12, 13, and 28 of *Principles*.

James graphically made his point about the a priori nature of what comparison yields for knowledge:

> First, consider the nature of comparison. *The relations of resemblance and difference among things have nothing to do with the time-and-space-order in which we may experience the latter.* Suppose a hundred beings created by God and gifted with the faculties of memory and comparison. Suppose that upon each of them the same lot of sensations are imprinted, but in different orders. Let some of them have no single sensation more than once. Let some have this one and others that are repeated. Let every conceivable permutation prevail. And then let the magic-lantern show die out, and keep the creatures in a void eternity, with naught but their memories to muse upon. Inevitably in their long leisure they will begin to play with the items in their experience and rearrange them, make classificatory series of them, place gray between white and black, orange between red and yellow, and trace all other degrees of resemblance and difference. And this new construction will be absolutely identical in all the hundred creatures, the diversity of the sequence of the original experience having no effect as regards this rearrangement. Any and every form of sequence will give the same result, because the result expresses the relations between the *inward natures* of the sensations; and to that the question of their outward succession is quite irrelevant. Black will differ from white just as much in a world in which they always come close together as in one in which they always come far apart; just as much in one in which they appear rarely as in one in which they appear all the time. (*Principles*, 2:642–43)

This argument challenged Herbert Spencer's "experience-philosophy," which made the relation of comparison into subjective duplicates of outer relations that obtain in the external world. But Spencer failed to explain, according to James, the necessity our thought finds in the way that black and white differ; James believed the source of that necessity resides not in accumulated experience but in the structure of the brain itself.

43. James's view is in some respects comparable to that of Noam Chomsky, who has revived the Cartesian concept of innate ideas and has argued against behaviorism such as B. F. Skinner's in favor of using the brain's structure to explain how we acquire and employ language. Compare James's thinking on serial orders with what Chomsky said in his review of Skinner's *Verbal Behavior* in *Language* 35 (1959):26–58.

Referring in this review to Karl S. Lashley's paper, "The Problem of Serial Order" (*Hixon Symposium on Cerebral Mechanisms in Behavior,* ed. Lloyd Jeffress [New York: Wiley, 1951], 112–36), Chomsky wrote:

> Lashley has implicitly delimited a class of problems which can be approached in a fruitful way by the linguist and psychologist, and which are clearly preliminary to those with which Skinner is concerned. Lashley recognizes . . . that the composition and production of an utterance is not simply a matter of stringing together a sequence of responses under the control of outside stimulation and intraverbal association, and that the syntactic organization of an utterance is not something directly represented in any simple way in the physical structure of the utterance itself. A variety of observations lead him to conclude that syntactic structure is " a generalized pattern imposed on the specific acts as they occur," and that "a consideration of the structure of the sentence and other motor sequences will show . . . that there are, behind the overtly expressed sequences, a multiplicity of integrative processes which can only be inferred from the final results of their activity." He also comments on the great difficulty of determining the "selective mechanisms" used in the actual construction of a particular utterance. (55)

James, if more directly oriented toward language and syntactics, could have suitably accommodated to those topics what he said about serial order.

44. See "Two English Critics," in *MT,* 284.

45. *Principles,* 1:331. This part of the discussion also draws upon "The Perception of Reality." Compare James's concept of judgment as a synthesizing or knitting operation (1:341n) with Russell's view of judgment in *The Problems of Philosophy* (London: Oxford University Press, 1912), 125–28.

46. "On Some Hegelisms," *Mind* 7 (1882):186–208; reprinted in *WTB,* 290. See also *Principles,* 2:630–33.

47. I had the opportunity in the 1950s of asking Russell what lay behind his one-time rejection of negative facts, and he replied that it was because he did not believe that nature contains logical complexes such as "p or q" or "not-p."

My interpreting James in line with Russell here is supported by the texts, with one exception: "The word 'or' names a genuine reality. Thus, as I speak here, I may look ahead *or* to the right *or* to the left" (APU, 146). He did not elaborate this point, and had he been queried, I think he would have agreed with Russell that "or" is needed not for physics but for psychology; it describes states of mind such as hesitation and weighing alternatives, but not anything nonmental.

48. *Principles,* 2:30. This part of my discussion is based largely upon "Reasoning," chapter 22 of *Principles,* which in turn is based on "Brute and Human Intellect," *Journal of Speculative Philosophy* 12 (1878): 236–76. Perry remarks in his annotated bibliography that the 1878 essay differs from the chapter in *Principles* by giving less emphasis to subjective interest and the relation of reasoning to formal logic. This is another instance of James's retaining in *Principles* a set of convictions formed before or at the time the book was begun.

On the distinction between animal and human intelligence, James wrote:

> We may . . . consider it proven that *the most elementary single difference between the human mind and that of brutes lies in this deficiency on the brute's part to associate ideas by similarity*—characters, the abstraction of which depends on this sort of association, must in the brute always remain drowned, swamped in the total phenomenon which they help constitute, and never used to reason from. If a character stands out alone, it is always some obvious sensible quality like a sound or a smell which is instinctively exciting and lies in the line of the animal's propensities; or it is some obvious sign which experience has habitually coupled with a consequence, such as, for the dog, the sight of his master's hat on and the master's going out. (*Principles*, 2:360)

Animals are deficient in the capacity to abstract recurrent or characteristic features, whereas humans have a greater capacity to associate by similarity. If several things—A, B, C, D—have the feature M in common, then because the presence of M in A will call up in rapid association B, C, and D, M will call attention to itself more than will the features that vary between A, B, C, and D. Being noticed on its own, M becomes an abstract character and a tool of reasoning.

49. *Principles*, 2:369. When two people are conversing, James said, "Before one of them is half through a sentence the other knows his meaning and replies" (2:370). He may have had his brother Henry in mind, since it was reported that Henry, if he knew what was coming, would stop a speaker from continuing.

50. Ibid., 2:360. James related his respect for genius to his philosophy of history. Calling himself a hero-worshipper, he disagreed with Herbert Spencer's evolutionist view that historical change is unaffected by great individuals doing great things. "The fermentative influence of geniuses must be admitted as, at any rate, one factor in the changes that constitute social evolution." "Great Men and Their Environment," *WTB*, originally published as "Great Men, Great Thoughts and Their Environment," *Atlantic Monthly* 46 (1880), 441–59. See also "The Importance of Individuals," in *WTB*, 255–62.

James certainly recognized the analogy between his principle of selectivity in thinking and Darwin's theory of selection.

10. KNOWLEDGE

1. *Principles*, 1:216. In his review of George T. Ladd's *Elements of Physiological Psychology*, James wrote about the mystery of cognition: "*Knowledge* is the miracle. . . . No physiologist can explain either [knowledge-by-acquaintance or knowledge-about] out of properties of the brain. The most the materialist can do is to borrow them and clap them on, as a ready-made addition, to the brain's other powers" (*The Nation* 44 [2 June 1887]:473); see also *Principles*, 1:480. He also wrote: "All schools refuse to admit the unmediated function of *knowing a thing*, and so incorrigibly do they substitute *being the thing* for it."

2. *Principles*, 1:196, 278, 353; 2:281. C. S. Peirce commented about James's description: "I do not get a clear notion from this passage [1:196] about the Psychologist's Fallacy" (question 19, "Questions on William James's *Principles of Psychology*"; from Peirce's notes. This manuscript, in the Widener Library at Harvard, is #1099, I CIA, 621.) The fallacy is one of mistakenly replacing the cognitive relation of a person to an object with a psychological theory of how that relation works.

3. *Principles*, 1:217–218.

4. Ibid., 1:218; see also 1:471. In view of James's statements in his development of pragmatism that the known is affected by the knowing (see, for example, "The Pragmatist Account of Truth And Its Misunderstanders," in *The Meaning of Truth*, 185–86), we might interpret him to mean here that the concept of the known as totally independent of the knowing is merely another mistake following from the mistaken doctrine of dualism. But in *Principles* he clearly subscribed to the claim that "the Thing remains the same whether known

or not. . . . I disregard *consequences* which may later come to the thing from the fact that it is known. The knowing *per se* in no wise affects the thing" (1:219 and n). This position was modified in the subsequent defenses of pragmatism.

In his notes on *Principles,* Peirce objected to the claim that the cognitive relation is irreducible but did not offer an alternative; see his question 28 in the manuscript cited in note 3 above.

5. *Principles,* 1:219, 501, and 687–89.

6. In a letter of 1907 to Charles A. Strong, James wrote: "I absolutely agree with you (and thought I had said so) that knowledge of reality is a *state of mind* that puts us into relation with a reality—any relation, almost, provided it be with *that* reality" (quoted in RBP, 2:544; first italics mine).

The discussion of knowledge in *Principles* reflects what James called in 1882–83 his "floundering in the morasses of the theory of cognition," from which he later escaped, he thought, by developing the philosophies of pragmatism and pure experience; see RBP, 2:72–80.

7. See John Grote, *Exploratio Philosophica,* pt. 1 (Cambridge: Deighton, Bell, and Co., 1865).

8. *Principles,* 1:274.

9. Because he believed that *"a pure sensation is an abstraction"* (*Principles,* 2:3), he did not include the chapter on sensation in the first volume of *Principles.* On the other hand, he wrote: "Somewhere our belief always does rest on ultimate data like the whiteness, smoothness, or squareness of this paper" (*The Meaning of Truth,* 47). Sensations are all-important in James's metaphysics, and indeed he reduced physical objects to sensations. But despite the ring of this sentence, he thought that sensations are always clustered rather than atomic, a belief which excludes any neat foundationalism of the sort that Russell and others envisaged. For James, there was little if any difference between objects and clustered sensations; indeed, a few sentences later he dropped the reference to sensations, referring instead to "the white paper or other ultimate datum of our experience" (48).

10. *Principles,* 1:189–90. James denied that acquaintance is really knowledge when he wrote: "True knowing is, in fine, not substantially, in itself, or 'as such' inside of the idea from the first" (*MT,* 175). In this context he wanted to emphasize that knowledge is a process or sequence of actions, not a momentary experience or acquaintance, yet he spoke often as if acquaintance were knowledge.

11. RBP, 2:77.

12. One of James's strongest statements of this view occurs in "On the Function of Cognition":

> In such pieces of knowledge-of-acquaintance all our knowledge must end, and carry a sense of this possible termination as part of its content. These percepts, these *termini,* these sensible things, these mere matters-of-acquaintance, are the only realities we ever directly know. . . . These sensations are the mother-earth, the anchorage, the stable rock, the first and last limits, the *terminus a quo* and the *terminus ad quem* of the mind. To find such sensational *termini* should be our aim with all our higher thought. They end discussion; they destroy the false conceit of knowledge; and without them we are all at sea with each other's meaning. (*MT,* 39)

But James never proposed a foundationalism of the sort that claims to reduce neatly physical-object statements to sense-datum statements. Observational testing discloses objects or clustered sensations. *"Sensible objects are thus either our realities or the tests of our realities. Conceived objects must show sensible effects or else be disbelieved"* (*Principles,* 2:301).

13. "A dream-candle has existence, true enough; but not the same existence . . . which the candles of waking perception have" (*Principles,* 2:290). See also 2:289, 291, and 294.

14. Ibid., 2:289; see also 2:288 and 319.

15. Ibid., 2:284. James refers his reader in a footnote to Benjamin P. Blood, *The Anaesthetic*

Revelation, and the Gist of Philosophy (Amsterdam, N.Y.: private printing, 1874). For a discussion of Blood, a mystic and a nonacademic philosopher, and James's interest in him, see chapter 83 of RBP. James reviewed Blood's work in 1874 and was affected by it throughout his life.

16. *Principles*, 2:296–97. This passage is reminiscent of Johann Fichte, although James did not mention him in this context. In the first volume of *Principles*, when discussing Kant's concept of the ego, James wrote: "It was reserved for [Kant's] Fichtean and Hegelian successors to call [ego] the first Principle of Psychology, spell its name in capitals and pronounce it with adoration, to act, in short, as if they were going up in a balloon, whenever the notion of it crossed their mind" (1:365). Oddly, James seemed in the second volume to be closer to Fichte on the significance of the ego, the thought of which seems to have had a ballooning effect on James as well.

What James said here seems to conflict with the express denial that "reflective consciousness of the self is essential to the cognitive function of thought" (*Principles*, 1:274). The reference to Descartes's cogito can be interpreted to mean that below the level of reflection or self-consciousness, the Ego, in a prereflective sense of its own life, instinctively believes what excites and interests it. Without some such interpretation, the passages in 1:274 and 2:297 threaten to clash.

17. *Principles*, 2:317. The final chapter of *Principles* reinforces this argument by asserting that our knowledge of reality cannot be explained as the effect of experience alone; there are also conditions or features, such as these postulates or requirements, that are native to us and that must be satisfied if knowledge or the recognition of reality is to take place.

18. Ibid., 2:312. James articulated this point of view earlier, in "Rationality, Activity, and Faith," *Princeton Review* 2 (July 1882):64–69; even earlier reviews and articles of the 1870s either state or suggest it. As he was about to finish Chapter 28 (and with it, *Principles*), he became more convinced that the budding science of psychology lent support to his "subjectivist-pragmatist" conviction. He connected this conviction, expressed as a proposition in theoretical philosophy, with the issues surrounding the resolution of moral, religious, and metaphysical doubts. He credited Royce's *Religious Aspects of Philosophy* with having supplied "the clearest account of the psychology of belief with which I am acquainted" (2:318n); see also 2:317 on materialism and religion.

An example of James's use of an emotion or attitude to explain the nature of some reality is his discussion of remorse in "The Dilemma of Determinism": "And what sense can there be in condemning ourselves for taking the wrong way, unless we need have done nothing of the sort, unless the right way was open to us as well? . . . I cannot understand the belief that an act is bad, without regret at its happening. I cannot understand regret without the admission of real, genuine possibilities in the world" (McDermott, 605). In James's view, nature abhors a functionless emotion or attitude; just as a twinge of pain indicates that something is wrong, moral regret points to the existence both of free will and of a wrong that might through free will be avoided or corrected in the future.

19. *Principles*, 1:644. This suggestion, James said years later, was in effect lost:

> Relations between invariant objects will themselves be invariant. Such relations cannot be happenings, for by hypothesis nothing shall happen to the objects. I have tried to show in the last chapter of my *Principles of Psychology* that they can only be relations of comparison. No one so far seems to have noticed my suggestion, and I am too ignorant of the development of mathematics to feel very confident of my own view. But if it were correct it would solve the difficulty perfectly. Relations of comparison are matters of direct inspection. As soon as mental objects are mentally compared, they are perceived to be either like or unlike. But once the same, always the same, once different, always different, under these timeless conditions. Which is as much to say that truths concerning these man-made objects are necessary and eternal. . . . The whole fabric of the *a priori* sciences

can thus be treated as a man-made product. As Locke long ago pointed out, these sciences have no immediate connection with fact. (*MT*, 84–85)

20. *Pragmatism*, 138; see also *MT*, 84, and *Principles*, 1:466–68, 2:641–44, and 2:661–69.

21. For more on James and Darwin, see Robert J. Richards, "The Personal Equation in Science: William James's Psychological and Moral Uses of Darwinian Theory," *A William James Renaissance, Harvard Library Bulletin*, 30 (October 1982):387–426.

22. *Principles*, 2:631; see also 2:629.

23. See Chomsky's review of Skinner's *Beyond Freedom and Dignity, The New York Review*, 30 December 1971, 18.

24. *Principles*, 2:641–42.

25. See C. I. Lewis, *An Analysis of Knowledge and Valuation* (La Salle, Ill.: Open Court, 1946); Sandra B. Rosenthal and Patrick L. Bourgeois, *Pragmatism and Phenomenology: A Philosophical Encounter* (Amsterdam: B. R. Gruner, 1980); Lillian Panchieri, "James, Lewis and the Pragmatic A Priori," *Transactions of the Charles S. Peirce Society* 7 (1971):134–46; Morton White, *Science and Sentiment in America* (New York: Oxford University Press, 1972) and *Pragmatism and the American Mind* (New York: Oxford University Press, 1973); A. J. Ayer, *The Origins of Pragmatism* (San Francisco: Freeman, Cooper & Co., 1968); Henry D. Aiken, "American Pragmatism Reconsidered: II. William James," *Commentary* 34 (September 1962):238–46; Sidney Hook, *The Metaphysics of Pragmatism* (Chicago: Open Court, 1927); John E. Smith, *The Spirit of American Philosophy* (New York: Oxford University Press, 1961); and Richard Rorty, *Consequences of Pragmatism* (Minneapolis: University of Minnesota Press, 1982).

26. David Hilbert and Wilhelm Ackerman, *Principles of Mathematical Logic* (New York: Chelsea, 1950), 136.

27. See, for example, *Principles*, 1:253.

28. "*The sense of our meaning is an entirely peculiar element of the thought.* It is one of those evanescent and 'transitive' facts of mind which introspection cannot . . . isolate and hold up for examination" (ibid., 1:472).

29. See, for example, "Some Metaphysical Problems Pragmatically Considered," in *Pragmatism*, 65–86.

30. *Principles*, 2:48–50.

31. See, for instance, *Principles*, 1:272, 1:459–60, 1:480–82, 1:532–33, and 2:650; *SPP*, 75–97; and "The Sentiment of Rationality," *Mind* 4 (1879):317–46.

32. James almost never mentioned the logic of identity and never analyzed judgments involving the identity of meanings. He simply asserted that the mind can mean the same thing in its meanings, even if sameness never appears elsewhere. He contrasted this psychological law that assumes the existence of minds and thoughts with an ontological law that everything is what it is (a statement he labeled a tautological truism) and a logical law that what is once true of the subject of a judgment is always true of that subject. The logical law is not truistic, for it assumes subjects that are unalterable by time (1:460n). Although James did not raise the issue, a seeming consequence is that a priori knowledge depends not only upon immediately intuited meanings and their relations but also upon the logical law with its existential assumption; the a priori judgment asserts that the predicate "differs from white" must universally and necessarily hold of the concept black, the logical and unalterable subject.

33. Perry, citing such sources as the 1878 article on Spencer and *Principles*, 1:288, wrote that James did not view the mind as essentially creative: "Its ideas are not of its own making, but rather of its own *choosing*. At every stage of its development, on every level of complexity, the mind is essentially a selective agency" ("The Philosophy of William James," *Philosophical Review* 20, no. 1 (January 1911):3). James's text clearly supports Perry's interpretation; however, James attributed considerable creativity to mental processes in saying that they are

responsible for new conceptions even though the original materials were selected rather than created; see 1:464–68 and 2:675–78.

34. In studying James's papers in the Houghton Library, I became aware of his keen interest in developing this notion of substitution, by which concepts substitute for percepts, into a fruitful technical concept. Perry aptly commented: "The towering importance for human life of this kind of knowing [knowledge-about or knowledge-by-description] lies in the fact that an experience that knows another can figure as its *representative,* not in any quasi-miraculous 'epistemological' sense, but in the definite practical sense of being its *substitute* in various operations" ("The Philosophy of William James," 9). Perry refers to chapters 1, 4, and 5 of *MT* for textual evidence.

35. *Principles,* 1:478; see also 2:49.

36. Although Perry was invaluable in explaining Locke's influence upon James (perhaps as early as 1863) and how it drew James to concrete particulars and molded his ideas about conception and his attitude toward nominalism, he does not explain the change to logical realism in *A Pluralistic Universe* and *Some Problems of Philosophy;* see RBP, chapter 33.

37. *SPP,* 107. As James developed the concept of pure experience and moved closer to Bergson's anti-intellectualism (notably after 1902), he may have felt the need to balance rationalism and an (empirically oriented) intuitionism such as Bergson's and to do justice to abstract concepts at a time when both he and Bergson were on the brink of denying a theoretical, as opposed to a purely practical, function of the intellect.

> I am quite willing to part company with Professor Bergson, and to ascribe a primarily theoretical function to our intellect, provided you . . . concede that theoretic knowledge which is knowledge *about* things, as distinguished from living or sympathetic acquaintance with them, touches only the outer surface of reality. . . . Concepts are realities of a new order, with particular relations between them. These relations are just as much directly perceived, when we compare our various concepts, as the distance between two sense-objects is perceived when we look at it. . . . We get those bodies of "mental truth" (as Locke called it) known as mathematics, logic, and *a priori* metaphysics. To know all this truth is a theoretic achievement, indeed, but it is a narrow one; for the relations between conceptual objects as such are only the static ones of bare comparison. . . . Nothing *happens* in the realm of concepts; relations there are "eternal" only. The theoretic gain fails so far, therefore, to touch even the outer hem of the real world, the world of causal and dynamic relations, of activity and history. To gain insight into all that moving life, Bergson is right in turning us away from conception and towards perception. ("Bergson," in McDermott, 570–71 and n)

The position stated here is indistinguishable from that in the final chapter of *Principles,* but in 1909, though not in 1885, James considered it logical realism.

If James had not said explicitly, in *The Meaning of Truth, A Pluralistic Universe,* and *Some Problems of Philosophy,* that he had adopted Platonism or logical realism, we might well wonder whether he actually had. In a letter of 1908 to H. N. Gardiner, he objected to the suggestion that ideas, concepts, or propositions are abstract entities that play the role assigned by logical realism. " '*That*' Caesar existed, *e.g.,* is not an intermediary between the objective fact 'Caesar existed' and the other objective fact 'someone's-belief-that-Caesar-existed.' . . . Surely truth can't inhabit a third realm between realities and statements of beliefs. . . . It seems to me the great merit of pragmatism to have stepped right over all such mongrel figments and to have put discussion on the solid ground of facts and relations-between-facts, that are also facts" (quoted in RBP, 2:485).

This statement resembles what he declared in "Two English Critics," in *MT,* 282–83, but it goes further. In both places he objected to the ambiguous term *proposition,* which sometimes means "the fact that" and sometimes "the belief that." In discussing Russell he conceded that "for certain logical purposes it may . . . be useful to treat propositions as absolute entities," but in the letter to Gardiner he appears to have discarded propositions and all abstract entities as a coordinate realm of reality intermediate between the fact of holding a belief and the fact that makes the belief true; nothing then remains of logical realism.

How can logical realism cohere with pragmatism? In the letter to Gardiner, the latter doctrine is said to require only the fact of a belief and the fact that disproves or verifies that belief. Since intentionality or self-transcendency is analyzed by pragmatism into actions or "leadings," it cannot be responsible for a need to postulate abstract concepts. James clearly wanted to discuss not only the fact that one holds a belief (sometimes equated with *idea*) but also the content of the belief; he may have meant that abstract concepts taken as Platonic entities are needed to identify that content. When we believe that black differs from white, the content of our belief consists of the abstract, ideal entities *white, black,* and *differs from.* But although these entities are real and form an order of their own, they exist only as long as they participate in the belief that black differs from white, and are thus more Aristotelian than Platonic; see *Principles,* 1:467 and *MT,* 203. This interpretation permits the reality of abstract entities as mandated by James's logical realism but limits those entities to being part of the fact or occurrence of belief. This limitation is seemingly demanded by the concreteness not of psychological prejudice but of pragmatic thinking.

This interpretation also suggests a way of reconciling James's assertions that "reality consists of existential particulars as well as of essences and universals [concepts] and class-names, and of existential particulars we become aware only in the perceptual flux" (*SPP,* 78) and that "abstraction is not insulation; and it no more breaks reality than the tube breaks the landscape. Concepts are notes, views taken on reality, not pieces of it, as bricks are of a house (*SPP,* 200). Although, as James noted, the latter sentence is taken from Bergson, he evidently agreed with it; in contrast to the first sentence, the quotation from Bergson suggests that concepts are views rather than parts of reality. But if concepts are mental realities—abstract entities which can be distinguished from states of consciousness or mental occurrences but which cannot exist except by particpating in them—then they can be seen as participating real entities that are also views or ways of understanding objective or known reality. This interpretation harmonizes with what James said in *SPP,* 58–61 and 76–86.

38. *Principles,* 2:335. See also "The Sentiment of Rationality," in *CER,* 86–87. This essay should be read alongside chapter 28 of *Principles,* for it is in many respects an anticipation of the latter. James himself qualified such assertions as this: "[Pragmatism] . . . agrees with nominalism . . . in always appealing to particulars" (*Pragmatism,* 47).

39. Perry remarked: "[James] never became a nominalist. In one way or another he always found a way to provide for universals, generals, and concepts, however much he might disparage them. This persistent retention of a modicum of Platonic realism, despite the general tendency of his thought to the contrary, was largely due to Peirce's insistence on the rights of thought as opposed to sensation" (RBP, 2:407).

40. *Principles,* 1:468. For other discussions of the issue, see *Pragmatism,* 47, 66, 87–90; *MT,* 83–85, 203–06, 234–42, 246–50; chapters 4–6 of *SPP;* "A World of Pure Experience," in McDermott, 196 and chapters 7, 13, 21, and 28 of *Principles.*

41. *Principles,* 1:472–80.

42. See, for example, *SPP,* 73–74.

43. Morton White writes: "James becomes fuzzy when he begins to speak of what can be achieved once science discovers those outer realities." White suspects confusion on James's part and possibly the influence of traditional rationalism. See *Science and Sentiment in America* (New York: Oxford University Press, 1972), 176–80.

44. See note 37 above.

45. This interpretation is beset by a difficulty in the attempt to see James's theory consistently. If, as he said, the eternal verities cannot, despite Kant, legislate for all possible

experience (1:662, 664), and if reality is always changing, with abstract concepts coming and going, then the coincidence between empirical phenomena and the idealized conceptions of mathematical physics may be only temporary at best; categorical a priori knowledge, as usually conceived in science, thus seems impossible. One problem in claiming a priori knowledge—which James may have thought was the scientist's rather than the philosopher's—is how to determine when a coincidence of phenomenon and concept actually occurs. He said that it was "for experience itself to prove whether its data can or cannot be assimilated to those ideal terms between which *a priori* relations obtain" (2:662), but he showed no interest in exploring whether the best that can ever be achieved is only an approximation yielding probabilistic instead of an a priori knowledge. Perhaps he did not want to rule out the possibility of actual coincidence, and thus concluded without much enthusiasm that science might somehow claim to show instances of it; there may come a point when an empirical formulation is so well established that we are justified in moving it into the category of the a priori.

James regretted that the question of whether some or all a priori knowledge is analytic or synthetic originated in Kant's vague distinction. He argued that such analytic judgments as "equidistant lines can nowhere meet" are not mere tautologies because the predicate amplifies the conception of the subject, which can happen even in mere truisms. To ask at what point the predicate amplifies the subject is too vague and subjective a question to answer.

> All philosophic interest vanishes from the question, the moment one ceases to ascribe to *any a priori* truths (whether analytic or synthetic) that "legislative character for all possible experience" which Kant believed in. We ourselves have denied such legislative character, and contended that it was for experience itself to prove whether its data can or cannot be assimilated to those ideal terms between which *a priori* relations obtain. The analytic-synthetic debate is thus for us devoid of significance. (*Principles,* 2:662)

46. *Principles,* 2:667. James called ideas or concepts that enter the mind through the senses *front-door effects,* and those of logic, mathematics, metaphysics, and the theoretical parts of the empirical sciences, which originate within the brain, *back-door effects.* In opposition to Spencer's evolutionary philosophy, which sought a universal correspondence between things inner and outer, James conceived of created concepts and insights as instances of Darwin's spontaneous variations—spontaneous and deviant enough to wreck Spencer's scheme.

G. S. Brett, a historian of psychology, called James's claim that science originates to such an extent from back-door effects his "most recondite doctrine. . . . James proceeds to elaborate what is in effect an interpretation of the *a priori* forms of judgment and in general that whole structure of scientific thought which enables us to anticipate experience. . . . A middle path between Spencer and Kant . . . beyond the limits of traditional naturalism without taking refuge in the . . . rationalism . . . [of] 'pure activity' and 'transcendent modes of thought'" ("The Psychology of William James in Relation to Philosophy," *In Commemoration of William James* [New York: Columbia University Press, 1942], 84–85).

47. *Principles,* 2:671. James seems somewhat disingenuous here. He could, by his own admission, impulsively overstate a point, and he was enough of a man of the world to want to sell his wares. Since he characteristically defended religion, morality, and metaphysics against logical or scientific explanations, preferring to explain them by subjectively pragmatic considerations or by outright faith, it is not likely that he believed that a metaphysical explanation could be modeled on a physical one. James never actually described metaphysical knowledge in his writings, but his claim to have done so helped to cement his view about the relation between mind and nature.

In a letter of 1910 to F. S. C. Schiller, James wrote:

> There may be an advantage, from the point of view of converting the public, in our working at different levels. For example, in a book for college use like mine (I want it to

sell) the "eternal" view of concepts can do no particular harm, for they are *relatively* eternal (and some of them actually so, so far as we yet know), and the distinguishing of them as such is a rather definite stage in thought, practically attained by opinion concerning them, on which the student can start easily and keep step with you. . . . It is important to show the public that the function of concepts is practical, but it disconcerts the beginner to be told that the very concepts you use in doing so are themselves delinquent. (Quoted in RBP, 2:511–12)

James was troubled by Schiller's polemical tone in his defenses of pragmatism and repeatedly begged him to approach his public more graciously. This attitude may explain in part why many readers wonder whether James really held a Platonic view of concepts and whether he was really convinced that metaphysical knowledge could be built upon the model of physics. See Patrick K. Dooley, *Pragmatism as Humanism: The Philosophy of William James* (Chicago: Nelson-Hall, 1974).

48. The earlier essays are: "Remarks on Spencer's *Definition of Mind as Correspondence*" (1878); "Quelques considérations sur la méthode subjective" (1878); and "The Sentiment of Rationality" (1879). James claimed that "On the Function of Cognition" is a "chapter in descriptive psychology,—hardly anything more" (*MT*, 3). That characterization might not have been misleading a hundred years ago, but today the essay seems unmistakably philosophical.

49. See the preface to *Pragmatism.*

50. "On the Function of Cognition," in *MT*, 22n.

51. In 1907 James wrote: "We can now describe the general features of cognition, tell what on the whole it *does for us,* in a universal way" (*MT*, 145). In 1904, while making notes for a course he was teaching, he jotted: "[Morris] Cohen [a graduate student then at Harvard] stands out for self transcendency in cases where the terminus is not presented. Admit it: but what is it *known-as?* What does it *do for us?* It is only *known* as knowledge when the terminus is reached, until then it is not known as *knowledge* but as tendency. Astonishing how much rubbish the pragmatic acct. of knowing scuffs away. E.g., Bert. Russell's diseased stuff in *Mind* Oct. '04."

See James's 1907 letter to C. A. Strong in which he calls "On the Function of Cognition" the *fons et origo* of all his pragmatism (RBP, 2:548).

52. This is a recurrent theme in James's pragmatism; see, for example, *MT*, 42, 46; *Pragmatism*, 49. A more effective formulation appeared in "The Knowing of Things Together," where James credited Dickinson S. Miller with having led him to it. "I hope you may agree with me now that in representative knowledge there is no special inner mystery, but only an outer chain of physical or mental intermediaries connecting thought and thing. *To know an object is here to lead to it through a context which the world supplies.* All this was most instructively set forth by our colleague Miller. . . . I owe him this acknowledgment" (*CER*, 377). See chapter 9, note 23.

53. For James's remarks on solipsism, see *MT*, 20–28, 38, 178, 212, 215; *Principles* 2:318n; and "The Compounding of Consciousness," in McDermott, 560–61. Among James's papers in the Houghton Library are notes from 1870 on idealism, which show an early interest in the problem of solipsism. He concluded then, as he did later: "We infer a mind from its physical concomitants just as we infer a property not actually felt in a mass of matter from those we do actually feel."

Little has been written about James on the topic of other minds. See Michael H. DeArmey, "William James and the Problem of Other Minds," *Southern Journal of Philosophy* 20 (Fall 1982):325–36.

54. *CER*, 410; see note 52 above.

55. *CER*, 412; see also *MT*, 42, 44, and 174–75.

56. *MT*, 174–79. James wrote confidently here about the ability of psychologists to define

the intentional tendency. "The idea has associates peculiar to itself, motor as well as ideational; it tends by its place and nature to call these into being, one after another; and the appearance of them in succession is what we mean by the 'workings' of the idea. According to what they are, does the trueness or falseness which the idea harbored come to light. These tendencies have still earlier conditions which, in a general way, biology, psychology and biography can trace."

But the question of whether these motor and ideational associations *are* the tendency or are only its accompaniments is not explored. In the case of a priori knowledge, for instance, intentionality may be impossible to identify in physiological terms. Consistent with the reduction of mental states to physiological ones in "The Stream of Thought" and "The Consciousness of Self," James might have insisted that such identification is always theoretically possible.

That he may have felt uncertain about the analysis of what is in an idea or belief that makes it refer or intend as it does is indicated by the fact that he never completely dropped the claim that when intentional reference or cognition occurs, some relevant resemblance exists between the idea or belief and the object intended or cognized. James remarked that he had overemphasized the role of resemblance in "The Function of Cognition," and that in his developed pragmatism he replaced resemblance with a functional analysis (*MT*, 41–42). Yet while clearly repudiating the so-called "copy" theory of knowledge that mandates resemblance and equates it with cognition, he always included resemblance as a possibly relevant component of a cognitive state of consciousness. The question of whether cognitive belief and object resemble each other did not disappear when James dropped dualism. In a letter of 1907 to C. A. Strong he explicitly included resemblance as one of the important factors in the cognitive process. He also wrote that he had never intended an exclusively sensuous or imagelike likeness but had wanted to include logical likeness as well (RBP, 2:545). James may have operated with the vague notion that what is in a cognitive state of consciousness and is responsible for its particular intentionality or reference is a logical or structural resemblance to the kind of thing that is believed or known. But this notion does not square with his view that intentional tendencies consist in motor and ideational events, since it makes no sense to construe logical resemblance in physiological terms.

For more discussion of resemblance between the cognizing and the cognized, see *Principles*, 1:471–74, 499–500, 2:634–35; *MT*, 6, 78–82, and *Pragmatism*, 139–40.

57. RBP, 2:463.

58. For James's most famous statements that pragmatism was designed as a method of philosophizing, see the first three lectures of *Pragmatism*. On James and pragmatism, see John Smith *The Spirit of American Philosophy* (New York: Oxford University Press, 1961).

59. The critics did not all seize upon this one passage (*MT*, 189–90) for their verdict. Other passages suggest the same conclusion. In fairness to James, his readers did not always appreciate that throughout *Pragmatism* he tried to identify the consequential differences between the rival hypotheses in philosophical disputes about such issues as monism, free will, reality, and religion. Readers sometimes spotted the element of subjectivism, the "tender-minded" feature of his philosophizing which he ceaselessly defended, but overlooked the pragmatic tracing and comparison of the consequences implied by conflicting propositions, which could also give reasons for choosing between the propositions. That we choose on subjective grounds does not disqualify the compared consequences as reasons. When consequences were admitted as reasons, James raised the question of whether in each particular context they were very good reasons.

One of the most acute criticisms of *Pragmatism* was that of A. O. Lovejoy, who urged James to distinguish more clearly between pragmatism as a theory of meaning and as a theory of truth. In addition, he seems to have caught a reason for James's having occasionally allowed pragmatism to slip into pure subjectivism: James sometimes failed to separate the consequences of a proposition from the consequences of believing the proposition. The confusion of the two was probably responsible for James's thinking that, even with cases such as the automatic sweetheart, the consequences of believing an impractical hypothesis are still pragmatic reasons; originally, he had said that only the consequences of the hypothesis itself could play that role.

In a letter to Lovejoy in 1907, James responded: "I have to frankly cry *peccavi*—you convict me of real sin. Consequences of true ideas *per se*, and consequences of ideas *qua believed by us*, are logically different consequences, and the whole 'will to believe' business has got to be re-edited with explicit uses made of the distinction. I have been careless here" (quoted by RBP, 2:481). On Lovejoy, see RBP, 2:480–82. James never did reedit or write in response to Lovejoy's criticism; if he had, it is not clear whether he would have formulated a sharper distinction between a belief that is pragmatically based and one subjectively based.

C. S. Peirce sensed that James advocated pragmatism as a way of opening one's mind to both sides of a philosophical debate but wrote to him in 1904: "Pragmatism solves no real problem. . . . When one comes to such questions as immortality, the nature of the connection of mind and matter . . . we are left completely in the dark. The effect of pragmatism here is simply to open our minds to receiving any evidence, not to furnish evidence" (quoted by RBP, 2:430). Peirce did not mention that James had dedicated *Pragmatism* to the memory of John Stuart Mill, "from whom I first learned the pragmatic openness of mind"; in view of the connection James made between being pragmatic and being philosophically tolerant, Peirce's criticism was certainly correct to a point. But he overlooked James's use of the pragmatic method for something more than merely being open to possible evidence. The method intended not to furnish new evidence but to give a person a basis for making up his mind in light of factual evidence too inconclusive to produce definite belief.

James's lectures at the Lowell Institute in Boston in 1906 and at Columbia University in 1907, published together as *Pragmatism* in 1907, were often regarded as too loose and popular in their formulations, confusing readers about James's exact intent. John Dewey wrote:

> A few considerations found in the *Principles*. . . disclose the nature of pragmatic empiricism better than do the popular lectures on *Pragmatism*. . . [such as] the importance of *analysis* in the procedures of knowing. . . . James brought out the way in which discrimination and disassociation are directed to human interests so that genuine distinctions in ideas and beliefs are what make a difference in behavior in a literal sense of "making" . . . [and] unifying functions of knowledge. . . . Reasoning, general ideas, definition, and classification are treated as "teleological weapons"; as means of attack upon the brute facts of existence in spite of the indifference of the facts in themselves to our "higher" interests ("James as Empiricist," *In Commemoration of William James* [New York: Columbia University Press, 1942], 50).

Dewey was especially impressed by the chapter "Discrimination and Comparison" in *Principles,* with its twin emphases upon analysis in knowledge and the teleological nature of cognitive concepts. Dewey's essay is a generous tribute to James, defending him from attacks that he had glorified the will at the expense of reason. Like Dewey, I think pragmatism was first formulated in *Principles;* but Dewey, like Peirce, may have missed the key point in Jamesian pragmatism, which appears conspicuously after *Principles:* its role in producing and sustaining belief. In any event, Dewey's praise of James was eloquent: "I think it could be shown that two contemporary schools, now exercising considerable influence, the British analytic school and the school of logical positivism, suffer greatly because of their dependence upon pre-Jamesian psychology" (54). Dewey was aware of the charges that James's *Pragmatism,* together with "The Will to Believe," seemed to license willful unreasonableness and that Jamesian pragmatism could resemble subjectivism pure and simple, and he thought that a return to the more scientific temper of *Principles* might help to mollify the critics. A careful but sympathetic reading of James's pragmatic writings can rebut the charges, but not without making assumptions beyond his literal words.

60. G. E. Moore was among those who took James to task for equating truth with "what is useful to believe." "Professor James' 'Pragmatism' " (1907–08; reprinted as "William James' 'Pragmatism' " in *Philosophical Studies* [London: Routledge & Kegan Paul, 1922]).

Bertrand Russell, in his review of *Pragmatism,* wrote that pragmatism can be summarized thus: "The truth is anything which it pays to believe" ("Transatlantic 'Truth,' " *Albany Review* 2 [1908]:393). (James noted in his copy of the review [now in the Houghton Library]: "The question being in every case whether it really *does* pay.") Russell went on to comment: "Now, if this definition is to be useful, as pragmatism intends it to be, it must be possible to know that it pays to believe something without knowing anything that pragmatism would call a truth" (399). (James's marginal note: "Can't it pay to believe in the pragmatist definition?")

Russell's main criticism was that it is difficult to determine whether a given belief pays; we must make an awkward estimation of the consequences of competing beliefs. "It is far easier, it seems to me, to settle the plain question of fact: 'Have Popes been always infallible?'—than to settle the question whether the effects of thinking them infallible are on the whole good. Yet this question, of the truth of Roman Catholicism, is just the sort of question that pragmatism considers specially suitable to their method" (399). (James's marginal comment: "The 'pay' is not a mark 'easy to find' of the truth in a given instance. It is the essence, if the belief is true, and very hard to find in many cases.")

James's published reply to Russell shows not only that he did not consider pragmatism to define truth, but that workability or utility is not even a criterion.

> We affirm nothing as silly as Mr. Russell supposes. Good consequences are not proposed by us merely as a sure sign, mark, or criterion, by which truth's presence is habitually ascertained, tho they may indeed serve on occasion as such a sign; they are proposed rather as the lurking *motive* inside of every truth-claim, whether the "trower" be conscious of such motive, or whether he obey it blindly. They are proposed as the *causa existendi* of our beliefs, not as their logical cue or premise, and still less as their objective deliverance or content. They assign the only intelligible *meaning* to that difference in our beliefs which our habit of calling them true or false comports. ("Two English Critics," in *MT,* 273)

The idea that good consequences are simply the motive for holding a belief—and not that the true is the useful or that the useful is a criterion of truth—was always the leading idea in Jamesian pragmatism. Pragmatism provided a motive for making up one's mind in the thicket of abstract philosophizing.

Morton White writes in his review of Ayer's *Origins of Pragmatism:* "If I were writing a book on James I should call attention to a strain in his thought which Ayer neglects, but which seems to me to be closer to the truth." White quotes from "The Sentiment of Rationality": "Pretend what we may, the whole man within us is at work when we form our philosophical opinion" (*WTB,* Harvard edition, 77). White adds: "I would remark that here intellect, will, taste, and passion are *all* said to cooperate in the formation of a philosophical opinion, and that intellect is not denied a part" (*The New York Review,* 30 January 1969, 26). I agree with White that the key phrase is "the whole man," which is important in understanding what I mean in calling James's view subjective pragmatism. The whole person constitutes the subjectivity that is legitimately enlisted in choosing a philosophical opinion.

Abraham Edel makes much the same point in his remarks about the "activist man" in James's psychology; see *Analyzing Concepts in Social Science,* 2 vols. (New Brunswick, N. J.: Transaction Books, 1979), 1:251, 255.

61. *Pragmatism,* 133; see also the first lecture, "The Present Dilemma in Philosophy," 22–37.

62. See RBP, 2:371, 447.

63. See "The Chicago School," in *CER,* 445–47.

64. "Humanism," in *CER,* 449.

65. *CER,* 449–50. See also "G. Papini and the Pragmatist Movement in Italy," in *CER,* 459–66.

66. See, for instance, "What Pragmatism Means" and "Pragmatism and Common Sense" in *Pragmatism.* The latter lecture is closely connected with the final chapter of *Principles.*

67. See note 56 above.

68. *Pragmatism,* 140. Bertrand Russell wrote of this passage:

> This language is rather metaphorical, and a little puzzling; to my mind it suggests nothing so much as being introduced to a personage at a garden-party. At least, that seems describable as being "guided either straight up to a reality or into its surroundings, and put into working touch with it." By the help of a little sycophancy, we can fulfill the rest of the definition, and "handle either it or something connected with it better than if we disagreed." But such behavior would not usually be identified with the pursuit of truth. ("Transatlantic 'Truth,'" 395)

James made no marginal note here, though he did elsewhere on his copy of this review of *Pragmatism.* Russell's was a typical though more amusing reaction of befuddlement, causing James to express continuing annoyance with his critics.

69. Letter of 28 April 1905; quoted by RBP, 2:489. For instances of the difficulty of trying to define clearly the opposition, see *Pragmatism,* 148, 167–68, 198–99; *MT,* 180, 221–22, 226, 238, 266.

In the preface of *The Meaning of Truth,* James conceded that much of the wrangling between him and his critics was mainly verbal. He began to justify his continuing defense of pragmatism on the grounds that it supported his radical empiricism, though in the preface to *Pragmatism* he had explicitly set the two apart.

> Most of the pragmatist and anti-pragmatist warfare is over what the word "truth" shall be held to signify, and not over any of the facts. . . . The difference is that when the pragmatists speak of truth, they mean exclusively something about the ideas, namely their workableness; whereas when anti-pragmatists speak of truth they seem most often to mean something about the objects. Since the pragmatist, if he agrees that an idea is "really" true, also agrees to whatever it says about its object; and since most anti-pragmatists have already come round to agreeing that, if the object exists, the idea that it does so is workable; there would seem so little left to fight about that I might well be asked why instead of reprinting my share in so much verbal wrangling, I do not show my sense of "values" by burning it all up. I understand the question and I will give my answer. I am interested in another doctrine in philosophy to which I give the name of radical empiricism, and it seems to me that the establishment of the pragmatic theory of truth is a step of first-rate importance in making radical empiricism prevail. (*MT,* xi-xii)

70. "Faith and the Right to Believe," *SPP,* 221. James occasionally referred to "vicious intellectualism," and in one place cited it as the denial of the leadings or intermediary steps, the series of actions and experiences that constitute any verifying process (*MT,* 147). Elsewhere he blamed intellectualism for using abstract concepts at the expense of concrete reality. See *MT,* 249–50, 255.

71. See *Pragmatism,* 53, 162–66.

72. *MT,* vii. In places James appeared to be explicitly offering definitions or criteria of truth (see *MT,* 200, 221, 266), but these passages should not be taken literally.

For helpful discussions of James on truth, see H. S. Thayer's introduction to *Pragmatism* and *The Meaning of Truth* in the Harvard edition, and his "On William James on Truth," *Transactions of the Charles S. Peirce Society* 13 (Winter 1977):3–19. See also Ellen Kappy Suckiel, *The Pragmatic Philosophy of William James* (Notre Dame: University of Notre Dame Press, 1982).

73. Letter of 21 August 1907; quoted in RBP, 2:543–47.

74. *Pragmatism,* 105. For statements about the past, see *MT,* 287–98. For typical remarks about relative and absolute truth, see *MT,* 89–92, 177–79, 221–25, 239, 265–66.

The question of what *satisfaction* means was especially annoying to James because he wanted to use it as a generic term, useful because it is vague; he never intended to define it precisely. Perry remarked in a review: "The greater the pomp and circumstance of knowledge, or the dramatic interplay of interests, the more important the element of satisfaction. But it is clear that this does not in itself determine truth" ("A Review of Pragmatism As a Theory of Knowledge," *Journal of Philosophy, Psychology, and Scientific Methods* 4 [1907]:373). James's marginal note in his copy (now in the Houghton Library) reads: "Of course it doesn't but what pragmatist ever said that it did? Truth is *the relation to reality* of those ideas which are satisfactory. It turns out that ideas that have no relation to reality practically do not turn out to be satisfactory and so do not count as true." See also *MT,* 195, 213.

In response to the charge that he could not know his own theory to be true, James wrote: "But whether what [pragmatists] themselves say about that whole universe is objectively true, *i.e.,* whether the pragmatic theory of truth is true *really,* they cannot warrant,—they can only believe it. To their hearers they can only *propose* it, as I propose it to my readers, as something to be verified *ambulando,* or by the way in which its consequences may confirm it" (*MT,* 213). This response is a natural inference from the way he characterized truth.

75. *MT,* 228; on meliorism, see *Pragmatism,* 84, 89, 185.

76. *MT,* 156–57. Perry, who customarily declared that there is a place for knowledge-by-acquaintance in James's epistemology (whereas there is not in Dewey's) let his own doubt show: "In addition to pragmatic 'knowledge-about,' James provides an alternative, namely, knowledge by acquaintance; and this, *however rare or impure it may be,* does at any rate afford a cognitive footing" (RBP, 2:514; my italics).

11. REALITY

1. G. E. Moore, "The Refutation of Idealism," *Mind,* n.s. 12 (1903):450.

2. "Does 'Consciousness' Exist?" in McDermott, 169.

3. Ibid. James credited Shadworth Hodgson with having made a similar argument in *The Metaphysics of Experience* and *The Philosophy of Reflection.* Hodgson was an early and important influence upon James, who called him and Renouvier "the two foremost contemporary philosophers" ("The Sentiment of Rationality," in *CER,* 133). For Hodgson's influence, see RBP, chapters 38–40.

In emphasizing James's contribution to the movement away from Cartesian dualism toward what Russell and others called neutral monism, commentators have overlooked James's disavowal that pure experience is a single kind of stuff from which all experience is made. If his concept of pure experience can be freed of idealistic overtones—a problematic endeavor—it might be called neutral pluralism, in that the basic units of reality or pure experience are the vast variety of sensations.

Russell, while missing the plural nature of what James should have referred to as pure experiences, recognized James's doctrine as revolutionary, influencing the development of realism, especially in America, yet retaining a distinct flavor of idealism nonetheless.

> The use of the phrase "pure experience" . . . points to a lingering influence of idealism. "Experience," like "consciousness," must be a product, not part of the primary stuff of the world. It must be possible, if James is right in his main contentions, that roughly the same stuff, differently arranged, would not give rise to anything that could be called "experience." . . . My own belief . . . is that James is right in rejecting consciousness as an entity, and that the American realists are partly right . . . in considering that both mind and matter are composed of a neutral-stuff which, in isolation, is neither mental nor physical. (*The Analysis of Mind* [1921; reprint, London: Allen & Unwin, 1949], 24–25)

See Andrew J. Reck, "Idealist Metaphysics in William James's 'Principles of Psychology,'" *Idealistic Studies* 9 (Spring 1979):213–21.

4. "A World of Pure Experience," in McDermott, 208. James clearly considered the idea that the distinction between consciousness and its content does not fall within the "instant field of the present" (pure experience) but is made only by later experience as a central doctrine in his radical empiricism; it recurs in "Does 'Consciousness' Exist?" (McDermott, 178), "The Notion of Consciousness" (McDermott, 187, 192), "How Two Minds Can Know One Thing" (McDermott, 229–30), and "The Place of Affectional Facts" (McDermott, 272). The idea had been stated in 1885 in "The Function of Cognition" (*MT*, 16), and occurred originally in early drafts of "The Stream of Thought" and "The Consciousness of Self."

James credited Hodgson with the notion that the minimum consciousness requires two subfeelings, of which the second retrospects the first; see "How Two Minds Can Know One Thing," in McDermott, 231n.

5. *Principles*, 1:189, 304.

6. "The Place of Affectional Facts in A World of Pure Experience," in McDermott, 272.

7. "How Two Minds Can Know One Thing," in McDermott, 227; see also "Does 'Consciousness' Exist?" 181.

8. See, for example, *Principles*, 1:163.

9. This manuscript in the Houghton Library is labeled the "Miller-Bode" notebook because it is a running reflection on the problem as it was put to James by Dickinson S. Miller and W. H. Bode, philosophy professor at the University of Wisconsin. For relevant details, as well as the text of most of this notebook, see RBP, 2:393–95 and 750–65. What Perry has reproduced of the Miller-Bode notebook conveys James's worries about the defensibility of radical empiricism, but until one reads through its more than three hundred pages, including jottings, diagrams, and questions, one cannot know how obsessed James was by the need to make his doctrine work and by the difficulties he faced. Entries were sometimes written in Cambridge, sometimes in Chocorua; the problem apparently went with him wherever he went. In an entry from November 1905 he wrote:

> I get lost here between the entitative and the functional points of view. If to be is to be experienced, then everything can be *immediately* only as it is immediately experienced. If not immediately experienced *as* the same or *as* other, how can it in its immediacy have been the same? Or other? If we meet this by the assumption that things are immediately as they are known to have been, isn't this naïf? Doesn't it abrogate the pure experience principle? Evidently Bode, Miller etc. suspect this to be the case. . . . This is as far as I can go consecutively today. Let me add some random considerations and memoranda.

On 22 November 1905 he wrote: "As regards Miller's first point, the difficulty relates again to the distinction between fact per se and fact as experienced, around which all my present writing has revolved." On the facing page he scrawled: "Fact vs. experience—methinks pure experience breaks down here definitively. We have to turn things by fact, which is virtually experienceable as having been etc." What he meant by this is obscure, but he was clearly concerned with the difficulty of trying to collapse the fact-experience distinction within the confines of pure experience.

In the Houghton Library is a letter, dated 23 August 1932, from Miller to Perry, who was then preparing *TCWJ*. Miller recalled the problem for radical empiricism that he had pointed out to James; after noting that his formulation of the difficulty had been mainly in letters to and conversations with James, he wrote:

> The objection as I made it is as clear in my mind now as then—if one says, the very object is immediately given, one implies that it may be given to you and to me, or an identical part or aspect of it may thus be given, at the same time. Now the *other* contents or present

objects of your mind and mine will *not* be the same. My objection has force only on one assumption, that what we mean by "consciousness" is a *relation* between the contents or objects of consciousness. The object O will stand in a relation of appearance with my *other* content of the moment, but, insofar as *you* are conscious of it, it will not stand in this relation (i.e. you are of course not conscious of my other content, my bodily sensation for instance). That is, the object O will stand in a certain relation and not stand in it at one and the same time—a self-contradiction. It will not do to say, it stands in that relation from *my point of view only,* not from your point of view. "From my point of view" here means for my consciousness and this fact has already been considered and embodied in the statement of the objection. My point of view or consciousness is a relation between my contents, and on the neo-realist theory a given content may stand in a certain relation and yet not stand in it.—This was a difficulty I had in accepting the neo-realist theory *if* the account of consciousness as a relation between contents is correct. I have not varied the present statement from the one I gave to him. . . .

James conceived consciousness as a relation between pure experiences rather than an inherent property of any one of them. See, for example, "The Notion of Consciousness," in McDermott, 193.

10. "Does 'Consciousness' Exist?" in McDermott, 179.

11. "The Thing and Its Relations," in McDermott, 215; for James's remarks about dizziness and pure experience, see "The Notion of Consciousness," in McDermott, 189.

12. Tilting with neo-idealism or absolutism, which conflicted with James's concept of relations, was a lifelong hobby; see in *ERE* "Does 'Consciousness' Exist?" "A World of Pure Experience," and "The Thing and Its Relations"; in *APU* "Monistic Idealism," "Hegel and His Method," and "Bergson and His Critique of Intellectualism"; and in *CER* "Bradley or Bergson."

13. See, for instance, the section "Conjunctive Relations" in "A World of Pure Experience," in McDermott, 196–99. For a valuable discussion of James on relations, see Marian C. Madden and Edward H. Madden, "William James and the Problem of Relations," *Transactions of the Charles S. Peirce Society* 14 (Fall 1978):227–46.

14. In the Houghton Library there is a small notebook, many pages torn out, which seems to date from 1903–04; one page comprises these entries:

> My system is like a Dyak's head (Furness, p. 60). Royce's like a crystal globe with goldfish, or aquarium.
>
> *Motto for my book.* "God help thee, old man, thy thoughts have created a creature within thee; and he whose intense thinking then makes him a Prometheus; a vulture feed upon that heart forever; that vulture the very creature he creates."
>
> Moby Dick, 1892, 192
>
> (I wonder if my notion of PE with all the other categories formed by additional relations among them may not be as fertile a principle in Ontology as Association has been in Psychology!
> Quien sabe?)

For James's description of what he meant by a Dyak's head, see "A World of Pure Experience," in McDermott, 197.

15. "Does 'Consciousness' Exist?" in McDermott, 175.

16. *SPP,* 235. James himself was troubled by the constant difficulties of trying to make radical empiricism and his general weltanschauung coherent. Besides the Miller-Bode notebook, other items among his unpublished papers bear witness to his travails. For his Philosophy 9 course lecture on 14 January 1905, his notes were as follows:

Go back to a theory of cognition
Your lamp & mind, your body
   & mine conterminous   because of activity passing
How represent the activities?
We have only one paradigm
Our inner life
Idea & percept are confluent
Percepts engender ideas
Ideas engender percepts
Activity, if *efficacious,* means creation
Desire—ideal

On the facing page is scrawled, "This stuff not examinable."

17. See, for instance, the argument in "The Notion of Consciousness," in McDermott, 190–91.

18. Ibid., 192.

19. "How Two Minds Can Know One Thing," in McDermott, 230–31. The idea that consciousness is a retrospective addition occurs throughout *ERE* and also in *Principles* and "On the Function of Cognition." See also "The World of Pure Experience" (McDermott, 202) for what may be a reluctance to call anything knowledge that is not in transition. Knowledge-by-acquaintance is presumably the end of a transition.

20. Perry, for one, tended in *TCWJ* to underestimate the problems whenever he discussed James's concept of knowledge.

21. *The Analysis of Mind,* 22. Hilary Putnam has criticized logical positivists for thinking it queer to state that the world consists of only sensations. "What is queer about it is *not* that it is unverifiable but that there cannot be a world consisting *only* of sensations." ("Logical Positivism and the Philosophy of Mind," in *The Legacy of Logical Positivism,* ed. Peter Achinstein and Stephen Barker [Baltimore: Johns Hopkins University Press, 1969]).

For another incisive criticism of James, see John E. Smith, "Radical Empiricism," *Proceedings of the Aristotelian Society* n.s. 65 (1966):205–18.

22. For a comparison of James's radical empiricism with the views of Renouvier, Mach, and the positivists, see RBP, 1:587–88 and 2:389–91. According to Mach's theory, sensations are neutral elements from which both mind and body are constructed. As Perry noted, Mach envisaged a construction modeled on physics. Perry described Mach's theory and James's response to it thus: "Thus we find him defining the domain of psychology as the dependence of the sensations or elements on the central nervous system. 'Decidedly *not,*' remarked James [marginal comment on his copy of Mach's *Analysis der Empfindungen*]—for this could only mean the reduction of psychology, through psychophysics, to physics; while for James psychology had its *own* categories, scientifically as authoritative as those of physics and metaphysically more fundamental."

Perry's interpretation, with which I agree, raises the question of why, given James's conclusion that everything experienced is physiological prior to being conceptualized in terms of pure experience, he did not, like Mach and Russell, attempt to accommodate sensations into an all-embracing framework of physics rather than conceiving of them as neutral pure experiences.

We must be careful in offering facile commentaries on Mach's view because it too presents interpretive problems. What he meant by *sensation* is controversial, so it is not immediately evident how his use of the term compares with James's. See, for instance, Thomas S. Szasz's introduction to Mach's *Analysis of Sensations* (New York: Dover, 1959), xiv–xv.

James met Mach during the academic year 1882–83, and they began a long and friendly relationship. Mach's book on sensations was published in 1886, years before James's essays in radical empiricism; there are numerous references to James's psychology in later editions of this book, but none to his metaphysics. In his preface to the second edition, Mach wrote: "This book was intended to have the effect of an *aperçu,* and if I may judge from the occasional utterances of Avenarius, H. Cornelius, James, Külpe, Loeb, Pearson, Willy, and others, it seems to have fulfilled its object." Although Carl Stumpf (another friend and strong influence upon James, especially in the psychology of space) was not mentioned by Mach, it may be more than a coincidence that in a letter to James Stumpf had described Mach's book as an aperçu. "Mach's work gave me much pleasure; but upon closer examination much of it is seen to contain *aperçus* that are more ingenious than true. In my review in the *Deutsche Literaturzeitung* I ventured to indicate this conviction as politely as possible, and was delighted to hear that Mach took no offence at my criticism. Instead he expressed his thanks to me." (See RBP, 2:66.)

Mach's several complimentary references to James's psychology emphasize his work on dizziness with deaf-mutes and his arguments (against Bain, Wundt, and Helmholtz) that no feelings of innervation occur. In a footnote, in the penultimate chapter of his book, Mach wrote: "With regard to the idea of concepts as labor-saving instruments, the late Prof. W. James directed in conversation my attention to points of agreement between my writings and his essay on 'The Sentiment of Rationality' (*Mind,* vol. IV, p. 317, July 1879). This essay, written with refreshing vigor and impartiality, will be perused by everyone with pleasure and profit" (Dover edition, 310). Elsewhere, Mach praised *The Varieties of Religious Experience* and *A Pluralistic Universe,* but seems to have been more reserved about *Pragmatism.* James immensely admired Mach and once wrote to his colleague, Hugo Münsterberg: "I am reading Ostwald's *Vorlesungen über Naturphilosophie,* and find it a most delectable book. I don't think I ever envied a man's mind as much as I have envied Ostwald's,—unless it were Mach's" (RBP, 2:288). Though, as Perry commented, this is typical Jamesian generosity, there is no doubt about James's respect for Mach's work. Despite its antimetaphysical tone, *The Analysis of Sensations* bears striking similarities in topics, approach, and general concerns to James's psychological writings.

23. "Loose Notes [A]" in the James Collection at the Houghton Library. James apparently jotted these notes while he was preparing the lectures published as *The Varieties of Religious Experience* in 1901.

24. *The Origins of Pragmatism,* 323. Ayer makes further references to metaphysics as picture-making in the final pages of his book.

References to "picture-thinking" are abundant in Wittgenstein's writings; he, perhaps more than any other thinker, appreciated that philosophy is typically subject to both the obvious and the sly invasions of picture-thinking.

> And as for the feeling of certainty: I sometimes say to myself "I am sure it's . . . o'clock", and in a more or less confident tone of voice, and so on. If you ask me the *reason* for this certainty I have none.
>
> If I say, I read it off from an inner clock,—that is a picture, and the only thing that corresponds to it is that I said it was such-and-such a time. And the purpose of the picture is to assimilate this case to the other one. I am refusing to acknowledge two different cases here. (*Philosophical Investigations,* 158)

25. "A World of Experience," in McDermott, 212–13. An amusing example of James's reliance upon spatial imagery occurs in his notes on how to make pure experience plausible: "I find that I involuntarily think of *co*-ness [simultaneously overlapping experiences of two persons] under the physical image of a sort of lateral suffusion from one thing into another, like a gas, or warmth, or light. The *places* involved are fixed, but what fills one place radiates and suffuses into the other by lateral movement, 'endosmosis'" (RBP, 2:757).

26. "The Types of Philosophical Thinking," in McDermott, 489.

27. "A World of Pure Experience," in McDermott, 195, 212.

28. Ibid., 195.

29. See, for example, "Bergson and His Critique of Intellectualism," in McDermott, 575.

30. "The Essence of Humanism," in McDermott, 308. Following the lead of his friend and fellow pragmatist, F. S. C. Schiller, James called his pragmatic/radical empiricistic view "humanistic." For the relation between Schiller and James, and the introduction of the term *humanism,* see RBP, 2:494–513.

31. "The Notion of Consciousness," in McDermott, 186.

32. "A World of Pure Experience," in McDermott, 209. In view of James's many favorable references to Berkeley and his own dedication to *esse est percipi* and its reduction of physical things to sensations, it is interesting that he criticized Berkeley more than Locke in a course taught in 1884–85. "Then came Berkeley, in whom he found more to criticize and less to accept. For the main contention of Berkeley he had no respect whatever, but the Roycian idealism he did respect" (course notes of R. W. Black, in the Houghton Library). James's objection to Berkeley in this course probably ran along lines similar to those in the quoted passage.

33. Letter to W. M. Salter, quoted in RBP, 1:578. Prior to the essays in radical empiricism, James had declared his willingness to accept the compounding of consciousness (in "The Knowing of Things Together" in 1895). Perhaps because of a lingering uncertainty or a confusion about the implications, he did not reassert that willingness until writing the essays for *A Pluralistic Universe* (1909).

34. RBP, 2:666; see also 1:543–85 for more on James's relation to Berkeley and to British empiricism.

Walter B. Pitkin expressed the sort of puzzlement that even James's most sympathetic readers, including Perry, have felt in trying to understand James's combination of natural realism and Berkeley's *esse est percipi.* "I am utterly unable to reconcile the common-sense realism . . . with the apparent idealism proclaimed in the remark that 'while one part of experience leans upon another part, experience as a whole leans upon nothing.' I can only conjecture that the reconciliation is to be found by showing that the word 'experience' is used in a different sense in each of the above passages" ("In Reply to Professor James," *Journal of Philosophy, Psychology, and Scientific Methods* 4 (1907):45). James's response does not illuminate matters much better. See "A Reply to Mr. Pitkin," *Journal of Philosophy, Psychology, and Scientific Methods* 4 (1907):105–06, as well as "Mr. Pitkin's Refutation of 'Radical Empiricism,'" *Journal of Philosophy, Psychology, and Scientific Method* 3 (1906):712.

Although Bertrand Russell was influenced by James's "Does 'Consciousness' Exist?" he never accepted it fully. In a letter of 30 August 1912 to Perry, acknowledging the receipt of a volume on new realism, he said he agreed with the logic of the new realists but found their metaphysics, which seemed to derive from James's radical empiricism, too problematic. His only decided opinions, however, were confined to logic. In a previous letter to Perry (16 November 1910) he had mentioned that he and G. E. Moore were the only realists in England, except for some "quite young men." See Box (K–Z) in the James Collection at the Houghton Library.

George Santayana was tentative in his judgment. "In ["Does 'Consciousness' Exist?"] James takes an important, if not the final, step in the phenomenalistic analysis of experience. If we reject matter with Berkeley and spirit with Hume, we have only data or phenomena with which to compose the universe. . . . The system has been worked out later by Bertrand Russell and the school of 'Logical Realists' or 'Logical Analysts,' and if it were found tenable would give William James a high place among modern philosophers" ("Three American Philosophers," *American Scholar* 22 [1953]:281–84). Santayana's article is an interesting estimate of James, Dewey, and himself. Given what Russell said in his letter to Perry, he would have had misgivings about being described by Santayana as working out James's phenomenalistic system.

James's response to Russell is clear in a letter of 24 December 1909 to C. S. Peirce: "Your essays in Vol. II and III of the Monist seem to me the most pregnant of all your work. But then I am *a*-logical, if not illogical, and glad to be so when I find Bertie Russell trying to excogitate what true knowledge means, in the absence of any concrete universe surrounding the knower and the known. Ass!"

For further references to Berkeley, see "Does 'Consciousness' Exist?" in McDermott, 172; "A World of Pure Experience," in McDermott, 196; *SPP*, 122–23; and "Humanism and Truth," in *MT*, 63, 88.

35. See *Principles*, 1:226, 346; and "Concerning Fechner," "The Compounding of Consciousness," and "The Continuity of Experience" in *APU*.

36. Notes of 29 April, 1 May, and 15 May 1898 for a seminar titled "Philosophical Problems of Psychology"; most of this is reproduced in RBP, 2:368–71. For the remainder, see Notebook N II in the Houghton Library. The concept of conterminousness which was being worked out here eventually appeared in the essays in radical empiricism, notably in section 6 of "A World of Pure Experience."

37. Emphasizing that entitative ontologies troubled James, some have called him a "process philosopher." After reading "Does 'Consciousness' Exist?" C. S. Peirce wrote to James on 28 September 1904:

> Your article about consciousness comes to me very *a propos* as I am writing about consciousness and have been reading up about it well as my library (!) permits. But your paper floors me at the very opening and I wish you would do me the favor (I suppose it to be a simple matter) of explaining what you mean by saying that consciousness is often regarded as an "entity." I do not think you capable of setting up a man of straw and have no doubt you can tell me just how any given writer regards consciousness as an "entity." But this word, in modern philosophy, has never conveyed to my mind any idea except that it is a sign the writer is setting up some man of straw whom he imagines to entertain opinions too absurd for definite statement.

According to Perry, James replied that he did not "understand a word." For Peirce's reply, and for other of his letters relevant to radical empiricism, see RBP, 2:430–40.

Alfred North Whitehead, too, was uncertain about James's use of *entity*. He praised "Does 'Consciousness' Exist?" as inaugurating "a new stage in philosophy," encouraged the reader to compare it with Descartes's *Discourse on Method* and to see that "James clears the stage of the old paraphernalia, or rather he entirely alters its lighting." Whitehead hailed James's radical empiricism as a "double challenge," to the Cartesian ego and to scientific materialism. Nevertheless, he was troubled by *entity*:

> James denies that consciousness is an entity, but admits that it is a function. The discrimination between an entity and a function is therefore vital to the understanding of the challenge which James is advancing against the older modes of thought. . . . But he does not unambiguously explain what he means by the notion of an entity, which he refuses to consciousness. . . . James is denying that consciousness is a "stuff." The term "entity," or even that of "stuff," does not fully tell its own tale. . . . The notion of "entity" is so general that it may be taken to mean anything that can be thought about. . . . In this sense, a function is an entity. Obviously, this is not what James had in mind. (*Science and the Modern World* [New York: Free Press, 1967], 143–44)

Despite the concerns voiced by Peirce and Whitehead, I think James made it plain that he meant that there was no discriminable item, thing, process, or noticeable property—no *entity*—discoverable by introspection. But in his ambivalent relation to Berkeley, more seems to have been built into *entitative* than into *entity*; the latter term designates anything at all, the former only what is discrete, separable, configured, or boundaried.

38. *A Pluralistic Universe* was originally given as the Hibbert Lectures at Manchester College, Oxford, in 1908 (see RBP, 2:583–98). James began writing *Some Problems of Philosophy*, planned as a historically oriented and technical introductory text, in 1909, but died before completing it. See the prefatory note by his son, Henry James, Jr. See also the valuable introduction by Richard J. Bernstein to the *APU*.

39. *SPP*, 113–14. For a helpful discussion of James's ideas and intentions in *SPP*, see Peter H. Hare's introduction in the Harvard edition (1979).

40. Notebook J, "Memoranda for Gifford Lectures, Original plan for a philos. 2nd volume." The inside cover gives two titles: "The Varieties of Religious Experience" and "The Tasks of Religious Philosophy." Many pages have been torn out of the notebook, which is dated "1900+." Here as elsewhere there is evidence of the intimate connections James saw between religion and radical empiricism.

41. James had long felt some uncertainty about the extent to which he could use the stream of consciousness for theoretical purposes; around 1893 he responded to Léon Marillier, a French critic who had reviewed *Principles*:

> Even if our thoughts *are* compounds of "ideas," they are at least superficially and practically also all that I say they are, namely, integral pulses of consciousness with respect to the multitude of facts of which they may take cognizance in a single passing moment of time. All you ought to accuse me of is *insufficiency*, not error. But I freely admit that in the vehemence of my argumentation in the chapter on the "Stream of Thought," I seem to be contending for the unity more as an ultimate and definitive truth than as a peculiarly advantageous methodological assumption. That chapter was really written as a bit of popular description, to show (first) the natural way in which our mental life would appear to a man who has no theories, and (second) to show certain omissions and difficulties involved in the account given by the theory of ideas. I should be sorry to have it taken as a "theory" of my own; and in particular . . . I have no definite theory whatever as to just how the consciousness of relations may arise. (Quoted in RBP, 2:102–03)

42. *SPP*, 127, 154, 172. See chapter 4.

43. *SPP*, 182–83. James's references are to Russell's *Philosophy of Mathematics*, especially to 1:260, 287, and 381.

44. *SPP*, 184–86; see also James's comments about the significance of Zeno's paradoxes in "Bergson," in McDermott, 562–66.

45. See Alfred North Whitehead, *Process and Reality* (New York: Macmillan, 1929), 365–67. See also Wesley C. Salmon, *Zeno's Paradoxes* (Indianapolis: Bobbs-Merrill, 1970). This is an excellent anthology, with a comprehensive bibliography. In Salmon's own contribution to the volume he writes:

> Experience does seem, as James and Whitehead emphasize, to have an atomistic character. If physical change could be understood only in terms of the structure of the perceptual continuum, then the mathematical continuum would be incapable of providing an adequate description of physical processes. In particular, if we set the epistemological requirement that physical continuity must be constructed from physical points which are explicitly definable in terms of observables, then it will be impossible to endow the physical continuum with the properties of the mathematical continuum. . . . We shall see, however, that no such rigid requirement needs to be imposed. (20)

Compare this with what Adolph Grünbaum argues in "Zeno's Metrical Paradox of Extension" and "Modern Science and Zeno's Paradoxes of Motion," both reprinted in Salmon's anthology.

See also Grünbaum's "Relativity and the Atomicity of Becoming," *The Review of Metaphysics* 6, no. 2 (December 1950): 143–86, especially sections 2, 3, and 7. Grünbaum concludes: "We reject the pulsational theory of becoming advocated by James, Whitehead and Weiss, since the rejection of their epistemological assumptions and the adoption of those of Einstein's theory cuts the ground from under their theory" (186).

46. RBP, 2:666; Perry here offered his own impression of what Jamesian continuity might be like.

47. "On the Notion of Reality As Changing," in McDermott, 303. James here credited the influences of Peirce and Bergson. He had previously been content to defend Peirce's tychism or idea of novelty as chance; here, enamored of Bergson's notion of the flux or *élan vital* as a "creative free evolutionary" process, he adopted also Peirce's concept of synechism or continuity. He said that Peirce had combined tychism and synechism into a higher-order agapasticism which is virtually the same as Bergson's evolution creatrice; see RBP, 2:411–12, 619, 663, 655–56, and 747–49.

48. "The Continuity of Experience," in McDermott, 295.

49. "Bergson and His Critique of Intellectualism," in McDermott, 564, 575.

50. *Principles*, 1:245–46. See Wittgenstein's remarks on this passage in *Philosophical Investigations*, 181–82.

51. See "The Thing and Its Relations," especially sections 4–6.

52. "A World of Pure Experience," in McDermott, 199.

53. Israel Scheffler points up the problem:

> James, emphasizing the flow of thought, stresses the importance of feelings of transition and relation. . . . Sensationalists, he says, have denied the existence of such feelings, juxtaposing substantive sensations "like dominoes," whereas intellectualists, on the other hand, have put our knowledge of relations into the realm of thought rather than sensibility. It is not, however, clear how James, in interposing *feelings of transition* between substantive sensations, avoids juxtaposing these transition-feelings with sensations like so many further dominoes. (*Four Pragmatists* [New York: Humanities Press, 1974], 142–43)

See also Marian C. Madden and Edward H. Madden, "William James and the Problem of Relations," *Transactions of the Charles S. Peirce Society* 14, no. 4 (Fall 1978):227–47. A work that emphasizes the role of relations in James's thought is Charlene Haddock Seigfried's *Chaos and Context: A Study in William James* (Athens, Ohio: Ohio University Press, 1978).

54. *SPP*, 218. See RBP, 1:492, 2:403–05, and 2:534–52 for more on James's relationship with Strong and the issue of panpsychism.

See also Marcus Ford, *William James's Philosophy* (Amherst: University of Massachusetts Press, 1982). Ford focuses on whether James was a panpsychist and concludes that he was. See chapter 14, note 74, below.

Perry, who later developed his own theory of neutral monism, always took James's neutralism at face value and did not see him as being heavily tilted toward Berkeleyan idealism. Perry never surrendered the possibility that James would have been able, had he lived to complete his labors, to harmonize most of his favorite ideas with neutral monism. I believe the Jamesian metaphysics was well on its way to panpsychism, propelled toward it by Berkeley's view of physical things.

55. See *Principles*, 1:196, 278, 353; 2:281.

56. "The Continuity of Experience," in McDermott, 296.

57. Ibid.

58. See Hannes Alfven, *Cosmic Plasma* (Boston: D. Reidel, 1981). Alfven, a physicist at the University of California at San Diego, won the Nobel Prize in physics in 1970.

59. For more on Fechner, see especially "The Continuity of Experience," "The Compounding of Consciousness," and "Concerning Fechner," all in *APU*.

Perry wrote of Fechner:

There were for James, as there were in fact, two Fechners. When James was writing the *Principles*, Fechner's *Psychophysik* was already a recognized classic in modern experimental psychology. From it James derived many suggestions bearing on imagination, attention, discrimination, and perception. But with the fundamental doctrine of the book he was in profound disagreement. Fechner was "a man of great learning and subtlety of mind," but as regards the great "psychophysical law" on which his fame as a psychologist mainly depended, it was a "patent whimsey" of "the dear old man," which had inspired a literature so dreadful that James refused even to admit it to a footnote. . . . The second Fechner was the metaphysical Fechner, who conceived the universe as a series of overlapping souls from God down through the earth-soul to man, and from man to the unobservable psychic states that lie below the threshold of his consciousness. This daring speculation excited James's imagination, and at the same time satisfied two motives of his thought: he had always been tempted by the panpsychistic view of physical nature, and his religious thought had steadily moved towards the hypothesis of superhuman consciousness. In 1905 he read with great relish Fechner's *Die Tagesansicht* and *Über die Seelenfrage*. Then, in 1907, he wrote to his friends in praise of *Zend-Avesta*, "a wonderful book, by a wonderful genius" (RBP, 2:586–87)

60. "The Compounding of Consciousness," in McDermott, 556. The reference here to "hundreds of sheets of paper" is in part to the Miller-Bode notes, many of which are reproduced in RBP, 2:750–65.

61. "The Compounding of Consciousness," in McDermott, 558.

62. For a valuable comparison of the philosophies of James and Bergson, see Horace M. Kallen, *William James and Henri Bergson: A Study in Contrasting Theories of Life* (Chicago: University of Chicago Press, 1914).

In unpublished papers titled "Notes After Strong's Book" (catalogued in the Houghton Library as [A] 10, n.d.) James wrote: "The difficulty of making Bergson's view unite with mine is that he posits a material world independent of subjective histories into which my subjective history 'inserts' itself, whilst for me the material world is a mess of subjective history not mine."

63. This was a handwritten note added to the original version of "The Sentiment of Rationality," apparently intended as one of several revisions for a new version to appear in *WTB;* for whatever reason, it did not appear in the later publication. It is listed in the Houghton Library as manuscript [O] 15. For more on James's thoughts on identity, see the first version of "The Sentiment of Rationality," especially sections 4–5, in *CER*.

The James Collection includes some unpublished notes titled "Identity." They bear no date but seem to be fairly early; Perry wrote on the cover "Belongs with Mill on Induction," emphasizing not so much the concept of identity in itself as its connection with James's other reflections about Mill on scientific method. In these notes James wrote: "Mill & Co.'s denial of identity to the same general character wherever found really falls back on the assumption of a noumenal essence of each phenomenally distinguishable event, separate and so to speak personal to it. . . . A true philosopher taking the phenomenon in its entirety will sacrifice no aspect to another. Time place & relation differ he will freely say; but just as freely admit that the quality as quality is identical with itself through all these differences."

Here James indicated his own thoughts on the puzzlement often expressed by philosophers about where and how to find identity in the world of space and time. But in the realm of mental events (not including abstract concepts) he was convinced that no state ever identically recurs; its temporary identity is given in the sensing of it, which is never literally repeatable. If the *esse est sentiri* doctrine is abandoned, as it was in *A Pluralistic Universe*, then a basic conviction underlying James's logic of identity vanishes also.

64. "Concerning Fechner," in McDermott, 533.

65. "The Continuity of Experience," in McDermott, 295–96.

66. An unpublished notebook in the Houghton Library, dated 1895–96, contains notes for a seminar in psychology and is titled: "Subject 'The Feelings': Beginning of Philosophy of Pure Experience." James wrote: "Why do we attribute an intrinsic plurality to the datum as thing, and a unity to it as feeling?—That is the great question." He does not answer the question in this notebook, and I am not sure that he ever did to his own satisfaction. Whereas any datum seemed to be clearly analyzable into various aspects or constituents, he thought that we experience it as an indissoluble unit so strongly that it defies any attempt to imagine it as dissectable.

The problem of how to conceive identity on radical empiricistic principles is indicated throughout the Miller-Bode notes. "The question is: can the same be in two ways? If 'to be' is to be experienced, how can it *be* the same, if experienced in two ways [by two people]—i.e., not *as* the same. (Is Lotze's and Bowne's attack on 'being' relevant here?)" The connection with the concept of being is clear here.

67. *Principles,* 2:290n.

68. Miller-Bode notes, 8 August 1906.

69. Unpublished notes titled "Notes on Heyman's Book," dated some time after 1905.

70. See "The Experience of Activity," in McDermott, 289–90n.

71. *SPP,* 189–207.

72. "The Experience of Activity," in McDermott, 288–89.

73. *SPP,* 218. James went on to conclude the book:

> If we took these experiences as the type of what actual causation is, we should have to ascribe to cases of causation outside of our own life, to physical cases also, an inwardly experiential nature. In other words, we should have to espouse a so-called "pan-psychic" philosophy. This complication, and the fact that hidden brain-events appear to be "closer" effects than those which consciousness directly aims at, lead us to interrupt the subject here provisionally. Our main result, up to this point, has been the contrast between the perceptual and the intellectualist treatment of it. (218–19)

74. "The Experience of Activity," in McDermott, 288.

75. Ibid.

76. From a notebook dated 1903; quoted in RBP, 2:699–700.

77. James's unpublished lectures, 1905–06; quoted in RBP, 2:444. The term *humanism* was proposed by F. S. C. Schiller, an English philosopher and James's colleague in promoting pragmatism to a movement; though James had some reservations about the term, he adopted it for expressing some of the essential aspects of the pragmatic position. Writing to James in 1903 and proposing *humanism* as a better word than *pragmatism,* Schiller declared:

> But why should we not call it HUMANISM? "Humanism" as opposed to scholasticism; "humane" as opposed to barbarous (in style and temper); human, living and concrete as opposed to inhuman, fossil, and abstract; in short, not "anthropomorphism" (horrid word!) but "humanism." Consider, *e.g.,* how much better your remark about "*re-humanizing* the universe" sounds! . . . Not that we need drop "pragmatism" on that account as a technical term in epistemology. Only pragmatism will be a species of a greater genus,—humanism in theory of knowledge. (Quoted in RBP, 2:499)

Philosophy professors who represented variations of idealism, monism, or absolutism that were often allied with conservative outlooks, and who were themselves often loyal to traditional religious viewpoints, were ensconced throughout the universities, but they were hardly organized into an ongoing movement. Bradley once wrote to James: "I had not so much as heard of either Royce or Taylor. . . . In any case I will look them up" (letter of 27 July 1904, in the Houghton Library). This comment is interesting, since James often associated A. E. Taylor and Josiah Royce with Bradley as an "intellectual group."

78. See, for instance, *SPP*, 221–31.

79. See, for example, "Hegel and His Method" and "The Continuity of Experience," both in *APU*.

80. *SPP*, 221–31.

81. "The Thing and Its Relation," in McDermott, 214–15; italics mine.

82. "The Sentiment of Rationality," in *CER*, 135. For more on radical empiricism, see *ERE*. McDermott's introduction to the Harvard edition (1976) and the historical materials compiled by the Harvard editors are particularly valuable.

12. SELF

1. Besides occasional references to the notion of self, we can turn for evidence to "Person and Personality" in *Johnson's Universal Cyclopedia,* 8 vols. (New York: D. Appleton, 1895), 6:538–40, and "The Hidden Self," *Scribner's Magazine* 7 (1890):361–73, which is largely about psychical research and about the work of Janet and Binet in abnormal psychology. Three pages of this article were incorporated into "The Consciousness of Self" in *Principles.*

2. James suppressed, for instance, the autobiographical nature of the famous description of what it is like to experience melancholy in the form of panic fear, in "The Sick Soul" chapter of *VRE.* He evidently considered it in bad taste to take the topic of self into highly personal areas.

Another explanation might be the fact that James sent to Croom Robertson, editor of *Mind*, the first half of "The Consciousness of Self," but Robertson decided not to use it (see RBP, 2:41–42). If it had been published as an essay, James might have been more confident about building further essays upon it. He was not easily discouraged, however, and given the topic's significance for him, this explanation seems dubious.

3. Diary entry dated 3 April 1868. James never decided what conditions must be met for a child to acquire a use of *I* or a sense of self. He mentioned here the claim that it is acquired by the child's imitative use of the pronoun, but he did not say whether he agreed with that claim, nor did he return to it in later reflections. He did not entertain the sorts of considerations, for instance, found in Bruno Bettelheim's *The Empty Fortress*; see note 67 to chapter 7 above.

4. Quoted in RBP, 2:112; see also 2:41–42.

5. See *Principles,* 1:337–40 and 359–60. On the nature of thinking as a synthesizing activity, see 1:331 and "The Knowing of Things Together." This essay, especially in its first section, is explicitly concerned with the synthetic unity of consciousness.

6. See, for example, *Principles,* 1:346.

7. Ibid., 1:304.

8. "The Experience of Activity," in McDermott, 284; see also "The Continuity of Experience," in McDermott, 297.

Compare James's statement here with Anscombe's interpretation of Wittgenstein: "In Wittgenstein's version, it is clear that the 'I' of solipsism is not used to refer to anything, body or soul; for in respect of these it is plain that all men are alike. The 'I' refers to the centre of life, or the point from which everything is seen" (G. E. M. Anscombe, introduction to Wittgenstein's *Tractatus 2,* 2d ed. [New York: Harper & Row, 1965], 168). See in the same volume *Tractatus,* 151; see also *Philosophical Investigations,* 123.

9. "Does 'Consciousness' Exist?" in McDermott, 170n.

10. For the continuing denial of the soul, see "The Compounding of Consciousness," where James wrote: "Souls have worn out both themselves and their welcome, that is the plain truth. Philosophy ought to get the manifolds of experience unified on principles less empty" (McDermott, 556–57).

11. "The Notion of Consciousness," in McDermott, 192–93.

12. From a notebook in the Houghton Library for an 1895–96 seminar in psychology. Its subject is given as "The Feelings," and it represents the beginnings of the philosophy of pure experience.

See RBP, 2:365. Perry omits both the sentence which recommends the use of *field* because of its convenient ambiguity and the remark that it would be philosophically simpler to admit that the *I* is given to introspection.

For an interpretation of James's application of *field* to the analysis of self, see Eugene Fontinell, *Self, God, and Immortality: A Jamesian Investigation* (Philadephia: Temple University Press, forthcoming).

13. Quoted in RBP, 2:99. Ward wrote this letter in 1892 and thus refers to the mixture of psychology and metaphysics about the self only in *Principles*.

14. Quoted in RBP, 2:100–01. James's letter is dated 15 November 1892, but the same sentiments were present in radical empiricism.

15. Quoted in RBP, 2:216. C. S. Peirce reacted curiously to James's concept of the self; see RBP, 2:107.

16. This letter is dated 14 December 1902. James refers to Bergson's lectures on immortality in *Human Immortality: Two Supposed Objections to the Doctrine* (Boston and New York: Houghton Mifflin, 1899).

17. "The Knowing of Things Together," in *CER*, 397.

18. Ibid., 398–99.

19. Ibid., 399–400.

20. See, for instance, *Principles*, 2:458–59.

21. "The Mind-Stuff Theory" in *Principles*, which stresses the *esse est sentiri* doctrine, was composed before 1883 (see *Principles*, 1:175n) and is thus one of the earliest written chapters of the book. It seems plausible that James's later reflections on emotion, sensation, discrimination, and consciousness of self were sufficient to produce his change of conviction.

22. "The Knowing of Things Together," in *CER*, 400.

23. *Loc.cit.*, p. 383.

24. In "The Compounding of Consciousness," James wrote that the *esse est sentiri* doctrine of *Principles* applies to an "enormous number of higher fields of consciousness. They demonstrably do not *contain* the lower states that know the same objects" (McDermott, 549n). Far from being jettisoned, then, the doctrine was said to be true for many states of consciousness. But James provided no clue here about how he would distinguish between those cases where *esse est sentiri* holds and those where the compounding of consciousness holds. He may have meant that an emotional state, unlike a thought, occurs to introspection as containing a variety of elements that indissolubly combine into a unified emotion. Thought, on the other hand, does not appear to introspection to contain any psychic variety; it is the best example one can imagine of a simple psychic unit. It does not follow from the fact that sentences have parts that the thoughts expressed by those sentences must have corresponding parts, or any parts whatever.

25. See, for example, "The Compounding of Consciousness," in McDermott, 556–59.

26. See *Principles*, 1:158–59.

27. "Concerning Fechner," in McDermott, 542.

28. Ibid., 544.

29. See, for instance, "Bergson and His Critique of Intellectualism," in McDermott, 576–81.

30. Appendix, *WTB*, 29–30.

31. "Bergson," in McDermott, 578–79.

32. Ibid., 580; italics mine.

33. *SPP*, 97.

34. Notebook in the Houghton Library for an 1895–96 seminar in psychology.

35. Letter of 14 December 1882, *LWJ,* 220.
36. Letter of 6 July 1891, *LWJ,* 310–11.
37. See, for instance, *Principles,* 1:139–42.
38. "The Experience of Activity," in McDermott, 289–90.
39. James wrote:

> If we aspire to strip off from Nature all anthropomorphic qualities, there is none we should get rid of quicker than its "Force." How illusory our spontaneous notions of force grow when projected into the outer world becomes evident as soon as we reflect upon the phenomenon of muscular contraction. In pure objective dynamic terms (i.e., terms of position and motion), it is the *relaxed* state of the muscle which is the state of stress and tension. In the act of contraction, on the contrary, the tension is resolved, and disappears. Our feeling about it is just the other way—which shows how little our feeling has to do with the matter. ("The Feeling of Effort," in *CER,* 214)

40. "The Experience of Activity," in McDermott, 289.
41. See, for instance, *Principles,* 2:105. This passage was used as a point of departure by G. N. A. Vesey in "Volition," *Philosophy* 36 (October 1961):352–65.
42. "The Experience of Activity," in McDermott, 283–84.
43. Ernest Jones, *The Life and Work of Sigmund Freud,* 3 vols. (New York: Basic, 1953–57), 2:57.
See James's essay "The Final Impressions of a Psychical Researcher," reprinted in *William James on Psychical Research,* ed. Gardner Murphy and Robert Ballou (New York: Viking, 1960), 325. This essay originally appeared in October 1909 in *The American Magazine* under the title "The Confidences of a 'Psychical Researcher' "; it was also reprinted posthumously under its second title in *MS.*
44. Quoted by Murphy and Ballou, *William James On Psychical Research,* 19. The book *Planchette,* written by Epes Sargent and named after the instrument or board used in automatic writing experiments, was a history and defense of the genuineness of spiritualistic or psychic phenomena. James's review (reprinted in Murphy and Ballou, 19–23), while criticizing Sargent for being too incautious and unanalytical, sympathized with the attempt to awaken the interest of the scientific community in such phenomena. In fact, the review is somewhat skeptical about the significance of those phenomena even if their scientific status were established: "The existence of the phenomena as a class once being granted, we fail to discover among all the facts given in *Planchette* a single one possessing either aesthetic beauty, intellectual originality, or material usefulness" (Murphy and Ballou, 22). But James never ceased to be intrigued by the literature on psychical research, and by the 1880s was decidedly more convinced of its significance.
A few references to psychical research appear in *Principles.* There are two entries for F. W. H. Myers and five for Edmund Gurney in the index, but such citations are much less frequent than those of the work done in abnormal psychology by Théodule Ribot, Alfred Binet, and Jules and Pierre Janet. Such discussions occur notably in chapters 8–10, 16, 25, and 27.
45. "The Sense of Dizziness in Deaf-Mutes," *American Journal of Otology* 4 (1882):239–54. Reprinted in *CER,* 220–43.
46. Ibid., *CER,* 230. See also "A Suggestion for the Prevention of Seasickness," James's letter to the editor in *Boston Medical and Surgical Journal* 116 (1887):490–91.
47. See, for instance, *Principles,* 1:666–68n.
48. "The Consciousness of Lost Limbs," in *CER,* 302. James was open to suggestions about psychical phenomena from every quarter, but in the end he remained skeptical about almost all of them. Nor did he entertain all hypotheses out of an excessive curiosity, as is evident from his criticism of phrenology in a review of Nicholas Morgan's *The Skull and Brain* (*Nation* 21 [1875]:185).

The consciousness of lost limbs is mentioned in relation to the illusion of willing something; see *Principles*, 2:105.

49. *Principles*, 1:97. See also "Reaction-Time in the Hypnotic Trance," *Proceedings of the American Society for Psychical Research* 1 (1887):246–48.

50. *WTB*, 294–95. For the relationship between Blood and James, beginning in 1874, see RBP, especially chapters 64 and 83.

On the connection between anesthetic revelation and James's view of Hegelian philosophy, see RBP, 1:728–30. Daniel Cook claims that James's opinion of Hegel was seriously affected by reflections upon the nature of nitrous oxide intoxication. Cook emphasizes the significance of the nitrous oxide experience in James's chapter on mysticism in *VRE*. He also provides a useful bibliography in his examination both of James's way of reading Hegel and of whether there is any basis for James's idea that mystical or intoxicating feelings were responsible for Hegel's key notions. See "James's 'Ether Mysticism' and Hegel," *Journal of the History of Philosophy* 15, no. 3 (July 1977):309–19.

James wrote of the nitrous oxide experience: "The keynote of it is invariably a reconciliation. It is as if the opposites of the world . . . were melted into unity. . . . I feel as if it must mean something, something like what the hegelian philosophy means, if one could only lay hold of it more clearly" (*VRE*, 379).

51. *Principles*, 1:398–99. The details of these cases had been published earlier in "Notes on Automatic Writing," *Proceedings of the American Society for Psychical Research* 1 (1889):548–64.

52. Quoted in John Malcolm Brinnin, *The Third Rose* (1959; reprint, Magnolia, Mass.: Peter Smith, 1968), 30. I am indebted to this work for the information about Stein and her relation to James. A vast amount of interesting material is assembled by Brinnin, including his treatment of B. F. Skinner's article about Stein, "Has Gertrude Stein a Secret?" *Atlantic Monthly* 153 (1934):50–57. Brinnin states that Skinner used Stein's first experimental report against her and that his article "came to be the handiest and most glib way in which to account for her more difficult works, or to dismiss them" (32). For more on the relation of Stein to James, see Donald Gallup, ed., *The Flowers of Friendship: Letters Written to Gertrude Stein* (New York: Knopf, 1953).

53. Quoted in Gardner Murphy, *William James on Psychical Research* (New York: Viking, 1960), 7. James's early interest in mental healing is clear from a review he wrote in 1868, titled "Moral Medication"; this was a notice of *Du Sommeil et des états analogues, considérés surtout au point de vue de l'action du Moral sur le physique*, by A. A. Liébault. The review appeared in *Nation* 7 (1868):50–52.

For the relation of James to mental healing or the mind-cure movement at the end of the nineteenth century, see Nathan G. Hale, Jr., *Freud and the Americans* (New York: Oxford University Press, 1971), especially chapters 6 and 9; and idem, *James Jackson Putnam and Psychoanalysis* (Cambridge: Harvard University Press, 1971), 67–81. These two volumes contain invaluable bibliographies. See also RBP, 2:318–19.

54. "The Hidden Self," *Scribner's Magazine* 7 (1890):373. The reader who wonders why the references to research on hysteria are to Janet rather than to Freud should note that it was not until four years later that James wrote his review of Breuer's and Freud's *Ueber den Psychischen Mechanismus Hysterischer Phänomene* (*Psychological Review* 1 [1894]:199).

55. Quoted in RBP, 2:121.

56. "Person and Personality"; see note 1 above.

57. Ibid., 539.

58. Ibid.

59. Ibid.

60. Ibid., 540.

61. Ibid.

62. James did not have Freud's work in mind when he formulated his own view here, but it

seems evident enough that he would have been unsympathetic to the unconscious as conceived by Freud. See *Principles,* 1:211, 227–29, 384–400.

In siding with Janet's position that whatever is unconscious to the primary or waking self is nevertheless conscious to an associated but hidden self, James remarked that Janet qualified his position by acknowledging that some thoughts can be so fragmentary and scattered that they do not belong to any synthesized personality whatever. "He admits, however, that these very same unutterably stupid thoughts tend to develop memory,—the cataleptic ere long moves her arm at a bare hint; so that they form no important exception to the law that all thought tends to assume the form of personal consciousness" (*Principles,* 1:229).

63. Freud, *An Autobiographical Study* (New York: Norton, 1963), 58–59. Freud advances a severe criticism of Janet (57). See also Freud's *Five Lectures on Psychoanalysis* (New York: Norton, n.d.), 21–22, 25–26. See again the discussion of the unconscious in chapter 2.

64. See, for instance, Gardner Murphy, "William James and Mrs. Piper," *William James on Psychical Research* (New York: Viking, 1960), 95–210.

65. In "The Stream of Thought," James explained that thought is "sensibly continuous" within each personal consciousness: "When Paul and Peter wake up in the same bed . . . each one of them mentally reaches back and makes connection with but *one* of the two streams of thought which were broken by the sleeping hours. . . . Peter's present instantly finds out Peter's past, and never by mistake knits itself on to that of Paul. Paul's thought in turn is as little liable to go astray" (*Principles,* 1:238).

The reader brought up on modern arguments that make it conceptually impossible for Peter's and Paul's thoughts to intersect in either mind may wonder why James did not question the intelligibility of such an assumption instead of being content to state it as a contingent or factual matter. Unlike many of us, he never considered such intersection to be logically impossible; indeed, he made every effort to discover how it might actually happen. Hence, some qualification of the view advanced in the paragraph quoted above is required to make it consistent with James's idea that in some fashion individual minds and selves can overlap.

That qualification is needed is confirmed by James's account of an experience he had with dreams in 1906:

> I awoke suddenly . . . in the middle of a dream, in thinking of which I became suddenly confused by the contents of two other dreams that shuffled themselves abruptly in between the parts of the first dream, and of which I couldn't grasp the origin. Whence come *these dreams?* I asked. They were close to *me,* and fresh, as if I had just dreamed them; and yet they were far away *from the first dream.* One had a cockney atmosphere, it had happened to some one in London. The other two were American. . . . Each had a wholly distinct emotional atmosphere that made its individuality discontinuous with that of the others. And yet, in a moment, as these three dreams alternately telescoped into and out of each other, and I seemed to myself to have been their common dreamer, they seemed quite as distinctly *not* to have been dreamed in succession, in that one sleep. *When, then? . . . I could no longer tell. . . .* I seemed thus to belong to three different dream-systems at once, no one of which would connect itself either with the others or with my waking life. I began to feel curiously confused and *scared. . . .* Cold shivers of dread ran over me: *am I getting into other people's dreams?* Is this a "telepathic" experience? Or an invasion of double (or treble) personality? Or is it a thrombus in a cortical artery? And the beginning of a general mental "confusion" and disorientation . . . ? ("A Suggestion About Mysticism," in *CER,* 506–07)

In commenting on this experience, James emphasized that its oddity lay in the fact that the three dreams both did and did not hang together intimately. "To this day I feel that those extra dreams were dreamed in reality, but when, where, and by whom, I can not guess" (511).

Instead of dismissing the intersection of different people's thoughts or dreams, here James clearly allowed its possibility.

Erik Erikson analyzed James's experience in "William James's Terminal Dream," *Identity: Youth and Crisis* (New York: Norton, 1968), 204–07. Erikson called James's dreaming on this occasion a case of terminal despair and identity confusion, emphasizing the importance of the date of the dream, which he took to be just prior to James's death. Saul Rosenzweig wrote an incisive correction, pointing out that James did not die in 1906 after this dreaming experience but rather in 1910; neither the dream nor the despair (if that is what it really was) qualified as terminal. What confused Erikson was the fact that James's publication "A Suggestion About Mysticism" did not occur until 1910. Rosenzweig's own brief remarks about James's experience are worth consulting, especially his comments about the Zen method of dealing with the sorts of doubts that James had about the origins of the three dreams. See his "Erik Erikson on William James's Dream: A Note of Correction," *Journal of the History of the Behavioral Sciences* 6 (1970):258–60.

66. Daniel N. Robinson, "Cerebral Plurality and the Unity of Self," *American Psychologist* 37 (August 1982):908. I am grateful to Dr. Charles H. Daly for bringing this article to my attention. Robinson makes some useful suggestions about a clearer use for terms such as *personal identity, self, self-identity,* and *person,* but in the end he says of the effects of split-brain and multiple-personality cases:

> The rest of the effects *may* be taken as evidence of multiple personal identities and the different self-identities ascribed to and adopted by a person may be shocking to that person when subsequently discovered. But the basic fact of existence as a conscious entity cannot be shocking, for this is never news. As of now logic, language, and data leave the "moi" intact and preserve the unity of self as an issue of continuing interest, and even of mystery. (910)

Thomas Nagel expresses an uncertainty to which James would probably have assented:

> The concept of a person might possibly survive an application to cases which require us to speak of two or more persons in one body, but it seems strongly committed to some form of whole numbers countability. Since even this seems open to doubt, it is possible that the ordinary, simple idea of a single person will come to seem quaint some day, when the complexities of the human control system become clearer and we become less certain that there is anything very important that we are *one* of. But it is also possible that we shall be unable to abandon the idea no matter what we discover. ("Brain Bisection and the Unity of Consciousness," in *Personal Identity,* ed. John Perry [Berkeley and Los Angeles: University of California Press, 1975], 243)

67. "Frederick Myers's Service to Psychology," in Murphy and Ballou, 219–20. Originally printed in *Proceedings of the Society for Psychical Research* 17, pt. 62 (May 1901):13–23, this article was reprinted in *MS.*

68. "Final Impressions of a Psychical Researcher," in Murphy and Ballou, 310. This essay originally appeared as "The Confidences of a 'Psychical Researcher,'" *American Magazine* 68 (October 1909), 580–89. It was reprinted in 1911 as "Final Impressions of a Psychical Researcher" in *MS.*

69. "A Record of Observations of Certain Phenomena of Trance," part 3, *Proceedings of the Society for Psychical Research* 6 (1890):651–59, quoted by Murphy and Ballou, 105. See Murphy and Ballou for the accounts that James gave of Mrs. Piper (95–210).

70. "What Psychical Research Has Accomplished," in *WTB,* 318–20. This essay was formed from parts of "The Hidden Self," from "What Psychical Research Has Accomplished," *Forum* 13 (1892):727–42, and from James's President's Address before the Society for Psychi-

cal Research, published in *Proceedings* 12 (1896):2–10 and in *Science,* n.s., 12 (1896):2–10. The final version appeared in the original edition of *WTB.*

In 1896 James also published "Psychical Research," in which the question of evidence is treated, in *Psychological Review* 3 (1896):649–52. In the same year "A Case of Psychic Automatism, Including 'Speaking With Tongues'" appeared in Proceedings of the [*English*] *Society for Psychical Research* 12 (1896):277–79.

71. Letter of 9 February 1906 to Theodore Flournoy, *LWJ,* 2:242; quoted in Murphy and Ballou, 111.

72. "Report on Mrs. Piper's Hodgson-Control," in Murphy and Ballou, 209. This article was originally published in *Proceedings of the* [*American*] *Society for Psychical Research* 3 (1909):470–589. Composed a year before his death, it represents James's final published views on the subject.

73. "Does 'Consciousness' Exist?" in McDermott, 179.

74. "Frederic Myers's Service to Psychology," in Murphy and Ballou, 218.

75. *Human Immortality: Two Supposed Objections to the Doctrine* (1898; reprint, New York: Dover, 1956), 23.

76. "Final Impressions of a Psychical Researcher," in Murphy and Ballou, 324.

77. Ibid.

78. "Frederic Myers's Service to Psychology," in Murphy and Ballou, 231.

79. "Concerning Fechner," in McDermott, 536. Perry wrote: "He suggested, following Fechner, that the individual might survive in traces of his action left in the outer world, and that the so-called 'spirit' might be a revival of the individual through a systematic excitation of these traces, as memory is revived from an excitation of cerebral traces. This speculation was at best an aid to the imagination" (RBP, 2:172).

Since James professed to be especially impressed by Fechner's analogies and their stimulative qualities, Perry believed that James read Fechner nonliterally, but whether that is the case is difficult to determine.

For an unappreciative assessment of Fechner, see G. S. Hall's 1879 letter to James (RBP, 2:18–19). For more appreciative opinions, some of which mention Fechner's idea of the earth-soul, see Ernst Mach's 1909 letter to James (RBP, 2:627–29) and F. H. Bradley's 1909 letter to James (RBP, 2:638).

80. "Report on Mrs. Piper's Hodgson-Control," in Murphy and Ballou, 208–09.

81. We should not, however, forget the occasional statements in James's metaphysics on behalf of the body's importance; see, for example, "The Experience of Activity." But these statements are always to be reinterpreted as the pure experience philosophy of radical empiricism demands, thus reducing the body to sensations.

13. MORALITY

1. Letter of 1 March 1958 to Edgar B. Van Winkle.

2. Quoted in Fredric Harold Young, *The Philosophy of Henry James, Sr.* (New Haven: College and University Press, 1951), 14.

3. William conveyed his father's remark about the moral character of college campuses in a letter of 18 September 1858 to Van Winkle.

4. This diary is partly reprinted in Allen, 149. James's mention of *"Vorstellungen* disproportionate to the object" might be an anticipation of T. S. Eliot's concept of the objective correlative. A few days later, on 27 May 1868, he wrote in his diary:

> About "Vorstellungen disproportionate to the object" or in other words ideas disproportionate to any practical application—such for instance are emotions of a loving kind indulged in where one cannot expect to gain exclusive possession of the loved person. In such a case the only proportionate ideas are those of mere delight as often as the lovable quality is displayed—but no pretention to earn a sort of right over it.

This passage suggests that the moral crisis of a few days earlier had a romantic or sexual element as well. Besides being worried about leading a morally wasted life, he may have been troubled by feelings aroused (by "Miss H's [Kate Havens's] magic playing"?) that seemed disproportionate in that they were futile. Was he saying in his diary that, lovable as Havens was, he should forget any thought of possessing her and simply settle for the delight that her presence afforded?

5. Although he was cautious about crediting Newman with bringing about his improvement, this was his tenth visit to her. Despite what has been said about James's failure ever to be helped by any of the mental healers whom he consulted, it appears that he was at times tempted if not totally prepared to attribute his recoveries, however transitory, to her.

6. The first paragraph of this diary entry is quoted in RBP, 1:323. Between the two paragraphs I have quoted occurs the following:

> After the first of January, my callow skin, being somewhat fledged, I may perhaps return to metaphysical study and skepticism without danger to my powers of action.
>
> For the moment, then, remember: Care little for speculation[,] Much for the *form* of my action. Recollect that only when habits of order are formed can we advance to really interesting fields of action—and consequently accumulate grain on grain of wistful choice like a very miser—never forgetting how one link dropped undoes an indefinite number.
>
> Today has furnished the exceptionally passionate initiative which Bain posits as needful for the acquisition of habits. I will see to the sequel. Not in maxims, not in Anschauungen, but in accumulated *acts* of thought lies salvation.

Some scholars point to this and other texts to suggest that Bain rather than Renouvier was the key influence upon James in his learning how to survive crises. But while Bain was certainly important in this regard, he did not have for James the crucial significance that Renouvier did (see chapters 1 and 14).

7. *Principles,* 2:672. Abraham Edel, in an especially perceptive and sensitive treatment of James's ethics, notes this feature in James's thinking and refers to it as a picture of the "lone individual on the frontier of decision as the moral situation" ("Notes on the Search For a Moral Philosophy in William James," in *The Philosophy of William James,* ed. Walter Robert Corti [Hamburg: Felix Meiner Vorlag, 1976], 253).

8. *Principles,* 1:288. Other writers have also connected James's ethics with existentialism. See, for example, Julius S. Bixler, "The Existentialists and William James," *The American Scholar* 28, no. 1 (Winter 1958–59):80–90, and John Wild, "William James and Existential Authenticity," *Journal of Existentialism* 5, no. 19 (Spring 1965):243–56.

9. John Stuart Mill experienced when he was in his twenties a crisis similar to James's. Mill titled chapter 5 of his autobiography "A Crisis in My Mental History: One Stage Onward"; in that chapter he wrote:

> During the later returns of my dejection, the doctrine of what is called Philosophical Necessity weighed on my existence like an incubus. I felt as if I was scientifically proved to be the helpless slave of antecedent circumstances; as if my character and that of all others had been formed for us by agencies beyond our control. . . . I often said to myself, what a relief it would be if I could disbelieve the doctrine of the formation of character by circumstances. . . . I pondered painfully on the subject, till gradually I saw light though it. . . . I saw that though our character is formed by circumstances, our own desires can do much to shape those circumstances; and that what is really inspiriting and ennobling in the doctrine of free-will, is the conviction that we have real power over the formation of our own character; and that our will, by influencing some of our circumstances, can modify our future habits or capabilities of willing. (*Autobiography* [New York: Liberal Arts Press, 1957], 109)

On how we should interpret such "intellectual crises," see again our discussion in chapter 1.

10. "The Dilemma of Determinism," in *WTB*, 152–53. James maintained this standpoint throughout his life; his earliest statements of it date to the 1870s, notably in "Quelques considérations sur la méthode subjective" (1878) and "The Sentiment of Rationality" (1879) as well as in earlier book reviews. See Perry's *Annotated Bibliography of the Writings of William James* (New York: Longmans, Green & Co., 1920).

11. "The Dilemma of Determinism," in *WTB*, 175. E. H. Madden emphasizes this element of the argument in his introduction to the Harvard edition of *WTB*.

12. "The Dilemma of Determinism," in *WTB*, 176. See also "Some Metaphysical Problems Pragmatically Considered," in *Pragmatism*, especially 81–86.

13. "The Dilemma of Determinism," in *WTB*, 149.

14. "Clifford's 'Lectures and Essays,'" in *CER*, 139. Clifford's views on the ethics of belief prompted James's attitudes in "The Will to Believe." James and Clifford appear to be the historical antecedents of Roderick Chisholm's influential writings on the ethics of belief today.

15. "Spencer's 'Data of Ethics,'" in *CER*, 148.

16. James characterized ethical discussion thus in his preface to John Edward Maude's *Foundations of Ethics* (New York: Holt, 1887), 1. James also edited the manuscript for posthumous publication, although his involvement seems minimal. Most of the preface was written by a Reverend Murkland and is a biographical sketch of Maude, who had been an undergraduate student of James's at Harvard and who, after a troubled life, died at the age of twenty-nine. Maude's book contains useful discussions of Kant, Sidgwick, and Spencer, with references also to what he clearly considered a significant psychological contribution to ethics, James's essay "The Feeling of Effort." James inserted a footnote, remarking that what he had written about mental "effort" was not intended to be quite as "mechanical" as Maude made it appear (149n). Whereas some of Maude's ideas appealed to James, his espousal of hedonism did not.

17. "Clifford's 'Lectures and Essays,'" in *CER*, 140–41.

18. "The Moral Philosopher and the Moral Life," in *WTB*, 184–85.

19. James delivered "The Moral Philosopher and the Moral Life" as an address to the Yale Philosophical Club, then published it in *The International Journal of Ethics* in April 1891. Thinking it the best essay in *WTB*, he was disappointed, he wrote to his brother Henry, that it was received so quietly at Yale (see RBP, 2:263, 274–75). John Dewey wrote to James praising the essay, especially for its claim that an a priori ethical theory formulated without trial-and-error experience is out of the question (see RBP, 2:517).

E. H. Madden, however, writes that James was not entirely consistent here because he was committed to the ethical principle, in advance of all experience, that we have an obligation to maximize the good (see Madden's introduction to the Harvard edition of WTB, xxxiii). I think that James supposed this idea to be too isolated and abstract to add up to a theory, for he remarked in the essay: "No single abstract principle can be so used as to yield to the philosopher anything like a scientifically and genuinely casuistic scale" (*WTB*, 201).

20. "The Moral Philosopher and the Moral Life," in *WTB*, 185.

21. Ibid., 187. See *Principles*, especially 2:624–29 and 672–75. In invoking Darwin's spontaneous variations while arguing against an evolutionistic theory of ethics, James was in essence pitting one evolutionist (Darwin) against another (Spencer). Because Spencer failed to appreciate the accidental features of natural selection that Darwin recognized, he concluded, mistakenly James felt, that experience can explain the origins of the entire range of our mental life.

22. Ibid., 188.

23. Ibid., 205–06.

24. Ibid., 188; italics mine.

25. Ibid., 205–08.

26. This passage occurs in an examination blue book entitled "Resume of My Lectures in Ethics 1888–89"; this and other passages are quoted in RBP, 2:263–64.

The notebook also contains this, not quoted by Perry: "I firmly believe that we have preferences inexplicable by utility or by direct influence of the environment, preferences for certain kinds of behavior, as consistency, veracity, justice, nobility, dignity, purity, etc. etc. Those who contend for an innate moral faculty are therefore right from a *psychological* point of view. . . . But assertions of *what* is ethically the best are subject to discussion and debate—an ethical proposition must be either *ultimate* or 'proved.' " James also wrote here: "*No psychological fact* by itself can prove ethical proposition, need another ethical proposition, too, in a proof. Ultimate question always: *Shall* I obey it? *Shall* it bind me? *Shall* I hold it good?"

This notebook is characterized by many changes and crossings-out and a fragmented manner of recording lecture notes, all of which seem to indicate an ongoing difficulty in James's search for a confident position.

27. "The Moral Philosopher and the Moral Life," in *WTB*, 199, 213.

28. "Clifford's 'Lectures and Essays,' " in *CER*, 140.

29. A great deal of confusion occurs over whether James was a utilitarian. Herbert Schneider's essay "William James As A Moralist" (*In Commemoration of William James* [New York: Columbia University Press, 1942], 127–39) contends that James was anti-utilitarian. Yet Schneider wrote to Perry on 12 January 1942: "I hope you noticed that I suggested that James' ethics was more Kantian than utilitarian. . . . [William] Montague says I am quite wrong, but the evidence which you yourself muster seems to me so overwhelming that I fail to understand on what grounds you emphasize his utilitarianism. Of course from the point of view of philosophical method and personal temper I understand your point, but I wonder whether in a technical doctrinal sense his ethics is utilitarian" (Papers of Ralph Barton Perry, Harvard Archives).

"The Moral Philosopher and the Moral Life" clearly rejects the traditional utilitarian goal of happiness, but it can be construed as advocating another version of utilitarianism, which declares the moral act as that which maximizes the good, which consists in satisfying the maximum number of moral beliefs. In this, I may be approaching Perry's interpretation of James as a utilitarian of sorts; see Perry's description of the respects in which James was indebted to the ideas of Chauncey Wright (RBP, 1:522).

30. "The Moral Philosopher and the Moral Life," in *WTB*, 203. James may have been prompted to reject hedonistic utilitarianism by having read Edmund Gurney; in his notes for a course on ethics in 1888–89, in the Houghton Library, he wrote: "Gurney on *meanness* of buying our pleasure with another's pain" (italics mine). Since James observed that consequences may teach us what is wicked but not what is mean or vulgar, we must wonder whether he wanted to call a universe that buys the general happiness with one person's pain a wicked or a mean one—and what really is the difference between the two terms. The phrase about Gurney is followed in his notes by this: "moral indelicacy—impropriety—marrying dead wife's sister. [Matthew] Arnold." Was he tempted to conceive of meanness as a case of moral indelicacy or impropriety? I think he concluded that buying the general happiness with another's pain is so mean that it must be wicked, not merely a moral indelicacy.

31. "The Moral Philosopher and the Moral Life," in *WTB*, 213.

32. Ibid., 213–15. It is in his description here of the "divine thinker," James noted, that his view most closely approached that of Josiah Royce's in *The Religious Aspect of Philosophy;* see *WTB*, 214n.

33. "Pragmatism's Conception of Truth," in *Pragmatism*, 145.

34. Eliseo Vivas, for instance, has noted the statement in contending that if one compares Henry and William James, "the contrast between Henry's moral vision and William's moral theory is sharp and shocking. For the beauty of character, faithfulness to the pledged word,

and scrupulous sensibility for the feelings and rights of others, which we have seen to be implicit in Henry's vision of life, we must now substitute a barely attenuated version of Darwinism in the moral life, which hardly conceals the doctrine that successful force is the right" ("Henry and William," in *Creation and Discovery: Essays in Criticism and Aesthetics* [New York: Noonday, 1955], 20–21). I hope that my discussion in this chapter, as well as throughout this book, is an adequate rebuttal to Vivas.

See Henry D. Aiken's "William James as Moral and Social Philosopher," *Philosophic Exchange* 3 (Summer 1981):55–68.

35. For information about the relationship of James and Holmes, see RBP, 1:504–19.

36. James acknowledged that "the religion of humanity" affords a basis for ethics "as well as theism does," but added that "whether the purely human system can gratify the philosopher's demand [for an objective, inclusive ethical system] as well as the other is a different question, which we ourselves must answer ere we close" ("The Moral Philosopher and the Moral Life," in *WTB*, 198. His answer in this essay, and indeed throughout his life, was an emphatic no.

37. Ibid., 190–91.

38. Ibid., 197.

39. Ibid., 195.

40. Ibid.

41. The idea that some desires are also imperatives appears to have been James's answer to what he had once jotted in his notes: "A man loses no sense of worth if he misses a pleasure; he does if he fails in his duty. Utilitarianism may explain how certain things come more than others to pertain to the sphere of conscience, but the psychological question is: What is the origin and the meaning of the particular *quality* of feeling which we call conscience?" (This note is tucked into notes on J. S. Mill, Heinrich Heine, Jacob Clarke, and Emil Harless in notebook #26 in the James Collection at the Houghton Library. The notebook spans the period from 1864 to 1890, making it difficult to date this entry. If it was made while James was reading Clarke and Harless and deliberately laid alongside the pages bearing their names [where I found it], then it could date as early as 1869. It seems more likely that it was written around 1890, when he was actively working out his ethical ideas.)

The idea that some desires become their own imperatives was even more clearly his answer to an entry in another notebook: "What is significant is *feeling of obligation*. What say about it? Kant calls notions of obligatory good 'imperatives' " (notebook titled "Resume of My Lectures in Ethics 1888–9"). The answer was that the feeling of obligation is not something apart from all other feelings and desires but is rather a feature of feelings or desires which have intensified into imperatives.

42. See, for example, the arguments against subjectivism in "The Dilemma of Determinism" and in the concluding pages of "The Sentiment of Rationality," both in *WTB*.

43. "The Moral Philosopher and the Moral Life," in *WTB*, 196. The same idea is expressed in one of James's notebooks from 1888–89: "Two minds, of whom one is authority for the other, are enough to constitute a systematic moral universe. But what constitutes authority itself? I can find nothing but the *claim* on the one part and the *submission* on the other. Where both elements exist the authority may be called *perfect*, otherwise imperfect" ("Resume of My Lectures in Ethics").

44. For sympathetic criticism of James's ethics, see John K. Roth's *Freedom and the Moral Life: The Ethics of William James* (Philadelphia: Westminster, 1969), especially 66–68, where Roth offers criticisms of James's demand principle. Roth emphasizes the significance of the topic of freedom for James's ethics in chapters 3, 5, 7, and 9. Some of these criticisms also occur in Roth's introduction to his edited volume, *The Moral Philosophy of William James* (New York: Crowell, 1969), especially 8–10.

A less critical but good summary of the main features of James's ethics is Bernard P.

Brennan, *The Ethics of William James* (New York: Bookman Associates, 1961). Brennan is particularly helpful in relating James's ethics to his religious and metaphysical ideas. See also Ayer, *The Origins of Pragmatism*, 198–202, for remarks on James's ethics. Ayer is troubled by James's view that ethical judgments are empirical and can be verified only by the total human experience.

45. This is the title of a review of Allen's biography of James in *The Times Literary Supplement*, 1 August 1968, 813–16. The review emphasizes James's spiritual crises and general susceptibility to depression and melancholy. See chapter 1.

46. For two prominent texts on this topic, see "The Sentiment of Rationality" and "Reflex Action and Theism," both in *WTB*.

47. *Talks* (Harvard edition), 4; see also my introduction to this edition, xxi–xxvii. For more on James's evaluation of this essay, see the editors' account of the history of the text of *Talks* (Harvard edition), 244.

48. William Frankena referred to this segment of James's essay, which praises the imaginative appreciation of the feeling of others, in asserting that the need to become aware of others as persons is a part of moral education ("Toward a Philosophy of Moral Education," in *Philosophy and Education*, ed. Israel Scheffler [Boston: Allyn and Bacon, 1966], 242). In the same volume, see Frankena's "Public Education and the Good Life," 305.

49. "What Makes a Life Significant," in *Talks* (Harvard edition), 155. This passage has often been quoted, as has James's letter to his wife in which the experience was originally reported. In that letter, dated 24 September 1882, he concluded his description of the peasant women as follows:

> Their poor, old, ravaged and stiffened faces, their poor old bodies dried up with ceaseless toil, their patient souls make me weep. "They are our conscripts." They are the venerable ones whom we should reverence. All the mystery of womanhood seems incarnated in their ugly being—the Mothers! the Mothers! Ye are all one! Yes, Alice dear, what I love in you is only what these blessed old creatures have; and I'm glad and proud, when I think of my own dear Mother with tears running down my face, to know that she is one with these. Good-night, good-night! (*LWJ*, 1:211)

This letter has understandably prompted speculations about the relationship between James and his wife (see chapter 1). I discuss James's attitude toward women later in this chapter.

50. James's discussion of Wright's challenge occurs in "Is Life Worth Living?" in *WTB*, 52.

51. "On a Certain Blindness in Human Beings," in *Talks* (Harvard edition), 134.

This is the kind of passage that ought to be cited by phenomenologists who adopt James's views, but they seem to have paid little attention to such texts, being almost totally absorbed by James's psychology, especially its treatment of the stream of consciousness, pure experience, and the consciousness of self.

52. "On a Certain Blindness in Human Beings," in *Talks* (Harvard edition), 138–39. In the same spirit he wrote: "A mere bare fraud is just what our Western common sense will never believe the phenomenal world to be. It admits fully that the inner joys and virtues are the *essential* part of life's business, but it is sure that *some* positive part is also played by the adjuncts of the show" ("What Makes a Life Significant," in *Talks* [Harvard edition], 159).

53. "On a Certain Blindness in Human Beings," in *Talks* (Harvard edition), 149.

54. Ibid., 148–49. Because of such statements, McDermott asserts: "More than James cared to admit, Emerson was his master" (introduction to *ERE* [Harvard edition], xxii). I discuss briefly the relationship between James and Emerson later in this chapter.

55. "What Makes a Life Significant," in *Talks* (Harvard edition), 159.

56. Ibid., 162.

57. Ibid., 163–64.

58. Ibid., 165; italics mine.

59. Ibid., 166.

60. In the James Collection in the Houghton Library is a page of notes titled "Optimism and Pessimism." James tore this page from a notebook and enclosed it in a letter of 7 June 1877 to Alice Gibbens, then his fiancée. He wrote in the margin: "This you see was written years ago when I was going through the pessimistic crisis." The crisis was presumably the one of 1869–70. The early letters to Alice (1876–77) reveal a man very much concerned about himself and life's prospects, a man wont to philosophizing about "the meaning of it all."

61. J. A. Passmore wrote: "Schopenhauer's pessimism has left a permanent mark on human culture, partly through its influence on von Hartmann and Freud. His depiction of thought as an *instrument* more immediately concerns us: According admirably with the new Darwinian biology, it came to be—as the 'instrumentalist' analysis of human thinking—the staple teaching of influential schools of psychology. In particular, William James is at this point in the direct line of succession from Schopenhauer." Recognizing that James, while usually very tolerant, was "extremely hostile" to Schopenhauer (he refused in 1883 to subscribe to a memorial to Schopenhauer; see RBP, 1:722–24), Passmore argued that "this, I should say, is precisely because [James] felt [Schopenhauer's] fascination" (*A Hundred Years of Philosophy* [London: Duckworth, 1962], 97). See also James's "German Pessimism" for comments both on Schopenhauer and on the merits of optimism over pessimism (*CER*, 12–19).

In the same essay James called the pessimistic controversy an "ethnic" affair (19), but he was not always disposed to equate German thought and pessimism. In one of his earliest book reviews (unsigned) he praised the novelist Hermann Grimm for being an exception to the tendency, not confined to Germany, to

> be too exclusively sensitive to the form and manner of things, and to have no perception of that inward breath of life and health which blows through them, and which, tending as it does to the future, is often the one point in their composition that has any significance. . . . In Herr Grimm . . . the result is liberalism in its best sense. . . . It will be indeed fortunate for Germany if . . . many men on the pattern of the author of these volumes . . . lend a hearty voice and helping hand to those who are immersed in the dust and sweat of practical labor. ("A German-American Novel," *Nation* 5 [28 November 1867]:433).

62. "German Pessimism," in *CER*, 18.

63. "What Makes a Life Significant," in *Talks* (Harvard edition), 159; "The Importance of Individuals," in *WTB*, 256–57.

64. "Great Men and Their Environment," in *WTB*, 232. This quotation is engraved in the lobby wall of William James Hall at Harvard.

65. Ibid., 222.

66. The unpublished manuscript in the Houghton Library is titled "Notes on Darwin" and bears no date, but James indicated that he made the notes while reading Darwin's *Variation of Animals and Plants under Domestication*. Since James published two reviews of this book in 1868, it seems safe to date the manuscript around that time. The reviews, both unsigned, appeared in *Atlantic Monthly* 22 (1868):122–24 and *North American Review* 107 (1868):362–68.

James liked to illustrate the dead-end nature of evolutionary theory in some cases by remarking that evolutionists "should not forget that we all have five fingers not because four or six would not do just as well, but merely because the first vertebrate above the fishes *happened* to have that number. He owed his prodigious success in founding a line of descent to some entirely other quality,—we know not which,—but the inessential five fingers were taken in tow and preserved to the present day. So of most social peculiarities" ("Great Men and Their Environment," in *The Will to Believe*, 238–39). James had made the same point a year earlier in "Spencer's 'Data of Ethics,'" in *CER*, 149.

This passage is in the spirit of the reviews of Darwin's book. For example, James wrote:

And even when the existence of a "law" is pretty certain, how can we be sure whether particular facts are instances of it or not? For example, Mr. Darwin seems to think, in one place, that the existence of extra fingers, in certain men, may be due to reversion, away back of the salamanders, to a fish-like ancestor; and elsewhere, that the case of a woman, with a breast developed in the groin, should be interpreted as a return to the cow-like condition of some antique progenitress. But it seems, to say the least, as reasonable to look on these as new and original variations. (*North American Review* [1868]:367)

In the other review James wrote:

The nature of the reasoning on which Darwin's hypothesis [about the concept of reversion] . . . is nowhere of strictly logical cogency, for the conclusions drawn from certain premises are assumed in their turn as true, in order to make those same premises seem more probable. Perhaps from the very nature of the case, it may never be any more possible to give a physically strict proof of it . . . than it is now to give a logically binding disproof of it. . . . At any rate it removes the matter from the jurisdiction of critics who are not zoologists, but mere reasoners (and who have already written nonsense enough about it). (*Atlantic Monthly* 22 [1868]:124)

James clearly had reservations as a young man about the scientific merits even of Darwin's own work, not to mention that of Darwin's followers.

James hinted at another criticism of Darwin years later, in a review of *The Ethical Impact of Darwinism,* by Jacob Gould Schurman, a professor of philosophy at Cornell. "Dr. Schurman, with much ability and success, takes Darwin to task for having abandoned the notion of primitive variations in his explanation of the moral sense, and tried to exhibit the latter as a necessary resultant of such preexistent mental traits as memory, reflection, and sociability" (*Nation* 45 [1887]: 376). In the 1890s James indicated continuing reservations about Darwinism, although the context makes them considerably more sympathetic than they appear alone: "[F. W. H.] Myers uses that method of gradual approach which has performed such wonders in Darwin's hands. When Darwin met a fact which seemed a poser to his theory, his regular custom, as I have heard an able colleague say, was to fill in all round it with smaller facts, as a wagoner might heap dirt round a big rock in the road, and thus get his team over without upsetting" ("Psychical Research," in *WTB,* 320). (Some scientists thought it damning to Darwin to compare his method to Myers's psychical research.) In the same essay James wrote "Even Lyell's, Faraday's, Mill's, and Darwin's consciousness of their respective subjects are already beginning to put on an infantile and innocent look" (326).

In an unsigned review in 1865 of Alfred R. Wallace's essay "The Origin of Human Races and the Antiquity of Man Deduced from the Theory of Natural Selection," James was more congenial to the concept of natural selection:

Natural selection then in its action upon man singles out for preservation those communities whose social qualities are the most complete, those whose intellectual superiority enables them to be most independent of the external world. . . . Such is Mr. Wallace's theory. It certainly seems most reasonable; indeed, so obvious; so that in this use as in the case of Darwin's original law, what most astonishes the reader is the fact that the discovery was made so late. Why may there not now be lying on the surface of things and only waiting for an eye to see it, some principle as fertile as natural selection or more so, to make up for its insufficiency (if insufficiency there be) in accounting for all organic change?" (*North American Review* 101 [1865]:263)

This review is not listed in McDermott's updated bibliography, nor is James's review of T. H. Huxley's *Lectures on the Elements of Comparative Anatomy,* also unsigned, in the same year, previous volume, of *North American Review*. James praised Huxley's book but was dismayed at its aggressiveness and hostility toward authors with whom Huxley disagreed. "To use the words of an English critic, people go to Prof. Huxley's lecture room with somewhat of the same spirit as that with which they would flock to a prize fight" (298).

Wallace probably met James in 1886. In the Houghton Library there are letters from Wallace to James during that year, while Wallace was staying in Boston. He wrote that he liked James's "Great Men and Their Environment" but doubted that it was an adequate reply to Herbert Spencer and Grant Allen (the latter was James's target in "The Importance of Individuals").

Two recent discussions of James and Darwin are useful. Robert J. Richards, "The Personal Equation in Science: William James's Psychological and Moral Uses of Darwinian Theory," in *A William James Renaissance: Four Essays by Young Scholars*, Harvard Library Bulletin, vol. 30, no. 4 (October 1982):387–426, is an interesting essay, and its notes contain references to important work by Richards on Darwinian interpretations in other contexts. Jacques Barzun, *A Stroll With William James* (New York: Harper & Row, 1983), gives an informed layman's reaction to the ongoing debate about how to interpret Darwinism and evolutionary theory (209–14).

67. "Great Men and Their Environment," in *WTB*, 226.

68. Ibid., 244. For a critical response to James's theory of great persons and history, see Victor J. Jerome, "Accident and History," *Philologica Pragensia* 6 (1963):337–42. Jerome places James and Thomas Carlyle in the Anglo-American tradition which interprets history as the result of accidental variations represented by great persons. James mentioned Robert Clive's role in India, and Jerome writes: "Actually, any serious examination of Clive's role in India will show him to have been, not demiurge creating history out of thin air, but the active, influential *instrument* of forces far greater than himself" (338).

In "Great Men and Their Environment" James made controversial remarks such as: "Would [England] be the drifting raft she is now in European affairs if a Frederic the Great had inherited her throne instead of a Victoria?" (228) and "Had Bismarck died in his cradle, the Germans would still be satisfied with appearing to themselves as a race of spectacled *Gelehrten*. . . . Bismarck's will showed them, to their great astonishment, that they could play a far livelier game" (228–29). Jerome protests vigorously against this view of Bismarck and against the "accidentalist" claim that the "chance facts" of Bismarck's birth and personality explain Germany's transformation from impotence to military strength (339).

In this connection, James commented on the Franco-Prussian hostilities in a letter to his mother in 1867: "Even I am beginning to have an opinion and one all in favor of Prussia's victory and supremacy as a great practical stride towards civilization. I think the French tone in the last quarrel deserved a degrading and stinging humiliation as much as anything in history ever did, and I'm very sorry they did not get it" (*LWJ*, 1:95).

Donald C. Williams has written an insightful if controversial essay, "William James and the Facts of Knowledge," in *In Commemoration of William James* (New York: Columbia University Press, 1942), 95–127. Williams covers a remarkable amount of ground. He comments on James's social views, saying: "But what now seems most unreal to us is the larger climate which nurtured him, the world of complacent bourgeois intellectualist liberalism, hardly faintly stirred by the rise of Prussia, with its 'wholesome animality' which the young James, in 1867, applauded 'as a great practical stride toward civilization,' whose consummation he saluted in 1910 as 'strong, calm, successful . . . *great*' " (96). Williams concedes in a footnote, but without quoting, that in an 1870 letter James "relented a little." The passage he refers to is this: "Now I feel much less interested in the success of the Germans, first because I think it's time that the principle of territorial conquest were abolished, second because success will redound to the credit of autocratic government there, and good as that may happen to be in the particular junctures, it's unsafe and pernicious in the long run. Moreover, if France succeeded in beating the Germans now, I should think there would be some chance of the peace being kept between them hereafter" (*LWJ*, 1:159). As for the 1910 letter to which Williams refers, James did briefly refer to German civilization in such words, but he hardly envisaged it as a consummation of Prussian militarism. Given his views on militarism (discussed later in this chapter), it is outrageous to suppose that he praised it in Germany. Indeed, after calling contemporary Germany great, he implied a criticism of it by praising the older ways: "But something of the old *Gemütlichkeit* remains, the friendly manners, and the disposition to talk with you and take you seriously" (*LWJ*, 2:341). Finally, we must remember that this letter was written on 4 June 1910 while he was very ill, two months before his death and not long after he arrived at Bad-Nauheim for the baths. This treatment seemed to afford him temporary relief, which may have contributed to his calling Germany great at that time.

69. "The Importance of Individuals," in *WTB*, 261–62.

70. "What Makes a Life Significant," in *Talks* (Harvard edition), 167.

71. "Pragmatism and Religion," in *Pragmatism*, 185.

72. Before pragmatism became his official mission, James still emphasized the sameness of the human condition. "Not the absence of vice, but vice there, and virtue holding her by the throat, seems the ideal human state. And there seems no reason to suppose it is not a permanent human state. There is a deep truth in what the school of Schopenhauer insists on,—the illusoriness of the notion of moral progress. . . . The final purpose of our creation seems most plausibly to be the greatest possible enrichment of our ethical consciousness, through the intensest play of contrasts and the widest diversity of characters" (*WTB*, 169).

73. "The Gospel of Relaxation," in *Talks*, 132–48. A main idea of this essay was expressed years before in a short piece, "Vacations," *Nation* 17 (1873): pp. 90–91.

Morris R. Cohen admired "The Gospel of Relaxation." See Leonora Cohen Rosenfield, *Portrait of a Philosopher: Morris R. Cohen in Life and Letters* (New York: Harcourt, Brace & World, 1962), p. 77.

74. "The Gospel of Relaxation," in *Talks*, 139. Both James and Dewey took an interest in techniques such as exercises in breathing and relaxation for physical and mental improvement. James paid particular attention to the techniques of Francois Delsarte, Dewey to those of F. M. Alexander.

75. "The Energies of Men," in McDermott, 673.

76. Ibid., 56–57.

77. James, however, qualified any claim that pragmatism is primarily an appeal to action; see, for example, *MT*, 184–86.

78. From an interview in the *Sunday Times of London*, 11 April 1926, quoted in RBP, 2:575. James H. Powers wrote an article on this interview in the *Boston Sunday Globe*, 25 April 1926.

79. H. W. Schneider, *Making the Fascist State* (New York: Oxford University Press, 1928), 341–63.

Perry went to great lengths in his correspondence to get to the bottom of the Mussolini-James question. An interesting reply to his inquiry is a letter of 8 December 1932, now in the Harvard Archives, written by Giuseppe Prezzolini, then director of the Casa Italiana at Columbia University. Prezzolini stated that James's influence in Italy was great during the first decade of the twentieth century, but that there was no connection between pragmatism and fascism. If any philosophical influence existed, it would have been Benedetto Croce's or Giovanni Gentile's. Mussolini, wrote Prezzolini, was interested in many thinkers, including Sorel, Bergson, and Einstein.

Perry wrote to Mussolini directly on 16 December 1932; the reply from the Royal Consul General of Italy, dated 11 May 1933, reported that "His Excellency read the principal works of the late William James, whom He remembers to have known personally." Both letters are now in the Perry Papers in the Harvard Archives.

Also in the Perry Papers is an extract from a letter of 24 March 1933 from H. W. Schneider to H. A. Larrabee: "There is nothing to that James-Mussolini partnership. You are quite right in supposing that Mussolini knows nothing about James except through Papini, and he never had much to do with Papini either. Mussolini was with the crowd of futurists with whom Papini flirted, but they never had much to do with each other. Every new reporter finds that Mussolini has a new 'master.' "

80. Horace M. Kallen, "Mussolini, William James, and the Rationalists," *Frontiers of Democracy* 4, no. 35 (May 1938):255. This article was provoked by a debate in the *Social Frontier*, between Sidney Hook on one side and Pitirim Sorokin and Brand Blanshard on the other, over the relations between metaphysical doctrine and social attitudes. Kallen quoted Blanshard as saying, "Mussolini is nearer to pragmatism than to any other philosophical creed," to which Hook replied that this was "a thoroughly exploded legend" (255). Part of the issue was whether, as Hook argued, rationalism or idealism tends to be socially and politically conservative.

Kallen had reported his interview with Mussolini in "Fascism: For the Italians," *New Republic* 49 (January 1927):211–12. He wrote that the discussion of pragmatism was "a fizzle" and that Mussolini was aware only of James's name; Kallen characterizes Mussolini's response to being asked what had converted him from socialism to Fascism as follows: " 'I gained the conviction,' he said, drawing himself up in his chair, and beating the desk forcefully and rhythmically with his forefinger, 'that there is no such thing as equality in life. We seek to bring out more and more the inequalities' " (212). Asserting his agreement with Machiavelli, Mussolini went on to say, Kallen added, that the state is above all and, if necessary, against all.

81. *LWJ*, 2:260. Louis Hartz wrote: "But in the world of Horatio Alger, where the compulsive power of Locke made both of these schemes [British Toryism and socialism] unthinkable, 'success' and 'failure' became the only valid ways of thought, which is what really lay behind William James's disgust with the 'bitch-goddess,' though his own pragmatism was by no means unrelated to it" (*The Liberal Tradition in America* [New York: Harcourt Brace Jovanovich, 1955], 219).

82. Unsigned review of H. R. Marshall's *Pain, Pleasure, and Aesthetics*, in *Nation* 59 (1894):49. See chapter 1 for a discussion of the artistic talent in the James family and in James himself.

An intriguing item in the James Collection is a typed memo by Henry James III that quotes La Farge as having said that William James could have been a great painter. La Farge apparently said that he still had some of James's paintings, although the only one known to exist is that of Katharine Temple, painted in Newport in 1860 (see illustration section). The same note, however, quotes a Mrs. Cadwallader Jones as saying in another context, "La Farge was always a conscienceless liar."

See also James's letter to Henry R. Marshall (*LWJ*, 2:86–87).

83. Review of Bernard Berenson's *Florentine Painters of the Renaissance with an Index to Their Works* in *Science* 4 (1896):318.

84. Unsigned review of George Santayana's *Sense of Beauty*, in *Nation* 65 (1897):75. See also the review of Marshall's *Pain, Pleasure, and Aesthetics*. Although James could be harsh in his judgments of Santayana, this sort of praise was not untypical. Altogether, his public and private comments about Santayana were laudatory.

85. Unsigned review of Grant Allen's *Physiological Aesthetics*, in *Nation* 25 (1877):186. Folder #4392 in the James Collection, titled "Notes on Aesthetics," contains notes that seem to have been made while James was preparing his review of *Pain, Pleasure, and Aesthetics* in 1894. The notes contain an extensive bibliography on aesthetics but are themselves fragmentary and tentative. He discussed whether desire is a pain or a pleasure and whether stopping pain is a pleasure and stopping pleasure a pain. He merely listed the ideas that pain goes with strong impressions, that cravings result when habitual stimulation ceases, that both pleasures

and pains are not easily localized, and that the "higher senses," especially vision, are more moderate (presumably in their sensations) and "don't threaten our self." The meaning of a reference to chords, flats and sharps, and the diatonic scale is difficult to decipher.

86. RBP, 2:250–62. The sentence written on James's copy of Kant is quoted in RBP, 2:256.

87. I agree with David A. Remley that James had a "three levelled hierarchy of ideality— the moral, the aesthetic and the scientific" ("William James: The Meaning and Function of Art," *Midcontinent American Studies Journal* 4, no. 2 [Fall 1963]:42). Remley's article is largely supplementary to Perry's discussion but adds some interesting observations, especially on *VRE*. I do not think it is correct to say, as Remley does, that James denied inherent goodness to aesthetic pleasure. Remley's examples, taken mostly from Perry, are relevant, but each has a twist which keeps it from being as clear a subordination of aesthetic to moral pleasure as Remley desires. For example, he says that James condemned "indulgence in music" (41), but James actually spoke only of "excessive indulgence" on the part of "those who are neither performers themselves nor musically gifted enough to take it in a purely intellectual way," and even this criticism is softened when James granted that excessive indulgence probably has "a relaxing effect upon the character" (*Principles,* 1:125–26).

For an early statement of James's thought about the character of art, in itself and as a career, see his letter of 24 August 1860 to his father, quoted in RBP, 1:198–200.

88. On Peirce, see Murray G. Murphey, *The Development of Peirce's Philosophy* (Cambridge: Harvard University Press, 1961), 361–64, and Elizabeth Flower and Murray G. Murphey, *A History of Philosophy in America* (New York: Putnam's, 1977), 11:617–18. In a letter of 25 November 1902, Peirce wrote to James:

> My own view [of pragmatism] in 1887 was crude. Even when I gave my Cambridge lectures I had not really got to the bottom of it or seen the unity of the whole thing. It was not until after that that I obtained the proof that logic must be founded on ethics, of which it is a higher development. Even then, I was for some time so stupid as not to see that ethics rests in the same manner on a formulation of aesthetics,—by which, it is needless to say, I don't mean milk and water and sugar.

Wittgenstein's words are from *Tractatus Logico-Philosophicus* 6.421 (New York: Harcourt, Brace & Co., 1947), 183.

For contemporary discussions, see Stuart Hampshire, "Logic and Appreciation," in *Aesthetics and Language,* ed. William Elton (Oxford: Blackwell, 1954), 161–69, and Philippa Foot, "Morality and Art," *Proceedings of the British Academy* 56 (London: Oxford Univ. Press, 1970), 1–15.

89. In a diary entry of 21 January 1910, James wrote: "To see St. Denis dance, at Mary Tappan's invitation. Exquisite!" Since Ruth St. Denis was a founder of American modern dance and by no means a dancer who appealed to established taste, James seems to have had an appreciation for the avant-garde. Given his own religious proclivities, St. Denis's spiritual dances may have charmed him more for this than for the avant-garde quality of the dancing.

James's appreciation of St. Denis's dancing may have had its roots in Schiller's *Essay on Grace and Dignity,* which he mentioned reading in his diary in 1868. Schiller argued that natural movements that are also graceful demonstrate a harmony between the natural and the moral person. James's critical response to Schiller's essay reveals his own inclination to run moral and aesthetic considerations together: "My old trouble and the root of antinomianism in general seems to be a dissatisfaction with anything less than grace. It is obvious how little facts are consulted throughout the above [notes on Schiller]—It is absurd to restrict grace to moral agents—animals are graceful and so are immoral people."

Having seen Sarah Bernhardt in a London performance the previous evening, he wrote a card, dated 19 June 1880, to his wife: "Bernhardt last night was the *finest* piece of acting I've ever seen—as if etched with the point of a needle—and altogether she is the most race-horsey high mettled human being I've ever seen—physically she is a perfect skeleton."

See James's criticism of J. S. Mill's aesthetic deficiency in *LWJ*, 1:144. See also Barzun, *A Stroll with William James*, 220–22.

90. "The Dedication of the Germanic Museum," *Harvard Illustrated Magazine* 5, no. 2 (November 1903):50.

91. Lowell Lecture notes in the Houghton Library, 68–71. See also "Degeneration and Genius," in *CER*, 401–06. In a different vein is James's review of Lucien Arreat's *Psychologie du peintre*, in *Philosophical Review* 2 (1893):590–94. James was harshly critical of this book's pretense to illuminate the psychology of painters, saying that it was mainly anecdotal rather than scientific and that it irrelevantly employed a vague statistical method. James suggested that the capacity to draw is the only essential condition for being a painter, that this ability is probably inherited, that paths of conduction in the brain probably explain the painter's special sensory-motor abilities, and that vivid visualization is not required. (According to his testimony, he himself was a poor visualizer, but that lack had not prevented him from pursuing painting.)

> The satisfaction of the lust of the eyes tends to beget a contentment with the concrete face of the world, and the peaceful occupation tends to produce a serenity of disposition, so that we should rather expect a painter, *ceteris paribus*, to be sociable and genial, as so many of M. Arreat's painters prove to have been. In fact a competent introspective critic could write a book on the deductive method, which might be really *explanatory* of such professional peculiarities as painters tend to show and have ten times the charm and value of M. Arreat's work. (593)

92. *Principles*, 2:315. See the rest of the chapter "The Perception of Reality," as well as "The Sentiment of Rationality," in *CER*; "Some Metaphysical Problems Pragmatically Considered," in *Pragmatism*; and "Necessary Truths and the Effects of Experience," in *Principles*.

93. I offer some ideas along these lines in an essay on capital punishment, "The Death Penalty," *Criminal Justice Review* 6, no. 1 (Spring 1981):48–54.

94. James noted at the conclusion of this manuscript that it was based upon an episode "which actually happened on Wednesday March 3rd." In April 1867 Emerson gave James a letter of introduction to Hermann Grimm for James's trip to Berlin; since James was interested in art and aesthetics at this time, the manuscript may date from 1867, when he was twenty-five (see RBP, 1:246–47).

95. James Elliot Cabot, who became Emerson's biographer, had also been criticized by James's father. According to a note in the James Collection, dated 16 May 1873, Henry, Sr., had criticized Cabot's concept of the ego. The son thus followed the father, although the particular point of criticism was different.

96. *LWJ*, 2:99. James recognized that the virulent forces of anti-Semitism and nationalism had influenced the Dreyfus vedict; like the others who had protested years earlier, he felt vindicated when Dreyfus was finally exonerated in 1906.

97. In a letter of 22 January 1908, for example, he wrote to Pauline Goldmark: "Thank Heaven, *I'm* [in contrast to Dickinson S. Miller, who had just been ordained as a priest in the Episcopal Church] an anarchist, and likely to remain so!"

Years before, he had expressed his reaction to the Haymarket Square massacre and riot in Chicago on 4 May 1886 (in which seven policemen were killed and many injured by a bombing during a protest held by anarchists) in a letter of 9 May to his brother Henry:

> Don't be alarmed by the labor troubles here. I am quite sure they are a most healthy phase of evolution, a little costly, but normal, and sure to do lots of good to all hands in the end. I don't speak of the senseless "anarchist" riot in Chicago, which has nothing to do with

"Knights of Labor," but is the work of a lot of pathological Germans and Poles. I'm amused at the anti-Gladstonian capital which the English papers are telegraphed to be making of it. See the Irish names are among the killed and wounded policemen. Almost every anarchist name is Continental. (*LWJ*, 1:252)

98. Letter of 27 January 1903 to Theodore Flournoy. Rockefeller was the father-in-law of James's friend, Charles A. Strong, a professor of psychology at Columbia, and was visiting at the home of the Strongs when James was. This attitude toward Rockefeller did not prevent James from asking him to contribute to a cause associated with Clifford W. Beers (see note 116 below).

99. "Robert Gould Shaw," in *MS*, 40–42. This essay was adapted from an oration delivered in the Boston Music Hall at the unveiling of a monument to Colonel Robert Gould Shaw. Shaw was commander of the Fifty-fourth Massachusetts Regiment, the first largely black regiment in the North. As James put it, after Shaw "led them up the parapet of Fort Wagner he and nearly half of them were left upon the ground" (41).

In addition to the issues of the Civil War, the problems of black Americans, and questions about war itself, James was also occupied in writing this oration with the fact that his younger brother Wilky had been a member of Shaw's regiment and had been badly wounded in the assault on Fort Wagner.

Booker T. Washington also spoke on this occasion. James's wife made it appear in her correspondence that James's speech was the highlight of the occasion, but a different version, drawn from the Boston papers, suggests that Washington's speech was the emotional climax of the day. See Louis R. Harlan, *Booker T. Washington: The Wizard of Tuskegee (1901–1915)* (New York: Oxford University Press, 1972), 236. Harlan notes that James, having become aware of the impact of Washington's speech, later wrote him a somewhat "abashed" message of congratulations.

In a letter of 22 March 1909, Washington wrote to James to request financial assistance for the Tuskegee Institute in Alabama. Citing the severe needs of Tuskegee (for example, one teacher and his family were residing together in a tiny cottage that would cost $6,500 to enlarge), Washington stated his funding goal to be $45,000. Although there is no record of James's reply, he was generally inclined to send generous checks in response to such requests.

McDermott notes that in a letter to his brother Henry, William reported the Shaw unveiling with this remark: "Read the darkey Washington's speech, a model of elevation and brevity." McDermott takes this to be a revelation of James's "condescension to the blacks of his time, a position strikingly inappropriate for a third-generation descendant of an Irish immigrant" (Introduction to *Essays in Religion and Morality* [Cambridge: Harvard University Press, 1982], xx). George A. Garrison and Edward H. Madden share McDermott's concern on the issue; see their "William James—Warts and All," *American Quarterly* 29 (Summer 1977): 215–16.

I interpret James's use of *darkey* differently. Intellectuals at the time were often ready to identify someone as being a Frenchman, a German, a Catholic, a Jew, and so on; it was only natural for James to refer to Washington's being black. Using *darkey* was James's way of trying not to be stilted, artificial, or sentimental, but to indicate that he was himself relating with respect and admiration to a person whom many described, whether endearingly or otherwise, as a "darkey." I think it was not condescension but rather James's show of confidence that in *his* use, a word like *darkey* could take on positive connotations. Because of this confidence, he could afford to show, to his brother anyway, a lack of fear toward a borderline epithet. Given his well-known penchant for embracing the underprivileged, James learned to protect himself from accusations of condescension by going to some lengths in his use of language to avoid the appearance of sentimentality, artificiality, or self-righteousness.

On James's nonparticipation in the Civil War, see chapter 1. For one black's feelings about James, see W. E. B. Dubois's statement in chapter 1, page 13.

100. Charles W. Eliot, Harvard's president, encouraged the presence of Jews in Harvard's undergraduate body. Leonora Cohen Rosenfield wrote: "Back in the days when Charles W. Eliot was an undergraduate, there were no Jews at Harvard. During his presidency, 1869–1909, their number swelled, according to *The American Hebrew,* from two to three to almost three hundred. President Eliot even expressed a wish to be succeeded by Louis D. Brandeis" (*Portrait of a Philosopher: Morris R. Cohen in Life and Letters* [New York: Harcourt, Brace & World, 1962], 67). James also played a part in effecting this change. Rosenfield provides a vivid account of his influence upon her father, Morris R. Cohen.

101. Walter Lippmann, "An Open Mind: William James," *Everybody's Magazine* 23 (December 1910):801.

102. For an excellent treatment of the attitude of Henry James, Sr., in these respects, see Jean Strouse, *Alice James: A Biography* (Boston: Houghton Mifflin, 1980), 45–48, 87–90, and 97–116. Strouse's book is invaluable for understanding how the influence of the father upon his children, especially Alice, can be construed regarding attitudes about gender.

103. The best example is James's letter of 24 September 1882, partially reproduced in *LWJ,* 1:210–11, but there are many such examples in James's personal correspondence, with his wife and with others, of what many would call the typical male attitude—typical then as now.

For Jacques Barzun's interpretation of the remark about an antisexual instinct, and for his defense of James, see *A Stroll with William James,* 276–77. See also Allen's response to the same matter in *William James: A Biography,* 213–14.

104. "H. Bushnell's *Women's Suffrage* and J. S. Mill's *Subjection of Women,* " *North American Review* 109 (1869):556–65.

105. Ibid., 563. This passage is quoted in RBP, 2:260, and is Perry's sole reference to this review.

106. Unsigned review of Henry T. Finck's *Romantic Love and Personal Beauty: Their Development, Causal Relations, Historic and National Peculiarities,* in *Nation* 45 (1887):238.

107. Letter of 23 March 1907. Four days later James sent Shaw a postcard urging him, "Pray postpone the reading of my poor Father's works till after you have tackled Jane Addams. I feel confident that in some respects it will *feed* your Genius—of which I am the chief American beneficiary in professional-ethical circles."

Shaw sent a postcard on 15 April 1907, promising to put Addams's *New Ideals of Peace* at the top of his reading list. See Morton and Lucia White, "Pragmatism and Social Work: William James and Jane Addams," chapter 9 of *The Intellectual Versus the City* (Cambridge: Harvard University and M.I.T. Presses, 1963).

108. In a 1928 letter to Henry James III, now in the Houghton Library, Wyatt recalled that the hiking episode occurred in 1901, but she may actually have had in mind the trip of July 1898, reported by James in a letter to his wife (*LWJ,* 2:75–78). James referred to Wyatt as the author of an "exquisite book of Chicago sketches" in "The Social Value of the College-Bred" in *MS,* 322.

109. Notably George R. Garrison and Edward H. Madden. Their short article contains much useful information about James's social views and puts them in a better perspective than do the accounts of Perry and Allen. Garrison and Madden are especially helpful in pointing to weaknesses in James's responses to American racism, feminism, and England's treatment of Ireland. They observe that James was much too insensitive to the economic, social, and political determinants of human behavior (212). In fact, they argue, while James had attitudes toward many social issues, he almost never translated them into the behavior of a social reformer. Garrison and Madden do not downgrade the significance of his social concerns, concluding only that "William James the man and philosopher is indeed impressive and important. He needs no useless embroidery of 'active citizen' and 'social reformer' " (221). I basically endorse this view, although to deny James the role of active citizen seems to go too far

in the reverse direction. James was quite an active citizen both at Harvard and in the wider world.

110. RBP, 2:290. Perry refers to James's letter of 24 December 1895 to E. L. Godkin (*LWJ*, 2:28) as support for this assertion; he undoubtedly also had in mind the sentiment expressed in "The Social Value of the College-Bred," in *Memories and Studies*, where James said that the best thing a college education can do is to *"help you to know a good man when you see him. This is as true of women's as of men's colleges; but that it is neither a joke nor a one-sided abstraction I shall now endeavor to show"* (309). In his briefer version of *TCWJ*, Perry inserted "practical" so that the passage reads: "The root of James's practical ethics is to be found not in his ethics and philosophy. . . ." This addition, I think, helps very little.

111. See RBP, chapters 67–68; Barzun, 142–80; Garrison and Madden.

112. Unsigned review of A. A. Liébault's *Du Sommeil et des états analogues, considérés surtout au point de vue de l'action du moral sur le physique*, in *Nation* 7 (1868):52.

113. "William James's Remarkable Plea for Medical Freedom," *Medical Freedom* 9 (May 1912):7, 9. The address was originally reproduced in *Banner of Light* on 12 March 1898. See also *LWJ*, 2:66–67, 72, and RBP, 2:303–04.

James's stand on this issue has been discussed more than the philosophy and psychology professions realize. Those on the side of "alternative" forms of medicine, or simply in favor of an open-door policy in medicine, think that James won a battle for their cause. An example is a letter written in 1944, which will remain anonymous.

> William James has been a sort of Hero to me for nearly 60 years. At that time the Massachusetts State Medical Society went before the Massachusetts Legislature to get a Medical Practice Act enacted to control the practice of medicine in the state. The control was to be exercised by a Board of Examiners, that was to be comprised of doctors of the various medical "Schools" of medicine, in proportion to their numerical strength, which would work out practically as one of each, of the homeopathic, eclectic, and physio-medical societies, and about 20 of the orthodox school. It was a cinch that it would pass the Legislature, as it *seemed* fair to the average man, but it was the intent of the Mass. State Soc. to strangle out the unorthodox gradually but surely. . . . When the matter came to [James's] attention he went before the Legislature and killed the bill by showing its manifest intent and the outrageous unfairness of it. I say it takes a real man to do that. . . . At that time I was a Freshman in Michigan Homeopathic Medical College, and our school had been through just such a fight, for existence, and naturally I would appreciate the work of James in Massachusetts.

James was not, however, against all legislation that would infringe upon the interests of some parties. In a letter to the editor of the *Nation*, he once complained about newspaper medical advertisements. Although some of his criticism is tongue-in-cheek and deliberately exaggerated, he evidently thought that legislation might be the only solution:

> Every product of social evolution inevitably proceeds to excesses until it has to be regulated by law for the better protection of the individual. Electric wires are the last case in point; cannot medical advertisements be the next? . . . Now they literally form the principal feature of our provincial newspapers, and in many of the "great dailies" of our cities play a part second only to the collective display of suicides, murders, seductions, fights, and rapes; while thousands of shameless persons are reputed to add materially to their incomes by selling for publication their portraits with descriptions, sincere or insincere, of their pretended cures. . . . The way in which a certain "kidney" nostrum . . . was worked, was truly diabolical. . . . We presently discover, coordinated with perhaps a change of ministry in England, the annexation of Hawaii . . . accounts of Mr. Mingo's kidneys, Mr. Hankshaw's bronchi, or Mrs. Hecla's skin—on which the grotesque pictures

of the sufferers set the seal. Like Ulysses, these worthies have become a part of all that we have met; and all experience is an arch where-through their entrails gleam as if it were iridescently upon us, until the world looms to our imagination in a sort of catarrhal vapor, or as if bathed in a cancerous and haemorrhoidal mist. . . .

The authors of these advertisements should be treated as public enemies and have no mercy shown. The first step towards such a society for agitation as I propose might well be made by the medical societies of the several States. . . . A generation will come after ours, so conscious of spiritual forces and of health as a public ideal, that when, in the chamber of horrors of their historic museum, they look upon a newspaper of our day, framed upon the wall to show the regime under which our generation lived, they will refuse to believe their eyes. [Appended to James's letter was an editorial response: "Prof. James will be glad to learn of the existence of a New York Act for the more effectual prevention of wanton and malicious mischief, and to prevent the defacement of natural scenery."] (*Nation* 58 [1894]: 84–85)

114. Notice of Morselli's *Manuale della Semejotica delle Malattie Mentali,* in *Psychological Review* 3 (1896):681.

115. Unsigned review of Henry Maudsley's *Responsibility in Mental Disease,* in *Atlantic Monthly* 34 (1874):365. The rest of this review reveals that James, unlike the author reviewed, did not believe that people can avoid going mad in stressful circumstances simply by being inwardly stoic and remaining in harmony with the world.

116. Letter of 1 July 1906 to Beers, quoted in *A Mind That Found Itself* (Pittsburgh: University of Pittsburgh Press, 1981), 197–98. Beers also reproduced a letter of 17 January 1910, in which James praised him for being a moral idealist and for being effective in promoting his cause. "I esteem it an honor to have been in any degree associated with you. Your name will loom big hereafter, for your movement must prosper, but mine [the academic one] will not survive unless some other kind of effort of mine saves it" (199).

Beers's book has been reprinted forty-one times since its appearance in 1908. The 1942 edition (Garden City N.Y.: Doubleday, Doran & Co.) included more letters from James and some from Booth Tarkington, as well as an epilogue on the mental hygiene movement. The 1908 letter by James referred to next in the text also occurs in *A Mind That Found Itself.*

See also RBP, 2:318–19; Perry reproduced part of James's letter to Rockefeller asking for money for Beers's cause.

117. See, for instance, *WTB* (Harvard edition), 52–53, 325; see also RBP, 2:268.

118. "Brute and Human Intellect," *The Journal of Speculative Philosophy* 12 (July 1878):262. This article, incorporated into the chapter on reasoning in *Principles,* argues that humans and animals differ in their abilities to associate and dissociate, but reasoning of a sort is clearly ascribed to animals.

119. *Journal of Philosophy* 46 (December 1949):829–38.

120. Unsigned article on vivisection, in *Nation* 20 (1875):129. James's unpublished Lowell Lectures include this entry: "anti-vivisectionist mania—one-idea." He was clearly distressed by the obsessiveness of many antivivisectionists.

121. The *New York Times* on 27 September 1983 carried an article by Bayard Webster titled "Should Vivisection Be Abolished?" Ever since the Australian philosopher Peter Singer published *Animal Liberation* in 1975, debates about animal rights have been heated. The difference between his antivivisectionist views and the position of the psychologist Neal Miller, as reported by Webster, is reminiscent of the exchange between James and Cannon.

122. RBP, 2:297; see also the rest of Perry's chapter 57.

123. James's letter was published in the *Congressional Record,* 1895, 28, pt. 1:399. The letter was written on 21 December 1895 in Cambridge.

124. Quoted in Samuel E. Morison, *Three Centuries of Harvard* (Cambridge: Harvard Uni-

versity Press, Belknap Press, 1963), 412. See also RBP, 2:304. For more on James's relations to Theodore Roosevelt, see RBP, 2:311–15.

125. Charles, Mary, and William Beard, *New Basic History of the United States* (Garden City, N.Y.: Doubleday, 1960), 320. I have drawn from their readable interpretation of this period in American history; see chapter 21, "The Breach with Historic Continentialism."

126. *LWJ*, 2:73. See also the frequently quoted letter of 17 June 1898 to Theodore Flournoy, quoted in full in Robert C. Le Clair (ed.), *The Letters of William James and Theodore Flournoy* (Madison: University of Wisconsin Press, 1966), 71–74, and in part in RBP, 2:307–08.

127. Notice of Gustave Le Bon's *The Crowd*, in *Psychological Review* 4 (1897):313–14. Freud had a higher opinion than James did of Le Bon's book, calling it a "deservedly famous work," and wrote sympathetically about many of its suggestions. But he too was finally critical, concluding that although Le Bon's contentions accorded well with his own psychology, "none of that author's statements bring forward anything new." See Freud's *Group Psychology and the Analysis of the Ego* (New York: Bantam, 1965), 6–8, 19–20.

128. Letter to Flournoy, in Le Clair, 73.

129. Ibid.

130. George F. Kennan, *American Diplomacy 1900–1950* (1951; reprint, New York: Mentor, n.d.), 17.

131. On these matters, see Lloyd Morris, *William James: The Message of a Modern Mind* (New York: Scribner's, 1950), 75–82.

132. *New York Evening Post*, 10 March 1899.

133. Address on the Philippine question, published by the New England Anti-Imperialist League in its report of its Fifth Annual Meeting (n.p., 1903), 23.

134. Letter to the editor, *Boston Transcript*, 2 May 1904.

135. George Santayana, *Persons and Places*, 3 vols. (New York: Scribner's, 1945), 2:169.

136. Ibid., 2:170.

137. Stuart Creighton Miller, *"Benevolent Assimilation": The American Conquest of the Philippines, 1889–1903* (New Haven: Yale University Press, 1982), 116. Miller also discusses the elitist bias of such anti-imperialists as E. L. Godkin, C. E. Norton, Charles Francis Adams, and James. James is included because of isolated statements and "The Social Value of the College-Bred" (in *Memories and Studies*, 307–25) and because of Perry's observations (RBP, 2:290–99). Despite such evidence, however, James usually emphasized the individual and democracy and sympathized at least somewhat with H. G. Wells's utopian socialism; as such, he was temperamentally antielitist. See Robert L. Beisner, *Twelve Against Empire: The Anti-Imperialists, 1898–1900* (New York: McGraw-Hill, 1968), especially chapter 1, and Daniel B. Schirmer, "William James and the New Age," *Science and Society* 33 (Fall–Winter 1969), 434–45. Beisner and Schirmer cover much of the ground mentioned here, including some references to Santayana. Both note that James differed from the Boston and New England elitist anti-imperialists; see Beisner, 37, and Schirmer, 436.

138. This point is made in Beisner, 51. Beisner gives an excellent treatment of American anti-imperialism between 1898 and 1900; his chapter 3, which discusses James, includes extensive information and interpretation.

139. Ibid., 51–52.

140. Address on the Philippine question, 22; quoted in Schirmer, 440.

141. Schirmer, 438.

142. In a letter of 21 April 1923, Henry James III, writing on behalf of the James family to the President and Fellows of Harvard to present much of his father's library, noted that the books fell into four groups: about four hundred on philosophy and psychology; about six hundred on abnormal psychology and psychical research, many not easily obtainable; approximately fifty on philosophy and religion; and about "a score of books, somewhat annotated, which my father placed together shortly before his death with the intention of working

up the subject of military psychology." James thought he might one day write a book called *A Psychology of Jingoism* or *Varieties of Military Experience* (see Schirmer, 441), but the closest he came was "The Moral Equivalent of War."

143. "Remarks at the Peace Banquet," in *MS,* 304–06.

144. "The Moral Equivalent of War," in *MS,* 272. This essay was first published by the Association for International Conciliation (Leaflet No. 27); it was reprinted in *McClure's Magazine* in August 1910, in *The Popular Science Monthly* in October 1910, and finally in *MS* in 1911.

There is in the Harvard Archives a letter written by Mrs. Bailey Aldrich, secretary to Perry, which states that in 1912 Frederick P. Keppel, the secretary of the American Association for International Conciliation, wrote a letter saying that James accepted seventy-five dollars for "The Moral Equivalent of War" and that neither the *Atlantic* nor the *American Magazine* wanted it. This is in part borne out by James's diary of 29 December 1909, which reads: "Six hours good sleep at last/[Wendell] Phillips [editor of the *Atlantic*] declines my war-article."

Also in the Harvard Archives is a letter to Perry, dated 30 January 1934, from Rabbi David Philipson of Cincinnati. Philipson stated that he had heard James read this essay at a summer school course in ethics at Plymouth, Massachusetts, in 1895. The summer school was under the auspices of Smith College, and the lecturers included James, Philipson, Felix Adler of Columbia, Crawford H. Joy of Harvard, and Henry Carter Adams of the University of Michigan. Perry does not mention Philipson's claim in *TCWJ,* probably doubting its accuracy.

I. K. Skrupskelis has shown that James made notes on hotel stationery for the essay in February 1906. See *Essays in Religion and Morality,* 251; the essay is reprinted on pages 162–73, with notes and historical information on 250–64.

145. "The Moral Equivalent of War," in *MS,* 273–74.

146. Ibid., 274.

147. Ibid., 276–77.

148. Ibid., 283. Schirmer notes this passage and remarks:

> In fact, it was against "the more or less socialistic future towards which mankind seems drifting" that he especially saw the need for an institution like universal conscription in the battle with nature to preserve in a new form the virtues of supreme effort and self-sacrifice which he identified with the old war-dominated and competitive way of life, for him already doomed. It was more with this interest and less as a means of checking war's outbreaks that James at this point put forward the idea of the moral equivalent. (444)

This conclusion is misleading. James was clearly concerned with developing a strategy for checking war's outbreak, and the moral equivalent was the strategy he offered. It kept alive even in socialist utopias the spirit of martial virtues, without which the justified claims of the military-minded would surface again.

149. "The Moral Equivalent of War," in *MS,* 290, 291.

150. In 1942, when the United States was bracing for another global war, Perry wrote:

> The two deepest moral sentiments of James were his humanity and his admiration of heroic action, and his conclusion was a union of the two in heroic action for humanity. This was the teaching of his "Moral Equivalent of War," which is now the Bible of the group of young Americans who have created the William James Camp at Tunbridge, Vermont. Members of the group have engaged in the settlement of Alaska and in the rehabilitation of parts of Mexico ravaged by earthquake. They have volunteered in the Canadian army or cheerfully accepted their military duties in America in order to prove that the conquest of the wilderness, brotherly help across national borders, or an idealistic defense of democracy against aggressors can command the same physical courage, the same self-forgetfulness, and the same élan as have hitherto been evoked by the primitive emotions of war. They find their inspiration in passages [from "The Moral Equivalent of War"]. ("If James Were Alive Today," *In Commemoration of William James,* 78)

See also in this volume Julius S. Bixler's discussion of James's essay, 58–71.

Personal experience may have motivated part of "The Moral Equivalent of War." Whereas James himself had been reared as a "gilded" youth, he encouraged his two eldest sons, Henry III and William, Jr., to get a taste of the moral equivalent by working in the summer for the United States Forestry Service in Washington. James's letters to Henry III during that time indicate that he thought the wilderness experience would do his sons good.

151. McDermott referred me to Jo Ann Boydston, general editor of John Dewey's *Collected Works*, for information about Dewey's reaction to "The Moral Equivalent of War." Dewey wrote, in a letter to Scudder Klyce on 29 May 1915, that James's essay

> on war seemed to me to show that even his sympathies were limited by his experience; the idea that most people need any substitute for fighting for life, or that they have to have life made artificially hard for them in order to keep up their battling nerve, could come only from a man who was brought up an aristocrat and who had lived a sheltered existence. I think he had no real intimation that the "labor problem" has always been for the great mass of people a much harder fight than any war; in fact one reason people are so ready to fight is the fact that that is so much easier than their ordinary existence.

I am grateful to Boydston for permission to quote this. She tells me that this is the only remark about James in Dewey's correspondence that might be construed as negative.

Lest we agree that Dewey's response shows that James's moral equivalent is only a Boston Brahmin's concoction, we should remember that James made it explicitly clear toward the end of his essay that the "gilded youths" especially needed to be sent to iron mines and road-building, a policy which might help to counterbalance the unfair advantages enjoyed by young people of the leisure class. While James's program would have included the entire youthful population, he presumably believed that his program would be more challenging than the usual humdrum existence even for underprivileged youths and that they, as well as the privileged, would acquire the military ideals of hardihood and discipline. James's notion is problematic and perhaps naive, but he protected himself against the charge that it was an aristocratic brainchild. He did not mean to make mere labor for its own sake function as the moral equivalent; rather, labor in the deliberate service of the nation and its best interests might instill in youth the moral and psychological equivalent of what only the military had accomplished previously.

I am grateful to Boydston and McDermott for bringing Dewey's reaction to my attention and for making me appreciate that James's essay might be criticized from his line of thinking.

14. RELIGION

1. "The Moral Philosopher and the Moral Life," in *WTB*, 211.

2. Ibid., 212.

3. Ibid., 213.

4. Ibid., 213–14.

5. Letter of 3 January 1898, reproduced in J. C. Kenna, "Ten Unpublished Letters from William James to Francis Herbert Bradley," *Mind* 75 (July 1966):316.

James edited the work of his father under the title *The Literary Remains of the Late Henry James* (Boston: Houghton Mifflin, 1884). His points of agreement and disagreement with his father's Swedenborgian views are outlined in his lengthy introduction to this volume. For more on the relation between the religious outlook of James and that of his father, see Perry, *TCWJ*; F. O. Matthiessen, *The James Family* (New York: Vintage, 1980), especially 136–89; Frederic Harold Young, *The Philosophy of Henry James, Sr.* (New Haven: College and University Press, 1951); William A. Clebsch, *American Religious Thought* (Chicago: University of Chicago Press, 1973); and Henry Samuel Levinson, *The Religious Investigations of William James* (Chapel Hill: University of North Carolina Press, 1981). Levinson's book is an excellent study of James's religious thought and must be consulted by anyone wanting a more comprehensive presentation of James on religion.

I agree with McDermott's statement: "In sifting through Henry James's [Sr.] writings, William repeatedly emphasizes certain themes. It is difficult to know whether these interests of William James are due to his father's influence or whether he arrived at his conclusions independently and thereby isolated them in his father's writings either as an anticipation of or as a foil for his own position" (Introduction to James's *Essays in Religion and Morality* [Harvard edition], xv; see also McDermott's succeeding observations.)

James liked to present his own position on any issue as a mediation between conflicting extremes. Strange as it may sound, he was a middle-of-the-road philosopher. On the relation of ethics to religion, he considered his own view to be the middle ground between his father's position and its opposite. As he read his father's conception, it entertained God as the only active principle; individual selfhood was really *"naught,* a provisional phantom-soul breathed by God's love into mere logical negation."* This view resulted in a contempt for societal values of moral achievement, that is, a contempt for moralism. The elder James's concern was exclusively focused upon the religious demand to secure the well-being that comes from the union with God. His absolute religion (which is monistic) was pitted against absolute moralism (which is pluralistic). William then queried: "Is the religious tendency or the moralistic tendency *on the whole* the most serviceable to man's life, taking the latter in the largest way?" (Introduction to *The Literary Remains of the Late Henry James,* in *Essays in Religion and Morality,* 63; italics mine).

If James had had to make an exclusive choice, he would have favored the moralistic tendency. But as letters such as the one to Bradley and essays such as "The Moral Philosopher and the Moral Life," "The Will to Believe," and "Some Metaphysical Problems Pragmatically Considered" reveal, he preferred a middle ground between his father's absolute religion and absolute moralism. On the whole, we achieve maximum well-being by intense moral performance, by fulfilling our moral demands through our religious ones. See Bernard P. Brennan, *The Ethics of William James* (New York: Bookman Associates, 1961), especially chapter 3, for a helpful commentary on James's writings as they connect ethics and religion.

6. See, for instance, "Pragmatism and Religion," in *Pragmatism,* 190–91.

7. For example: "The problem I have set myself [the defense of religion in *VRE*] is a hard one: *first,* to defend (against all the prejudices of my 'class') 'experience' against 'philosophy' as being the real backbone of the world's religious life" (letter of 12 April 1900 to Frances P. Morse, in *LWJ,* 2:127).

8. "The One and The Many," in *Pragmatism,* 97–98.

9. Understanding this point enables us to appreciate more fully why James (to the distress of many academic philosophers) devoted so much of *Pragmatism* to a defense of concrete religion against the abstract version offered by neo-Hegelians. Virtually all of *Pragmatism* defends James's pluralistic religion. (Only lecture 5, "Pragmatism and Common Sense," does not.) James saw a connection between concrete, popular religion and his concept of pluralism, which he identified as a respect for the method of experience in opposition to a priori abstract theorizing. Indeed, he thought the tension between monism and pluralism should be called the deepest issue in philosophy (see, for instance, *SPP,* 114). James was sincere, for instance, in "Abstractionism and 'Relativismus,'" chapter 13 of *MT,* in claiming that criticisms of the concept of a will-to-believe stemmed from a vicious abstract way of thinking which had lost touch with concrete realities.

John Macy, a student of James, wrote the following account:

One day, with his curious mixture of nonchalance and alertness, James was reducing a word to its meanings, trying to find the heart of it by pulling away some of its connotations. There was no heart in it. One student, who had not quite followed the game and still mistook the faceless abstraction for the god of his fathers, grew aghast at the process of verbal denudation and cried out: "But I do not see how that takes away my God."

Professor James paused for a puzzled moment and then replied, "It doesn't. Your God stands on his own hind legs." Then he pursued the idea, found often in his books, that the metaphysical Absolute is like an anatomist's mannikin. It can be taken apart and put together; it may be a useful diagram of a living being, but it is itself dead. ("William James as Man of Letters," *Bookman* 33 [April 1911]:206-07)

10. "Some Metaphysical Problems," in *Pragmatism*, 76, 77-78. The rest of this essay elaborates James's contention.

11. "Is Life Worth Living?" in *WTB*, 57-58. This passage casts light upon our discussion of James's views on vivisection in the preceding chapter. The experimental animal's suffering can be justified not only for its contribution to medical science but also for its admirable illustration of heroic redemptiveness.

12. "The Will to Believe," in *WTB*, 7-8. James's references are to W. K. Clifford's *Lectures and Essays* and to T. H. Huxley's "The Influence upon Morality of a Decline in Religious Belief," *Nineteenth Century* 1 (April 1877):331-58. See *WTB* (Harvard edition), 255-56.

13. See Peter Kauber and Peter H. Hare, "The Right and Duty to Will to Believe," *Canadian Journal of Philosophy* 4 (December 1974):327-43. For further discussion of James's ethics of belief, see Kauber's "Does James's Ethics of Belief Rest on a Mistake?" *The Southern Journal of Philosophy* 12 (Summer 1974):201-04, and idem, "The Foundations of James's Ethics of Belief," *Ethics* 84 (January 1974):151-66. Kauber's essays indicate the relevance of James to contemporary discussions of the ethics of belief.

See also Peter H. Hare and Edward H. Madden, "William James, Dickinson Miller, and C. J. Ducasse on the Ethics of Belief," *Transactions of the Charles S. Peirce Society* 4 (Fall 1968):115-29. Madden's introduction in *The Will to Believe* (Harvard edition) is valuable.

See James L. Muyskens, "James' Defense of a Believing Attitude in Religion," *Transactions of the Charles S. Peirce Society* 10 (Winter 1974):44-54; Stephen T. Davis, "Wishful Thinking and 'The Will to Believe,'" *Transactions of the Charles S. Peirce Society* 8 (Fall 1972):231-45; and Patrick E. Dooley, "The Nature of Belief: The Proper Context for James' 'The Will to Believe,'" *Transactions of the Charles S. Peirce Society* 8 (Summer 1972):141-51.

A recent and ingenious discussion, which represents a novel approach to James's essay "The Will to Believe," is Richard M. Gale's "William James and the Ethics of Belief," *American Philosophical Quarterly* 17, no. 1 (January 1980):1-14.

14. "The Will to Believe," in *WTB*, 26. Jay Newman reminds us that James said in "The Will to Believe" that faith-vetoing absolutism is a weakness of our nature from which we must free ourselves. See Newman's *Foundations of Religious Tolerance* (Toronto: University of Toronto Press, 1982), 58.

15. For James's mention of Blaise Pascal, see "The Will to Believe," in *WTB*, 5-6, 11. Pascal's wager is the idea that the stakes are such that we are advised to bet that there is a god; we win eternal life if the bet is won, we lose little if the bet is lost.

16. A. O. Lovejoy, for example, held that James had confused the consequences of a proposition itself with the consequences of believing in that proposition. James atypically agreed that he had been guilty of this confusion and needed to revise his formulations accordingly, but he never made such revisions. On the exchange between Lovejoy and James, see RBP, 2:480.

17. "The Will to Believe," in *WTB*, 25-26.

18. The questionnaire, formulated and distributed by James B. Pratt, was known as the Pratt Questionnaire. The questions and James's responses are reproduced as an appendix to *The Varieties of Religious Experience*, enlarged edition with appendixes and an introduction by Joseph Ratner (New Hyde Park: University Books, 1963), 529-31.

19. James referred in passing in "The Will to Believe" (*WTB,* 21n) to Wilfrid Ward's essay "The Wish to Believe," in his *Witnesses to the Unseen* (New York: Macmillan, 1893). Brand Blanshard's essay "The Ethics of Belief" focuses on religion in James. He writes:

> But the situation as regards religion is different. . . . Every person of common sense must feel the force of this. It seems to present us with an unwelcome dilemma: we must give up either serenity or intellectual honesty, either the peace that goes with confident beliefs on ultimate things or else that saving salt of skepticism that is needed for integrity of mind. Is there any way out? We should be merely deceiving ourselves if we thought there was any wholly satisfactory way out. Something valuable must go. (*Philosophic Exchange* 1 [1971]:90)

20. See RBP, chapters 63–64.
21. "The Will to Believe," in *WTB,* 11.
22. Ibid., 9.
23. Letter of 30 August 1896, in *LWJ,* 2:49. See also James's letter of 17 August 1897 to E. L. Godkin, in *LWJ,* 2:64–65.

James stressed the influence of Renouvier in a letter of 30 March 1897 to Peirce, to whom he had dedicated *The Will to Believe:* "[Renouvier's] form is atrocious, but I am thankful to him for a number of points of view rather vital to me. The whole of my essay 'The Will to Believe' is cribbed from him."

The temperamental differences between Peirce and James are clear in a letter of 13 March 1897 from Peirce to James. Peirce wrote:

> I have learned a great deal about philosophy in the last few years, because they have been very miserable and unsuccessful years,—terrible beyond anything that the man of ordinary experience can possibly understand. . . . A new world of which I knew nothing . . . has been disclosed to me, the world of misery. . . . I would like to write a physiology of it. . . . Many days did however go at a time without a morsel of food or any idea where food was coming from, my case at the moment for very near three days. . . .
>
> Probability is simply absurd . . . in reference to a matter of "supreme interest," and any decision of such a question on probable grounds is illogical. But wherein does the illogicality lie? Simply in considering any interest as supreme. No man be logical who reckons his personal well being as a matter of overwhelming moment.
>
> I do not think suicide springs from a pessimistic philosophy. Pessimism is a disease of the well-to-do. . . . Men commit suicide because they are personally discouraged. . . . There was Mrs. Lunt who drowned herself in a well. I often talked to her when she was coming to that resolution. It wasn't the universe that she thought intolerable, but her own special condition.
>
> As for any form of belief in a future state being cheering to anybody, I can't conceive of it. At any rate I am quite sure that it is generally a source of dread. "Phantasms of the living" to those who believe it must add greatly to its horrors. The old fashioned heaven wasn't half so degraded as existence,—bad as it was.
>
> Religion *per se* seems to me a barbaric superstition. . . . The clergymen who do any good don't pay much attention to religion. They teach people the conduct of life, and on the whole in a high and noble way.

24. James's remarks on the science of religions occur in the preface to *WTB* and in *VRE.* See also Levinson, *The Religious Investigations of William James,* 58–59, 71–94, 156–59.
25. "The Will to Believe," in *WTB,* 16.
26. George Santayana, *Character and Opinion in the United States* (Garden City, N.Y.: Anchor Books, 1956), 47. Santayana seems to me right in saying: "[For James] the degree of authority

and honour to be accorded to various human faiths was a moral question, not a theoretical one'' (47).

Dickinson S. Miller wrote: "The man [James] who said again and again, in different classes and years, 'If there *is* a God . . .' (I suppose many former students can hear his voice saying it), was not at that moment an example of the will to believe. The truth was that the man's mind was so big, there were so many elements present in it, that it was almost riven asunder'' (Review of J. S. Bixler's *Religion in the Philosophy of William James*, in the *Journal of Philosophy, Psychology and Scientific Method* 24 (April 1927):206.

27. Letter of 17 April 1904 to James H. Leuba, included in Ratner's edition of *VRE*, 538. For more on James's personal faith, see RBP, chapter 71; Ratner's appendixes to *VRE*, 531–39; and *LWJ*, 1:145 and 2:171.

That James was reluctant to venture into interpretation is borne out by this statement: "I am as convinced as I can be of anything that this experience of ours is only a part of the experience that is, and with which it has something to do, but *what* or *whose* or *where* the other parts are, I cannot guess. It only enables one to say, 'behind the veil, behind the veil!' more hopefully, however interrogatively and vaguely, than would otherwise be the case'' (Letter of 17 October 1908 to Charles E. Norton).

28. *VRE* (Ratner's edition), 161. James offered this account of his own experiences anonymously.

29. "Reflex Action and Theism," in *WTB*, 120, 141. On feelings of remorse and regret, see "The Dilemma of Determinism.''

30. Josiah Royce, *William James and Other Essays on the Philosophy of Life* (New York: Macmillan, 1912), 19–23. For biographical details, see RBP, Matthiessen, Allen, and Barzun.

In a notebook dated 1862, James made notes on Jonathan Edwards on original sin. Henry James III has noted on the manuscript that most of the entries were written later than 1862, but the earlier entries seem to be in pen and the later ones in pencil. Since the notes on Edwards are in pen, they may be closer to 1862 than the others.

31. "The Sentiment of Rationality," in *CER*, 84–85. See also chapters 9 and 10.

32. "The Sentiment of Rationality," in *WTB*, 82, 86. This is the second essay bearing the title "The Sentiment of Rationality" (the first is reproduced in *CER*). The later essay is a combination of the earlier one and the essay "Rationality, Activity and Faith." See also "The History" of "The Text of *The Will to Believe*" in the Harvard edition, 299–311.

James praised the practical grasp of rationality thus: "When the cosmos in its totality is the object offered to consciousness, the relation is in no whit altered. React on it we must in some congenial way. It was a deep instinct in Schopenhauer which led him to reinforce his pessimistic argumentation by a running volley of invective against the practical man and his requirements. No hope for pessimism unless he is slain!'' ("The Sentiment of Rationality," in *WTB*, 85).

33. See James's letter of 8 January 1882 to Thomas Davidson, in RBP, 1:736–38.

34. "Reflex Action and Theism," in *WTB*, 127.

35. Ibid., 134.

36. See RBP, 2:592. See also chapters 11 and 12.

37. "Pragmatism and Religion," in *Pragmatism*, 190.

38. "Reason and Faith," in *Essays in Religion and Morality*, 125. For the occasion of this brief essay, see also 243–47. Similar presentations of faith's argument or the faith-ladder occur in *SPP*, 224, and in *APU*, 148.

39. These notes are very brief and are mostly reproduced (though not what is quoted here) in RBP, 2:327–28.

40. Henry F. May writes about this stage in American history:

More than we used to realize, in the period of social upheaval social critics made natural and fervent use of religious terminology . . . like Edward Bellamy but also of Populists. . . . It is true and important, that on the top intellectual level various people challenged . . . dominant religious assumptions. But one cannot understand William James, Thorstein Veblen, or John Dewey without remembering the agonies and struggles of doubters in an age when religious commitment was taken for granted. (*Ideas, Faiths, and Feelings* [New York: Oxford University Press, 1983], 157)

41. "The Sentiment of Rationality," *WTB,* 110.

42. William A. Clebsch, *American Religious Thought: A History* (Chicago: University of Chicago Press, 1973), 153. Clebsch also remarks that "nobody exerted a wider influence [than James] on the palliative-peddlers of twentieth-century American popular religion" (165), and refers the reader to Louis Schneider and Sanford M. Dornbusch, *Popular Religion: Inspirational Books in America* (Chicago: University of Chicago Press, 1958).

43. Russell's reference to Wittgenstein is in a letter of 20 December 1919 to Lady Ottoline Morrell, included in *Wittgenstein's Letters to Russell, Keynes, and Moore,* ed. G. H. von Wright (Ithaca: Cornell University Press, 1974), 82; Russell's own reaction to *Varieties* occurs in the first volume of *The Autobiography of Bertrand Russell* (Boston: Little, Brown, & Co., 1967), 252.

Russell made only one reference to James in his famous *Mysticism and Logic* (London: Allen & Unwin, 1910). In the first chapter he asserted: "The hope of satisfaction to our more human desires—the hope of demonstrating that the world has this or that desirable ethical characteristic—is not one which, so far as I can see, a scientific philosophy can do anything whatever to satisfy" (29). In the same vein he wrote: "A philosophy which does not seek to impose upon the world its own conceptions of good and evil is not only more likely to achieve truth, but is also the outcome of a higher ethical standpoint than one which . . . is perpetually appraising the universe and seeking to find in it an embodiment of present ideals" (31). These statements apply directly and negatively to James, though Russell mentions only Bergson by name. The only direct reference is in the sixth chapter, "On Scientific Method in Philosophy": "As regards our present question, namely, the question of the unity of the world, the right method, as I think, has been indicated by William James [*SPP,* 124]. 'Let us now turn our backs upon ineffable or unintelligible ways of accounting for the world's oneness, and inquire whether, instead of being a principle, the "oneness" affirmed may not merely be a name like "substance" descriptive of the fact that certain *specific and verifiable connections* are found among the parts of the experiential flux'" (100). Although Russell takes up James's pragmatism, he does not seem to have realized that pragmatism recedes behind mysticism in *Varieties* and *A Pluralistic Universe* when James confronted the unity of the world. This concept can never be grasped rationally or pragmatically in Jamesian metaphysics; at best it is an object for mystical appreciation.

44. Santayana, *Character and Opinion in the United States,* 49–50.

Writing in 1950 to Corliss Lamont, Santayana said: "Your book on immortality [*The Illusion of Immortality*] has made me think of what I thought of William James's Religious Experiences, that he had been on a slumming tour in the New Jerusalem" (*The Letters of George Santayana,* ed. Daniel Cory [New York: Scribner's, 1955], 394).

45. Dickinson S. Miller, "Mr. Santayana and William James," *Harvard Graduate's Magazine* 29 (March 1921):358. Miller added later in the article: "[James's] mind was larger than any known system. Mr. Santayana has 'the completeness of limited men'" (362).

46. Letter of 21 September 1910 to Henry James III. Another distinguished admirer of *Varieties* was Ernst Mach (see RBP, 2:341).

47. Letter of 12 April 1900 to Frances R. Morse, in *LWJ,* 2:127.

48. RBP, 2:323.

49. This letter to Holmes is quoted in RBP, 1:512–18.

50. *APU,* 138, 149; *VRE* (Modern Library edition), 512.

51. *VRE,* 21.

52. *VRE,* 22. See also *MT,* 189–90.

53. *VRE,* 403. Some commentators argue that the recognition of this complexity of an emotional experience in *Varieties* represents a clarification of James's theory of emotion as described in *Principles* and elsewhere (see chapter 7). Levinson, for instance, thinks the "reductively physiological" view of emotions in James's earlier works is altered in *VRE* to include beliefs among emotions and to see religious emotions as "total" views resulting from experiences of the divine (*The Religious Investigations of William James,* 104–05). I agree with Levinson that readers of "What Is an Emotion?" may conclude that James considered emotions only physiological phenomena; such readers may be impressed, as Levinson is, by those passages in *Varieties* which emphasize the complexity of emotional experience and integrate faith, belief, and revelation with emotion. Although that connection may be more explicit in *Varieties,* James assumed it even in his initial writings on emotion. In expounding the James-Lange theory, he never thought that the whole of an emotional experience excludes the element of belief. If he gave this impression, it was only because he concentrated upon the bodily aspect of emotion and because the associated beliefs, changes in consciousness, cultural conditioning factors, and expectations were not his main concern. His focus is clear, for instance, in his replies to critics in "The Physical Basis for Emotion," which Levinson does not mention in this context. Given the considerations that occur in discussing religion, it is hardly surprising that faith and belief are conspicuous concepts in relation to emotional experience, but that conspicuousness represents no shift in the James-Lange theory of emotion.

Given the amount of attention to emotion in *Varieties,* it is surprising that the James-Lange theory is not mentioned and that its relation to religious emotion is never explored at all. In "The Reality of the Unseen," for instance, James noted that trying to locate the organic seat of an emotion would form a "pretty problem," but "with such vague conjectures we have no concern at present, for our interest lies with the faculty rather than with its organic seat" (*VRE,* 62–63).

54. *Principles,* 2:453; see chapters 7, 11, and 12.

55. *VRE,* 163; see also 77–125. James borrowed the terms *once-born* and *twice-born* from Newman's *The Soul: Its Sorrows and Its Aspirations.*

56. *VRE,* 157. In a footnote James observed that his father had once experienced a similar sudden attack of panic. Using Swedenborgian terminology, Henry James, Sr., had labeled his experience a *vastation.* See Frederic Harold Young, *The Philosophy of Henry James, Sr.* (New Haven: College and University Press, 1951), 6–9.

The fact that it was James's own experience came out when he wrote on 1 June 1904 to Frank Abauzit: "The document on p. 160 is my own case—acute neurasthenic attack with phobia. I naturally disguised the *provenance!* So you may translate freely." See also *LWJ,* 1:144–48.

James cited two cases at the end of lectures 4 and 5 on the religion of healthy-mindedness in *VRE.* A friend surmised that the accounts were autobiographical, and James responded: "Is it that the 'divine shamelessness' which you say I exhibit refers to the two 'cases' at the end of the Chapter on healthy mindedness, the which possibly you may have taken (as others have) to be confessions of my *own?* Heaven forfend!" ("A Packet of Wendell-James Letters," ed. M. A. DeWolfe Howe, *Scribner's Magazine* 84 [1928]: 682). Given James's identification with the sick soul, it must have struck him as ironic to have to deny that he thought of himself as a paragon of healthy-mindedness.

57. Cushing Strout has observed with some justification that *Varieties* is striking in its lack of variety, that the focus throughout is on a single type of religious experience, the twice-born conversion of the sick soul; see "The Pluralistic Identity of William James: A Psycho-Historical Reading of *The Varieties of Religious Experience,*" *American Quarterly* 23 (May 1971):136–39. There is genuine variety in the book, however, if we consider the variety of emotions that

characterize religious experiences, as well as the variety of attitudes about and interpretations of such experiences. The mixture of attitudes sought by James is a case in point.

This article is one of several by Strout that seeks to explain James's thought through a diagnosis of his relation to his father. Strout is one of the more sensitive, sympathetic, and informed interpreters of James in this regard. A sample of his diagnosis: "In modern terms what can we conclude about James's crisis in relation to his theory? Certainly his own conversion was connected with 'deeper forces,' deriving from an over-identification with a disturbed father. Such a son, with less suffering today, might 'work through' a similar problem with the sustained and expensive help of a psychoanalyst or a psychiatrist. But James lived between the two cultural worlds of religious conversion and psychoanalytic therapy" (148).

James named most of his sources for the reports of religious experience in *VRE;* some were friends he had asked to send accounts. While in Europe he wrote, for instance, to his friend George Dorr on 22 July 1900:

> I have just written a Gifford Lecture on the religion of optimism or "healthy-minded-ness," in which I have given a somewhat emphatic account of the American Mind-Cure movement, broadly so called.
>
> I sadly need a few personal documents, as *traits rifs,* to redress so much abstraction.
>
> Would it be possible for you to set down in two pages your own experience of regeneration? Or do you think you might induce Mrs. Sears, Mrs. Warren or Mrs. Shaw or any other friend to put themselves down on paper in a similar way? . . . I have only one such document as of yet, to quote, and I ought to have five or six. Of course absolute *anonymity* is assured.
>
> What I especially should like is some account of the transition from the tense moral-istic state of mind to that of passivity of expectant faith. Also of course the sort of regenera-tion, spiritual or physical, experienced. . . . I really think it is worthwhile to make an effort for the sake of these lectures, for in them Mind Cure is for the first time presented to Court Circles.

James was in a weak mental and physical condition when he wrote this, adding, "My own condition baffles me, going up and down as it does. On the whole there is little durable change of level, and I can *do* nothing."

See John Baillie, *Our Knowledge of God* (New York: Scribner's, 1959), 88–89, on the variety of James's religious experiences. For references in a different context to James on religious experience, see Wendy Doniger O'Flaherty, *The Origins of Evil in Hindu Mythology* (Berkeley and Los Angeles: University of California Press, 1976), 8, 138.

58. Letter of 22 July 1909. Russell had been reading James's *Pluralistic Universe* and ex-pressed this reservation: "With regard to religion, I notice one purely temperamental dif-ference: that the first demand you make of your God is that you could be able to love him, whereas my first demand is that I should be able to worship him. I do not desire familiarity lest it should breed contempt." Although Russell responded favorably to the pragmatic defense of religion in *Varieties* insofar as religious experiences seem to be rewarding and thereby encour-age faith, he was put off by James's semitheological interpretations, which struck him as nonpragmatic.

59. Compare these remarks with those of John E. Smith on James's philosophy of religion and its contrasts with other dominant philosophies of the time; see *Themes in American Philoso-phy* (New York: Harper Torchbooks, 1970), 152–60. See also Don S. Browning, *Pluralism and Personality: William James and Some Contemporary Cultures of Psychology* (Lewisburg, Pa.: Buck-nell University Press, 1980), 237–70, for a discussion of James's philosophy of religion and of the respects in which it is both phenomenological and pragmatic.

60. *VRE,* 437. See also "What Pragmatism Means," in *Pragmatism,* 41–62, as well as James's answers to the Pratt Questionnaire, in *VRE* (Ratner edition), 529–31.

61. Letter of 22 January 1908 to Pauline Goldmark. In this letter James separated himself from Miller's impulse to join, remarking, "Thank Heaven, *I'm* an anarchist, and likely to remain so!" He pointed out the irony of Miller's joining the Church, since Miller had been one of the chief critics of "The Will to Believe." "The beauty of this is that M[iller] will still as obstinately as ever denounce my 'Will to Believe.'"

In a later letter to Pauline Goldmark, dated 22 June 1909, James wrote that he had declined an invitation to the Jubilee at the University of Geneva, "where I understand confidentially that I was to be made a Doctor of *Theology!!!* The temptation was strong to go, so as to crow over Royce, and listen to his sarcasm in return—Irving Street would be more lively as a result." In notes titled "Theological School Lectures" (1902) James wrote: "Doctrinairism in general—the philosophic sin."

In the Houghton Library is a letter from David A. Pfromm to James's wife, Alice, dated 27 August 1913, Pfromm enclosed a photostatic copy of the following manuscript:

XXXV Jan. 15

Predestination has existed in all religion. It draws its assurance from the conceptions of God rather than from metaphysical principles. God was omnipotent. He created and has control of the world. The same idea is found in nature study to-day. Everything seems predestined.

XXXXI Jan. 22

Wm. James
Good Bye Harvard!
January 22, 1907

In his letter Pfromm said that he had the original of this manuscript framed and under glass. He also wrote:

The circumstances under which Professor James wrote these lines were those of his last lecture of his last course at Harvard. . . . The course was Philosophy D dealing with general problems etc.—an introductory course. I was a Junior at the time. At the end of the lecture I asked him to favor me with an autograph. It is the last page of my notes for the course. The "Good-bye Harvard" was written without any suggestion from me. And it is for that alone that I have communicated with you. It seems so indicative of his thought on that last day of his long and active service in the university.

It is difficult to tell from Pfromm's notes about God and predestation exactly what James was saying in the lecture, but there is the suggestion, consistent with what James wrote elsewhere, that the notion of an omnipotent God (which he opposed) is like the notion of omnipotent nature in that both lead to the idea of predestination.

62. Max Weber, *The Protestant Ethic and the Spirit of Capitalism,* trans. Talcott Parsons (New York: Charles Scribner's Sons, 1958), 232.

James attended Harvard's chapel on a daily basis; his son Henry wrote: "At twenty minutes before nine in the morning he could usually be seen going to the College Chapel for the fifteen-minute service with which the College Day began" (*LWJ,* 2:7).

63. See James Leuba, "Studies in the Psychology of Religious Phenomena," *American Journal of Psychology* 7 (1896):309–85.

64. F. W. H. Myers, "The Subliminal Consciousness," *Proceedings of the English Society for Psychical Research* 7 (1891–92); quoted in *VRE,* 502. See also chapters 11 and 12.

65. See *VRE,* 230. Unfortunately, the index to *Varieties* does not include the names of Binet,

Janet, Breuer, Freud, Mason, and Prince. But Myers's name shows up in the index as well as in the text.

66. "The Energies of Men," *Philosophical Review* 16 (January 1907):2–3. This article gives a fuller statement of James's belief that the subconscious can revitalize one's energies, and that therefore laboratory psychologists and not only clinicians like Janet and Binet ought to investigate it. James was in the avant-garde in interpreting the action of the subconscious upon consciousness. Jung praised James's contributions in this regard in *Two Essays on Analytical Psychology*, 2d ed. (Princeton: Princeton University Press, 1972), 175; see also 54 and 288–89. Ninian Smart notes that James anticipated Jung's view that recurrent patterns of religious experience well up from subconscious levels; he also says that James was more interested in the experiences as such, whereas Jung was intrigued by their myths and symbols; see *The Philosophy of Religion* (London: Oxford University Press, 1979), 182.

67. *VRE*, 498–99. As the draft and page proofs preserved in the Houghton Library show, James originally wrote the italicized section of this quotation differently. Instead of *"He becomes conscious that this higher part is conterminous with a* MORE . . . " he had written: "The sense of salvation seems to be describable as the consciousness that one's higher and better part is in working contact with a MORE. . . ." Since James retained the word *salvation* in the preceding part of the quotation, the reworking does not seem to have been due to a desire to avoid what might be associated with that word, although he sometimes expressed incredulity at the Christian idea of selective salvation. He may have rephrased this passage in order to insure that the sense of salvation would be understood as something additional to the consciousness that our higher part is conterminous with a *more.*

Although James used the term *over-belief*, he avoided the oversoul of Emerson and others. "Transcendentalists are fond of the term 'Over-soul,' but as a rule they use it in an intellectualist sense, as meaning only a medium of communion. 'God' is a causal agent as well as a medium of communion, and that is the aspect which I wish to emphasize" (*VRE*, 507n).

68. The tension in James's mind between religion as a matter of faith different from science and religion as a respectable discipline related to science is clear in his writings. "If asked just what the differences in fact which are due to God's existence come in, I should have to say that in general I have no hypothesis to offer beyond what the phenomenon of 'prayerful communion' . . . immediately suggests" (*VRE*, 513). But this rationale makes things rest upon the consequences of being prayerful rather than upon the consequences of God's existence, and it is hardly a scientific claim. When James considered Fechner's admittedly bizarre scheme, he claimed that it was "not without direct empirical verification" and that the evidence gave it "a decidedly *formidable* probability" ("Pluralism and Religion," *Hibbert Journal* 6 [1908]:724, 725). But Fechner's speculations, as described by James in "Concerning Fechner," are hardly supported by evidence. What others thought was Fechner's major contribution to psychology—his quantitative psychophysics, which was backed by evidence—James dismissed as "moonshiny." He wrote on 16 January 1880 to G. Stanley Hall: "Your description of Fechner is entertaining enough. You know I always thought his psycho-physics as moonshiny as any of his other writings, fundamentally, valuable only for its rich details." James's later praise of Fechner did not include the psychophysics, though it showed an enthusiasm toward Fechner's other writings that was absent in the letter to Hall. James wrote to Bergson on 28 July 1908: "Are you a reader of Fechner? I wish that you had read his Zend-Avesta. . . . He seems to me of the real race of prophets." Curiously, Fechner is not mentioned in *Varieties;* James's discussions of him occur in *A Pluralistic Universe* and other places.

69. See, for instance, *APU,* 131. For further textual sources that are relevant here, see also 60–61, 80–82, 92–100, and 140–41.

70. "Concerning Fechner," in *APU,* 71. See note 68 above.

F. H. Bradley wrote to James on 3 February 1910 that while he was generally skeptical, "I have just been reading your paper on Fechner which I find very interesting." Fechner's ideas, for all their bizarre quality, were not merely dismissed by the philosophers of the time. See William R. Woodward, "Fechner's Panpsychism: A Scientific Solution to the Mind-Body Problem," *Journal of the History of Behavioral Sciences* (October 1972):367–87.

71. "Concerning Fechner," in *APU,* 80–81.

72. "Conclusions," in *APU,* 140.

73. Notes in the Houghton Library, titled "Philosophy 1904–5." See Perry's reference to them, which includes part of this quotation (RBP, 2:443–44). See also *VRE,* 29, 515.

74. "Conclusions," in *APU,* 141–44. The question arises of whether James was committed to panpsychism, especially in his philosophy of religion. Marcus Ford, arguing that James's metaphysics is panpsychistic, takes issue with such Jamesian interpreters as Perry, Ralph Ross, Edward Madden, and Peter Hare; see *William James's Philosophy: A New Perspective* (Amherst: University of Massachusetts Press, 1982), especially 75–89.

I agree with Ford that James defines pure experience so that panpsychism, if one means by it that everything is of the nature of sensations and feelings, seems to be the natural implication (see section 5 of "Does 'Consciousness' Exist?"). As Perry pointed out, however, James never actually accepted C. A. Strong's version of panpsychism (RBP, 2:405, 534–52). It was therefore an error on the part of Wendell T. Bush, Ford says, to have written that James's pronouncements on panpsychism, while scattered and tentative, were yet "full of personal confidence" (quoted in Ford, 113). James never expressed such confidence. Ford has concluded that James's panpsychism "is never systematically developed nor is it very sophisticated. Nonetheless, he is a panpsychist" (6). James may not have fully realized that he was, however.

Perry noted two points in Strong's panpsychism upon which James hesitated: first, to say as Strong did that *psychic* suggests the primal quality of existence was unclear; second, to say that the real physical object can be directly presented only to itself, or is only what it feels itself to be, was to contradict James's commonsense view that the physical object is presented directly to human perception. Nevertheless, James's published and unpublished remarks on panpsychism suggest that he never settled on a precise meaning of the word and that its unresolved ambiguity in his mind made him reluctant to use it as a technical term for his own views. (He had enough trouble with *pure experience* and its uncertainties.) James called Fechner's system panpsychic even though it was clearly dualistic in holding that vaster psychical systems attach to vaster physical systems. Psychism is *pan* by being everywhere but not by being everything. If James's world of pure experience is panpsychic, however, then since the physical is defined in terms of pure experience, which in turn is defined as sensation, panpsychism cannot be dualistic.

Among James's unpublished notes are three brief sets of entries on panpsychism: "Panpsychism," in a notebook titled "Seminary in Metaphysics, 1903–4"; "Notes on Panpsychism" and a notebook dealing with the writings of Gerardus Heymans and C. A. Strong. For a discussion of the issues, see RBP, 2:394–405. The first lists eleven propositions that might represent panpsychism, beginning with this: "The only Realities are Minds with their thoughts—psychical facts," a statement which James in his radical empiricism might have accepted. Other propositions, such as "All I can truly know is *what* some other thinker is thinking," are problematic at best and are left undiscussed in the notes. One assumes that they were part of panpsychism as he understood it and that they struck him simply as problematic.

It is hard to make much of the second set of notes, which pits panpsychism against something called substantialism. The note says, "[Panpsychism] admits reality *extra mentem meam*," suggesting that we know something about it. "The . . . phenomenon it supposes, instead of reducing the phenomenon to unreality, as substance does, corroborates, confirms, reinforces the reality of the phenomenon." The third set includes this: "The real existents are psychic facts which form a system of which we individuals only realize patches, the rest being conceptual fillings in for those individuals . . . but real experiences for other real experients. Some of *our* patches are physical phenomena, others concepts of the same, others again bits of subjective feeling."

James found his own attempts to identify panpsychism almost as obscure as we find them; given the absence of any evidence that he resolved such obscurities, we must infer that he dropped the question. If panpsychism meant nothing more than what he called pure experience, he would probably have called himself a panpsychist; if it meant what others meant by it, however, he was at least uncertain about it if not against it.

75. See RBP, 2:355–59. James's interest in psychical research had many facets, including a curiosity as to what it might reveal about life after death. In 1901, James was present when Myers died; Alex Munthe recounted the episode:

> William James told me of the solemn pact between him and his friend [Myers] that whichever of them was to die first should send a message to the other as he passed over into the unknown—they both believed in the possibility of such a communication. He was so overcome with grief that he could not enter the room, he sank down on a chair by the open door, his note-book on his knees, pen in hand, ready to take down the message with his usual methodical exactitude. In the afternoon set in the Cheyne-Stokes respiration, that heartrending sign of approaching death. The dying man asked to speak to me. His eyes were calm and serene.
>
> "I know I am going to die," he said, "I know you are going to help me. Is it to-day, is it tomorrow?"
>
> "Today."
>
> "I am glad, I am ready, I have no fear. I am going to know at last. Tell William James, tell him . . ."
>
> His heaving chest stood still in a terrible minute of suspense of life.
>
> "Do you hear me?" I asked, bending over the dying man, "do you suffer?"
>
> "No," he murmured. "I am very tired and very happy."
>
> These were his last words.
>
> When I went away William James was still sitting leaning back in his chair, his hands over his face, his open note-book still on his knees. The page was blank. (Alex Munthe, *The Story of San Michele* [New York: Dutton, 1931], 372–73.

On James and Myers's death, see also *LWJ*, 2:141, 151, 157.

76. "Human Immortality: Two Supposed Objections to the Doctrine," in *WTB*, 24.

This discussion of human immortality was originally given as the Ingersoll Lecture at Harvard in 1897 and published in 1898; a second edition, with a preface containing replies to criticisms of the first edition, was published in 1899.

Although James did not refer to Fechner in *Varieties*, the Ingersoll Lecture on immortality and *A Pluralistic Universe* both include many references to him. For other remarks by James on Fechner's significance, see "Introduction to Fechner's *Life After Death*," in *Essays in Religion and Morality*, 116–23. (This essay was originally published in 1904 as the introduction to M. C. Wadsworth's translation of Fechner's *Little Book of Life After Death* [Boston: Little, Brown & Co.], vii–xix). See also "A Suggestion About Mysticism," in *CER*, 500–13.

77. "Introduction to Fechner's *Life After Death*," *Essays in Religion and Morality*, 118–19.

78. "Human Immortality," in *WTB*, 37.

79. Ibid., 40–41.

80. "Final Impressions of a Psychical Researcher," in *Memories and Studies*, 204.

81. "A Suggestion about Mysticism," in *CER*, 503. In this essay James described his experiences which seemed to resemble true mystical ones. See also Leonard H. Bridges, *American Mysticism: From William James to Zen* (New York: Harper & Row, 1970).

82. "A Suggestion about Mysticism," in *CER*, 504–05. Whitehead sympathized with James's sense of the inability of words to describe certain features of experiences and of the

inevitable incompleteness that this inadequacy represents for any philosophical theory. Lucien Price has reported a discussion with Whitehead in which the latter said of *Varieties:*

> The difficulty of communication in words is but little realized. If I had to write something about your personality, of course I could—but how much would remain that couldn't be put into words. So when the rare balance of knowledge and perception appears, as in William James—one who could communicate so much more than most—it is perhaps an advantage that his system of philosophy remained incomplete. To fill it out would necessarily have made it smaller. In Plato's *Dialogues* there is a richness of thought, suggestion, and implication which reaches far. Later, when he came to be more explicit concerning some of those implications, we have a shrinkage. . . .
>
> Consider John Dewey. In carrying out the philosophy of William James, I think he enormously narrowed it. With James the consciousness of the ever-present complexity and possibility in human experience is always implicit in his writing. Dewey is without it. William James's awareness of the wide scope and the interrelations of all questions made him one of the great philosophic minds in history. (*Dialogues of Alfred North Whitehead: As Recorded by Lucien Price* [Boston: Little, Brown & Co., 1954], 337–38)

For a philosophical symposium on mystical experience and the value of mystical reports, see the discussions by Nelson Pike, Paul Schmidt, and Ninian Smart in W. H. Capitan and D. D. Merrill (eds.) *Art, Mind and Religion,* Proceedings of the 1965 Oberlin Colloquium in Philosophy (Pittsburgh: University of Pittsburgh Press, n.d.), 133–58. Pike refers to James on p. 146. See also James M. Edie, "William James and the Phenomenology of Religious Experience," in *American Philosophy and the Future,* ed. Michael Novak (New York: Charles Scribner's Sons, 1968).

83. See, for instance, "Quelques considérations sur la méthode subjective," in *CER,* 69–82, which was originally published in *Critique philosophique.* The question James discussed was this: "Il s'agit de savoir *si l'on est en droit de repousser une théorie confirmée en apparence par un nombre très considérable de faits objectifs, uniquement parce qu'elle ne répond point à nos préférences intérieures*" (69).

84. "A Pluralistic Mystic," in *MS,* 410–11.

INDEX

This index lists the major persons and topics, but for the latter the table of contents should also be consulted. Titles of works are cited selectively, especially *The Principles of Psychology*, which is referred to copiously in the text. Names of the James family are abbreviated as follows:

AHGJ = Alice Howe Gibbens James (wife)
AJ = Alice James (sister)
HJ Sr. = Henry James, Sr. (father)

HJ Jr. = Henry James, Jr. (brother)
HJ III = Henry James III (son)
WJ = William James